# Becoming and Belonging in Ireland AD *c.*1200–1600: Essays in Identity and Cultural Practice

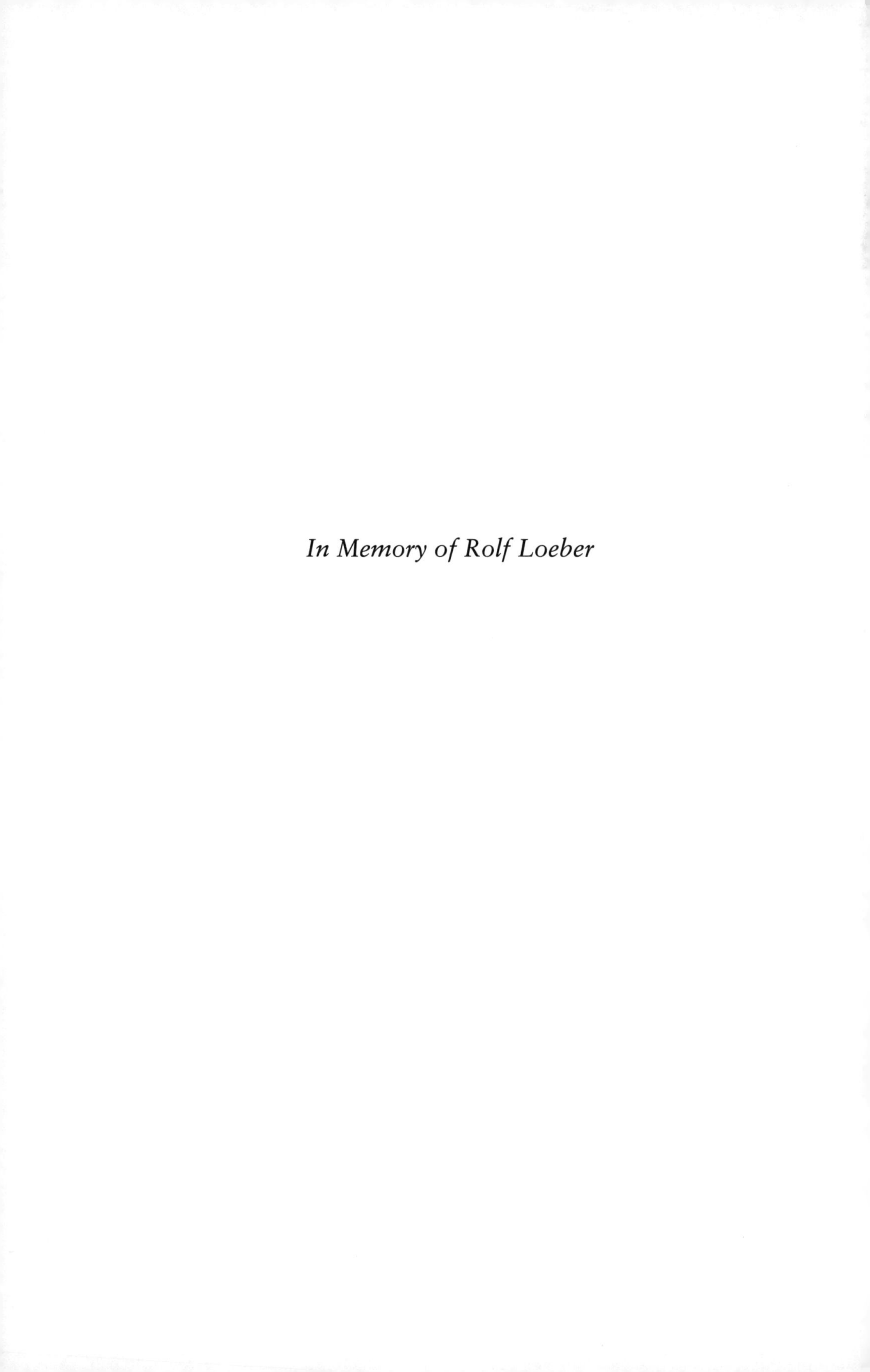

*In Memory of Rolf Loeber*

# Becoming and Belonging in Ireland AD *c.*1200–1600: Essays in Identity and Cultural Practice

EVE CAMPBELL, ELIZABETH FITZPATRICK,
AUDREY HORNING

First published in 2018 by
Cork University Press
Youngline Industrial Estate
Pouladuff Road, Togher
Cork
T12 HT6V
Ireland



**British Library Cataloguing in Publication Data**
A CIP record for this book is available from the British Library.

ISBN: 978-1-78205-260-9

This publication was grant-aided by the Publications Scheme of the Senate of the National University of Ireland.

Printed in Poland by Hussar books
Print origination & design by Carrigboy Typesetting Services

www.corkuniversitypress.com

# Contents

# Preface

Research on individual, group, gendered, community and national identities, and the links between identity and cultural practice, is central to many disciplines within the humanities. It is an area of enquiry that has been especially active over the past twenty years and continues to develop in archaeology and history. For those disciplines, identity is an important conceptual framework for unlocking the meanings of landscape and place, relationships between human communities and material culture, and for decoding expressions of ethnicity and nationalism. *Becoming and Belonging in Ireland* is very much based within that endeavour.

The sixteen essays in this collection address how peoples on the island of Ireland constructed and transformed self and group identities between AD *c.*1200 and 1600, and how they expressed their senses of belonging in the ways they went about living their lives.

The idea for the book arose from a conference held at the Clinton Centre, Enniskillen, County Fermanagh in October 2013 during which there was robust discussion between the contributors and audience about predicaments of identity and cultural practices among Gaelic, Old English and New English peoples of later medieval and early modern Ireland. The essays are substantially revised and reviewed versions of the ideas presented and discussed at Enniskillen.

Collections that bring scholars from different disciplines together, to write on a particular theme, often represent schools of thought. *Becoming and Belonging* is, in a sense, a companion to and development of a previous collection of essays, *Gaelic Ireland* c.*1250–1650: Land, Lordship and Settlement*, edited by P. J. Duffy, D. Edwards and E. FitzPatrick (Dublin: Four Courts Press, 2001). Five of the contributors to that volume – Colin Breen, Colm Donnelly, Elizabeth FitzPatrick, Audrey Horning and Kieran O'Conor – feature again in this collection alongside some of their former PhD students – Eve Campbell, Paul Logue and Paul Naessens – now established scholars working on the archaeology of later medieval and early modern Ireland. Several of the aspirations for future research in this key period, set out in *Gaelic Ireland*, have since been addressed and appear in *Becoming and Belonging*. The continuities from one volume to the next, together with the new contributors from archaeology, history and English literature in this volume, are testimony to the considerable work and results that have been achieved in the field through dedicated scholarship over many years. New insights from archaeological survey and excavation, from landscape analyses, and from material culture studies and archival research, run through the chapters. The most important development between the first volume and the next is the strong theoretical framework that *Becoming and Belonging* has attempted to forge in order to facilitate understandings of lives lived in Ireland in the period AD *c.*1200 to 1600. In Chapter 1, Audrey Horning introduces the book and the emic approach that frames it.

The theme of this anthology is regarded as prescient because we live in a time of great change in which group identities and boundaries are being variously contested and reasserted, threatened and augmented. It is hoped that readers will find insights, surprises and challenges in this book that will help to enlighten some of the critical issues of our contemporary world.

The editors would like to thank Nick Brannon, David Edwards, Rolf Loeber†, Siobhán McDermott and Tadhg O'Keeffe, who facilitated the conference sessions and debate at the Clinton Centre, Enniskillen in 2013. Special thanks to Councillor Alex Baird, former Chair of Fermanagh District Council, who opened the conference, and to the staff of the Clinton Centre for their professionalism on that occasion.

We are indebted to our contributors for their scholarship, dedication and patience during the making of this book, and to the staff of Cork University Press for their guidance and support.

The editors
May 2017

# Illustrations

## COLOUR SECTION

FITZPATRICK

2 The *baile biataigh* holdings of the Ó hÁgain, Ó Doibhlin, Ó Cuinn and Ó Donnghaile on the *lucht tighe* lands of Ó Néill, which extended between the Ballinderry River and the River Blackwater. The inset highlights the varied bedrock geology of the *lucht tighe* along the Elagh and Clogher Faults, and the Enler Group of sandstones that may have been the source of the Ó Néill stone chair at Tulach Óg (drawing: Eve Campbell).

CAMPBELL

6 Drawing of the Clonyn demesne after the first-edition Ordnance Survey map (1837) (image: author).

O'NEILL

2 (1) The Irish shot engaged and halted the head of the column but were eventually forced to give ground due to a determined English pike charge. (2) Irish shot forced in the English loose shot and disordered the pikemen. (3) Irish pikemen and Scots charged into the disordered rear forcing it into the main battle and then the van. (4) The English army made it to low ground. Under fire from the surrounding heights, the English attacked south but were forced to cross further upstream. (5) Incongruously, the Irish horse played no part in the battle (image: author).

3 An extract from a drawing of the Battle of the Yellow Ford, 14 August 1598. (A) Irish shot supported by targeteers. (B) Irish targeteers surround the lead English regiment. (C) Irish pike. (D) Irish horse (TCD, MS 1209/35).

# Conventions

The practices adopted in this book in respect of chronology, orthography and terminology are set out here.

## Chronology

The following scheme is used to refer, broadly, to particular periods of time in Ireland, which the authors refer to in their chapters:

| | |
|---|---|
| Early medieval | AD 400 to 1000 |
| High medieval | AD 1000 to 1350 |
| Late medieval | AD 1350 to 1550 |
| Early modern/early post-medieval | AD 1550 to 1750 |

## Orthography and Terminology

Gaelic rather than English forms of personal names, family, sept and historical territory names are used, where appropriate, in referring to Gaelic peoples and their polities. This has been done in order to reflect the largely emic perspective adopted in the chapters of this book and to offset the challenges that may otherwise arise, for the reader, from using multiple variants of anglicised name forms. Gaelic terminology is also used in reference to settlement forms, territorial denominations, cultural practices, professions and offices of that society. A referenced glossary of terms used in the text is provided at the end of the book.

## Territories and their Names

The primary polity in the territorial matrix of Ireland up to the late sixteenth century, and in some instances as late as 1600, was the *oireacht* or lordship. A map of the lordships as they had matured by the sixteenth century was prepared, applying the Gaelic name forms for the territories and their ruling families where appropriate. This is the geography within which the individuals, families and communities explored in the book lived. The map is based on K. W. Nicholls, 'Lordships, *c.*1534', which was first published in T. W. Moody, F. X. Martin and F. J. Byrne (eds), *A New History of Ireland, vol. 3: Early Modern Ireland 1534–1691* (Oxford: Oxford University Press, 1976), and a new version reproduced in P. J. Duffy, D. Edwards and E. FitzPatrick (eds), *Gaelic Ireland* c.*1250–1650: Land, Lordship and Settlement* (Dublin: Four Courts Press, 2001), pp. 24–5.

# Abbreviations

| | |
|---|---|
| *AC* | P. Bambury (comp.), *Annála Connacht* (University College Cork: CELT, 2008), [http://www.ucc.ie/celt/published/T100011/index.html]. |
| *AFM* | J. O'Donovan (trans.), *Annals of the Four Masters*, comp. E. Ryan (University College Cork: CELT, 2002), [http://www.ucc.ie/celt/published/T100005A/index.html]. |
| *ALC* | D. Ó Corráin (comp.), *Annals of Loch Cé A.D. 1014–1590* (University College Cork: CELT, 2002), [http://www.ucc.ie/celt/published/G100010A/index.html]. |
| *AT* | G. Mac Niocaill (trans.), *The Annals of Tigernach*, comp. E. Purcell and D. Ó Corráin (University College Cork: CELT, 2010), [http://www.ucc.ie/celt/published/T100002A/index.html]. |
| *AU* | M. Balé and E. Purcell (comp.), *The Annals of Ulster* (University College Cork: CELT, 2010), [http://www.ucc.ie/celt/published/T100001C/index.html]. |
| *BL* | *British Library* |
| *Cal. Carew MSS.* | J. S. Brewer and W. Bullen (eds), *Calendar of the Carew Manuscripts preserved in the Archiepiscopal Library at Lambeth*, 6 vols. (London: Longmans Green and Co., 1867–73). |
| *Cal. S.P. Ire.* | *Calendar of the State Papers Relating to Ireland*, 24 vols. (London, 1860–1911). |
| *Cal. S.P. Scot.* | J. Bain, W. K. Boyd, A. I. Cameron, M. S. Giuseppi, H. W. Meikle and J. D. Mackie (eds), *Calendar of the State Papers Relating to Scotland and Mary, Queen of Scots, 1547–1603*, 13 vols. (Glasgow, 1898–1969). |
| *HHA* | *Hatfield House Archive.* |
| *MIA* | S. Ó hInnse, *Miscellaneous Irish Annals, Fragment I* (Mac Carthaigh's Book), comp. B. Färber and P. Bambury (University College Cork: CELT, 2010), [http://www.ucc.ie/celt/published/T100013/index.html]. |
| *TCD* | *Trinity College Dublin.* |
| *TNA* | *The National Archives, Kew.* |
| *NAI* | *National Archives of Ireland.* |
| *NLI* | *National Library of Ireland.* |
| *NMM* | *National Maritime Museum, Greenwich* |
| *PRONI* | *Public Record Office of Northern Ireland.* |

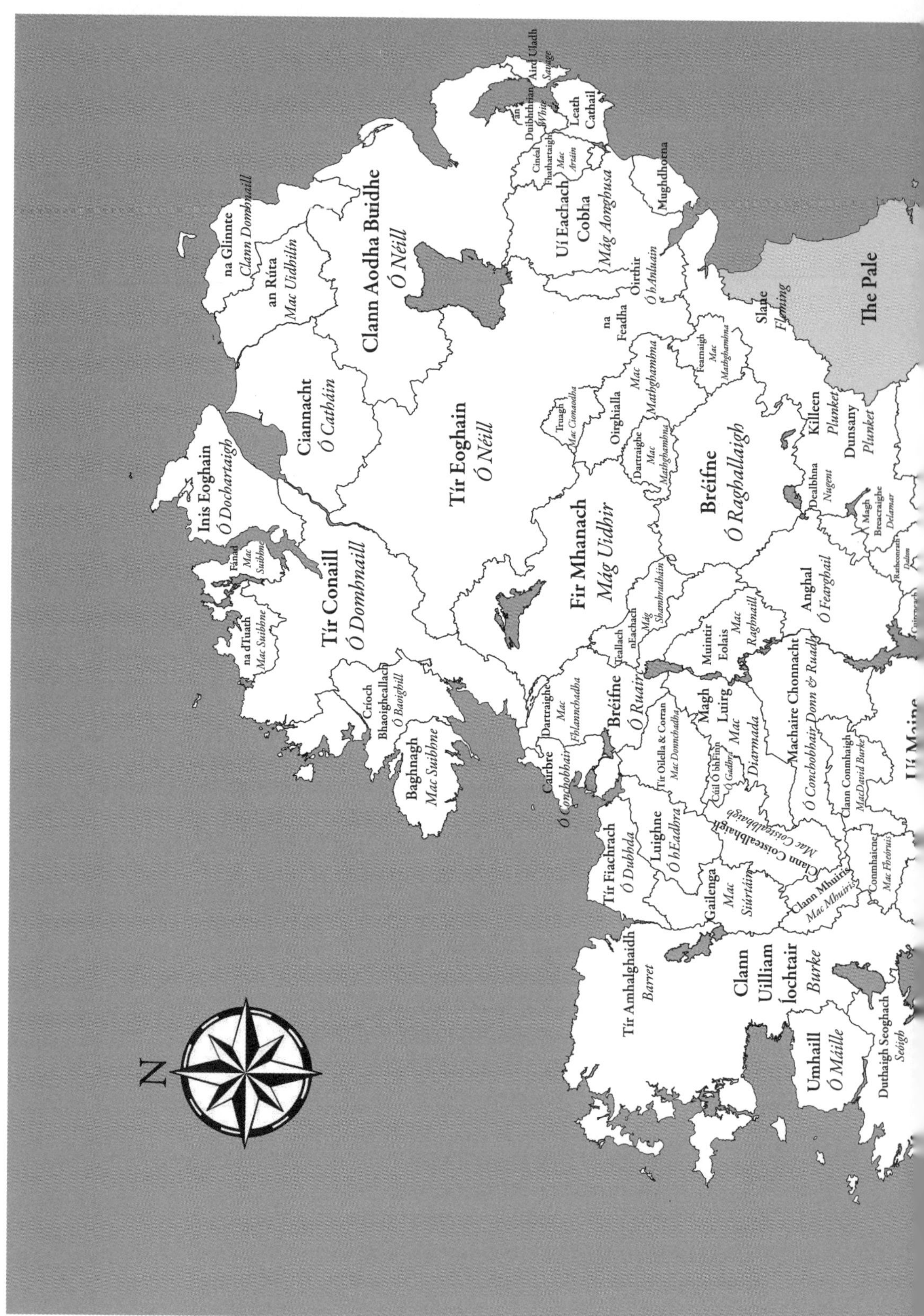


Map 1. The lordships of Ireland in the sixteenth century (FitzPatrick and Campbell, after Nicholls, 1976).

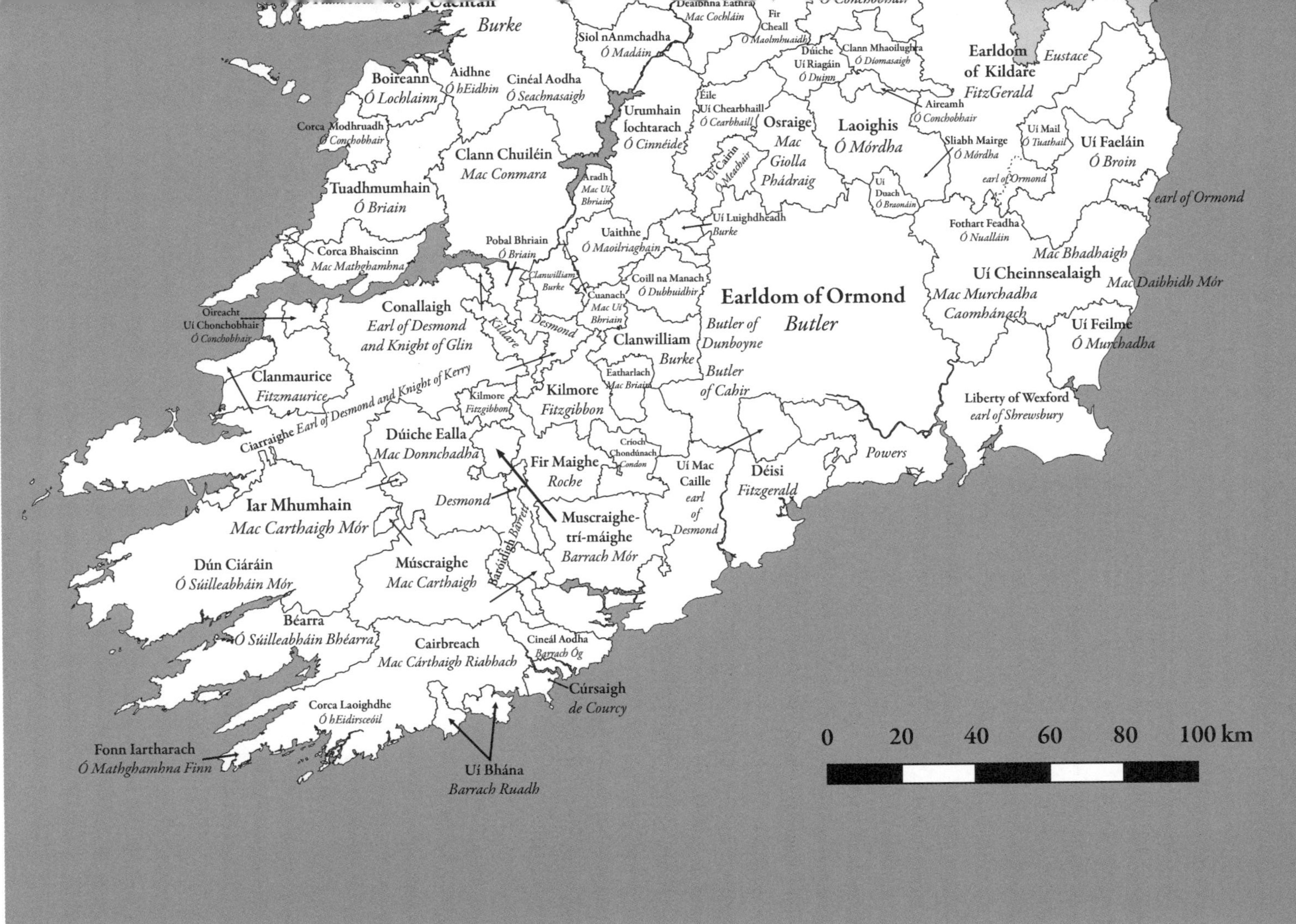
Burke
Siol nAnmchadha
Ó Madáin
Mac Cochláin
Fir Cheall
Ó Maolmhuaidh
Dúiche Uí Riagáin
Ó Duinn
Clann Mhaoilughra
Ó Díomasaigh
Earldom of Kildare
FitzGerald
Eustace
Boireann
Ó Lochlainn
Aidhne
Ó hEidhin
Cinéal Aodha
Ó Seachnasaigh
Éile
Uí Chearbhaill
Ó Cearbhaill
Urumhain Íochtarach
Ó Cinnéide
Aireamh
Ó Conchobhair
Corca Modhruadh
Ó Conchobhair
Osraige
Mac Giolla Phádraig
Laoighis
Ó Mórdha
Uí Mail
Ó Tuathail
Uí Faeláin
Ó Broin
Sliabh Mairge
Ó Mórdha
Uí Cairín
Ó Meachair
Clann Chuiléin
Mac Conmara
Aradh
Mac Uí Bhriain
Uí Duach
Ó Braonáin
earl of Ormond
Tuadhmumhain
Ó Briain
Uí Luighdheadh
Burke
Fothart Feadha
Ó Nualláin
Uaithne
Ó Maoilriaghain
Pobal Bhriain
Ó Briain
Corca Bhaiscinn
Mac Mathghamhna
Clanwilliam
Burke
Coill na Manach
Ó Dubhuidhir
Mac Bhadhaigh
Uí Cheinnsealaigh
Mac Murchadha
Caomhánach
Mac Daibhidh Mór
Earldom of Ormond
Butler
Cuanach
Mac Uí Bhriain
Conallaigh
Earl of Desmond and Knight of Glin
Kildare
Desmond
Oireacht Uí Chonchobhair
Ó Conchobhair
Clanwilliam
Burke
Butler of Dunboyne
Uí Feilme
Ó Murchadha
Eatharlach
Mac Briain
Butler of Cahir
Clanmaurice
Fitzmaurice
Ciarraighe
Earl of Desmond and Knight of Kerry
Kilmore
Fitzgibbon
Kilmore
Fitzgibbon
Liberty of Wexford
earl of Shrewsbury
Dúiche Ealla
Mac Donnchadha
Críoch Chondúnach
Condon
Fir Maighe
Roche
Uí Mac Caille
earl of Desmond
Déisi
Fitzgerald
Powers
Iar Mhumhain
Mac Carthaigh Mór
Desmond
Muscraighe-trí-máighe
Barrach Mór
Baróidigh Barrett
Dún Ciaráin
Ó Súilleabháin Mór
Múscraighe
Mac Carthaigh
Béarra
Ó Súilleabháin Bhéarra
Cairbreach
Mac Cárthaigh Riabhach
Cinéal Aodha
Barrach Óg
Cúrsaigh
de Courcy
Corca Laoighdhe
Ó hEidirsceóil
Fonn Iartharach
Ó Mathghamhna Finn
Uí Bhána
Barrach Ruadh
0
20
40
60
80
100 km

# Contributors

COLIN BREEN Centre for Maritime Archaeology, Ulster University, Coleraine

EVE CAMPBELL Achill Archaeological Field School

TRACY COLLINS Aegis Archaeology Limited

COLM J. DONNELLY School of Natural and Built Environment, Queen's University Belfast

THOMAS FINAN Center for Medieval and Renaissance Studies, Saint Louis University

ELIZABETH FITZPATRICK School of Geography and Archaeology, National University of Ireland, Galway

SUSAN FLAVIN Department of Humanities and Social Sciences, Anglia Ruskin University

MARK GARDINER School of History and Heritage, University of Lincoln

AUDREY HORNING College of William and Mary and School of Natural and Built Environment, Queen's University Belfast

BRENDAN KANE Department of History, University of Connecticut, Mansfield

PAUL LOGUE Historic Environment Division, Department for Communities, Belfast

EILEEN M. MURPHY School of Natural and Built Environment, Queen's University Belfast

PAUL NAESSENS Western Aerial Survey, Oughterard, Galway

KIERAN O'CONOR School of Geography and Archaeology, National University of Ireland, Galway

JAMES O'NEILL School of History, Anthropology, Philosophy and Politics, Queen's University Belfast

PATRICIA PALMER Department of English, National University of Ireland, Maynooth

COLIN RYNNE Department of Archaeology, University College Cork

1

# Constructing selves, constructing others: Becoming and belonging in Ireland

AUDREY HORNING

## Introduction

Understandings of Irishness and the place of Ireland in the modern world are indelibly rooted in popular conceptions of the political upheavals and cultural negotiations of the period AD *c.*1200–1600. But how much do we actually know and understand about how individuals and communities in that period framed their own senses of identity? And to what extent is the historiographical emphasis upon upheaval, conflict and change really the most appropriate lens through which to understand community and individual experiences and self-perceptions? In this volume, authors explore and expose the myriad and meaningful ways in which individuals and communities understood themselves in a process labelled 'becoming and belonging'. This phrasing is deliberately employed in acknowledging that the processes of identity-making are never complete. Contrary to the way in which contemporary political agendas often present national and ethnic identities as essentialised and fixed, identities can instead be seen as constantly shifting and fluctuating. At a broader level, senses of belonging are fundamental to human society and to the maintenance, and construction, of communities of interest.

This volume is an explicitly interdisciplinary project that brings together a range of perspectives to consider the nature of identity and its relationship to cultural practices in Ireland during the period from the zenith of Anglo-Norman influence, to the refashioning of Gaelic elite identities after 1300, to and through the warfare and Plantations of the sixteenth century.[1] Combining approaches from history, literature, archaeology, architecture and material culture studies, the sixteen chapters in the book explore the complexities of identity formation, presentation and reconstitution from multi-scalar perspectives, drawing upon a wide range of source materials. While focusing on Ireland, the discussions are of relevance to all scholars concerned about theoretical approaches to identity, debates over the character and nature of the emergence of modernity, European social and political relations in the late medieval and early modern worlds, and the genesis of European Atlantic expansion.

Until recently, researching late medieval Ireland, and particularly Gaelic Ireland, was considered very much a minority pursuit. However, over the last decade, scholarship into this complex yet key period began to expand exponentially, albeit in disparate fashion.[2] For example, new studies have explored the landscape archaeology and organisation of Gaelic lordships; the cultural associations and chronologies of site types such as *crannóga*, enclosed settlements, moated sites, castles and tower houses, and assembly places; material culture and trade; and politics and political economy.[3] This volume evolved out of a successful effort to bring together scholars working individually or separately on the period to, in essence, construct a new community of interest to share insights and to bring greater coherence to the study of Ireland between the thirteenth and sixteenth centuries.

## Language Matters

In her poem 'Ceist na Teangan' (The Language Question), Nuala Ní Dhomhnaill writes: *Cuirim mo dhóchas ar snámh i mbáidín teangan* ('I place my hope in the water in this little boat of the language', as translated by Paul Muldoon).[4] As expressed by Ní Dhomhnaill, who herself composes her poetry only in Irish, language matters and must be respected. It is an indicator of identity, a facilitator of communication and a barrier to understanding. Language was (and is) a serious matter and has the capacity to obscure, undermine and even be wielded as a weapon. So in writing about the complex identities of the period AD *c.*1200–1600, it is imperative to be as true as possible to the manner in which people understood and presented themselves in the past. This desire for empirical honesty presents some challenges. How should the personal and family names of Gaelic people and the names of Gaelic territories and places be expressed today? Should the original Irish be employed or the more familiar anglicised forms, or should it be reproduced exactly as written in sixteenth-century documents? Many of those sources, of course, were written by English commentators unfamiliar with, and at times unsympathetic to, the Irish tongue. Names were misheard and rendered into something new, and alien.

With the support of all the authors in this collection, it was agreed that the best course of action was to employ Irish spellings for selected place-names, people and titles that would originally have been spoken and recorded in Irish, rather than rely upon the, perhaps, more familiar but arguably less honest and certainly less accurate English renderings (see Conventions). Some readers may find this challenging or even alienating, but de-familiarising the English version serves a critical purpose in striving towards an emic understanding and presentation of past peoples, to the extent that such a portrayal is possible given our temporal remove and the constraints of the available evidence. Emic approaches, as developed in anthropology in the 1960s, seek to understand the practices and behaviours and understandings of a group of people from their inside perspective, on their terms, utilising their own concepts and understandings.[5] This is opposed to an etic perspective, from the standpoint of an outside observer, which of necessity characterises much historical scholarship. Implementing the decision in practical terms was often far from straightforward. What is to be done with Aodh Ó Néill/Hugh O'Neill, who self-presented as both a Gaelic chief and an English lord, as explored in depth by Paul Logue (Chapter 13). Or those *ceatharnaigh* or kern whose names are only ever recorded on the margins of English documents, rendered in such improbable transliterations that the original form becomes unknowable, as may be the case with the 'Daniel McUillimet' as discussed by Patricia Palmer (Chapter 15).[6] In those instances, a poorly translated name is better than no name at all.

## Theoretical concerns

Clearly, the ongoing legacies of the conflicts and political re-orderings that emerged in late medieval Ireland and coalesced in the early modern period continue to impact how we view and employ language. But there is an even more fundamental consideration. Any work produced in the twenty-first century that purports to be able to address past concepts of being, belonging and identity in Ireland must also address the philosophical context for understanding identity, and the impact of the Enlightenment on Western categorisations of the self. If we are truly seeking to achieve an emic understanding, then we must accept that people in the past, people in Ireland AD *c.*1200–1600, are likely to have understood themselves in a very different way to how we conceptualise ourselves. Overemphasising individual autonomy and assuming a desire for individual rights are difficult to avoid when socialisation in much of the modern Western world emphasises the centrality of the individual. The prevalence of agency approaches in archaeology since the 1990s, which emphasise the ability of self-aware individuals in the past, acting with intentionality on their worlds, illuminates the challenge of not back-projecting contemporary understanding of individualism.[7] Society in later medieval Ireland was clearly characterised in part by its hierarchical nature and by the importance of communal and kin-group identities. It would be folly to ignore those structures and the constraints placed upon individuals and groups. Further complicating this issue is that the latter part of the period we are examining is itself foundational to the development of the concepts that underpin notions of modernity. The dichotomisation of culture and nature, and of mind and body, inherent to Cartesian understandings of the world which emphasised empirical observation, emerged from the fifteenth- and sixteenth-century rejection of medieval scholasticism. Ireland was as affected by this fundamental philosophical shift as any other European country, with a concomitant impact upon individual and communal conceptions of what Heidegger would later label 'being' and 'being in the world'.[8]

Some of the key thinkers of the day were politically involved with the transformation of Ireland in the sixteenth century, as perhaps best exemplified by Francis Bacon (1561–1626). In his philosophical writings, Bacon concerned himself with the foundations of reason and the value of induction in scientific observation. In his political writings on Ireland, he emphasised ideas of improvement, making both the land and its people more productive and 'civilised' through both individual action and collective responsibility. Unlike more hard-line colonial theorists, Bacon was content to extend participation in this new Ireland to the Irish, provided they accepted and adhered to a new set of cultural beliefs and practices presented as more rational and modern.[9] However, focusing too much on Bacon's perspective on the Irish would obscure and indeed fundamentally misconstrue the level of engagement by Gaelic and Old English elite with the same new ideas of science and rationalism that inspired Bacon. Long connected within continental networks, these elites were immersed in discourses on humanism, discourses that emphasised individualism and intellectual curiosity.[10]

Without doubt, the influence of Renaissance thinking on identities and politics in Ireland was multi-directional. The result was that core notions of identity and cultural practices were in considerable flux, a situation addressed by many of the authors in this collection. Crucially, such identity negotiations were not uniquely a characteristic of the Renaissance period. The emergence and transformation of patterns of lordship from the thirteenth century onwards can also be understood as an outcome of similar political strategising and active employment of allegiances and associations. While the transformation from kingship to lordship in the wake of the Anglo-Norman incursions has long been recognised as one of the most significant aspects of the period, the process was neither instant nor uniform at any point in time, nor were lordships ever wholly stable or impermeable to external influences.[11]

A key concern of the studies in this volume is considering how individuals and groups constructed, presented and understood themselves, and the manner in which we can intuit those understandings from the very different types of sources left to us. Authors consider the extent to which the evidence may suggest a relational character to identities in Ireland, whereby senses of being are constructed through engagements with others. At the same time, the power of the past in both framing and providing stability in identity formulations becomes explicit when we see the ways in which groups intentionally call upon their own histories and connections to place, to reaffirm and bolster identity and solidarity. Groups and identities can define themselves in multiple ways. For example, in Chapter 4, Tracy Collins presents a focused consideration of one particular gendered identity, that of the nuns whose lives became defined and identified with the new monastic orders introduced to Ireland in the twelfth century. Her research demonstrates that while their monastic identity was clearly pre-eminent in structuring daily life, individual nuns also actively balanced a number of other significant identities that linked them with patrons and communities outside of the nunneries themselves, identities linked to economic engagement as well as to kinship ties.

In Chapter 2, Tom Finan provides a close-grained consideration of the ways in which the Mac Diarmada lords shaped their identity in the thirteenth century. Subordinate to the Uí Chonchobhair, the Mac Diarmada lords of the thirteenth century focused their energies upon retaining and strengthening their economic and political base in and around Loch Cé. In Chapter 5, Paul Naessens considers the ways in which another lordship consciously reconstructed its own identity. The Uí Fhlaithbheartaigh of Mag Seóla and Iarchonnacht recast themselves from an inland lordship – which was (like Magh Luirg) subordinate to the Uí Chonchobhair, with territories on the east side of Lough Corrib (County Galway) – into a dynamic maritime lordship capitalising upon the increased Atlantic trade activity of the late medieval period. The chapters by Finan and Naessens illustrate the variable responses and strategies employed by Gaelic elites in negotiating power struggles between lordships, Anglo-Normans and Atlantic traders. Through these considerations, Gaelic elites emerge as both self-aware and highly strategic, often manipulating seemingly timeless cultural practices in order to retain or enhance political power in the face of new challenges. Active strategising rather than static complacency was clearly the norm, but importantly, it should be recognised that each lordship shaped their own solutions to their own problems. Diversity across and within lordships has increasingly been recognised as a fundamental element of late medieval culture and society throughout Ireland.[12] There was no uniform response to external challenges.

Another significant cultural influence on the island of Ireland during this key period was Scotland, most notably via the activities of Clann Domhnaill in north Ulster. In Chapter 7, Colin Breen overtly challenges traditional views of north and northwest Ulster as culturally isolated in the late medieval period by exploring the actions and influences of both Clann Domhnaill and Clann Suibhne, which clearly linked the north of Ireland with Argyll, the Western Isles and the wider world. Moving from regional to individual identities, Paul Logue (Chapter 13) then presents a complex reconsideration of the ways in which Aodh Ó Néill actively utilised the built environment as part of his transcultural strategising. Ó Néill consciously deployed his familiarity with both English and Gaelic defensive and settlement forms, shifting between his *crannóga* and his castles depending upon his audience. In Chapter 12, Eve Campbell shifts the focus from Gaelic identities to the ways in which the Anglo-Norman Nugents materialised their power in Delvin. The Nugents endeavoured to surmount their newcomer status by deliberately employing archaic architectural features in their new castle in a bid to claim ancestry and legitimacy. Such a strategy would be widely repeated in later centuries by incoming English planters who, rather than building anew as directed, more often than not refurbished and reclaimed existing buildings.[13] Exploring elite identities on the island of Ireland is not simple, but it is undeniably aided by the survival of associated structures and landscapes, and documentary sources ranging from bardic poetry to official English government records. Extrapolating the experiences and identities of the non-elite is a far more difficult task, and is the issue taken up in Chapter 15 by Patricia Palmer. Through painstaking examination of documentary sources, she finds tantalising evidence for both quotidian and extraordinary activities undertaken by the poorly documented, but resists the temptation to relegate these shadowy figures to mere representatives of an undifferentiated underclass.

What actions, places and things reflect or even embody culturally distinct practices? Food-ways, material culture, landscapes, warfare and politics have always been seen as central to the construction and negotiation of identity, yet interpretations of these cultural expressions are seldom as straightforward as they might seem. Can we actually intuit anything about the identity of a group of people from their pottery, houses and foodstuffs? Archaeologists have long endeavoured to do just that, but have struggled with some of those same Cartesian concepts which also impede understandings of personal identities. Objects become alienated from their use history and multiple meanings and become merely representational of some kind of fixed association. However, as many of the chapters in this volume reveal, those same items also reflect, and indeed materialise and make manifest, identity transformations. For example, in Chapter 6, Colin Donnelly and Eileen Murphy focus their attention on violence, often presumed to be a key feature of the Gaelic experience in the late medieval period. Working from the evidence uncovered at five late medieval cemeteries, they argue for a more nuanced understanding of the extent and character of internecine conflict, noting a relative dearth of physical evidence for traumatic injuries and questioning the historiographical focus on violence. The role of the *crannóg* as a distinctively Gaelic site type is the topic of Chapter 8, by Kieran O'Conor. Here he asks a key question: what is the meaning of the continued use of seemingly archaic forms like the *crannóg* and slight, post-and-wattle buildings by the Gaelic elite, particularly when viewed in light of the widespread uptake of other more 'modern' forms of architecture, such as the tower house or, earlier, impressive ecclesiastical structures that clearly reference up-to-date continental architectural design? The answer lies in recognising the conscious decision-making practices of the builders and users of these forms, and what they were seeking to achieve. There appear to be no uniform patterns across Gaelic lordships in terms of the use, reuse, and/or abandonment of these forms.

Issues of continuity and change also permeate Chapter 3, by Colin Rynne, who draws upon archaeological and documentary sources in relation to milling practices in order to address the complex interplay between food-ways, technology and identities. As he notes, Anglo-Norman and Gaelic food-ways and practices overlapped, but differed in subtle yet important ways, which can be elicited through careful interrogation of evidence relating to technological change and continuity. Moving from material culture to landscape, in Chapter 9 Elizabeth FitzPatrick provides an in-depth exploration of the manner in which hereditary Gaelic service families employed the landscape, and their hereditary claims to mensal lands, as a significant form of place-making and identity construction. Chapter 10 continues the theme of landscape interpretation, as Mark Gardiner explores the tantalising yet ephemeral evidence for non-elite settlement forms. Presenting the results of recent fieldwork in the Antrim uplands, he reminds us that while such fieldwork is critical in uncovering new evidence, what is first needed is a much better understanding of the economic system under which the non-elite operated, modified and understood their environments.

In Chapter 11, Susan Flavin turns our attention to the material practices of the Gaelic, Old English, and New English elite in the sixteenth century. Her focus is upon consumption practices and, in particular, the extensive circulation of luxury items in Ireland as revealed through extant port books. Like so many other of the chapters in this volume, her research makes it absolutely clear that late medieval Ireland was very well connected to the continent and far from being insular and static, elite society on the island were active contributors to the expansion of trade relations and the adoption of new fashions in food, drink and material culture. Such an outward-looking attitude is similarly reflected in the evidence presented by James O'Neill in Chapter 14, where he argues for a particularly military revolution in the late sixteenth century in terms of the strategies and tactics employed by forces under the command of Aodh Ó Néill. Combining up-to-date continental weaponry with an intimate knowledge of the Irish landscape (and how best to move around in it) served the forces well at iconic battles, such as at Yellow Ford. While in the end the troops were defeated, it was not for lack of innovation and creativity. But what of other less tangible practices? In the final chapter of the volume, by Brendan Kane, political awareness and action can be thought of as a form of identity-making, as the non-elite can be seen, through careful interrogation of the documentary records, to be both challenging and shaping political structures in late medieval and early modern Ireland. The emergence of popular politics in Ireland, he argues, is a phenomenon very much linked to the period of the sixteenth century, and one which comes to characterise early modern Ireland.

## Exploring identity

Identity as a theoretical concept is core to contemporary historical, anthropological and archaeological discourse. Identities can be ascribed, achieved, performed and subverted over the course of an individual's life, while remaining always subject to biological and societal constraints. Identity, and particularly identity transformation, must be fundamental to any consideration of lived experience in Ireland during the period AD *c.*1200–1600. Those 400 years encompassed the zenith of Anglo-Norman influences; the transition from Gaelic kingship to lordship; the ideological, religious, political and physical conflicts associated with Reformation; and the forcible reassertion of English control that ultimately culminated in the implementation of Plantation projects that brought new people and ideas to the island. The political legacies of these four centuries live on and the period remains central to current debates about Irishness and about the place of the island of Ireland in the modern world. How can we best characterise and understand the nature of identity and identity transformation during this crucial timeframe in such a way as to both do justice to the people of the past while remaining ever aware of the contemporary ramifications of our discussions?

To start with, approaching any identities anywhere in the past invariably occurs through the lens of the present, as we construct, deconstruct and reconstruct past peoples' meaningful existences for our own purposes. We seek heroes and heroines, identify and excoriate villains, empathise with victims and, by and large, overlook the lazy, the confused, the conflicted – the human. On a broader scale, nations have long based unified national identities on the often shaky foundations of the past. Examples are well known and not hard to find: we could look back at the collapse of the Ottoman Empire, when archaeological notions of a Mesopotamian culture were used by British imperial diplomats, including the archaeologist Gertrude Bell, as the explicit foundation for the construction of the new nation of Iraq.[14] Or we could consider the significance of renaming a newly postcolonial nation after a significant indigenous archaeological site, as in the case of Zimbabwe;[15] or at the continual wrangling between Greece and the Former Yugoslavian Republic of Macedonia over claimed links to ancient Macedonia and Alexander the Great.[16] Irish archaeology has long been implicated in similar identity politics, from its antiquarian origins to de Valera's notion of the authentic, to the international marketing of Irish heritage today, to the centrality of the past in the contemporary peace process – all collectively rendering our current efforts to comprehend past experiences so much more challenging, if so much more worthwhile.[17] Of particular relevance to this collection is the fact that the common conception of a fourteenth- and fifteenth-century Gaelic resurgence cannot be divorced from its historiographical framing within the twentieth-century debates over the construction of an Irish national identity. Essays in this volume interrogate the notion of Gaelic revival, usefully moving us beyond the dichotomous opposition between Anglo-Norman and Gael by highlighting mutual entanglements.

We have stock figures from late medieval Ireland essentialised in memory, from war leaders to mercenaries, to clerics, to merchants, to peasants; characters all presumed to have held dearly to fixed ethnic identities: Gaelic, Anglo-Norman/Old English, New English, Scottish. Yet invariably, on a closer look, the edges of our sharply drawn caricatures begin to blur, to fade, to blend into the opposition. To take one example that Paul Logue explores (Chapter 13), Aodh Ó Néill is conventionally remembered as a Gaelic chieftain and heroic war leader, requiring us to forget his time growing up in the Pale, to dismiss his ability to converse easily in English, to overlook his insistence on employing an English tutor for his children, and to dismiss the intelligence that lay behind his active manipulation of his own cultural identity.[18] Or we might reflect upon English military man Captain Thomas Lee, who in 1594 posed for a portrait wearing a stylised version of Irish soldiers' clothing,[19] while, as James O'Neill (Chapter 14) considers, Gaelic military leaders readily adapted up-to-date continental weaponry and tactics, a far cry from romanticised nationalist imagery of heroic Gaelic warriors bravely clinging to weapons as archaic as their ideals.[20] These mutations beg explanation and challenge our collective yearning for a straight story. The easy way to address these contradictions is simply to acknowledge complexity in the past, a not-uncommon conclusion in historical research. However, it is just not good enough, or satisfying enough, to simply pepper all of our descriptions and discourses with handy words such as 'complicated', 'nuanced', 'multi-faceted' and leave it at that, as if all of our transcultural actors had no individual sense of self or of others and as if by acknowledging the complexity of the past we are relieved of the need to closely examine its construction and its uses in the present.

So how might we best explore becoming and belonging in Ireland from AD *c*.1200–1600? If we take our lead from the social sciences, there are a number of ways in which to frame considerations of identity and particularly ethnicity. The fundamental distinctions come down to primordial versus instrumentalist approaches.

Primordial identities are fixed: you are born into a family and a community with a set of beliefs and practices which define the group and therefore define the individual. A belief in primordial identities underlies the normative, functionalist model of culture derived from the late-nineteenth-century studies of the French sociologist Emile Durkheim, and the early-twentieth-century work of social anthropologists such as Bronislaw Malinowski and A. R. Radcliffe-Brown.[21] In a functionalist model, cultures are bounded groups that seek stability and reproduction; cultures are discernible through their own distinct set of practices, behaviours and material culture. Few anthropologists today would adhere to a purely functionalist model of culture, but the idea of fixed cultural identities still holds sway in some areas of archaeology. For example, the increasing application of DNA analysis to address past identities represents a variant of primordialism, whereby the most important element of an individual's identity is their genetic code. Genetic heritage serves as a proxy for identity but, in reality, it reveals little about an individual beyond the origins of their ancestors. In aggregate, DNA studies are certainly very useful for understanding past demography and mobility, but tell us nothing about lived experience and the multitude of ways in which an individual may have self-identified over their life course. More problematic are the ways in which scientific research into genetic heritage can be readily politicised in the present to both promote and disenfranchise contemporary interest groups in the service of territorial disputes and national claims.[22] Primordialism is clearly implicated in nineteenth-century framings of the Gaelic Irish, as once summarised by Katharine Simms thus: 'the descendants of the original population of Ireland who preserved their own culture after the Norman invasion and remained socially and politically distinct from the colonists' "Anglo Irish" community'.[23]

By contrast to such primordial framings, instrumentalist approaches position humans as active strategists, capable of altering circumstances and opting in and out of groups. So instead of conceptualising Gaelic Irish and Anglo-Norman individuals as members of utterly separate communities with distinct cultural traditions, we can begin to explore the blurring at the edges of these identities, the meshworks of relationships that actually bound groups together and the ways in which individuals and groups intentionally constructed senses of self and other. Arguably, instrumentalism was even institutionalised in late medieval Ireland, through the practices of *gossiprid*, as discussed by Susan Flavin in Chapter 11, and fosterage. Although fostering was condemned in the Statutes of Kilkenny, aspirational Anglo-Norman elites recognised the strategic value of affiliated kinship with Gaelic lordly families. Peter Parkes notes the case of Gerald, earl of Desmond, who acquired a royal licence in order that his son be fostered by Conchobhar Ó Briain. Beyond the political value of customs of fosterage, it would be folly to overlook the cultural implications of the practice, and of *gossiprid*, which could link lords and clients together across apparent cultural boundaries.[24] A child's daily exposure to customs, language, food-ways and material culture provides for an embodied perception of social worlds that is foundational to what Bourdieu referred to as the *habitus*, a set of socialised norms and tendencies that while not fixed, provides an often unconscious structure to daily life and perceptions.[25] An individual who has undergone a fosterage experience as a child carries aspects of those embodied dispositions throughout life, invariably impacting upon engagements with self and others, and contributing to the emergence of hybrid cultural practices and understandings.

Other forms of instrumentalist strategising can even include a group actively promoting the notion of their own primordial identity, as Elizabeth FitzPatrick discusses (Chapter 9) in relation to the ways in which hereditary Gaelic service families endeavoured to materialise and normalise their offices and attendant identities by identifying with the antiquity of the lands on which their settlements were located. Similarly, Kieran O'Conor's discussion (Chapter 8) of the use of seemingly archaic forms of buildings by the Gaelic elite reveals this practice to be a deliberate strategy intended to display the ancient pedigree of the lord, thereby normalising their reign.

The Norwegian anthropologist Fredrik Barth was the classic proponent of an instrumentalist approach, arguing that ethnic groups in particular are not the result of geographical or social isolation, nor are they bearers of discrete cultural entities, but instead they are effectively interest groups. Barth emphasised the significance of boundaries as the essence of 'ethnicity', focusing not upon essentialised characteristics of groups, but rather upon how groups define themselves and negotiate their identities in relation to others. For Barth, an ethnic identity is not a fixed, static construct, an understanding of ethnicity echoed in that provided by Sîan Jones (1997, 100): '... a variable social phenomenon; it is created and recreated constantly'. Key to Barth's formulation is the construction of difference through the active maintenance of boundaries. In essence, you know who you are because you know who you are not. Boundaries serve as the foundation for group identification and as such, groups, and by extension boundaries, persist because of particular advantages, but can be rejected or reconstituted as circumstances and needs change. Such processes are considered by Tracy Collins (Chapter 4), when she looks at the establishment and maintenance of distinctive female monastic communities, communities very much defined by their boundaries.[26]

Building on instrumentalist approaches, scholars have increasingly emphasised individual agency and the ways in which past people consciously fashioned their own identities and directed their own engagements with the world. For example, discussions of creolisation, hybridity and ethnogenesis fall into this category, with their interpretative focus upon the emergence of new forms of identity through both conscious and unconscious means. However, such emphasis on agency and individual freedom may be as problematic as our essentialised stock characters with their static identities fixed at birth. Characterising past actors as all self-aware and individually responsible for constructing selves risks effectively imposing the contemporary western cult of the individual onto the past, force-fitting past individuals like the late sixteenth-century Munster planter and Atlantic adventurer Sir Walter Raleigh into the guise of a self-made Marlboro man; even given his legendary role in popularising New World tobacco, this characterisation overlooks the constraints on his ability to control his own destiny. Everything was not possible in the past, just as it is not in the present.

So when we struggle to intuit past senses of identity and what it meant to continually become and belong, or shift how one became and belonged, we have to consider structure and agency: the influence of communities of practice, communities of belief, external forces and individual negotiations, both conscious and unconscious. Critically, how do we address or 'see' the relational nature of structure and agency through material culture? What does material culture have to say about identity? What does it mean that *crannóga* continue to be a significant locus for activity, as considered by Kieran O'Conor (Chapter 8) and Paul Logue (Chapter 13), or that Ireland continued to rely on private mills long after the Anglo-Normans introduced new technologies, as Colin Rynne ponders (Chapter 3)? Such examples could easily be taken at face value as evidence for cultural atavism, but that explanation is not wholly plausible given the documented character of extensive political and social transformation wrought by the engagements between disparate interest groups over this period, demonstrable also through the innovation displayed in the construction of new types of buildings within Gaelic settlements. Instead, what emerges from the studies in this volume is a sense of the very active and dynamic role played by material culture, architecture, landscape and settlements in the constant negotiation and construction of identities by all the communities and interest groups on the island. Perspectives that stress dynamism and ambiguity in considering the impacts of encounters thus seem to provide the most productive avenue for approaching the entanglement of identity and material culture, as such approaches are all founded on the assumption that change is a constant for all human cultures. Material culture then becomes less a reflection of primordial identities – 'this is a Gaelic Irish object' – and more of an active constituent in dynamic processes of identity formation, with all parties acting upon one another and objects capable of holding multiple meanings. Material culture, and the way it is altered through encounter, can facilitate and structure communication.

The well-known Dungiven costume serves as a point of departure to consider the interplay between objects and identity, and also of how contemporary preoccupations can warp our engagement with material evidence.[27] While chronologically the costume falls into the tail-end of the period considered in this volume, the issues it raises are pertinent to our considerations of identity in the centuries before its production, use and deposition. Consisting of a scattered set of clothes of late sixteenth- to early seventeenth-century date, the Dungiven costume was found by accident in 1956 when a ditch was being mechanically excavated in Flanders townland, just outside of Dungiven in County Londonderry. Incorporating a woollen mantle, woollen doublet, tartan trews, leather shoe fragments and a length of leather belt, the clothing was acquired by what is now the Ulster Museum and a replica made for display.

Until recently, the clothing was interpreted by the museum as associated with a Gaelic Irish identity, an association supported by the presence of the mantle (Gaelic *brat*): a large semi-circular woollen garment that wrapped around the body and was worn by all classes of society.[28] Sixteenth-century characterisations of the mantle as quintessentially Irish in its usage and character trace their parentage back to Cambrensis, who described Irish clothing in this fashion: 'Their clothes are also made after a barbarous fashion ... They use woollen rugs instead of cloaks, with breeches and hose of one piece, or hose and breeches joined together, which are usually of some colour.' The integral and powerful relationship between clothing and identity led to continual efforts to legislate who could wear what apparel and when. Clothing was understood to mark ethnicity, class, status, age and gender. Transcending or subverting sumptuary laws, as well as culturally accepted norms, served as a fundamental source of anxiety through the entire late medieval period. The 1367 Statutes of Kilkenny ordered the English to adhere 'to their own custom, fashion, mode of riding and apparel', just as the 1537 Act for the English Order, Habit, and Language insisted that 'no person or persons ... shall use or wear any mantles, coat or hood after the Irish fashion'.[29] The continued need for such decrees makes it clear that individuals routinely adopted and subverted what were intended to be understood as culturally specific articles of clothing. Evidence for the strategic use of fashion in the latter end of our period of interest can be found in the code-switching employed by the Earl of Desmond and his wife Eleanor. Between 1567 and 1573, the pair were held under house arrest in London and while there, sported English-style clothing. Upon return to Munster, however, they reportedly changed into clothing described as 'Irish rayment' to better facilitate their re-engagement with their tenants and local peers.[30]

While the Museum displayed the Dungiven clothing as an exemplar of Gaelic fashion, a conflicting interpretation was posited by the former chairman of the Ulster Scots Agency, emphasising the Scottish nature of the outfit as attested to by the presence of tartan cloth in the trews (Gaelic *triubhas*). While tartan is not uniquely Scottish, the cut of the trews may well support an origin in the Scottish Isles or Highlands, but not the Scottish lowlands most commonly associated with a contemporary Ulster Scots identity, given the influx of Presbyterian immigrants from the Lowlands who came to the north of Ireland in the later seventeenth and eighteenth centuries.[31] As yet no claim has been made for the English identity of the garments and their former incumbent, despite the woollen doublet being derived from documented English fashion of the 1570s, while the shoes (of an Irish brogue style) employ an intriguing mixture of English stitch and Irish thong construction. Closer examination of the elements of clothing makes it obvious that the outfit was not designed as a 'costume', intended to be worn together in an early example of fusion fashion. All of the elements exhibit considerable wear and tear and careful patching and repair. Far from being a designed outfit, it is clear that this is a mismatched set of second-hand, if not fifth-hand, garments worn by someone whose life ended in a bog in the patrimonial lands of the Ó Catháin lordship of Ciannacht.

So what was the identity of the wearer? Irish, Scottish, English? The multi-ethnic pedigrees of the individual elements of clothing reflect the diversity of peoples present in the later medieval landscape of Ulster, including Gaelic Irish and Old English, English servitors and planters, Scots *gallóglaigh* and those descendants of the Scottish Clann Domhnaill and Clann Suibhne, discussed by Colin Breen (Chapter 7), who had settled in Ulster in the thirteenth century. The gender-specific nature of the clothing suggests that the wearer was male, but without the body we will never know much about his embodied experience, what labours, illnesses or injuries may have left tell-tale traces on his bones, as Eileen Murphy and Colm Donnelly (Chapter 6) are able to explore in their thought-provoking consideration of the osteoarchaeological evidence for limited violence in late medieval Gaelic society. Exactly how the wearer perceived his hybrid attire in relation to his own perceived cultural identity is impossible to know, but it is unlikely to reflect any of today's efforts to assign an exclusive Irish or Ulster Scots label. However he self-identified, his life was undoubtedly constructed below the level of political manoeuvring and negotiation documented for more elite members of society, such as the lordships that are analysed in depth by Brendan Kane (Chapter 16) and Thomas Finan (Chapter 2). Instead, our protagonist is as fleeting as the fugitives that Patricia Palmer (Chapter 15) discusses, individuals who accidentally intrude into the documentary record as one-off references, then fade again into anonymity.

While these barely documented individuals were self-evidently not political decision-makers, they were equally affected by those decisions; such people were often the first brokers of cultural change through the sheer necessity of working alongside unfamiliar others to perform the labour and service required by an ever-changing succession of leaders and overlords. The pragmatism and creativity implied by the mixed and matched Dungiven ensemble exemplifies the character of non-elite entanglements, raising the key question of the extent to which material blending may well have been the norm in the late medieval Irish landscape, as unfamiliar items gained new meanings in juxtaposition with the familiar. Individual elements of the outfit would have been familiar to any observer; the 'Irish' mantle or *brat*, the 'English' doublet, the 'Scottish' trews, provide a starting place from which to communicate with and understand the wearer. The totality of the ensemble, however, and the juxtaposition of its individual parts, would inevitably confound efforts to readily pigeonhole the identity of the incumbent. The ambiguity of the cultural associations of the Dungiven costume challenges Barth's understanding of boundaries as central to the construction and maintenance of ethnic identities because it so clearly transcends those boundaries by demonstrating both their contingent nature and their permeability. Instead, it may be better understood as occupying what the postcolonial scholar Homi Bhabha labelled as 'third space': a zone of ambiguity, contestation and negotiation where multiple and contingent meanings can exist simultaneously.[32]

A similar 'third space' may be represented by those enigmatic beehive-shaped houses found on maps of Carrickfergus dating to 1560 and 1567, which Mark Gardiner explores (Chapter 10). As an English garrison, Carrickfergus was supposed to be a culturally exclusive zone, but the shadowy presence of clearly non-English dwellings within the settlement serves as a clear reminder that intention and reality are often very different. First established as an Anglo-Norman stronghold, Carrickfergus later served as a key stronghold for the Crown in the northeast, but in reality it was never a wholly English enclave. In addition to the cartographic evidence for Irish dwellings within the town, the principal patron of the Franciscan friary at Carrickfergus was not an Old English family, but rather the Gaelic Clann Aodha Buidhe Uí Néill. Furthermore, in the sixteenth century, Carrickfergus was situated at the interface between territory controlled by Clann Aodha Buidhe and that of the Scottish Clann Domhnaill. The English constables assigned to hold the castle and town for the Crown therefore had to negotiate their positions very carefully. Carrickfergus was not only a military stronghold, but a key entrepôt. The merchants of the town invariably engaged in trade with Irish and Scots as well as Old and New English.[33]

The constable of Carrickfergus from the late 1550s into the 1570s was Captain William Piers, who maintained his own tenuous control by carefully cultivating his relationship with the Scots and especially Clann Aodha Buidhe, while claiming to the Crown that he held sway over both powers. This strategy ultimately backfired when Piers was arrested in 1573 and accused by the Earl of Essex of performing espionage on behalf of the Uí Néill and their then-allies. Essex lent weight to the accusation by alleging in a letter to the Privy Council that Piers' 'wife's brother was one of the Scots', further underscoring the complexity of cultural and political relationships in sixteenth-century Ulster, when (much as today) the personal could also be political.[34]

Piers' active strategising, invariably influenced in some manner by his own daily familial engagements, relied upon the same type of creativity and pragmatic exchange exemplified by the Dungiven costume, while his success in attaining sufficiently in-depth knowledge of his enemies clearly carried the demonstrated risk of being perceived as alien to, or betraying, his own cultural identity. A consideration of the process of mimesis can be of particular value in interpreting such actions. Mimesis involves the interpretation and imitation of behaviour, and it occurs across cultural boundaries. It is not simply a coping strategy engaged in by oppressed others, but a strategy employed by those in authority endeavouring to understand the behaviour of those over whom they sought to wield power, as well as those struggling to gain ascendancy when lines of authority are unclear, as in Carrickfergus. Copying can be flattering and reflect fascination and admiration, but can also be insidious, insofar as the act of copying ultimately takes power away from the original.[35]

One example of mimetic practice in later medieval Ireland involves English efforts to replicate Irish forms of behaviour regarding hospitality, whereby lavish displays underpinned lordly status for Gaelic and some Old English elites.[36] Rather than investing in architecture, Irish nobles directed their wealth towards feasting and conspicuous consumption. Political power was reflected in the ability of the host to attract noble guests and to demonstrate generosity through abundant food and drink, itself extracted as tribute from the tenantry. Given that the acceptance of hospitality entailed acceptance of obligation, hospitality served to cement social ties and reify socio-political hierarchies.[37] Generosity had to be acknowledged, however, which meant that it had to be recorded and proclaimed by bards and chroniclers, whose critical role in the maintenance and promotion of lordly power is considered by Thomas Finan (Chapter 2) as one component in the political toolkit of a Gaelic lord. Catherine O'Sullivan provides many examples of literature celebrating lordly generosity, such as a thirteenth-century poem that extolled the hospitality of Brian Mág Shamhradháin ('numerous are the gold cups' that Brian provided for his guests); and a fourteenth-century description of Donnchadh Mac Conmara as 'a handsome purveyor of the wine feast'.[38] The late sixteenth-century poetry of Tadhg Dall Ó hUiginn similarly proclaimed the munificence of Cú Chonnacht Óg Mag Uidhir: 'I sat on the right-hand of the champion of Tara, till the circling of goblets was over; although it had its due of nobles the king's elbow never disdained me.'

As explored by Bernadette Cunningham and Raymond Gillespie, annalistic reports also highlight hospitality practices. One of many examples can be found in a chronicle of the generosity of Ruaidhrí Mac Diarmada: 'it is not possible to count or over-reckon all that he gave to the poets, and professors, and learned men of Erinn, and to all men besides'.[39] While O'Sullivan argues that 'by the late medieval period, little had changed for Irish nobles in the way of publicly staged hospitality', we should not presume that just because hospitality remained a key means of marking status in Gaelic Ireland, that the specifics of the hospitality rituals themselves were unchanging or archaic. The increasing availability of continental commodities, both comestible and material, undoubtedly played a role in ensuring the dynamism of such practices. As considered in depth by Susan Flavin (Chapter 11), sixteenth-century Gaelic nobles incorporated an increasingly wide array of imported continental, as well as English, luxury goods and consumables into their own repertoires. Gaelic hospitality could be both understood as a deeply rooted tradition while at the same time serving as a powerful vehicle for proclaiming the broader, up to date cultural knowledge of the lordly purveyor.

Facilitated by nodes of convergence between elite practices, such hospitality rituals were selectively imitated by English servitors, and may have been employed by Piers in his tactical dealings with Clann Aodha Buidhe Uí Néill, given his assertion to the Queen that he had been compelled to entertain 'all strangers, captains and gentlemen' in his 'house in Knockfergus' because of the lack of other suitable facilities. While we do not have evidence for how Piers looked after his visitors, we do have an extensive account of the hospitality rituals employed by another military man, Sir Richard Moryson. In 1602, Moryson was visited by Josias Bodley and a group of his compatriots. Bodley penned an extensive and revelatory account of the hospitality provided by Moryson within his Lecale, County Down castle:[40]

> Master Moryson himself leads us by wide stairs into a large hall where a fire is burning the height of our chin … and afterwards into a bed-chamber, prepared in the Irish fashion … In the midst of supper Master Morrison ordered to be given to him a glass goblet full of claret … and drank to the health of all and to our happy arrival. We freely received it from him, thanking him, and drinking, one after the other, as much as he drank before us. … And behold now the great kindness that Master Morrison shows towards us! He gives up to us his own good and soft bed, and throws himself upon a pallet in the same chamber, and would not be persuaded by anything we could say to lie in his own bed … But how can we now tell about the sumptuous preparation of everything? How about the dinners? How about the suppers? How about the dainties? For we seemed as if present (as you would suppose) at the nuptial banquet to which some Cleopatra had invited her Antony; so many varieties of meat were there; so many kinds of condiments, there would be no end of writing were I to recount all our grave and merry doings in that space of seven days.[41]

Bodley was writing about Moryson's abilities in a very bardic style betraying both knowledge of and a certain fascination with Gaelic practices. Over the week that Bodley and his men stayed with Moryson, they not only were plied with food and drink but were entertained by Irish masquers and also taken to see nearby sites of interest including 'the Well and Chair of St Patrick', a reference to the pilgrimage site of Struell Wells, situated some three miles outside of Downpatrick.[42] Moryson's behaviour as a munificent host replicated practices that he witnessed during his military service in Ireland, even though his own status was conferred not through his abilities as a host, but via his standing as a successful military leader. Moryson may or may not have consciously acknowledged his borrowings from Gaelic culture, but he is unlikely to have recognised where his understanding of ritual and use of material culture deviated from that he mimicked.

By contrast, the Offaly planter Mathew de Renzy was overt and directed in his mimicry of Gaelic practices. During the Plantation of Dealbhna Mhic Chochláin, which commenced in 1610, de Renzy set himself up in a tower house at Clonony More, to learn Irish and concoct an Irish pedigree, all in a bid to normalise and justify his position in the landholding society of County Offaly. At the same time, de Renzy exhibited considerable anxiety over what he perceived to be the historical readiness of outsiders to assimilate into Irish culture. The ambiguity of de Renzy's enthusiastic immersion in Gaelic learning, while at the same time condemning Gaelic culture, demonstrates the role of mimesis as a tool for control rather than merely evidence for admiration or assimilation. While de Renzy perceived himself as holding the upper hand over his Gaelic Irish neighbours, his incomplete efforts to ape the practices of those same neighbours must have also been a source of some local amusement whenever he failed to grasp a particular nuance of Gaelic culture.[43]

Another case in point – both of the mutability of identity and the self-aware and strategic adoption of new cultural practices – brings us back to the circumstances that saw William Piers ousted as constable of Carrickfergus by the Earl of Essex. As noted above, Piers had cultivated positive connections with Clann Aodha Buidhe Uí Néill, in whose territory Carrickfergus was situated. Key to the cordiality was Piers' relationship with Sir Brian McPhelim Ó Néill, who like many other native leaders had accepted an English knighthood and title to lands through submitting to the authority of Queen Elizabeth. However, Ó Néill soon found his position undermined when the Queen granted tracts of Ó Néill's own lands to the English planter Sir Thomas Smith in 1570. In response, Ó Néill defended his lands and reclaimed his Gaelic standing by burning out the newcomers, ordering the murder of Smith's son and ensuring that the Plantation venture was an embarrassing debacle.[44] The Queen's response was to grant Ó Néill lands to Walter Devereux, the Earl of Essex, albeit with the requirement that Essex subdue the Irish lord in order to take possession. According to Essex, Piers informed Ó Néill about Essex's designs, leading the earl to strip Piers of his constableship.[45] Essex then went in pursuit of the native leader, marching to Ó Néill's Belfast tower house in the autumn of 1574. The precise details of what next transpired are unclear, but the outline clearly indicates how Essex employed his own understanding of Gaelic hospitality practice to engineer the capture of Ó Néill.

On arrival, Essex did not seek to attack, but instead he requested entry and hospitality for himself and his men, knowing that it would be granted lest Ó Néill diminish himself through refusal. As recorded in the *Annals of the Kingdom of Ireland* (M1574), three full days passed during which Essex and his men enjoyed the company and entertainment of the Ó Néill household:

> Peace, sociality, and friendship, were established between Brian, the son of Felim Bacagh O'Neill, and the Earl of Essex; and a feast was afterwards prepared by Brian, to which the Lord Justice and the chiefs of his people were invited; and they passed three nights and days together pleasantly and cheerfully. At the expiration of this time, however, as they were agreeably drinking and making merry, Brian, his brother, and his wife, were seized upon by the Earl, and all his people put unsparingly to the sword, men, women, youths, and maidens, in Brian's own presence. Brian was afterwards sent to Dublin, together with his wife and brother, where they were cut in quarters. Such was the end of their feast. This unexpected massacre, this wicked and treacherous murder of the lord of the race of Hugh Boy O'Neill, the head and the senior.

Essex's version of events, however, was rather less colourful than that of the annalists, noting that he met Ó Néill and his accomplices outside of Belfast, and that the company 'after their dissembling manner welcomed me into the country'. Later, 'with the advice and consents of all the captains in the camp, I gave order to lay hold of Brian in the castle of Belfast where he lay ... Sir Brian and his wife, Rory Óg and Brian Mac Revelin were taken'.[46] If the account from the *Annals of the Kingdom of Ireland* is correct, or even close to correct, Essex's plan to infiltrate the castle succeeded because he understood the seriousness of proffering hospitality, while his reference to Ó Néill's 'dissembling manner' suggests he was not naive enough to believe that entertainment came without a price, even if he and his men were content to enjoy the rituals of entertainment for three full days. Essex's knowledge would have been incomplete, however, exacerbated by his inability to speak Irish. Conversations may have been mediated by the liminal figure of a translator, or conducted in Latin.[47] As such, the potential for miscommunication or the unintentional violation of a cultural norm was considerable, and may have tipped the balance towards violence rather than negotiation.

As underscored by the readiness of many Gaelic elites, like Sir Brian MacPhelim Ó Néill, to accept English titles and feign allegiance while plotting acts of resistance, mimetic practice was clearly not the sole province of the English. At the same time that Richard Moryson imitated Irish hospitality rituals in his tower house, some elite Gaelic and Old English families began to move away from a reliance on munificence and hospitality as a means of demonstrating their status. A case in point is provided by Eve Campbell (Chapter 12), where she explores the overt decision of the Nugents to abandon their medieval castle and withdraw to a manor newly built, to reflect emerging notions of privacy and increased separation between social classes. Similarly, as researched and argued by James Lyttleton, the Gaelic elite of sixteenth-century County Offaly began to construct English-style manor houses and implement the types of agricultural improvement schemes introduced through Plantation. Such actions on the part of the native Offaly elite were deliberate and intended to facilitate communication and convey their standing as equal to that of the incoming English planters. But however closely they may have copied English styles and economic practices, Offaly's Gaelic elite still found themselves subjected to land confiscations and the ultimate erosion of their political power.[48]

The examples discussed in this chapter and those presented throughout this volume serve to illustrate the dynamism of identity and its material expressions in late medieval Ireland. Critically, these studies allow for scholars to begin the very necessary process of discerning change over time during this period. While studies may pinpoint aspects of continuity through the four centuries herein examined (for example, the centrality of hospitality), overall the true constant that emerges is cultural and political dynamism. We are still just beginning to piece together the evidence needed to produce a much more nuanced understanding of each century, each half century, and each decade under consideration. Arguably, at no point within the 400-year span considered in this volume (this temporal framing being itself a somewhat arbitrary selection) were identities ever fixed in the manner that historical memory might imply. Political structures were volatile; the boundaries, hierarchies and internal structures of lordships fluctuated, and the degree to which partisans evoked the past, as well as the future, mutated according to need. Applying theoretical insights drawn from postcolonial scholarship, as considered above, provides one means of interpreting the often bewildering range of personal and interest-group behaviours chronicled in the array of sources available to scholars of the period, be it architecture, landscapes, official state records, personal letters, bardic poetry, annalistic references or portable material culture. The critical interrogation of these sources promises to significantly challenge our accepted views of Ireland between AD *c.*1200 and 1600 by shining light on contradictions and incongruities. But we must do more than just acknowledge complexity in the past. In addition to critically analysing that complexity towards an understanding of lived experiences, we should also draw lessons from the conflicts, the accommodations, the admixtures, the ad hoc solutions, the transgressions, the boundary crossings and the third spaces that host and materialise cultural discourses. We should use these lessons to confront and confound efforts to construct essentialised differences in the present on a false belief in primordial identities in the past.

## Towards the future

The study of Ireland in the period AD *c.*1200–1600 is clearly vibrant and is benefitting from productive discussions across a range of disciplinary divides. At the same time, it must be acknowledged that the period has historically been understudied, as a consequence of twentieth-century politics and perspectives on the fraught relationship between Ireland and Britain. In the first half of the twentieth century, archaeologists in the new Irish Republic intentionally prioritised the examination of early sites, as underscored by statements made by R. A. S. Macalister: 'as we review the products of medieval Ireland, we see everywhere a sad decline from the achievements of Celtic Ireland'. Furthermore, 'in speaking of the antiquities of the period ... their extension to Ireland is much more a matter of English than of Irish interest'.[49] While few would now agree with Macalister, his words and attitudes clearly stifled interest in the period and overtly situated the centuries of experiences of the descendants of the Anglo-Normans as de facto unimportant to the history of the island. At the same time that Macalister was dismissing the value of medieval archaeology, others were actively seeking evidence for untarnished Gaelic continuity as a means of identity-making in the new republic. Their work was facilitated by the establishment of the Irish Folklore Commission, whose mission was to chronicle rural Ireland as a means of bolstering Irish identity as Celtic, Catholic and rural. This perspective was given political legitimacy through the constitution drafted under the leadership of Éamon de Valera in 1937, which specifically emphasised the purity of rural life, economic self-sufficiency and adherence to the precepts and faith of the Catholic Church.[50]

We have come a long way from the essentialist perspectives of the last century in conceptualising Irish identity in all periods, and especially AD *c.*1200–1600, but there is far more work to be done. Many of the topics addressed by the authors in this volume have seldom, if ever, been tackled in any depth previously. We still lack basic, fundamental understandings of the experiences and lifeways of the non-elite, whether it is of an English-speaking craftsperson in later medieval Dublin or a transhumant Gaelic herder in Connacht. Even more well-known and visible site types, such as *crannóga*, tower houses and hall houses, have revealed themselves to be far less straightforward and understandable, the closer we look. Historical figures, on closer examination, are far less predictable in their actions and their motivations than we assumed, or hoped. Sites and site types we did not even know existed are beginning to emerge, not because they were ever hidden, but because we never looked. A case in point are the extensive traces of ports and havens that dot the Irish coastline and materialise the continental trade relations and engagement of Gaelic maritime lordships with the broader North Atlantic sea trade.[51] A traditionalist view of Gaelic society, as atavistic and insular, does not provide space for the complexities we are now recognising and exploring; neither does it allow for the ways in which communities of interests formed and dissolved, reformed and recalibrated throughout this 400-year period. As illustrated in the chapters that follow, Ireland in the period AD *c.*1200–1600 was home to individuals, families, communities and interest and kin groups who were constantly engaged in ongoing processes of becoming and belonging. Exploring the ways in which historically situated identities were defined, contested, redefined and transformed over time helps to complicate and challenge understandings of how our own contemporary society was shaped and influenced by the experiences of all those who made their lives on the island of Ireland between the thirteenth and sixteenth centuries.

2

# Identity among the Mac Diarmada lords of Magh Luirg in the thirteenth century

THOMAS FINAN

## Introduction

By the beginning of the fourteenth century the Mac Diarmada lords of Magh Luirg enjoyed a pre-eminent status in Connacht in relation to their Ó Conchobhair overlords. That relationship was formally defined as follows:

> And the ancient books of Ireland say it was in return for the kingship of Connacht that Clann Maol Ruanaigh obtained these gifts from [the kings of Connacht] as well as every other emolument they received from the kings of Leath Cuinn and from their nobles and from the chief lords of the whole of Connacht besides. For no king is entitled to be inaugurated king of Connacht except the king who is inaugurated by Mac Diarmada, king of Carrick [the Rock], as the poet, Mac an Duais, attests: When the king of Connacht is inaugurated on Carnfree, a royal assembly, no king dare approach him until the fair-headed one of Fál come with power.[1]

The thirteenth century is one of the most dynamic and curious in Ireland, and an indicator of that dynamism was, perhaps, the transition of the Mac Diarmada lords to a status second only to the Ó Conchobhair. Recent work at sites around Loch Cé has also shown that the thirteenth century was dynamic in terms of building construction. Excavations conducted at Kilteasheen in northern County Roscommon were guided by a number of research objectives from the outset, but, at heart, one lingering question is how and why an Ó Conchobhair bishop of the diocese of Elphin, a cousin of the reigning Ó Conchobhair king of Connacht, Feidhlimidh, built a fortified hall house prominently overlooking both the entrance to Loch Cé and the Romanesque church that had been built perhaps half a century earlier.[2] And how is it that a decade before the hall house was built in 1253, we find a reference to Kilteasheen, not as an ecclesiastical site, but as a staging point for Ó Conchobhair cavalry before raiding into Bréifne?[3]

This is also the century when the creation of bardic poetry begins in earnest, particularly because of patronage by the highest-level lordships.[4] It is also a century where we see an increasing shift to new families of historians, particularly in the west of Ireland, in Connacht.[5] Recent works on the various Irish annals have reminded us that the great narrative of the thirteenth century was something very new, primarily because the narrative was composed for a purpose different from that of earlier chronicles.[6] It is, perhaps, easy to consider Gaelic lordships such as the Ó Conchobhair lordship of Machaire Chonnacht as model, if only because the sources seem to give the Uí Chonchobhair priority of place, and they were one of a few dynasties able to make a claim to the high kingship when the Anglo-Normans settled in Leinster. Like all Gaelic lords, they patronised both poetry and history and, as Terry Barry has noted, they were quite adept at the construction of military fortifications along the Shannon frontier before the Anglo-Normans even arrived in Ireland.[7] On the other hand, as noted at the outset, Ó Conchobhair lords, duly inaugurated, were part of a network of political allies whose status was ritualised as part of inauguration ceremonies and hence we might ask ourselves how that network of vassal lords, in particular, negotiated their identity in an increasingly complex, violent and turbulent century.

The basic question that I propose is, what role did the Mac Diarmada lords play within that dynamic political world of thirteenth-century Machaire Chonnacht and what evidence might we provide to answer that particular question? The Ó Conchobhair and Mac Diarmada dynasties, as we know, were connected by a formal political relationship, with the Mac Diarmada lord sometimes playing the role of principal vassal and inaugurator to the Ó Conchobhair at inauguration. That particular role was not static, however, and as has been alluded to by Katharine Simms and Elizabeth FitzPatrick, the role of Mac Diarmada seems to change over the course of the thirteenth century, or at least the description of that role changes.[8] In other words, while it is almost impossible to conceive of Mac Diarmada without Ó Conchobhair, can we answer the basic question: who did the Mic Dhiarmada think they were and did that identity play into their actions in the thirteenth century?

Strategy, as in the idea of the 'Grand Strategy' described by Geoffrey Parker in his treatment of Philip II, and Edward Luttwak in his heavily criticised work on the later Roman and Byzantine empires, is a helpful guide in this process.[9] I used this model in considering the Uí Chonchobhair of the thirteenth century in *Medieval Lough Cé*; one of the reasons I moved to this model was that, increasingly, I found a disconnect between the twentieth-century historiography of Gaelic Connacht and the actual Uí Chonchobhair actions during the thirteenth century, and the results of those actions.[10] Extending all the way back to Edmund Curtis and Goddard H. Orpen, the Ó Conchobhair lords were seen as failures in the thirteenth century because they were never able to unite under one king for very long, or because they traded alliances with both Gael and Gall regularly, or because by the end of the century they had lost control of Connacht and were left with a space roughly comparable to modern County Roscommon.[11] Orpen stated directly that the imposition of English law and politics in Ireland was a good thing for these very reasons. My counter-argument was that the Ó Conchobhair lords most certainly practised some complex strategic planning, and while that strategic planning looks very different from the typical modus operandi of Anglo-Norman lords and English kings, it was nevertheless a cohesive strategy that included military tactics that preferred the use of the natural landscape as opposed to overt offensive thrusts, the patronage of historians and poets to bolster support among their own populations, external political alliances with Gaelic lords and marriage alliances that brought the first waves of Scottish mercenaries to Ireland.[12] Whether the strategy worked is, in a sense, immaterial, but to a certain extent it did work. Outside of major castles in the King's Cantred, Anglo-Norman settlement never took hold.[13] Like the Romans in the post-Octavian imperial period, the Uí Chonchobhair could never quite figure out a clean, smooth method of transition from one leader to the next but they certainly tried, as with Cathal Croibhdhearg's failed attempt to pass his title to his son Aodh.[14]

The language of strategy as employed by Gaelic lords might be seen as a tool kit, with some tools commonly employed by all Gaelic lords and some selectively used more than others. In the thirteenth century, not all Gaelic lords patronised bardic poets; the evidence clearly shows that some recognised the benefit of the poetry earlier than others.[15] In the thirteenth century in particular, the Mic Dhiarmada do not seem to have invested in the production of bardic poetry, unlike other Gaelic lords.[16] One lord used the *crannóg* as his main settlement form, while another built a moated site and yet another may have had both. One lord built new monasteries and friaries, while another ensured that his daughters married the right Gaelic lord in Ulster or in Scotland.[17] As, ultimately, the strategic goal of all of those lords was effectively the same – the maintenance of power and control over their lordships and stability within them – individual identities can only be better understood by examining the respective tool kits employed by particular lords.

This consideration of strategy might enlighten our understanding of the main focus of this chapter, the Mac Diarmada lords of Magh Luirg in the thirteenth century, because for all intents and purposes, they continued to ally themselves with the Uí Chonchobhair time and time again. The Mac Diarmada lords never tried to seize the kingship of Connacht or of the King's Cantreds from the Uí Chonchobhair. They may have selected the weaker Ó Conchobhair a few times, but usually they were able to align themselves with the ultimate winner of the Uí Chonchobhair civil wars. If we accept the *Rights of Mac Diarmada* as the fourteenth-century text that it likely is, the Mic Dhiarmada seemed to take the position of highest-status vassal with a great deal of pride. That status, alone, might cause us to pause and ponder just how a second-tier lord might behave within the context of medieval Roscommon, Connacht and Ireland, and whether he would employ the same set of tools as his Ó Conchobhair overlords. What might be more interesting to consider, however, is the fact that a century earlier, when Cathal Croibhdhearg was inaugurated, the person who gave the rod of kingship to Ó Conchobhair was not Mac Diarmada but Ó Maoilchonaire, historian to the dynasty.[18] So, in short, over the course of the thirteenth century, there is a transition in the role of the Mic Dhiarmada from one of a number of client lords to the pre-eminent client who gave the rod to Ó Conchobhair.

For the remainder of this chapter I will consider how the Mac Diarmada lords created their political identity, and I will then turn to recent field work at Mac Diarmada settlements around Loch Cé, because their settlements around the lake were, in fact, one of the most important ways in which they expressed their identity. The support of learned families might be construed as a form of internal, domestic politics, in that bardic poets and professional historians – two of the more prominent learned classes in north Roscommon – played a direct role in maintaining the pedigrees, ancestries and prowess of Gaelic lordships. In the case of bardic poetry, we can see how bardic poems were used as means of publicly creating political and historical relationships, enhancing genealogical backgrounds, and bluntly describing just how pre-eminent the patron might be.[19] In thirteenth-century Connacht we also witness the increasing significance of historians, especially the Uí Mhaoilchonaire who not only became prominent and pre-eminent historians in north Roscommon, but are the likely main sources for what should be best called the Connacht Chronicle. While the Mac Diarmada lords of the thirteenth century do seem to have patronised the learned classes, the extent of that patronage was much more limited.

In *A Nation in Medieval Ireland*, I considered the corpus of bardic poetry as literature and as a quantitative historical source.[20] Because bardic poetry can be localised temporally and physically, it is a unique source that can show particular trends in terms of thematic development, when particular families tended to patronise poets and even the travel patterns of the poets themselves. The explosion in bardic poetry production takes place across the thirteenth century, but what is more important is that the production in that century is nearly exclusively found in Connacht and the west of Ireland, and more particularly that production is sponsored by members of the Ó Chonchobhair dynasty.[21] What is also interesting is that other families, like the Uí Dhomhnaill, who began to use bardic poetry rather early, were related to the Uí Chonchobhair through marriage alliances. Yet, with all that, very little bardic poetry exists for the

Mic Dhiarmada. It could be the case that we have a somewhat distorted view of the survival of poetry by poets patronised by the Uí Conchobhair because of, for instance, the *Book of the O'Conor Don* and other *duanairí*. However, it does not seem to be the case that the Mac Diarmada lords employed bardic poets to the same extent as the Uí Conchobhair in the thirteenth century. It is difficult to imagine that the Mic Dhiarmada, who rode with the Uí Chonchobhair on more than one occasion in the thirteenth century, would not have found poet patronage to be a useful political tool. Yet, it is the fifteenth and sixteenth centuries before extensive Mic Dhiarmada bardic patronage, particularly in relation to the Ó hUiginn poets, is seen.

Gaelic lords, like their English and continental counterparts, were known for building, supporting and enhancing religious foundations within their territorial borders. Uí Chonchobhair patronage of houses in Roscommon, Cong and elsewhere is well noted.[22] The great Mac Diarmada-sponsored monasteries of northern Roscommon are also well known, especially the Cistercian abbey at Boyle and the Premonstratensian abbey at Trinity Island, Loch Cé.[23] While Boyle abbey was originally endowed by the Méig Riabhaigh at its foundation in the 1160s, the Mic Dhiarmada quickly supplanted them as the abbey's main benefactors in terms of landed wealth.[24] Most references to deceased elite Mic Dhiarmada state that they were duly buried at Boyle, as befitting the kings of Magh Luirg. Mic Dhiarmada also served in episcopal positions, for example Tomás Mac Diarmada, archdeacon of Elphin in the 1250s, and Tomás mac Fearghal Mac Diarmada, bishop of Elphin (noted as also having previously been abbot of Boyle and having followed Tomás Ó Conchobhair, the bishop who constructed the hall house at Kilteasheen) in the 1260s. The increased patronage of religious houses and the increasing references to Mac Diarmada clerics rising to episcopal office only takes place after the rise of Cormac Mac Diarmada in 1218.

Gaelic lords did not have secretaries of state or foreign affairs, but they most certainly considered their position *vis-à-vis* foreign and external political entities. Cathal Croibhdhearg and his son Feidhlimidh Ó Conchobhair were quite adept at striking a balance between local needs and the practical realities of working with the Anglo-Norman feudal structure; as tenants of the Crown both served feudal levies at one time or another, with Feidhlimidh bringing a band of his men to Wales for a short time at the service of the king. But there were other, far more practical ways to manage such foreign relations. Emmett O'Byrne has called attention to the way Leinster Gaelic lords used marriage as a political tool, and this was also the case with the Mic Dhiarmada.[25] A cursory scan of the chronicles bears this out:

> 1229.4: 'Duibessa daughter of Ruaidri O Conchobair, wife of Cathal Mac Diarmata, died a nun.'[26]
>
> 1231.2: 'Dubhchabhlaigh, daughter of Conchobar Mac Diarmata and wife of Muirchertach Muimnech son of Toirrdelbach Mor O Conchobair, died this year.'[27]
>
> 1243.2: 'Tadc son of Aed mac Cathail Chrobdeirg, after being released by O Raigillig, came to Boyle and led a company to Mac Diarmata's house. He captured Cormac mac Tomaltaig and brought away his own mother, Etain daughter of Mac Carthy, Fingen to wit, who was Mac Diarmata's wife, and gave her as wife to Cu Chonnacht O Raigillig as ransom for himself.'[28]
>
> 1269.9: 'Christine, daughter of O Nechtain and wife of Diarmait Midech Mac Diarmata, fairest of form, most bounteous and just, prudent and pious of all the women of her time, and who conferred the most benefits on the Cistercian Order, died after a triumph of repentance.'[29]

The first wife of Cormac Mac Diarmada was an Ó Dubhda, while his second wife was Étaín, the daughter of Finghin Mac Carthaigh of Desmond. What often goes unrecognised, though, is that his second wife was also the wife of Aodh mac Cathail Ó Conchobhair. This particular twisted family tree proved problematic in 1243. Tadhg Ó Conchobhair, Étaín's son by Aodh Ó Conchobhair, had been captured by the Ó Raghallaigh of East Bréifne in that year. Upon his release, he decided to raid Magh Luirg and managed to capture both Cormac Mac Diarmada and his mother, whom he later ransomed to the Ó Raghallaigh. Tadhg was seized again by the Ó Raghallaigh, who imprisoned him on Lough Allen, where he was summarily blinded and castrated. This particular narrative was the underlying cause of Uí Chonchobhair and Mic Dhiarmada raids into East Bréifne in the 1240s and 1250s, and may have had a part to play in the construction of the hall house at Kilteasheen at that strategic point where the Boyle River enters Loch Cé.[30]

A lord's capacity to freely and easily wage war when necessary would be considered another type of foreign policy. Beginning with the reign of Cormac Mac Diarmada in 1218, there is a much clearer and decisive military relationship between himself and particular members of the Uí Chonchobhair dynasty, that is those who were related to Cathal Croibhdhearg. Aodh mac Cathail, a Gaelic king who suffered from some sort of paternal anxiety, could never claim the same sort of dominance in Connacht as his father, and despite his bold attempts at exerting himself as a fiery Gaelic king of the 'old style', his style ultimately led to the encastellation of Roscommon by the Dublin government. Yet, he enjoyed the support of Cormac Mac Diarmada. At Aodh's death and with the ensuing civil war between the sons of Ruairí Ó Conchobhair, Aodh and Toirdhealbhach Ó Conchobhair, efforts concluded with Feidhlimidh Ó Conchobhair being made king by de Burgo. De Burgo and Feidhlimidh raided into north Roscommon where Cormac Mac Diarmada and Aodh mac Ruairí had brought their cattle and folk into the forests around Lough Key and ultimately fled northward. The army camped on the shore opposite the Rock of Loch Cé, and stayed there for nine nights, after which they left, 'full of gaiety and high spirits'. The following year Feidhlimidh fell out with the de Burgos, and his first, immediate ally that he sought once he escaped prison was Cormac Mac Diarmada. In 1233 Feidhlimidh and Cormac encamped at Lough Gara and afterwards attacked and killed Aodh mac Ruairí.[31]

In 1235 the frustration felt by the Dublin government and by the de Burgos led to one of the great feudal hostings of thirteenth-century Ireland, when a large force of Anglo-Normans pursued Feidhlimidh and Cormac in north Roscommon. The Anglo-Normans proceeded south from the Curlews and managed to catch Feidhlimidh and Cormac on the Rock of Loch Cé. The justiciar and the army granted general protection to all the clerics on Trinity Island and did reverence to the church. They then brought a fleet of ships with galleries and *perriers* to the lake, and mounted one *perrier* on a ship platform that they then used to attack the island. The attack was ineffective, however, so they went to the nearby town of Ardcarne, dismantled the houses there, and brought the wood to the lake in order to build fire boats. This was more than effective at drawing out the inhabitants of the Rock, who surrendered and were theoretically exiled from Connacht by de Burgo.[32] The withdrawal of Mac Diarmada to the Rock is not surprising, but what is somewhat surprising is that Feidhlimidh also resorted to the Rock as his last refuge; he certainly had access to a number of other *crannóga* that could have provided a comparable amount of protection. Could it be that the Rock was a harbour of safety unparalleled in north Roscommon at that time? After all, this was a *crannóg*, not with a wicker timber wall, but a stout, circular stone enclosure, strong enough to stand up to stones cast at it.[33]

As mentioned earlier, Cormac Mac Diarmada was joined by Feidhlimidh and Aodh mac Feidhlimidh Ó Conchobhair in exacting revenge upon the Ó Raghallaigh lords of Bréifne in the 1240s and 1250s. These strikes were not just vengeance. The Uí Raghallaigh were in a precarious position with newer settlements of Anglo-Normans popping up in Longford and Westmeath. The strikes into Bréifne must have been fairly large affairs, because it is within that context that we hear about Aodh Ó Conchobhair using Kilteasheen as his staging point for cavalry, and also as a spot where he left his cavalry to attack East Bréifne on foot. This particular incident might further explain why an Ó Conchobhair hall house was built in what can best be described as Mac Diarmada territory on the shores of Loch Cé. By the time the hall house was built in 1253, the alliance between Ó Conchobhair and Mac Diarmada was more than solid. Bréifne was a common foe and was dealt with by a combined army, stemming from Mac Diarmada lands where there was also an Ó Conchobhair fortified house, looking directly down at the Boyle river. Unlike the other ecclesiastical hall houses in Connacht, such as Kilmacduagh, the hall house at Kilteasheen was constructed outside of the main ecclesiastical enclosure on the highest land. This position enhanced the height of the hall house and the house became a significant symbol of Ó Conchobhair authority, placed directly on the Boyle river before entering Loch Cé.

The results of recent survey work carried out by Kieran O'Conor (see Chapter 8) at the Rock of Loch Cé and at Port na Carraige (a moated site across from the Rock near Lough Key Forest Park) have shown that the Rock has three distinct phases within the structure, including an earlier medieval stone enclosure, a later medieval tower house and a nineteenth-century folly.[34] The resistivity and gradiometry surveys were very inconclusive, no doubt because of significant amounts of metallic surface debris.[35] While disappointing, two resistivity tomography surveys were also conducted in the interior of the tower house, with the hope of identifying the nature of the subsurface soils upon which the tower house was constructed.[36] Figure 1 shows the sloping bedrock, which might confirm the hypothesis that the front portion of the island was added to the site at a later date than the enclosure, which itself was constructed directly on stone foundation in most parts of the island. This is an important point, because it means that sometime after the thirteenth century the Mic Dhiarmada added a tower to the enclosure, and that the tower was facing the mainland settlement.

Recent research into the nature of *crannóga* by O'Sullivan, Naessens, O'Conor and Brady has shown that later medieval *crannóga* rarely existed on their own, despite their seemingly isolated appearance in lake and riverine landscapes.[37] What this means is that there is usually a landward component of the settlement that may have been occupied by the residents of the site most of the time, with the *crannóg* used for defensive or, perhaps, hospitality purposes (see Logue, Chapter 13). As noted, the Rock of Loch Cé is deceptive because, at first glance, it appears to be a nineteenth-century folly. Once that veneer is removed and it is understood that the Rock is a well-fortified and defended *crannóg*, it makes sense to assume that there is a landward component to the Mac Diarmada *caput*.

The moated site identified by the Archaeological Survey within the Rockingham estate in the 1980s fits this description precisely, for a number of reasons. First, the Rockingham moated site is located directly opposite the pier on the Rock. It was also likely located directly opposite the main entrance to the earlier stone wall enclosure, but this is supposition given that the later medieval tower likely replaced that entrance. The two sites are connected visually and physically, in that individuals could see one site from the other, and boats could have easily moved back and forth between the sites.

Second, and perhaps most importantly, are the various references to Port na Carraige after around 1231. The term describing Port na Carraige in *The Annals of Loch Cé* is *baili marcaid*, or 'market town', which is curious as it is rarely, if ever, used within a Gaelic context before or after that mention in 1231.[38] The reference is also important because the one who built the market was a Mac Diarmada. Throughout that decade, though, the settlement was the scene of a number of attacks by Anglo-Normans, again most notably the siege of the Rock in 1235.[39] But there is a perplexing problem in that event that often goes unmentioned, despite the unambiguous narrative regarding siege weapons, fire boats and surrender of the Rock. The chroniclers say, without ambiguity, that the Anglo-Norman army had collected timber and wood at the nearby ecclesiastical settlement of Ardcarne, *c.*5 kilometres away. It seems that they were unable to secure sufficient amounts of timber from around the lake itself to construct their fireboats.

However, it could be considered that a moated site, with ancillary buildings both within and without the main structure, would provide such timber. It could be the case that the moated site was being defended, which does not seem likely, or that the Mic Dhiarmada burned Port na Carraige, which does not seem likely either as it would have been, no doubt, referenced in the annals. In addition, in both this incursion and several others in the thirteenth century, the chroniclers state that the Uí Chonchobhair drove their cattle to the forest around Loch Cé to keep them hidden from the invaders. That forest could have been located to the north of the lake, between it and the Curlew mountains, but later seventeenth-century maps of the region clearly show forest surrounding the entire lake. Why was none of this timber used in the assault on the Rock? It could be that the Anglo-Normans approached the Rock from a direction that is not obvious to the modern visitor, perhaps from the direction of the Boyle river. This too seems doubtful. The narrative of the siege describes siege engines launching from the shore, then those engines being placed on platforms on the water. It seems possible that they could have launched from the north-northwest, which would have required transporting the timber from Ardcarne through bogland.

In a separate foray into north Roscommon in 1230 the Anglo-Normans stayed on the shore opposite the Rock of Loch Cé for nine days; when they departed they were 'full of gaiety and high spirits'.[40] At the conclusion of the siege of 1235, though, the chroniclers state that the Anglo-Normans placed a garrison in the Rock with provisions, and while they held out for three weeks, they were apparently duped into opening the gate. They were forced to seek sanctuary on Trinity Island.[41] Another point to consider is that Anglo-Norman armies followed particular routes into and out of Roscommon, following what were likely roads between major ecclesiastical settlements. When they invaded from the south, for instance, they moved from Athlone, to Roscommon, to Elphin, to Boyle/Loch Cé. While Athlone had grown because of the bridge and castle constructed there, Roscommon, Elphin and Boyle were effectively ecclesiastical towns. Nevertheless, these were the centres of economic activity along those invasion roads and in that sense, after the Rock of Lough Key was suppressed, Port na Carraige was significant enough to warrant the attention of the army.

The Rockingham estate has been surveyed and studied for over a century and most of the obvious archaeological features have been noted. Yet, none of these features could conceivably be construed as Port na Carraige, given the prominence that the site is given in the historical sources. Furthermore, the connection between the Rock of Loch Cé and the moated site in Rockingham, by virtue of their visual orientation, is undoubted. The lands of the estate that are now occupied by the Lough Key Leisure Centre (formerly Rockingham House) did not show any evidence of archaeological activity. Further from the shore, the only features that were noted are a series of ringforts to the south of the Rock. The ringforts located within the present forest of Lough Key Park were surveyed as part of this project in 2014. They appear to be agricultural enclosures, possibly associated with the church at Kilbryan or perhaps tenants of Mic Dhiarmada. Furthermore, given that they were likely used as pastoral enclosures, these ringforts would seem typologically distinct from what is referred to in the name Port na Carraige. Future survey of the estate may prove this point incorrect, but there is simply no other place in Rockingham where the landward element of the Rock might be located.

In 2006 a topographical survey and gradiometry survey were conducted at the moated site.[42] The survey clearly identified the moated site and an additional enclosure to the west of it in the same field. The platform of the moated site is 34m north–south by 33m east–west and is bounded on the east side by a field wall. Half-metre scarps were identified to the west and north, while an outer moat was located on the south side of the platform (Fig. 2). The enclosure 15m to the west is oblong with dimensions of around 40m northwest–southeast and 30m northeast–southwest. These measurements

2. Gradiometry survey of Rockingham moated site (image: author using Google Earth).

and the landscape setting of the moated site would define it as a 'Category 1' moated site, using a designation defined through the use of statistical cluster analysis.[43] The qualities that put it in this category are, in order of importance, proximity to a *crannóg*, the dimensions, the presence and size of external earthworks, the proximity of the moated site to modes of transportation, the position of the moated site within the townland and the proximity of the site to ecclesiastical settlement. Another notable Roscommon moated site in this category is the Ó Conchobhair site at Cloonfree (see O'Conor, Chapter 8 and FitzPatrick, Chapter 9).[44]

A survey campaign at the site began in the summer of 2013 in order to augment the findings of the original survey completed in 2006 and to delineate any additional features through other means of archaeological and geophysical survey. A second gradiometry survey was completed on the moated site proper; the findings essentially confirmed those found in 2006, with several additional caveats.[45] To the north of the moated site is a trackway, seen only in the gradiometry, extending from the moated site to the shore and, if one were to follow the line, to the Rock of Loch Cé. A small anomaly appears in the central area of the platform. Several other potential enclosures were noted, but none were as completely discernible as the one identified in 2006 to the east of the moated site.

A resistivity tomography survey was completed on the platform from east to west across the anomaly mentioned (Fig. 3). On the far end of the resistivity section the beginnings of the ditch are just about visible to the west of the platform, an area of very high moisture. At the bottom of the section there is an area of very high resistivity. This could be the natural topography, as this spot is located on the highest land in the surrounding fields; in other words, the site could have been located here because of the natural rise which is then identified by the zone of high resistivity. Near to the surface is a small zone of relatively low resistivity surrounded by two zones of higher resistivity. A two-dimensional resistivity survey was completed in 2014, with results that detailed the ditch on the south and west sides of the square platform and that accentuated a prominent pathway crossing the ditch on the southwest corner. This two-dimensional survey also highlighted the same area of very high resistivity noted earlier.

Through the generous support of Alpha XRay and Bruker Scientific, our team was able to use a hand-held XRF analyser in the field to identify trace elements in the soil on site. XRF (x-ray fluorescence) hand-held analysers show extremely great promise for future archaeologists, as they can identify the chemical composition of soils, mortar, stone, artefacts or art very quickly, without compromising the sample or the item studied.[46] In 2013, we were keen on testing whether there was an appreciable difference in levels of phosphorus in the area where we performed the gradiometry survey.[47] The resulting map shows that there is a clear difference between phosphorus levels on the top of the platform and outside of the surrounding ditch (Fig. 4). Phosphorus is generally considered an indicator of human activity and higher levels would generally relate to areas where organic waste has been deposited or perhaps where nearby pastoral activity is taking place.

As mentioned, several ringforts are located in the surrounding townland of Rockingham, and a number of smaller *crannóga* are

4. Phosphorous analysis survey of Rockingham moated site (image: author using Google Earth).

located all around Loch Cé. A walk-over survey of the landscape surrounding the moated site leads to the suggestion that the settlement at Port na Carraige is much larger than initially assumed, and that it is likely to extend east beyond the fence and field boundary. While the Rockingham estate modified the coastline around the harbour used by most boats today, it remains to be seen to what extent the area between the moated site and the shore has been disturbed.

To conclude, I return to the two documents that refer to Uí Chonchobhair inauguration ceremonies: the first recorded as the inauguration of Cathal Ó Conchobhair, the second recorded in what is, no doubt, a fourteenth-century list of the entitlements of a Mac Diarmada lord. What has changed significantly is the position of the Mac Diarmada over the preceding hundred years or so. They moved from having the status of an important ally among many, to pre-eminent right-hand men over the course of that century. The claims found within the Rights of Mac Diarmada were bold and the fact that they supplanted the historians of Ó Conchobhair as the one to place the rod into the hands of the chief-elect shows that a new sort of relationship had developed between the lordships, one that was effectively made by Cormac Mac Diarmada and Feidhlimidh and Aodh Ó Conchobhair.

The later part of the thirteenth century saw fourteen successive Ó Conchobhair kings following the death of Aodh mac Feidhlimidh. Only one experienced a natural death and nearly all were killed by kinsmen. This put the Mic Dhiarmada in an equally precarious position, as the four Mac Diarmada lords of the late thirteenth century would have needed a score-card to manage who to support at any given time. Yet, throughout that period, they continued to maintain their support for religious houses and they continued to be buried at Boyle abbey. The fourteenth century proved to be even more complicated for Mic Dhiarmada, with the changing environment, famine, the Bruce invasion and other calamities.

Our general histories of medieval Ireland, going back to Orpen, characterise the utter failure of the Uí Chonchobhair to maintain a unified political structure over and against intrusive Normans. Phrases like 'incessant civil war', 'inability to support a single heir', 'questions of Uí Chonchobhair identity' often pop up in scholarship. My approach, instead, has been to track how the Uí Chonchobhair thought of themselves, how they presented themselves and how they used those ideas to achieve the end of political control over Connacht and especially over Machaire Chonnacht. In the Mac Diarmada lords, we can see a similar sort of strategy with a much different use of the toolbox. The Mic Dhiarmada of the thirteenth century were every bit as shrewd in their political alliances as the Uí Chonchobhair, as evidenced in the records of their marriages and their military exploits. To a certain extent, all of the other aspects of Gaelic lordship were perhaps overshadowed by one, single identifying characteristic of the Mac Diarmada of Magh Luirg: the Rock of Loch Cé and the landward settlement related to it. For it was there that Feidhlimidh and Cormac held out against the Justiciar's army and where, according to the chronicles, a 'market town' had been built by a Gaelic lord.[48] We do not hear about the cattle of Mic Dhiarmada as we do the cattle of Uí Chonchobhair.

That is probably because Loch Cé was of significant economic value to Mic Dhiarmada and while it was not as comparable an asset as the great herds of Connacht cattle that moved north and south in the thirteenth century, it was certainly profitable and strategic enough to aid the Mac Diarmada in becoming the only one allowed to grant the rod of lordship to Ó Conchobhair.

# 3

# Milling of cereals in Gaelic and Anglo-Norman Ireland *c.*1200–1500: Technology and cultural choice

COLIN RYNNE

## Introduction

The introduction and imposition of seigneurial monopolies on the milling of cereals (multure) by the Anglo-Normans created an important but seldom acknowledged conflict effecting cultural and individual choice in Ireland. In effect, multure prohibited both the ownership and use of private mills, which in many parts of Europe (including England) led to the widespread abandonment of hand querns and horizontal mills. However, whereas in later medieval Ireland the use of horizontal and other forms of 'private' milling technologies comes to symbolise, in many respects, 'resistance' to feudal law, in southern France, Iberia and Italy, certain forms of horizontal mills actually became *the* seigneurial mill. In Ireland, therefore, the continued use of private water-mills would appear to be a cultural rather than a technological choice. Consumption preferences also appear to be at play. The variety of stone used for millstones was the key determinant of the type of flour or meal produced. In the pre-Anglo-Norman period there is, as yet, no evidence for the importation of millstones into Ireland. However, the Anglo-Normans began to import these from both Wales and the continent to produce flour and meal of a distinctive flavour and quality. In Gaelic and Anglo-Norman Ireland, therefore, as will be

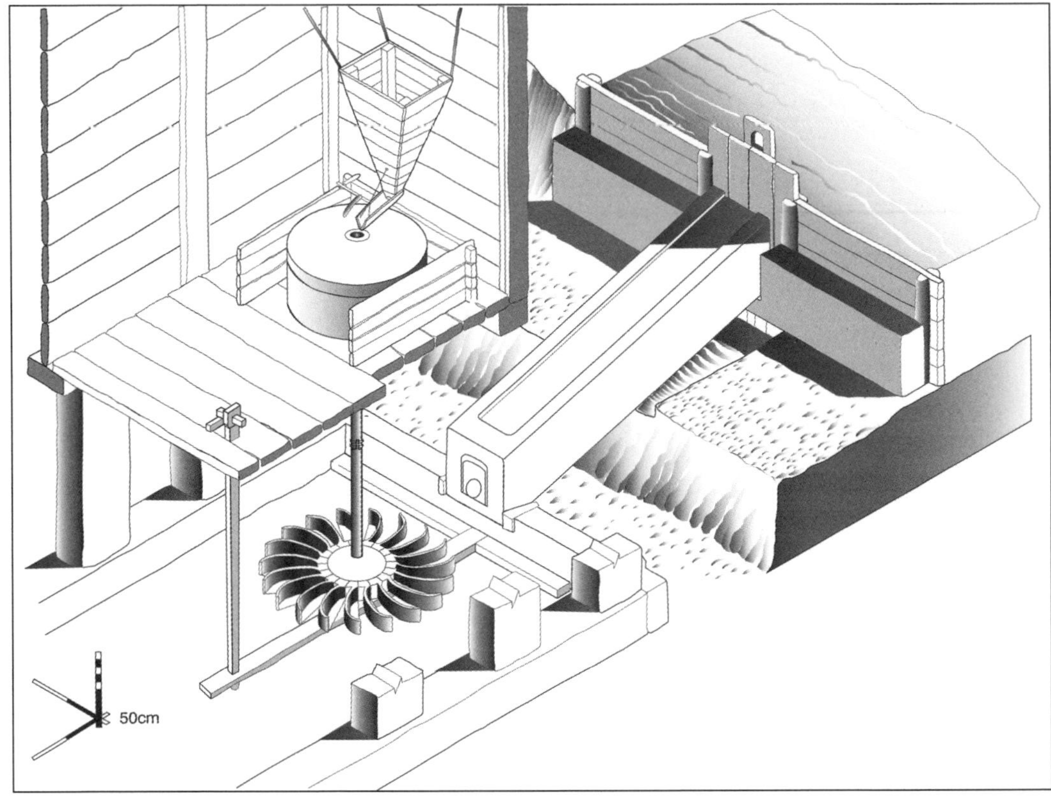


1. Reconstruction of horizontal mill from Cloontycarthy, Co. Cork, *c.*AD 833 (image: author).

argued here, continuity in the use of native milling practices and the introduction of new ones became important facets of the group identities of both native and colonist.

In order to understand the differences in the types of milled cereals produced in Gaelic and Anglo-Norman Ireland, we must begin by comparing the technologies employed. While these were largely similar, it was the purposeful choice and use of one item of the mill's mechanism – the millstones – which essentially determined the final product. In essence, the type of stone selected for grinding, its diameter, weight and speed of rotation were the key determinants in the production of a type of flour or meal required to meet the expectation of a particular ethnic grouping. As Olivia Remie Constable has recently noted, in relation to how Christians in later medieval and early modern Spain understood Muslim food-ways:

'Foodstuffs and eating traditions have always been complex in the ways they have the ability to build, define and separate communities.'[1] To this end, in order to maintain a cultural practice common in mainland Europe from the Roman period and to create the grades of flour to which they were accustomed in their homeland, Anglo-Norman communities within Ireland were prepared to engage in the long-distance importation of millstone blanks.

In early and later medieval Gaelic Ireland, by way of contrast, only native millstones were employed and in sizes which strongly suggest that bread wheat was less commonly processed than either oats or barley. This latter hypothesis will be further explored in a comparison between the types of millstones employed in Irish and European medieval horizontal and vertical watermills. Following on from this, the use of larger millstones and imported forms into Anglo-Norman Ireland will be located within a wider European context. Finally, it will be argued that the apparently exclusive use of vertical-wheeled mills within the colony, and the association of larger millstones with these, was a distinctive feature of Anglo-Norman food-ways.

## Water-powered milling in later medieval Gaelic and Anglo-Norman Ireland

Both horizontal and vertical-wheeled mills were widely employed in pre-Norman Ireland, although the former appears to have been much more common than the latter (Figs 1 and 2). Of the 153 known watermill sites recorded thus far, and dated to the period AD *c.*612–1124, only six were vertical undershot mills (Fig. 3).[2] However, a later legal commentary on the eighth-century text on land values, *Tír Cumaile*, makes explicit reference to mill weirs, the *lánsód muilinn*, or full mill weir, and the *lethsód muilinn*, or half mill weir.[3] Weirs are used to provide a suitable hydraulic head only for vertical waterwheels, and if these were being legislated for in the pre-Norman period then this suggests that watermills of this type were more common than the archaeological record would currently indicate. Within the Anglo-Norman lordship vertical-wheeled grain mills and horse-powered mills, from the late twelfth century onwards, are likely to have been almost universally employed.

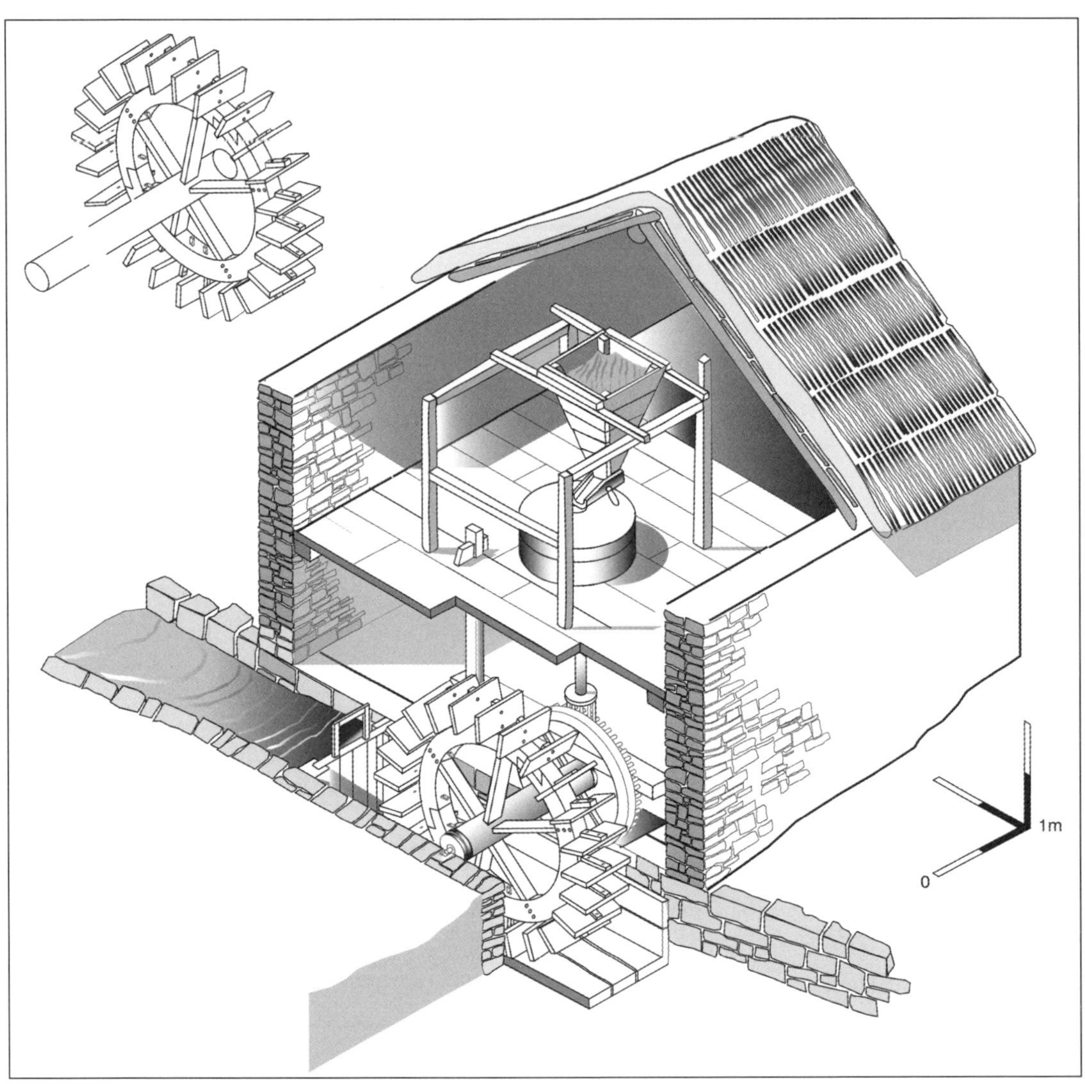


2. Reconstruction of tenth-century vertical undershot mill at Chapelizod, County Dublin (image: author).

Nonetheless, at no stage during the later medieval period in Ireland did manually operated rotary quernstones go out of use in either Gaelic or Anglo-Norman Ireland.[4]

To date, only three examples of Anglo-Norman water-powered grain mills have been excavated: two rural examples at Ballyine, County Limerick (later medieval); Twomileborris, County Tipperary with a dendro date of AD 1199–1217, and a fourteenth-century urban example at St Patrick's Street in Dublin (Fig. 4).[5] Nonetheless, while larger mills may well have been constructed within the lordship from the fourteenth century onwards, as the documentary record would suggest, none of the excavated examples exhibit any real advance on those of the pre-Norman period. Indeed, where individual mill outputs are available in Anglo-Norman sources, there is little evidence to suggest that these were in excess of many pre-1169 Irish mills, whether vertical or horizontal. Moreover, keyhole-type corn-drying kilns, the same type widely used by the Anglo-Normans to parch the grain to facilitate de-husking, was one of five types used in the pre-Norman period.[6] The technologies of milling in both the pre- and Anglo-Norman periods were, therefore, very similar. Yet, they differed in one key respect. Based on what was essentially an ethnic preference in the Anglo-Norman realm for wheaten flour, larger-diameter millstones were used in the colony almost from the outset. In pre-Norman Ireland, the predominant cereal crops were barley and oats. By way of contrast, wheat, while grown, makes up only a small part of archaeobotanical assemblages from early medieval Ireland, while the documentary evidence also suggests that it was a high-status crop more commonly given to a lord as a render.[7] Furthermore, in order to ensure the production of a particular type of flour, Anglo-Norman settlers began to import millstones from both Wales and France, and for the first time the varieties of flour produced in Britain and the continent since the Roman period began to be both manufactured and consumed in Ireland. Millstones of around 0.8–1m in diameter, which in medieval Europe as a whole would have generally been used for processing wheaten flour (see below) are rare within the Irish corpus of early medieval/pre-Norman examples (which is also the largest number of recorded examples from any region of either Europe, Africa or Asia). This would tend to confirm what other sources, archaeological and documentary, appear to be telling us about the limited consumption of wheaten flour in the pre-Norman period. As will be argued below, the preferences for certain types of cereals, and the means by which they were milled with water-powered stones, closely followed ethnic divisions in later medieval Ireland. Thus, key differences in the ways in which flour and meal were manufactured and consumed in societies where cereal foodstuffs formed a substantial component of everyday diet could at once define and separate communities in later medieval Ireland.

## The milling process

Owing to the nature of the type of flour or meal produced with millstones, milling had to be conducted regularly by the early medieval Irish household; whereas grain could be stored, stone-ground flour could not. The friction created by the grain passing between the millstones had two principal effects on the finished product. In the first, the heat generated by this process caused damage to the endosperm, which affected both its keeping quality and the performance of the ground product when baked. The second involved the inclusion of grit, becoming detached from the stone (and especially sandstones), in the flour or meal. Thus, as milling with stones seriously impaired the keeping quality of the ground product, members of the household, generally women, and of monastic communities, were obliged to use the mill on a regular basis. This, in turn, required that millstone surfaces be dressed at least twice a year, a process which itself wore down the thickness of the stone. The rate of attrition was conditioned by a number of factors, principally the type of stone involved, its hardness, tenacity (resistance to crumbling) and the volume of grain processed. The type of millstones employed in pre-Norman Ireland clearly lacked the hardness and uniformity of structure of German lava stones and French 'burr' stones widely employed elsewhere in medieval Europe. The most common variety in the Irish corpus, sandstone, had a tendency to crumble, while its quartz crystals reduced the integument of grains passed through them.[8] Granite millstones, on the other hand, while harder, tend to become polished more easily when in regular use and were therefore likely to require more frequent dressing.[9] In general this variety of stone would have created less efficient grinding surfaces than sandstone.[10] The widespread use of water-mills in early medieval Ireland strongly suggests that specialist millstone quarries existed to supply their needs. Apart from the construction of new mills, the millstones of existing ones (and especially runner stones) would also have to be replaced a number of times during the working life of the mill.

## Horizontal millstone assembly in pre-twelfth-century Ireland and Europe

The millstone assembly consisted of an upper revolving stone and a lower, stationary stone.[11] Although only one matching millstone set has been recovered to date in Ireland, that from Nendrum Mill 2, County Down, where the runner stone was 0.84m in diameter and the bedstone 0.82m, it can be reasonably inferred that the upper and lower stones in any given assembly would have been of similar diameters.[12] It has recently been suggested that 'any stone over *c*.55cm and certainly any over 60cm, unless having strongly diagnostic features to suggest otherwise, should be viewed as a probable millstone'.[13] However, caution is clearly needed here as the estimated diameter of the stones from the vertical undershot mill at Killoteran, County Waterford (AD 612) was 0.53cm, while the size of individual millstones cannot be taken as indicative of either a particular period, or even whether or not the mill was horizontal- or vertical-wheeled (see below).[14] The vast majority of the recorded examples were carved out of some variety of sandstone (usually a conglomerate), although the well-preserved millstone set from the Mill 2 at Nendrum was of granite, while a small number of further examples have come to light in the northeast and in Leinster. However, as McErlean has recently shown, early granite horizontal-wheeled millstones in Ireland are more common than has previously been supposed.[15] Nonetheless, only a handful have, thus far, been recovered outside Ulster, which include one of two massive bed-stones from Desert, County Cork, that appears to have been fashioned out of a glacial erratic of Galway granite.[16] Yet owing to their tendency to take a polish, millstones made from granite would have been of very poor quality, requiring frequent re-dressing (see above).

In most of Ireland during the early medieval period, the transportation of millstones from the quarry to the mill site would have occurred overland. The difficulties involved in quarrying and transporting a millstone are described, at length, in the late seventh-century life of St Brigit of Kildare, by Cogitosus, which in this instance required the miraculous intercession of the saint to safely bring it down from the mountainside.[17] It is often assumed that this occurred in the Wicklow Mountains, some 30km to the east of the monastery at Kildare; however, there are also good sources of both granite and red sandstone within County Kildare itself. Regardless of whether such activity was conducted on land or by sea it is likely to have required, in relative terms, considerable resources. Yet, in a wider European context, where long-distance trade in lava millstones from the Mayen-Niedermendig, in modern Germany, existed from Roman times, and continued throughout the medieval period to supply the needs of water-mills throughout Europe, the early medieval Irish millstone industry appears parochial.

On the basis of their diameters, the recorded Irish millstones can be divided into five main groups (Fig. 5). In each group there are examples which exhibit not only close similarities in size but also a wide geographical spread. This grouping also includes the Nendrum examples (0.84cm), and there is another stone in a Wicklow graveyard at Dunboyke with a diameter of 0.87m. The final group contains three millstones in excess of 1m in diameter, from Milverton, County Dublin (1.07), Mashanaglass, County Cork (est. 0.84–1.02m) and Kilturra, County Sligo (*c.*1m).[18] By reference to Table 1 it will be seen that the Irish corpus of early medieval horizontal millstones, in terms of overall diameter and the diameter of the eye, bears close comparison with the small number of examples which have come to light in Britain, Europe and North Africa. The ninth-century Tamworth site, in particular, provides a good chronological parallel for Boherduff, County Galway and Cloontycarthy, County Cork, while the Kilturra, County Sligo bedstone is comparable to that recovered from the tenth-century Valencia mill.[19] The Catalonian examples from the tenth to the thirteenth centuries, which lie in the range 1–1.2m in diameter, are also similar in size to Milverton, Kilturra and Mashanglass. An early description of a *cubo* (arubah penstock) mill near Jaén, in the Muslim kingdom of Al-Andalus, in a lease of AD 1114, which states that 'There are two pairs of flat millstones, formed of eight pieces of Arnedo stone, 31 cm thick and 1.06m in diameter', also compares well with those listed in Table 1.[20]

A further comparison with Table 2 below will demonstrate that there is no appreciable difference between the size of the millstones recovered from vertical undershot mill sites throughout the entire medieval period and those recorded at early medieval horizontal mills. As the size of the millstones is a key determinant in a mill's

Table 1. Millstones from early and later medieval horizontal mills in Europe and Africa.

| Site | Max. stone Ø M | Max. thickness cm | Form of rynd sockets | Eye Ø cm | Stone type | Date |
|---|---|---|---|---|---|---|
| Tamworth, England | RS 0.60–0.80<br>RS c. 0.70<br>c.0.80 | c. 3–7<br>c. 3–7<br>1.7–4.5 | Dovetail<br>Dovetail | | Coal measure sandstone<br>Keuper sandstone<br>Mayen-Niedermendig lava stone | AD 855 |
| Bosra, Syria | 0.80–1.20 | 12 | | | | 7th–8th centuries |
| Sohar, Oman | 1–1.08 | | | | | 9th–10th centuries |
| Valencia, Spain | BS 1.10 | 12 | | 13 | Red sandstone | 10th century |
| Church of Sant Esteve de Castellar, Catalonia | c. 1 | | | | | 10th century |
| Els Molins de la Vila, Montblanc, Catalonia | 1.10–1.2 | 16 at centre, 10.5 at rim | | | | 13th century |
| Sant Maria de Lavit, Catalonia | c. 1 | | | | | 13th century |
| El Molí de laVolta Montblanc, Catalonia | c. 1.30–1.35 | 26.5 | | | | 14th century |
| Torre Baldovina de Santa Coloma de Gramenet, Barcelona | 1.18–1.32 | 8–18 at rim. 9–20 at centre | Dovetail | | | 14th century |

productive capacity, this latter circumstance raises important questions about the relative efficiencies of horizontal and vertical watermills.

To begin with, the stones in the 0.80m–0.87m range, and in excess of 1m in diameter, are not only larger than those recorded from early medieval vertical watermills in Europe, but also from examples that remained in use up to recent times. It may well be that they had a specialist purpose such as grinding wheat (for which larger, heavier stones were preferred), or for grinding malt. The speed of rotation of the upper millstone also determines the finished product; in general, the faster the wheel turned, the finer the flour. However, when the millstone is larger, its speed of rotation is slower, and this generally produced the finest flour.

In the Irish corpus there are at least nine millstone diameters which have been recorded at least twice, and which exhibit a wide geographical distribution across the island (Fig. 5).[21] This suggests that, while these sizes were unlikely to have been regionally distinct forms, certain shared milling practices (relating to the products involved) were clearly in existence. On the contrary, the manufacture of set, predetermined millstone sizes would indicate that each diameter was intended for a specific purpose. This latter might have involved either a particular variety of milled product and/or a volume of production appropriate to local needs. There are, however, two County Cork sites, Mashanaglass and Glenwood, from which stones of different diameters were recovered, as was also the case at the Tamworth mill site. The same phenomenon has also been recorded at a number of early medieval vertical undershot mill sites, such as Dasing, Germany (seventh century) and Audun-le-Tiche, France (mid-ninth century).[22] There are two possible explanations for this practice. In the first, it may well be that the volume of production at any given mill site might either expand or contract during its working life, necessitating either the installation of larger or smaller diameter stones. The second is, in essence, a corollary of the first, where the installation of millstones of reduced diameter could have occurred on a seasonal basis to accommodate lower water levels. Similar practices have also been recorded in the traditional horizontal mills of Morocco, where the 'winter' runner stone (0.70m in diameter and 10cm thick) was replaced in the summer time with one 0.60m in diameter and some 5cm thick.[23]

A corresponding degree of continuity is also evident in the size of millstones used in horizontal mills to recent times, as is also the case with those associated with vertical-wheeled grain mills (see below). Indeed, there is no appreciable increase in the size of water-powered millstones in either horizontal or vertical forms before the fourteenth century (Rynne forthcoming, see Table 1 above and 2 below). In Portugal, the types of millstones still used in the twentieth century have the same basic characteristics of Roman and medieval forms, in terms of size and dressing.[24] For the fine grinding of flour, in the larger mills, quartzite or limestone was commonly used, whereas granite millstones were often considered suitable for only corn and rye, although this may be a reflection of recent practice. In later medieval sources, granite stones are referred to as *mós triguerias* and *mós secundeiras*. The dimensions of individual stones vary from region to region. In the north, for example, and in small mills, diameters of 0.8m–0.9m are common, although in some cases it comes down to the type of stone employed. Limestone and quartzite types (*mós alveiras*) can be around 0.8m, whereas *negreiras* (granite) can vary between 0.9m and 1m in diameter. A lease of 1358 also records a *mós triguerias* runner stone 17cm thick, and a bedstone 25cm thick.[25] Thicknesses of 21–25cm for runner stones of traditional Spanish *rodezno* (horizontal) mills are also recorded in a document of 1400, from Murcia, Spain.[26] As Sergi Selma has demonstrated, the millstones employed in the medieval mills of Sharq al-Andalus (the Muslim kingdom of northeastern Spain) shared the same basic dimensions with those recorded elsewhere in the contemporary Muslim world and, indeed, in certain regions up to quite recently.[27] Even the basic elements of Sicilian watermills, including the means of impounding the water, its intake and the ratio in size between the millstone and the water-wheel (which were heavily influenced by Arab settlement), remained substantially unchanged in the twelfth to fourteenth centuries.[28]

One of the most enduring and persistent myths about horizontal-wheeled mills in general is that they were only capable of powering millstones of small diameter and were, in effect, no more than mechanised querns. As Table 2 below will demonstrate, there is virtually no difference in the diameters or thicknesses of the recorded examples of millstones associated with either horizontal or vertical mills. In point of fact, there are a number of instances where the millstones of undershot vertical mills, as at Killoteran, County Waterford (AD 612), Dasing, Germany (AD 744) and Omgård, Denmark (AD *c*.940), were actually smaller than those recorded in association with horizontal mills. Furthermore, when larger-diameter millstones (*c*.1.2m–1.3m) become more common in Europe in the fourteenth century, horizontal mills throughout the Mediterranean were adapted to operate with them. In later medieval Spain this usually involved the installation of a larger diameter water-wheel and, not infrequently, the enlargement of the grinding room.[29] Such transformations were commonplace in former Muslim-controlled territories after the Christian *reconquista*. However, the change in millstone size was influenced more by consumption preferences than increased production. Christian settlers were accustomed to finer flour, which required a larger grinding surface and thus millstones of an increased diameter. The descendants of Arab and Berber colonists, on the other hand, preferred semolina flour for the preparation of dishes such as *couscous*, which could be processed using lighter millstones of up to 1m in diameter.[30] Similar considerations are likely to have influenced the introduction of larger millstones into Ireland after the Anglo-Norman conquest, to accommodate the newcomers' preference for wheaten flour (see below). On the Iberian Peninsula, therefore, the horizontal mill, by scaling up, made the transition to a new preference for a culturally specific form of milled product and by this means ensured both its continuity and social relevance. At the same time, however, drop-tower penstock-fed grain mills retained their technological advantage over all forms of their vertical-wheeled equivalents, in terms of both their product and output.

## Millstones in early and later medieval vertical watermills

With regard to the manufacture of water-powered millstones, pre-Anglo-Norman Ireland stands apart from almost the rest of medieval Europe in one key respect. The island as a whole had no apparent engagement with the international millstone trade and, in particular, with that in German lava stones. These latter were imported into pre-Norman England and were demonstrably employed in the ninth-century horizontal mill at Tamworth, Staffordshire. The introduction of millstones of non-Irish origin and the use of stones of larger diameter appears not to have occurred in Ireland until the advent of the Anglo-Normans. However, all of the recorded examples from Anglo-Norman contexts, while clearly of larger diameter than those of pre-Norman manufacture, were fashioned from varieties of native sandstone conglomerates. It also seems clear that the watermills built by the Anglo-Normans in Ireland were of the geared, vertical-wheeled variety, which in the Anglo-Norman lordship (as in most of northern Europe) became, exclusively, the seigneurial mill.

As in most other aspects of medieval water-powered milling, the manufacture of millstones displays, in most respects, the same continuity from the Roman period in terms of form, size and in the long-distance trade in certain volcanic stone types. This also appears to extend to the manner in which the stones were extracted in quarries. A recent study of a millstone quarry at Claix, in southwest France – noted for a type of porous, abrasive limestone that is eminently suitable for grinding wheat – concluded that the techniques involved in the manufacture of Roman and Merovingian millstones appear to have been generally similar.[31] Indeed, Roman millstones manufactured from certain varieties of basaltic lava actually formed part of a long-distance trade in sizes varying from 0.55–0.90m in diameter.[32] Larger stone sizes have been recorded from the Roman and the early and later medieval period (see below). Yet from Table 2, it is evident that the same general size-range in vertical-wheeled mills in the post-Roman period was common throughout most of Europe. As we have already seen, the same is also true of horizontal-wheeled mills in early medieval Ireland, England and Spain. We must, therefore, be careful to avoid any technologically deterministic or progressivist assumptions about the size of millstones being related to any specific period or, rather, that the diameter of water-powered millstones gradually and uniformly increased in size as the medieval era progressed. Irish horizontal millstone diameters compare very favourably with those of recorded pre-AD 1000 vertical-wheeled mills in Britain and Europe, while there are also millstones from early medieval European vertical-wheeled mills that are larger than those excavated at high medieval sites.

For the most part, the study of medieval water-powered millstones associated with medieval vertical mills has been neglected. There are now, however, a number of excellent site-specific studies, based on the mills at Dasing and Elfgen in Germany and West Cotton and Castle Donington in England, which have provided important insights into the extent of the regional and continental trade in medieval water-powered millstones.[33] Nonetheless, there are some scholars who have suggested that the use of volcanic rocks for millstones actually declined in the medieval period. Amouric, for example, has observed that in the post-Roman period, in southeastern France, volcanic

Table 2. Millstones from early- and later-medieval vertical water-mills in Europe.

| Millstone | Max. Diameter (m) | Max. Thickness (cm) | Eye (Dia.) cm | Rynd socket form | Stone type and source | Date |
|---|---|---|---|---|---|---|
| Le Paludi, Italy | 0.70 | | | | Lava stone | Late sixth/early seventh century |
| Killoteran, Ireland | 0.53 | | | | Old grey sandstone | AD 612 (d) |
| Dasing, Germany | 0.50–0.60, 0.80 | 3.4 | | Rectangular | Conglomerate sandstone, from Lechbruck; quartz mica sandstone from Reiselsberg; garnet mica slate from Alps | AD 744–789 (d) |
| Gimbscheim, Germany | 0.88 | | | Dovetail | Ignimbrite, from area between Nahe and Saar rivers | AD76c (C14) |
| Reigoldswil, Germany | 0.85–0.90 | 4.5 | | Rectangular, two arms | Sandstone | 8th century |
| Rotbachtal | | | | | Rhenish basalt | AD 832–3 (d) |
| Audun-le-Tiche, France | 0.66m, 0.70, 0.80 | | | | Lava stone, Eifel, Germany | AD 840–51 (d) |
| Omgård, Denmark | 0.45 | | | | Coarse-grained schlieric gneiss (Britain?) | AD 915–45 (C14) |
| Belle Eglise, France | 1.30 | 2.5 | | | | AD 930–80 (d) |
| West Cotton, England | 0.90–1 | 6.4 | | | Lava stone, Eifel, Germany | c. AD 950–1000 |
| Kirke Værløse, Denmark | | | | | Mica schist with garnets | Early medieval |
| London | c.1.2 | | | | | 11th century |
| West Cotton, England | 0.90–1 | 12 | 14 | Rectangular, two arms | Millstone grit, English North Midlands, probably Derbyshire | c. AD 1000–1150 |
| Castle Donington | 0.55–0.60, 0.90–1 | | | | Millstone grit, Medbourne, Derbyshire | AD 1130–50 (d) |
| Elfgen, Germany | c.1 | 5 | | | Basalt, Mayen and Niedermendig | Second half of 11th century |

| Millstone | Max. Diameter (m) | Max. Thickness (cm) | Eye (Dia.) cm | Rynd socket form | Stone type and source | Date |
|---|---|---|---|---|---|---|
| Løgumkloster, Denmark | | | | | Rhenish basalt; garnet schist (from Norway or Slavic regions) | AD 1175 (d) |
| Twomileborris, County Tipperary, Ireland | 1.2 | 26 | | | Coarse grained quartz conglomerate sandstone | AD 1199–1217 |
| Verjeslev, Denmark | 0.98 | | | | Mica schist with garnets | AD 1210 (d) |
| Verjeslev, Denmark | 0.98 | | | | Rhenish basalt | AD 1210 (d) |
| Lejre, Denmark | | | | | Mica schist | c. AD 1200 |
| Dons Mølle, Denmark | | | | | Mica schist with garnets | c. AD 1200–1300 |
| Kolding Bygrunde, Denmark | | | | | Basalt millstones from Andernach, Rhineland | c. AD 1200–1300 |
| Rathmullan, County Down, Ireland | 1.06 | 5 | 15 | X-shaped, slight curvature | Sandstone, possibly from Scrabo, County Down | 12th/13th century |
| Rathmullan, County Down, Ireland | 0.95 | 10 | 14–18 | X-shaped, slight curvature | Sandstone | 12th/13th century |
| Glanworth, County Cork, Ireland | 1.2 | 13 | | | Sandstone | 13th century |
| Kells Priory, County Kilkenny, Ireland | 1.3 | 12-13 | | | Sandstone conglomerate | Mid-late 13th century |
| Borup, Denmark | c.1 | | | | Imported mica schist with garnets | 1200s to c.1450 |
| Tovstrup, Denmark | 0.80–1 | | | | Gneiss | AD 1407–1531 |
| Tovstrup, Denmark | 1.22 | | 7–8 | | Mica slate from either Kverstein Bjerget, Norway or Slavic regions | AD 1407–1531 |
| Ahrensfelde, Germany | | | | | Rhenish basalt | |
| Elsdorf-Desdorf, Germany | 1.1 | | 13.5 | | | High medieval |

rocks began to be substituted with conglomerates, while others have noted a similar change occurring in the south of the Iberian Peninsula.[34] Amouric also suggests that the alleged changeover from volcanic to sedimentary rocks could possibly be associated with the introduction of new cereal types in the early medieval period. This, he posits, may have challenged existing millstone technology with regard to the shape, size and speed of rotation.[35]

The introduction of water-powered milling could also have assisted the transition from volcanic to conglomerate forms in which 'larger, flatter, pebble-incrusted, tight-fitting millstones permitted grain to transit once through the mill contrary to the earlier slow rotating installations [i.e. querns] where grains had to be ground in repeated passages'.[36] It has even been suggested that water-powered volcanic stones could even have 'burnt' the flour.[37] By reference to Table 2 it is clear that the assertion that millstones of volcanic origin were replaced by conglomerates in the medieval period bears little scrutiny. Furthermore, it seems highly unlikely that those responsible for constructing the mills at Audun-le-Tiche (France), Tamworth and West Cotton (England), and Verjeslev (Denmark) would have gone to the trouble of acquiring expensive millstones from Germany if these in any way impaired the flour or, more to the point, if appropriate conglomerate substitutes were available locally. Just over 50 per cent of the millstones listed in Table 2 were sourced from distant locations, from quarries that had been exploited since the Roman period. Of these, nine were acquired from German sources of volcanic origin. These include the German mill sites at Gimbscheim (ignimbrite, from the region between the Nahe and Saar rivers), Rotbachtal (Rhenish basalt) Elfgen (basalt from Mayen and Niedermendig, in the Eifel hills of Germany) and Ahrensfelde.[38] But even within central Europe, this would still have involved transportation across considerable distances. The export of large millstones from German quarries to sites further afield, such as Audun-le-Tiche, West Cotton, Løgumkloster, Verjeslev and Kolding Bygrunde in Denmark, in the period AD *c*.840–1300, thus assumes a significance that has barely been touched upon. Querns of basalt lava stone had been imported into England from at least the first century AD, but by the third and fourth centuries these were somewhat less common. Until recently it was believed that the trade in Mayen quernstones was not revived until the seventh and eighth centuries, but it is now clear that lava querns can be dated to the earliest period of Anglo-Saxon settlement in Britain.[39] In Britain, therefore, this trade appears to have been largely uninterrupted. The absence of either imported lava querns, or millstones blanks, in northern England and Scotland has been interpreted as self-sufficiency in these regions in stone suitable for milling.[40] Likewise, there was no shortage of either conglomerates or volcanic stones (of either granite or basalt) in Ireland, but the absence of imported quern and millstones blanks in both regions appears to suggest that they did not form part of the trade routes from which they originated. The importation of English and continental millstones into Ireland in the later medieval period, therefore, suggests an important change in newcomer/immigrant food-ways.

It seems likely that stone from the Mayen quarry was transported to Andernach on the Rhine (via the River Nette) and thence to Denmark, via Deventer, and to Britain via Utrecht.[41] Finds from early medieval wrecks indicate that blanks for quernstones, of between 20–25kg (50kg for a full set), were being shipped to destinations throughout Europe.[42] However, the tenth-century Mayen and Niedermendig millstones from West Cotton, England which were, on average, 64mm thick, weighed around 80–85kg each, a millstone set weighing *c.*160–170kg.[43] While approximately half the weight of the Derbyshire grit millstones later employed on the same site, the transportation of the German lava millstone blanks to Northamptonshire must have been a considerable undertaking. Why, then, did mill owners in medieval Denmark, England and France go to such lengths to import volcanic lava stones from Germany? The answer would appear to lie in a cultural rather than a technological preference for a particular type of flour, which could only be produced when these stones were employed.[44] Similar considerations, it will be argued below, appear to have obtained in the later medieval lordships of Ireland.

Nonetheless, given the weight of quern and millstone blanks, and the fact that these would have to be replaced, in relative terms, quite frequently, they were clearly considered an essential commodity, regardless of the distances involved. They were not, therefore, in any sense a by-product of a trade in another commodity.[45] French millstones (probably 'burr' stones from the Seine basin) were also imported, at considerable expense, into England and Ireland in the thirteenth and fourteenth centuries.[46] German lava millstones, which were one-half to two-thirds the price of French stones, were also often preferred over cheaper native conglomerates. Not until the second half of the fourteenth century, after the Black Death when the profits from manorial milling were in decline, did millstones from Wales and Derbyshire become more common.[47] But was the selection of millstone type in medieval Europe simply a triumph of necessity over convenience? While on the one hand, as Table 2 would suggest, we may have underestimated the lengths to which millers were prepared to go to acquire the grinding stones that they considered best suited to their needs, it is perhaps too easy to assume that the use of more geographically accessible sources might be an indication that they were somehow being less selective. The eighth-century Dasing undershot mill is a case in point. The millstones recovered from this site included stone types acquired over a wide area: conglomerate sandstone from Lechbruck, Bavaria; quartz mica sandstone from Reiselberg, near Murnau, and even a garnet mica slate from near Landeck-Paznauntal in the Austrian Tyrol.[48] Doubtless, the attractions of using a more convenient source of stone would have been evident to early and later medieval millers but even if the millstone blank was acquired from a quarry within, say, a 20km radius of the mill site, this need not necessarily imply that convenience was the overriding factor in the selection of the grinding stones. The provision and replacement of millstones in the medieval period as a whole was probably the largest single expenditure incurred in mill construction and maintenance.[49]

Although the size and type of millstone employed is one of the key determinants of both the quality and output of the flour or meal produced by a mill, rarely has this association been linked to consumption preferences.[50] The closely comparable size between Roman and most medieval millstones has already been alluded to. However, the fact that medieval horizontal millstones, especially from Ireland, were manufactured in similar sizes has received virtually no comment (see above). There is even one example of an upper millstone from a tenth-century horizontal mill at Madinat Balansiya (Valencia) which was 1.10m in diameter.[51] Until recently the diameters of many Roman millstones were generally believed to fall within the range 0.55–0.85, but there is an increasing number of larger examples coming to light.[52] There are, in addition to the Selsey, West Sussex millstone (diameter 1.09m), further examples from the Palatine Hill which are 0.87–0.93m in diameter, and the Domus Tiberianus (0.83–90m) in Rome.[53] A millstone of 1.30m diameter also survives in the collections of the Musée St Germain.[54] This latter bears comparison with that from the tenth-century mill at Belle-Eglise (1.30m), and with the later medieval discoveries from Twomileborris, Ireland (1.20m, AD 1199–1219) and Tovstrup, Denmark (1.22m, AD 1407–1531).[55] By reference to Table 2, it is clear that the same general range of millstone diameters was also in evidence in early and later medieval Europe.

On present evidence, therefore, millstone size cannot be considered specific to either period or mill type (horizontal or vertical). The early seventh-century millstone from Killoteran, at 0.53m diameter, is actually smaller than any of the recorded forms from any early medieval Irish horizontal mill. Yet, some three centuries later we find an even smaller example (0.45m diameter, a bedstone with a distinctive hour glass perforation similar to those recorded on Irish bedstones) associated with an undershot vertical mill at Omgård, Denmark.[56] Small-diameter millstones were also in evidence at Dasing, Bavaria (seventh century, 0.50–0.60m) and Castle Donington, England (first half of twelfth century, 0.55–0.60m), while at each site these were found in association with stones of larger diameters.[57] By reference to Table 2 it will be seen that recorded millstone sizes from undershot vertical mills, from the late sixth century to around AD 1000, vary quite considerably from 0.50m to 1.30m in diameter. And, while a broadly similar range of diameters is evident in the period AD 1000–1531, the larger-diameter examples recorded at Twomileborris, Ireland and Tovstrup, Denmark (see above and Table 2) are still slightly smaller than the 1.30m diameter millstone from Belle Eglise (see above and Table 2). Indeed, the Belle Eglise example is similar in diameter to those described in 'hands' in fourteenth-century English documents, in which diameters of the equivalent of 52–56 inches (*c*.1.32–1.42m) are recorded.[58] Again, this overall pattern in millstone sizes also occurs across a wide chronological and geographical spectrum (see Table 2) where also, as in the Roman period, the size and type of millstone would appear to be linked with both the type of flour or meal preferred and a specific level of output required.

By way of summary of the main points developed thus far, the Irish corpus of early medieval water-power-driven stones, the largest from anywhere up to the end of the twelfth century, fits in well with developments elsewhere in Europe in terms of millstone size and dressing. In pre-Norman Ireland millstones over 0.8m diameter are rare, which suggests they were not used, generally, for processing bread wheat. Elsewhere in Europe the long-distance trade in basaltic millstones from Mayern-Niedermendig continues uninterrupted and, while millstone sizes change little from the Roman period, in the thirteenth and fourteenth centuries examples of 1.2m diameter and upwards become noticeably more common in archaeological assemblages. This change, as we will now see, is reflected in Anglo-Norman Ireland.

From Table 2 above, there is a clear correspondence between the sizes of water-powered millstones recovered from Anglo-Norman sites in Ireland and those recorded in Britain and the continent. Of the four recorded examples only Rathmullan, County Down has produced millstones of less than 1.2m in diameter but which were, nonetheless, larger than 0.9m diameter and thus within the range of stones likely to have been used to process bread wheat.[59] At the other sites, Twomileborris, County Tipperary (1.2m), Glanworth, County Cork (1.2m) and Kells Priory, County Kilkenny (1.3m), the excavated examples were actually larger than contemporary recorded forms from most of Britain and Europe (see Fig. 4).[60] All of the Irish stones were, in addition, fashioned from local sandstones, mostly conglomerates. Although the number of Irish Anglo-Norman stones is small it does, nonetheless, represent around one-third of the current corpus of later medieval water-powered millstones, and we may infer that the use of larger-diameter examples within the colony, and throughout Europe, is a reflection on cultural behaviours associated with the milling of cereals.

In Ireland, millstones were imported from England, Wales and France from at least the fourteenth century (but probably earlier) to meet demand for wheaten flour in the Anglo-Norman colony, of a quality experienced at home. An account of the King's Mills, near Dublin Castle in 1306, refers to an 'old' French millstone and an English one, while in 1313–14 documented repairs to these same mills involved an expenditure of 28s 9d on a Welsh millstone, most probably sourced from Penmon on Anglesey.[61] When the two mills at Leixlip, County Kildare were let to Robert Leyngenour from 1323–27, he purchased two French millstones for £7 13s 4d, along with a third stone worth £1 13s 4d, which also seems likely to have been imported.[62] Later on, in around 1330, two French millstones (*molaribus Gallicanus*) were acquired for the royal mills at Leixlip, for £7 6s 8d, and transported to the site at a cost of 6s 8d (a distance of just over 24km).[63] The importation into Ireland of what appears to have been French 'burr' stone, quarried in the La Ferté-sous-Jouarre (Seine et Marne) region of the Paris basin, as its use in the royal mills at Dublin and Leixlip might suggest, could be an indication that imported stones were associated with high-status mills. Indeed, the contemporary importation of foreign building stones, such as Dundry stone from the Bristol area, along with Bath stone and Purbeck marble, for architectural purposes and domestic use in mortars, is also generally associated with aristocratic patrons.[64] At the time of writing, there are upwards of seventy-four sites at which these imported stones have been recorded in Ireland, mostly in Leinster and Munster, but with no known examples in Ulster.[65] The importation of millstones into Anglo-Norman Ireland is likely to have been much more common than the generally poor survival of manorial records from the lordship would suggest. Nor, for that matter, need this trade have been exclusively conducted to meet the needs of aristocratic tastes. Such was the extent of this trade that by the fifteenth century a large crane was installed on the Dublin quays to unload millstones, while there is also a directive of the municipality of Dublin, of 1467–68, which ordered anyone who cluttered up the quay with millstones to remove them or face a fine of 3s 4d.[66]

The introduction of feudal monopolies into the lordship is also likely to have reinforced Anglo-Norman cultural practices governing the way in which cereals were milled. The seigneurial control of mills not only compelled the lord's tenants to bring their grain to the manorial mill for grinding, but also imposed a toll known as multure (*multura*). In Ireland, as a whole, this was normally about one-sixteenth of the final milled product.[67] Nominally, at least, private mills were banned, but in certain well-documented instances, as on the de Burgh manors in Munster held by Elizabeth de Clare, the betaghs of Lisronagh, County Tipperary were permitted to use their own hand mills on payment of ½d per acre. Elsewhere, tenants at Cloyne, County Cork paid a *pro molendio* payment which enabled them to process their grain in rotary querns.[68] In the main, however, this restriction in Anglo-Norman areas would not only have heavily influenced the type of mill employed but the type and diameter of the stones used by it. This, in turn, fundamentally changed the quality and taste of flour and meal processed in such mills. At the same time, individual choice of milling technology was removed, along with the obvious convenience of where and when this may have been undertaken. Furthermore, multure is also likely to have reinforced Anglo-Norman weights and measures for grain, especially in urban areas. The introduction of larger millstones fashioned from native sandstone conglomerates, along with the importation of Welsh, English and French millstones, therefore, can be seen as cultural markers. Within the Anglo-Norman immigrant community, the higher-grade flours produced by these met a specific, ethnically defined preference.

While both the archaeological and documentary sources for areas under Gaelic control remain largely silent, traditional practices (the use of horizontal mills and rotary querns) seem certain to have continued uninterrupted. Both technologies were widely employed in western Ireland, well into the twentieth century. Indeed, technical terms for horizontal mills used in a seventh-century Old Irish text on distraint, *De Ceithri Slichtaib Athgabalá* ('On the four sections of distraint'), were still employed near Carna, County Galway in the 1860s.[69] As has been seen, both horizontal and vertical forms were at work in pre-Norman Ireland, although both appear to have been largely involved in the milling of oats and barley, and used millstones of less than 0.8m in diameter. If one assumes technological and cultural continuity in the food and food-ways associated with the processing of cereals in later medieval Gaelic Ireland, then this represents a clear ethnic division between these communities and those of the Anglo-Norman lordship. And although by no means a 'dietary frontier', it would have been as distinctive as dress and language in separating and defining each community. Elsewhere in contemporary Europe cereals were as important in Muslim as in Christian diet. Even the nomadic and sedentary populations of Muslim North Africa consumed between 600–800 grams/day, the same as the inhabitants of medieval Baghdad: in medieval England this total was 680–790 grams/day.[70] However, as in later medieval Spain, where closely comparable milling technologies were employed, it was the essential differences in the finished product in which ethnic choices and cultural behaviours became physically manifest.

## Conclusion

Food-ways have long been understood as central to the performance and maintenance of identity. But while these can be imitated and adopted, they are not necessarily transformative. From the foregoing consideration of the archaeological evidence for milling in Gaelic and Anglo-Norman Ireland, it seems clear that what was involved here was not an all-embracing technological change, but rather an adjustment to accommodate a cultural preference. In what were two essentially Christian societies, perceived differences in the preferences for particular foods can be much more subtle, although just as demanding to maintain (for example, the need to import costly millstones) as those separating and defining Christian and non-Christian communities. These can be explicitly religious indicators of identity (as, for example, the avoidance of alcohol and pork amongst Muslims or Christians fasting during lent), or non-religious, such as the Anglo-Norman preference for wheaten bread or the custom of sitting on the ground to eat in Muslim Spain.[71] However, while these practices can be adopted by nominally different ethnic groups out of necessity, rather than as a conscious transgression of the perceived norms or codes of behaviour of one's community, as is evident from milling practices in Anglo-Norman Ireland, some cultural preferences will be stubbornly adhered to. Indeed, considerable effort and expense appears to have been incurred to ensure that these were not abandoned. So what might this tell us about the group identity of Anglo-Norman settlers?

In one sense, the way in which certain cereals were not only privileged over others, but also in the way in which they were processed and consumed in later medieval Ireland, reflects two culturally distinct customs. As has been seen, the essential milling technologies, in the form of both vertical- and horizontal-wheeled watermills already existed in Gaelic Ireland. Crop processing – threshing, winnowing and the drying of the grain – was also very similar in both Gaelic and Anglo-Norman areas. Yet a clearly defined cultural difference emerges in the main type of cereals preferred in the immigrant communities and the type of millstones – stones of increased diameter and of non-Irish origin – employed to reduce these to both flour and meal. Immigrants of all social classes and, in particular, those of the largest, the peasant communities transplanted to Irish manors from the English west midlands, had a by no means unreasonable expectation of being able to consume the same types of bread they had been accustomed to in their homeland. Nevertheless, this is likely to have had as much to do with taste as a need to fulfil a sense of difference from the natives. The consumption of native foods may not have been frowned upon and the maintenance of a group identity could have been as much governed by what one was seen to be eating as by individual taste.

When viewed in the wider context of the material culture of the period, during which the newcomers readily intermarried with the natives (something which would have been unthinkable between Christians and Muslims in contemporary Spain), adopted the Irish mode of dress, their language, and the distinctively Irish custom of fostering their children, the rigid maintenance of certain food-ways suggests that these were perceived as defining and immutable characteristics of their group identity. While others might be adjusted, diluted or abandoned, some proved destined to be adhered to regardless of the expense. Similarly, while imported ceramics from England and France became increasingly used in Gaelic Ireland, there is nothing to suggest that they abandoned their horizontal-wheeled mills, which continued to employ native conglomerate sandstones and granite millstones of sub-1m diameter to process their oats and barley. Indeed, there is little evidence that English millwrighting traditions became widespread in Ireland up to the period of the English Plantations of the late sixteenth and early seventeenth centuries. The size and types of millstones employed in later medieval Ireland, therefore, can provide important insights into often subtle, rather than explicit, differences between immigrant and native groups, even when one of these appears to have been eager to adopt, for political reasons, the customs of the other.

4

# Archaeologies of female monasticism in Ireland: Becoming and belonging *c.*1200–1600

TRACY COLLINS

## Introduction

The singular archaeological 'master narrative'[1] of European medieval monasticism has, until relatively recently, considered religious women as the lesser partner and adjunct to male monasticism.[2] Male monasticism and, in particular, the Benedictine and Cistercian orders, has become the 'standard' form of medieval monastic life, architecture and archaeology. It is by this standard that all forms of monasticism, including female nunneries, are commonly measured and compared. However, this perception is being challenged in modern archaeological and historical scholarship, through the use of different, sometimes novel, approaches. I have adopted an engendered approach to the study of female monasticism in medieval Ireland, one that was first set out in archaeological studies of monasticism by Roberta Gilchrist.[3] The basic premise of this approach is that nunneries were not deviant to the male monastic standard but different from male religious houses in their function. Moreover, all medieval nunneries were not the same. One of the challenges of this research is to acknowledge and identify essential differences between male and female houses, and indeed between female houses (Fig. 1), by asking new questions. In this chapter, important research themes, such as the purpose

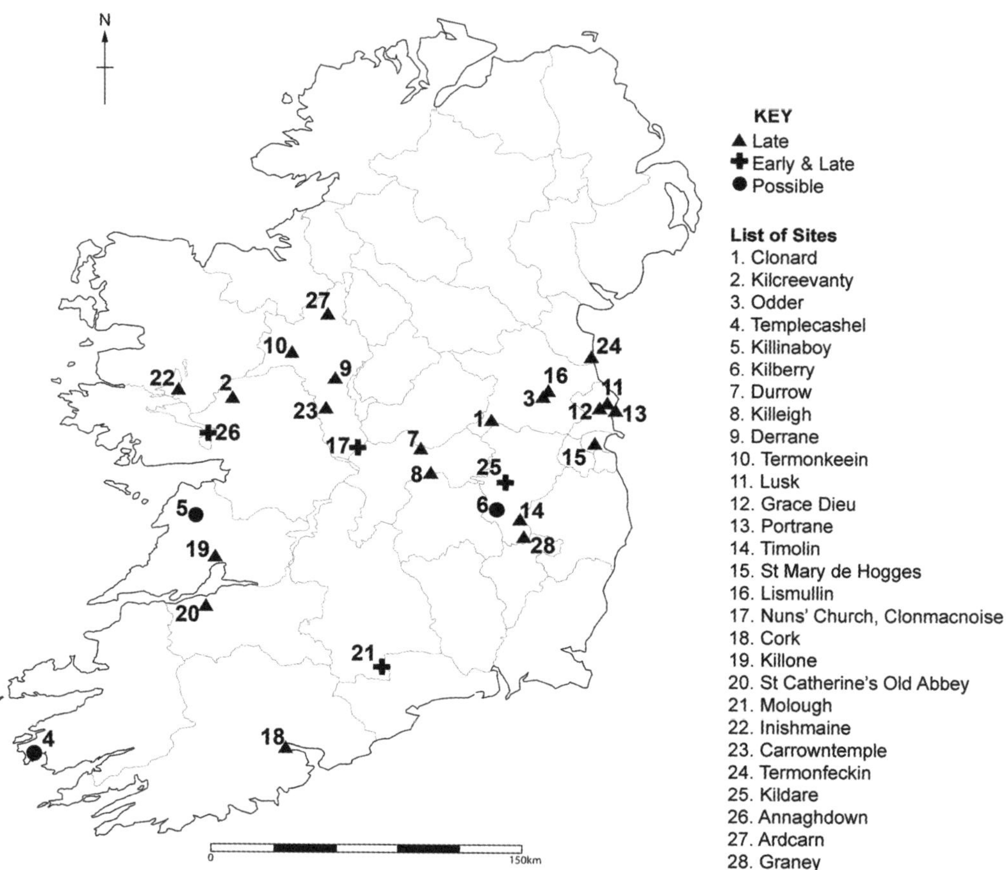


1. Location map of later medieval nunneries mentioned in the text (image: author).

of nunneries, predicaments of identity in relation to nuns and the repositioning of female monastic houses in the social world of medieval Ireland, *c.*1200–1600, are explored. By expanding the current view of medieval monasticism in Ireland to include those women who became nuns and belonged to a religious life, the complex and nuanced landscape of gender in medieval Ireland might be better appreciated.[4]

A review of the historiography of female monasticism in Ireland has shown that popular and modern perceptions of religious women may have been projected onto their medieval pasts and identities, which in turn narrows interpretation of them in the present.[5] Such perceptions require scrutiny and reassessment.[6] This point can be illustrated by the example of Clonard, County Meath, which was an important religious site throughout the medieval period. Clonard was founded in the sixth century by Saint Finnian, and by the late eighth century it was one of the most prominent churches in the Irish midlands.[7] It was the diocesan centre of Meath until the transfer of that function to Newtown Trim in 1202.[8] The early medieval ecclesiastical foundation at Clonard is not directly associated with religious women or nuns. However, it is recorded in the *Life* of Finnian that his mother, Ríoghnach (his sister), along with St Ciaran's mother,[9] lived in an adjacent *cella*.

By the 1140s, there was both an Arroasian male religious house, St Peter's, and a female religious house, St Mary's, at Clonard.[10] The nunnery was of particular importance because, in the first instance, it was established in 1144 through Saint Malachy's influence and, secondly, it was confirmed as the mother-house of the Arroasian canonesses in Ireland by Pope Celestine III, in a bull of 1195.[11] By the thirteenth century, Clonard's importance had waned because many of its dependencies were transferred to Kilcreevanty in what is now County Galway. Kilcreevanty became the head of the Arroasian nunneries in Connacht while Clonard was superseded by the nunnery at Odder and reduced in status to a cell during the fourteenth century.[12]

There is no upstanding trace of the later medieval nunnery, or the male religious house, at Clonard. A nineteenth-century church, with a medieval stone head incorporated into its tower, stands on the site today. Several enclosures, burials, a graveyard, an Anglo-Norman motte and bailey and medieval fields are recorded nearby.[13] The main point about Clonard is that more recent investigations of the site have failed to take account of, or sometimes even mention, the fact that an important nunnery once existed there. Excavations of human remains near the site of the male and female religious houses in the 1970s, and a later very successful geophysical survey, both overlooked the historical presence of Arroasian canonesses at the site.[14] Likewise, studies of material culture relating to the site, such as the Clonard crosier and reliquary, and the later medieval font (now in the Roman Catholic church at Clonard), exclude interpretations that might otherwise have connected them with Clonard nunnery.[15] Significant early medieval artefacts would have been re-used in the later medieval period and it can be reasonably suggested that the nunnery community may have done so. A crosier, for instance, is a symbol of authority for both abbots and abbesses throughout the medieval period, and examples of abbesses with crosiers, represented in paintings, grave-slabs and burials, are known from medieval England.[16] Therefore, new archaeological interpretations at sites such as Clonard should include the important female monastic element.

## The evidence

Some 114 medieval nunneries are known to have existed in Ireland, forty-nine of which date to the early medieval period (*c.*450–1100) and sixty-five of which are attributed later medieval foundation dates (*c.*1100–1540). The interpretations offered in this paper are based on this latter group of sixty-five sites. In addition, there are *circa* seventy-six sites that can be proposed as nunneries as a result of a dedication to a female saint or local folk tradition: for example Templecashel, County Kerry,[17] Killinaboy, County Clare,[18] and Kilberry, County Kildare.[19]

Not all later medieval nunneries were in use at the same time in the later medieval period and communities of nuns are known to have moved location. The religious communities of Clonard moved to Odder, County Meath in the 1380s,[20] the Durrow community moved to Killeigh, County Offaly sometime after 1195,[21] and the nuns at Derrane transferred to Termonkeelin, County Roscommon sometime after 1223.[22] The community of nuns at Lusk first moved to Grace Dieu and then much later to Portrane, County Dublin in 1539.[23] Documentary evidence for these female communities in medieval Ireland is sparse and this makes it difficult or impossible to assess the size and status of many of the communities of nuns by the time of the Dissolution in the sixteenth century.[24] Therefore, 'looking for traces of medieval women's religious activities in medieval Ireland means looking with eyes trained for omissions, ellipses and small clues'.[25]

Knowledge and preservation of nunnery sites ranges from a documentary reference, with no known nunnery location, through to substantial archaeological remains. As has been realised elsewhere, in England, Scotland and Wales, the study of female monasticism has been somewhat thwarted by the opinions and considerations of earlier scholarship, which may have been overly concerned with the *best* medieval architectural detail or the *best* historical evidence. As such, nunneries have tended to lose out in academic investigations, as they have been unfairly compared to both male architecture and its history, and were found wanting. More recently, attitudes have been changing and female monasticism is now considered for what it is.

## Founders and benefactors

Perhaps the first port of call in any study of the identities of monastic houses is a consideration of their founders and patrons. It has been demonstrated for England and Wales that nuns were related to their patrons who, for the most part, came from the aristocratic and gentry strata of medieval society.[26] The same is true of medieval Ireland, with families from the higher echelons of both Gaelic and Anglo-Norman society establishing and patronising nunneries over time.[27] For example, the important nunnery at Kilcreevanty, County Galway was founded by the Uí Chonchobhair *c.*1200,[28] and Timolin, County Kildare was founded, adjacent to his castle, by John Robert FitzRichard, Lord of Narragh. The first prioress of Timolin, Lecelina, was a relation of the founder.[29] St Mary de Hogges, situated immediately outside the town walls of Dublin, was initially founded by Diarmait Mac Murchada, King of Leinster *c.*1146, and later its benefactors were Anglo-Norman.[30] As the nuns were close relatives of members of society's elite and indeed came from this background themselves, the nunnery's communal identity and the individual identity of the nuns were inextricably linked to their elite patrons. Therefore, a complex interaction between individual and community identity must have been forged, rather than one notion of identity replacing the other upon a woman's entry into the nunnery.

Moreover, it has been noted that medieval women who became nuns in Scotland retained their original surnames. This helped to maintain links with their families and the local communities of which they were part before entering the nunnery. Fortunately, this fact has made them more recognisable in the historical records. The names of 232 nuns have been identified for later medieval Scotland.[31] From the records of later medieval Ireland, 189 names of religious women are known.[32] These numbers must represent a mere fraction of all professed nuns in those regions in the later medieval period.

A popular perception surrounding monastic patronage is that nunneries were founded usually by women for women. This certainly did occur, although rarer than is commonly thought. In England, women from aristocratic or royal backgrounds did establish nunneries. The *Regularis Concordia*, a tenth-century agreement between English monasteries and the Crown, named the Queen as the special protector and patron of all nuns. This agreement held into the later medieval period, but it seems to have been more of a tradition rather than showing widespread practical support.[33] However, for later medieval Ireland where the nunnery founder is known, the patronage pattern is distinctly male, with only three women patrons identified: Avicia (Alice) de la Corner, sister of the Bishop of Meath founded Lismullin, County Meath, in about 1240 with her brother's assistance;[34] Derbforgaill, the 're-builder' of the Nun's Church at Clonmacnoise, County Offaly, in 1167;[35] and the recluse Agnes de Hareford, instigator of one of two nunneries in Cork in 1297.[36]

However, it should also be considered that patronage figures for later medieval Ireland may actually obscure female agency in foundation. Sally Thompson has noted that in medieval England women's wishes may have been carried out by their husbands and therefore recorded in terms of male patronage. The nunneries themselves, however, were located on the wife's dowry land, which Thompson has interpreted as indicating an underlying female agency in their establishment.[37] Karen Stöber has revealed for medieval Wales (through a detailed study of documentary sources including wills) that monastic patronage was diverse and that wealthy families founded and sponsored a wide variety of religious houses.[38] A similar pattern can be concluded for later medieval Ireland. Elite families patronised religious houses, including nunneries, for a variety of reasons. Patronage facilitated the creation of family identity and was a clear, visible demonstration of links to the Church. On a more practical level, patronage provided a religious life, home and career for female members of the extended family, such as those that were widowed or who did not marry for various reasons. However, on this point Marie Therese Flanagan has stated that she has found no evidence of a surplus of high-status females in the population in later medieval Ireland for whom provision had to be made in nunneries, and so this reason does not fully explain the founding of nunneries in that period. Nunneries were not intended as retirement homes for elderly women; in fact, deaths of high-status women are often recorded at major ecclesiastical centres rather than female houses.[39]

There is little doubt that later medieval monasticism and the founding of religious houses had profound effects on medieval Irish culture and society in general. The early twelfth century saw reform of the Irish Church which laid the groundwork for the re-organisation of Irish monasticism based on the earlier continental church reform movement.[40] Female monasticism was an intrinsic part of that reform. By the close of the twelfth century, many religious houses were already established by both native Gaelic lords and Anglo-Norman colonisers alike.[41] It has been suggested that the foundation of female religious houses in England and Ireland were the 'second generation' of monastic foundations, after an initial phase of establishing male houses in order to colonise and then consolidate the new lands.[42]

While this may have generally been the case, when foundation dates and locations of later medieval female houses in Ireland are considered, a significant number, almost 22 per cent (fourteen of a total of sixty-five) were actually established as the first monastic house in a locality, prior to the foundation of any male religious house (Table 1). In a further two cases, nunneries were founded at an early date in the overall monastic development of their localities. The nunnery of Killone, County Clare was founded in 1189 at the same time as the Augustinian male house of Clare Abbey.[43] St Mary de Hogges, an Arroasian female house at Dublin, was founded in 1146 and was only predated there by the male religious house of St Mary's, founded in 1139.[44] This suggests that for at least fourteen locations in later medieval Ireland the first monastic presence in the locality was female.

This is particularly interesting when it is considered that the historic towns of Dublin, Waterford and Limerick (based on dates of foundation) had established nunneries very early in their monastic development, sometimes even before any male religious house. These examples serve to illustrate that female houses, at least in some

Table 1. Foundation date of nunneries that pre-date male religious houses in a locality.

| Date of Nunnery Foundation* | Nunnery Name | Townland | County (modern) |
|---|---|---|---|
| 1123 | Ardcarn | Ardcarn | Roscommon |
| 1144 | Addrigoole | Addergoole | Laois |
| 1144 | Caltragh | Collinstown | Westmeath |
| 1144 | Killevy | Ballintemple | Armagh |
| 1151 | Aghade | Aghade | Carlow |
| 1151 | St Mary de Bello Portu, Kilculliheen | Abbeylands | Waterford |
| 1171 | St Brigit's, Kildare | Kildare | Kildare |
| 1171 | Taghmon | Taghmon | Wexford |
| 1171 | St Peter's Cell | Limerick historic town | Limerick |
| 1195 | St Mary's Grace Dieu | Grace Dieu | Dublin |
| 1218 | St Mary's Derry | Derry historic town | Derry |
| 1223 | Termonkeelin | Moor | Roscommon |
| 1240s | St Catherine's | Old Abbey | Limerick |
| 1450 | Ballymacdane | Old Abbey | Cork |

*Foundation dates taken from Gywnn and Hadcock, *Medieval Religious Houses,* 310–311 and Hall, *Women and the Church,* 207–210.

localities, were the first monastic identities encountered by the local populace. Indeed, they were established there by family patronage to fulfil a variety of needs for the founding family but also for the local community. Significantly, the figures reveal that in over a fifth of cases in later medieval Ireland, it would appear that the need for a female religious house in a particular locality was more immediate than for a male house.

## Affiliation

Nunnery affiliation, unlike most male houses, is sometimes difficult to ascertain for female religious houses in medieval Ireland. This is also the case with nunneries in Britain and the continent.[45] Janet

Burton, among others, has suggested that analysing nunneries by order is particularly unhelpful, as it attempts to 'squeeze' women into categories that were originally designed for male congregations.[46] In medieval Ireland, the vast majority of nunneries are considered Augustinian of Arroasian observance, perhaps a legacy of the flexibility of that Rule and its introduction by the influential St Malachy.[47] Furthermore, it should be considered that perhaps the ethos of a particular religious order may have been a deciding factor in the identity of a monastic house.[48] For nunneries in later medieval Ireland, this is difficult to prove definitively due to the lack of contemporary historical documentation.[49] Penelope Johnson notes a dichotomy in the identities of nuns and their communities. Firstly, there is the 'corporate' identity of a nunnery as a female religious house, with its negative 'sacramental disabilities', meaning that the nunnery required a male priest to perform the Mass. This situation placed nunneries at a distinct disadvantage to male religious houses, as male clerics had to be paid, and so nunneries could not generate the same amount of income as male houses in the provision of Masses and other sacramental services. Secondly, however, and in stark contrast to the negative corporate identity, the 'personal' identity of an individual nun, removed from the trials and tribulations of secular life (albeit an elite one), could allow her to follow a life of both spiritual and professional fulfilment.[50] While high-status women who chose to become professed nuns did undergo some transformation of identity in their journey to become religious women,[51] the historical evidence that is available also suggests that many of these nuns still managed to maintain strong links with their families through visits (both visits to and away from their nunneries), gift giving and correspondence, management of family land and assets, and as guardians of family histories.[52]

## Relative wealth

The relative economic and architectural 'poverty' of nunneries in Ireland and abroad is commonly cited as the reason why they have not been studied and why they may have ultimately failed as going concerns.[53] However, this conclusion is based on a direct comparison with male houses, which has been challenged as a false dichotomy.

Male religious houses were generally expected to be self-supporting, although poverty was particularly important to friars who were entirely dependent on patrons and benefactors.[54] The Church accepted the *cura mulierum* (care of women) with the proviso that women's houses were sustainable.[55] Eileen Power, in her economic history of nunneries in England, postulated that they were expected to be self-sufficient and produce a surplus for sale,[56] and in some larger nunneries this was achieved.[57] However, overall, nunneries in much of England were still considered poor.[58]

When analyses are undertaken of the documentary records of nunneries in England, in regard to production and consumption, it is difficult to demonstrate surpluses, even at the larger houses.[59] Indeed, where records are extant, it is clear that many nunneries were not endowed at foundation with the means to become self-sufficient, even though it was a major tenet of medieval monasticism. It is unusual that such a tenet was not adhered to, in at least certain larger nunneries. This leads to the conclusion that self-sufficiency was not as important a consideration for female monastic houses as for male houses, and it is on this basis that the suggestion has been made that nunneries may not have ever been required to be self-sufficient and produce a surplus, like their male counterparts.[60]

In Ireland the debate on the relative poverty of nunneries also continues. Some suggest that nunnery founders seemed to favour self-sufficiency, so that the nuns could continue a life of prayer,[61] while others have suggested that nuns in medieval Ireland were entirely dependent on the father abbot and his monastery.[62] Despite these varying opinions, there is no strong evidence to suggest that nunneries were expected to be self-sufficient to the same degree as male houses, particularly in foodstuffs. In many cases, nunneries might be considered mainly consumers, rather than actual producers.[63]

Indeed, poverty may have been an active ascetic *choice* for medieval nuns as part of their religious identity; it was, after all, a third of the monastic vocation and vows, together with chastity and obedience.[64] While many nunneries in Ireland would appear to have been of lowly status – which now might be considered deliberate – there are some distinctive exceptions. Killone, County Clare, for example, possesses a sophisticated under-croft structure beneath its church, along with some fine architectural details, and

St Catherine's, Old Abbey church, County Limerick has an elaborate west doorway. The survival of this architectural richness is rare in nunnery architecture in Ireland. Perhaps it reflected the wealth of their benefactors and their connections to the Church, while also serving as a constant reminder to the nuns of their patrons.

## Layout and architecture

The layout and architecture of nunneries can be considered as a possible manifestation of identity. The layout and architecture of monastic houses is a particular archaeological concern with the 'standard' template of any monastic house stemming from the male, and specifically Cistercian, ideal of a church and buildings arranged neatly around a square cloister; the expectation is that the plan of nunneries will conform to this rule too.[65] As can be seen, however, from the three remaining claustrally planned nunneries in Ireland, at Killone, County Clare, St Catherine's, County Limerick and Molough, County Tipperary, there are exceptions. All three are Augustinian and yet all show flexibility in layout, which was not observed in earlier scholarship on nunneries. These layouts may put some concrete form to Archbishop Alen's comment relating to the nunneries of Timolin, County Kildare and Grace Dieu, County Dublin, that they were 'cloistral without a cloister and regulars without a rule'.[66]

There is no clear explanation for this variety in layout, although modes of initial foundation may provide a clue. It has been accepted in continental studies of nunnery foundation that their establishment was in many cases more organic or informal than that of male houses. Female religious houses tended to emerge from informal groups of women who wished to become nuns; they may have initially been donated secular buildings for their use, which may or may not have later been developed into claustral arrangements. This mode of establishment goes some way to explaining the variety of layout seen in the archaeological record in Ireland. Notwithstanding the fact that many may have had cloisters long destroyed or have been constructed in timber, there is a significant number of nunneries that are clearly only represented by churches with or without attached accommodation, such as Inishmaine, County Mayo and Carrowntemple or perhaps Termonkeelin, both in County Roscommon. It is also interesting to note that in the Dissolution surveys of nunneries, which provide details of eleven female religious houses, only in a single case, that of Lismullin, County Meath, is a cloister listed.[67] An explanation may be that a cloister was such a ubiquitous nunnery feature that it did not warrant mention in the surveys. However, considering the inventory detail of other structures, rights and customs afforded at other nunneries and the fact that a cloister is mentioned at one nunnery, it might not have been such a common feature.

The 'non-conformance' and exception to standard plans, described above, at female religious houses is also now recognised in male monastic architecture, most notably in that of the Augustinians.[68] Tadhg O'Keeffe has identified substantial variation in the architecture of Augustinian male houses in later medieval Ireland, concluding that 'there is then no such thing as a typical Augustinian monastery, within Ireland or without, and so a study of Augustinian monastic architecture in Ireland would thus be nothing less than a study of the entire spectrum of architectural forms and sculptural motifs used in the ecclesiastical environment of medieval Ireland'.[69] Indeed, this statement could be equally applied to the corpus of later medieval nunneries in Ireland. No distinct architecture of nunneries can be distinguished. Rather, they use the wider vocabulary of monastic architecture in the formation of their architectural identity. The flexible architecture and layout identified at nunneries in later medieval Ireland has been noted elsewhere. For example, the lack of uniformity of English and Welsh nunneries has been considered their most distinctive characteristic.[70] However, this flexibility and lack of uniformity is based on variation within a claustral plan.

The diversity in the Irish archaeological evidence extends to changes in arrangement over time in the life of the nunnery and these alterations can be clearly seen in the extant remains, usually in the form of blocked or inserted doors and windows, as archaeological investigations at St Catherine's, Old Abbey, County Limerick have shown (Fig. 2). However, what is more unusual is the identification of changes of plan at construction stage, as has been found in the excavations there. An east range appears to have been planned and commenced, at the northeastern corner of the cloister, only to have been abandoned at an early phase of construction and an

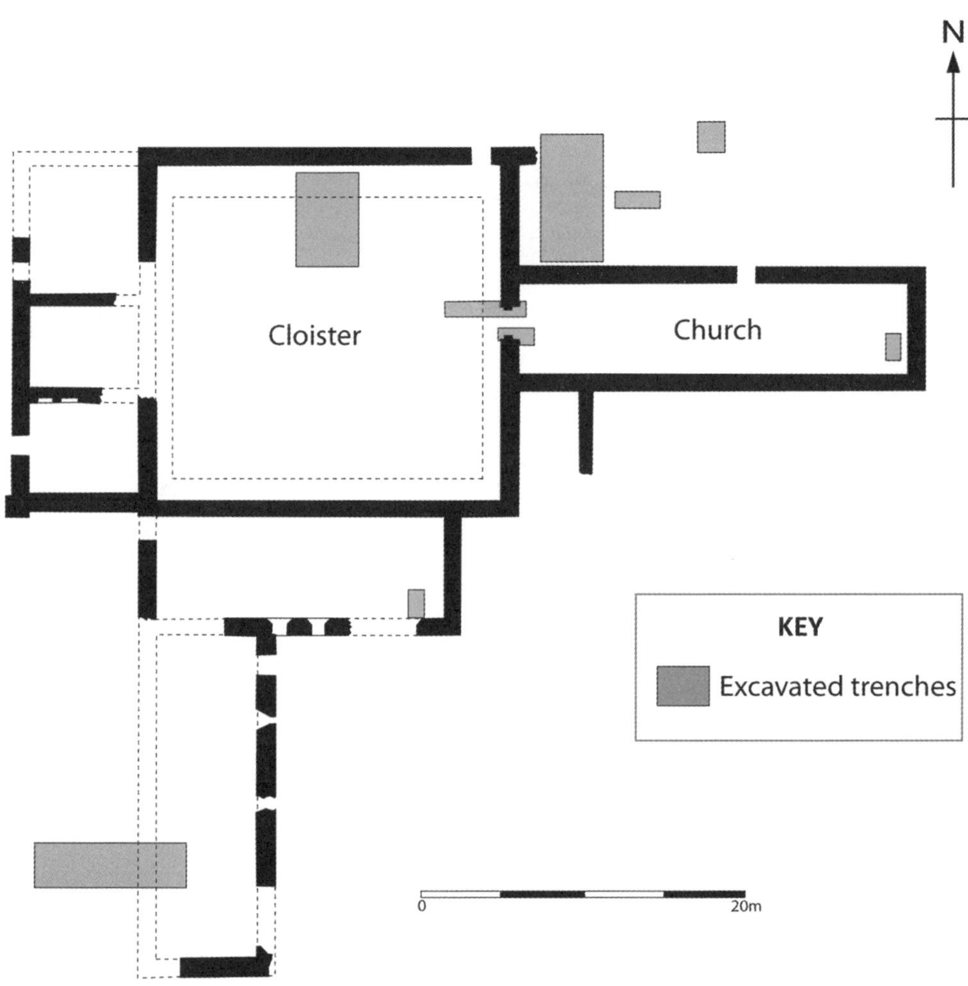


2. Ground plan of St Catherine's, Old Abbey, County Limerick showing main features and excavated trenches (image: author).

unusual projecting church constructed in its place, which utilised the fine doorway to provide access to and from the western cloister ambulatory.[71] This diversity can also be extended to patterns of patronage. For instance, four Augustinian houses in County Clare, Canon Island, Killone, Clare Abbey and Inchicronan, thought to have had the same patron (Domhnall Mór Ó Briain), all have notable differences in design (Fig. 3) and no two are alike.[72]

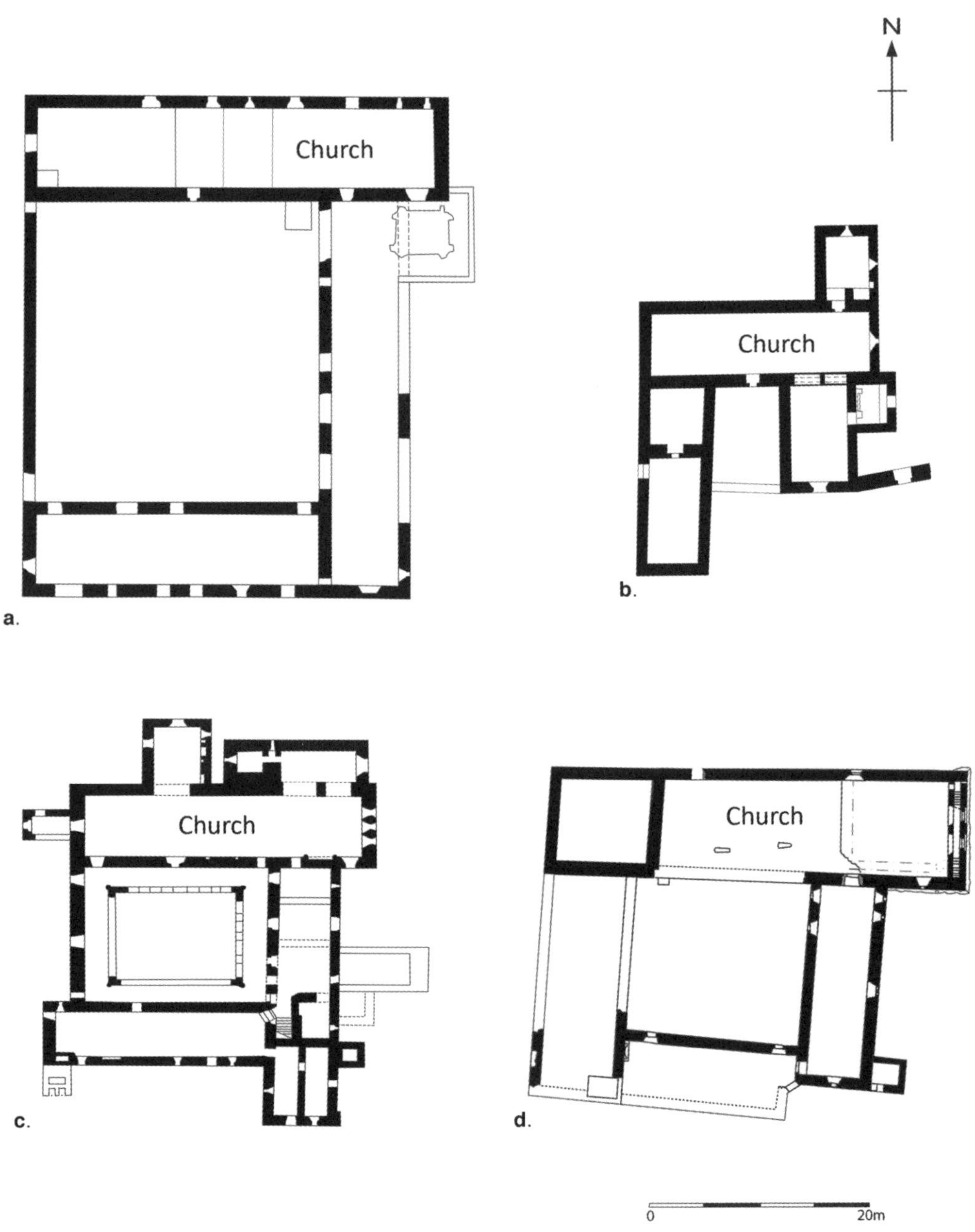


3. Diverse plans of Augustinian houses in County Clare.
**a.** Clare Abbey, **b.** Inchicronan, **c.** Canon Island, **d.** Killone
(image: author after Westropp 1900 and Salter 2009 with additions).

## Enclosure and segregation

Design and layout of any monastic house can be considered a physical manifestation of its various functions. One of these functions was monastic enclosure and separation from the secular world. Enclosure was particularly important for religious women and has been described as a fourth vow, in addition to chastity, poverty and obedience.[73] But what, if anything, can the variability of layout of nunneries in Ireland show with regard to how these spaces might have been used and how can this be related to notions of female monastic enclosure and identity? Surprisingly, at nunnery sites that have standing remains, there is no indication of masonry precinct walls. A contemporary account by Gerald of Wales states that only permeable hedges were employed at nunneries in Ireland and it has been suggested that he was specifically referring to the nunnery at Termonfeckin, County Louth.[74] Moreover, in his *Topography of Ireland* (*c*.1188), he shows the enclosure around the nunnery at Kildare as a hedge (*sepem)* rather than a wall.[75]

Therefore, perhaps female monastic enclosure in medieval Ireland might be considered more conceptual and theoretical, though not any less powerful as a result. This conclusion has ramifications for the consideration of female monastic identities for the medieval period as a whole. A modern instance serves to illustrate the point. In 1921, Benedictine nuns established a new house at Kylemore Castle, County Galway, the first Benedictine house founded in Ireland since the Reformation. Having purchased the castle they did not have the funds to build an enclosure wall. In consultation with the archbishop it was agreed that the mountains surrounding their new nunnery would be their enclosure, a perfect example of the archaeology and symbolism of 'natural places'.[76]

Despite the fact that modern scholarship has a tendency to view the actual or conceptual enclosure of medieval nuns to have been a predominantly negative force, there are no contemporary accounts by nuns themselves that show their dissatisfaction with enclosure, which suggests that it was generally accepted.[77] Therefore, enclosure could be considered as a positive force, drawing the female religious community together in a shared environment through the structure of codified behaviour of the nunnery's chosen rule and ethos. As has already been considered above, enclosure may not have been a positive force in the overall corporate identity of nunneries, but it may have been a positive influence on individual nuns as it facilitated them reaching their objective of getting closer to God.[78]

While enclosure is an important theoretical concept for all monastics and their identities, as has been seen, it can be widely interpreted in practice. There are many historical examples of abbesses leaving the confines of their cloisters to conduct business on behalf of their communities. One such business would have been the management of the nunneries' estates. In the case of St Catherine's, County Limerick, the nunnery's known holdings were close to the nunnery complex and it is easy to imagine various interactions between the nuns and their tenants. Indeed, it is likely that the nuns came from the locality. The numerous contemporary later medieval features – such as settlements, enclosures, castles and moated sites – which are in the vicinity of the nunnery were probably very familiar to the nuns and formed part of their world view and wider familial identities.

There is also a general perception leading from enclosure that strict segregation also applied at later medieval nunneries. Although true 'double-houses', in the English or French sense,[79] were not established in medieval Ireland, perhaps with the exception of Kildare,[80] there are several places – such as the Augustinian foundations of Annaghdown, County Galway and Ardcarn, County Roscommon – where co-location may have occurred, with canons, monks and nuns sharing facilities, perhaps even the church.[81] Similarly, nuns are historically recorded at male Cistercian houses by Stephen of Lexington in 1228 during his visitations.[82] He ordered the immediate removal of nuns from Mellifont, County Louth, Inishlounaght, County Tipperary and possibly Jerpoint, County Kilkenny. Although the precise location of the nuns and the nature of their accommodation at these sites remain unknown, it must have been sufficiently close to the male monasteries to cause serious concern. Perhaps these sites might also be considered in this group of co-located religious houses, despite it being officially irregular for nuns to be in such close proximity to male Cistercian houses.[83]

While there is some evidence for co-location of religious male and female houses, what of the notion of later medieval enclosed nuns sharing their church with parishioners and the laity? This may seem at odds with modern conceptions of female religious life, but it is the case that several nunneries in medieval Ireland probably did share their church. Although for Ireland there is scant evidence as to how this might have been achieved, evidence from elsewhere proves that it was quite common. Nuns employed galleries or screens in their churches to separate them from both the priest and the lay congregation. In some cases, the nuns' space was actually at the west end of the church, as shown in a sixteenth-century drawing of the church at Marrick nunnery in Yorkshire.[84] At St Catherine's, an incised ship – a recognised Christian religious symbol usually located near an altar – is located on the southern wall, near the west end of the church.[85] Perhaps this indicates the location of a dedicated nuns' altar.[86] Alternatively, Mark Gardiner has noted that several graffiti ships in churches in England are associated specifically with the location of the baptismal font, traditionally placed at the west end of the church, for example at Broomhill church, Sussex. These ships may also have had an apotropaic or evil-preventing function.[87]

## Burial

Is female religious identity expressed through burial and, if so, how? Historical accounts of burial at some religious houses are believed to be quite prescriptive as to where a member of a religious house or a patron might be buried. However, archaeology reveals that in most cases burial rules were seldom adhered to in practice, especially at prestigious houses.[88] To date, there has been just one research investigation of later medieval burials at a nunnery in Ireland. The excavations at St Catherine's, County Limerick confirmed the presence of burials of men, women and children in the church, cloister ambulatories and immediately to the north of the church (Table 2). Most of these burials are contemporary with its use. Surprisingly, the earliest burial was of a three- or four-year-old child (burial 2), dated to AD 1170–1270, buried in the northern cloister ambulatory. There were also two burials of females, one from the northern cloister ambulatory (burial 4), dated to AD 1440–1640, and the other (burial 8) was dated to AD 1280–1400 and located outside and to the north of the western end of the church. These burials afford a very rare glimpse of some members of a medieval nunnery community in Ireland, as there is just one other excavated nunnery burial recorded, from Graney, County Kildare.[89] The burials

Table 2. Data on radio-carbon dated excavated human remains from St Catherine's, County Limerick, according to date.

| Date (calibrated sigma 2) | Sex | Age | Burial Location | Skeleton Context/ burial numbers | Beta Analytic reference lab number |
|---|---|---|---|---|---|
| AD1170–1270 | undetermined | 3–4 years | N ambulatory | 909 burial 2 | 322858 |
| AD1280–1320<br>AD1340–1390 | undetermined | Adult | NW of church | 163 burial 9* | 322865 |
| AD1280–1400 | female | Middle Adult | NW of church | 160 burial 8 | 322864 |
| AD1290–1410 | male | Older Adult | N ambulatory | 914 burial 3 | 322859 |
| AD1300–1360<br>AD1380–1420 | female | 30–40 years | N ambulatory | 908 burial 1 | 322857 |
| AD1440–1520<br>AD1590–1620 | female | 20–25 years | NW of church | 128 burial 7 | 322863 |
| AD1440–1640 | female | 20–25 years | N ambulatory | 917 burial 4 | 322860 |
| AD1470–1650 | undetermined | *c.*5 years | NW of church | 114 burial 6 | 322862 |
| AD1500<br>AD1510–1600<br>AD1620–1660 | female | Older Adult | NW of church | 112 burial 5 | 322861 |

from St Catherine's suggest that the nunnery was possibly used as a burial place for the wider local community as well as the nuns themselves, highlighting its importance in this locality, even before its change in status to a parish church.

## Conclusion

Nunneries in later medieval Ireland had predicaments of identity on several levels. Within the nunnery, the individual identity of a woman of high status was transformed into a community identity by performing the ritual of profession. However, 'community' is a term laden with aspirations and contests and is sometimes contradictory, constructed through overlap and interactions of networks of communities.[90] Therefore, community identity in a nunnery was certainly not stagnant and fixed, and a shared identity could change over time.[91] Indeed a woman religious could be a member of several communities or networks. A particularly important factor affecting this identity was patronage. The families or individuals who supplied the funding for such monastic enterprises had their own agendas and so their agency cannot be discounted. Benefactors' agendas were varied and they may have supported a nunnery for status or prestige, for the benefit of close female family members (wives, sisters, daughters and granddaughters are all historically recorded), or to be prayed for and remembered to ensure the ultimate safe passage of their souls from Purgatory to Heaven.

On a corporate level, to use Penelope Johnson's term, nunneries were different from male houses because they were founded and supported for different reasons and they performed various functions for their respective local communities. Indeed, it can also be argued that nunneries differed from each other in flexibility of layout and uses. They were founded by their patrons to support them in prayer and, in some cases, to be the parish church and to provide services to the local community within which they were based. In these instances, nunneries were an important form of local monasticism. Most notably, a significant number, over a fifth of nunneries established in later medieval Ireland, were founded in locations prior to any male religious house. This suggests that initially the need for a female house in those locations was more immediate than for a male house. It is suggested from historical evidence that the nuns themselves were an intrinsic part of the patron's family and community, whom they served and interacted with in a variety of ways, such as through estate management, parish church functions and burial.

Therefore, rather than considering nunneries as foundations in an unwelcoming alien environment and subservient to their male counterparts, they are likely to have been founded in the midst of a willing and supportive patron and laity. The nuns themselves came from and belonged to this wider local community. In addition, they retained a multiplicity of identities, in addition to their religious role as Brides of Christ, as mothers, sisters, daughters, granddaughters, landlords and estate managers.

# 5

# The Uí Fhlaithbheartaigh of Mag Seóla and Iarchonnacht: From inland kings to sea-lords

PAUL NAESSENS

## Introduction

Along with a number of powerful dynasties on the west coast of late medieval Ireland, such as the Uí Mhaille, the Uí Fhlaithbheartaigh were renowned for their seamanship and for their exploitation of the burgeoning maritime trade and fisheries on the Atlantic seaboard (Fig. 1). They did not always hold this position, however: archaeological and historical evidence for the period before the thirteenth century shows that they originally ruled the inland kingdom of Mag Seóla on the eastern shores of Lough Corrib, while their early medieval *caput* at Loch Cimbe was about twenty-five kilometres from the shores of Galway Bay. The process by which the Uí Fhlaithbheartaigh transformed from early medieval inland kings to later medieval sea-lords, and the changes and continuity in settlement forms associated with that transformation, are the subject of this chapter.

## The emergence of the Uí Fhlaithbheartaigh and the kingdom of Mag Seóla

The Uí Fhlaithbheartaigh of Mag Seóla emerged in the later ninth century as the dominant sept among the tribes known as the Uí

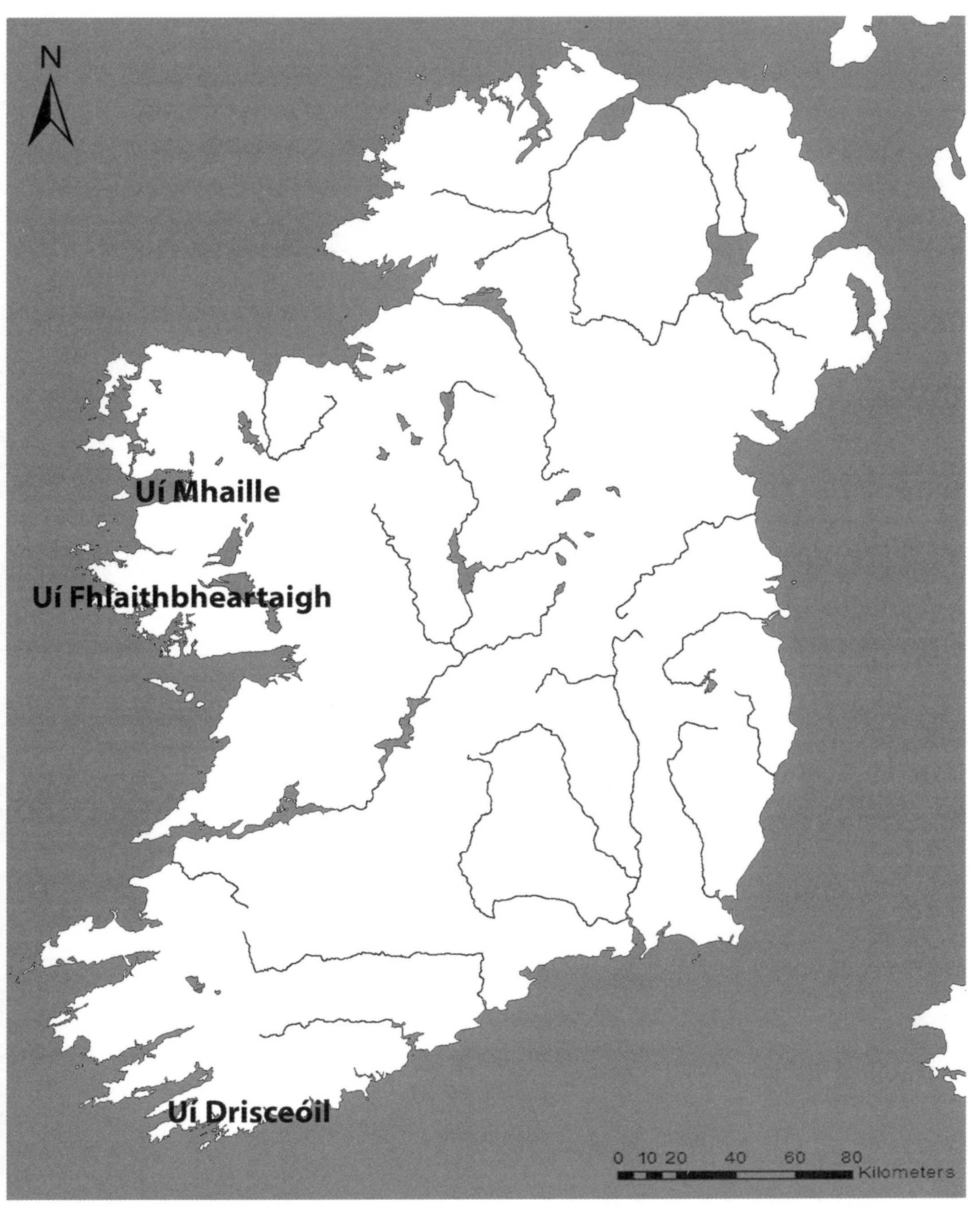


1. Location of the Uí Fhlaithbheartaigh lordship of Iarchonnacht and other later medieval Gaelic maritime elites discussed in the text (image: author).

Briúin Seóla, who occupied the eastern shores of Lough Corrib. From that time until their expulsion into Iarchonnacht during the thirteenth century, they controlled territories that were for the most part coterminous with the later barony of Clare in County Galway.[1] The borders of the Uí Fhlaithbheartaigh Mag Seóla lands were defined by the Black River to the north, the Clare River to the east, the north shore of Galway Bay and the territories of the Medraige to the south, and by Lough Corrib to the west (Fig. 2). From their emergence in the eighth century to their expulsion in the thirteenth century, they played a fulsome role in the political affairs of the region and emerged in the twelfth and thirteenth centuries as a major naval force while also being influential in the dynastic struggles of the Uí Chonchobhair that characterised much of the thirteenth century.

The rise of the Uí Fhlaithbheartaigh should be viewed through the filter of the major shifts in early Irish politics that took place from *c.*800. The specifics of the emergence of the Uí Fhlaithbheartaigh as kings of Mag Seóla are historically vague, but they appear to have been one of three major lines to emerge from the seventh-century division of the Uí Briúin of Dumha Selga, at Ard Caoin in County Roscommon.[2] By the eighth century, one of the resultant groups, the Uí Briúin Seola, had settled the lands directly to the east of Lough Corrib. By the ninth century the Uí Fhlaithbheartaigh, also known as the Muintir Murchada, had emerged as the dominant sept in that grouping and from then until the thirteenth century they ruled their vassals from their island *caput* at Loch Cimbe near Headford. In 990, 'The wind sunk the island of Loch Cimbe suddenly, with its *dreach*[3] and rampart, i.e. thirty feet'.[4] By the middle of the eleventh century the Uí Fhlaithbheartaigh were sufficiently powerful to embark on a campaign against the ruling Connacht dynasty of the Uí Chonchobhair. Muintir Murchada 'invaded Loch Oirbsean (Corrib) and deposed Aodh Ua Conchobhair' in 1061.[5] Their hegemony was short-lived, however, as 'the victory of Gleann-Phadraig was gained by Aodh Ua Conchobhair over the people of West Connaught, where many were slain, together with Ruaidhrí Ó Flaithbheartaigh, lord of West Connaught, [who] was beheaded, and his head was carried to Cruachain in Connaught'.[6] Ruaidhrí's death did not go unavenged, however, as in the following year 'Tadg son of Aed ua Conchobuir was treacherously killed by the Clann Choscraigh and the west of Connacht'.[7]

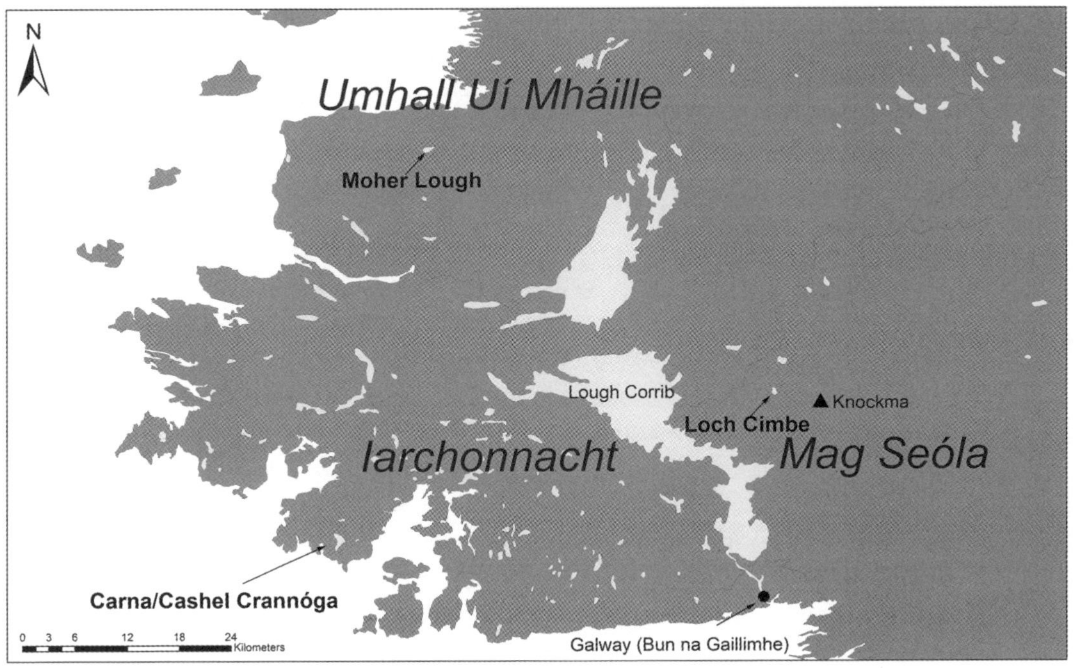


2. Location of Mag Seóla and significant sites of the Uí Fhlaithbheartaigh and the Uí Mháille (image: author).

The Uí Fhlaithbheartaigh continued to oppose the Uí Chonchobhair, suffering the loss of another of their kings in 1065.[8] Their efforts culminated in a final endeavour in 1092 when 'Ruaidhrí Ua Conchobhair, chief king of Connacht, was blinded in treachery by Ua Flaithbhertaigh, king of the West of Connacht'.[9] They were thwarted on this occasion by Muircheartach Ó Briain who seized the kingship for himself and installed Giolla na Naomh Ó hÉidhin, of the Uí Fhiachrach, as puppet ruler of Connacht. The blinding of the Ó Conchobhair king was also avenged in 1098 when 'Flaithbheartach Ua Flaithbheartaigh ... was slain by Madadhan Ua Cuanna, in revenge for the blinding of Ruaidhrí Ua Conchobhair'.[10] With the restoration of Ó Conchobhair hegemony in the early twelfth century, the Uí Fhlaithbheartaigh seemed to accept their fate as sub-kings of the Connacht kingdom under the competitors for provincial and national kingship and, for the most part, they are noticed in the chronicles as military supporters of the reigning, or contending, Connacht kings. Many of the subsequent entries in this vein have a decidedly naval or nautical aspect, perhaps indicating the developing maritime power of the Uí Fhlaithbheartaigh.

Later Ó Flaithbheartaigh kings found, however, that support for the Uí Chonchobhair did not necessarily bring about a change in their fortunes, an example being when Muireadhach Ó Flaithbheartaigh was killed in 1121 on a cattle raid in support of Toirdhealbhach Ó Conchobhair.[11] Conchobhar Ó Flaithbheartaigh suffered the same fate at the hands of Cormac Mac Carthaigh at the battle of An Cloidhe,[12] after Cormac sacked the town and Caisleán Bhun na Gaillimhe.[13]

For the next hundred years the fate of the Uí Fhlaithbheartaigh remained closely knit with one or more of the Ó Conchobhair kings or claimants to the Connacht kingship. They continued to guard the western flank of the province through their control of Lough Corrib and its fortifications at Bun na Gaillimhe, Iniscremha and Caisleán na Circe (Castlekirk), until their displacement from Mag Seóla in the mid-to-late-thirteenth century. While some chronicle references throughout this period testify to Uí Fhlaithbheartaigh involvement in provincial power struggles, little is revealed about their demesne lands, or *capita*. The Uí Fhlaithbheartaigh are not unique in their treatment by native chroniclers, who were more interested in recording the great events of the day than the minor details of settlement. In the case of the Uí Fhlaithbheartaigh, however, there is a manuscript (TCD MS 1319) that provides a detailed, and perhaps unique, early account of the mensal lands (*lucht tighe*) of Mag Seóla. The document names the service families of the Uí Fhlaithbheartaigh on their mensal lands, records their duties and lists the estates that they controlled in return for their respective services to their chief. The manuscript was translated by O'Donovan in his Ordnance Survey letters for County Galway and also published by Hardiman in his notes in O'Flaherty's *West or h-Iar Connaught*.[14]

The greater part of the chronicle entries relating to Connacht in the first half of the twelfth century are concerned with the efforts of Toirdhealbhach Ó Conchobhair to gain and consolidate his position as high king of Ireland. The Irish sources are replete with evidence for grand land battles and naval expeditions in support of his efforts and the counter-campaigns of the other regional kings. Not only was the scale and duration of the wars greater, there is also much evidence for innovation in the way in which strategy was conceived and carried through. Toirdhealbhach's strategy, from the 1120s at least, appears to have been based on enhancing the defence of Connacht as a prelude to embarking on campaigns of consolidation into the remaining provinces. Having successfully forced the submission of a province, he would then appoint at least two or more kings of his choosing to divide the conquered territory.[15] The practical implementation of such a plan involved three main military policies. The tactics consisted of (a) the construction of key fortifications to guard his Connacht kingdom, (b) the deployment of major armies to harry the other provinces and (c) the use of naval fleets to support his land forces on rivers, lakes and the sea.

The Uí Fhlaithbheartaigh of Mag Seóla appear, from copious notices in the various chronicles and from archaeological evidence, to have played a substantial part in all three tactical strands. In 1121 they are to be found raiding into Munster, with Ó Conchobhair, as far as Lismore, suffering the loss of their king Muireadhach Ó Flaithbheartaigh in the process.[16] The *Annals of Tigernach* record the building of three major fortifications on the borders of the Ó Conchobhair kingdom in 1124.[17] For the first time in the Irish chronicles the term *caistél* (castle) or *caisleán* is used to describe these three fortifications at Galway, at Ballinasloe, County Galway and at Collooney, County Sligo, perhaps indicating that they were new structures of a greater scale and complexity than the *dún* that had gone before.[18] Caisleán Bhun na Gaillimhe, on the site of present-day Galway city, lying as it did on the southern borders of Mag Seóla, was most likely built and garrisoned by the Uí Fhlaithbheartaigh and their vassals.[19] Caisleán Bhun na Gaillimhe, along with other major strong-points on Lough Corrib such as Iniscremha, Caisleán na Circe and Caisleán na Cailligħe on Lough Mask, defended the western flank of the Uí Chonchobhair against naval attack. Recent archaeological investigations of the substantially intact *caisleán* at Iniscremha have demonstrated that the scale and morphology of such sites was indeed innovative. Moreover, the radiocarbon date (AD 1020–1180) obtained for the construction of the enclosing wall at Iniscremha supports the chronicle evidence.[20]

The Uí Fhlaithbheartaigh, along with other Connacht families such as the Uí Dhubda, the Uí Fhiachrach and the Uí Mháille of Fir Umaill, served as naval officers to the Connacht kings and are recorded as such in a late thirteenth- or early fourteenth-century tract on the inauguration of the Ó Conchobhair.[21]

The Uí Fhlaithbheartaigh, although it is not explicitly stated in the chronicles, appear to have supported Cathal Carrach Ó Conchobhair in his successional dispute with Cathal Croibhdhearg in the closing decade of the twelfth century. In 1196 'Ruaidhri O'Flaithbheartaigh, king of the West of Connacht, went on the sea, to escape from Cathal Croibhderg, and from the men of Connacht also, and went to O'Briain'.[22] Croibhdhearg expelled him once more from the protection of the Uí Bhriain, and Ó Flaithbheartaigh was found later that year raiding the tribes of the Conmaicne-mara and the Umhall, whether out of spite or necessity is unclear.[23]

The Uí Fhlaithbheartaigh submitted to de Burgh's forces in 1235 and assisted the English in their campaigns against Maghnus Ó Conchobhair, bringing their boats overland from Lough Corrib through the Maam valley to Killary Fjord and onward by sea to Westport bay.[24] Ó Flaithbheartaigh support of the English on this occasion, however, was not rewarded when the subinfeudation commenced two years later.

The end of the power struggle of the Uí Fhlaithbheartaigh with their Connacht over-kings coincides closely with the date normally assigned to TCD MS 1319. The content of the manuscript suggests that it may have had some connection with the defeat of the Uí Fhlaithbheartaigh in 1092 and was, perhaps, intended as a document reaffirming their power within their own mensal lands and throughout their Mag Seóla patrimony. Analysis of MS 1319 has allowed for a partial reconstruction of the Uí Fhlaithbheartaigh mensal lands in Mag Seóla, in the period just prior to their expulsion to Iarchonnacht in the thirteenth century. The location of many of the landholdings occupied by Uí Fhlaithbheartaigh vassals can be identified among the names of the townlands recorded in the manuscript. Further cross-analysis of MS 1319 with the OS six-inch maps, O'Donovan's *Letters* and the national Record of Monuments and Places (RMP) has been undertaken to also identify the possible core settlements of the vassals of the Uí Fhlaithbheartaigh. This identification has led to the conclusion that the *caiseal* form may have been favoured over the *ráth* by high-status vassals of the Uí Fhlaithbheartaigh in the early second millennium.

The final failure of the Uí Fhlaithbheartaigh to usurp the power of the Ó Conchobhair kings left them guarding the western flank of the province, through their control of Lough Corrib and its fortifications, until their eventual expulsion from Mag Seóla in 1273. They were accompanied on their migration to Iarchonnacht by several of their vassal families, the most important of whom were the Uí hAllmhuráin (O'Halloran). Indeed, the frequent references to service families such as the Uí Cheanndubháin (Canavans) and the Uí Laoidhigh (O'Lees), also known as Meic an Leagha, and the survival of those surnames in the Moycullen area today, and of Uí Cathasaigh (Casey) further west, suggests that the household officers of the *lucht tighe* of the Uí Fhlaithbheartaigh in Mag Seóla migrated *en masse* to Iarchonnacht.[25]

The settlement model of the mensal lands developed for Mag Seóla with the aid of MS 1319 has been used here as a comparative tool in the identification and analysis of the post-expulsion high medieval settlements of Iarchonnacht.

## Establishment of the Uí Fhlaithbheartaigh in Iarchonnacht

The Uí Fhlaithbheartaigh territories of Iarchonnacht comprised Conmaicne Mara, Gnó Mór and Gnó Beg (the later baronies of Ballynahinch and Moycullen).[26] The Uí Sheóigh (Joys or Joyces), in the barony of Rosse and to the north of Gnó Mór, appear to have become important vassals to the Uí Fhlaithbheartaigh only at some time in the sixteenth century, while the Uí hAllmhuráin were probably their chief vassals in Gnó Mór and Gnó Beg from a much earlier period, as suggested by their role as clerics in the lordship and their later possession of the tower houses of Barna and Oghery.

The position of the Uí Fhlaithbheartaigh and the Uí Mháille as naval chiefs serving the Ó Conchobhair kings in the early fourteenth century is alluded to in a tract on the inauguration of Ó Conchobhair:

> *Do longa ag Ua Flaithbheartaigh agus ag airdrígh Umhaill*
> (Your ships with Ó Flaithbheartaigh and the high-king of Umhall).[27]

The chronicles for the fourteenth and fifteenth centuries reinforce this notion of the Uí Fhlaithbheartaigh and the Uí Mháille as seafarers, as most of the references to the Uí Fhlaithbheartaigh for this period are in relation to sea-borne raids on or by the Uí Mháille.[28] In 1384 a parley between the neighbours went disastrously wrong when 'a meeting took place between O'Flaherty and O'Malley but a quarrel arose between them in which Owen O'Malley, Cormac O'Malley (i.e. Cormac Cruinn)[29] and many others besides these were slain by the people of O'Flaherty'.[30] In 1417 the Uí Fhlaithbheartaigh suffered a major loss in Uí Mháille waters when 'Ruaidri son of Murchad O Flaithbertaig and Ruaidri son of Diarmait Dub O Flaithbertaig and sixteen other Uí Flaithbertaig with them were drowned in Clew Bay'.[31] Whether this major loss of life through drowning, also recorded in the Annals of Ulster, was the result of an abortive raid on the Uí Mháille of the Owles or a trading expedition, is not recorded.

From the close of the thirteenth century to the mid-sixteenth century, the Gaelic lords of Iarchonnacht remained relatively isolated from the Anglo-Irish political world and are hardly noticed at all in the native chronicles from the mid-fifteenth to the early sixteenth century. Their greatest contact with the 'Old English' was probably as a result of trade in goods such as hides, fish and agricultural produce. Thus, we know little about this crucial period when trade and fishery exploitation appears to have developed and financed the building of coastal tower houses along the western seaboard.[32] It was probably at this time that the divergence between the eastern and western septs of the Uí Fhlaithbheartaigh became more pronounced, with the eastern septs identifying to a greater degree with the merchants of Galway, while the western chiefs saw their future in the control and exploitation of the increasingly busy sea-lanes of the Atlantic coast.

## The Carna/Cashel medieval lakeland settlement complex

The nature of secular settlement and housing in high medieval Gaelic Ireland is among one of the most poorly understood aspects of Irish archaeology, despite the increased amount of attention that it has received of late. O'Conor has recognised that the Gaelic-dominated regions of Ireland, which included much of west Ulster, Connacht and west Munster, were not consistent in their relationships with the

Anglo-Norman lordships. Factors such as proximity to the English lordships and the limited agricultural potential of some Gaelic lands ensured that the relationship between Gaelic lords and the English varied from almost total independence in some cases, such as that of Iarchonnacht, to one of tenant status in others.[33] The virtual autonomy of many Gaelic lordships, together with the failure on the part of the chiefs to maintain administrative records of their decrees and financial affairs, has meant that a much greater understanding has been reached of settlement patterns in the English-controlled regions in the later medieval period.

The case for the continued occupation of *crannóga* throughout the later medieval period rests on much firmer ground. Copious entries in the native documentary sources refer to Gaelic Irish lords dying on island sites which could be assumed to be their main residences. FitzPatrick has suggested that many of these *crannóga* were located on the landholdings of service families, continuing the tradition of the *crannóg*-based monastic hostels or hospitals serving as retreats where kings or lords could recuperate from illness or die.[34] Kelleher has suggested that private island sites were favoured by lords throughout the later medieval period, a theme that is echoed in other regions.[35] Davies' excavation of Island MacHugh, County Tyrone produced some evidence for thirteenth- and fourteenth-century occupation, while Fredengren has identified some distinctive features of later medieval *crannóga* on Lough Gara, County Sligo.[36] Fredengren's argument is based on the dating of one *crannóg* on the lake that is topped by dense stone packing which she believes may be a feature of later medieval *crannóga*. Evidence from sites such as Ardakillen, County Roscommon, which is also enclosed by a *caiseal*-type wall, provides further support for her theory.[37] Artefactual evidence, much of it from Ulster, adds further support to the case for the continued widespread use of *crannóga* into the later medieval period.

Island or *inis* sites are also well attested to in both native and English sources from the high medieval period. These sites are usually distinguished by their status as natural or partly natural islands, which have been substantially fortified and are mentioned by Giraldus Cambrensis in the 1180s as the habitations of many Irish lords.[38] Some of these sites were riverine, such as that of Inis Samer in the estuary of the Erne at Ballyshannon, County Donegal.[39]

The term *longphort*, meaning stronghold, is often used in the native sources to refer to fortified island sites such as Iniscremha, County Galway and Caisleán na Cailligh, County Mayo, but it also has a more general application. It has been applied to temporary military camps and was used to describe elite settlement forms of the Uí Chonchobhair at Cloonfree and Ardakillen, County Roscommon and at Fasa Choillidh, County Sligo in the fourteenth century.[40] It has also been shown by O'Conor that other moated sites besides Cloonfree were occupied by Gaelic Irish lords of high rank in north Connacht,[41] and FitzPatrick (Chapter 9) has shown how service families of the Uí Chonchobhair were living at Cloonfree as late as the end of the sixteenth century.

It has been shown how MS 1319, a composite manuscript, can provide sufficient detail for a partial reconstruction of the Ó Flaithbheartaigh mensal lands in Mag Seóla in the period just prior to the thirteenth-century expulsion of the Uí Fhlaithbheartaigh to Iarchonnacht. The results of the Mag Seóla survey show that the principal high-status settlements of the Uí Fhlaithbheartaigh were concentrated, in the pre-expulsion period, in the northwest of Mag Seóla and lay for thc most part between their *caput* at Lough Hackett and Lough Corrib to the west and south. As already noted, their choice of *caput* was lacustrine despite the paucity of suitable lakeland landscapes to the east of Lough Corrib. It is suggested here that the Ó Flaithbheartaigh kings and later lords were probably inaugurated in the vicinity of Knockmaa (but perhaps not on its summit) given the hill's outstanding presence on the flat plains of the Mag Seóla landscape and its location in a boundary place between the parishes of Kilower and Belclare. The hill of Knockmaa was central to a medieval hunting ground and adjacent to a later deerpark at Castle Hackett demesne. A folly, immediately west of two cairns, on the summit of Knockmaa is called 'Finbarra's castle'. The Ó Flaithbheartaigh kings of Mag Seóla exploited the natural and cultural resources of the landscape of Knockmaa, as did the later proprietors of the Castle Hackett estate through emparkment and the setting of the folly. It is possible that a locally significant prehistoric site served as the inauguration venue of the Ó Flaithbheartaigh kings. A cairn on a low hill in the townland of Kildrum, west of Knockmaa, has the perfect profile for an inauguration place, set against the backdrop of the hill of Knockmaa.

The pre-expulsion distribution map of the core of the Ó Flaithbheartaigh lordship was compared with possible settlement sites directly west of the Mag Seóla *caput* in Gnó Mór. A model for high medieval settlement west of Lough Corrib was subsequently developed, the results of which are presented here.

The gradual pressure exerted on the Uí Fhlaithbheartaigh by the Anglo-Normans from the early thirteenth century may have led to the consolidation of their hold over the lands to the west of Lough Corrib prior to their final expulsion in 1273. A striking feature of the pattern of settlement in Iarchonnacht is the high concentration of settlements of possible high medieval date situated directly across the narrows of Lough Corrib to the southwest of Mag Seóla. Possible island sites of high medieval date were the later tower house sites of Oghery on Ross Lake, Fough on the Oughterard River, Aughnanure on the Drimneen River and the *crannóg* situated on Lough Naneevin in Rosscahill, 150m to the south of the modern N59. While no evidence of any high medieval activity has been found at Fough or Aughnanure, both of which were later developed as tower house sites, the *crannóg* on Lough Naneevin and the island site of Oghery on Ross Lake remain strong candidates for the initial Ó Flaithbheartaigh *capita* following their expulsion. Lough Naneevin's similar landscape location to Lough Hackett, its proximity to the route preserved in the modern N59 and its close spatial relationship to the probable Ó Flaithbheartaigh inauguration site at Carn Gégáin all support its candidacy.[42]

The island was investigated by Kinahan in 1865 when he surveyed the site and carried out six small excavations.[43] The site (41m × 25m) was joined to the mainland by a narrow causeway, traces of which remain underwater today. A row of oak piles were observed to the south and southwest while an irregularly laid floor, consisting of oak beams, ash and sallow, was observed to the east. A structure described as a long rude bench of stone was noted west of the centre of the island, although it was remarked that it could be the remains of wall foundations.[44] While a hearth was uncovered, based on a large flagstone, few finds, and none diagnostic of a high medieval date, were recorded.

The island of Oghery on Ross Lake, in contrast, has substantial remains of a 1m-wide enclosing dry-stone wall throughout its *c.*110m circumference. The island is also the site of a later tower house recorded in a 1574 list of Galway castles and owners, although very little remains of the fabric of that tower.[45] A stone-lined circular well (diam. 1.5m) survives in the northeast quadrant of the island, which may also be of high medieval date. A harbour or docking bay is also visible on the northern shore of the island.

The contrast between the high density of *ráth*, *caiseal*, island sites, churches and enclosures of possible high medieval date adjacent to, and also to the northeast of, the modern N59 is quite striking when compared to the evidence from the west of the lordship. There, the overall levels of settlement appear to be lower, while the predominant settlement site-type of pre- tower house date appears to be the *crannóg*. Two significant clusters of lacustrine settlement stand out as possible Ó Flaithbheartaigh *capita* of high medieval date. The first of these is centred on Ballynahinch Lake where the island tower house was later erected, while the other is in the Carna/Moyrus region. In the sixteenth century Ballynahinch became the only site of an inland tower house in the western half of Iarchonnacht. It was perhaps the *caput* of the western Sliocht Eoghan sept of the Uí Fhlaithbheartaigh from the time of their arrival in the thirteenth century. It seems highly significant that the area should be the location for the only two later medieval monastic foundations in the entire lordship. A Carmelite friary was founded here in 1356 although nothing remains of the site today.[46] A second foundation was endowed by the Uí Fhlaithbheartaigh in 1427 as part of the expansion to the west of the Dominican order.[47] This foundation was suppressed in the mid-sixteenth century and the masonry of the priory was reputedly used in the construction of the tower house at Ballynahinch, although close inspection of the fabric of the castle has failed to identify any evidence to support that tradition. The fact that both foundations and the island *caput* of the Uí Fhlaithbheartaigh are either on or adjacent to the river and lake reflects the great richness of the Ballynahinch fishery, which underpinned much of the economy of the area and also its significance as a fording point on the route to Bunowen, another major Sliocht Eoghan *caput*. Castle Island, on Ballynahinch Lake, appears to be partially artificial, as is the case at the Rock of Lough Cé, where a natural island was consolidated into a more substantial land mass through the addition of substantial amounts of loose stone and earth.[48] The collapsed remains of what was probably a retaining wall, encompassing the garth of the island, are still visible throughout, while a semi-submerged stone jetty is visible to the north of the island.

A more general distribution of possible high medieval settlement sites, including those classified as *ráth*, *caiseal*, *crannog*, and a promontory fort, was plotted to identify possible settlement concentrations or clusters. This information was then compared with the location of firmly dated high medieval and late medieval churches. In order to fulfil their pastoral function, the churches would have been built in the vicinity of, or at least be easily accessible to, the greater concentration of their parishioners, while secular control of those institutions and their dues by Gaelic lords might also predicate proximity to lordly settlements. This information was then plotted in relation to the tower houses that were built in the later fifteenth and early sixteenth centuries. By examining the distribution of possible high medieval sites through the filter of earlier secular settlements, contemporary and later ecclesiastical sites and also later tower house sites of the Uí Fhlaithbheartaigh, some broad patterns can be identified. A general archaeological survey of all possible high medieval settlement in Iarchonnacht was undertaken using the same methodology, while a more focused study was undertaken at Carna and Moyrus in southwest Connemara where there is abundant evidence for high medieval lacustrine settlement, a high medieval parish church and also a later coastal tower house and bawn.

Perhaps the most significant cluster of lacustrine sites of possible high medieval date in Iarchonnacht is the Carna/Cashel group. A total of eight *crannóga* or island *caisil* have been identified in that area, three of which are located on Lough Skannive. The largest of these, Oileán an Chaca, shows evidence for quite extensive settlement and would appear to have been a high-status site (Fig. 3). The enclosed island (60m N–S × 35m E–W) is trapezoidal in plan. The walls of the northwest area of the island have collapsed, exposing, in section, the large boulders of the inner and outer facing and the inner rubble core. The enclosing walls are for the most part in a state of collapse and are difficult to discern along some of the shoreline. They are best preserved at the northern end of the island where a stone quay (4m deep × 2m wide) is situated on the north-northwest shore. A level platform area is discernible to the south of the harbour feature before the island rises to a low peak of about 5m in height in its south central portion. A round structure (diam. 5m) represented by a single grass-covered course of stones, which may possibly be the remains of a house or hut, covers much of the crown of the hill. A short wall extension of two courses runs for two metres from the west of this structure, while a possible keyhole-shaped kiln was identified to the west of the island. The kiln bears a striking resemblance to that excavated at the thirteenth- or fourteenth-century ringwork at Ballysimon in County Limerick.[49] To the south the remains of several walls can be traced with at least two enclosures that may also represent the remains of buildings. The first of these is in the southwest corner of the island where a low wall curves in a semicircle to meet the exterior walls of the island, enclosing an area of about 4m in diameter. This area is abutted to the east by a long rectangular enclosure (9m E–W × 2m N–S). An area of stone collapse at the southeast edge of the island may also be the remains of a feature or may just represent the collapsed outer wall.

The island is connected to two smaller islands to the west by a stone causeway (2.5m × 1.5m). A smaller circular *caiseal*, Oileán an Bhalla, lies 100m to the west of Oileán an Chaca (Fig. 4). This very well preserved island *caiseal* appears to have been constructed by consolidating the stone from a shallow area close to the southwest shore of Lough Skannive and is enclosed by a substantial stone wall that is broken at the north to house a quay of the same dimensions and style as that of Oileán an Chaca (Fig. 5). The interior of the *caiseal* is heavily overgrown with vegetation, and no man-made features can be discerned within it apart from a small robber trench that appears to be a recent feature. A third *crannóg* (18m × 16.5m) is situated in the northwest arm of Lough Skannive. Traces of dry-stone walling survive but the site does not appear to have been as substantial as the other two. The interior rises towards the centre and is also very overgrown with vegetation and apparently featureless.

These sites, and four additional *crannóga* to the west on Lough Bola, Lough Athrohaunderg, Lough Keamnacally and Lough Sheedagh, constitute the most significant *crannóg* cluster in Iarchonnacht. The parish church of Moyrus lies 2.5km to the west of this cluster while the later tower house of Ard lies approximately 5km to the west of Lough Skannive. There are a number of other island *caisil* and *crannóga* to the west of Ballynahinch including the artificial stone-circled, raised peat island in the north of Lough Fadda,

4. The island *caiseal* of Oileán an Bhalla, Lough Skannive (Carna/Cashel *crannóg*)(image: author).

5km south of Clifden. This *crannóg* is notable for the remarkably well-preserved stone causeway (1.5m × 23m) which joins the island to the western shore. The island *caiseal* on Lough Doonloughan, 3km northwest of Bunowen, has a similarly well-preserved causeway connecting it to the mainland to the north. A further small island *caiseal* in the east of Courhoor Lough near Claddaghduff is also joined to the shore to the south by a stone causeway.

Although it cannot be proven without excavation that any of the sites were occupied from the thirteenth to the sixteenth century, many Gaelic Irish of the high medieval period made a conscious choice to place their *capita* on or near water. While it is often stated that sites are located near rivers or coasts, in the case of the Uí Fhlaithbheartaigh it seems to have been imperative that the sites were actually physically placed as near as possible to water. From

5. The enclosing wall at the northwest (boat dock) side of Oileán an Chaca (Carna/Cashel *crannóg*)(image: author).

their island *caput* at Lough Cimbe in Mag Seóla, through to the later tower houses such as Aughnanure and Fough in the east, and Ard and Bunowen in the west, there is no known Ó Flaithbheartaigh power centre that is not placed on, or directly adjacent to, water. It would seem that water and its presence had more than a purely practical role to play for Gaelic maritime lords, and that tradition and their heritage as seafarers was expressed in a very public way through bardic poetry that featured motifs such as naval warfare, sea-voyage, storm at sea, the importation of wine in ships and swimming.[50]

Evidence that lacustrine sites were of greater significance is also found in other Gaelic lordships in Ireland and Scotland. Both the Clann Domhnaill lords of the Isles and the Uí Drisceóil of Baltimore chose to retreat to lacustrine sites.[51] It appears that the principal septs of the Uí Fhlaithbheartaigh of Iarchonnacht continued to occupy lacustrine and river-island sites from their arrival in the thirteenth century through to the late fifteenth or early sixteenth century, when they adopted the tower house form of architecture. Although there is some evidence to suggest that a late occupation of promontory forts may have been a feature of high medieval settlement in Iarchonnacht, the evidence for this on mainland sites is less than compelling. A possible exception, however, may be the 'Doon' at Bunowen, 1km west of the later tower house of the same name. O'Flaherty recorded that 'There is an old fortress of a down on the top of the hill, which gives its name to Balyndown'.[52] Doon Hill is a steep-sided volcanic plug rising directly to the west of the former medieval parish church of Ballindoon. The crown of the hill was the location for post-medieval follies built by the Geoghegan family in the eighteenth century and was also later used as a Second World War lookout post. The sea was reached from the summit by a shallow sloping depression to the south, which leads to the northern shore of Bunowen Bay. No surface trace of the 'Doon' survives today but the possibility that it was a high medieval *caput* of the Sliocht Eoghan remains.

## The Ó Máille *caput* on Moher Lough

The Uí Fhlaithbheartaigh and the Uí Mháille shared a territorial boundary in the later medieval period that ran along the line of Killary Fjord on the modern Galway–Mayo border. The Ó Máille lordship extended northwards from this boundary encompassing the numerous islands, shores and sea lanes of Clew Bay, which appear to have constituted the core of their estates. While the large number of promontory forts concentrated in the Clew Bay region appears to suggest that the pre-tower house *capita* in the Ó Máille lordship were of this settlement form, there are a number of island sites that may also have served this function in the high medieval period. One such example is the island *caiseal* on Moher Lake in the townland of Carrowmore to the southeast of Croagh Patrick. This island (*c.* 28m E–W x 30m N–S) was originally enclosed by a dry-stone wall, three courses of which survive in parts. The footings of a substantial, rectangular stone house occupy much of the centre

6. The boat quay on the southeast side of the island *caiseal* on Moher Lake (image: author).

of the island while a sizeable stone-lined quay or dock, 2m wide by 5m deep, survives at the southeast of the island (Fig. 6). The scale of the island, the boat dock and the presence of a substantial stone building in the interior of the island all point to a similarity in morphology and use with the island *caiseal* of Iarchonnacht to the south. While it may be simplistic to suggest that this pattern is replicated throughout the lordships of the Atlantic coast in the later medieval period, it has been noted that private island spaces were seen as significant features beyond Iarchonnacht.

## Conclusion

The ninth-century Ó Flaithbheartaigh kings of Mag Seóla might seem to have been unlikely candidates for a major maritime force, but there are strong indicators proceeding from that time which suggest that they commenced their transition from inland kings to sea-lords at quite an early date. Their choice of Loch Cimbe (Lough Hackett) as their *caput* is one such indicator. The location of Mag Seóla on the eastern shore of Lough Corrib left it and the Ó Conchobhair kingdom vulnerable to incursions by Viking raiders in the tenth century. The short-lived occupation of Lough Corrib by Limerick-based Vikings in the early tenth century may have been a catalyst towards the development of Ó Flaithbheartaigh naval power. The gradual loss of their inland kingdom and the assumption of direct rule of Iarchonnacht, to the west, during the thirteenth century cemented the process. The part played by the Uí Fhlaithbheartaigh as naval admirals serving the Uí Chonchobhair, in the dynastic and inter-provincial struggles of the twelfth and thirteenth centuries, left them in a strong position to assert their authority over the sea lanes of the Atlantic coast following their migration to Iarchonnacht. While there is no direct documentary evidence supporting the idea that they continued to favour island sites as their *capita* prior to the construction of tower houses on the coast of Iarchonnacht, the archaeological evidence presented here is quite compelling. It seems likely that together with their households and vassals, they established similar patterns of settlement in Iarchonnacht to those implied in MS 1319 for Mag Seóla, with their *capita* once again occupying island sites. Island sites such as Oileán an Chaca and Oileán an Bhalla in Iarchonnacht, and the Ó Máille island *caiseal* on Moher Lough in County Mayo, clearly functioned as high-status *capita* in the later medieval period. The adoption of the tower house architectural form, combined with an upsurge in coastal trade in the late medieval period, saw them relocate to the littoral zone of the Atlantic coast. The verticality of the tower house, with its practical applications to the control of fisheries, and its symbolism as a marker of power, probably predicated a move from inland island *caput* to coastal castle in the Gaelic lordships of the Uí Fhlaithbheartaigh and the Uí Mháille in the west of Ireland. This pattern of migration to the shore was most likely replicated in other lordships such as that of the Uí Drisceóil of Baltimore in Cork.

6

# Violence in later medieval Ireland: The osteoarchaeological evidence and its historical context

COLM J. DONNELLY AND EILEEN M. MURPHY

## Introduction – Ireland in the later medieval period

In 1515 a document was compiled for Henry VIII that provided the English king with an overview of the current state of Ireland, with plans for how the monarch might, in essence, reconquer the island. Authorship of the document may rest with John Kite, Archbishop of Armagh, in consultation with key figures within the Anglo-Irish community in Ireland.[1] Leaving aside the fact that it provided a draft blueprint for what actually happened as the sixteenth century progressed and the Tudor government's involvement in the country became increasingly interventionist, the text provides a view of how politics worked among the indigenous aristocracy. The document states that Ireland was made up of some sixty countries of the 'Kinges Irishe enymyes', each with their own 'Chyef Capytaynes'.[2] These 'enymyes' of the Crown were the Gaelic Irish lords whose names the document goes on to list, men who:

> lyveyth onely by the swerde, and obeyeth to no other temperall person, but onely to himself that is stronge: and every of the said Capytaynes makeyth warre and peace for hymself, and holdeith by swerde, and hathe imperiall jurysdyction within his rome,

> and obeyeth to noo other person, Englyshe ne Iryshe, except only to suche persones, as maye subdue hym by the swerde.[3]

Clearly in the eyes of the king's advisors these were dangerous men who were beyond the pale, both literally and metaphorically, but what has the document to say about the 'Middle Nation', as they evidently called themselves,[4] those lords descended from the Anglo-Norman adventurers who had arrived on the island from the late twelfth century onwards? The assessment of the Crown's advisors in London was that this category of aristocrat had indeed become and belonged to Ireland, and the 'more then 30 greate captaines of thEnglyshe noble folke' were described in similar form to those of their Gaelic Irish neighbours, to the point that they:

> folowyth the same Iryshe ordre, and kepeith the same rule, and every of them makeith warre and pease for hymself, without any lycence of the King, or of any other temperall person, saive to hym that is strongeyst, and of suche that maye subdue them by the swerde.[5]

For the purposes of the current study the 1515 text is relevant since it provides a fairly accurate, if somewhat basic, assessment of how Ireland was politically organised in the period prior to the Tudor Reconquest; it is a text that emphasises a lack of central government and a resultant devolution of political control among ninety-odd power brokers, each competing for domination over their 'countryes' against internal and external competition, but with 'an acknowledgement that the "Englishry" and "Irishry" formed a single political nation'.[6] While ancestral distinction still existed between *Gaedhil* and *Gaill*, the Anglo-Irish were viewed by the former as clearly distinct from the 'Saxon' English of England, the implication being that in Gaelic eyes they may still have been considered as foreigners. However, they were 'their' foreigners[7] and by the late medieval period the elites within both ethnic groupings had been brought close together through intermarriage and fosterage, with a shared common culture. Examples of this would be the adoption of defensive armour by the Gaelic nobility[8] and the advent of the tower house as the status symbol and defensive home used by both Gaelic and Anglo-Irish lords in the period between *c.*1400 and *c.*1600.[9]

In addition, language now united both populations. As Bliss has noted, one of the key aspects of the Statutes of Kilkenny of 1366 is the fact that it presupposed the existence of people of 'English' origin who were monoglot speakers of the Irish language.[10] Indeed, by the late medieval period Irish had become the sole language in use throughout the country, with the exception of the towns (where it was used in conjunction with English), Fingal in north County Dublin and south-east Wexford. This is perhaps the strongest indicator of how the Anglo-Irish had become and belonged to Ireland.

There is a temptation, however, to read the 1515 document as evidence to indicate that Ireland was in a perpetual state of strife during the later medieval period, portraying, as it does, a political landscape that was dominated by local warlords, men who held power through their own strong-arm methods, and men who evidently were not to be trifled with. But does it follow that the 'Chyef Capytaynes' had reduced Ireland to a land of violence to the unhappy detriment of all its inhabitants? The study of documents, architecture and material culture can be of use as a means of assessing the impact of warfare and violence, particularly within elite society; this chapter also uses osteoarchaeological data in the form of the weapon-trauma that has been identified among skeletal populations in both Gaelic and Anglo-Norman areas of Ireland, in order to assess something of the scale and nature of violence within society during the later medieval period. At the core of this study are the large human skeletal populations recovered from two rural sites in particular. The first of these is from Ardreigh in County Kildare, an Anglo-Irish region during the period we are reviewing, while the second assemblage is from Ballyhanna and represents a Gaelic population from the southern shore of the River Erne in County Donegal (Fig. 1).

## The nature of warfare in later medieval Ireland

Katharine Simms has noted that the primary forms of warfare in Gaelic Ireland during the later medieval period were harrying and cattle-raiding, but such tactics were not restricted to the Gaelic population and were used to equal effect by the Anglo-Irish.[11]

1. Map showing the location of the Irish sites mentioned in the text (map: authors).

The objective of such warfare was not to exterminate an enemy population and seize their lands; it was to force the submission of the lord of that territory in order that they – and their people – might then provide their new overlord with tributes and services.

We see the political framework behind this situation in documents such as *Ceart Uí Néill* which, however, relates to a much earlier time (see Chapter 9). It sets down the claims of the Ó Néill lordship of Tír Eoghain to the tribute and services of the other lordships in Ulster, including the Ó Domhnaill lordship of Tír Conaill.[12] How enforceable such a claim might have been is debatable and it should be viewed as historical and aspirational. To make it a reality would have required the prosecution of a successful campaign in the Ó Domhnaill territory and then it would only have been binding for as long as the Ó Domhnaill lordship remained in a weakened condition. The objective of these raids, therefore, was to destroy crops, steal livestock and burn houses, thereby forcing a political submission by the ruling lineage; the Church, however, frowned heavily on attacks on women, children and clerics.[13]

Such warfare was certainly not about killing on a grand scale and late medieval Ireland was spared the general political turmoil – and associated violence – experienced in England during the second half of the fifteenth century and the 'Wars of the Roses' (1455–87), with its associated battles such as that at Towton, Yorkshire, 29 March 1461, where as many as 28,000 combatants may have been killed in one day and where perhaps as many as 76,000 soldiers were present on the field of battle.[14] An osteoarchaeological perspective on the slaughter that occurred that day was provided through the discovery in 1996 of a mass grave containing thirty-nine soldiers, who displayed an age-at-death range of sixteen to fifty years, and a mean age-at-death of about thirty years.[15] A notable proportion of these individuals had attained weapon injuries at, or around, the time of their death; some 33 per cent (13/39) displayed peri-mortem injuries on the post-cranial skeleton, while such injuries were apparent on 96 per cent (27/28) of skulls. The wounds were classified as sharp force, blunt force and puncture injuries that had been made with a variety of weapons, including swords, the top-spike of a poleaxe, the beak of a war hammer and arrowheads. Nine (32 per cent; 9/28) of the crania also displayed well-healed sharp force and blunt force injuries that appear to have arisen as a consequence of previous battles or incidents of armed conflict and are suggestive of the presence of professional soldiers in this mass grave.[16] The common grave was located one mile from the battlefield and it has been suggested that those buried in it had either been massacred by the victorious Yorkists during the rout of the Lancastrian forces that happened following the initial engagement of the battle or that Towton Hall had been a place where injured Lancastrians had been taken, only to then be killed.[17]

While Irish lords might hold their power by the sword, the scale of warfare was small in comparison to contemporary England. The Battle of Knockdoe in August 1504, for example, was one of the largest battles in Ireland during the late medieval period, yet the combined total for both armies involved may have been as low as 10,000 men.[18] As many as 4,000 of this number may have died on the battlefield, however, and Edwards has highlighted how the carnage of that day seems to have traumatised those involved and left Irish lords reluctant to engage in any similar ventures: 'The next battle of any real size did not occur until September 1520 [at Mourneabbey, County Cork], when the new earl of Desmond and his enemies came to blows in south-west Munster.'[19] The annals indicate that raiding remained the principal form of military activity after Knockdoe and in the period from 1501 to 1550 a total of ninety-five raids are reported;[20] it would seem that Ireland had returned to low-level conflict. Edwards, however, has highlighted that it was not only combatants who were affected as a result of these raids. Just because you do not kill a farmer during a raid does not mean that you have not placed his life, and that of his family, in danger. As noted above, raids were a form of economic warfare, waged with the intention of impoverishing a neighbouring lord to the point that he would be forced to become your vassal, but the raids themselves involved the stealing of cattle and possessions, the destruction of crops and the burning of homes belonging to that lord's tenant farmers and their labourers. As a consequence, it was the lower orders within society who were 'driven towards destitution, and faced serious malnourishment and even death from starvation, because of the military methods of their social superiors'.[21]

## Aodh Ruadh Ó Domhnaill: a case study in Gaelic political power

From the writings of contemporary English authors such as John Hardying, it is apparent that law and order in England had effectively broken down in the fifteenth century as a consequence of the ongoing dynastic struggles between the Yorkists and the Lancastrians. Politically motivated murder was also rife and continued to be used as an effective means of dealing with opponents (even only potential opponents) well into the reigns of Henry VII and Henry VIII;[22] it is at the level of the political elite, however, that we find comparability between England and Ireland with regards to the use of violence as a means of achieving personal political goals. Within Gaelic society the medieval annals enable us to track the dynastic power struggles that occurred among the great lineages during a comparable time to the 'Wars of the Roses', and a consideration of the life of Aodh Ruadh ('Red Hugh') Ó Domhnaill (*c.*1427–1505), *taoiseach* (leader) of Tír Conaill (Fig. 2), provides a suitable case study to illustrate this point.

The death of Neachtan Ó Domhnaill in 1452 at the hands of his nephews Domhnall and Aodh Ruadh Ó Domhnaill, the sons of Neachtan's brother and former ruler of the lordship, Niall Garbh Ó Domhnaill, threw Tír Conaill into 'great war and dissentions'. Evidently there had been dynastic tensions in the run-up to this event, since we are informed that Neachtan had previously banished his two nephews 'some time before',[23] but this was evidently part of a more longstanding enmity between the branches of the lineage. Niall Garbh had become lord of Tír Conaill following the abdication of his father, Toirdhealbhach 'an Fhíona' ('of the wine'), in 1422, but by 1434 he was campaigning against his brother Neachtan, as a consequence of the death of their brother Éigneachán;[24] no explanation is provided by the annals as to why Éigneachán was killed, and it is not explicitly stated who killed him, but it was an event that commenced a cycle of raid and counter-raid between the two brothers and their forces; and it was while Niall Garbh was involved in a raid in Oirghialla and Meath that year that he was captured by a party of English cavalry, in an encounter in which his son and *tánaiste* (heir) Toirdhealbhach was killed. Niall Garbh was handed over to Sir Thomas Stanley, the Lord Lieutenant, who seems to have dispatched him first to Dublin and then to London in 1435.[25] He was taken to the Isle of Man in 1439 'that he might be ransomed from the English; and one hundred marks were paid for information of the price of his ransom'.[26] Who paid the money for this information is not detailed, but it is hard to imagine that it would have been Neachtan; a more sinister note is sounded in the

2. The statue of Aodh Ruadh Ó Domhnaill erected at the quay in Donegal Town in 2007. The work of sculptor Maurice Harron, it commemorates the close connection that Aodh Ruadh had with the origins of the settlement in the late fifteenth century, through his foundation of the friary and the construction of the castle (image: authors).

fact that Niall Garbh rather conveniently died in captivity in 1439, and his place as the overlord of Tír Conaill then formally passed to Neachtan.

From his obituary in 1505 we are informed that Niall Garbh's son, Aodh Ruadh, died 'in the seventy-eighth year of his age',[27] which would indicate that he was born *c.*1427, that he was about twelve years old when his father died on Man, and that he was around twenty-five years old when he joined with his brother, Domhnall, in the murder of their uncle, Neachtan. How Aodh Ruadh and indeed Domhnall had passed the intervening years between 1439 and 1452 is not known, but their action should be seen as an effort by them to regain power for their branch of the lineage from that of their uncle and his sons. When this activity commenced is not known either, but Simms has highlighted how their grandfather Toirdhealbhach 'an Fhíona' had endured political exile in north Fir Mhanach with a small warband engaged in guerrilla-style attacks against his kinsman and *taoiseach*, Seán Ó Domhnaill, prior to his own coming to power in 1380.[28] Might it be possible that Toirdhealbhach's grandsons took a similar path when Neachtan had his two nephews banished?

With Neachtan dead, however, the Ó Domhnaill lordship did not pass to Domhnall but was retained by the dead lord's son, Ruaidhrí. Cousin now fought cousin. Following the capture of Domhnall by the Ó Dochartaigh in 1454 he was imprisoned within the former's castle on Inch Island in Lough Swilly. Learning of this, Ruaidhrí and his forces attacked the castle but Domhnall, now freed by his captors, dropped a rock down from the top of the castle onto Ruaidhrí that 'fell on the crest of his helmet, on the top of his head, and fractured it, so that he instantly died'.[29] Domhnall then assumed the lordship for two years until 1456 when he was killed by Énrí Ó Néill, lord of Tír Eoghain. Political power now transferred back to the sons of Neachtan, and Toirdhealbhach Cairbreach became lord of Tír Conaill, while Aodh Ruadh – captured by Énrí Ó Néill in the same encounter which had seen the death of his brother Domhnall – now became a prisoner. Upon his liberation in 1460, Aodh Ruadh recommenced his struggle against the sons of Neachtan; in a battle near Kilmacrenan in 1461 Toirdhealbhach was captured and maimed, reputedly having one of his hands and one of his feet cut off according to the account in the *Annals of Ulster*.[30] Political power within Tír Conaill then passed to Aodh Ruadh.

All of this action had occurred within a period of nine years and this must have been a tumultuous period in the history of the lordship. That said, while Aodh Ruadh's reign was to last forty-four years, there were further episodes of dynastic turmoil, such as in 1488 when Domhnall's son (also Domhnall) was executed, presumably because he had become a threat to Aodh Ruadh's power,[31] while in 1497 Aodh Ruadh abdicated in favour of his son Conn – presumably at the instigation of the latter – only to resume the lordship later that same year upon Conn's death, fighting against Énrí Óg Ó Néill who had attacked Fánad.

Evidently, Conn had faced a challenge to his leadership from his brother, Aodh Dubh, which had resulted in the latter being kept a prisoner with the de Burghs in Connacht. With Conn now dead, however, Aodh Ruadh set his house in order. Aodh Dubh was released and his father offered him the lordship; his son refused, but both 'commenced governing their principality, and humbling their neighbours and borderers, who began to resist their authority, by reason of the contests of O'Donnell's sons with each other'.[32] The last vestige of this conflict was played out in 1503 when Donnchadh na nOrdóg ('of the thumbs'), another of Aodh Ruadh's sons, died after having been maimed by his brother, Domhnall, *tánaiste* to Aodh Dubh. Aodh Ruadh, in his mid-seventies, was part of the Ulster Gaelic contingent on the side of Gerald, eighth Earl of Kildare, at the Battle of Knockdoe near Galway in 1504. He died on 11 July 1505 and was buried at his monastery in Donegal. His son, Aodh Dubh, was inaugurated as the new Ó Domhnaill on 2 August. He ruled Tír Conaill for the next thirty-two years.

The obituary for Aodh Ruadh contained in the pro Ó Néill *Annals of Ulster* stated that 'there came not from Brian Borumha, or Cathal Red-hand, down a king, or lord, that was of better sway and rule and was of more power than that king'.[33] High praise indeed for a Tír Conaill lord, but matched by the contents of his obituary in the *Annals of the Four Masters* which stated that he was:

> the full moon of the hospitality and nobility of the North, the most jovial and valiant, the most prudent in war and peace, and of the best jurisdiction, law, and rule, of all the Gaels in Ireland in his time; for there was no defence made of the houses in Tirconnell during his time, except to close the door against

> the wind only; the best protector of the Church and the learned; a man who had given great alms in honour of the Lord of the Elements; the man by whom a castle was first raised and erected at Donegal … and a monastery for Friars de Observantia – in Tirconnell, namely, the monastery of Donegal; a man who had made many predatory excursions around through Ireland; and a man who may be justly styled the Augustus of the north-west of Europe.[34]

## Violence and power in later medieval Ireland

Within the Anglo-Irish lordships in the late medieval period the succession of a new ruler rested on the concept of primogeniture, whereby a lordship passed from father to eldest son. This, however, was not always the case. During the early years of the fifteenth century, for example, the earldom of Desmond was surrounded by hostile forces, both Gaelic (Mac Carthaigh and Ó Briain) and Anglo-Irish (the Butlers of Ormond). The lordship required a strong leader to withstand such pressures and it received this through James, the seventh earl, who ruled from 1411 to 1463. The ascent of James to this position, however, did not happen through primogeniture; the sixth earl, Thomas, was James' nephew but he was deposed by his uncle and forced into exile. Although his claim to the earldom was not secure until the death of Thomas in 1420, James proved to be an astute and powerful magnate and no military weakling; the available sources would certainly suggest that his claim to the title was not questioned by any other members of the lineage and that he retained a strong grip over the earldom until his death.

There is a sharp difference, however, in the events in Desmond (and the usurping of the lordship by an uncle for the good of the earldom in 1411) when compared to the dynastic struggles within a Gaelic polity, such as has been outlined during the career of Aodh Ruadh Ó Domhnaill. At the core of these Gaelic power struggles lay the membership of the ruling lineage from among whom a lordship's new *taoiseach* would be selected. Aodh Ruadh's grandfather, Toirdhealbhach an Fhíona, had eighteen known sons by ten different women, and fifty-nine grandsons.[35] All of these individuals had, at least in theory, a call on being made the next *taoiseach*. That this struggle could lead to violence was an issue acknowledged by James Hogan some eighty years ago, who noted that the 'chief sufferers in all this were the dynasts themselves' who lived dangerous lives and often met with violent deaths.[36]

The reason advanced by Hogan was the nature of the succession process within the hierarchy of a ruling lineage since it created tension for those members of the hierarchy who found themselves at the outer margin of eligibility for the role of *taoiseach*. If they did not secure the lordship then they ran the risk of falling out of the succession and, as a consequence, they would drop down the social order, thereby incurring economic and social losses.[37] As such, securing the leadership of their *sliocht* ('division') became an all-consuming affair for such nobility which, as we have witnessed in Aodh Ruadh's story, could, and did, lead to bloodshed. In addition, however, Hogan cheerfully noted that 'behind the dynastic turmoil, which looms so largely in the annals, the people, clergy, and lower ranks of the nobility lived unchronicled but comparatively peaceful lives'.[38] Nothing is provided by Hogan, however, in support of this statement, but the *Annals of Ulster* recount how in 1492 during a Mág Uidhir raid on the Mac Maghnusa, two 'inoffensive farmers' were slain by the raiding party:

> But themselves were taken in their pride and the Lord visited their iniquity. And they were turned to flight and fourteen of their elect sunk as lead in the waters and went down like a stone into the depth.[39]

In a text that is dominated by accounts of raid and counter-raid and the actions of political elites, the passage is of interest since it highlights that the author clearly thinks that this divine retribution is appropriate for those who might harm inoffensive members of society, albeit that such references to this class of folk are rare indeed within the annals.

## Violence in Medieval Ireland: The osteoarchaeological evidence

In 2012 a research paper was published by Jonny Geber on the results obtained from his osteoarchaeological study of the skeletons excavated from two early medieval Irish cemetery sites at Mount Gamble in Dublin and Owenbristy in Galway. The former site dated to AD 500 to AD 1150 and comprised 176 skeletons, of which six males displayed evidence for weapon trauma, representing 3.4 per cent (6/176) of the adult and adolescent population. The Owenbristy cemetery dated to between AD 550 to AD 1000 and comprised fifty-six adult and adolescent individuals but with 17.9 per cent, or ten individuals, displaying weapon injuries, some of which were of a particularly frenzied nature.[40] Geber also noted that 12.9 per cent (eighteen sites) of the 140 early medieval burial grounds excavated in Ireland have skeletons with evidence of peri-mortem trauma. This osteological evidence for weapon injuries was achieved through his review of the information included in the on-line database of the INSTAR Mapping Death project.[41] However, the details for the seven sites that Geber quoted specifically in his text represent a total of 873 early medieval skeletons and only thirty actually displayed peri-mortem weapon trauma, representing an overall percentage of 3.4 per cent. The implication is that while eighteen sites out of the 140 excavated cemeteries have individuals with evidence for weapon trauma, the overall frequency of individuals displaying weapon trauma within these cemetery populations is actually low. It is also improbable that soft-tissue injuries associated with violence – and invisible in any case within the osteoarchaeological record – would be numerable or the cause of death. As such, one can surmise that death caused as a consequence of interpersonal violence does not seem to have been particularly prevalent in the early medieval period in Ireland.

Over the course of recent decades human skeletal assemblages have also been retrieved from a number of late medieval cemeteries and these can be used as a means to generate and compare frequencies of peri-mortem violence between the early and late medieval periods (Table 1). The late medieval assemblages include those from Kilroot, County Antrim (AD 1022–1440),[42] St Patrick's Church, Armoy, County Antrim (AD 1400–1700)[43] and the major assemblage from the graveyard associated with Ballyhanna church (AD 1200–1650) on the outskirts of Ballyshannon in County Donegal, and located on what was an *airchinneach* estate of the bishop of Clogher.[44] To this corpus we can add the information published on skeletons associated

Table 1. Details of the osteological assemblages discussed in the text.

| PERIMORTEM DEFINITE TRAUMA ONLY | | | | | | | | |
|---|---|---|---|---|---|---|---|---|
| Site | Period | Total adults | Total adults + adolescents | Total adult males | Total adult females | Total adults unsexed | Total adolescents | Source |
| Early Medieval | | | | | | | | |
| Mount Gamble | AD 500–1150 | 6/172 (3.5%) | 6/176 (3.4%) | 6/56 (10.7%) | 0/77 | 0/39 | 0/4 | Geber 2012 |
| Owenbristy | AD 550–1000 | 8/47 (17.0%) | 10/56 (17.9%) | 6/25 (24%) | 2/16 (12.5%) | 0/6 | 2/9 (22.2%) | Geber 2012 |
| Late Medieval – articulated | | | | | | | | |
| Ardreigh | 12th–16th century | 0/820 | 0/882 | 0/365 | 0/401 | 0 | 0/62 | Troy 2010; Carty 2013 |
| Ballyhanna | 13th–16th century | 13/869 (1.5%) | 15/938 (1.6%) | 10/322 (3.1%) | 2/333 (0.6%) | 1/214 (0.5%) | 2/69 (2.9%) | McKenzie 2015; Murphy 2015 |
| Kilroot | AD 1022–1440 | 1/46 (2.2%) | 1/50 (2%) | 1/19 (5.3%) | 0/5 | 0 | 0/4 | Murphy and Russell 2011 |
| St Patrick's Church, Armoy | 15th–17th century | 0/27 | 0/31 | 0/10 | 0/16 | 0/1 | 0/4 | Murphy 1998 |
| Cistercian Abbey, Newry | AD 1460–1660 | 3/38 (7.9%) | 3/38 (7.9%) | 3/20 (15%) | 0/11 | 0/7 | 0/0 | Dawkes and Buckley 2009 |
| *Totals* | | *17/1773 (1.0%)* | *19/1939 (1.0%)* | *14/726 (1.9%)* | *2/766 (0.3%)* | *1/222 (0.5%)* | *2/139 (1.4%)* | |
| | | | | | | | | |
| Wharram Percy | 11th–16th century | 2/360 (0.6%) | 2/395 (0.5%) | 2/211 (0.9%) | 0/140 | 0/9 | 0/35 | Mays 2007 |
| Late Medieval – disarticulated | | | | | | | | |
| Armagh | 11–12th century | 1/1 | | | | | | Gilmore and Murphy 2001 |
| Greencastle | 14–15th century | 1/4* | | | | | | Lynn 1988; Murphy 2013 |
| Carrick-fergus | 16–17th century | 1/1 | | | | | | Murphy 2012 |

* A fragment of juvenile cranium with evidence of a probable puncture injury was also recovered from Greencastle, County Down.

with the Cistercian Abbey at Newry in County Down (AD 1460–1660),[45] while the study of 882 late medieval adult and adolescent skeletons from Ardreigh in County Kildare (AD 1100–1600)[46] provides evidence from Leinster, which can be used to compare and contrast the data from Ulster. To ensure comparability with Geber's findings for early medieval Ireland the same methodology was used for the current study.[47] The prevalence rates are based on the numbers of adolescents (thirteen to seventeen years) and adults, while only sharp force or puncture peri-mortem injuries caused by weapons around the time of death are considered in the study.

Before dealing with the analysis of the skeletons from these late medieval cemeteries, however, mention must be made of the remains of four individuals with peri-mortem weapon trauma that were discovered in non-cemetery contexts and, specifically, ditch (or near ditch) features. These include an eleventh- to twelfth-century disarticulated skull of an adult male with clear evidence of decapitation, found in one of the *trían* ditches in Armagh city;[48] two skull fragments, one from an adult and one from a juvenile, with puncture injuries, recovered from fourteenth- to fifteenth-century contexts in the ditch of the castle at Greencastle, County Down;[49] and an adult skull fragment with evidence of a probable puncture wound from a probable medieval or later medieval layer at Carrickfergus, County Antrim.[50] Barra O'Donnabhain has considered similar remains from early medieval to early modern contexts across Ireland and he is of the opinion that they represent heads which were displayed in public arenas, largely as a deterrent towards anyone else who might transgress the power of an area's ruling authority.[51] The recovery of the cranium from Armagh, in a ditch near the entrance to Trían Saxan, certainly fits with the idea that the severed head may been displayed. However, no definitive evidence for this was visible on the cranium. The recovery of the two crania in the ditch at Greencastle is similarly suggestive, particularly since they displayed puncture injuries. The skull fragment with a probable puncture wound from Carrickfergus was recovered from a layer near the inner line of the medieval town's defences. As such, the contexts for all of these finds – at high-profile boundaries – seems to correlate well with the idea that the heads were deliberately displayed for socio-political reasons.[52]

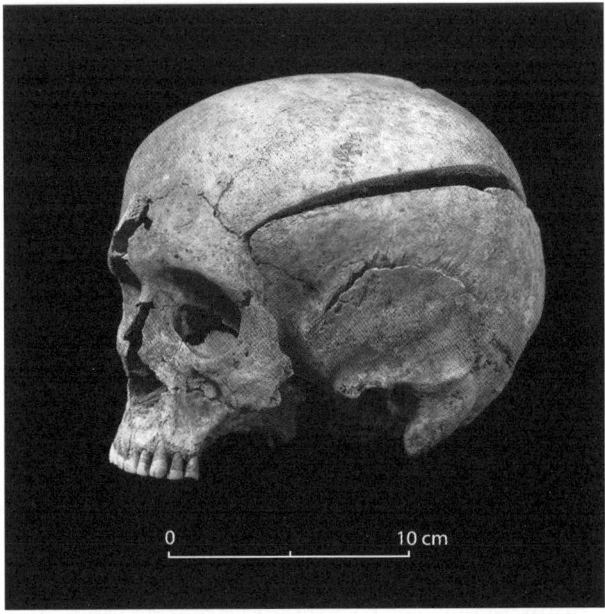


3. Peri-mortem trauma in the skull of 35–50 year-old adult male from Kilroot, County Antrim (SK 199). While the injury in this individual is very dramatic and undoubtedly caused his death it should be noted that he was the only individual with such an injury from this population of fifty adults and adolescents. The occurrence of two healed weapon injuries in the individual's cranium, along with other joint lesions, are suggestive that he may have been a professional soldier (Murphy and Russell 2011, 38). (Crown Copyright).

The analysis of the data from the Gaelic *airchinneach* burial ground at Ballyhanna has revealed that only fifteen of the 938 adults and adolescents displayed definite evidence of peri-mortem weapon trauma, representing a prevalence rate of 1.6 percent. Twelve of the individuals displayed peri-mortem sharp force injuries that had been attained as a result of a sword (1.3 per cent; 12/938). The affected individuals comprised nine males, one of whom was a teenager, two adult females and an adult of indeterminable sex. A further adolescent and two adult males (0.3 per cent; 3/938) displayed dagger or *scian* injuries. One of the adults had his throat cut (SK 81), while the other appears to have attained a defence wound and had been stabbed in the hand (SK 852), while the teenager (SK 35) had been stabbed at least twice in the chest. When the numbers of adult males (3.1 per cent; 10/322) and females (0.6 per cent; 2/333) with peri-mortem injuries was compared to the numbers of individuals without evidence of injury by sex, the male preponderance is clear.[53]

None of the individuals from St Patrick's Church, Armoy, County Antrim displayed evidence of weapon trauma,[54] while a single middle-aged adult male (SK 199) from the burial ground at Kilroot, County Antrim displayed sharp-force injuries. A large peri-mortem wound was visible on the left side of the cranium (Fig. 3). Two long-standing and well-healed, non-fatal wounds were also present on the cranium and the degree of healing would tend to indicate that both injuries may have been attained during a single event. It is probable that the individual had been able to survive the two blows because they had failed to fully perforate the cranium.[55] Three individuals with clear evidence of peri-mortem weapon injuries were recovered from the precinct of the Cistercian Abbey at Newry. Some ten injuries, nine sharp-force and one puncture, were visible on the incomplete cranium of a young adult male (SK 4), while another adult of indeterminable sex (SK 14) displayed a further sharp-force injury. Both of these crania were recovered from a late medieval charnel pit. An adult male recovered from a contemporary individual grave displayed at least four sharp-force peri-mortem wounds on his cranium.[56]

When the adults and adolescents from Armoy, Kilroot and Newry are amalgamated they make a total of 119 individuals, with the one individual from Kilroot and three cases from Newry displaying peri-mortem weapon trauma, providing a prevalence rate of 3.4 percent (4/119). If the figures from these three sites are added to the data from Ballyhanna we get a total Ulster population of 1,057 individuals, with a peri-mortem weapon trauma rate of 1.8 per cent (19/1,057).

Clear cases of ante-mortem sharp-force trauma were identified in the crania of four adult males and two adult females from Ardreigh, County Kildare (0.7 per cent; 6/882); no examples of weapon trauma were identified in any post-cranial remains. In all cases the injuries had been made using either a sword or an axe. For the individuals to have survived such blows – some of which had caused considerable damage to the cranium – suggests that they had access to a high standard of medical care.[57]

Since all of the injuries from Ardreigh were healed, they do not increase our count of individuals who died as a result of weapon trauma. As such, the addition of the Ardreigh population to the individuals from the Ulster assemblages generates a total population of 1,939 adult and adolescent skeletons, and an overall trauma rate of 1.0 per cent (19/1,939). The osteological evidence is therefore indicative of a rate of 1.8 per cent for Ulster, and just 1.0 per cent for Ardreigh and the Ulster sites combined. To put this into context, at any given time in the late medieval period in Ireland it is possible that perhaps over 98 per cent of the entire population died for reasons that were not definitely associated with violence caused by weapons. Obviously, a degree of caution has to be exercised in reaching this conclusion given that violent death does not have to involve weapons. It can also be caused, for example, by strangulation or poisoning, and these are traumas that are normally impossible to detect in the osteoarchaeological record. Suffice to say it is probable that such murders would have been rare, however, and it is highly unlikely that they would significantly alter the overall figures generated through the current analysis. As might be expected, adult males (1.6 per cent; 12/726) displayed greater levels of weapon trauma compared to females (0.3 per cent; 2/766).[58] The only adolescents with evidence of peri-mortem trauma were two possible male individuals from Ballyhanna, while apart from the juvenile skull fragment recovered from the ditch at Greencastle, we have no evidence at all for children displaying weapon trauma.

The peri-mortem trauma rate of 1.0 per cent for the late medieval Irish assemblages also represents a decrease in the rate of 3.4 per cent for similar trauma that was obtained by Geber's study of 873 early medieval adults and adolescents in Ireland.[59] The late medieval Irish trauma rate is more in keeping with what has been calculated for contemporary cemetery sites in England. The eleventh- to sixteenth-century rural population of 395 adult and adolescent skeletons from the graveyard at Wharram Percy in Yorkshire, for example, had a peri-mortem weapon trauma frequency of 0.5 per cent, which represents two people out of the entire population.[60] Although the use of peri-mortem weapon injuries might be considered to be a rather crude measure of levels of violence, it is a definitive one. If a person displays an unhealed weapon injury, then we can be confident that the individual's death was related to this trauma. The inclusion of blunt force injuries may have increased the overall prevalence values to some extent but the data would be less definitive; while some blunt force injuries may well have been caused by weapons, others could have arisen as a result of everyday accidents. It could also be suggested that certain peri-mortem injuries might be invisible in the skeleton but there are specialised cemetery populations where notable concentrations of peri-mortem injuries are evident, such as in the individuals from the mass grave associated with the Battle of Towton, where some 110 sharp force or puncture peri-mortem wounds were identified in the remains of thirty-nine men.[61] It would seem unlikely that very high levels of injuries would originally have existed that are now invisible in the skeleton. As such, the very low prevalence for definitive unhealed weapon injuries can only lead us to conclude that death at the end of a sword, axe, arrow, or other cutting or puncturing weapon, was a relatively rare occurrence in later medieval Ireland.

## Conclusion

It is probable that the vast majority of the skeletons excavated and studied as part of the current exercise represent the mortal remains of 'ordinary folk'. If we wanted to analyse the bodies of those who died in raids or during dynastic struggles then this would require archaeological excavations to be conducted at the traditional noble burial places of the elite (for example, Assaroe Abbey or Donegal Friary for the Ó Domhnaill lineage). As yet, no common burial pit associated with Irish medieval battles, such as Knockdoe, has been recovered. The results of the current study, however, would certainly suggest that Hogan's statement that 'the people, clergy, and lower ranks of the nobility lived unchronicled but comparatively peaceful lives' finds support in the osteoarchaeological record, but that this was not just restricted to the Gaelic territories, and life in late medieval Ireland, both in the Gaelic and Anglo-Irish territories, was less violent than in the early medieval period. Why might this have been the case? Could it be that the ninety-odd 'Chyef Capytaynes' of both Gaelic and Anglo-Irish background who are listed in the text prepared for Henry VIII in 1515 actually did exert such power over their lordships that violence in society was kept in check? Perhaps having gained control by the sword, these individuals could then apply the same control as strong rulers over their people and bring stability to their land? In his study of violence in thirteenth-century Ireland, based on the contents of the *Annals of Connacht*, Finan notes that in 1224 when Áed Ó Conchobair became king of Connacht he severely punished two individuals – a robber and a rapist – who had engaged in their wrongdoings 'at the moment of his accession'.[62] As Finan concludes, Áed was asserting his authority through his actions in dealing with these criminals, since it was his duty as the new overlord to administer law and justice within his jurisdiction.[63]

Hogan's 'peaceful lives' may, however, be a relative concept.[64] It is one thing to enjoy peace, and not be the direct target of violence, but if we return to Edwards' observation regarding the impact of raids on the life of the ordinary people, these are the individuals who will be most affected directly by the actions of the combatants.[65] They are the ones who have their livestock stolen and their houses burned down and they are the ones who have to manage in the aftermath of an attack, facing economic hardship, perhaps leading to malnutrition for themselves and their families and even starvation. The evidence of high rates of young adult death and physiological stress markers, in addition to low statures, witnessed in the skeletal population from Ballyhanna, for example, is indicative of a community enduring poor health and malnutrition.[66] One is forced to consider this small *airchinneach* estate's location on the River Erne in proximity to Ballyshannon and the crossing points on the Erne that provided access routes between Connacht and Ulster. As such, the inhabitants would have witnessed and encountered armed forces moving through this landscape on raid and counter-raid.[67] While physical violence leading to death may not have been visited upon the inhabitants of Ballyhanna, evidently life was tough and one has to wonder was this because, as a frontier population, they were at the mercy of those raiders stealing their livestock and possessions? Furthermore, was life made all the more harsh for them by the fact that this was a community whose overlord was the bishop of Clogher and not a secular warlord? The medieval registers of the archbishops of Armagh would certainly indicate that ecclesiastical censure through excommunication was the only real weapon that was available to use against the excesses of the Uí Néill with regard to their cattle raids and harassment of church tenants on the archbishop's landholdings *inter hibernicos*.[68] Presumably it was the case that similar measures were available to the bishop of Clogher, although how effective these would be in protecting his interests and those of his tenants must remain questionable.

A weak lord would evidently be seen as an easy target for raiding by an ambitious neighbouring ruler. As such, the best way for a lordship and its people to remain safe would be for that population to be ruled by a competent warlord. In short, having a tough and capable *taoiseach* such as Aodh Ruadh Ó Domhnaill as your overlord may have been viewed as a great boon by the people of medieval Tír Conaill. It is certainly the case that when we read Aodh Ruadh's obituary in the *Annals of the Four Masters*, we could be forgiven for forgetting the dynastic violence and turmoil associated with the early years of his career. His obituary extols him as a jovial, valiant man who had the 'best jurisdiction, law and rule of all the Gaels in Ireland in his time; for there was no defence made of the houses in Tirconnell during his time, except to close the door against the wind only; the best protector of the Church and the learned'.[69] The temptation is to read this obituary and view it as being full of hyperbolic praise. Perhaps, however, it really *was* safe to leave the door of your house open under his long reign, and perhaps the dynastic struggles really did achieve their objective of ensuring that the best man for the role of *taoiseach* actually succeeded to the inheritance of a lordship.

## Acknowledgements

Thanks are due to Libby Mulqueeny, Archaeology and Palaeoecology, School of Natural and Built Environment, Queen's University Belfast, for preparing Figure 1 and to Ruairí Ó Baoill, Centre for Archaeological Fieldwork, Queen's University Belfast, for his information about the context of the cranium from Carrickfergus.

# 7

# Scottish, Irish or other? Negotiating identity in late medieval north Ulster

COLIN BREEN

## Introduction

Traditional narratives from the nineteenth and twentieth centuries implied that medieval Gaelic Ireland was an insular and remote place.[1] It was a place perceived as being somewhat apart both from the anglicised eastern half of the country and western Atlantic society.[2] By extension, the peoples who inhabited the northern and western coasts of Ireland were isolated communities with their own distinctive set of cultural traditions and values. They were viewed as distinctly Irish, centred in an exclusively Gaelic culture and localised world. Such forms of overly romanticised societal constructs emerged initially in the eighteenth century, but continued to be commonly expressed in both popular and academic literature following the establishment of the Irish state, and into more recent times.[3] However, a closer examination of medieval society across the island very quickly establishes that this notion of an exclusive and isolated Gaelicness does not bear scrutiny.

The Gaelic world of the western seaboard was not an isolated region but a culturally dynamic area. It was a region that was subject to continual western European influences through mercantile activity and intensive fishing activity along the coasts, with fishing fleets sailing from Spain, the Basque region and other parts of the continent.[4] In particular, the notion of an exclusive Irish Gaelicness can be challenged in north Ulster where this landscape was accustomed to the continual movement and settlement of people from Scotland and the Western Isles and Argyll in particular.[5] This movement of peoples took place over millennia but is strongly attested to, historically, from the early medieval period onwards. The continual migrations across this region challenge the notion of an exclusive Irishness, certainly in terms of the contemporary nationalistic construct of the term. It also challenges the concept of an insular society bound by the natural borders of the island. The communities from this northern region were engaged in continual negotiation of their place through territorial movement and socio-political aspiration. By extension, they were also engaged in the continued reimagining of their identity and allegiance, not necessarily on a national stage but within their local maritime world.

This chapter looks at two distinct lordships in north Ulster, those of Clann Domhnaill in north Antrim and Clann Suibhne of County Donegal, from the fifteenth to the early part of the seventeenth century (Fig. 1). Both groups camc originally to Ulster from the Western Isles and Argyll during the thirteenth and fourteenth centuries, before settling permanently.[6] During the later medieval period they consolidated their presence across Ulster and emerged as powerful social and political forces. In particular, this chapter examines how they utilised cultural and architectural expressions to further their own socio-political and economic aspirations and how they came both to see themselves and how they wished others to see them.

## 'High Irelanders'

This particular chronological emphasis on the late medieval period needs to be contextualised against the previous centuries of close political and social contact between the two regions of west Scotland and Ulster throughout the historic period. A continuum of connection and contact is probably best exemplified from the fifth to the ninth centuries when north Antrim and Argyll were encompassed within the maritime kingdom of Dál Riata.[7] This was also a maritime region intrinsically bound by early Christianity centred on Colum Cille and Iona. However, it was the Scots' skills in the art of warfare and conflict that were in special demand. While it is likely that there were Scottish groups fighting in Ulster for Irish chieftains from at least the early part of the thirteenth century, the first chronicle references to the use of Clann Domhnaill *gallóglaigh* were recorded during the Ó Domhnaill succession conflict of the late thirteenth century.[8] The subsequent familial connections and use of marriage to consolidate alliances further strengthened the link between both groups. At the close of the fourteenth century Marjory Bisset from the Glens of Antrim married Eóin Mór Mac Domhnaill of the Isles, which in turn encouraged extensive settlement of the Glens by Clann Domhnaill.[9]

In the 1540s an extended branch of Clann Iain Mhór arrived in north Antrim, following an invitation from the Mic Cuilinn to fight for them. The former quickly usurped the Mic Cuilinn to establish a powerful lordship across the region.[10] Marriage had become a key political tool to facilitate and encourage these alliances but military force remained their primary political tool and commodity. The use of marriage to create alliances was similarly deployed by the Uí Dhomhnaill of Donegal. Of particular interest in this regard was Aodh Ó Domhnaill's association with Clann Suibhne of Knapdale, Argyll. By the close of the fifteenth century Clann Suibhne had come to hold three sub-chieftaincies in Donegal within Ó Domhnaill territory – including Fanad, Trí Tuatha and Tír Boghaine – having been expelled from Scotland in the early part of the fourteenth century.[11] They quickly established themselves as a considerable force of *gallóglaigh* in Ireland, a position they retained into the sixteenth century when they continued to command a strong military capability.[12] During the Nine Years' War (April 1593 to March 1603), for example, both Mac Suibhne of Fanad and Mac Suibhne na Trí Tuatha owed service of 120 *gallóglaigh* each, while Mac Suibhne of Tír Boghaine owed sixty.[13] The Clann Suibhne lordships emerged from the Nine Years' War in varying states of health but had essentially collapsed with the onset of Plantation by the second decade of the seventeenth century. By contrast, Clann Domhnaill, through astute leadership and ambitious vision, survived both events and successfully negotiated their family's transition from Gaelic lords to landholding servants of the Crown. There is a range of evidence with which we can reveal the nature of late medieval identity in this region.

## Architecture as identity

Architecture is strongly imbued with meaning and, whether through the medium of stone or other building materials, it has been used repeatedly in the past to make statements. Castles and high-prestige residences in the landscape were constructed as symbols of power and control and were also used to express allegiance and identity.[14] Architecture was also expressive of social and political change, as buildings were continually adapted to reflect changing circumstances, technologies and fortunes. This was especially true in the central chiefry places of these lordships, at Dunluce, Rathmullan or Doe.

### *Tower houses and friaries*

Most of our present understandings of the settlement places of the Ulster lordships are derived from the residences of the elite. This is an inherent problem when studying such groups, as effectively it is often only high-end settlement that is visible in the archaeological record, which results in a skewed and unbalanced view into past settlement and building practices. The situation is seemingly less biased across the Western Isles of Scotland where a range of house types and settlement clusters have been recorded and dated to the late medieval period through a combination of historical analysis, field survey and excavation.[15] There also appears to be continued association with fortified sites dating from earlier periods, while castles, or at least heavily fortified masonry sites, are present in varying numbers across the Western Isles. In Ireland there is a less diverse range of evidence due in some part to the more intensive land management practices of recent centuries, when many sites were lost following improvement and intensive agriculture. The element of continuity in the Irish landscape should, however, not be underestimated; the continual resettling and rebuilding of settlement clusters and house sites has rendered late medieval house survival very rare.

The predominant architectural form associated with Gaelic Ireland is the tower house.[16] This is, however, a ubiquitous monument that is present across the island as a whole, dating from the late fifteenth century through to the early part of the seventeenth century. Tower houses would also have been a common feature of the towns and rural landscapes of eastern Ireland and are therefore not restricted to the territories of the Gaelic lords. One of the striking aspects of their distribution in the context of this study is their relative paucity across northeast Antrim and the northern coastline of Derry. A number of the sites that are labelled as tower houses are actually other forms of monuments dating to the thirteenth and fourteenth centuries, or later fortified house types. This is an interesting anomaly compared to landscapes of a similar socio-political structure and form elsewhere in Ireland. Their relative paucity does not reflect agricultural practice or differing landscape management structures but must instead be related to the preferences of the inhabitants of this region and their own set of dynamic cultural traditions and changing demographics. There are also few tower houses in County Donegal. While this can be associated with marginal agricultural lands and relatively low population levels, it must also be associated with the hierarchical structures present in that society and variation in the cultural expressions of its population.

One of the interesting research questions that arises in this regard is the continued usage of the *ráth* and *caiseal* across this landscape of north Ulster. Certainly, primary historical sources, such as *Leabhar Chlainne Suibhne*,[17] contain a number of references to the use of such settlement forms across north and south Donegal during the period under discussion here. Similarly, both the Mic Cuilinn and Clann Domhnaill are associated with a number of *crannóg* sites in particular, although Clann Domhnaill appear to have had only a limited interest in using this site type. Both Kieran O'Conor[18] and Elizabeth FitzPatrick[19] have argued for reuse or continued usage of native enclosed settlement forms, and the frequent appearance of *caiseal* and *ráth* sites in historical sources relating to the Clann Suibhne lordships lends support to their findings elsewhere in Ireland.

An examination of the known sites from the Clann Domhnaill lordship area suggests a greater degree of settlement types and building variation than might be found in other parts of Ireland. Some of the buildings that survive show clear architectural influences from the Scottish regions. They also demonstrate a degree of cultural fluidity in terms of architectural fashion and building usage. The sixteenth-century branch of Clann Domhnaill that first settled in northern Antrim from 1544 onwards initially fortified a headland at Kinbane, a chalk promontory west of Ballycastle.[20] They constructed an enclosing wall around the headland with a small squat tower at the edge of its landward approaches (Fig. 2). The morphology of this site has clear affinities with similar fortified sites across the Western Isles. From the close of the fifteenth century a number of small towers were constructed across the Western Isles including examples at Castle Mac Leòid on Barra and at Eilean Bheagram in South Uist. Both towers are similar to Kinbane in terms of size and the absence of fireplaces, and both were associated with other domestic structures. The construction of this type of tower at Kinbane may have subsequently served as a prototype for similar site-types, such as the refortification of the early medieval stronghold of Dunserverick by Ó Catháin in the sixteenth century and the later enclosure of Ballyreagh headland, immediately west of Portrush. Such fortified headlands are known from other sixteenth-century contexts in Ireland and it is not claimed here that the Antrim examples are unique. They do, however, have a closer affinity to the forms of fortified hierarchical sites along the western Scottish seaboard than other parts of the Gaelic world. The paucity of tower houses highlights a clear difference in the Clann Domhnaill lands. Even the tower house at Ballylough, south of Bushmills, is associated with these Islay arrivals, but Ballylough tower house was a previously standing structure built originally in the fourteenth century and later rebuilt by the Mic Cuilinn. The strongest architectural expression of the Clann Domhnaill lordship was their refurbishment of Dunluce castle, again originally built by the Mic Cuilinn at the close of the fifteenth century. Their initial changes to the structure consisted of an extension to the fortified headland area and the addition of further residential and service quarters. Later in the century they rebuilt a strong gatehouse structure with clear Scottish architectural expressions including two small corbelled projections, common features on many Scottish buildings of the period. The extent to which it can be suggested that they were making statements of political affiliation or power through architecture is debatable. It does appear clear that their forms of building were firmly rooted in Scottish built-heritage traditions and that their outward projection of identity was embedded in this tradition. This building style does

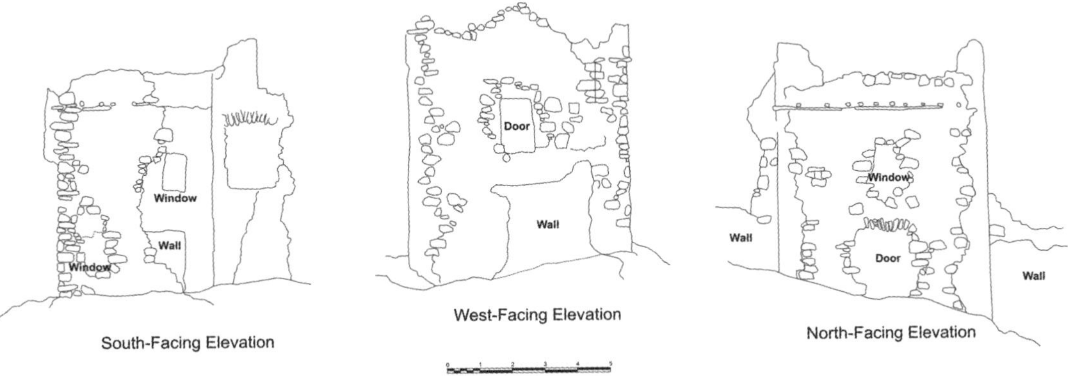


2. Elevations of the small tower at Kinbane, County Antrim (image: author).

3. Doe Castle, County Donegal (image: author).

not feature in structures south of Ulster, and the eastward-looking connections contained within this style were a clear statement of continuing cultural and political associations with the lands of Scotland to the east.

The lordship territories of Clann Suibhne across Donegal present a more typical pattern of late medieval Gaelic settlement. The use of the term 'typical' is used advisedly here as it is certainly not clear as to whether these lordships had a high degree of structural commonality. A range of socio-economic and environmental variables existed across the Gaelic territories, and individual lordships did not respond in a singular fashion to the diversity of factors influencing their area. However, our existing, albeit limited, knowledge base would suggest that the maritime lordships of the western seaboard shared a degree of similarity. Each had central lordship centres focused on particular bays or sections of coastline within a distinctive bounded geographical area. Three primary chiefry places can then be identified in the Clann Suibhne territories following a pattern that corresponds, for example, to the lordships of west Cork, Kerry and parts of Connacht. The best surviving and originally preeminent site is the probable early sixteenth-century, four-storey tower house at Doe, contained within an enclosing bawn wall and later extensive modifications (Fig. 3).

First mentioned in the historical sources in 1544,[21] Doe tower house overlooks a sheltered bay and adopts a typical position for these maritime tower houses along the western seaboard of Ireland.[22] It served as the centre of the Mac Suibhne na dTuath lordship, functioning both as a place of lordly residence and as an administrative and political centre. Similarly, a probable tower house was located at Rathmullan immediately south of the friary. This would originally have been built on a rocky eminence right on the water's edge, with commanding views across Lough Swilly. Although now destroyed, the site is shown on an early seventeenth-century map source illustrating Docwra's early seventeenth-century campaign and has the appearance of a typical late medieval tower house.[23] It served as the territorial centre for the Mac Suibhne Fánad lordship which was also served by the small squat tower built on a rock outcrop in the sheltered marine inlet of Moross. Its architecture suggests that this was the tower of a subgroup or individual within the lordship. This has been traditionally ascribed a building date of 1532,[24] a date broadly in keeping with an escalation of building across Donegal undertaken by the Clann Suibhne in the early decades of the sixteenth century. The third lordship centre of the Mac Suibhne of Tír Boghaine was at the tower house of Niall Mór Mac Suibhne (d.1524), built on a fortified promontory at Rahan Near.

In constructing these buildings, Clann Suibhne were expressing their sense of lordship in accepted contemporary terms and were following the societal and political norms prevalent across Gaelic society in western Ireland. While retaining a historical sense of coming from another place, they further embedded themselves in traditions of Irish lordship through the patronage and continued sponsorship of religious orders, and the Franciscans in particular. Eóin Ruadh Mac Suibhne is recorded as having founded the Carmelite house at Rathmullan in 1516 while the Mac Suibhne of Tír Boghaine is attributed with the founding of the Franciscan third order friary at Fan an Charta in south Donegal. Additional sites include the now destroyed Franciscan third order site of Ballymacswiny at Magheraroarty founded by the Mac Suibhne na dTuath. This patronage differs somewhat from the experience of Clann Domhnaill in north Antrim who arrived in Ulster after the primary era of patronage. Ballycastle friary had been established by the Mic Cuilinn decades earlier, but Clann Domhnaill continued to support it.

## Grave-slabs

One of the most distinctive expressions of identity across Argyll and the Isles, during the late medieval period, was the use of elaborate, carved grave-slabs depicting individuals and representative symbols of their society.[25] The *bìrlinn* or galley appears frequently as an illustration of their dependence on sea travel, while swords signify the militaristic nature of west Highland society and serve as expressions of power and status within the clan-based hierarchies. A number of slabs from this same tradition are known from Ulster but are far less frequent than in Scotland. This relative paucity may possibly be explained in part by the preference of many Gaelic lords to be buried, or at least commemorated, at Iona, but it is also clear that as these groups became embedded in Ulster society they were buried there too.

Four late medieval grave-slabs are known from Donegal.[26] One of the slabs from Clonca church in Inishowen carries an inscription in memory of Magnus Mac Orristin, as well as a sword and *camán*. The foliate patterning and layout of the slab bears a strong resemblance to a number of slabs from both Kilarrow churchyard and Finlaggan on Islay, and to an example from St Oran's churchyard on Iona. A further more complex slab is known from the Franciscan tertiary friary, Ballysaggart, now removed to Killybegs, and is traditionally associated with one of the Mac Suibhne of Tír Boghaine, of Rahan Near Castle. It contains a depiction of an armed man with an axe and sword, while his head is topped by a fan-shaped plume. This head-wear feature is reminiscent of the form of head-wear worn by the Mac Suibhne in a number of sixteenth-century illustrations discussed below. A series of panels contain interlace design and a number of animals. A second slab from Doe Castle, dated to 1544 by Bigger[27] and traditionally associated with Mac Suibhne na dTuath, features a number of animals including a boar as well as an elaborate cross with a *fleur de lis* head (Fig. 4). Both of these slabs differ in a number of ways from the examples known across western Scotland and could be considered here as an Irish form, or at least an adaptation, of the tradition. The Doe Castle example, in particular, appears to draw from other medieval slabs across Ireland on stylistic grounds, and it shows a fusion between the two traditions. The final slab from Clonmany graveyard features extensive foliage patterns and could be seen as representing a hybrid between both traditions.

A note of caution is advised at this point. There has been a temptation to view the Highland sculptures as representative of a single seamless tradition, but a more nuanced examination of the stones would suggest a variety of temporal and stylistic groups. The occurrence of a small number of slabs from Donegal is hardly coincidental given the ancestral narratives of Clann Suibhne, and this group of slabs demonstrates continued connections and the sharing of cultural traits between both regions. Just three of the slabs are directly associated with Clann Suibhne and the presence of the Inishowen slab at Clonca is illustrative of further interconnections associated with temporary or semi-permanent movement of groups and individuals. The absence of this type of commemorative marker from north Antrim is perhaps surprising then in that regard. Certainly the later sixteenth-century Clann Domhnaill lords were buried at Ballycastle but there is no evidence of this form of marker there. It could be that this form of commemoration was embedded within certain Highland families who were associated with certain activities like soldiering, and that Clann Domhnaill had adopted

4. Bigger's illustration of 'The MacSwyne grave slab', published in the *Ulster Journal of Archaeology*, vol. 9, 3, 1903.

more conventional approaches to death and memory by the late sixteenth century. It is probably also the case that this form of commemoration had come to be seen as out-dated by the middle of the sixteenth century; the Clann Domhnaill arrivals from Islay, after 1544, effectively post-dated this tradition.

## Material culture as identity

It is overly simplistic to interpret past perceptions of identity solely on the use and proliferation of particular forms of material culture.

Just because a community or society uses the same pottery does not necessarily mean that they were kin groups or had a shared sense of identity. Forms and styles may change, but this may or may not reflect change or the manner in which these objects were consumed within society. Similarly, societies may interact or assimilate but this may not be apparent in their material cultural-set, rendering themselves partially invisible in the archaeological record.[28] However, many objects are indicators of cultural interaction and similarities, but archaeological analysis needs to also focus on social agency behind the processes of their production and distribution in order to develop a more interrogative approach to understanding objects. Jones[29] has cautioned against using comparative material cultural studies as a straightforward tool for examining past societal interaction. This is a loaded and subjective process that is littered with potential obstacles.

One of the key analytical difficulties lies in the nature of the record itself across the territories of Gaelic Ireland. A limited level of data will only allow for superficial analysis and this highlights one of the central issues when it comes to the research of late medieval Gaelic societies. Firstly, a relatively small number of sites have actually been investigated, although this situation is slowly changing as demonstrated by a number of excavations that have taken place over the last decade (for example, Comber's excavations at Caherconnell[30] and the Discovery Programme excavations at Carns and Tulsk[31]). Where artefactual records exist for these communities they tend to be limited. Even where sites have been investigated, the stratigraphic contextual record of objects is often not of a high enough resolution to allow for tight temporal analysis, while most reports will group the artefactual material together in a single collective analysis and thus ignore the dynamic nature of societal change on a temporal basis. In many archaeological reports, artefacts have been grouped into traditional and unchallenged category-based narratives that do not allow for detailed cultural analysis. For example, most of the tower houses that have been investigated archaeologically in Ireland were occupied for well over a century. Attempts to differentiate the material culture of their past occupants, between centuries, is very difficult, while attempting to tie this down further to decadal divisions, or even to particular event horizons, is often impossible. Even then, the range of finds recovered further limits interpretation due to the poor preservation of certain artefact types. Few house sites have been investigated from this period, and the limiting factors mentioned above are of relevance here as well. It is now accepted that *crannóga* played an integral part in the settlement patterns of past Gaelic landscapes. The preservation conditions offered by these sites has produced significantly more diverse ranges of material culture but again the problems of extended occupation, coupled with often complex stratigraphy, has rendered tight temporal contextualisation difficult. In order then to instigate a more nuanced approach to the study of late medieval Gaelic material culture, we need to not only examine the limited archaeological record, but also look to both written and illustrative sources. These are also both limited and limiting in their content and have to be approached with a degree of caution.

Interestingly, there is one striking difference between the material culture of Ulster sites and those Gaelic sites that have been excavated from the rest of the country: the presence or absence of locally made pottery. Ulster has a distinctive local tradition recently labelled medieval Ulster Coarse Pottery (UCP) by McSparron,[32] whereas communities elsewhere in the country do not appear, on present evidence, to have engaged in pottery production. UCP is ubiquitous across the sites excavated east of Lough Foyle in Ulster, but its distribution west of the Lough remains largely unknown due to the paucity of excavations. Western Scotland shares a similar ceramic tradition, and future research will probably document morphological and typological similarities between both. In terms of personal items, there is a distinct dearth of recovered evidence and the limited nature of this material militates against generalised statements that are inclusive of the Gaelic territories as a whole.

We can get some insights into the military attire and equipment of the groups and this is especially relevant for Clann Suibhne, given their pre-eminence as *gallóglaigh*. It is perhaps no coincidence then that the majority of swords of west Highland character have been found in Ireland,[33] reflective of the many groups from the islands and Scottish mainland who were involved in internecine conflict. Halpin has suggested that by the sixteenth century a distinctively Irish open-ringed pommel had developed, but that sword usage had been common across Irish society from the fourteenth century.[34] The Gaelic *ceatharnach* would probably have carried a bow, and two bows are shown in the West Highland sculpture tradition from a late fifteenth-century grave-slab at Arisaig and from Alexander Mac Leòid's tomb on Harris dated to 1528. Spears were in common usage across the region, but throwing darts was more common amongst the Irish. Targes – large circular shields averaging 0.5m in diameter – were used in both areas and were carried across the back when not in use,[35] while the Irish groups certainly wore aketons under mail shirts, from the fourteenth century onwards. Again, the extent to which we can make informed comparative or group-specific analyses of their military attire is constrained by the range of evidence available. One interesting aspect of the Clann Suibhne group is the apparent distinctiveness of headwear worn by the Mac Suibhne, as depicted in John Derrick's (1581) *The Image of Irelande* (Fig. 5). These illustrations show the group feasting and demonstrating loyalty. The Mac Suibhne wears a high hat made from the same fabric, or at least decorated in the same manner as his tunic, with a series of 'tufts' at the apex of the 'hat'. Interestingly, this piece of headwear is positioned beneath the Mac Suibhne's seat at the table next to a ring-pommel sword. This appears to be a distinctive and possibly unique badge of rank amongst this group, in addition to the more usual rod of power. Could this headwear be a bascinet (a type of metal helmet) that is possibly covered in fabric, or is it a felt hat fashioned in a similar manner to the bascinet? This form of helmet was commonly shown on West Highland grave-slabs and was a common component of the *gallóglaigh* military kit in Ireland.[36] The similarity in shape and style may be reflective of this continued cultural affinity with Scotland.

## A Gaelic Mindset

But to what extent can we get inside the Gaelic *mentalité* of Clann Suibhne and the Uí Dhomhnaill? One avenue is to examine their cultural practices and social activities. We know, for example, that during the sixteenth century the Mac Suibhne chief-elect of Fanad was inaugurated by the Ó Domhnaill at Kilmacrenan.[37] This direct association with an established Irish regional succession practice clearly indicates the kindred group's cultural position at this time. Through inauguration at the symbolic kingship site of their Ó Domhnaill overlords, Mic Suibhne of Tír Boghaine were not

5. Detail of an illustration taken from John Derrick's *The Image of Irelande*, published in 1581 (and reproduced by John Small in Edinburgh, 1883) showing the Mac Suibhne lord feasting.

only demonstrating their loyalty and special relationship with the Uí Dhomhnaill but were also making a highly visual statement of their place within Gaelic society in Ulster and further afield. The traditional scene of the Mac Suibhne's feast is another indicator of their perceptions of their place in late medieval society. In that image Mac Suibhne is shown entertaining in a local fashion and outwardly demonstrating both a sense of importance and sense of place within Ulster society.

Another useful means of examining the ways these groups thought about and regarded their situation is through an analysis of contemporary poetry. While we recognise that there are difficulties with these sources in terms of their politically loaded meanings and the partisan nature of their production, they do reflect the formative narratives of the period.[38] They can illustrate the changing nature of allegiances, show how varying groups negotiated their place within society and the aspirations and ambitions that individuals and families had. Both groups under discussion here have a number of extant poems associated with them. A number of poems make particular reference to the developing relationship that Clann Domhnaill had with Ulster society as their place within that society changed and evolved. Tadhg Dall Ó hUiginn's late sixteenth-century address to Brian na Múrtha Ó Ruairc talks of Clann Domhnaill as an 'excellent and wondrous band of the soldiery of Fódla, the mercenaries of Islay'.[39] The poet has created a clear association of ancestral place here, between the Clann Domhnaill and Islay. Elsewhere, an anonymous late sixteenth-century poem written for Aonghus Mac Domhnaill of Dunyveg states:

> You won the Route with a single day's offensive
> From the Mac Uilíns, despite their royaly blood;
> And I would not mention this to your curly ringlets
> That you have deprived me of my native place

The poet was almost certainly from Ulster and while this form of mock combative poetry was written to praise the subject, the poet is making a clear differentiation between his native place and that of the arrivals from Islay. McLeod[40] also notes the repeated references in bardic poetry to the Hebridean groups campaigning (albeit in a mythical sense) around the Boyne and Tara, the effective spiritual and emotive centre of Gaelic power. This connection to Tara was effectively promoting an ancestral linkage to the ancient tribes of Ireland and a sense of entitlement to landholding. A series of poems also appeared in the late sixteenth century urging a number of Scottish chiefs to effectively return to Ireland in order to re-establish their ancestral rights over that place against the yoke of English oppression. A poem dedicated to Giolla Easpuig, Earl of Argyll, makes reference to his ancestors holding possession of 'tribute over Tara of the Three men'. Tadhg Dall Ó hUiginn composed a similar piece in praise of Somhairle Buidhe Mac Domhnaill entitled 'Long has Ireland had a claim upon Scotland', in which Somhairle is compared to Caesar returning to claim his ancestral lands centred again on the Boyne. Elsewhere, Séamus mac Aonghuis Mac Domhnaill of Knockrinsay is asked to return from Islay to Ireland ('to unite the kingdom grasp thy blue blade') in order to fulfil a prophecy of Finn mac Cumaill. Finally, a number of poems developed the notion that the groups from the Western Isles were merely exiled from Ireland and that it was their destiny to ultimately return home. Tadhg Dall Ó hUiginn urged Somhairle Buidhe to return to Ulster by making reference to the three Collas of Clann Somhairle:

> It is strange that they allowed themselves
> the stately men of destructive weapons
> Colla and his ancient lineage ever since
> to be deprived of their inheritance

Fear Flatha Ó Gnímh's particularly political poem, 'These Hebrideans are Irishmen indeed', was composed in 1620 for Randal MacDonnell, the first earl of Antrim.[41] In it he begins:

> These Hebrideans are Irishmen indeed
> Owing to their springing from the fair-bright Collas,
> The noble, well-spoken band
> That stayed not in Eamhain of the wave-grit estuaries
>
> For long, under the yoke of military service
> that lion-band stayed far from Flann's land
> an upturn in fortune for the royal assembly;
> and happy, too, the end of their exile

The poet goes on to state that the land of Scotland was not their original motherland and they were always going to be foreigners there. In many ways these later poems composed for Clann Domhnaill epitomise the fluid and dynamic nature of identity amongst these familial groupings. This branch of Clann Domhnaill had arrived in Ulster in the 1540s and had set about rebuilding the centre of power in an architectural style common across the castles and homes of the leading Scottish lords. They sided with the Ulster chieftains who rose in rebellion against English rule in the 1590s but later changed sides and realigned themselves with the Crown. Randal was at pains to demonstrate his loyalty in the opening decades of the seventeenth century and had effectively reimaged himself as an English lord. As his confidence increased and he set about establishing himself in the mode of a semi-autonomous lord across his northeast Antrim estates, he began to once again remould himself as a Gaelic chieftain and used poetry to propagate this new identity.

## Conclusion

Ultimately then, we are left partially frustrated in our attempts to understand later medieval senses of identity across north Ulster. Was there a sense of nationhood? In contemporary terms the answer is 'No', but when one considers medieval notions of nationhood and belonging, an argument can be forwarded that these peoples were rooted in a broader cultural concept of nation and a wider sense of connection and belonging. Such a nation was, however, not defined by a singular aim of unity but was instead constructed around geography, shared traditions and local aspirations. Both language and material culture represent this set of cultural traditions, while architecture and landscape responded similarly but in a more fluid and politically nuanced way. Tom Finan has argued that the peoples of Gaelic Ireland shared 'a common history', but that they did not have a sense of a unified Irishness in terms of the contemporary nationalistic connotations of that term.[42] Yes, they shared notions of similar pasts and a sense of a common set of experiences and this does, to a certain extent, constitute a shared history. It could then be labelled a pseudo-history, best expressed in the *Leabhar Gabhála Éirin*.[43] However, their sense of a shared history did not necessarily translate into a unified set of political goals but was instead constructed around the primacy of kinship and familial relationships. Ellis has argued that any notion of a national history was essentially a propagandist tool propagated through poetry and, instead, argued that loyalties were familial and local.[44] Connections and familial binds through a shared and distinct geographical space further enhanced this concept of a local belonging, where people were tied to their leading family groups and local territory. These were often very distinctive and recognisably bound territories delineated by physical geography and the sea. It should also be recognised that family group relationships were hierarchical, where the kindred or sept group was defined primarily by its leaders rather than by the majority of its members or followers. Social mobility was limited if not absent from these societies and therefore it is important to differentiate between identities propagated by these hierarchies and the way in which the lower social groups perceived themselves and their sense of identity.

This study has concerned a number of kindred or sept groups with different histories and ambitions. Clann Domhnaill had a long presence in the Glens of Antrim before the Islay branch settled in north Antrim from the 1540s. While they were later viewed as a Gaelic Irish entity by some of the early antiquarians and historians, they were originally viewed as interlopers and as a threat to societal stability by the English administrations in Dublin and London. They did not share many of the features of the more established Gaelic lordships across Ireland but continuously repositioned themselves strategically within both Ulster and Scottish society in pursuit of their individual ambitions. Their identity negotiations were ultimately about the promotion and furtherance of Clann Domhnaill power and influence rather than any notion of national identity and political unity. They successfully negotiated the myriad political arenas of the late medieval world to emerge stronger in the seventeenth century as a landholding and social elite.

Clann Suibhne shared strong Scottish origins with Clann Domhnaill but negotiated a far clearer collective identity rooted in Ulster Gaelic traditions, while maintaining a history and strong association with Argyll and the islands. Over a period of centuries they emerged as an intrinsic part of the Ulster political landscape and their fighting services were much in demand across Ireland. As a group, they successfully integrated into the complex entity that constituted late medieval Gaelic society, but they retained a degree of cultural autonomy and expression. They, in effect, represented a creolised group firmly centred in the wider Gaelic regions of Scotland and Ireland.

What both of these groups illustrate is that Gaelic Ireland was not an isolated insular world but one which stretched beyond the borders of Ireland. This wider world requires us to look beyond the shores of the island of Ireland and take a broader view of the past, of an island that did not look inwards but was instead positioned within a culturally dynamic and outward-looking region, firmly centred in the northwest Atlantic social world.

# 8

# *Crannóga* in later medieval Ireland: Continuity and change

KIERAN O'CONOR

## Introduction

It is argued in this chapter that the continued use of *crannóga* as a settlement form by many members of the Gaelic elite, beyond the early medieval period down to the first years of the seventeenth century, was not due to innate conservatism. The motivation to occupy *crannóga* was more likely linked to the cultural practices of later medieval Gaelic society, one of the manifestations of which involved the deliberate use by the elite of anachronisms and references to the past in order to provide political power and social prestige in the present.

Ordinary Gaelic Irish people, living under their own laws and apparently in separate settlements, were a major component of the tenantry on Anglo-Norman manors in the east and southeast of Ireland during the thirteenth and fourteenth centuries, living alongside peasants of mainly English origin.[1] This aspect of Gaelic settlement on Anglo-Norman manors is clearly a priority for future research, although there are difficulties in actually recognising these places, archaeologically.[2] Furthermore, it would appear that the vast majority of tenants on the manors of the Anglo-Norman lordship of Ulster, whose heartland consisted of the lowland parts of modern County Antrim and County Down, were Gaelic Irish. The conquest of this part of east Ulster merely saw the removal of the Gaelic Irish elite and their replacement by Anglo-Norman lords.[3] It has been suggested that the great majority of the peasant population living on manors in peripheral areas of the Anglo-Norman colony, such as parts of western Westmeath and Longford, were also mainly of Gaelic Irish stock.[4] However, while acknowledging the fact that the indigenous Irish were a substantial part of the population, if not in fact a majority, in lowland regions of eastern and southeastern Ireland, the term 'Gaelic Ireland' is taken here to mean the parts of Ireland that saw the large-scale survival of the Gaelic elite[5] during the whole later medieval period.[6]

During the late twelfth, thirteenth and early fourteenth centuries, these regions included most of Ulster west of the Bann (importantly, this included the drumlin and lakeland areas of modern Counties Monaghan, Cavan and Fermanagh), much of Connacht, parts of west Munster and the bogland and mountain zones of Meath and Leinster.[7] Using the example of the modern County Sligo, I have drawn attention to the fact that there was large-scale survival of the Gaelic elite in many parts of Ireland that political historians have argued were core areas of the Anglo-Norman colony. While the Gaelic lords in such districts had Anglo-Norman overlords, actual settlement by the latter was not as intensive on the ground as political historians have implied in the past.[8] The area under Gaelic cultural and political domination was to expand during the course of the fourteenth century to include areas, such as lowland Carlow, which had been in the heartland of the Anglo-Norman colony in the previous century. Most of Ireland remained under the control of Gaelic and, indeed, Gaelicised lords down to the Tudor and Stuart reconquest of Ireland in the later sixteenth and early seventeenth centuries.[9] This quick review of the geographical extent of later medieval Gaelic Ireland shows it to have been fluid and not fixed. Importantly, this discussion shows that later medieval Gaelic Ireland, as defined in this paper, consisted of a large part of the island of Ireland at any one time, even at the height of Anglo-Norman power in the mid-thirteenth century.

It comes as a surprise to learn, therefore, that later medieval Gaelic Ireland, given its geographical extent, did not receive the same degree of attention from archaeologists over the twentieth century in comparison to the parts of Ireland that were heavily settled by the Anglo-Normans/English and their descendants, such as the urban centres of eastern and southeastern Ireland and their hinterlands.[10] For example, the archaeology of later medieval Gaelic Ireland is barely discussed in Barry's ground-breaking 1987 book *The Archaeology of Medieval Ireland* and, arguably, not in any great detail in O'Keeffe's *Medieval Ireland: An Archaeology* (2000). These were and are important textbooks used by students in Irish universities and elsewhere to understand the archaeology of later medieval Ireland.[11] There were a number of reasons for this lack of archaeological work on later medieval Gaelic Ireland that have been rehearsed over the years by various scholars.[12] The lack of detailed surviving economic and social information about Gaelic Ireland until the late sixteenth century and the lack of archaeological excavations in the various parts of Ireland that remained under the control of the native elite meant that it proved difficult in the past to identify and pinpoint medieval Gaelic secular settlement in the modern landscape. This was particularly true of the centuries before Gaelic Irish lords began to adopt the tower house form of castle from the late fourteenth and early fifteenth centuries onwards.[13]

This situation has changed since the late 1990s. The longest chapter in *The Archaeology of Medieval Rural Settlement in Ireland* (1998) discussed the archaeology of later medieval (particularly high medieval) Gaelic Ireland in detail.[14] A large section of *Gaelic Ireland, c.1250–c.1650: Land, Lordship and Settlement*, edited by Duffy, Edwards and FitzPatrick (2001), dealt with aspects of the physical remains of the later medieval Gaelic past in Ireland.[15] FitzPatrick's (2004) *Royal Inauguration in Gaelic Ireland,* c.*1100–1600* examined later medieval Gaelic inauguration sites in their landscape settings, and aspects of the material culture of the indigenous Irish during the latter period.[16] Breen's (2005) *The Gaelic Lordship of the O'Sullivan Beare: A Landscape Cultural History* was the first major archaeological and landscape study of a later medieval Gaelic lordship ever to be published.[17] The *Medieval Lough Cé: History, Archaeology and Landscape* volume, edited by Tom Finan (2010), can be described as a multi-disciplinary study of the later medieval Mac Diarmada lordship of Magh Luirg (see Finan, Chapter 2, this volume), with a very strong archaeological component.[18]

A major aspect of the work of the Discovery Programme's Medieval Rural Settlement Project, which was directed by Niall Brady, examined the archaeology of later medieval north Roscommon, a region dominated throughout the latter period by the Gaelic Uí Chonchobhair.[19] The ongoing excavation of the *caiseal* at Caherconnell, County Clare, directed by Michelle Comber, has clearly demonstrated that this site, while first constructed in the tenth century, continued to be intensively occupied throughout later medieval times, throwing further light on the material culture of Gaelic Ireland during the latter period.[20] The excavation of burials from a forgotten graveyard at Ballyhanna, County Donegal has uncovered considerable information about the lifestyles, health and diet of ordinary people in later medieval Gaelic Ireland, amongst other things.[21] Archaeological fieldwork and further research since the year 2000 has identified, discussed and analysed further Gaelic Irish elite centres, ordinary habitation sites, assembly sites and cultural landscapes of later medieval date.[22] This research has been substantially aided by the work of Simms and, to a lesser extent, Finan, who have reminded us of the value of using bardic poetry, not only in helping archaeologists recognise such centres, or informing us as to how they looked when in use or providing information about indigenous material culture, but also in allowing us an insight into the nature and mindset of Gaelic Irish lordship during the whole later medieval period.[23] Bardic poetry helps us understand the things that were important to the poets, their elite patrons and the audiences that listened to their poems. Such work is a reminder to archaeologists that a multi-disciplinary approach to the study of the later medieval past in Ireland – using evidence from archaeology, the historical sources, early maps and the literary evidence – is necessary in order to gain a better understanding of the sites and material culture under investigation.[24] In all, this discussion indicates that much more is known about the settlement archaeology and material culture of later medieval Gaelic Ireland than was the situation twenty years ago.

## *Crannóga*

Gaelic *crannóga* are mostly artificial islands, completely surrounded by water, which were constructed of layers of soil, brushwood, peat, rubbish and stone dumped onto relatively shallow parts of lakes. In reality, based on fieldwork carried out across north Connacht (or Lower Connacht, as it was known historically) and County Longford, it seems that the great majority of them were constructed of a dump of stones. Whatever the material used to build these artificial islands, the *crannóg* matrix was generally held or anchored in place (to stop movement caused by storms and currents) by submerged upright timbers sunk into the lakebed. The dumped material created a usually circular, dry occupation platform that was generally between 15m and 30m in diameter. Excavation evidence (and, indeed, very late pictorial sources) indicates that houses were built on these artificial occupation platforms and that post-and-wattle or plank-built palisades occurred around their edges, indicating that they were also defensive.[25] At least 1,500 *crannóga* have been recognised to date, the majority of them located on the small or relatively small lakes of the drumlin belt that runs across north Connacht and south Ulster, regions shown above to have been dominated by members of the Gaelic elite throughout the later medieval period.[26] Furthermore, it is also clear that quite a number of small, natural islands on lakes or occasionally in rivers – such as the high medieval Ó Domhnaill residence of Inis Saimer, which is located in the estuary of the Erne at Ballyshannon, County Donegal – effectively functioned as *crannóga*.[27] Some *crannóga* are, in fact, part-natural and part-artificial islands, such as the one on Inchiquin Lough, County Clare.[28] The Rock of Loch Cé, which was a Mac Diarmada fortress during the later medieval period, was mostly a natural island, but some artificial material was added to it to give it sufficient height to produce a dry habitation area. Also, the southeastern third of this site seems to be wholly artificial.[29] The word *crannóg* is rarely used in the sources. Instead, these sites were mostly referred to as *inis* (island) by contemporaries.[30]

Irish scholars over the course of much of the last century or so have, until recently, tended to view *crannóga* as being high-status, often royal, residences dating to the early medieval period, seeing this settlement form as beginning to be built in numbers from the fifth and sixth centuries AD onwards, basically at the same time that ringforts began to appear in the Irish landscape.[31] However, work in the Lough Gara area by the Swedish archaeologist Christina Fredengren has shown that some *crannóga* date to the late prehistoric period and are earlier than was once commonly thought.[32] However, one clear conclusion of the work of various scholars over the last twenty years or so has been to remind us that *crannóga* were also commonly used as residences by the Gaelic elite in lakeland Ireland, particularly across the drumlin belt of south Ulster and north Connacht, during the whole later medieval period.[33] Regional studies in south Ulster have further reinforced the view that *crannóga* were a common feature of the landscape throughout large parts of later medieval Gaelic Ireland. For example, despite their article being placed in the early medieval section of a 2006 Festschrift dedicated to the late Ann Hamlin, Foley and Williams, using radiocarbon-dating evidence and dendrochronology, clearly demonstrated this fact for later medieval Gaelic Fir Mhanach.[34] The conclusion that *crannóga* were commonly occupied by the elite of Fir Mhanach during later medieval times was reinforced by the work of Jacqui O'Hara in her thesis on the Mág Uidhir lordship of Fir Mhanach. Combining all the evidence from excavation, stray finds, dendrochronology, radiocarbon dates and the historical and literary sources, she argued that anything up to two-thirds of recognised *crannóga* in County Fermanagh, today, show some evidence for having being occupied during later medieval times.[35] The identification of *crannóga* occupied, if not built, during the later medieval period is ongoing. It is clear that they were a relatively common feature of the landscape of thirteenth- and fourteenth-century Roscommon. There also seems to be quite good evidence for the use of *crannóga* among the Gaelic elite in late sixteenth- and very early seventeenth-century north Roscommon.[36] For example, a detailed late sixteenth-century account survives of an English attack on an Ó Conchobhair *crannóg* in the northwest of the modern county.[37] 'Innsi Achaidh in Chairthe', 'inche aghochare' and 'Incheaghechare' are referred to in Gaelic and colonial sources during the early 1580s; these references can be translated as meaning the 'island' of Aghacarra, which appears to have been the centre of a Mac Diarmada landed estate at that time, consisting of at least two quarters of land.[38] It has been suggested that this site is represented today by the semi-submerged *crannóg* off Drumdoe townland in Lough Arrow.[39] However, it has been argued that a better fit for this site may be the *crannóg* extant on Cornacarta Lough today, as this lake bounds the modern townland of Aghacarra.[40] In 1610 there is a reference to 'de insula de Ballemacmanus', which was at that time the centre of quite a considerable landed estate owned by one Rory Roe MacManus.[41] Ballymacmanus in Tír Tuathail was the old name for Keadue, County Roscommon.[42] It would appear that one candidate for this *insula* or 'island' is the *crannóg* at the eastern end of Lough Meelagh, which lies off Keadue West townland (Fig. 1). It is constructed of a large dump of stones held in place at times by submerged wooden posts. The occupation platform (which is today covered by trees and bushes) is *c.*20m in diameter. The remains of the oaken planks of a collapsed palisade can be seen in the water in places around the *crannóg*.[43] The ruined parish church of Kilronan, probably of fourteenth century date (although it seems to have replaced an earlier Romanesque church), can be seen above the lake to the north of the site.[44]

It is clear from this discussion that *crannóga* were a feature of the landscape for many centuries. A further point that can be made from examining these late references to what appear to be *crannóga* in places like north Roscommon is that they indicate that they were not (or, at least, were not usually) isolated refuge sites located in wild landscapes. Instead, these quite detailed, late references are a reminder that *crannóga* throughout the later medieval period were mostly elite residences and centres of landed estates and, in some cases, lordships. Giraldus Cambrensis informs us in the late twelfth century that the Irish, while they did not have castles (or what he considered to be castles), did use 'islands' on lakes (presumably *crannóga*) for 'safety and refuge' and, importantly, 'habitation'.[45] For example, the part-natural and part-artificial Rock of Loch Cé, as noted, was the centre of the Mac Diarmada lordship of Magh Luirg, a chiefry estate, throughout the later medieval period (see Finan, Chapter 2). The combined archaeological and historical evidence suggests that the Rock had an associated enclosure, in this case a moated site, on the shore near it.[46] This moated site presumably housed the agricultural and at least some of the administrative buildings associated with farming the estate and running the lordship of Magh Luirg. The remains of pre-modern field systems, possibly linked to this later medieval estate, can also be seen in the vicinity. Furthermore, a nucleated settlement with market functions and a substantial pier may have existed to the immediate east of the moated site.[47] Dry-land enclosures, either some form of ringfort or moated site, and churches have been noted on the shores opposite various *crannóga* known to have been occupied during later medieval times.[48] The work of the Discovery Programme's Medieval Rural Settlement Project has shown that Ardakillen *crannóg* in County Roscommon, historically attested to as being an Ó Conchobhair residence during

1. The *crannóg* at the eastern end of Lough Meelagh, County Roscommon. It seems to have been the residence of the Mac Maghnusa lords of *Tír Tuathail* during later medieval times (image: author).

later medieval times, seems to have been associated with a dry-land enclosure, best classified as a ringfort, a church and a relatively small, unplanned nucleated settlement on the shore opposite.[49] The main point here is that most *crannóga* in later medieval times functioned as central points in ordered, seemingly prosperous, agricultural landscapes. In all, despite the fact that they were different as regards their appearance and architectural complexity, in terms of their functions as fortified lordly residences and estate centres, their siting, and general importance in the settlement hierarchy of their areas, *crannóga* have a lot in common with contemporary castles.[50]

It has been noted, however, that there has been a reluctance in places to fully engage with the fact that the available archaeological, historical, literary and late cartographic evidence suggests that *crannóga* were a common feature of the later medieval landscape in those parts of Ireland where lakes, particularly small drumlin lakes, were plentiful.[51] This is, perhaps, understandable simply because, as shown, the *crannóg* was a settlement form long in existence in Ireland and particularly associated in Irish scholarship with the early medieval period. To suggest that an archaic or seemingly archaic settlement form was in common use throughout Gaelic Ireland beyond 1169 is in a way embarrassing, as it could be seen as agreeing with the views of medieval Anglo-Norman and English commentators from Giraldus Cambrensis down to Edmund Spenser and modern Anglo-Irish scholars such as Goddard Orpen, who believed that later medieval Gaelic Ireland was conservative, backward and anarchic.[52] In this scenario, it is better to emphasise changes and similar developmental trends to what is seen in the so-called feudalised, core countries of contemporary Western Europe.[53]

Scholars who are somewhat uneasy with this widespread evidence for *crannóg* use in later medieval Ireland may be somewhat placated by the views of Donnelly, Logue and O'Neill that at least some sixteenth-century *crannóga* may have had quite complex timber towers, something akin to wooden tower houses, within their defences.[54] Here, perhaps, we have something similar to FitzPatrick's pedigree-of-place theory, where older Gaelic sites continued to be occupied due to their powerful association with the past but within which contemporary-style buildings were erected or, at least, older structures refitted and re-built to suit developing social and political needs.[55] Such scenarios are perhaps reassuring to some, as they indicate development – not stagnation or conservatism – in later medieval Gaelic Ireland.

Something like this occurs on the Rock of Loch Cé (Fig. 2; see also Finan, Chapter 2). It was shown above that the site emerges in the twelfth century as the centre of the Mac Diarmada lordship of Magh Luirg and that the Rock itself is a part-artificial and part-natural island. An analysis of the standing remains on the site indicated that the first identifiable architectural phase, presumably dating in its construction to the late twelfth century, consisted of a *caiseal*-like, mortared stone enclosure that was quite simple in design, although high-walled, the internal diameter of which was about 35m.[56] At a distance and even quite close up, this enclosure must have looked quite similar in morphology to earlier, substantial, high-walled *caiseal* enclosures of early medieval date; the fact that its stones had mortar between them would not have been immediately obvious to the observer.[57] At some stage in the late medieval period, however, a tower house was built on the eastern side of this enclosure, again showing development on an existing Gaelic lordly site, with all its ancient and powerful associations.[58] The site continued to be occupied as a residence, and a green-field site on dryland was not used. We have other examples of *crannóga*, such as the Mac Fhlannchadha one at Ros Clochair (Rosclogher) on Lough Melvin, upon which tower houses were built in late medieval times.[59] In these scenarios, development and modernisation is seen on older sites, and accusations of conservatism and backwardness on the part of the Gaelic Irish who lived in such places are harder to make.

Moving back to the Rock of Loch Cé, however, it is not at all certain as to when the tower house there was erected. Given the fact that there is quite detailed surviving documentation for this site, one interpretation of the historical references is that this tower house may have been erected as late as the last decades of the sixteenth century.[60] It took time for tower house building to take root in Gaelic Ireland and in many cases, as Breen has shown in the west Cork lordship of Ó Suilleabháin Bhéara, it was not until the late fifteenth and sixteenth centuries before they were built in numbers in many lordships.[61] In other words, sites like the Rock of Loch Cé, with its mix of *caiseal*-like defences and *crannóg*-type foundations, and proper *crannóga* that later saw tower houses built on them, may have arguably presented quite an archaic-looking face to the world until quite late in their occupation. Furthermore, even when tower houses, whether timber- or masonry-built, were constructed on *crannóga*, their siting, their defences and the other buildings on them must have continued to make these places look quite old-fashioned. For example, it has been argued that the rectangular wooden (see Logue Fig. 3) framework visible on Richard Bartlett's *c.*1602 famous depiction of an Ulster *crannóg* under attack by English forces may have been an unfinished wooden tower house.[62] However, its simple post-and-wattle palisade and the three other buildings on the *crannóg* – which appear to be small, oval, possibly window-less, post-and-wattle, *creat*-like houses of general Gaelic-Irish type – would have made the site quite archaic-looking to English observers, despite the existence of a possible wooden tower house. Such places differed in scale and complexity to the Renaissance-influenced fortified houses being put up at that time in different parts of Ireland, often (but not always) by the New English.

Furthermore, the available fieldwork and pictorial evidence suggests that the majority of *crannóga* occupied in late medieval times did not undergo the change of having tower houses built on them, wooden or otherwise, during the course of the fifteenth and sixteenth centuries. At least some of Bartlett's drawings depict certain *crannóga* in south Ulster as being defended by simple, undifferentiated post-and-wattle palisades with relatively small ovoid, *creat*-like buildings within their interiors. For example, much is made of Bartlett's depiction of the lower of the two *crannóga* at Rooskey Lough, near Monaghan town, as it has a large, modern English-style timber-framed house on it, although it is still girdled by a simple, arguably old-fashioned looking post-and-wattle palisade.[63] The other *crannóg*, however, again defended by a post-and-wattle palisade, has a small, oval, possibly post-and-wattle built house within it. At least some *crannóga*, if not the great majority, in use during the whole later medieval period, even in the late sixteenth and early seventeenth centuries, presented, at a first glance, a seemingly conservative, almost timeless appearance.

This does not mean that later medieval Gaelic Ireland was a stagnant place, as it shows many of the trends seen elsewhere in Europe throughout the whole period. For example, a recent study of the Dominican priory at Roscommon, which was founded by Feidhlimidh Ó Conchobhair in 1253, shows that this Gaelic king was patronising a new and vibrant religious order in much the same way as other members of the European elite were doing at the time. Furthermore, the large-scale nature of the priory and its rapid erection are all proof that the necessary wealth and technical expertise were there in mid-thirteenth-century Roscommon, as elsewhere in Gaelic Ireland, to build large, complex masonry structures (Fig. 3).[64] The fact that this priory was rebuilt on a massive scale in the mid-fifteenth century is evidence that Roscommon continued to be a wealthy place under the Uí Chonchobhair in late medieval times too.[65] However, given that Roscommon Priory, as built in the mid-thirteenth century, was as architecturally complex as any contemporary priory in Europe, it comes as a surprise to learn that the available historical and archaeological evidence suggests that Feidhlimidh's residence at Roscommon in the 1250s was a *crannóg*.[66]

3. Daniel Tietzsch-Tyler's 2010 reconstruction drawing of Roscommon Priory around the year 1265 (Roscommon County Council).

During the late twelfth and thirteenth centuries (and for the rest of the later medieval period), the Mic Dhiarmada of Magh Luirg patronised the Cistercian monastery of Boyle, the Premonstratensian foundation on Holy Trinity Island, and the Augustinians on Inchmacnerin. All these sites occur close to the Rock of Loch Cé, on the southern side of the lough. The buildings at these monasteries are complex, up-to-date structures that were either built or re-built during this period. Such patronage is indicative of major wealth and technological skills within the lordship of Magh Luirg at this time. Yet the Rock of Loch Cé (the secular centre of the lordship), at the time that these ecclesiastical sites were built, consisted of a relatively simple, rather archaic-looking enclosure, morphologically similar to an impressive *caiseal*, which was built on a partly artificial, *crannóg*-like island. This is all part of a wider observation made by scholars, such as McNeill, which argues that there is little evidence for Gaelic lords building complex masonry castles over the island of Ireland before the late fourteenth and early fifteenth centuries and in some areas (such as Fir Mhanach), up to the early seventeenth century. A few examples of Gaelic-built masonry castles can be recognised that date before the advent of tower houses, but these are relatively simple in design.[67] Alternatively, however, right from the late twelfth century until the seventeenth century, Gaelic Irish forces constantly showed that they had the ability and the technical knowledge to both besiege and take the most well-defended Anglo-Norman and later English fortresses and, on many occasions, to defeat them in battle.[68] This must again be indicative of wealth, technological know-how and good military organisation within later medieval Gaelic Irish kingdoms and lordships.

On the other hand, leaving aside traditional-looking *crannóga*, the literary references in bardic poetry to elite feasting in post-and-wattle-built halls are another indication of seemingly conservative building choices being made in elite Gaelic Irish secular contexts.[69] The conundrum is trying to understand this mix of modernity and conservatism in later medieval Gaelic Ireland. How do we balance accusations of Gaelic Irish barbarity and backwardness by contemporary observers (mainly biased Anglo-Norman and English chroniclers from Giraldus Cambrensis onwards, but also outsiders with less justification for bias such as the Catalan Raymond de Perelhos, in the fourteenth century and the Spaniard, Captain de Cuellar in the sixteenth century),[70] with clear archaeological and historical evidence for development and modernity in many aspects of Gaelic-Irish culture? Why do archaic settlement forms such as the *crannóg*, the post-and-wattle hall or, for that matter, the *caiseal* exist in the same landscape as up-to-date, modern and impressive friaries, abbeys and later tower houses, built and used by the same people? So, for example, we have the situation where high medieval and, to a certain extent, some late medieval Gaelic lords had the resources and technical knowledge to build complex masonry castles and yet did not do so in any numbers. How can this situation be explained? Relatively pragmatic reasons have been given to explain this. Periodic land redistribution, partible inheritance among the extended kin group and lack of the use of primogeniture in matters of inheritance to lordship have been suggested as reasons why few complex stone castles were built by the Gaelic elite before the late fourteenth century and in some areas, like Fir Mhanach, up to the early seventeenth century.[71] The very efficient use of the landscape in war by the Gaelic elite is another reason given why expensive fixed fortifications like masonry castles were not used to any degree.[72] This was a mobile method of warfare and territorial defence that suited a society whose main wealth was cattle. It might be added that research in France has noted that the adoption of primogeniture in that country during the twelfth century, by knightly families, saw a massive rise in castle-building there.[73] Partible inheritance in its various forms and the restrictions of Irish law must be at least partly responsible for this lack of stone castles, and for that matter Hen-Domen type timber castles, throughout later medieval Gaelic Ireland before *c.*1400, and in some areas far later than this date.

These are pragmatic reasons and explanations as to why older settlement forms, such as *crannóga* and wattle halls, continued to be used in later medieval Ireland by members of the elite. Nevertheless, research consistently shows that there are different levels of meaning in medieval architecture. Castle studies in recent years emphasises this point. Research over the last two decades, especially in England, has suggested that many castles were primarily erected as vehicles for social display, rather than defence (although this was still important), and were often set within deliberately manipulated landscapes – that included such things as deerparks, rabbit warrens, fish-ponds, planned settlements and ecclesiastical structures – to reinforce this impression. The combined effect of these great castles, set within these landscapes, was to impress all observers with their owners' status, importance and control of economic resources.[74] Furthermore, this research into the social context of castles has emphasised the fact that buildings – and rooms within these places – were often designed to be the 'theatres' for lordly display, the architectural elements and contrived settings within them acting as 'props'.[75] Indeed, in an attempt to downplay the debate over the primacy of either 'military' or 'social' functions of castles, it has been argued that such displays of lordly power were also important in turbulent border areas, as they could be seen as a pedagogic propaganda exercise designed to send out the message that it would be unwise to try to undermine the power of the castle's owner, as all the resources that were needed to build such structures and landscapes could be used to crush opposition.[76] It was a form of what Orser calls 'symbolic violence'.[77]

Creighton has noted that much academic literature on castles and their landscapes, right up to the present, has concentrated on sites that were at the forefront of architectural and landscape design for their time.[78] New and imposing architecture at such castle sites is seen by scholars as having formed a major part of lordly display – modernity representing power. Of course, it is also easier to study change, as change is more tangible. Nevertheless, Creighton argues that this emphasis amongst scholars across Europe on developing, contemporary design and sophistication in great castles has created a situation where scholarship has underestimated the extent to which medieval builders, and for that matter medieval communities, had a strong sense of the past.[79] To a certain extent, this has allowed us to ignore or understudy examples of where certain buildings were built to look older than they were, or where existing structures had features added to them to falsify a sense of antiquity. For example, arguably, Restormel Castle in Cornwall was deliberately re-built in the late thirteenth century (after 1268), probably by Richard, earl of Cornwall, to look archaic from a distance but actually had first-rate, state-of-the-art domestic apartments within it (Fig. 4).[80] Again, so much literature on Caernarvon Castle in north Wales emphasises the modernity of its defences and accommodation for the late thirteenth century. It is sometimes forgotten that its design, in the form of its polygonal towers and its embellishments of banded masonry and eagle sculptures, was meant to link its builder, Edward I, back to the great days of Rome and, also, King Arthur.[81] A false motte was thrown up around a rebuilt tower at Lydford Castle, Devon, in the second half of the thirteenth century apparently by Richard, earl of Cornwall, to purposely make the place look older (Fig. 5).[82] Such deliberate anachronisms emphasised not only the power but the permanence and immutability of lordship and kingship, according to Creighton. In these circumstances, it would appear that the long memories of local communities were being manipulated by these castle builders to add to their own power in the present.[83] In particular, in a recent article looking at the castle-building strategies of Richard, earl of Cornwall, in mid- to late thirteenth-century England, Creighton has again reminded us that the contrived feigning of antiquity was one method, amongst others, by which the elite demonstrated high status. He shows that anachronism (making something look older than it really was) was often an important

4. Restormel Castle, Cornwall, re-built in the second half of the thirteenth century deliberately to look archaic from a distance (image: Oliver Creighton).

5. Lydford Castle, Devon, deliberately modified in the late thirteenth century to look archaic (image: Oliver Creighton).

means by which great magnates, such as Richard, communicated rank and privilege to different audiences in certain circumstances.[84]

Returning to later medieval Gaelic Ireland, such situations were commonplace there. Later medieval Gaelic culture has been shown by FitzPatrick to be purposely anachronistic in its choice of religious and inauguration sites, and in its service family settlements (see FitzPatrick, Chapter 9).[85] It has been suggested that the same anachronisms were applied to the placement of the principal chamber or hall within Gaelic and Gaelicised tower houses of late medieval fifteenth- and early sixteenth-century date. The location of this room in the uppermost chamber of these tower houses allowed a central, communal hearth to be used, with the room open to the rafters, an attempt to reconstruct the old feasting halls of antiquity.[86]

With these observations in mind, let us return to bardic poetry and the continued and widespread use of *crannóga* and post-and-wattle halls in later medieval Gaelic Ireland. While realising that bardic poetry has to be used carefully, the deliberate choice of archaic words within these poems and the constant reference to ancient heroic figures and the eponymous ancestors of the poets' lordly patrons is interesting.[87] For example, poets often compared their patrons to particular mythological heroes, like Cú Chulainn or Conn of the Hundred Battles.[88] This is, at least, partly done to set both the patron and his dwelling place into a timeless heroic context, the poem in question comparing the lord more than favourably to the great figures of myth and legend that he often claimed as ancestors (Conn of the Hundred Battles, for example, was the supposed ancestor of the Ó Conchobhair kings of Connacht and the Mac Diarmada of Magh Luirg), so as to give him power in the form of 'cultural capital' and to further justify his right to rule in the present.[89] In this respect, combining the observations made by Creighton in an English context and this evidence, can it be suggested that while the continued use of *crannóga* and post-and-wattle halls can be partly understood for pragmatic and legal reasons, these choices can also be explained as deliberate anachronisms to reinforce lordly power in the present? Archaic-looking *crannóga* and post-and-wattle halls were deliberately chosen, built and occupied as the physical 'theatres' within which a specific type of lordly display took place, one that, perhaps more than elsewhere, tied itself to the ancient, heroic past, as the bardic poems suggest. Looking at it this way, it can be argued that the continued use of *crannóga* up to the early seventeenth century in Gaelic Ireland can be seen as a sensible, politically driven choice for its time. It helps explain this mix of modernity and conservatism that seems to be a feature of later medieval Gaelic society.

If *crannóga* and post-and-wattle halls can be seen as physical, three-dimensional living 'theatres' for the display of later medieval Gaelic princely and lordly power and the actors were the lords themselves, aided by their poets and harpers, who then was the audience? It certainly was not Anglo-Norman lords or later English colonial officials, soldiers and administrators or, for that matter, foreign visitors such as Raymond de Perelhos. One is reminded of the Englishman Stephen of Lexington and his contemptuous remarks in 1228 when he stated that Gaelic princes did not live in stone castles or substantial timber houses but instead lived in 'huts of wattle, such as birds are accustomed to build when moulting'.[90] As late as the sixteenth and seventeenth century, English officials and, indeed, continental visitors are making disparaging remarks about many Gaelic Irish residences, including those of the elite. They seem to have missed the point. The audiences for this display of archaism were clearly Gaelic Irish – including other Gaelic lords, sub-chiefs, possible rivals within the extended family group of the lord in question and local freeholders – whose long memories of the past and the landscape in which they lived were being manipulated for contemporary political reasons.

This discussion also suggests that the Anglo-Normans and the English, in particular royal officials linked to the Dublin government, did not understand later medieval Gaelic Ireland and the power of the past in that particular society and saw what is argued in this paper to be deliberate anachronisms as evidence of barbarity and backwardness. They often failed to see what was in front of their eyes. For example, the picture of the royal hall of Aodh Ó Conchobhair at Cluain Fraoich around 1300, provided in two extant praise poems, is that it was quite large and built of post and wattle (see FitzPatrick, Chapter 9, for its landholding context). The interior is described as being full of warriors drinking and feasting, flashing weapons and beautiful maidens – at first glance, a timeless picture of lordship not unlike the great ancient halls of mythological Tara. However, on closer inspection it appears that this antique-looking, deliberately old-fashioned post-and-wattle hall had a completely up-to-date, state-of-the-art cruck roof system to hold up its heavy roof.[91] In a way, this hall at Cluain Fraoich can stand as a metaphor for later medieval Gaelic Ireland. At one level, it was a society that constantly referred back to the past to give power in the present to its elite, but at another level it was one where new ideas from the outside, if appropriate, could be absorbed, developed and used to advantage in the continuation of that power.

## Conclusion

It has been argued that the continued use and occupation of *crannóga* by the later medieval Gaelic elite was at least partly done for political reasons linked to a particular display of power that referenced the past. Does this conclusion have any wider implications? In this regard, it is interesting from an Irish perspective, and for the discussion in this paper, that the examples of anachronisms in Britain, given above, occur in castles that are situated in Cornwall, its borders and Wales. It is noteworthy, in this respect, that Richard, earl of Cornwall, when building in England proper, chose instead to erect state-of-the-art castles, as at Wallingford in the period 1247–1256, where he re-modelled the castle there and gave it concentric defences. This made it one of the earliest concentric castles in western Europe. There was nothing at all anachronistic or old-fashioned looking about this castle, which lay relatively close to London and was situated on the Thames.[92] Modernity in castle design, power and privilege were one and the same at Wallingford. One question for further research in Britain, therefore, will be to enquire into the possibility that the medieval Welsh, Cornish and Gaelic-speaking Scots, particularly their elites, with their origin-myths placing their lineages deep into antiquity, were more susceptible to and impressed by displays of elite power that involved anachronisms and references to the past than was the case with their Norman and later English contemporaries.

# 9

# Gaelic service kindreds and the landscape identity of *lucht tighe*

ELIZABETH FITZPATRICK

## Introduction

My aim in this chapter is to place service kindreds of the Gaelic court in their landscape settings between *c.*1200 and 1600, and to show that the pedigree of their landholdings underpinned their roles as people with often long histories of hereditary service to ruling families. The kind of intense synonymy between identity and place expressed by the relationships between service kindreds and their landholdings is important to understanding how land was organised in Gaelic lordships.

Land organisation and the complex system of customs associated with it in Gaelic cultural practices was considered peculiar, if not incomprehensible, by successive English administrations in Ireland. However, an imperative to understand that system, so that resources could be transferred to subjects loyal to the Crown, produced a particular and informative kind of English record of Gaelic landholding and land use. The traditional historians and brehon lawyers of later medieval and early modern Gaelic Ireland are not known to have made or curated maps of the land denominations that constituted the lordships that they served. However, records of rights and dues in relation to landholding seem to have been kept by the *ollamh*[1] in law of the Gaelic court. This is suggested by an early seventeenth-century encounter between the Attorney-

General, Sir John Davies, and the Ó Breasláin, *airchinneach*[2] of Derryvullan parish church and *ollamh* in law to the Mág Uidhir lord of Fir Mhanach, when Davies was investigating landholdings in pre-Plantation Ulster. In a letter (1606) to Robert Cecil, the Earl of Salisbury, Davies explained that in order to find out 'how many vessels of butter, and how many measures of meal, and how many porks, and other such gross duties did arise unto M'Guire out of his mensal lands', a manuscript kept by Ó Breasláin was viewed and subsequently translated into English for Davies' benefit. The manuscript that Ó Breasláin produced when pressed to do so, and which he continually carried with him, was described by Davies as a roll which was 'not very large, but it was written on both sides in a fair Irish character; howbeit some part of the writing was worn and defaced with time and ill-keeping'.[3]

The landholding arrangement that prevailed in the lordships of Gaelic Ireland provided for four major categories of inheritable land that included (1) personal demesne land attached to the office of the chief; (2) *lucht tighe* or mensal land, also attached to the office of the chief, and populated with service families; (3) sept lands of vassals who owned their lands; and (4) termon or church lands.[4] All of those land categories were organised in an orderly system of estates generally termed *baile biataigh*.

Davies' meeting with Ó Breasláin concerned the *lucht tighe* of the lordship of Fir Mhanach. Katharine Simms has shown that during the fifteenth century the meaning of the term *lucht tighe*, literally 'people of the house', changed. The origins of *lucht tighe* lies in the formation of early medieval royal lands whereby the king's troops were granted parcels of land in return for providing military services to the household. Originally, the term meant household troops, but by the late fifteenth century it was used for mensal or household lands.[5] Mensal land was the place that resourced the lord's household, administrative, ceremonial and military needs.

## DEFINING THE *LUCHT TIGHE* AND ITS OCCUPANTS

The geography of the late medieval *lucht tighe* can be identified in many, but not all, instances as a relic of the early medieval arrangement of the lands of a king's householders, in the form of sometimes contiguous but more usually scattered blocks of estates occupied by service families. It is a feature of lordship mensal lands that they were usually situated in a boundary place of an earlier constituent territory such as a *trícha cét* or *túath*. The *lucht tighe* of Ó Néill occupied what was the southeastern extent of the earlier *trícha cét* kingdom of Tulach Óg, lying between the Ballinderry and Blackwater rivers and bordered by Lough Neagh to the east (Fig. 1). *Lucht tighe* lands were normally given to food-production and were fundamentally concerned with resourcing the lord's table (Latin, *mensa*), but the archaeology of the *lucht tighe* lands of Ó Néill indicates that *lucht tighe* also served elite threshold activities such as inauguration, predation, feasting and conflict.[6] The hill of Tulach Óg, which was situated on the service family lands of the Ó hÁgáin stewards to Ó Néill, hosted lordly and earlier royal inaugurations and there was seasonal feasting at An Chraobh, now Stewartstown, County Tyrone, on the estate of the service family of Ó Cuinn (Fig. 2).[7] The use of An Chraobh for that purpose is poetically recorded by Tadhg Dall Ó hUiginn in a eulogy for Toirdhealbhach Luineach Ó Néill, in which the poet writes: 'At Christmas we went to Creeve, / the poets of Ireland to a man, / on the smooth side of the little hillock, / where O'Neill was at Christmas'.[8] The hillock referred to by the poet is Crew Hill in Tamnylennan townland on the northeast side of Stewartstown. A *crannóg* on Stewartstown Lough, in Gortatray townland, was probably the residence of Ó Néill during hospitality events hosted on Ó Cuinn's estate.

In theory, *lucht tighe*, with a pedigree that underpinned the authority of the lord, could not be alienated from his family or given to another purpose. Centuries after the formation of the lands of a king's householders, some service kindreds with the family names of original household troops are still found on those lands. This is especially true of several of the service kindreds of the Uí Néill of Tír Eoghain, who are found living around the assembly place of Tulach Óg to *c.*1600. It is the case too with the service families of the Síol Muireadhaigh branch of the Uí Chonchobhair of Machaire Chonnacht, who were located around the old *pailís* of Cluain Fraoich as late as the close of the sixteenth century.

The types of service providers that served the courts of Gaelic lords included the steward or overseer of the household, the spenser in charge of distributing food, the marshal, horsemen or cavalry, huntsmen and keepers of hounds, horn-blowers, cup bearers, keepers of toilets, among many others, and a range of learned families that included poets, lawyers, physicians and surgeons, musicians and traditional historians and craftsmen.[9] Within the different groups of functionaries that served the courts of Gaelic lords, the learned professions constituted a very particular elite class, who were hereditary and male and both secular and church officials. Their geographies within lordships tended to be consistently marginal, with poets and traditional historians, in particular, holding lands on old kingdom boundaries. Learned families, who were appointed to the office of *ollamh* in their respective professions to the Gaelic court, could not always claim the same degree of longevity on their landholdings as stewards, spensers, foot-soldiers and huntsmen. The geographies of several of the learned kindreds attached to later medieval Gaelic courts were the result of migrations after the gradual collapse of the monastic schools in the twelfth century, which had been caused by a combination of Church reform and the introduction of the parochial system during Anglo-Norman settlement.[10] While some learned men who were *comharba* remained on their termon lands, others, especially *airchinnigh*, were slotted into different church lands and sometimes episcopal mensal lands, after the twelfth century.[11] They attached themselves to the cult of the saint associated with the church, in addition to running schools and guest houses and serving their lords in the professions of law, poetry, traditional history and genealogy, music, medicine and high-level crafts. Typical of such families were the Uí Dhuibhgeannáin, the leading representative of which was both the *comharba* of St Lasair of Kilronan and *ollamh* in traditional history (*senchas*) to the Mac Diarmada lord of Magh Luirg. The church land of the Uí Dhuibhgeannáin overlooked Lough Meelagh (in north County Roscommon) where they also kept a house of hospitality.[12]

Service kindreds are enumerated in native prose and verse and in English administrative records. A prose tract that accompanies a fifteenth-century inauguration ode to the Ó Conchobhair of Machaire Chonnacht, and the prototype of which, Simms suggests, may have had its origins as early as the twelfth or thirteenth century, notes, among others, the respective roles of Ó Taidhg as chief of the lord's household ('*taoiseach teaghlaigh*') and marshal of his house ('*a mharusgál tighe*'), Ó Floinn as steward of his horses

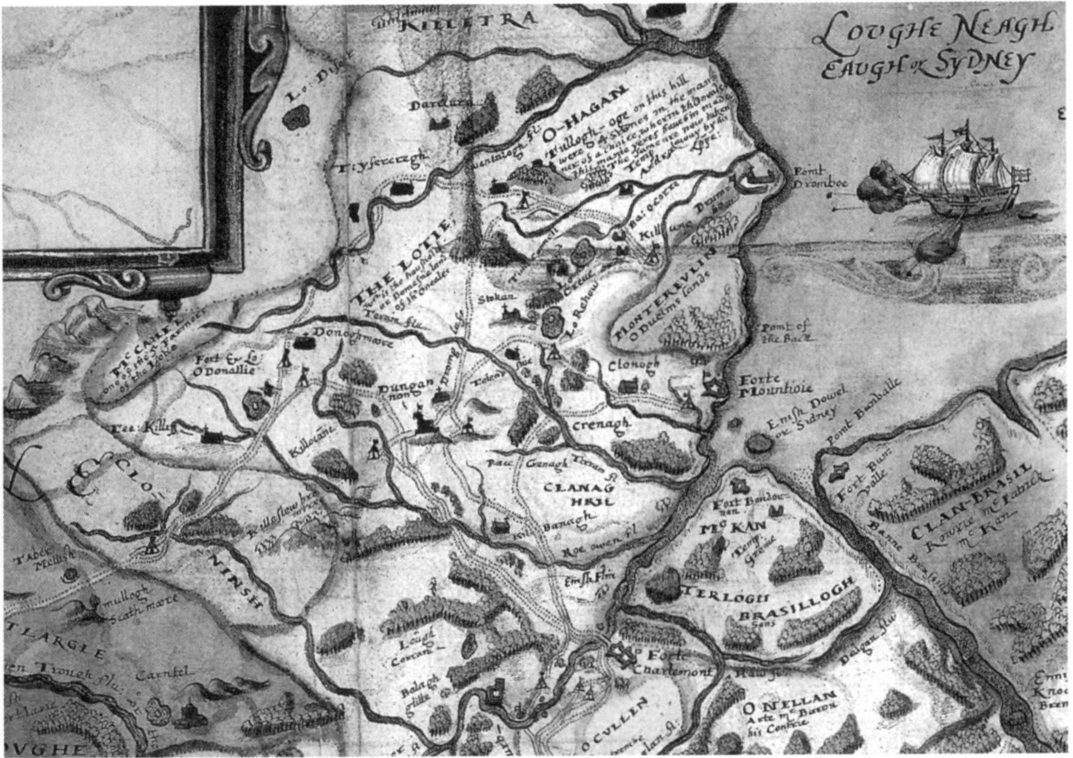


1. Richard Bartlett's portrayal of the *lucht tighe* of Ó Néill, which he designated 'The Lotie' on his map of Southeast Ulster, 1603 (TNA, MPF1/36).

(*'maoraigheach each'*) and Ó Dochraidh who was responsible for the privy, the benches and beds in Ó Conchobhair's house.[13]

The late medieval *Airem Muintiri Finn*, a fictive list of the people of the house of the quasi-mythical hero Finn mac Cumaill, reflects, in the roll-call of householders – that includes officials such as two stewards of Finn's hounds (*'da maer a chon'*), his spenser (*'a rannaire'*), his three cupbearers (*'a tri dáilemuin'*), his physician (*'a liaig'*), and his smith (*'a goba'*) and metalworker (*'a cerd'*) – the contemporary practice of placing service providers on mensal land.[14] The late fifteenth- or sixteenth-century tract *Ceart Uí Néill*, an historical recollection of tributes and provisions due to Ó Néill from the other kings of Ulster and relating to a much earlier time when the Uí Néill had mensal land in Inis Eoghain, mentions several service families.[15] Among them is Muintir Dhoibhlín who are defined as *fírcheithearnn* (literally 'true *ceatharnaigh*'). Although free of normal billeting, they had duties to provide 'twenty wholemeal loaves in the spring from each half-quarter [of land], and a meadar of butter with each loaf: and four pecks of malt in the spring, or a barrel from each half-quarter, and a meadar of butter per week. Four pence of Easter money per half year'.[16] In return for their professional services, families of the *lucht tighe* were immune from paying *cíos* or tribute, which was generally an annual payment.[17] However, as inhabitants of the *lucht tighe* they were obliged to produce food for the lord's household on particular occasions, hence the historical springtime expectations of Muintir Dhoibhlín.

The fact that mensal lands were occupied in perpetuity by hereditary service families was regarded as a peculiar practice by Tudor administrators. The early modern English elite genre of writing about Irish customs, laws and people generated ethnic stereotypes of the Gaelic Irish in particular, so that 'native conduct and customs, refracted through incomprehension and hostility, emerge as deviations'.[18] That the hereditary nature of their positions was alien to the office-holding norms of English officials in Ireland was observed by Davies (1609) when he described the principal inhabitants of Gaelic mensal lands thus:

> The chief had certain lands in demesne which were called his loughty [*lucht tighe*], or mensal lands wherein he placed his principal officers, namely his brehons, his marshal, his cupbearer, his physician, his surgeon, his chronicler, his rhymer, and others, which offices and possessions were hereditary and peculiar to certain septs and families …[19]

The hereditary status of service families was emphasised in native and English literature and it was clearly important to the families themselves. In this chapter, precedence is given to the biographies of the respective lands that service families occupied, because their archaeologies, geologies and topographies were integral to the hereditary nature of service kindred roles in lordly and earlier royal households. What *lucht tighe* meant, and the services provided by families on those lands, were, of course, not immutable, nor is it the case that all *lucht tighe* families could claim deep roots on their landholdings. Learned families were, in some instances, relative newcomers to the mensal lands of lordships after the twelfth century. Hereditary service families, or kindreds, presupposes the presence of women and children too, but in the historical and literary records, service providers are invariably cited as men. Future archaeological inquiry has an important role to play in broadening and gendering the identities of later medieval service families who, in the written word, are known only through their male representatives.

## Mensal Lands in Tír Eoghain

A deeper understanding of the cultural meaning of service kindreds in later medieval and early modern Gaelic society to *c.*1600 is found in the landscape history and archaeology of their *lucht tighe* holdings. In order to convey some of that meaning, mensal lands with early origins in Tír Eoghain and Machaire Chonnacht have been selected for discussion.

The *lucht tighe* of Ó Néill in the lordship of Tír Eoghain incorporated blocks of land in the area extending from the Ballinderry River south to the River Blackwater, and from Lough Neagh westward to the uplands around Pomeroy. The combined personal demesne of Ó Néill around Dungannon tower house and the *lucht tighe* occupied much of the landmass of the southeastern area of the early medieval kingdom of Tulach Óg (Figs 1, 2).[20] The antiquity of that kingdom is not known, but it appears to have been formed between AD 900 and 1000 from the greater part of the lands of the Uí Thuirtri. It was named after the territory's major landmark, Tulach Óg ('hill of assembly of warriors'),[21] which became the royal centre of the kingdom. After the formation of the lordship of Tír Eoghain, Tulach Óg lay in a boundary zone between Tír Eoghain and the northwestern extent of the lordship of Clann Aodha Buidhe to the east.[22] The importance of the hill to the identity of the *lucht tighe* and to its Gaelic community endured into the pre-Plantation years of the seventeenth century.

Recorded *c.*1603 by Richard Bartlett as 'The Lotie' [*lucht tighe*], on his map of southeast Ulster[23] and on his 'Generalle Description of Ulster',[24] the mensal lands of Ó Néill incorporated, among others, the estates of household officials described by Bartlett as 'the five farmers of the Lotie'.[25] Bartlett's description of the *lucht tighe* community is augmented by a sixteenth-century Tudor document and by *Ceart Uí Néill*, both of which provide the names of the five 'farmers' noted by Bartlett, as well as other service providers. Those named were all representatives of long-standing hereditary service families to the Uí Néill including the Ó hÁgáin, who had multiple roles as *reachtaire* (steward) and as an *ardfheadhmontaigh* (sheriff) and *ardmhaor* (tax collector); Ó Cuinn, who also held office as an *ardfheadhmontaigh* and *ardmhaor*;[26] Ó Donnghaile, *marasgál* (marshall); Mac Cathmhaoil, Mac Murchaidh and Ó Doibhlín, *fírcheithearnn* (leaders of *ceatharnaigh*); Ó Goirmleaghaigh, master of stud and chandler;[27] and Ó Corragáin, who is noted in the Carte manuscript but without a record of his roles.[28] Ó Doibhlín is distinguished in the Carte manuscript as the leader of Ó Néill's *lucht tighe* and his lands bordering the western shoreline of Lough Neagh are marked on Bartlett's map of southeast Ulster with the legend, 'Monterivlin O Duelins lands'.[29] Their estate was coterminous with the parish of Arboe (Fig. 1).

Mensal land must have been carefully chosen, or annexed, from the outset during the composition of royal lands. The greatly varied bedrock of the area covered by the *lucht tighe* of Ó Néill (Fig. 2) between the Ballinderry and Blackwater rivers in Tír Eoghain, predicates different types of physical and cultural resources in terms of pasture and arable land, woodland, bog, building-stone, mineral/metal ores, hunting grounds and prehistoric antiquities. The *lucht tighe* landscape is marked by two major faults – the Elagh Fault and the Clogher Valley Fault – which run due southwest from the vicinity of Ardboe Point on the western shore of Lough Neagh.

Tulach Óg is an expansive low-lying hill that commands extensive views, especially north to Slieve Gallion. The hill and its immediate hinterland is a point in the landscape where no less than eight different types of bedrock meet along the line of the Elagh Fault (Fig. 2). The presence of limestone, basalt, chalk, dolerite, marl with gypsum, coal measures, millstone grit and different types of sandstones, including red-brown sandstone with conglomerates, siltstone and breccia,[30] distinguishes Tulach Óg and its environs as a locus of transitions and a place of resource potential. The extent to which stone might have been exploited as a resource in the *lucht tighe* landscape between 1200 and 1600 is, as yet, unknown. However, the central role of 'Leac na Ríogh' ('flagstone of the kings') in Uí

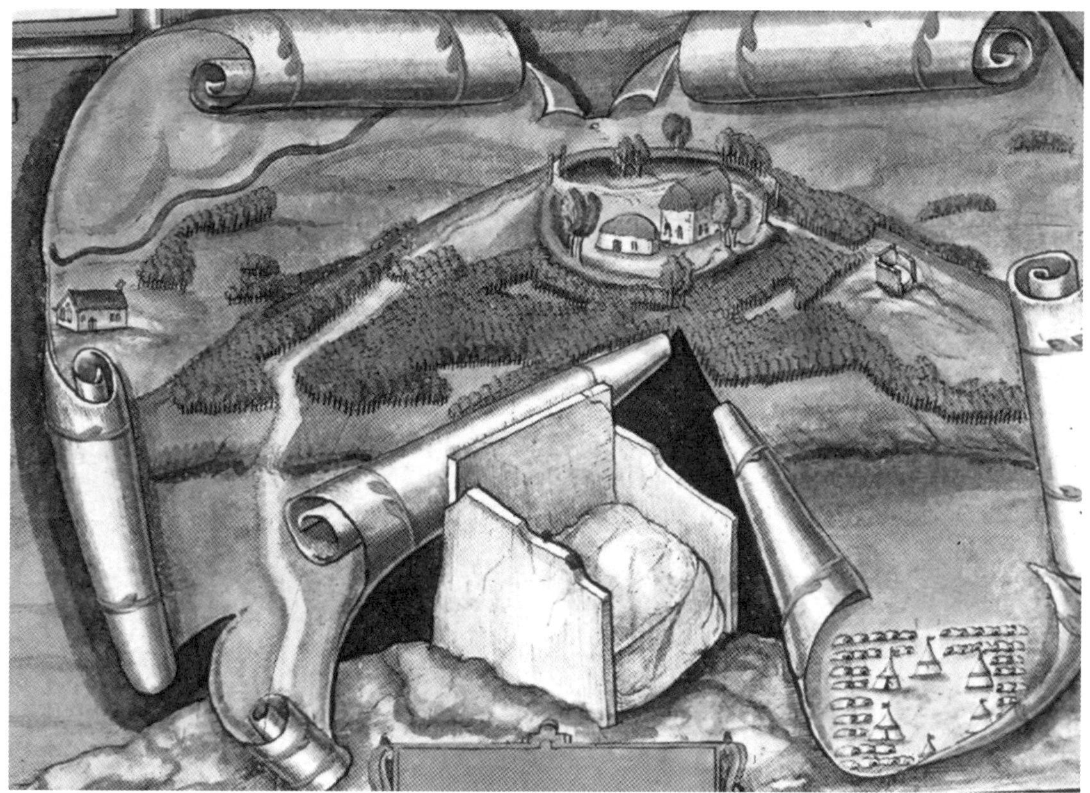

3. Richard Bartlett's map picture of Tulach Óg showing Ó hÁgáin's residence on the hill summit, woodland, and the inauguration chair of Ó Néill in a clearing on the southeastern downslope of the hill. His enlarged view presents the stone chair as a crude base with cut-stone sides elevated on a rock outcrop or a mound of clay (NLI, MS 2656, v: Courtesy of the National Library of Ireland).

Néill inaugurations at Tulach Óg might suggest that the diversity of bedrock in that landscape was important to the perception of the hill as, at once, a liminal landmark and a topography of power in the eastern boundary zone of the lordship of Tír Eoghain, 5km south of where it adjoined the neighbouring lordship of Clann Aodha Buidhe. The hill was the foundation of the *lucht tighe*.

It has been observed that landforms that occur in contact zones between different rock types, and which were used as boundary markers of Gaelic territories, often allude to the mythical warrior-hunter Finn mac Cumaill in the place-names Suidhe Finn (Finn's Seat) and Formaoil na Fiann ('bare place of the *fían*').[31] There is no surviving Finn lore associated with Tulach Óg but the implicit reference to an assembly of warriors in the place-name could be an allusion to early medieval young aristocrats classed as *féinnidi* and *díberga* who, having not yet come in to their inheritance, lived outside of society in threshold places given to hunting and wilderness lifeways.[32] There are intimations in Gaelic and English sources that Tulach Óg and its hinterland was a sylvan landscape to some degree. It is recorded in the chronicles as the site of venerable trees (*biledha*) which were cut down by the Ulaid during their attack on Cinéal Eoghain in AD 1111.[33] However, for the early medieval period there is conclusive evidence that arable farming took place on the hill, or at least in its immediate hinterland, over a prolonged period. Two cereal-drying kilns excavated at Tulach Óg were in use in the early to middle seventh century, and in the eighth to tenth century period.[34] This evidence advises against any characterisation of the hill as a wilderness, at least in the period between the seventh and tenth centuries and suggests, instead, a mixed-use landscape in keeping with a farmed estate. Bartlett's map-picture of Tulach Óg several hundred years later (*c.*1602) presents the hill as a semi-wooded place (Fig. 3). As Thomas Herron has convincingly argued, the woodland appears to be shaped in the figure of a satyr,[35] Pan, the Greek god of the woodland. Herron suggests that, here, Bartlett uses the tree-figure of the satyr to parody the venerable trees of Tulach Óg and to refer to the 'uncivilized state of Ireland's native inhabitants, who throughout the medieval and early modern periods frequented Ireland's plentiful woods for ambuscades, escapes and more mundane purposes such as firewood and cattle-grazing'.[36] The extent to which this image should be interpreted as a parody by a cartographer who was 'creatively satirizing the Irish'[37] is a matter for debate (see Logue, Chapter 13), but the possibility that Bartlett chose the satyr as a device to convey the genuinely liminal aspect of the hill and its setting is worth considering as a counterpoint to the view of the map-picture as a condescension of brutish Arcadians.[38]

The kaleidoscope geology of the greater landscape of the hill (Fig. 2) may bring a new perspective to bear on 'Leac na Ríogh', on which successive kings and lords of Tír Eoghain were inaugurated and which in its latest recorded manifestation was a stone chair.[39] The most detailed record of the form and location of the chair is Bartlett's map-picture (Fig. 3), which features the object composed of four separate pieces of stone, in a clearing in woodland on the southern declivity of the hill where it abided until 1602.[40] The geology of the rough seat, the cut sides and back of the chair, as portrayed by Bartlett, will never be known because the object was 'taken away' at Lord Deputy Mountjoy's command in September 1602.[41] Nor can the archaeology of the chair ever be fully understood from Bartlett's drawing. It is possible that the recumbent stone that formed the seat of the chair was a reused megalith. There is a single standing stone and a standing stone pair at the foot of the hill, to the north in Grange townland, which is a reminder that the Tulach Óg landscape has a prehistoric horizon which may prove to extend to the hilltop if some of the features recovered through recent geophysical survey are ever excavated.[42] A particular rock type is likely to have been selected for the chair because of its special qualities, whether a reused megalith or a freshly quarried block of stone. It is speculation, but the red-brown sandstone with conglomerate, siltstone and breccia, classified in modern geology as the 'Enler Group' and found in thin bands immediately south and east of the hill (Fig. 2),[43] may have been the source of the stone because it is speckled, but also because it expressed the place of transition represented by the hill and its hinterland. Some support for this idea can be found in the choice of speckled stone for inauguration furniture elsewhere. The basin stone at Magh Adhair (Fig. 4a), the assembly place of the early medieval Dál Cais dynasty and their descendants, the Ó Briain overlords of Thomond, is a large conglomerate boulder with porphyritic and quartzite inclusions,[44] while the probable inauguration chair of the Clann Aodha Buidhe branch of the Uí Néill (housed in the Ulster Museum) is composed of indurated, coarse sandstone of pinkish-brown hue, the sediment texture of which varies from a medium grain to a pebble-grade conglomerate (Fig. 4b). The front of the seat of the chair has a particularly conspicuous pebbly layer,[45] giving the otherwise rough object an ornamental or bejewelled appearance.

The keepers of Tulach Óg were the service kindred of Ó hÁgáin who lived there between the eleventh century and the early years of the seventeenth century and performed the roles of steward or overseer for the Ó Néill household and sheriff to Ó Néill.[46] The consolidation of the household lands of the Uí Néill of Cineál Eoghain in the early medieval kingdom of Tulach Óg is understood not to have occurred until after the partition of Tír Eoghain in 1166,

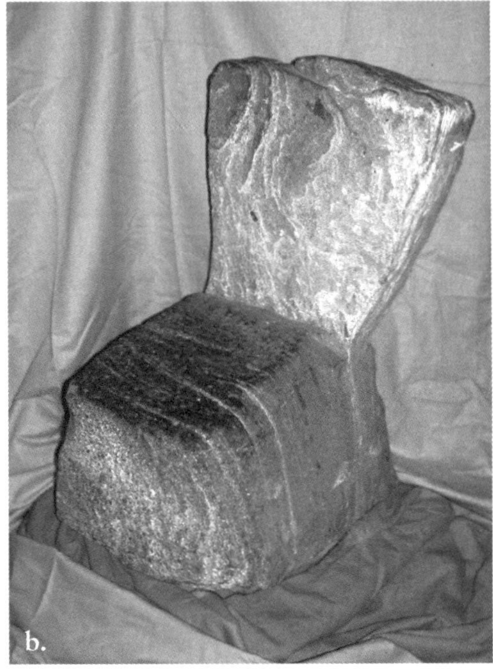

4a. The Magh Adhair basin stone at the inauguration place of the Ó Briain, Toonagh, County Clare, is a large conglomerate boulder with porphyritic and quartzite inclusions, an ornament in the predominantly limestone bedrock of the area (image: author). 4b. The coarse pinkish-brown sandstone with clasts of quartz, dark red sandstone, possibly jasper and mudstone, on the front of the seat, gives the Clann Aodha Buidhe chair a bejewelled appearance (image: BELUM. A305. 1911. © National Museum NI, Collection Ulster Museum).

during the reign of Aodh Ó Néill,[47] but the chronicle record of the death of Gilla Mura, son of Ócan (Ó hÁgáin), the *reachtaire* of the king of Cineál Eoghain, at the royal centre of Tulach Óg in AD 1056, suggests that the formation of the lands of the royal household had begun by the eleventh century.[48] The hereditary office came with a *baile biatagh* of *lucht tighe* land, an estate of *c.*1,000 acres, recorded as 'Bally O Hagan' (Baile Uí Ágáin), the place of O Hagan, which incorporated Tulach Óg (Fig. 2).[49] The use of *baile* in combination with a service family name is a common cultural practice relating to the place-names of later medieval service family landholdings throughout Ireland, but not one exclusive to those officers.[50] The Ó Donnghaile, as marshal to Ó Néill, held an estate of *lucht tighe* land called Baile Uí Dhonnghaile *c.*9km southwest of Baile Uí

Ágáin (Fig. 2).[51] Baile Uí Chuinn, the equally large estate of Ó Cuinn, chief administrator to Ó Néill, was coextensive with the medieval parish of Donaghenry (Fig. 2).[52] The estate centres of both of these service families were *crannóg* settlements (see Logue, Chapter 13). As hereditary office holders of the position of household overseer, the Uí Ágáin had their residence within a large earthen enclosure on the summit of Tulach Óg, captured in detail by Bartlett in his picture map of the hill (1602; Fig. 3). They also held the privilege of inaugurating Ó Néill until that role was passed in the sixteenth century to the Uí Chatháin of Ciannacht who emerged in that period as Ó Néill's principal vassals.[53]

By 1602, the year in which the Ó Néill stone chair was removed from Tulach Óg, the hill and its landscape setting was a persistent and mnemonic place. The Ó hÁgáin kindred had already lived there in a hereditary capacity for over 500 years. The traditional knowledge that they and the *lucht tighe* community must have had of Tulach Óg can only be imagined. Little has survived of its history, and almost nothing by way of folklore. The fracturing of the landscape and oral tradition of Tulach Óg, just before and during the Plantation period, greatly reduced the transmission and therefore the survival of the social memories of the long-lived Gaelic service family culture of the *lucht tighe*.[54]

## Hangers-on at the Palace in Machaire Chonnacht

The unique locus of *lucht tighe* families, which informs their cultural practices as service providers, can be recomposed by placing them in the landscape. What comes through in particular is the way that they closely identified and engaged with the antique world of early medieval royal lands which, mostly, they occupied in perpetuity from one generation to the next. This pattern of hereditary status and longevity of landholding in an enduring place is seen again in Machaire Chonnacht, on what can be proposed as the mensal lands of the Ó Conchobhair lords of Síol Muireadhaigh, even after their breakdown into two factions and the corresponding split of the territory of Machaire between them in 1384.[55] Identification of *lucht tighe* lands in Machaire is complicated, however, by the considerable movement of the *caput* of the Ó Conchobhair ruling family in the century after the Anglo-Norman subinfeudation of Connacht *c.*1235, and especially by the sept split of 1384 when the descendants of Aodh, son of Cathal Croibhdhearg divided into factions of Uí Chonchobhair Ruaidh (red) and Uí Chonchobhair Dhuinn (brown). The former were supported by the Mac Diarmada of Magh Luirg (see Finan, Chapter 2) and Clann Uilliam Uachtair, while the latter allied with the Ó Ceallaigh of Uí Maine and Clann Uilliam Íochtair.[56]

In the prose tract of probable twelfth- or thirteenth-century origin that prologues the fifteenth-century inauguration ode to the Ó Conchobhair king-elect of Connacht, the service family of Uí Bheirn are described as holding the position of *ronnadóir* or spenser in Ó Conchobhair's household, 'Ronnadóir Í Chonchobhair Ó Beirn'.[57] The Uí Bheirn are attributed a landholding, Cloonybeirne (Cluain Uí Bheirn) in Machaire Chonnacht, in the triangle extending from the modern County Roscommon settlements of Elphin, southwest to Tulsk and from there east to Strokestown and Slieve Bawn (Fig. 5). This was the core of the territory of Uí Chonchobhair Ruaidh after the split of 1384, but prior to that it was very much borderland between the *trícha céit* of Síl Máelruanaid to the west and Mag Aí to the east.[58] As early as the late eighth or ninth century, the ancestors of the Uí Chonchbhair, the Síol Muireadhaigh, had emerged as the most politically dominant family among the Uí Briúin Aí dynasty of Mag Aí.[59] Síl Máelruanaid and Mag Aí were incorporated into the later lordship of Machaire Chonnacht.

Two key high-status sites of the Uí Chonchobhair can be found in the lordship landscape of Machaire Chonnacht (Fig. 5). These are the *pailís* of Cluain Fraoich ('palace of Fraoch's water-meadow') and the assembly place of Ard Caoin (the fair height) crowned by the inauguration mound of Carn Fraoich (Fraoch's mound), which had an alternative name (Dumha Selga) and, probably, a role as a hunting mound.[60] Celebrated in two bardic poems composed in the fourteenth century, the *pailís* was built for Aodh Ó Conchobhair, lord of Machaire Chonnacht, between 1293 (when he first assumed power) and 1306 when it was attacked and burned (see O'Conor, Chapter 8).[61] The Irish *pailís* is variously translated as a palisade or stockade, a castle and a palace, but where associated with Gaelic elites in fourteenth-century Ireland, it appears to imply an elaborate timber hall which, I have argued elsewhere, probably combined the roles of hunting lodge and feasting hall in a boundary place.[62]

Table 1. The family names represented in the fiant of 1594, with their lands and hereditary functions where identified or inferred. They are tabulated in the sequence in which they occur in the fiant.

| SERVICE FAMILY NAME | LANDHOLDING | ROLE |
|---|---|---|
| Mac Branáin | *Cluain Finnlocha*<br>Cloonfinlough | *ceatharnach* (foot-soldier) |
| | *Cluain Fhéireach*<br>Cloonearagh | *stocaire* (horn-blower) |
| | *Pailís Cluain Fraoich*<br>Cloonfree Palace | *ceatharnach* |
| | Portnern<br>(unidentified) | *ceatharnach* |
| Ó hAinlidhe | *Cluain Coneadh*<br>Clooncony | *stocaire* |
| Mac Dubhghaill | Clooncony | *ceatharnach* |
| | Cloonfinlough | *ceatharnach* |
| Ó Donnabhair | Cloonfinlough | scholar |
| Ó Maolchonaire | Cloonfinlough | not stated (probably poet/chronicler) |
| | *Cill Ríogh*<br>Kilreagh | not stated |
| Ó Maoltuile | *Ail Finn*<br>Elphin | not stated (probably physician) |

Cloonybeirne, 'the meadow of Ó Beirn', was situated southwest of the *pailís* (Fig. 5). The combination of the family name with the place emphasised the important role that the Uí Bheirn played in the court of the Uí Chonchobhair, and the synonymy between genealogy and landholding that often characterised the geography of the *lucht tighe*. Brian Shanahan's work for the Discovery Programme has revealed that Cloonybeirne is rich in settlement, including a moated site that incorporates part of an earlier *ráth* and a settlement cluster of eight houses, the chronology of which is as yet unknown.[63] At the time of the Composition of Connacht (1585), Cloonybeirne constituted two quarters of land and was the estate of Aodh Mac Toirdhealbhach Ruaidh Ó Conchobhair, the *tánaiste* (heir apparent, second in rank to the chief)[64] of Uí Chonchobhair Ruaidh.[65]

A fiant of 1594 lists pardons granted to individuals who, by virtue of their names and occupations, are recognisable as service providers of the Uí Chonchobhair. Most of the fiants or warrants, directed to the Irish Chancery were pardons that required those persons concerned to ensure their good conduct and to appear at the next court sessions. They are an invaluable source for revealing personal details of members of Gaelic society in the sixteenth and seventeenth centuries, not least because their subjects range in status from lords to *ceatharnaigh*. The fiant of 1594 includes learned men, *ceatharnaigh*, horn blowers, huntsmen and keepers of hounds, the forebears of some of those named in the Ó Conchobhair inauguration ode and prose tract.[66] Their domiciles, as cited in the fiant, indicate that the majority of them were clustered in the vicinity of the old *pailís* of the fourteenth century (Fig. 5), on the landholdings of Cloonfinlough, Cloonearagh, Clonconny and Cloonfree, the correct name of the last of these the fiant reveals as 'Palishclonfrey' (Pailís Cluain Fraoich). It is the massing of a wide range of service families in the hinterlands of the *pailís* and the inauguration site of Carn Fraoich that confirms the former role of those lands as *lucht tighe*.

The landscape across which the land denominations are spread is rich in settlement archaeology, with the *ráth*, *crannóg* and moated site especially plentiful. The identification of some of the *lucht tighe* families of Machaire Chonnacht with the landholdings in which those monuments are distributed invites interpretation of the possible roles of those settlement forms for the kindreds concerned. The content of the 1594 fiant dealing with Machaire is as follows:

> Pardon to ... Dermot M'Ferrdorraghe M'Bronane, of Clonfinlag, freeholder, Conn m'Hughe oge M'Bronan, of same, kern, Shane m'Donowgh M'Brownan, of Cloynerany, stokagh, Thady m'Ferrall M'Brownan, of Palishclonfrey, kern, Cormack m'Wm. M'Brownan, of Portnern, kern, Melaghlin M'Anloghie, of Cloncony, stokaghe,[67] Cormack M'Andowalty, of same, kern, Conn M'Andowalty, of Cloynfinglagh, kern, Cormack O Downever, of Cloynfinglaghe, scholar, Mullmory O Mulconery, of same, Moyllyne O Mulconery, of Killreaghe, Loghtney O Mulconery, of the same, Arrhully m'Cach M'Multolly of Olfine ...[68]

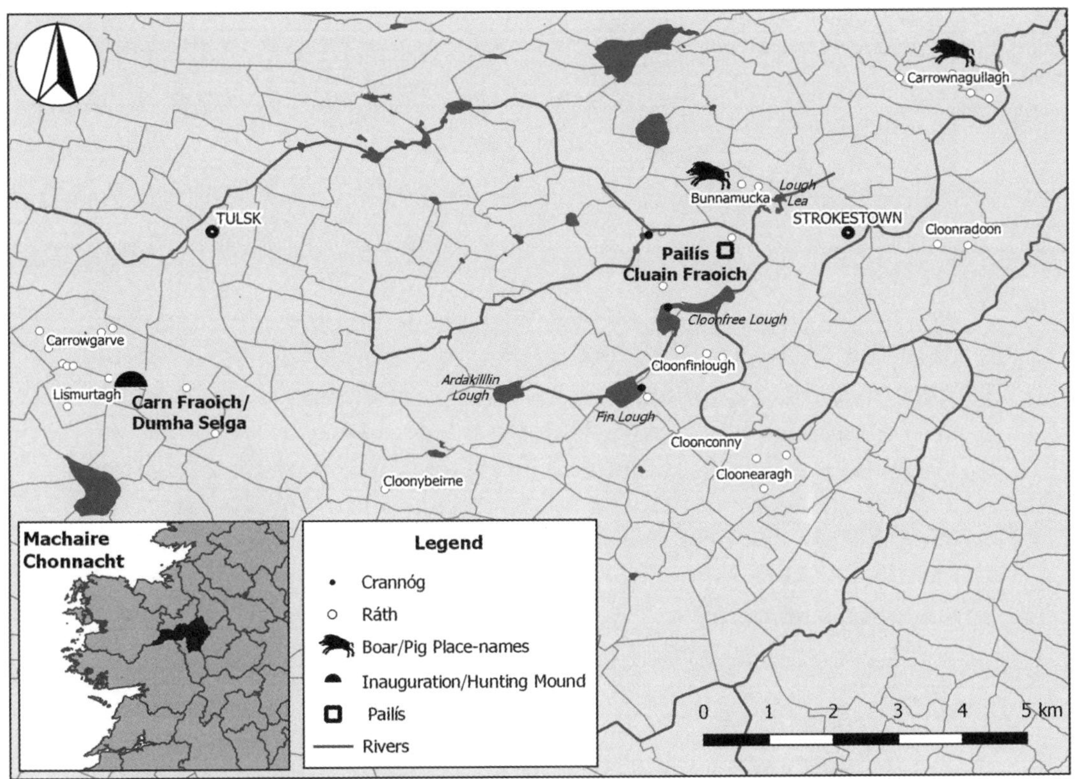


5. As late as the end of the sixteenth century, service families of the Uí Chonchobhair of Machaire Chonnacht were recorded living around Pailís Cluain Fraoich and Carn Fraoich in the townlands of Cloonfree, Cloonfinlough, Cloonearagh, Clonybeirne and Cloonradoon. The presence of huntsmen and keepers of hounds as well as pig-related and hunt-associated place-names suggest that predation was an elite activity in the *lucht tighe* terrain (drawing: Eve Campbell).

The fiant refers to the renowned Connacht learned families of Uí Dhonnabhair and Uí Mhaoilchonaire who are represented in the townlands of Cloonfinlough and Kilreagh. Giolla na Naomh Ó Donnabhair is cited as chief poet of Connacht in 1101,[69] and in 1594 a 'scholar' of that name is found living in Cloonfinlough just south of the high medieval *pailís* of Aodh Ó Conchobhair (Fig. 5). While the roles of two members of the Uí Mhaoilchonaire, living in Cloonfinlough and Kilreagh, are not recorded in the fiant, they are likely to have been members of the poetic family who also held the privilege of inaugurating the Ó Conchobhair on Carn Fraoich at Ard Caoin until *c.*1310.[70]

Tadhg Mac Branáin, described in the fiant as a 'kern', was living at Pailís Cluain Fraoich in 1594. His kinsmen, who also include *ceatharnaigh* and a horn-blower, were based in the neighbouring townlands of Cloonfinlough and Cloonearagh and in the unidentified Portnern. Another horn-blower, 'Mac Anloghie' (Ó hAinlidhe), is provenanced to Clooncony (Fig. 5). The role of the Ó hAinlidhe in the period from the twelfth/thirteenth century to the fifteenth century is communicated in the Ó Conchobhair tract and inauguration ode as 'the guarding of Ó Conchobhair's hostages' and 'the command of his foot soldiers' ('*Coimhét giall agus brághad Uí Chonchobhair cona sochar agus cennus a chosi* ...').[71] Horn-blowers were generally *ceatharnaigh*. In Albrecht Dürer's image of Irish warriors and peasants he shows two *ceatharnaigh* distinguished by their hairstyle and bare feet, one of whom carries a *stoc* or horn. German artists of the sixteenth century used dress and images of clothing to 'imagine identifications' and therefore Dürer's pen and watercolour drawing made at Antwerp in 1521 cannot be taken as an eye-witness record,[72] but it has been suggested that Dürer believed that 'human variety' could only be understood if it was 'well observed and visualised'.[73]

The combination of roles as *ceatharnaigh* and keepers of hounds, and *ceatharnaigh* and horn-blowers, suggests that *ceatharnaigh* were not simply foot soldiers but involved in hunting too. They were associated in the minds of high medieval commentators with early medieval *díberga* and with the mythological Finn mac Cumaill and his *fían*.[74] As Alan Harrison and Katharine Simms have observed, by the end of the sixteenth century *ceatharnaigh* were considered outlaws and popularly referred to as *cioth Ifrinn* ('a shower of hell'),[75] which possibly explains why they occur so frequently in the fiants.

The various Meic Bhranáin *ceatharnaigh* named in the fiant of 1594 were descendants of the hereditary leaders of Ó Conchobhair's *ceatharnaigh* and keepers of his hounds. The Mac Branáin is found in that role at least as early as the thirteenth century, since the family are mentioned in that capacity in the prose tract that prologues the Ó Conchobhair inauguration ode: 'Mac Branáin has the rear-guard of Ó Conchobhair and the stewardship of his hounds and the leadership of his kernes' ('*Cúlchoimét Í Chonchobhair agus conmaoraigheacht agus taoisigheacht cheithirne ag Mac Branáin*').[76]

6. The landscape of Ard Caoin, showing (at centre) Carn Fraoich, alias Dumha Selga 'the mound of the hunt', where Mac Branáin, keeper of Ó Conchobhair's hounds, died in 1448. The role of the route running north–south and curving around the mound is not known. It may have been processional or possibly used for coursing (photo: Gerry Bracken, courtesy of the Rathcroghan Project).

The ode itself compares Mac Branáin's role to that of Finn mac Cumaill and his *fían* in their wilderness hunting ground.[77] There are other insights into the cultural practices of the Meic Branáin as hereditary huntsmen to their lord on the lands of the *lucht tighe*. In 1448, Seán Mac Branáin, keeper of Ó Conchobhair's hounds and leader of his *ceatharnaigh*, died at Dumha Selga ('the mound of the hunt').[78] The circumstances of his death are not explained but Dumha Selga is located on Ard Caoin, the assembly place of Machaire Chonnacht.

The archaeological identity of Dumha Selga among the three known mounds on the ridge at Ard Caoin has been discussed by John O'Donovan and others,[79] but writing in 1649 the traditional historian and genealogist Duald Mac Firbhisigh was of the view that Dumha Selga and the inauguration mound of Carn Fraoich on Ard Caoin were synonymous, the former being its original name (Fig. 6).[80] The fact that Dumha Selga was the subject of a twelfth-century topographical poem (*dindshenchas*) in which it is defined, in origin, as a royal barrow (*ríg-duma*), the grave of Fer Fota, and subsequently as a hunting mound 'since the chase of Drebriu's six swine',[81] seems to strengthen Mac Firbhisigh's historical interpretation of the hybridity of the monument name and the dual role that it played as both an inauguration mound and a hunting platform. There is an implication in the *dindshenchas* attached to the site that hunting of wild pig/boar may have been conducted on Ard Caoin.

Swine-related place-names in the *lucht tighe* landscape, especially around Pailís Cluain Fraoich, lends some support to the idea that the mensal lands given to the threshold activities of the Ó Conchobhair, incorporating the inauguration site and *pailís,* included hunting. The townland of Bunnamucka (Bun na Muice), immediately north of the *pailís* and the Cloonfree River, refers to the bottom or low place of the pigs,[82] while Carrownagullagh (Ceathramhadh na gCullach[83]), northeast of Pailís Cluain Fraoich, is translated as the 'quarter of the boars'. Within it lies the local field-name 'Boarfield' and modern Boarfield Grove House. It is also worth mentioning that a large deer park occurs in the townland of Cloonradoon within Strokestown House demesne, which lies east of Pailís Cluain Fraoich. Later deer parks on country house estates are often found in landscapes previously given to hunting.[84]

The literary and historical references that intimate predation in the *lucht tighe* landscape, together with the place-names alluding to hunted species, give some physical context to the scene of Mac Branáin's death in 1448 at Dumha Selga, the 'mound of the hunt'. It is not inconceivable that he died there while coursing his hounds. Dumha Selga (alias Carn Fraoich, after Mac Firbhisigh) sits on the highest point of the ridge of Ard Caoin (OD 119.5m). The limestone bedrock of the ridge is very close to the surface and outcrops in several places, most notably on the crest of the ridge where Dumha Selga/

Carn Fraoich sits. As an inauguration mound and hunting platform, the celebrated monument could not be more inconspicuous, but the commanding view from the slightly dished summit compensates for its small size (2m in height and 11m in diameter at base). It would have been an ideal stand from which to engage with a ritualised hunt or ceremonial coursing of wild animals during an assembly. From the air, a route (15–20m wide) can be seen running in a north–south alignment on the immediate east side of Dumha Selga/Carn Fraoich and which respects the curve of the mound (Fig. 6).[85] Theorising this route, it might be interpreted as some kind of processional way, but it could also have been a run, along which prey were coursed by hounds into the sight of an archer or a spear-caster positioned on the mound, in the manner of bow-and-stable hunting. Coursing with sighthounds in an open environment where the spectacle could be viewed by an audience was a well-established hunting practice of European medieval elites and, in some instances, courses were made to make the chase more observable.[86]

The predominance of *ceatharnaigh*, keepers of hounds and horn-blowers in the *lucht tighe* landscape extending between Ard Caoin and the hinterland of Pailís Cluain Fraoich, combined with the abundance of lakes, underwood, rocky pasture and place-names that reference hunted species, strongly suggests that large parts of the *lucht tighe*, including the assembly place on Ard Caoin, were given to hunting. The family names associated with those roles in the fiant of 1594 were among the original household troops of Ó Conchobhair.

## Conclusion

I have attempted to show how enumerations of *lucht tighe* peoples in Gaelic and English written sources, which contain their names, roles and abodes, can be animated by reconstructing the landscape contexts of their lives. It is possible to interpret settlement in the *lucht tighe* and to populate it with meaningful communities of people by a total landscape approach that works different bodies of evidence together.

The landscape, language and history of the Gaelic *lucht tighe* is a complex set of codes, at the heart of which lies the identity of the service families who lived and worked in that specialised land category. Hereditary status was the principal identifier of service families and what conferred that standing was the sense of antiquity and permanence that their positions gave to them. They consciously affiliated themselves to the past, a practice that was underpinned by the fact that their *lucht tighe* landholdings were for the most part inherited from royal household lands of early medieval kingdoms. Those lands contained, among other natural and cultural resources, assembly venues and hunting grounds in prehistoric landscape settings. It is certain that *lucht tighe* lands were carefully chosen for their resources and threshold geographies and that there was considerable traditional knowledge of their importance among the people who provisioned the *lucht tighe* in Gaelic lordships.

# 10

# Buildings, rural landscape and space in sixteenth-century Gaelic Ulster

MARK GARDINER

## Introduction

The present landscape of Ulster bears little resemblance to its late medieval predecessor. It has yet to be shown that the existing farms are built on the sites of those of the sixteenth century, the field pattern is certainly different and much of the current road system has little relationship to that of 400 years ago. This is an unusual situation and quite different from the history of landscape in England and parts of Scotland and Scandinavia where the modern structure is based upon medieval roots. This paper examines the nature of the built landscape in sixteenth-century Ulster and considers why so little of it remains. Understanding something which has largely disappeared poses considerable problems. It is necessary to deploy a range of evidence to try to identify surviving remains. The study begins with drawn and written sources, then considers field evidence and finally offers a tentative interpretation of the character of the landscape of Gaelic Ulster in relationship to its economy and society.

By the mid-fifteenth century the lordship of Ulster had largely slipped out of the control of the English crown. The southern and eastern coastal margins of Ulster – particularly around Carlingford, Greencastle, Dundrum, Ardglass and Carrickfergus – remained to some degree in Anglo-Irish hands, albeit somewhat tenuously. Lands here had been granted to the Earl of Kildare in 1506 and he was successful in recovering some former possessions, or at least to extract a portion of the rents, which effectively serves as a measure of lordship. The position of the Anglo-Irish in the area was strengthened after the campaign of 1539, and on the north coast the castle of Coleraine was captured in 1542 and garrisoned to protect the Bann fishery, an important source of revenue.[1] The interior and west of Ulster remained almost entirely beyond the control of the Anglo-Irish, but there was no sharply drawn line between the lands under Gaelic control. Indeed, there must have been considerable interaction between the coastal towns of Carlingford, Ardglass and Carrickfergus, and the interior of the country. Those towns could not have existed without the produce of their hinterlands to supply them with food, or without opportunities for trade, as Shane Ó Néill demonstrated effectively when he briefly denied Dundalk commerce with the surrounding area in the mid-sixteenth century and was acknowledged by the constable of Carrickfergus in 1592, who encouraged all tenants from a broad region to use the market in the town.[2]

## Drawn and written sources

The starting point for an examination of the cartographic evidence for the landscape is the town of Carrickfergus. In the late sixteenth century the town was a mixed society containing elements of both Anglo-Irish and Gaelic-Irish, while the Scots occupied nearby townlands.[3] It had been founded as an Anglo-Norman town but in the sixteenth century the surrounding area increasingly fell under the control of the Uí Néill, while other parts were held by Scottish settlers. Robinson has characterised Carrickfergus as 'a bulwark against Gaelic expansion' and gives the impression it survived in a small enclave only a few kilometres in extent.[4] This idea is not correct since, as we have noted, the town would hardly have been able to operate as a commercial centre with such a minute hinterland. The reality must have been that the town served both Anglo-Irish and Gaelic Irish populations in the district and acted as a common place for trade. The town was certainly not wholly under Dublin's control, but acted in its own interest, whatever that happened to be. An indication of the town's opportunistic attitude is suggested by its trade with a Breton ship which was chased away in 1523 by an Anglo-Irish naval patrol while off-loading wine at the port. The same naval vessel also sought to intercept a Scots vessel in Belfast Lough seeking to trade with Carrickfergus.[5] The burgesses of Carrickfergus were happy to trade even with merchants of those nations with which England was in conflict. The role of the town began to change in the 1570s as the English Crown began to adopt a bolder policy in Ulster. It became a base from which English forces might be dispatched into areas under Gaelic control and a centre for Sir Thomas Smith's and, subsequently, the Earl of Essex's, ill-conceived plans for the Plantation of eastern Ulster.[6] Yet, as the cartographic evidence suggests, Carrickfergus remained a town of mixed cultures.

A number of sixteenth-century maps of the town survive, three of which need to be considered here.[7] These are all notable because they not only depict the masonry buildings of the town, but also show the other, slighter structures. The earliest, attributed to *c.*1560, shows seventy-three oval-shaped buildings, plus a further four outside the town beside the friary.[8] They are depicted with rounded roofs, no windows or chimneys and with a single door. Unlike the masonry buildings, which are largely set in rows lining the streets, the oval buildings have an irregular distribution, many near the seashore or in otherwise unoccupied spaces. The map may be compared to another drawn shortly after by Robert Lythe and dated to September 1567 when he surveyed the town.[9] Rather oddly, this does not show all the masonry buildings, but only the tower houses. It also depicts oval buildings with a single doorway of similar form to those in the earlier map. However, the most informative for the present purpose is a third map made *c.*1596 (Fig. 1).[10] It pays particular attention to land boundaries, depicting not only the churchyard, but also the burgage plots behind the terraced buildings. Each of the terrace houses along the town's streets had a rear door leading to an area of land shaded to show cultivation; the same applies to the tower houses, which had similar, but broader plots. These can be contrasted with the oval-shaped houses which did not occupy burgage plots or other bounded property. Most of these buildings do not lie on the street frontage, but were situated in peripheral positions. Some

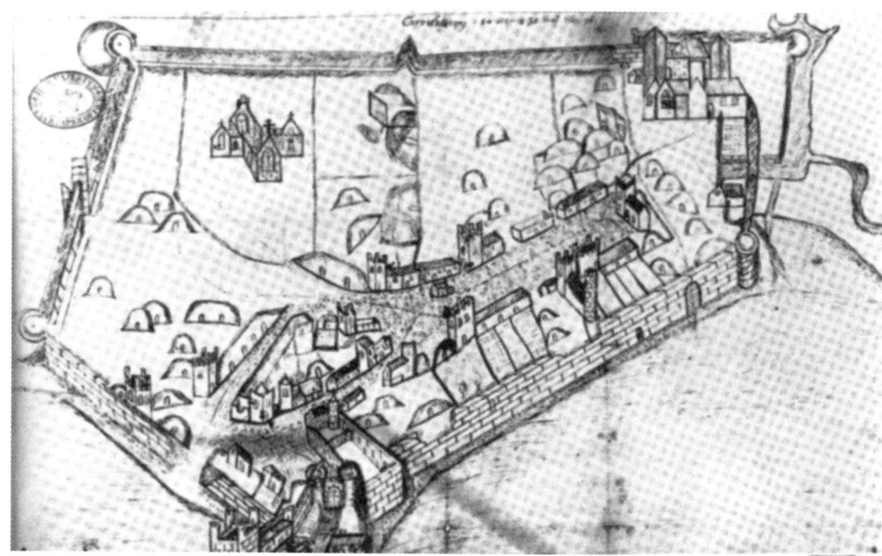

1. 'The Plat of Knokefergus': plan of Carrickfergus *c.*1596 (TNA, MPF 1/98).

of the oval buildings were depicted as if they had been constructed together as large structures.

These three maps are consistent in showing that Carrickfergus had terraced buildings of masonry, together with oval-shaped buildings with no windows and a single door. The latter had a less formal arrangement and apparently did not occupy the burgage plots which stretched back behind the masonry buildings and were used for gardens. A map of Newry made by Robert Lythe, possibly in November 1568, appears to show three similar buildings in the inner enclosure of the fort, two in the outer enclosure and many more outside the fort on the roads leading to Iveagh and to Tyrone. These last seem to correspond to the tenants mentioned in the rent roll of 1575 at 'Irish Street without the fort'.[11] However, the best-known and perhaps most informative depiction of oval-shaped buildings is in a map of the war-ravaged city of Armagh made in *c.*1600 by Robert Bartlett. The precise observation which informed this map has been discussed by Paul Logue.[12] Amongst the ruins of masonry buildings are a cluster of six buildings carefully depicted with wattled walls, possibly plastered and with rounded roofs covered with straw. Five of the buildings have only a single door, but a sixth is shown with two windows.[13]

Other oval-shaped buildings in the maps by Bartlett of Mount Norris, Dungannon, Inishloughan Fort and Monaghan are rather different. They are depicted with windows and generally with chimneys, but these were all likely to have been occupied by English soldiers; if they were built by the Gaelic Irish, they had been adapted to suit the requirements of the garrison.[14] They suggest a process of hybridisation – defined here, following Bhabha, as the outcome of encounters between social collectives – in which the form of the house is clearly not typically English in either plan or materials, but neither is it entirely characteristic of the Irish buildings.[15] The same hybrid buildings can be seen in the maps made by Thomas Raven in 1621–22 to accompany Sir Thomas Phillips' report on the progress of the London companies' settlements; one was partially excavated at Movanagher.[16] Contemporary records distinguish between the 'English-style' buildings constructed of stone, or timber-framed, and those erected in 'Irish style'. The latter were evidently constructed by the Irish for English or Scots settlers, or indeed for the Irish who continued to live on the planted land.[17] These were oval or sometimes rectangular, but most had windows and many of them chimneys.

The oval-shaped buildings were evidently ubiquitous in Ulster and the adjoining area. Bartlett shows them in a small-scale map at Dundalk and nearby in the Cooley peninsula at Grange and Whitestown, where they cluster around tower houses.[18] Similar buildings are also depicted on maps made by Thomas Raven in 1634–35 of the Farney estate in County Monaghan for the Earl of Essex. Duffy has shown that the vast majority of buildings depicted on the Raven maps (423, excluding Carrickmacross) were cabins, with only twenty-three of them shown as two-storey 'houses'. These cabins, he says:

> in the main are shown as single-storied structures with a door and, occasionally, windows although sometimes neither door nor window. Their roofs are coloured yellow indicating thatch. They most often were in formless clusters of from two to six in number, without any accompanying features.[19]

The oval-shaped buildings were evidently the most common type of house *c.*1600 in both urban and rural situations in the northern part of Ireland.

The second significant aspect of Gaelic settlement identified in the *c.*1596 map of Carrickfergus was the absence of property boundaries associated with Irish buildings. This was not just a feature of the urban areas occupied by the Gaelic Irish, but was also common, though not ubiquitous, in the Ulster countryside, even where arable crops were grown. English commentators drew attention to the absence of hedgerows or other boundaries. Sir Henry Docwra commented that Inishowen in Donegal 'lies all open and without any manner [of] inclosures', though flax, oats and barley were grown there. Equally, Lifford was said to have the richest soil of all the north, but 'the country about is champaign', meaning it was unhedged. The country around Ballyshannon was similar.[20] This must have been particularly notable to deserve comment by Docwra who had been brought up in Berkshire and Warwickshire, which were themselves areas of open fields with few hedgerows. However, as Horning has noted, the descriptions of the Ulster countryside were part of the broader English discourse about the supposedly uncivilised nature of the Gaelic Irish.[21]

Even if we set that aside, we cannot doubt that the Ulster countryside was largely unenclosed, and where boundaries were constructed for fields, they were only temporary. 'Dead hedges', or barriers of cut scrub were staked around fields to keep the stock out, but these were removed in the winter, evidently to allow the animals to graze, and were burnt.[22] The cultivated landscape taken over by the seventeenth-century Plantation settlers in Ulster was largely open. A frequent requirement in their leases was to fence the boundaries of their land, though often the individual fields within the farmstead remained unenclosed for many decades.[23] Work in the 1960s and 1970s tended to connect the absence of fences with rundale, a form of open-field agriculture, but more recent scholars have been rather more cautious.[24] Yager has pointed out that the evidence for rundale is largely from the nineteenth century and has warned against projecting the evidence backwards in an unconsidered manner. Currie, however, has established that Plantation lands in Ulster in the early eighteenth century were often leased jointly to groups of tenants, perhaps perpetuating earlier practices.[25]

The Ulster landscape of the late sixteenth century, though largely open, still had a considerable area of arable cultivation. Sir Henry Sidney found that corn was growing over an area of twenty-four miles in perimeter around Clogher. The area of corn planted in Gaelic localities became fully apparent during the Nine Years' War when the English forces practised a scorched-earth policy, attempting to destroy the crops to starve the Irish into submission, a policy which is unlikely to have been adopted if the economy had been mainly pastoral.[26] Bartlett illustrated a rare detail of the arable landscape: a field of corn with five rows of crops, evidently planted on ridges that had been cut by a road, perhaps made by the army camped around Inishloughan Fort (County Antrim). Significantly, there is no enclosure around the corn.[27]

We have, so far, considered two aspects of Gaelic settlement in Ulster: the types of buildings and the absence of permanent field boundaries. The third feature discussed here is the degree to which the population of the north of Ireland was permanently settled in one place. The alleged unsettled character of the Irish was a theme in contemporary English writing and used as evidence of lack of 'civility'. In an often-quoted account, Sir Arthur Chichester in 1610 proposed that the Irish should be 'drawn from the course of running up and down the country with their cattle which they term "creatinge" [*caoraigheacht*] and are to settle themselves in towns and villages, where they must be enforced to build houses like those of the Pale and not cabins after their wonted manner'. The 'cabins' to which he referred were evidently the oval-shaped buildings discussed above. Sir Thomas Phillips considered such practices to be 'the nursery of all idleness and rebellion'.[28] We need to treat with caution contemporary comments on this matter. English writers confused any such movement of peoples with two other factors: the movement of refugees consequent upon the military campaigns and the seasonal movement of livestock into the uplands – the practice of transhumance or booleying. It was, for example, almost certainly the activities of Docwra's forces and the destruction of crops which drove people to seek refuge on Inch Island in Lough Swilly, where a large population was sheltering in 1600.[29]

Yet, even if we set aside this English testimony, both Ken Nicholls and Katharine Simms are inclined to view the Gaelic Irish population throughout the later medieval period as relatively mobile.[30] Their argument is based on four strands. The first is that the historical descriptions of the buildings in Ulster, limited as they are, suggest that they were relatively slight structures and therefore unlikely to serve for long-term occupation. This issue is considered further below. The second strand is based on the evidence for the large-scale movement of cattle, the Gaelic practice known as *caoraigheacht*, anglicised as 'creaghting'.[31] According to Simms, it occurred either when groups were expelled from their territory, or as an act of aggression by which herds were moved into neighbouring lands to graze pasture there. If the herds were itinerant in this way, then the population may have had to move around as areas of grazing were consumed. The third point of argument turns upon an account given by Sir Toby Caulfield in 1610, of the rent formerly paid to the Earl of Tyrone. These rents were of different types. Some was given in the form of oats, oatmeal, butter, pigs and mutton, but this seems to have been paid only from the mensal lands (*lucht tighe*), as it was on the nearby land of the Mág Uidhir in the lordship of Fir Mhanach (see FitzPatrick, Chapter 9).[32] Other money rents, perhaps from the remaining land, were levied on the number of cattle grazed. From this it has been inferred that tenants were relatively mobile and therefore it was easier to levy rent, not on the land itself, but on the most valuable of their possessions, their livestock.[33] This is not a necessary conclusion, but it leads into the final element of the argument for the mobility of the Gaelic Irish population. The Caulfield rental notes that the rent demanded on livestock was particularly difficult to collect because tenants would drive their cattle into adjoining lordships where they were welcomed. The implication is that peasants, heavily weighed down with burdens of rent, would simply seek alternative lands in which to settle, a feature also noted in Antrim and Down by Sir William Weston in 1593.[34]

The difficulty for Gaelic lords was, as Canny has noted, that '[L]and was plentiful in Ulster, but manpower was at a premium'.[35] One response was to attempt to tie tenants to the land and even to enserf them. Serfdom was not an established feature of late medieval Gaelic Ireland and attempts to introduce it in the sixteenth century seem to have been a reaction to both the considerable mobility of and the increased demand for labour.[36] The Scottish migration to the east coast of Antrim in the sixteenth century should also be considered in the context of this labour shortage.[37] The movement of peoples was not limited to Ulster. Sir Richard Bingham, governor of Connacht, complained that the tenants were liable every May to remove themselves to another landlord so areas which were occupied might be left 'waste'.[38] Whether people were more transitory in this period than previously is difficult to determine, but as agriculture expanded in Ulster, as it seems to have done in the second half of the sixteenth century, the demand for labour increased, creating new opportunities for peasants.[39] Yet all this is very far from suggesting that the Gaelic Irish were typically nomadic. Migration in search of better conditions, seasonal transhumance and even the temporary removal of cattle to avoid rent should be clearly distinguished from the habitual nomadry that Nicholls and Simms were inclined to suggest characterised late medieval Gaelic Irish society.

The cartographic and historic evidence for the Gaelic Irish buildings and consequent sense of place can only advance our understanding so far. We lack both the volume of written records and the type of sources that would shed light on the problem as English sources provide a view of the Gaelic world refracted through a lens coloured by a belief in the barbarity of native Irish practice. It is necessary to turn to field evidence to consider first, the nature of the buildings and second, the broader context of space in which these were set.

## Field evidence

The cartographic evidence for building types in sixteenth-century Ulster was largely drawn from urban situations. By contrast, all the sites located in field survey and examined in excavation come from rural locations. This disparity reflects the nature of the evidence. Towns were the subject of most of the large-scale maps of this period, but late medieval Gaelic buildings have simply not survived in such situations, or have yet to be recognised in excavation in urban conditions. This in itself says something about the character of those houses, which were of slight construction. However, we face some fundamental problems in our interpretation of rural sites. The first is that any small building found in the countryside tends to be labelled as a booley hut. The term derives from the Irish *buaile*, referring specifically to buildings connected with cattle-herding, and is commonly applied to the small structures in the uplands which were occupied on a seasonal basis. This is not a useful appellation for most structures since it pre-judges whether they were connected

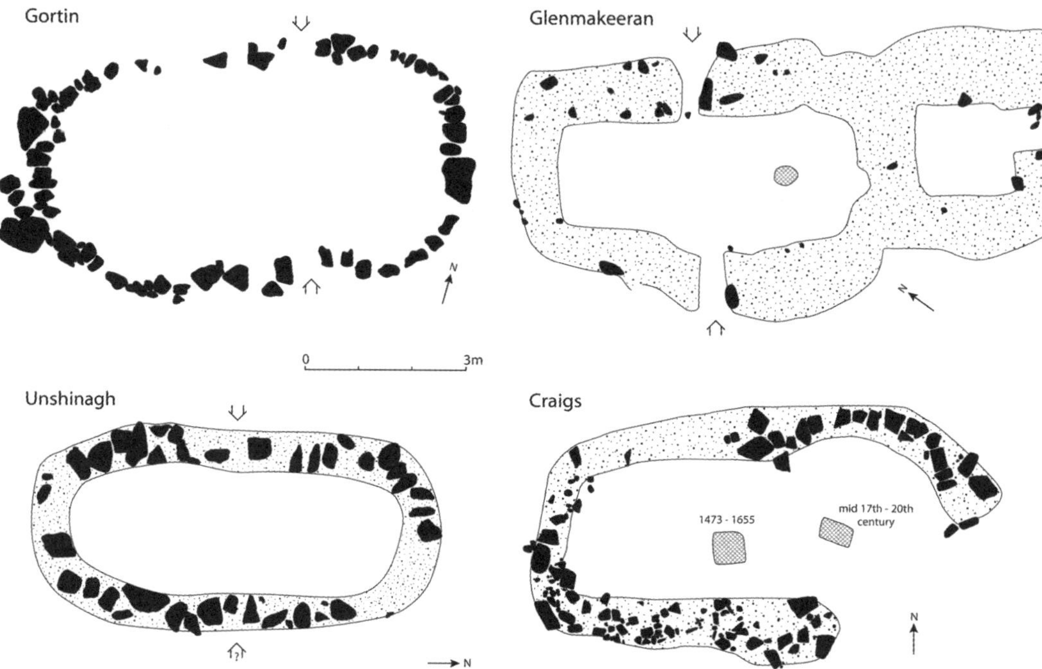


2. Four oval-shaped buildings (Glenmakeeran and Craigs after Williams). The probable entrances are marked by broad arrows and the hearths by cross-hatching (image: author).

with pastoral farming and were used for transhumance. All the buildings discussed here are significantly larger than the booley huts identified in the uplands of the Mourne Mountains; there is good reason to believe these huts were occupied on a seasonal basis as they were simply too small to be lived in by a family and were in such inhospitable locations that it is hard to imagine them being used in winter. The buildings discussed below are larger and often carefully located in sheltered spots, but not necessarily by streams, a distinguishing feature of the Mourne huts.[40] The second problem is associated with the first: all the building remains have so far been discovered on areas of poorer soils, often in the uplands; the remains are so slight that they have rarely survived on improved land. However, if these are similar to the oval-shaped buildings depicted in the cartographic sources, they would have been ubiquitous at the end of the sixteenth century.

One such building was excavated by James Mallory in 1982 in Gortin townland on the north side of the Carnlough valley (County

Antrim) before the land was improved in 1985–86. No trace now remains of the building. The excavated structure was rectangular with rounded corners and measured approximately 7.4m by 3.6m (Fig. 2). The walls were marked by a slightly raised bank which was revetted with close-set stones. Traces of charcoal were found in the interior, but apart from some residual worked flint, no artefacts were found. Aerial photographs taken by the RAF suggest that the excavated building was one of a number and around the buildings were faint traces of cultivation ridges.[41]

Two buildings of similar type and size have been excavated by Brian Williams. The first site, at Glenmakeeran near Ballycastle (County Antrim), was recorded in advance of quarrying and was unusual in comprising two conjoined elements: a main room with cross-entry and a smaller room entered from the end. It had a sod wall 0.2m high and the excavator believed that it was unlikely that it was ever much taller. The entrance to the main room was marked by schist slabs set at right-angles to the wall. A hearth was recorded towards one end of the room. The only dating evidence was provided by a few sherds of Ulster Coarse Pottery found in the entrance way and others found in the body of the sod wall. Two other buildings with identical plans were found close by, both with circular annexes, though the plan of one suggests that the smaller room might be later and partially overlie a simple, oval-shaped building.[42]

The second site excavated by Williams was at Craigs near Dunloy (County Antrim) and also lay in an area of rough pasture. It measured 6.2 by 2.6m internally and the walls were formed by a low bank 0.25m high, upon which angular stones had been laid. Again, Ulster Coarse Pottery was found both in the make-up of the walls and within and outside the house. Charcoal within the wall provided a calibrated date of AD 1473–1655 at two sigma, while charcoal from a second hearth provided a very broad calibrated date of the mid-seventeenth to twentieth century. The shape of the building might be interpreted to suggest that it had been rebuilt. Cultivation ridges enclosed by low stone-revetted walls were recorded nearby. There was no date evidence for these agricultural features.[43]

A number of similar buildings have been found in detailed survey work in two areas in particular, on the Antrim Plateau to the west and south of Garron Point, and on Leean Mountain (County Leitrim). The surveyed area of the Antrim Plateau lies near the excavated site at Gortin. Extensive work over nearly 40km² has identified the site of numerous buildings, including prehistoric or early medieval round houses and rectangular cottages of early modern date. These can be readily distinguished from the oval-shaped buildings, which usually lie on slopes, often just below sharply rising ground which provides protection from the wind. The building shown in Fig. 2 was recorded at Unshinagh townland and is typical of the others found in the survey area, with walls marked clearly by a series of stones which lie towards the edge of a low mound. It is one of a cluster of three buildings, one of which is built at the end of low field boundary of uncertain date. Similar clusters of oval buildings have been recorded just outside Ulster in County Leitrim, on Leean Mountain. A variety of buildings were noted there, but those in the group called Cluster A seem to have all been of the same type. They had a common orientation, lying on platforms set at right-angles to the slope. The recorded external dimensions were 7.7m by 3.9m for the largest and 5.9m by 3.4m for the smallest (Fig. 3). The buildings were marked by low banks with a few stones and each had opposed entrances in the long walls. The walls at the entrances were revetted with stone, exactly as at Glenmakeeran.[44]

A number of these sites were associated with areas of cultivation. We have already noted that the building at Gortin stood near cultivation ridges, but further study of these is not possible as they have now been removed in improvement works (Fig. 4). Elsewhere on the Antrim plateau similar areas with low cultivation ridges remain. The ridges are very slight and can often only be observed in oblique light or on aerial photographs. Therefore, they cannot be confused with later potato beds, such as those which remain to the northeast of Gortin farm. The low ridges usually have a width of 3.0 to 3.5m and are separated by very shallow depressions. Their length is often difficult to determine because they are not well marked and tend just to fade out. The areas of cultivation rarely form clear fields, but rather are small areas of ridging confined to pockets of better soil. There can be no doubt that the areas cultivated in the upland are much more extensive than has been identified so far, because they can only be seen in favourable conditions, and in the late spring and summer months they are hidden beneath bracken (*Pteridium aquilinum*) that appears to flourish on soils which have been disturbed by cultivation many centuries previously.

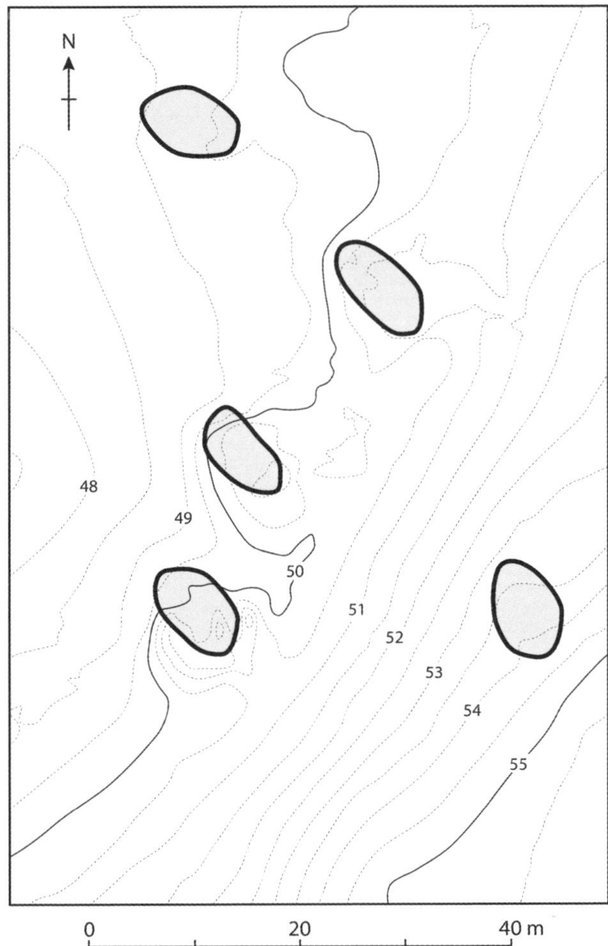


3. A group of oval-shaped buildings (shaded), Cluster A, on Leean Mountain, County Leitrim. The contours are in metres and are measured from an arbitrary datum. (image: author after Belton, 'An experimental study').

Areas of cultivation have been found across many of the areas of better soil towards the edge of the Antrim plateau, for example in a number of small patches in Unshinagh townland. They also occur in the uplands in County Londonderry. One patch lies at the 250m elevation to the southeast of a circular prehistoric barrow in Gortcorbies townland.[45] It is bounded on the north by a slight bank, which appears to be of prehistoric origin and seems to be unrelated to the cultivation ridges because it runs for several hundred metres beyond the cultivated area. There is a sod-walled building to the northeast of the barrow. A second area is found a few kilometres to the north at an altitude of 290m on the slopes of Binevenagh Mountain in Croaghan townland.[46] No associated buildings have been noted here.

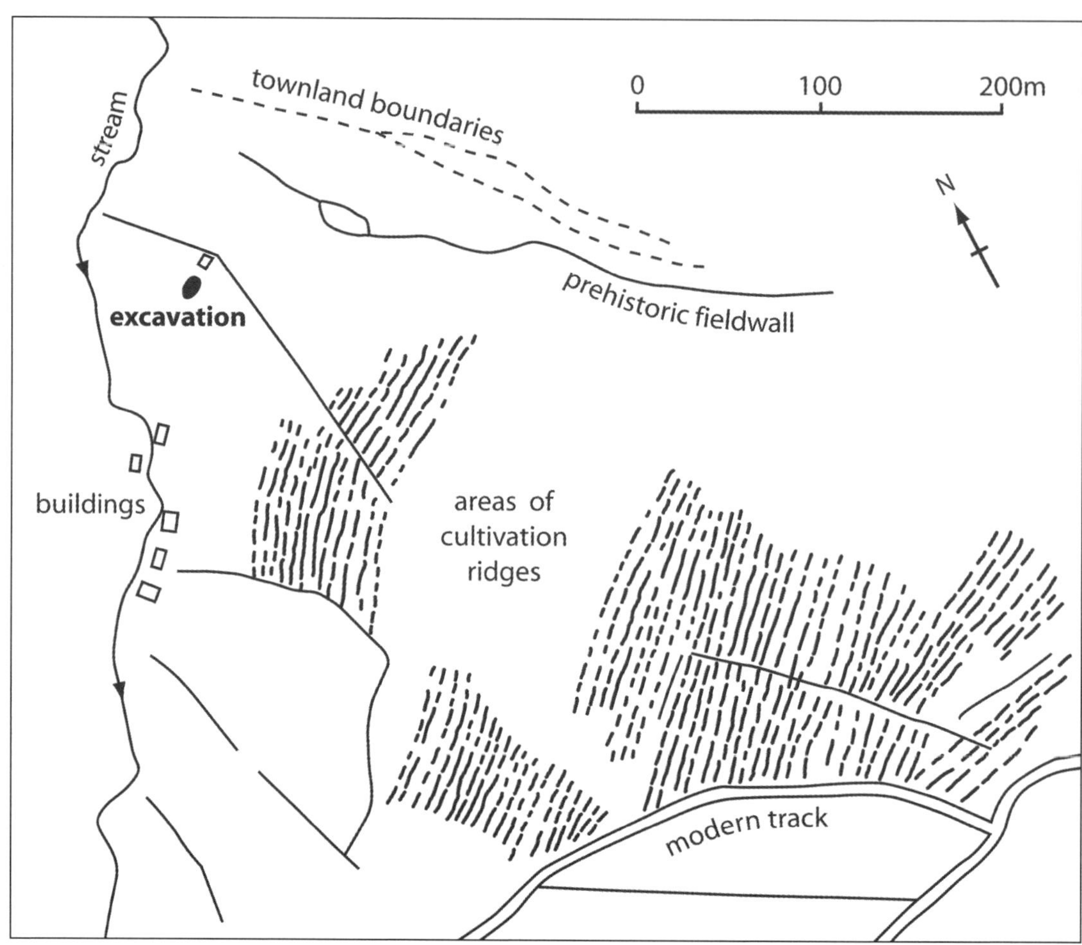


4. Cultivation ridges adjoining the excavated site of Gortin, County Antrim plotted from aerial photographs (image: author).

The areas of cultivation have a number of features which might suggest that they belong to the same period. They are rarely enclosed by any boundaries (except possible prehistoric banks), have a similar width and generally are found close to places in which oval-shaped buildings are located. In a more extensive area of cultivation above Garron Tower (County Antrim), there are bands of ridges with slightly different alignments and different widths, suggesting a number of separate phases of cultivation.[47] Some of the ridges there and elsewhere are overlain by oval-shaped buildings, providing a relative date.

## Discussion

There are good reasons to identify oval-shaped houses depicted on the maps with those found in excavation and field survey. The sites recorded in archaeological work had a central entrance, were small and rounded at the corners and so seem to match closely those depicted on maps. It is not difficult to imagine how the low walls could have been the base for a wickerwork superstructure, roofed either with straw or with sod as the maps show. Such buildings are also described by Fynes Moryson as 'a cabin made of boughs of trees, and covered with turf'.[48] Only one of the excavated sites is dated – Craigs – and the hearths there gave rather different dates, but sufficient to suggest that one phase of occupation of that building belonged to the end of the medieval period or the early modern period. The buildings had a number of features in common. They were of similar dimensions, rarely more than three metres wide and five metres in length. The walls are slightly raised banks, often reinforced or revetted in stone. The walls in some buildings are inward-turning at the entrance. Some of the excavated buildings had hearths set to one side of the entrance passage.

These oval-shaped, apparently ubiquitous buildings are the missing element in late medieval Gaelic Irish settlement: the houses of the common people. Although it is clear that other more substantial timber house-types existed, specifically those built with cruck posts, the field evidence supports the impression from the documents that these other methods of building were less common.[49] The oval buildings fit into a long Irish tradition of wicker construction, which can be traced from at least the early medieval period onwards. The adoption of rectilinear forms for buildings in the tenth century did not prevent the continuing use of wickerwork because the corners were simply rounded and the work was continued from one wall to that adjoining. Such buildings are known not only from urban contexts in Dublin and Waterford, but also in rural situations such as at Knowth (County Meath) and Dunsilly (County Antrim).[50] These were commonly built with low wall-footings of sod and dry stone and presumably had wicker superstructures. Traces of the vertical rods or sails have not been identified on non-waterlogged sites because they were set into the low sod walls and have been difficult to detect in excavation.

The use of comparatively thin, earthfast timbers in the wall must have limited the period before the wood rotted and the building's superstructure had to be repaired or replaced. One of the reasons for the use of a low wall into which the feet of the wicker sails were set may have been that it raised them above the ground and ensured that they stayed a little drier, though inevitably the sods would have drawn water upwards and the benefit must have been limited. Experimental work on a reconstructed round house suggested that the post and wattle walls had deteriorated significantly after twenty to thirty years.[51] The evidence from the early medieval site of Deer Park Farms led the excavators to suggest that each building could have only been used for a period of ten to fifteen years. The buildings from Viking-Age Dublin had a suggested period of usage of between ten and twenty years.[52] There is no reason to believe that the timberwork of the oval buildings would have lasted any longer. Yet, when we examine either the excavated evidence or the earthworks, only a few show any sign of rebuilding. This stands in contrast to the circular booley huts recorded in the Mourne Mountains which, though probably contemporary in date, often stand on raised sites apparently formed from the debris of successive buildings constructed on the same site.[53] However, it would have been quite possible to replace the decayed superstructure of an oval-shaped building without any change to the ground structure. The booley huts in the Mournes had to be rebuilt quite frequently because they were only occupied for a small number of months in the summer and were not maintained at other times of year. We should be cautious about drawing inferences about the length of usage of the oval-shaped houses without more excavation particularly examining the evidence for rebuilding.[54]

We need to consider the evidence for these buildings alongside that of the fields. Just as we are only able to trace the evidence for those buildings which were set on poorer lands, so the earthworks for cultivation ridges are only identifiable on land which has not been cultivated since. They are only found in peripheral locations and it could be argued they were not typical of cultivation practices on the better soils. Such upland areas may have been cultivated only briefly before the soils were exhausted and the yields declined. Nicholls envisages such a system of shifting or long-fallow cultivation may have operated in parts of sixteenth-century Ireland, though this seems to have been speculative and not supported by any clear evidence.[55] If there was such a practice of short-term cultivation, we might expect to see a series of small separate plots, each put under crop for a couple of years before the soils were allowed to recover. The field evidence does not seem to show this. Instead, we find areas of cultivation ridges, generally rather small, sometimes adjoined by low cairns formed of stones cleared from the fields. Whether stone-picking would have occurred on land which was only to be cultivated for a year or two is impossible to say, though it would have been particularly worthwhile if the field was in use for longer.

The field evidence does not provide any certain evidence for a transitory population, but mobility needs to be considered at various levels. There was a seasonal mobility or transhumance for which there is reasonably good written and field evidence.[56] There was also a long-term migration of people over greater distances to seek better conditions or because they were attracted by lower rents. This also seems to be attested to by various sources, including English observers of sixteenth-century Ireland. But evidence for a permanently unsettled and mobile population seems to be lacking, and indeed the presence of the well-built oval-shaped buildings, and particularly the cultivated fields, does not support a view of a population constantly on the move. However, to shift the argument forward in a more decisive way, we need to employ other lines of evidence. One approach would be to consider the degree of development of the cultural or conceptual landscape. This thought-about landscape may be defined as the way that the physical landscape is given shape and meaning by ascribing to it various cultural attributes. These might include the association of places with events, real or otherwise, the attribution of place-names to both physical and/or settlement features and knowledge of the line of boundaries and zones.[57] We can assume that the cultural perception of nomadic peoples will be strikingly different from that of settled populations because the knowledge of place by the former will necessarily cover many areas with a less intimate acquaintance of any one locality. This, then, provides a means by which we can investigate the degree of mobility of the Gaelic Irish population. A landscape with a rich network of boundaries, place-names and associations is likely to reflect occupation by sedentary inhabitants.

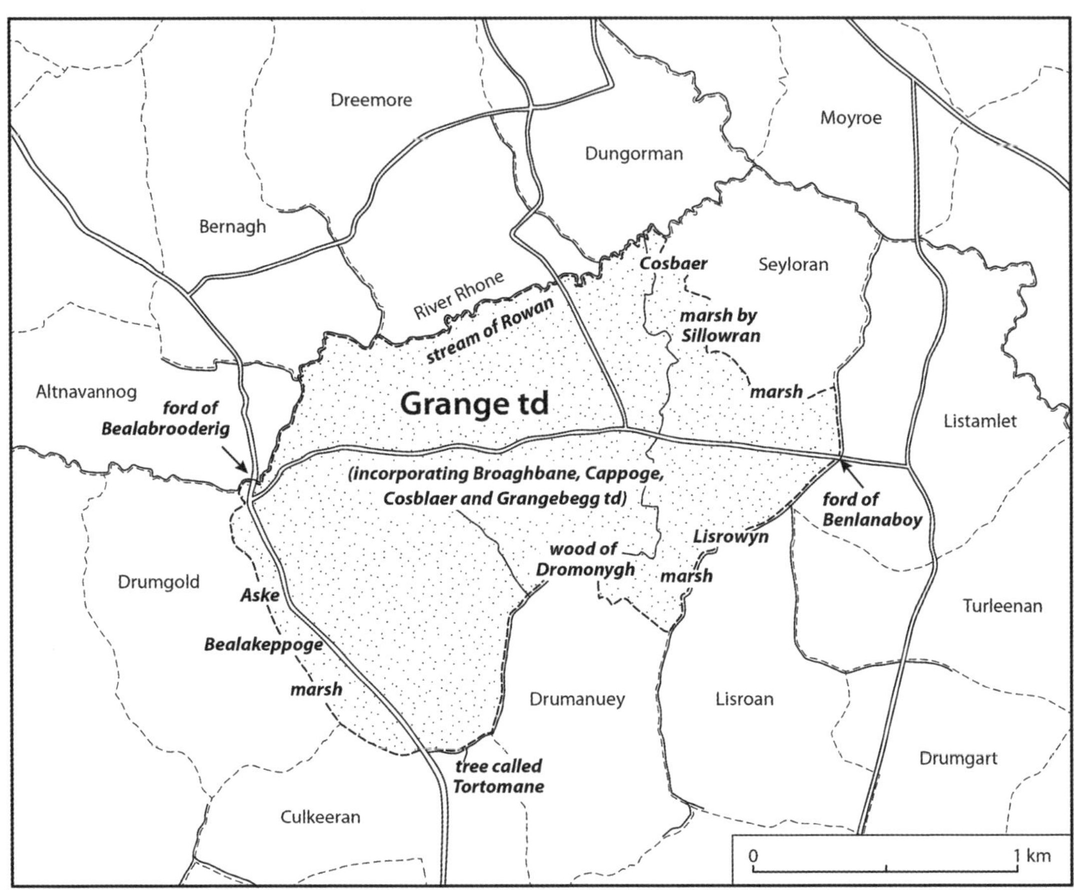


5. The four townlands – Broaghbane, Cappoge, Cosblaer and Grangebegg – constituted the lands of the grange of *Dromgenif*, now Grange townland, lying to the north of Moy (County Tyrone). The bounds, indicated by placenames in italics, were described in a grant of 1614 and suggest a thoroughly encultured landscape. Since so many boundaries followed watercourses, it is possible to suggest the line of the boundaries of the four constituent townlands within the present Grange townland (image: auhtor).

If we apply this measure, it rapidly becomes clear that the greater part of Ulster's population must have stayed in one locality. The extraordinary network of townlands, many covering only a few hundred acres and with roots in the early medieval period, reflects a deep and enduring sense of place, suggesting a persistence of orally transmitted knowledge of boundaries over many generations.[58] It is difficult to get access to the detail of the cultural inheritance of place. In the absence of Gaelic sources, we can use the boundary surveys drawn by the English authorities within twenty years of the end of the Nine Years' War with the help of 'very ancient men', as one source describes them. A single example may be used to illustrate this. Figure 5 shows the boundaries of a group of four townlands which formed the grange of Dromgenif (now the single townland of Grange, near Moy, County Tyrone), a property of Armagh Abbey.[59] It was bounded by the River Rhone to the north, and elsewhere by a notable tree, bogs and woods, some of which can still be identified. Boundary banks are not mentioned at all. There is an abundance of place-names, some of the adjoining townlands and others of particular features on the boundary. It is impossible to conceive that this type of local knowledge, with its detailed acquaintance with place and specific features, could have existed and been transmitted except in a sedentary society.

## Conclusion

Perhaps the most striking feature about the landscape of Gaelic Ulster in the sixteenth century was the lack of substantial investment in the construction of physical structures. This included not only houses, other buildings and fields, but also the construction of material boundaries of all sorts, including those of the farms and townlands. There was relatively little intervention to alter the natural environment and to create an infrastructure. Bogs remained undrained and rivers were not canalised. Fords served for the most part instead of bridges, only a small number of which had been constructed in Ulster by 1600. The paucity of travellers meant that few ferries operated.[60] Sir Henry Sidney commented that he had to cross with his army over the rivers of 'Omagh', Derg and Finn in 1566 without bridges or boats, though he did note a bridge at Dungannon.[61] It was not until 1611 that a ferry was provided over the River Finn between Strabane and Lifford.[62] There were a few causeways across bogs, but these seem only to have existed on major routes, such as the Gap of the North leading from Dundalk to Newry.[63] Generally, there were not many major roads and these were not well defined, so travellers might lose their way.[64] Only lordly dwellings – *crannóga* and tower houses – and ecclesiastical buildings provide evidence of more substantial landscape features.

The exceptional character of the northern part of Ireland needs to be emphasised. The absence of landscape features in Ulster contrasts with the situation in the Pale at this time, where the landscape was altogether more thoroughly exploited and managed. Excavation in the Dublin area has indicated that medieval fields were often bounded by banks and drainage channels. Transport was facilitated by a number of bridges and roads, some of which were metalled and delimited by ditches.[65] Many other European countries had better-developed networks of roads and bridges by the sixteenth century. England, for example, had an intensely exploited landscape, and a network of roads with numerous bridges.[66] So why was the landscape of Ulster so lightly marked by human features?

There is no reason to attribute the limited impact on the landscape to the lack of labour or of materials. Although the population of Ulster was low and land was abundant, this would not explain the paucity in investment of labour in individual buildings and field boundaries. Equally, Ulster was sufficiently provided with timber, though the distribution was patchy, and with other types of fuel.[67] Land quality was variable, but in places it was sufficiently good that substantial areas were under cultivation. There was extensive pasture land and numerous head of cattle were grazed. Unlike lands in Scandinavia, it was not necessary to make hay to sustain livestock through the winter. There was an extended season for pasture in Ireland and if we can extrapolate from modern conditions, then it is likely that only between early November and mid-March was there little grass growth.[68] Livestock during those winter months could be grazed on uncut pasture. None of these factors therefore constrained the development of the infrastructure of Ulster.

This makes the contrast between the physical impact on landscape and the cultural penetration of the countryside more puzzling. The example given of the grange of Dromgenif has shown that the density of place-names in boundary surveys indicates very clearly that sixteenth-century Ulster was far from a wilderness (Fig. 5). This is equally true for other areas covered by contemporary boundary surveys. Even in the rather poor lands at the edge of the Mourne Mountains in the Barony of Iveagh, County Down, witnesses in 1618 had an intimate knowledge of the bounds of territories, suggesting permanent settlement.[69]

The solution to the apparent paradox between a resource-abundant, culturally rich territory and the paucity of physical features marking human activity would appear to lie in the social and economic character of Gaelic Ireland. The relatively low density of population, lack of opportunity for disposing of agricultural products and of any means of storing surpluses, except on the hoof, tended to produce an approach in which there was no emphasis on maximising production. Land for the peasants had little value in itself since it was abundant. There was no benefit in building in a more enduring manner or in seeking to get a higher return from cultivated land or livestock. Such a response was entirely rational given the economic conditions. The situation for the Gaelic Irish lords was different only in part. They too had limited means of accumulating wealth and limited scope for exchanging commodities for imported goods.[70] Since the amount of food any one human can consume is restricted, the means by which wealth could be demonstrated and status marked was by entertaining or 'feasting' guests, and maintaining soldiers – *gallóglaigh* and *ceatharnaigh* – on the lords' lands and those of their tenants.[71]

We have little experience of societies of this sort, and relatively few Gaelic sources to illuminate the economic conditions in the sixteenth century, particularly the working of the economy below the level of the elite. Instead, to understand the possible economic and social system in Gaelic Ireland it is useful to think about comparable conditions elsewhere. Rosamond Faith, in a wide-ranging paper which included consideration of early medieval England and pre-modern Scotland, captured something of the essence of such a situation:

> While the peasant economy continued in a state of abatement and technological inertia it would remain difficult to appropriate much peasant surplus, or to exploit peasant traction power, or to establish a viable inland [approximating in Ireland to the mensal land, though this last point of comparison is less relevant]. Violent appropriations like cattle raids into another territory, or conquests resulting in captives who were enslaved, would be an easier route to wealth. ... Peasants supported the

> dominant elites of the time from their own fields and flocks, but the form in which they did this, food rents, were limited in extent and were essentially part of a culture of feeding a chieftain, not paying rent to a landlord. Land was conceptualized in terms of common use-rights rather than ownership.[72]

No two historical situations are identical and the description based on early medieval England and Scotland is not applicable to late medieval Ireland in every detail. However, Faith was not seeking to describe a particular place or time, but rather to identify a mode of production, a general economic pattern. Her analysis may help to illuminate some aspects of economic conditions in sixteenth-century Gaelic Ireland, which had many of the features she has outlined for England and Scotland, as well as setting Ireland in a broader economic context. Faith's description suggests that property rights may have been conceived of in an entirely different way from how we perceive them in the present. The absence of physical boundaries in Gaelic Ulster may have been the result of an approach to land which saw it in terms of use, rather than ownership. Possession was determined both by usage and by an investment in the cultural landscape. A similar form of possession has been suggested for early medieval England, in which acquaintance with local place-names provided a demonstration of the occupation of a locality.[73]

The lack of economic development can be interpreted as reflecting a system in which capital accumulation was difficult and was not a goal towards which people were working. The features of the landscape identified above are a reflection of a society with an abundance of resources but little capital, and few ways of accumulating and storing capital. The ephemeral archaeological traces left by the Gaelic Irish peasants are a sufficient statement of these difficulties.

From this perspective we can now return to Carrickfergus where we started. What we see implied by the sixteenth-century maps was different cultures living alongside each other, but seemingly with a limited degree of integration. One had a strong sense of property and of capital expressed in the investment in buildings and in the operation of commerce; the other had an alternative set of values which did not recognise property rights in the same way and made no attempt to invest in the construction of long-lived buildings.

Hybridity, it would seem, had yet to develop very far, but this is not to say that Gaelic Irish society was unaffected by its contact with the Anglo-Irish world. The expansion of arable agriculture, which seems to have taken place in the sixteenth century, may mark a society already in transition to a different economic system. This remains unclear because any indigenous change was cut short by English military intervention and the subsequent Plantation of settlers.[74]

The landscape of sixteenth-century Ulster is not elusive because archaeologists have failed to look for it or because later changes have entirely eradicated all traces. It is difficult to find because human intervention was comparatively light. Archaeological traces from this period are present, but they are difficult to locate. Instead of merely proposing more fieldwork as the solution, it is necessary first to develop a perspective with which we might begin to think about the nature of non-elite society in Gaelic Ireland and the approaches that might illuminate it. Our understanding of the landscape of that part of the Pale around Dublin is much better because we have a social and economic framework in which to set the discoveries.[75] Careful thought about the common people and their society in the Gaelic areas of Ireland is a pre-condition for understanding the historic landscape there.

## Acknowledgements

I am grateful to Libby Mulqueeny for preparing the illustrations and to Laura Belton for allowing Fig. 3 to be reproduced from her unpublished dissertation. I am grateful to Audrey Horning for her editorial comments which have helped to improve this paper.

11

# Food, drink and society in sixteenth-century Ireland: Cultures of consumption

SUSAN FLAVIN

## Introduction

In February 1576, Giles Wiggers of Antwerp set out on a voyage from Lisbon to Calais with a cargo of sugar and spices. En route, while most of the crew was sleeping, eight of the company 'fell upon' the rest, killing six. The master surrendered and was forced to bring his ship into the bay of Rosscarbery, in west Cork. Coming into the bay, he was greeted by Bishop Cornelius Brenner, who agreed, with the help of local fishermen, to bring the ship safely ashore to Glandore Haven, in return for thirty ducats. This, they agreed, was to be paid with 60 lbs of spices, in lieu of money. Trusting the kindly bishop, the master asked for help in dispossessing the murderous mariners and reclaiming his ship and cargo. The bishop, in turn, promised him 'great friendship' and 'took him to his house'. Instead, the bishop held the captain hostage for four days, releasing him only when he agreed to pay a ransom of 732 lbs of spices: 200 lbs each of nutmeg, cinnamon and pepper and 132 lbs of cloves.[1] How the bishop disposed of his extorted spices is unfortunately unknown, but it is clear from this and from the evidence to be explored in this chapter that there was a market for such luxury foodstuffs even, it would appear, in less commercialised parts of sixteenth-century Ireland.

In recent years both the social and cultural significance of food and drink have begun to receive significant historiographical attention. According to Edward Muir, 'No rituals are more widely practiced [sic], more formative of social identity or more differentiating of social groups than the daily habits of dining. The distinction between eating merely to consume food and dining as a form of sociability inhabits the very core of what we call culture'.[2] The growing interest in the material culture of food and drink has begun to influence studies of early modern Europe and England and, in particular, the sixteenth century has become acknowledged as a period of important changes in consumer demand and taste. European voyages of discovery to the 'new worlds' meant direct contact with new foods and culinary practices, while the desire to profit from expanding trade encouraged the development of new markets. At the same time, renaissance humanist writers opened up a range of debates regarding what and how to eat; table manners became formalised and more elaborate; and the printing press made both culinary and courtesy literature available to mass audiences.

In England, historians have found evidence of these changes in many aspects of food consumption and a number of important themes have recently emerged in food historiography.[3] In Ireland, historians for the large part ignore the field. This 'telling contrast' between explorations of the subject in Ireland and elsewhere relates mainly to the lack of appropriate source material for Ireland, which means that it still remains necessary to fully establish the fundamentals of food consumption – 'what was grown, imported and eaten and how the staples changed' – before engaging in more detailed studies of hospitality and of the preparation and presentation of food.[4] It is also likely that there is an element of ideological resistance to such topics in Ireland. In a society where many died of famine, the materials of life, often not sufficing for subsistence, are assumed to be unworthy or too sparse to warrant investigation.[5]

Certainly, the Irish diet has long attracted historiographical attention. Work, however, has traditionally focused predominantly on the Irish dependence on the potato from the eighteenth century and in particular on the Great Famine (1845–1852), which occurred as a result of crop failure in the 1840s.[6] This is a trend, however, that appears set to change and of late there has been a slowly growing emphasis on food in Irish historiography with attempts to explore the social and cultural significance of the Irish diet.[7] As yet, however, there has been very little work on the sixteenth century.[8] There are a number of reasons for this. First, of course, is the severe lack of documentary evidence for this period, which makes any serious consideration of changing consumption patterns very onerous. Another problem is the persistent belief that the Irish economy remained chronically underdeveloped during this period. It is the standard narrative of Irish economic and political development for the sixteenth-century economy that regressed even further at the end of the century due to the disastrous effects of the Nine Years' War (1594–1603).[9] Indeed, the basis for Louis Cullen's pioneering work on the emergence of modern Ireland was the assumption that Ireland was 'the last western European country to abandon the medieval world'. Cullen assumed that in 'anthropological terms, sixteenth-century Ireland had affinities with Europe two centuries previously'.[10] Given such perceptions, it is unsurprising that Ireland is not seen as the most likely place to find significant changes in consumption patterns, dietary or otherwise, and that Irish scholarship on the subject lags behind current wider historiographical trends.

Recent work at the University of Bristol, culminating in a major three-year Economic and Social Research Council (UK) funded project on Ireland–Bristol trade, has done much to abrogate these problems in Irish historiography. This project, which entailed the data capture and analysis of import and export accounts for eleven individual fiscal years, over the course of the century, was undertaken to examine changes in the size and structure of southeast Ireland's trade with Bristol during the sixteenth century and to illuminate the economic development of southern Ireland during this period.[11] The project also highlighted the potential use of the customs accounts to explore the evolving nature of Irish consumption and material culture during this period and to expand the methodology for future customs account based studies. Of particular significance is the fact that the Bristol port books of the late sixteenth century were found to include details regarding the exact port of arrival or departure of ships and also the domicile of the merchants that laded goods on them. These are very important details, since they throw light on the probable diffusion of goods after their arrival in Ireland, thereby allowing an exploration of the commercial relationships between ports and their hinterlands of a form that cannot be conducted using surviving Irish sources.

It may seem unusual to approach the study of Irish economic development or consumption through the use of Bristol's records, but there are valid reasons for this. First, it is generally agreed that trade between Bristol and Ireland had long been the most important branch of Ireland's overseas trade and that England remained Ireland's principal trading partner during the Tudor period.[12] Second, no comparable set of accounts have survived from Ireland or any continental port for this period, and it is only after 1565 that the quality and value of customs accounts from other English ports, such as Chester, start to match those of Bristol. Even these, however, tend to aggregate shipments under general terms such as 'wares', which means they cannot be used to examine the minutiae of the import trade like the Bristol accounts.

The Bristol accounts, then, form the only hard set of quantitative data that exists for investigating the economic development of any part of Ireland across the course of the century and they can be used to develop a very detailed picture of Ireland's import trade in the period. Specifically, they facilitate the chronological identification of major changes in the consumption of goods that were intended for everyday use; goods that were relatively inexpensive, had a short life-span or were produced for fairly immediate consumption and which, therefore, do not survive well in inventories, wills or indeed the archaeological record: items such as children's bibs, bottles and manners books, table napery, various herbal remedies, cooking ingredients and domestic utensils. They therefore permit a thorough examination of the evolving use of a broad range of commodities that relate very directly to the activities of daily living and present a picture of changing patterns in the consumption of goods that were not necessarily the preserve of people of a particular age or income scale. As such, they can shed light on the changing rituals and material culture of the table, the preparation and presentation of food, and evolving food fashions and tastes in sixteenth-century Ireland.

This chapter will, firstly, summarise some key major findings of the analysis of Ireland's import trade and participation in the emerging sixteenth-century world of goods.[13] In this regard, it will highlight two important trends in this trade: the geographical diffusion of import goods and the pace and chronology of change. Secondly, it will explore the social and cultural significance of this participation, with reference to the consumption and material culture of food and drink, by focusing on a small sample of everyday import commodities: knives, beer, wooden trenchers and babies' bottles. These will be used as a framework to explore some important themes in Irish food-related consumption, including the impact of continental trade on Irish material culture; the comparative nature of taste and consumption in Britain and Ireland; the impact of Plantation on dining practices and manners; and finally, the connection between material culture and colonial ideology.

## The Irish import trade

With regards to the statistical analysis of the Bristol accounts, the most immediate finding is the dramatic increase in the range of goods imported by Irish merchants over the course of the century. At the beginning of the century, Irish imports consisted of a range of just sixty individual items, including rather prosaic foodstuffs such as peas and beans, a narrow range of spices and a minor selection of domestic utensils, cloth and haberdashery. As Fig. 1 illustrates, the dissimilarity between the accounts from the beginning and end of the century is immense. By the last decade of the century, almost 400 different specified commodities were imported to Ireland from Bristol, with significant developments notable in almost every area of consumption.

The expansion of Irish imports occurred in two main areas. First, there was growing diversification of product types, for example the evolution of items like buttons, looking glasses and knives from a single category to a range of sub-types. This is notable in terms of both the variety and grade of such items. The later accounts, for example, distinguish knives by their place of origin, including knives from Flanders and Germany (specifically Cologne), as well as by their type, including, for example, fine, paring, pocket, cap, coarse and eating knives. There was also further diversification in terms of the grade of the item, with the appearance of half-penny, penny and two-penny knives. Secondly, there was a great increase in entirely new products in the trade, including for example various types of

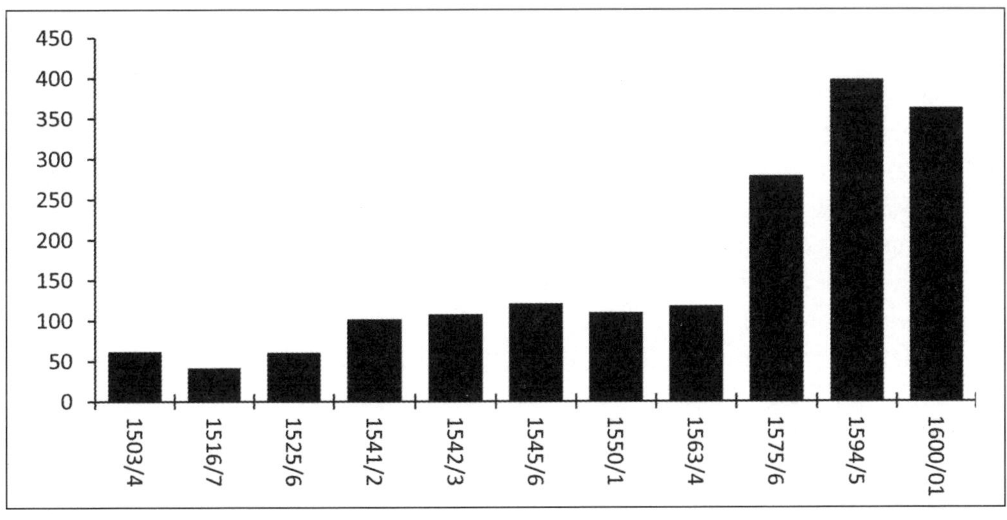


1. Range of individual commodities.

Source: Susan Flavin and Evan Jones, Bristol's Trade with Ireland and the Continent, 1503–1601 (2009), pp. 1–942.

luxury sarcenet, taffeta and fustian along with numerous types of new haberdashery items; dyestuffs, including indigo; domestic utensils such as drinking glasses and infant feeding bottles; new types of apparel for children and adults such as bibs and stockings; personal items including spectacles and tobacco pipes and luxury foodstuffs, including comfits and sugar.

There was also a growing volume of many items, including those that would previously have been classed as luxury goods, like looking glasses. A dozen of these, for example, are found in the accounts as early as 1526; by 1550 this had increased to 396, and by 1594 there are 882 looking glasses, of varying values, found among Irish imports. Also, items like woollen stockings, which according to Thirsk were lodged mainly at the lower end of the social scale, first occur in small quantities in 1575 but by 1594 become a regular import.[14] Likewise, imports of hats of widely varying values and descriptions, for men, women and children, which first appear in the accounts from 1541, grew significantly during the later sixteenth century, to the extent that, by 1594, they accounted for 10 per cent of Irish imports by value. There is a similar picture with luxury foods, with items like sugar and currants increasing significantly in volume in the later century. Tables 1 and 2 summarise specific changes in the nature of Irish imports by comparing the importation of food-related goods over the course of the century. Some important points can be made regarding the pace and extent of these changes in Ireland. First, regarding the geographical diffusion of goods, the Port Books, after 1565, record the exact port at which commodities were arriving in Ireland, along with the domicile of each merchant. If it is assumed that goods imported by merchants domiciled in inland towns were mainly intended for transport overland to those towns and their commercial hinterlands, this data gives a clear sense of inland trade connections in Ireland, unavailable from other sources.

The port of arrival of Irish imports in 1594 is plotted in Fig. 2, and the further distribution of the goods that arrived at Waterford, which received two-thirds of the value of the trade that year, is shown in Fig. 3. This data shows that the much-diversified range of consumer wares imported from Bristol entered Ireland not only through the southeastern ports but also through ports in the west and northeast of the country. Such wares were distributed across a wide area, with goods travelling well beyond the primary areas of English control, to towns stretching from Tipperary and Kilkenny in the southeast, up to Limerick and Galway in the west, likely indicative of Gaelic as well as Anglo-Irish consumption. It is notable that the shipments into the western ports and into the southeast by western merchants contain a similar range of import commodities as those imported by merchants from the southeast. This is of particular significance since it suggests a comparable demand for new consumer goods within the Pale and in the areas of Anglo-Irish control most geographically removed from the centre of government in Ireland. The Anglo-Irish consumers of these commodities, to some extent, shared a material culture, despite the fragmented nature of their society and economy and the geographical isolation of their more western communities.

Regarding the timing of these changes, it is notable that there appears to have been two significant periods of growth in consumption: one between 1526 and 1541, when the accounts show a 60 per cent rise in the range of commodities and a second between 1563 and 1575, when there was a dramatic acceleration of the trend, with an increase of 140 per cent in the range of goods imported, peaking in 1594, with a further 43 per cent increase. These two marked periods of growth occurred under distinctly different political and economic conditions.

Table 1. Volume of Imported Domestic Utensils (1503–1601)

| | 1503 | 1516 | 1525 | 1541 | 1542 | 1545 | 1550 | 1563 | 1575 | 1594 | 1600 |
|---|---|---|---|---|---|---|---|---|---|---|---|
| Bellows | | | | | | | | | | 16 | |
| Bellows, Pairs | | | | | | | | | | 24 | 25 |
| Bottles, Glass | | | | | | | | | | 36 | 36 |
| Bottles, Leather small | | | | | | | | | | 18 | |
| Bottles, Pewter | | | | | | | | | 12 | | |
| Bottles, Sucking | | | | | | | | | | 36 | |
| Boultel Bewpers | | | | | | | | | | | 1 |
| Boxes, Black | | | | | | | | | | | 12 |
| Boxes, Nest | | | | | | | | | | 24 | 7 |
| Boxes, Painted | | | | | | | | | | | 36 |
| Boxes, Painted, Nest | | | | | | | | | | 26 | 14 |
| Brushes | | | | | | | | | | 486 | 96 |
| Brushes, Heath | | | | | | | | | | 90 | |
| Brushes, Rubbing | | | | | | | | | | 12 | |
| Brushes, Small | | | | | | | | | 12 | | |
| Candlesticks | | | | | | | | | 4 | | |
| Candlesticks | | | | | | | | | | 42 | |
| Candlesticks, Brass | | | | | | | | | | 14 | 18 |
| Candlesticks, Pewter | | | | | | | | | 14 | | |
| Candlesticks, Small | | | | | | | | | | 138 | 18 |
| Canikine | | | | | | | | | | 1 | |
| Cauldrons, Brass | | | | | | 1 | | | | | |
| Chafing Dishes | | | | | | | | | | 2 | |
| Chest locks | | | | | | | | | | 24 | |
| Chests | | | | 8 | | | | | | | |
| Chests, Small Painted | | | | | | | | | | | 3 |
| Cruses, Stone | | | | | | | | | 12 | 120 | 24 |
| Cups | | | | | 12 | | | | | | |
| Cups, Earthen | | | | | | | | | | | 48 |
| Cups, Wooden | | | | | | | | | | 624 | 564 |
| Cutts | | 18792 | 23796 | 4392 | 4320 | 7848 | 576 | 17280 | 17119 | | 56 |
| Cutts (1d) | | | | | | | | | | 240 | |
| Cutts (ob) | | | | | | | | | | 72 | 42 |
| Diaper Napkins | | | | | | | | | | 6 | |
| Dishes, Iron chafing | | | | | | | | | | | 5 |
| Drinking Cans | | | | | | | | | | | 12 |
| Drinking Horns | | | | | | | | | | 120 | |
| Earthen Ware | | | | | | | | | | ? | |
| Flasket | | | | | | | 92 | | | | |
| Funnels | | | | | | | | | 48 | | |
| Glasses (1d.) | | | | | | | | | | | 804 |
| Glasses (ob) | | | | | | | | | | 48 | |
| Glasses and Stone Pots | | | | | | | | | | | 72 |
| Glasses, Coarse Drinking | | | | | | | | | | 1638 | 1410 |
| Glasses, French Drinking | | | | | | | | | | 624 | |
| Glasses, Green | | | | | | | | | | 288 | |
| Glasses, Unspecified | | | | 1872 | 552 | 684 | | | 54 | 168 | 456 |
| Graters | | | | | | | | | | | 60 |
| Grid Irons | | | | | 2 | | | | | | |
| Horns | | | | | | | | 2000 | | | |

Table 1. Volume of Imported Domestic Utensils (1503–1601) *(continued)*.

| | 1503 | 1516 | 1525 | 1541 | 1542 | 1545 | 1550 | 1563 | 1575 | 1594 | 1600 |
|---|---|---|---|---|---|---|---|---|---|---|---|
| Knives | 3708 | 648 | 756 | 45216 | 31788 | 24308 | 39996 | 12 | 312 | 1512 | 1068 |
| Knives (1d.) | | | | | | | | | 348 | 7788 | 8280 |
| Knives (2d) | | | | | | | | | 216 | 1656 | 72 |
| Knives (ob) | | | | | | | | | | 1728 | 60 |
| Knives, Almaine | | | | | | | 144 | 2838 | 72 | | |
| Knives, Brazil | | | 12 | | | | | | | | |
| Knives, Bumbard | | | | | | | 360 | 1320 | | | |
| Knives, Cappe | | | | | | | | | 24 | | |
| Knives, Coarse | | | | | | | | | | 96 | |
| Knives, Cullen | | | | | | | | | 216 | | |
| Knives, Cuttlers | | | | | | | | | | 696 | |
| Knives, Fine | | | | | | | | | | 24 | |
| Knives, Flanders | | | | | | | | | 12 | | |
| Knives, Flemish | | | | | | | | | 120 | | |
| Knives, in Pairs | | | 60 | 5178 | 3108 | 5916 | 4560 | 1800 | 312 | 192 | |
| Knives, in Pairs (2d.) | | | | | | | | | 24 | | |
| Knives, Paring | | | | | | | | | 6 pair | 48 | |
| Knives, Pocket | | | | | | | | | | 2736 | 696 |
| Knives, Prage | | | | | 24 | | | 288 | 12 | 252 | 108 |
| Knives, Shope? | | | | | | | | | 2 | | |
| Knives, Small | | | 24 | | 30 | | | | | | |
| Lanterns | | | | | | | | | | 31 | 57 |
| Mouce Snatches | | | | | | | | | | | 6 |
| Pans, Brass | | | | | | | 8 | | 5 | | |
| Pans, Dripping | | | | | 2 | | | | | | |
| Pans, Frying | | | | | | | | | | 48 | 12 lb |
| Pans, Plate Dripping | | | | | | | | | | 6 | |
| Pots, Brass | | | 4 | | | 1 | | | 2.5C, 120 lb | 238 lb | |
| Pots, Iron | | | | | | | | | | 6 | |
| Pots, Stone Uncovered | | | | | | | | | | | 220 |
| Pottle | | | | | 12 | | 150? | | | | |
| Serches | | | | | | | | | 24 | 12 | 78 |
| Setting Sticks | | | | | | | | | | 18 | |
| Skillets, Small | | | | | | | | | | | 6 |
| Sleek Stone | | | | | | | | | | | 4 |
| Snuffers | | | | | | | | | | | 24 |
| Table Cloths and Diapers | | | | | | | | | | 170 | |
| Table Napkins | | | | | | | | | | | 12 |
| Tables, pairs | | | | | | | | | | | 4 |
| Taps | | | | | 72 | | | 216 | | 1440 | |
| Taps and Cannells | | | | | | | | | 1320 | 2520 | 11104 |
| Taps, Small | | | | | | | | | | 2400 ? | |
| Tobacco pipes | | | | | | | | | | | 756 |
| Trenchers | | | | | | 2880 | | 648 | | 4032 | 16632 |
| Trenchers, Coarse | | | | | | | | | 5568 | | |
| Trenchers, Common | | | | | | | | | | 16512 | 6264 |
| Trenchers, Painted | | | | | | | | | | 24 | |
| Trenchers, Wooden | | | | | | | | | | 1008 | |
| Vials | | | | | | | | | | 288 | |

Source: Flavin and Jones, *Bristol's Trade*, pp. 1–942; Flavin, 'Consumption', p. 1157.

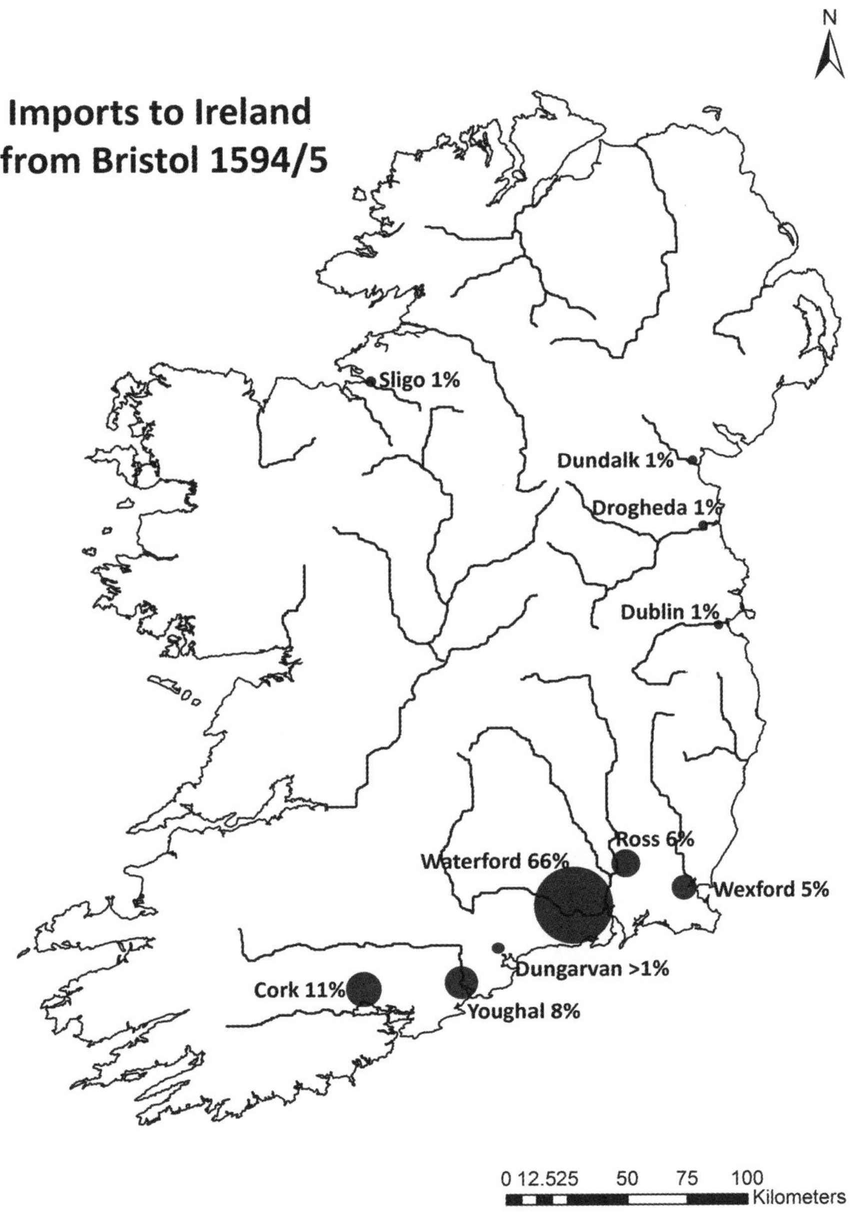


2. Imports to Ireland from Bristol 1594/95.

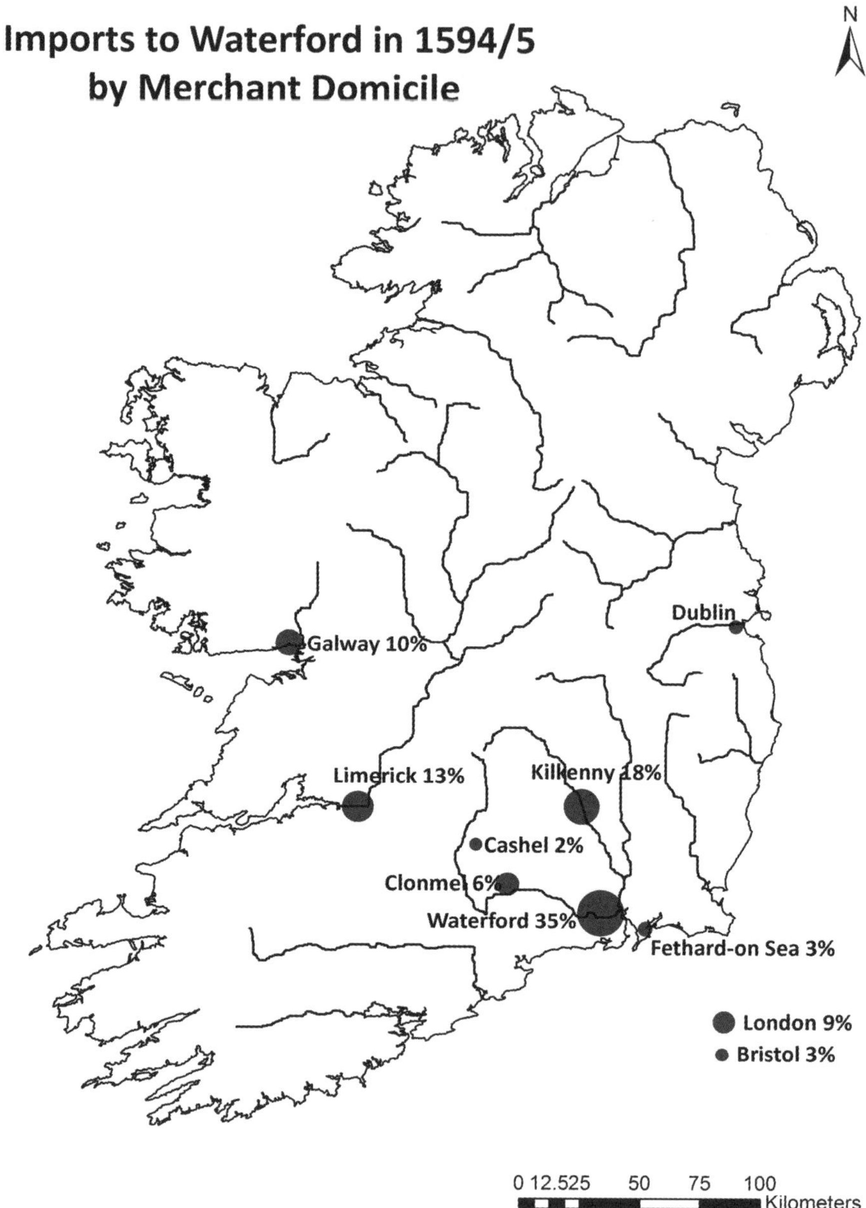


3. Imports to Waterford in 1594/95 by merchant domicile.

Table 2. Volume of Food and Drink Imports (1503–1601).

| | 1503/4 | 1516/7 | 1525/6 | 1541/2 | 1542/3 | 1545/6 | 1550/1 | 1563/4 | 1575/6 | 1594/5 | 1600/1 |
|---|---|---|---|---|---|---|---|---|---|---|---|
| Almonds (lb) | | | | | | | | | 36 | 148 | 0 |
| Aniseed (lb) | 1000 | 1618 | 3550 | 2847 | 12038 | 11682 | 464 | 3248 | 118 | 5826 | 112 |
| Apples barrel | | | | | | | | | | 0 | 4 |
| Aqua Vitae (gallon) | | | 94.5 | | | | | | | | |
| Arsenic (lb) | | | | | | | 2 | 1 | 28 | 0 | 0 |
| Bacon (flege) | 4 | | | | | | | | 1.5 | 0 | 0 |
| Barley/Malt/Peas/ Beans (wey) | 228.75 | | | 71.5 | 9.33 | | | | 3 | | |
| Beans (wey) | | 367.5 | 38.5 | 13 | | | | | 3 | | |
| Beans/Malt (wey) | | 24 | | | | | | | | | |
| Beans/Peas (wey) | | | 7 | | | | | | | | |
| Beer (barrel) | 215 | 27 | | | | | | | | | |
| Benedict's Laxative (lb) | | | | | | | | | | | 1 |
| Biskett (lb) | | | | | | | | | 11 | | |
| Bole Armeniac (lb) | | | | | | | | | 20 | | |
| Candy, Brown (lb) | | | | | | | | | | | 2 |
| Candy, White (lb) | | | | | | | | | | | 8 |
| Cider (gallon) | | | | | | | | | | 670.32 | |
| Cinnamon (lb) | 5 | 1 | 1.5 | 20.5 | 22.25 | 24.5 | 16 | 0.5 | 5.5 | | 2 |
| Cinnamon/Cloves (lb) | | | | 14 | 14 | 4 | 1 | | | | |
| Cinnamon/Cloves/ Mace (lb) | | | | 9 | 2.5 | | | | | | |
| Cinnamon/Mace (lb) | | | | 3 | 1.5 | 2 | | | | | |
| Cloves (lb) | | | 1 | 9.5 | 35 | 34.75 | 13 | 36.5 | 21 | 5.5 | |
| Cloves/Mace (lb) | | | | 8.5 | 3.5 | 10 | | | | | |
| Comfits (lb) | | | | | | | | | 10 | 25 | 21 |
| Comfits, Spice (lb) | | | | | | | | | 2 | | |
| Currants (lb) | | | | | | | | | 7 | 500 | 1342.5 |
| Figs (lb) | | | | | | | 672 | | | 112 | |
| Figs barrel | | | | | | | | | | | 2 |
| Fish New-Foundland (piece) | | | | | | | | | | | 12000 |
| Fruit (lb) | 3.75 C | | | 560 | 1306.6 | | | | | | |
| Ginger (lb) | 4 | 2 | 4 | 20.5 | 8.75 | 90 | 2 | 13 | 2 | 23 | 50 |
| Honey flasket | | | | | | | | | | | 1 |
| Honey-barrel | 12 | 1 | 9 | 10.5 | | 2.75 | 18.5 | 1 | 3 | 1 | 0 |
| Hops (lb) | 336 | 1498 | 2931 | 5908 | 1890 | 14220 | 8470 | 952 | 8981 | 34300 | 31892 |
| Isinglass (lb) | | | | | | | | | | 6 | 8 |
| Liquorice (lb) | 26 | 58 | 23 | 489 | 281 | 656 | 82 | 264 | 1386 | 48 | 616 |
| Mace (lb) | 1.25 | 1 | | 10.25 | | 9.25 | 0.5 | 1 | | | |
| Malt (wey) | | 42 | 307.75 | 64.16 | 12 | | | 10 | | | |
| Malt/Barley (wey) | | | 8.5 | | | | | | 19.25 | | |
| Malt/Rye (wey) | | | 22 | | | | | | | | |
| Marmalade (lb) | | | | | | | | | | | |
| Meal (barrel) | | | 1 | | | | | | | | |

Table 2. Volume of Food and Drink Imports (1503–1601)(*continued*).

| | 1503/4 | 1516/7 | 1525/6 | 1541/2 | 1542/3 | 1545/6 | 1550/1 | 1563/4 | 1575/6 | 1594/5 | 1600/1 |
|---|---|---|---|---|---|---|---|---|---|---|---|
| Nutmeg (lb) | | | | 4 | 6.5 | 14.5 | 4 | 6 | 0 | 3 | 1 |
| Oil, Olive (lb) | | | | | | | | | | | |
| Onions barrel | | | | | | | | | | | 1 |
| Peas (wey) | | | 2 | | | | | | | | |
| Pepper (lb) | 18 | 2 | 22.5 | 76 | 98.25 | 61 | 50.5 | 108.5 | 5 | 13 | 10 |
| Prunes (lb) | | | | | | | | 12 | 98 | 210 | 4172 |
| Raisins, Great (lb) | | | | | 373.33 | | 24826 | 93.33 | | 2623 | 1810 |
| Raisins, Malaga (lb) | | | | | | | | | | | 224 |
| Raisins, of the Sun (lb) | | | | | | | | | | | 392 |
| Raisins, Rotta (lb) | | | | | | | | | | | 728 |
| Rice (lb) | | | | | | | | | 56 | 826 | 348 |
| Rye (wey) | | | 126.5 | | | | | | | | |
| Salt (lb) | | 14000 | | | 284480 | 193088 | 22400 | 5040 | 15680 | | |
| Seed, Caraway (lb) | | | | | | | | | 4 | | |
| Seed, Coriander (lb) | | | | | | | | | 2 | | |
| Seed, Cumin (lb) | | 15 | 74 | 404 | 189 | 397 | 114 | 126 | 238 | 12 | 64 |
| Seed, Fennel (lb) | | | | | | | | 2 | | | 4 |
| Seed, Leek (lb) | | | | | 8 | 1 | | 122.5 | 4 | 18 | 12 |
| Seed, Onion (lb) | | | | 27 | 75 | 48 | 136 | 110.5 | 14 | 101 | 682 |
| Seed, Porcelic (lb) | | | | | | | | 2 | 0 | 0 | 0 |
| Senna (lb) | | | | | 2.5 | 3 | | | 10 | 14.5 | 13 |
| Succado/ Marmalade (lb) | | | | | | | | | | 4 | |
| Sugar (lb) | | | | | 6 | 188 | | 54 | 89 | 871 | 461 |
| Sugar Candy (lb) | | | | | 1 | 1 | 2 | | 4 | 3 | |
| Sugar of Roses (lb) | | | 2 oz. | | | | 0.5 | | | | |
| Terra Sigillata (lb) | | | | | | | | 1 | | | |
| Tobacco (lb) | | | | | | | | | | | 2 |
| Vinegar (gallon) | | 27783 | 2961 | 14112 | 3843 | 7938 | 9198 | 810.61 | 2047.5 | 126 | 63 |
| Wheat (quart) | | 117 | 2868 | 299 | 20 | | | | | | |
| Wine (gallon) | 756 | | 203 | 126 | 126 | 8316 | 2268 | | | | |
| Wormseed (lb) | | | | | | | | | 1 | | |

Source: Flavin and Jones, *Bristol's Trade*, pp. 1–942; Flavin, 'Consumption', pp. 1155–56.

The first half of the sixteenth century was a relatively stable and prosperous period in southeast Ireland. A number of factors contributed to this. Perhaps the most significant was the liberties and privileges accumulated by the towns as a result of the Crown's desire to nurture the 'traditional harmonious relations with the towns in Ireland'.[15] This was also, of course, a period when Anglo-Irish merchants faced few restrictions in engaging in commerce with the resurgent Gaelic Irish.[16]

The customs accounts shed significant light on Irish economic development in this period and indeed suggest a major transformation between the late fifteenth century and the mid-sixteenth century, with a significant rise in the percentage of the trade conducted on Irish ships, which rose from 50 per cent in 1503/04 to 75 per cent by the 1540s; a growing diversity in import commodities and, most importantly, a major increase in the export of manufactured Irish cloth and clothing. This rose from about a tenth of total exports in the late fifteenth century to half of exports by the 1540s. By the 1540s, the majority of Ireland's export trade to England consisted not of fish and hides, as is generally assumed, but of manufactured goods. It is difficult to overemphasise the significance of this finding. This was a state of affairs that Ireland would not enjoy again until modern times and it is of particular note that there appears to be a strong correlation between the growth in Irish exports of cloth and the increasing importation of new consumer goods. The rise in manufacture occurred between 1526 and 1541, in line with the first period of apparent growth in Irish imports, suggesting that there was a dynamic link between increasing domestic production and the desire and ability to purchase a growing range of consumer goods.

Looking at the second period of growth, which occurred between 1563 and 1575, a number of important issues arise. First, there is a tendency amongst historians to view changing trends in Irish consumption or material culture as a by-product of, or reaction to, wider British developments. A major concern of historians of eighteenth-century Irish material culture, in particular, is the extent to which the assimilation of 'English' habits or the circulation of English goods reveals dependence on or independence from Britain, or shows Ireland being subordinated and assimilated to British standards.[17] For the sixteenth century, Thirsk has argued explicitly that rising Irish consumer imports in the Pale were purely a function of English colonialism and, specifically, that luxury goods were not intended for Anglo-Irish or Gaelic Irish consumption at all but for the 'new English elite' and the English military.[18]

The timing of the changes in the accounts strongly suggests that this was not the case. The most significant influx of New English settlers to this region occurred during the Munster Plantation in 1586–87, and the data indicates that major changes were underway well before this, even from as early as the 1540s. Also, while it is

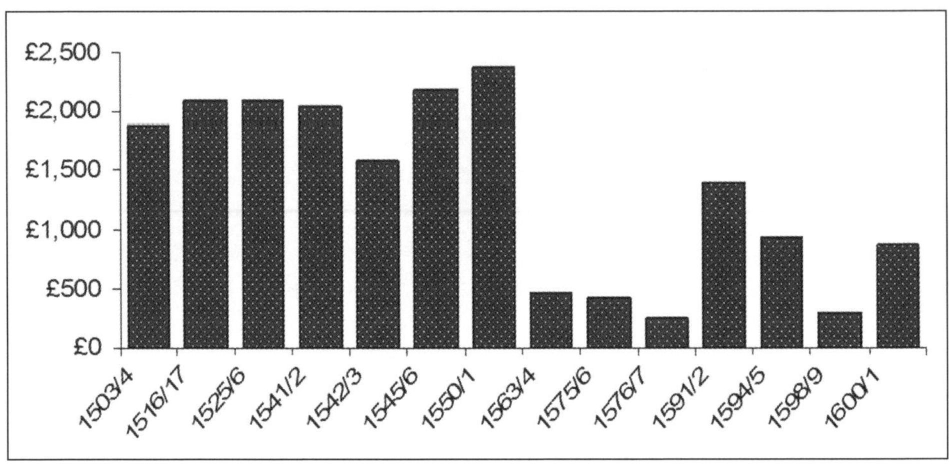


4. Gross value of Irish imports (deflated).

Sources: Flavin and Jones, *Bristol's Trade*, pp. 1–942; with the addition of gross import values for three additional fiscal years: 1576/77, 1591/92 and 1598/99 (TNA E190/1129/23, E190/1131/4, E190/1131/8, E190/1132/8).

likely that the further growth noted in 1594 and 1600 was in part related to the influx of settlers, the Plantation met with disaster in 1598, and was not re-established until after 1601, yet there was no significant difference in the type and range of goods or the gross value of the trade in the 1595 and 1600 accounts. It is clear, then, that we need to look at these changes in terms of Ireland's wider social, political and economic integration, rather than purely through the lens of English influences.

Secondly, what is striking about the diversification of goods in the last quarter of the century is that it is not related to the rising value of Anglo-Irish trade. Indeed, the reverse is true. While the range of commodities was rising, the value of the trade collapsed. Comparing the data in Fig. 1 and Fig. 4, it will be noted that the evidence is in fact pointing in opposite directions. The 1575 account, paradoxically, records both the greatest increase in terms of the range of goods imported, but also, with the exception of the 1591/92 account, the lowest recorded gross value for trade over the course of the century.

It is also of note that, along with the decreasing value of trade with England, the accounts also suggest the decreasing control of Irish merchants of that trade towards the end of the century. As Table 3 and Fig. 5 show, in 1575, Irish merchants controlled a massive 97 per cent of the value of imports from Bristol. By 1600, this had fallen to 76 per cent; Irish merchants still very much dominated the trade, but the 22 per cent decrease in their activity on this route indicates, perhaps, that their interests were moving elsewhere.

5. Percentage of gross value of trade imported by merchant domicile.

Source: Flavin and Jones, *Bristol's Trade*, pp. 672–942; with the addition of gross import values for: 1576/77, 1591/92 and 1598/99 (TNA: E190/1129/23, E190/1131/4, E190/1131/8, E190/1132/8).

Table 3. Percentage of gross value of trade imported by merchant domicile.

| Year | Ireland | Bristol | London | Other |
|---|---|---|---|---|
| 1575/6 | 95.28 | 0.71 | 2.36 | 1.65 |
| 1576/7 | 97.28 | 0.79 | 0.74 | 1.19 |
| 1591/2 | 85.98 | 4.34 | 8.47 | 1.21 |
| 1594/5 | 79.42 | 4.91 | 14.91 | 0.76 |
| 1598/9 | 96.12 | 3.88 | 0.00 | 0.00 |
| 1600/1 | 76.61 | 18.21 | 3.91 | 1.28 |

Source: Flavin and Jones, *Bristol's Trade*, pp. 672–942; with the addition of gross import values for: 1576/77, 1591/92 and 1598/99 (TNA: E190/1129/23, E190/1131/4, E190/1131/8, E190/1132/8).

There is certainly evidence, beyond increasing luxury consumption, to suggest that the falling values for trade are not representative of the health of the economy. The most important evidence comes from the accounts themselves, which, as noted above, show a transformation in the nature of Irish trade from around the 1540s. Other evidence for the health of the economy has been noted by Raymond Gillespie, including coin hoards, which suggest a large influx of English coin in the 1570s and 1580s, along with the relative stability of the Irish pound's exchange rate with sterling. According to Gillespie, Irish prosperity was related to the remarkable price stability which prevailed in the later sixteenth century, in contrast to the inflation occurring in England.[19]

Why then are we seeing this collapse in the figures for Ireland's trade with England at the end of the century? Examining the changing nature of the Irish import trade sheds more light on the reasons for this apparent prosperity. It is notable that while the variety and in many cases the volume of certain items was increasing – in luxury European cloth, foodstuffs, spices, items of clothing, domestic utensils and other small manufactured goods, for example – there was a significant corresponding fall in the traditional staple bulk Irish imports (specifically English woollen cloth, saffron and worked silk), which together comprised about 70 per cent of the gross value of Ireland's import trade in the first half of the century. The importation of English cloth and worked silk fell steadily towards the end of the century, in line with the increasing availability of new ranges of lighter cloths, silks and silk mixes, a significant proportion of which (in common with the vast majority of haberdashery and luxury foodstuffs) were still of continental rather than English origin. The quantities of these new items being imported to Ireland via Bristol, it appears, was not significant enough to maintain the gross value of the trade at the levels noted in the earlier accounts and it therefore seems that Irish merchants were sourcing a greater proportion of commodities elsewhere, either via another English port or, most likely, directly from the continent.

There is certainly ample documentary evidence to indicate the continental interests of Irish merchants in this period. Ireland's trade with Spain, in particular, was of major concern to the English administration. A letter from the Privy Council to the Lord Deputy in 1602, for example, noted the need to select and limit the Irish

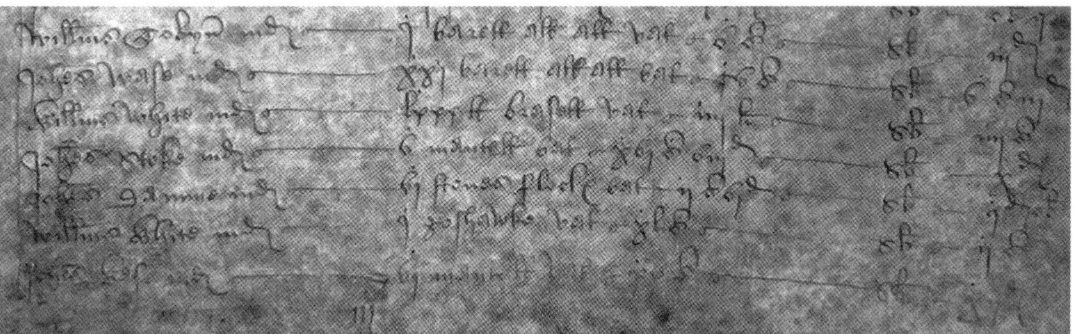

6. Image from the 1503/04 'particular account' showing Irish re-exports of Brazilwood (TNA E122/199/1, f42r).

Table 4. Percentage of gross value of imports comprised by English cloth, saffron and silk.

| Year | English Cloth | Saffron | Silk |
|---|---|---|---|
| 1503/4 | 50 | 11 | 8.52 |
| 1516/17 | 42 | 11 | 9.50 |
| 1525/6 | 20 | 12 | 9.47 |
| 1541/2 | 33 | 13 | 16.56 |
| 1542/3 | 30 | 17 | 15.21 |
| 1545/6 | 22 | 19 | 13.80 |
| 1550/1 | 16 | 16 | 15.52 |
| 1563/4 | 33 | 9 | 5.49[1] |
| 1575/6 | 10 | 1 | 4.84[2] |
| 1594/5 | 8.5 | 0 | 1.41[3] |
| 1600/1 | 5.6 | 0.07 | 0.50[4] |

Source: Flavin and Jones, *Bristol's Trade*, pp. 1–942; Flavin, 'Consumption', p. 1160.

1 This is raw silk as opposed to the 'worked silk' that occurs in every account prior to 1563/4.
2 Paris silk makes up 4.52% of this figure. Small quantities of Flanders and raw silk account for the remaining.
3 Comprised of small quantities of Paris, coloured, nobs, raw and slewe silk.
4 Spanish, Bruge, slewed and black silks.

merchants trading with Spain, which was 'exceedingly hurtful and dangerous'.[20]

The forensic analysis of the customs data sheds much further light on the extent and significance of Ireland's economic integration in this period. Looking first at Ireland's exports to England, it is clear that even at the beginning of the century, Irish merchants were dynamic participants in emerging continental markets. In 1500, for example, the Portuguese 'discovered' dyewood trees in Brazil, which produced a highly valued bright crimson dye, until then obtained only from India, Malaya and Sri Lanka. Two years later, King Manuel awarded a monopoly of the brazilwood trade to a consortium of Lisbon merchants, who immediately began felling trees and exporting the dye to Europe. The immediacy of the Portuguese exploitation of this new resource is evident in the Bristol accounts. In 1503, 9,500 lbs of 'New World' brazilwood was exported to Bristol by two Portuguese merchants. Notably, however, there was no time-lag between the 'discovery' and exploitation of brazilwood and its introduction to Ireland. In the same year, it appeared as a re-export to Ireland, when four merchants each imported 10 lbs of the dye, presumably to test the market. There appears to have been a growing market for the luxury dye. In the 1540s, imports grew to an average of 312 lbs per annum and by 1600, this had multiplied threefold, to 952 lbs. Much more significant, however, is the fact that even at the earliest stage in the trade, Irish merchants were capitalising on the re-export of brazilwood. In 1503, 80 lbs (worth £4), was re-exported from Ireland to Bristol by William White.[21]

This re-export of luxury continental goods to England was of significant economic importance to Irish merchants. In 1594, for example, Dominic Copinger, a Kinsale merchant, exported a significant quantity of expensive Spanish hat wool to Bristol.[22] This amounted to four times the total value of Irish wool exports to Bristol that year, and indicates the well-developed Irish mercantile contacts with Spain for commercial raw materials and also that Irish merchants were capitalising on new fashions, in this case the late sixteenth-century fashion for felt hats in England. Also found among Irish exports in 1594 were marmalade and wine, which comprised almost a quarter of the total value of Irish exports. Likewise, in 1600, Seville oil comprised 11 per cent of Irish exports to Bristol.

It is probable, then, that Irish merchants were being increasingly drawn towards European markets towards the end of the century. This may be because English access to continental commodities was limited due to war. Pauline Croft has noted that Hiberno-Spanish trade flourished during wartime.[23] She argues that while the Irish had always been distinguished from the English merchants in Spain and Portugal, and before the war had enjoyed separate and often greater privileges, their Catholicism and hostility towards the English ensured that they continued to be allowed to freely enter Spanish ports after 1585. Indeed, such was the freedom of Irish merchants in Spain that large numbers of English ships tried to pass themselves off as Irish in order to gain access to Spanish trade.[24]

## Cosmopolitan Consumption

Irish integration in European trade had an impact and influence on what was eaten in Irish towns and also on how it was cooked and consumed. Surprisingly, examining the nature of Irish imports from Bristol sheds some light on Ireland's continental trade and indicates, rather unexpectedly, the extent to which Ireland relied on European rather than English trade for everyday essentials. This is well illustrated by trends in the importation of knives from Bristol in the sixteenth century.

A large variety and volume of knives were imported to Ireland from Bristol and also from Chester, in this period. In the latter part of the century the range of knives imported diversified further to include continental knives from Germany, France and Flanders. At the same time, as noted earlier, imported knives became increasingly differentiated by variety, price and quality. This trend is of particular significance with regards to cutlery since these were items intended for mass consumption and were not exclusively for the rich.

A number of points can be made about trends in Irish knife imports from England. What is particularly notable is that despite the increasing diversification of knives, there was a major overall decline in the volumes imported to Ireland from Bristol. Imports peaked in 1541/42, when almost 55,000 knives were imported, and then fell steadily from the middle of the century until by 1600/01, they had fallen to around 10,000 knives, a decrease of 81 per cent of the peak volume. Knives were an essential commodity and since there is no evidence that they were manufactured in Ireland or that there was any increase in the volumes imported on other routes – such as the Dublin–Chester route – it seems likely that Irish merchants were obtaining increasing volumes via direct continental trade. Certainly in the 1540s, when Irish imports from England peaked, English merchants were still relying predominantly on foreign imports to meet consumer demand. Thirsk has noted that foreign knives filled the windows of fashionable shops in London and that 'even the poorest country folk insisted on buying foreign makes'.[25] As such, it is likely that a large proportion of the knives imported to Ireland from Bristol in the first half of the century were re-exported from the continent. From the 1560s, however, significant developments occurred in the English knife industry. By the early seventeenth century, English and, in particular, London knives had advanced significantly in reputation.[26] In 1615, Edmund Howes, in his revision of Stow's *Annales*, wrote that 'there were made in diverse parts of this kingdom many coarse and uncomely knives', whereas 'at this day the best and finest knives in the world are made in London'.[27]

The question, then, is why Irish knife imports from England declined at a time when English domestic production increased in volume and improved in quality. It may be that for reasons of conservatism or snobbishness Irish consumers continued to favour 'foreign' varieties of knife over new domestically produced English versions. It may also be that European and, in particular, Dutch knives were still more competitively priced than English versions. Either way, the falling importation of this essential commodity from England is evidence of Irish reliance on continental imports for everyday items.[28] This trend is of both economic and cultural significance, indicating again the well-developed trade networks of Irish merchants and raising questions, in this case, about the extent to which such foreign, rather than English, connections influenced Irish food tastes, table manners and perceptions of 'civility' during this period.[29] The knife was, after all, the principal eating utensil in this period and played a key role in dining rituals as well as being an important means of displaying refinement and elegance at the table.

While it is impossible to quantify continental imports, the examination of other records suggests a buoyant trade in luxury foodstuffs. Examinations of the High Court of Admiralty, for example, show the types of commodities sourced and laded directly on the continent. In 1596, Cork merchants in Middleburg bought brass pans, hand irons, damask and diaper (used to make table cloths), earthen fruit plates and Dutch ovens.[30] The ovens were presumably an earlier version of the cast iron Dutch ovens produced from the seventeenth century, which were used for cooking with an open fire and which had a huge market in England and in the American colonies. They consisted of a heavy pot with a lid. Food was placed inside the pot, the lid was put on, and hot coals were heaped over it. The ovens were used for baking bread, biscuits and cakes, as well as for roasting meat and other cooking. Their presence indicates Irish engagement with developing food technology in the sixteenth century.

Perhaps the best example of Ireland's direct access to exotic luxury goods in this period is the intended shipment of 1,400 lbs of sucket and marmalade to Waterford on the *Mary of Waterford* in 1592.[31] Suckets, or candied fruit, were a very fashionable foodstuff among the middling sort and the upper classes in the late sixteenth century, but are not found among Irish imports from Bristol in any of the accounts examined before or after 1594, when just 4 lbs was imported. Based on the customs accounts alone, it would appear that there was little market for such luxuries in Ireland. In reality, it appears that Irish merchants were catering to the sweet teeth of their customers via direct trade with Portugal. Such exotic and fashionable treats were, most likely, available in Irish towns well before they turned up among imports from England.

## Comparative Tastes

While it is clear then that we need to look beyond England to develop a full picture of the factors that influenced Irish desire to consume new foods in this period, there is much to be gained from the comparative study of changing consumption patterns in Britain and Ireland, and perhaps the best representative import commodity in this regard is hopped beer. Comparing the dietary components of England and Ireland during the sixteenth and seventeenth centuries, Clarkson and Crawford noted that beer was in short supply in Ireland. Army victuallers apparently found it difficult to buy hopped beer in Ireland and English soldiers disliked the local un-hopped ale. In 1580, for example, Lord Burghley instructed a Bristol merchant, John Bland, to ship 2,000 lbs of hops to Ireland, telling him that there was the 'gravest want of hopps in that country'.[32]

Contemporary evidence also suggests that the taste for hopped beer was slow to develop in Ireland. Fynes Moryson noted that the

Table 5. Volume of hops imported, 1503–1601 (lbs).

| Year | Volume (lb) | Year | Volume (lb) |
|---|---|---|---|
| 1503/4 | 36 | 1550/1 | 8470 |
| 1516/17 | 1498 | 1563/4 | 952 |
| 1525/6 | 2931 | 1575/6 | 8981 |
| 1541/2 | 5908 | 1594/5 | 34300 |
| 1542/3 | 1890 | 1600/1 | 31892 |
| 1545/6 | 14220 | | |

Source: Flavin and Jones, *Bristol's Trade*, pp. 1–942.

'common sort' of 'English-Irish' drink was 'not English beer made of malt and hops, but ale'.[33] While he noted that the Gaelic Irish did not have:

> ... any beer made of malt and hops, nor yet any ale – no, not the chief Lords, except it be very rarely; but they drink milk like nectar, warmed with a stone first cast into the fire, or else beef broth mingled with milk.[34]

Nevertheless, Gaelic Irish literature suggests that beer was consumed by the Gaelic Irish elite and was even considered to have restorative properties. In 1592, the *Annals of the Four Masters* records the escape of Aodh Ruadh and Art and Éinrí Ó Néill from prison in Dublin and their subsequent adventures in the Wicklow mountains, where:

> Fiagh immediately ordered some of his servants of trust to go to them, taking with them a man to carry food, and another to carry ale and beer ... As to Hugh, after some time, he retained the beer; and, after drinking it, his energies were restored.[35]

Clearly then, by the 1590s, the taste for hopped beer had to some extent penetrated even the most 'secure and impregnable' parts of Gaelic Ireland.[36] Certainly, as shown in Table 5, the customs records show a massive increase in the importation of hops towards the end of the century, with enough imported in 1594 to brew approximately 720,000 gallons of beer.[37] It is likely, however, that its use was restricted to the upper classes initially. Luke Gernon, writing *c.*1620, noted a distinction between the drinking habits of different classes in Ireland, remarking that in the 'baser cabins … you shall have no drink but bonyclabber, milk that is sowred to the condition of buttermilk'. In the castles, however, 'you shall be presented with all the drinkes in the house, first the ordinary beere, then aquavitae, then sacke, then olde-ale'.[38] Shortages of beer then were probably due to differing regional economies, class preferences and taste.

This actually compares well to trends in England in this period. Wilson has noted that apart from London, beer was 'fairly slow to gain ground in many parts of Britain' and that in the north and west the bitter flavour of the hops was not liked. By the Elizabethan period well hopped beer, while bitter, continued as the favourite drink in the south of England, the sweeter less hopped ale was 'long preferred' in the north and in Scotland.[39] Andrew Boorde shows the early ambivalence to beer in England. According to him, ale was a 'natural drink' for an Englishman, while beer was 'a natural drink for a Dutchman … for the drynke is a colde drynke: yet it doth make a man fat, & doth inflate the bely, as it doth appere by the dutche mens faces & belyes'.[40] Even by the eighteenth century, local differences in drinking were legion in England. In Yorkshire in the 1790s foreign visitors were struck by the fact that they saw ale everywhere but little beer, while in Cheshire and Gloucestershire, cider was the everyday drink.[41]

Taken in the context of comparative trends in England then, the social and economic significance of certain time lags in the adoption of new tastes in Ireland should not be overstated. Army victuallers in places as diverse as Cornwall and Lincolnshire would have had as much trouble sourcing beer in this period as those in parts of Ireland. Dietary regimes were regionally distinctive in the early modern period and provincial tastes were often slow to give way to new fashions.

These comparative trends are of wider significance, particularly given the contested nature of culture and society in sixteenth-century Ireland. An ongoing aspect of this research is the examination of tastes and practices in the British Isles to establish how consumption functioned in the integration or differentiation of societies. Examining the variety of exotic spices imported to southeast Ireland from Bristol from the middle of the century, for example, reveals a similar range of spices to those being used by the citizens of Southampton in the same period, a town that, due to its trading position, was very much up-to-date with current food fashions. Taken further, it seems that to a certain extent food choices were influenced in a similar way by the liturgical calendar in England and Ireland. Dried fruit, for example, was a particular feature of the Lenten diet in England and certainly the importation of raisins into Ireland shows a distinct seasonal trend with imports peaking in each year before the beginning of the Lenten season. This is interesting as it suggest similar links between food and religious identity in parts of Ireland and England.

In addition, it has been found that both elite and, to some extent, non-elite trends in the use of domestic utensils evolved along similar lines in England and Ireland. New types of items such as beer tankards, porringers, drinking glasses and specific styles of salt cellars seem to have entered elite English and Irish use around the same time. There also appear to have been similarities in the interpretation of such objects and certain rituals of the table were shared in Irish and English societies. The qualitative evidence indicates, for example, that both the English and Irish used specific drinking vessels for different types of drink. Likewise, drinking vessels and cutlery served similar symbolic functions in both societies; they displayed the wealth and social status of their owners; had ritual ceremonial functions, were given as items of commemoration, such as at weddings and christenings; and were regular items of bequest.[42]

## Planting Manners

Thus far, this chapter has focused on apparent similarities in the pre-Plantation dietary practices of England and Ireland. That is not to say, however, that the arrival of English and Scots planters had no impact on consumption practices in Ireland, and there is much to be learned from examining the pace at which certain domestic items were adopted by the populace. Perhaps the most interesting item in this regard is the humble or 'common' wooden trencher, the rapid acceptance of which raises interesting questions about consumption choices and social identity in Ireland.

It has been widely noted that in the sixteenth century, the use of wooden trenchers became increasingly common on English tables.[43]

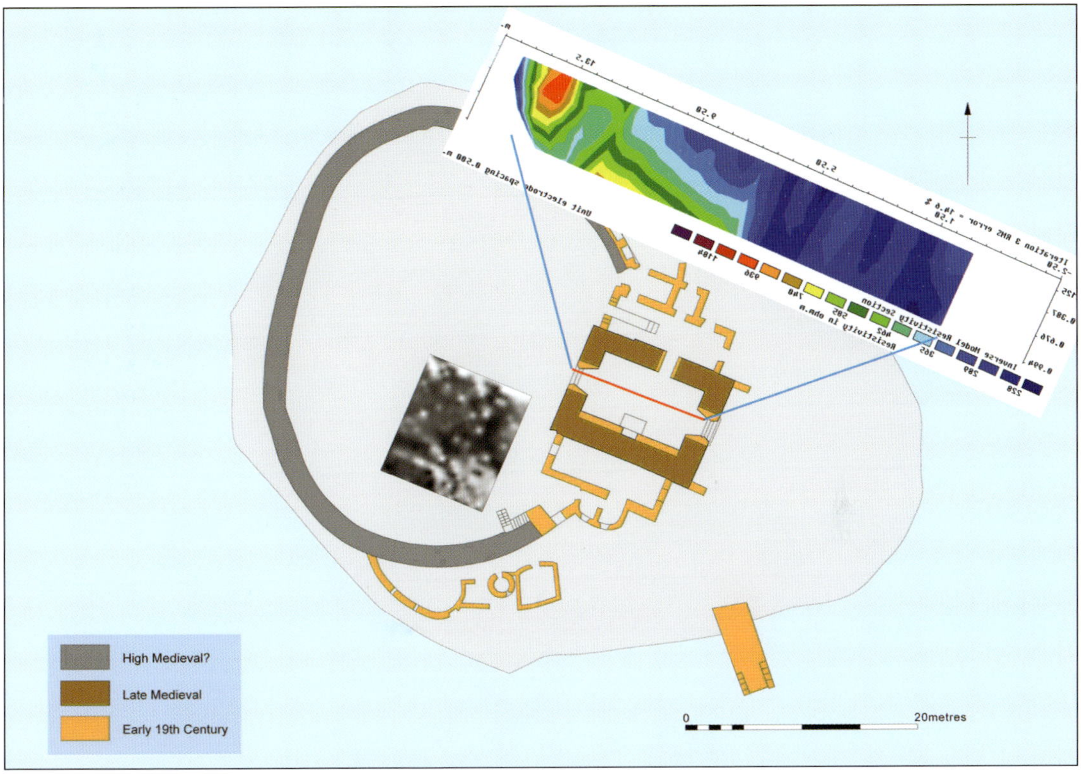

Finan 1. Geophysical survey on the Rock of Lough Cé (image: author).

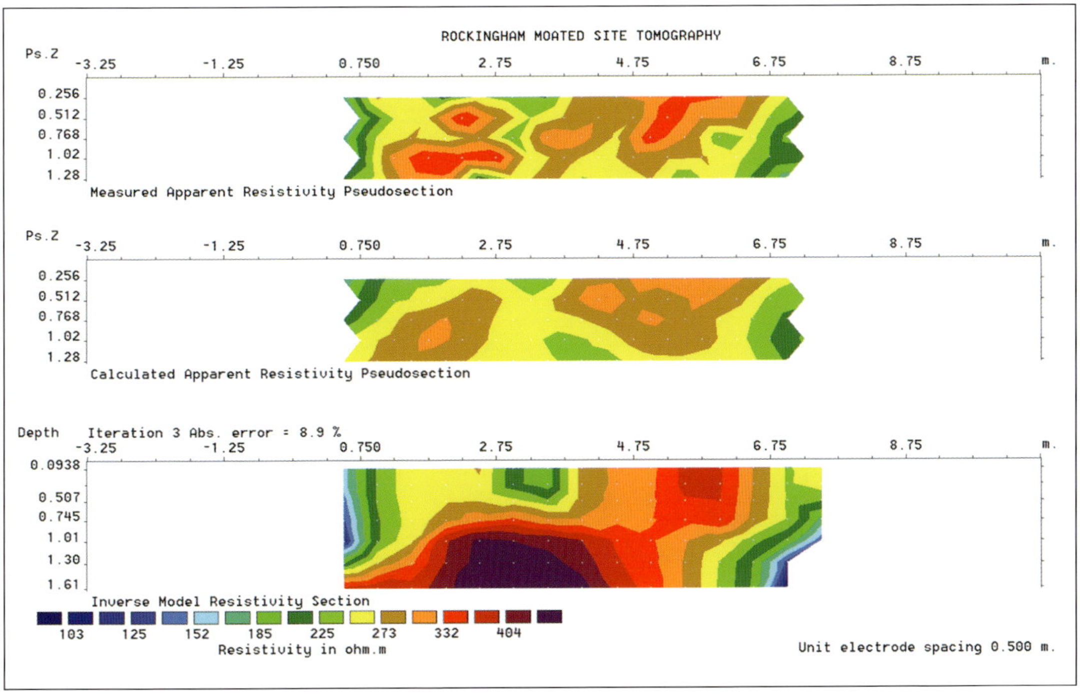

Finan 3. Resistivity tomography of Rockingham moated site (image: author).

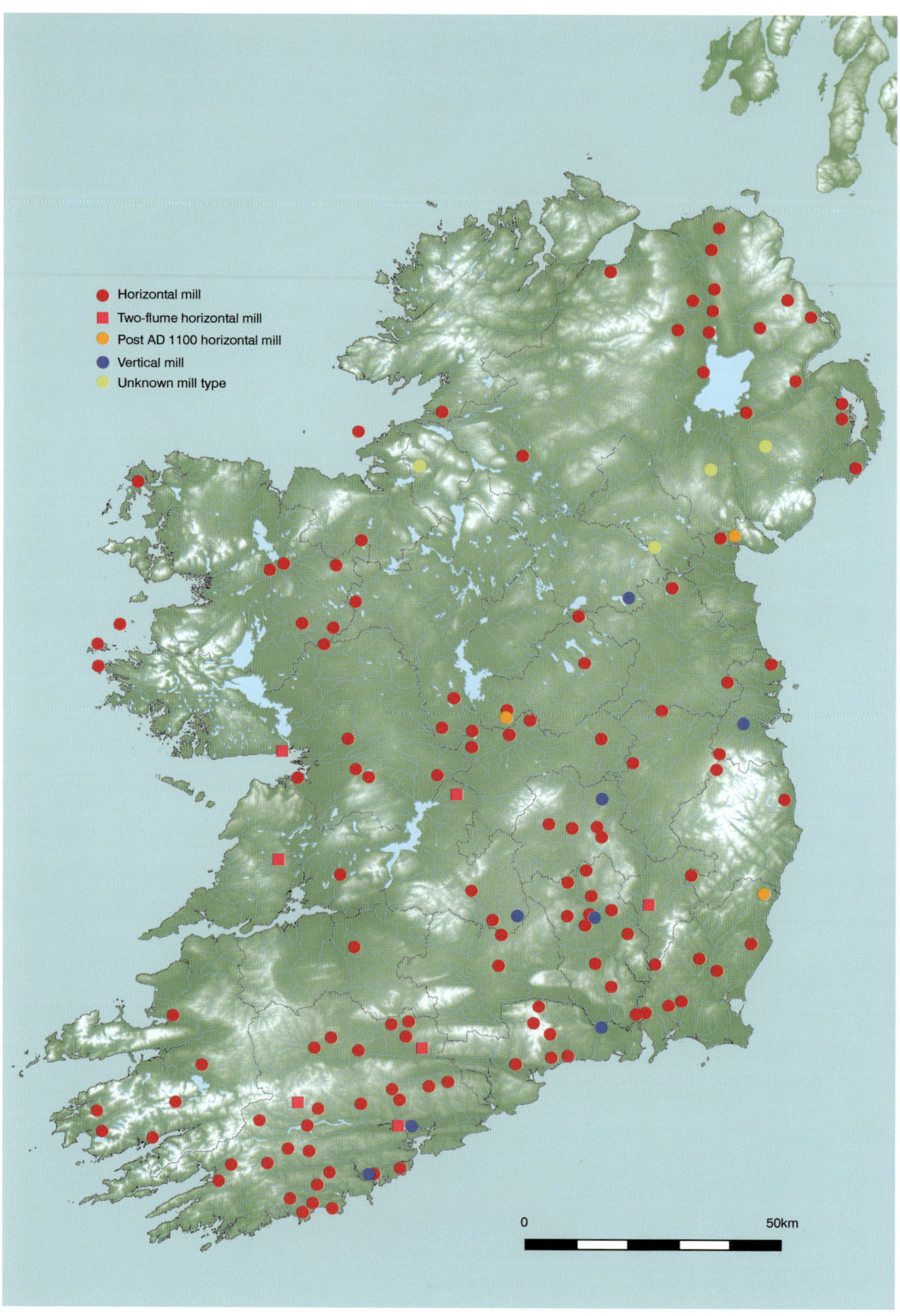


Rynne 3. Distribution of pre-Norman water-powered mill sites in Ireland (image: author).

Rynne 4. Distribution of excavated Anglo-Norman watermills and millstones in Ireland (image: author).

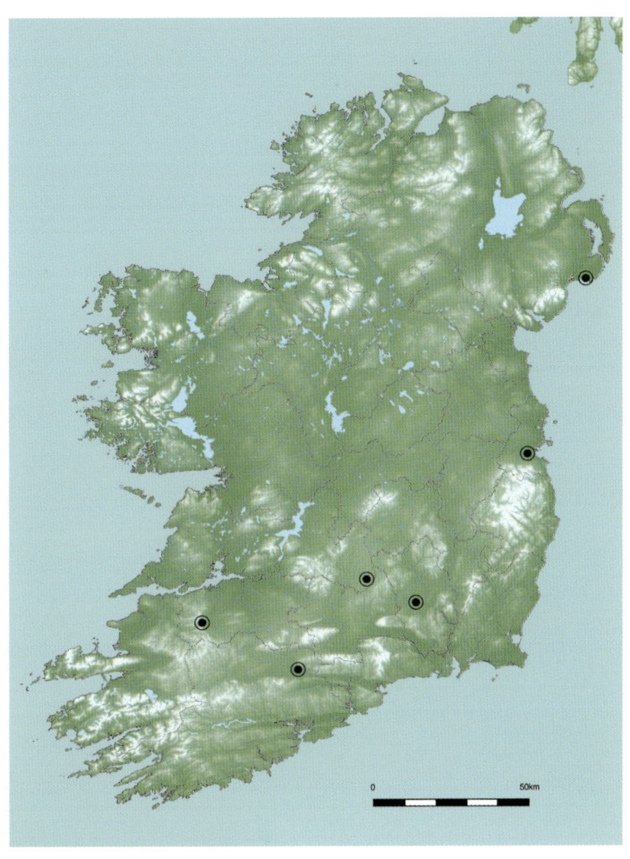


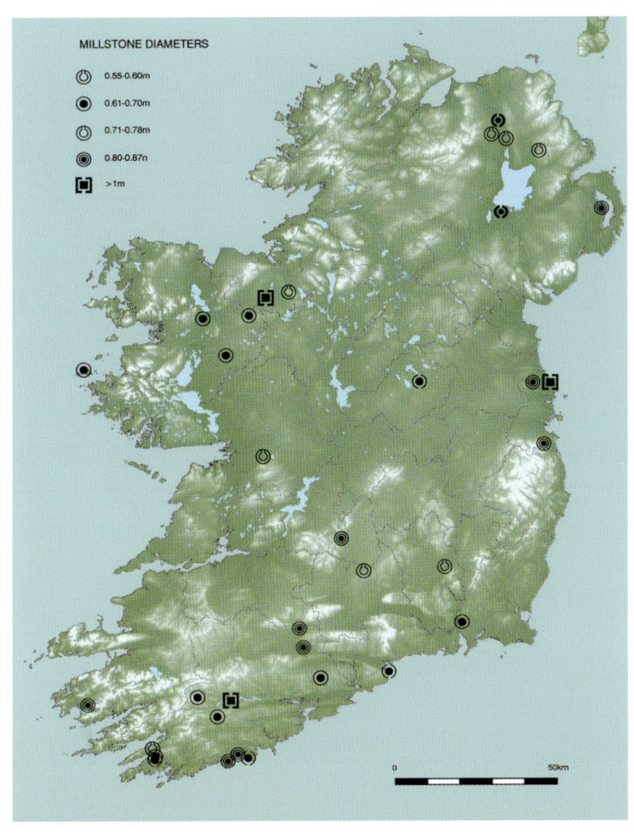


Rynne 5. Distribution of pre-Norman water-powered millstones in Ireland, by diameter (image: author).

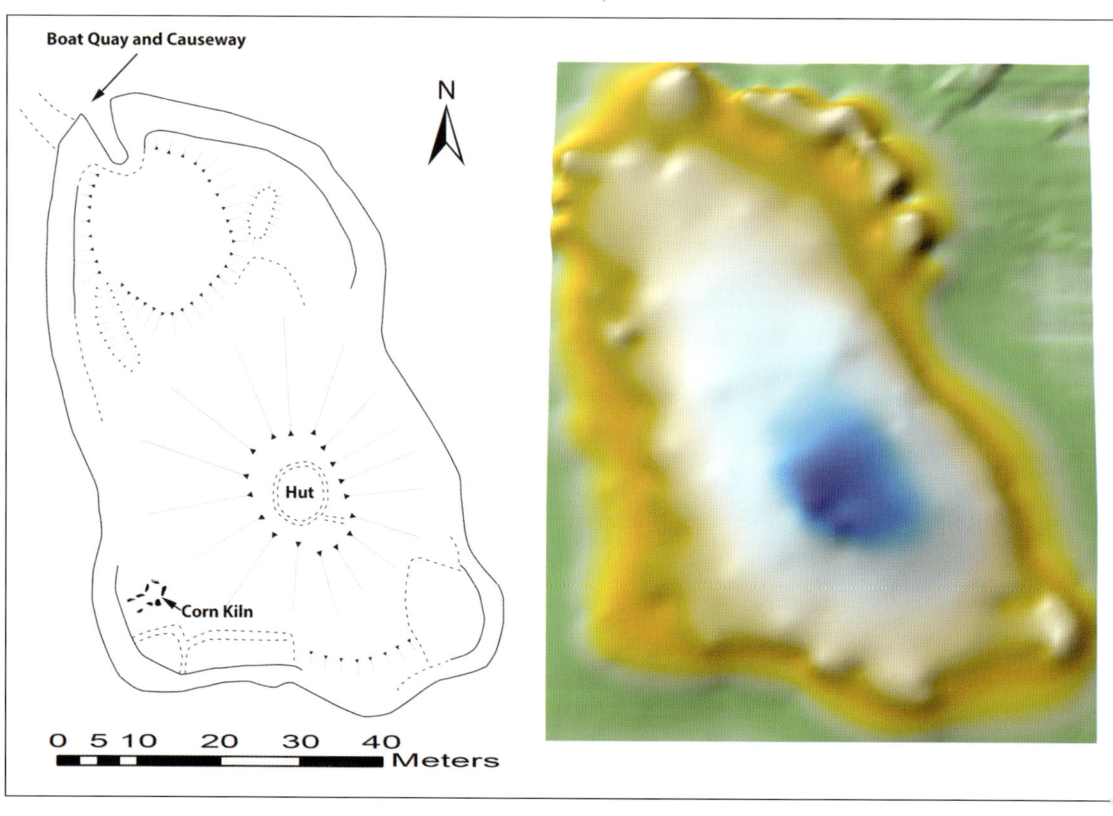


Naessens 3. Plan and Digital Surface Model of Oileán an Chaca, Lough Skannive (Carna/Cashel *crannóg*)(image: author).

Breen 1. Detail of Norden's late sixteenth-century map of Ulster showing the principal Gaelic lordship territories (TNA, MPF, 31–1).

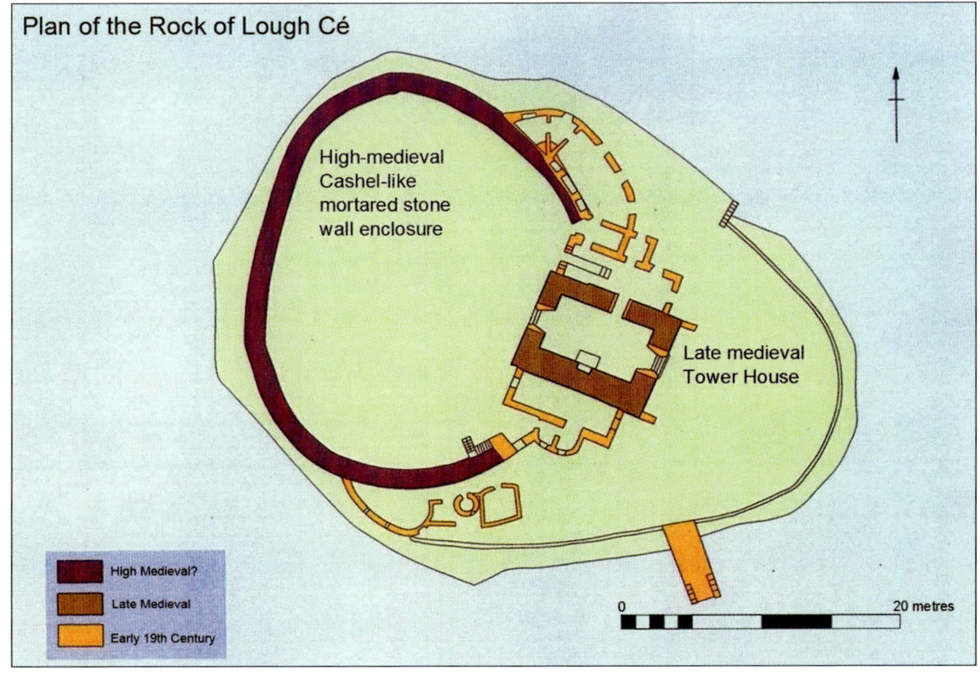


O'Conor 2. Phased plan of the Rock of Lough Cé, County Roscommon (after O'Conor, Brady, Connon and Fidalgo-Romo, 2010), showing its evolution over time.

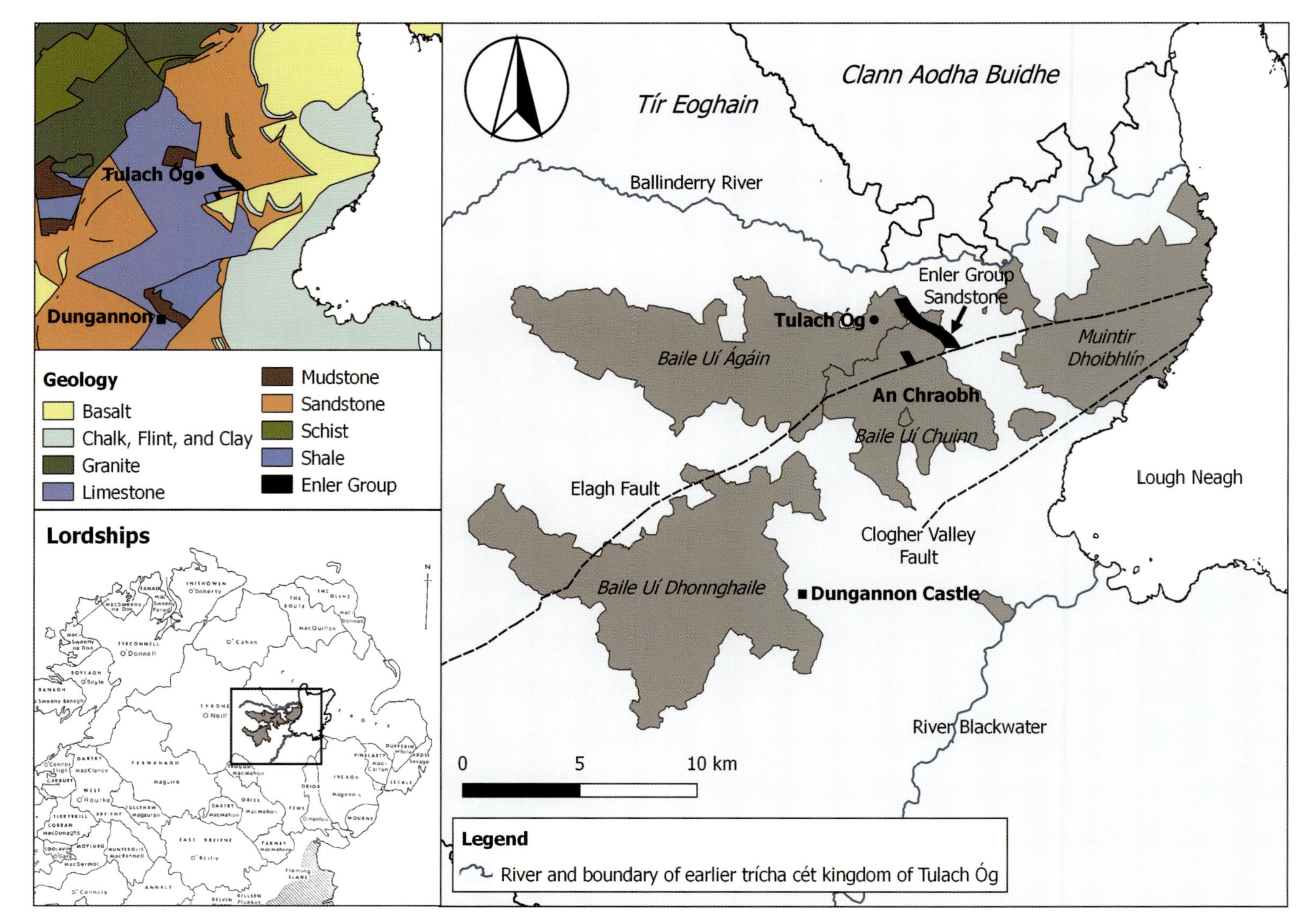
Tulach Óg
Dungannon
Geology
Basalt
Chalk, Flint, and Clay
Granite
Limestone
Mudstone
Sandstone
Schist
Shale
Enler Group
Lordships
Tír Eoghain
Clann Aodha Buidhe
Ballinderry River
Enler Group Sandstone
Tulach Óg
Baile Uí Ágáin
Muintir Dhoibhlín
An Chraobh
Baile Uí Chuinn
Elagh Fault
Lough Neagh
Clogher Valley Fault
Baile Uí Dhonnghaile
Dungannon Castle
River Blackwater
0
5
10 km
Legend
River and boundary of earlier trícha cét kingdom of Tulach Óg

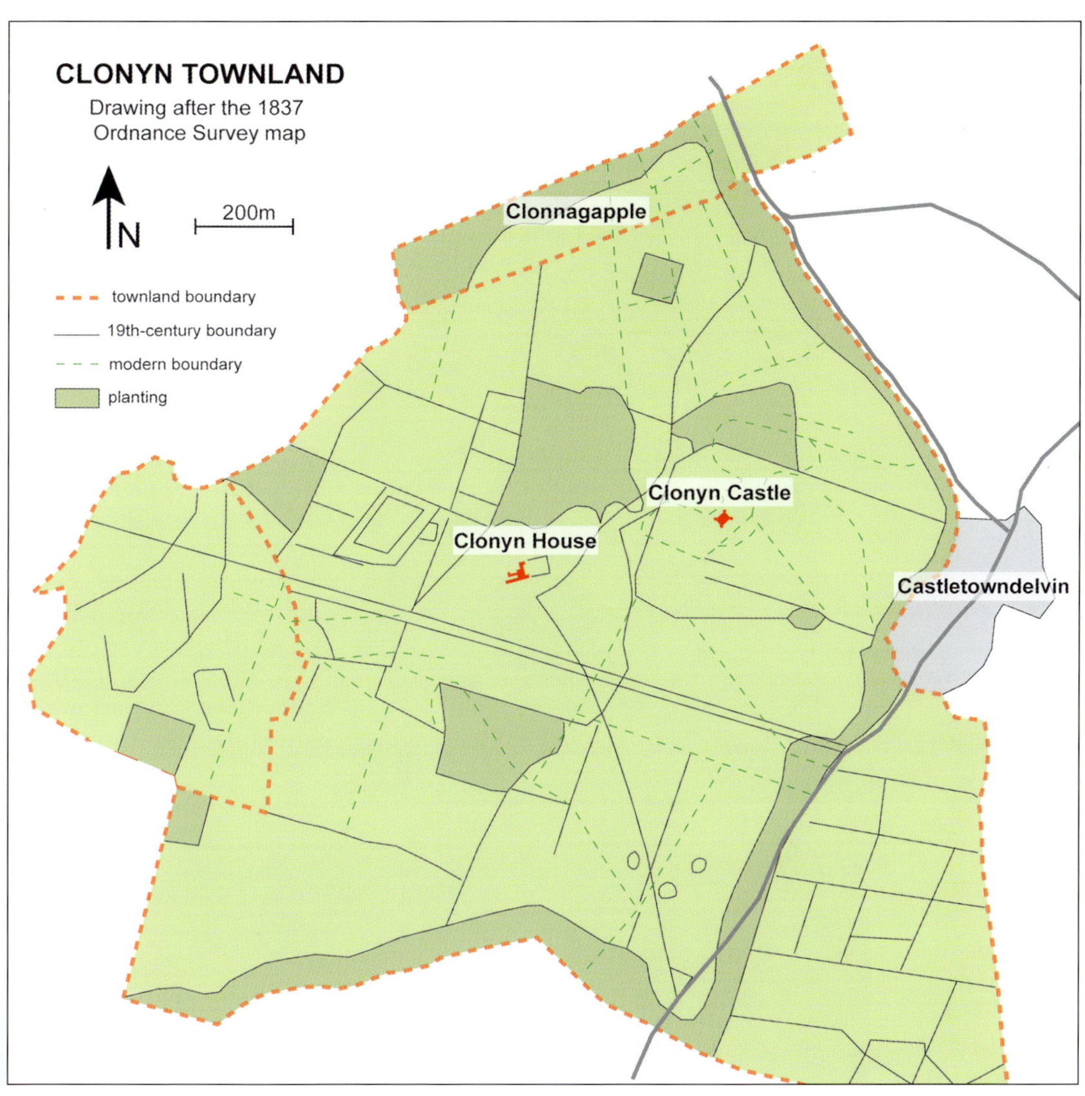


Campbell 6. Drawing of Clonyn demesne after the first-edition Ordnance Survey map (1837) (image: author).

FitzPatrick 2. *(left)* The *baile biataigh* holdings of the Ó hÁgain, Ó Doibhlin, Ó Cuinn and Ó Donnghaile on the *lucht tighe* lands of Ó Néill, which extended between the Ballinderry River and the River Blackwater. The inset highlights the varied bedrock geology along the Elagh and Clogher Faults, and the Enler Group of sandstones that may have been the source of the Ó Néill stone chair at Tulach Óg (drawing: Eve Campbell).

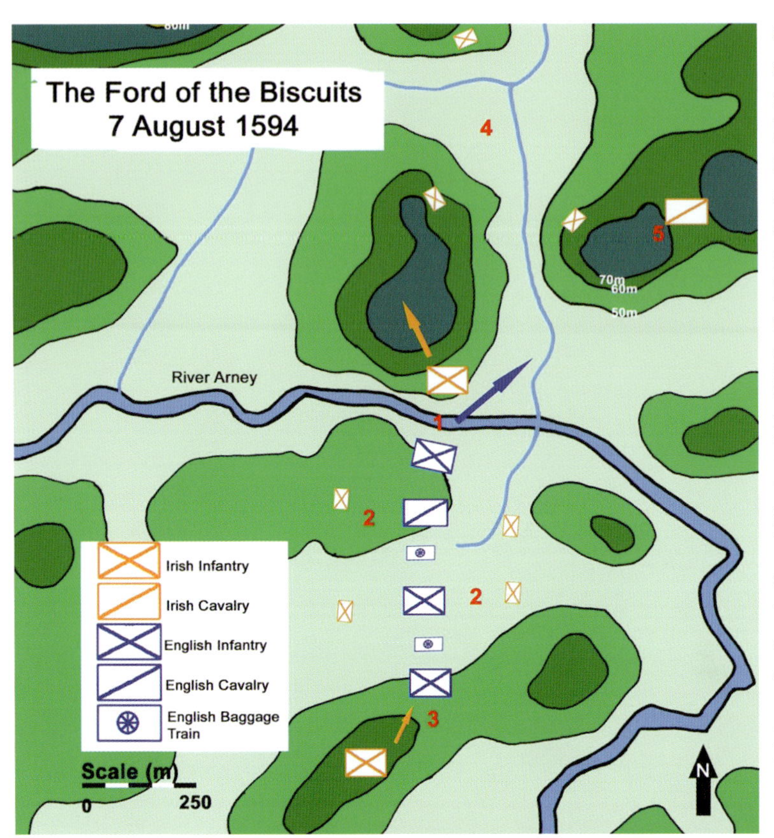


O'Neill 2. (1) The Irish shot engaged and halted the head of the column, but were eventually forced to give ground due to a determined English pike charge. (2) Irish shot forced in the English loose shot and disordered the pikemen. (3) Irish pikemen and Scots charged into the disordered rear forcing it into the main battle and then the van. (4) The English army made it to low ground. Under fire from the surrounding heights, the English attacked south but were forced to cross further upstream. (5) Incongruously, the Irish horse played no part in the battle (image: author).

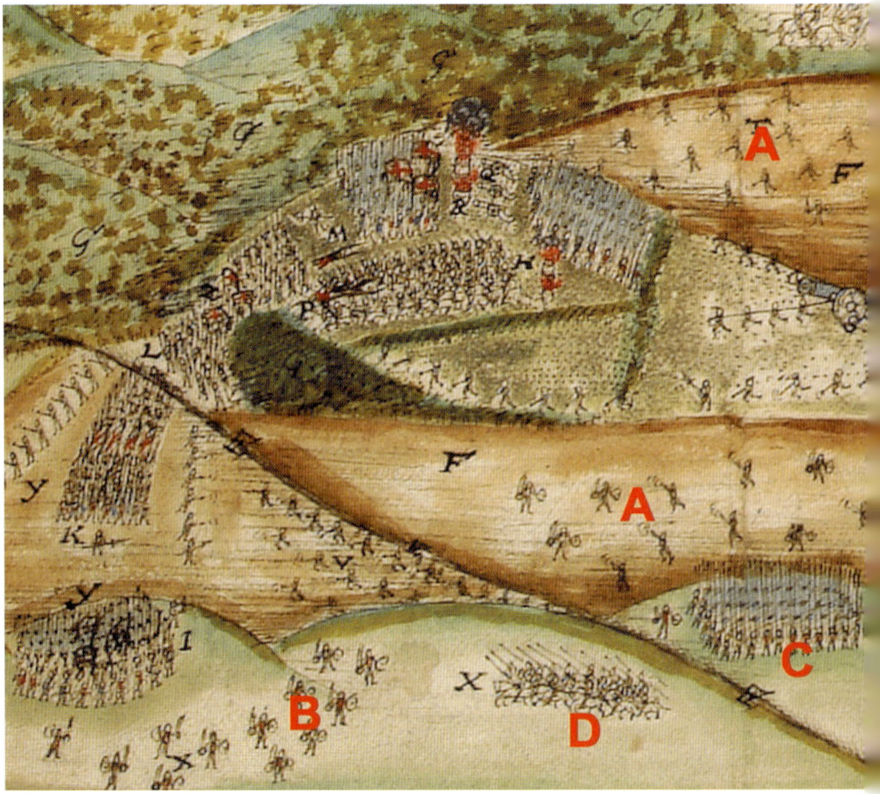

O'Neill 3. An extract from a drawing of the Battle of the Yellow Ford, 14 August 1598. (A) Irish shot supported by targeteers. (B) Irish targeteers surround the lead English regiment. (C) Irish pike. (D) Irish horse (TCD, MS 1209/35).

Before about 1500, a trencher was a piece of stale bread, cut into a square shape by a carver, and used as a plate.[44] Diners filled their trenchers with food from large platters placed in the centre of the table. By the end of the fifteenth century, particularly in northern Europe, trenchers had evolved into more durable utensils, made predominantly of wood or pewter.[45] It is unclear why the trencher became more commonly used in this period. The trend may perhaps relate to the rising price of food, which made the daily use of bread trenchers unfeasible, even among the upper classes. Wooden trenchers also had other practical functions. Pewter was an easily damaged metal and wooden trenchers may have been placed in the bottom of pewter dishes, in order to protect them.

The customs accounts suggest that from 1594/95, wooden trenchers became an item of mass consumption in Ireland. In that year a total of 21,576 trenchers were imported from Bristol to the southeast, with a similar figure noted in 1600/01. The vast majority of these were described as 'common' trenchers, which were made from a hardwood such as beech or sycamore that was 'non-porous, did not transmit its taste or odour to the food and turned well'.[46] While small volumes of trenchers were found in the accounts from 1545, the massive increase in the use of this item of tableware may well have been stimulated by the arrival of settlers with the Munster Plantation. Certainly, in 1630, Planters intending to go to the New England colonies were advised by Thomas Graves – an 'Engynere' who had gone there the previous year – to bring with them 'such needefull things as every Planter doth or ought to provide to go to New-England', including victuals, apparel, arms, tools, spices and various household utensils, in particular, 'wooden platters, dishes, spoons'.[47]

As noted earlier, the Munster Plantation added only around 3,000–4,000 settlers to the population of the region, and the fact that such large numbers of trenchers were imported, and continued to be after the collapse of the enterprise, suggests that demand for this particular type of wooden dish developed quickly in Ireland. The reasons are, of course, unclear, but it would be rash indeed to suggest that diners in Ireland chose to use these in order to emulate the more civilised practices of the New English settlers. Emulation is a very slippery concept and it is clear from the evidence in the accounts that many items, including things like knitted stockings and drinking glasses, even if novel, desirable and indicative of 'civility', were very slow to find a market in Ireland, most likely because in practical terms they did not meet the needs of Irish society.[48] Trenchers, on the other hand, were practical, useful, durable and cheap and would, no doubt, have appealed to a wide range of people.

Whatever the motivations for their acceptance, their use is of wider social and cultural significance since it suggests engagement with evolving rituals of the table in this period, including the growing individuality in eating practices; the movement away from communal dining; the standardisation and formalisation of eating habits; perhaps even what Norbert Elias identified as increasing 'thresholds of shame and repugnance' and 'self-restraint' relating to the 'civilising process'.[49] Certainly, along with trenchers, there is other evidence of a growing interest in table manners and etiquette in Ireland during this period, the importation of children's manners books and bibs, for example. 'Small books for children' – most likely referring to the popular late medieval *The Little Children's Little Book*, and also Francis Seager's manual, *The School of Virtue* – were imported from at least 1576, and perhaps before.[50] Both of these contained specific advice to children regarding table manners and food hygiene and included detailed instructions on hand-washing before and after eating.

## Objects and Ideologies

The evidence considered so far suggests that the material culture of food and the rituals of eating and drinking may have served a role in the integration of societies and maybe even in mediating social boundaries between natives and newcomers in Ireland. The final object chosen for discussion here, the infant feeding bottle, represents, on the other hand, how food and eating practices could distinguish and alienate communities.

From the late century there is a notable growth in the importation to Ireland of objects for children: bibs, hats and books, for example. Infant feeding bottles, however, are a particularly interesting import, because the history of infant nutrition in Ireland and England is entirely obscure. It has been noted that there was little mention of artificial feeding in the medieval period, babies being suckled by either their mother or a wet nurse for up to the first three years of life. Furthermore, as late as Tudor times, specially designed feeding bottles were not known in England: cow's milk was considered unsuitable for infants, partly due to superstition and partly because of the 'high degree of contamination in an unsanitary world'.[51]

Evidence suggests, however, that hand-feeding utensils were indeed known and used in sixteenth-century Europe, and by this period, specially designed upright 'sucking-bottles', similar to the one depicted in the woodcut in Fig. 7, were introduced in Germany and Italy. These bottles, which Haskell and Lewis noted, sometimes made their way to England from the continent and co-existed with another feeding device used from the sixteenth to eighteenth centuries in Europe: the pap-boat, which was used to feed pap, a semi-solid alternative or supplementary substance to milk.[52]

In 1594, thirty-six of these 'sucking bottles' were imported to Ireland by William Halley, a Limerick merchant.[53] Obviously, it would be unwise to reach any conclusions about the significance of such a small quantity of utensils. It is, for example, likely that as in Europe, some form of hand-feeding utensil was already known in Ireland before the sixteenth century. An alternative to breastfeeding would have been required for children who were ill, or born with congenital deformities (such as cleft lip and palate) and who therefore could not breastfeed effectively. Nevertheless, the chronology of imports is highly suggestive. These are not found among imports in any account apart from 1594/95, and then only in a small quantity. As such, their use is very likely to have been a function of new settlement due to the Munster Plantation.

This trend may well reflect broader social and cultural ideologies during the period. *The Boke of Children,* written by Thomas Phayre *c.*1545, suggests that by this date it was still fashionable and acceptable, for those who could afford to do so, to hire a wet nurse to feed their infants. Phayre preferred that mothers should nurse their own infants, 'Whyche yf it maye be done it shal be most commendable and holsome' but if not, 'ye must be well advised intaking of a nource, not of vil complexion and of worse maners, but such as shal be sobre, honeste and chaste [sic], well fourmed, amyable and chearefull, so that she may accustome the infant unto myrth, no dronkard, vycyous nor sluttyshe, for suche corrupteth the nature of the childe'.[54]

7. Woodcut illustration showing a child feeding from a bottle, Regiment der Gesundtheit (1549), Wellcome Library.

The growing disapproval of the practice of wet-nursing is clear in *The Treatise on Children*, published in 1577 by the Italian Omnibonus Ferrarious, who noted that infants would 'savour of the nature of the person by whom they are suckled'.[55] Likewise, the French physician Jacques Guillemeau, whose book on the nursing of children was published in English in 1612, suggested that the wet nurse should be:

> neither squint-ey'd, lame, nor crump shouldred: she must be one that is healthfull, and not subiect to any disease: the complexion and colour of her bodie, must be liuely, and rosie: she must not be spotted with rednesse, and especially she should not haue red haire: and therefore, such as are of a browne complexion, are held to be best, whose haire is of a chest-nut colour, betweene yellow and blacke.[56]

He also claimed that the nurse may communicate imperfections of her body or her character into the child and he commented on the loss of affection between the mother and the child sent out to be nursed.

It is interesting to note the manifestation of similar ideas in Irish colonial discourse during this period. Discussing the Gaelic Irish practices of fosterage and *gossiprid*, which were seen as 'exceedingly evil and full of mischief in this realm ... For they made strong parties and factions, whereby the great men were enabled to oppress their inferiors and to oppose their equals', Moryson and Good agreed that 'All who have suck'd the same breasts are very kind and loving, and confide more in each other than if they were natural brothers'.[57] According to Spenser, children were like apes that would imitate and 'draw into themselves, together with their suck' the nature and disposition of their nurses. He noted that the child would learn its first speech from the wet nurse and if the speech was Irish, the heart would be Irish.[58]

The choice between breastfeeding, wet-nursing and hand-feeding obviously varied over time and between social classes, depending on complex social and economic conditions, and it would therefore be unwise to draw any conclusions about the significance of a small quantity of infant feeding bottles in Ireland. Nevertheless, the presence of this commodity raises important questions about the decisions facing English parents arriving in Ireland during this period. Given the prevailing cultural ideas regarding the dangers of wet nurses on infant well-being, mothers would perhaps have hesitated to procure a nurse from a race variously described as 'sluttish', 'unclean', 'rude', 'drunken', and 'dull witted'.[59] For those English women unable or unwilling to breastfeed their own infants, the risk of illness or infection from artificial feeding was perhaps deemed preferable to the 'dangerous infections' of employing an Irish nurse.[60] Therefore, while many imported items suggest comparable consumption practices, which perhaps helped to integrate societies, this is an example of how material culture could differentiate social groups in Ireland.

## Conclusion

The analysis of the Bristol customs accounts suggests that southeast Ireland witnessed significant changes in consumption in the late sixteenth century. This demonstrates that whether or not Ireland was as 'backwards' as many contemporaries felt, parts of it were gaining access to the increasingly sophisticated and diversified range of consumer goods produced and traded in England and mainland Europe at this time. Ireland was able to participate in an evolving European consumer culture during this period, even if it was not at the forefront of it. The picture emerging here is not one of a backward colonial economy dependent on England and isolated from wider European developments. Rather, the evidence suggests that the southeast, at least, played an active, independent part in the early expansion of the European Atlantic economy.

Approaching trends in Irish consumption as a reaction to British developments might be a valid concept for studies of the eighteenth century, by which time the island was fully under English rule and integrated into the mercantilist English economy, with any potential for independent economic growth stunted by trade restrictions and competition from English industries. However, it must be borne in mind that conditions, even after the initial waves of Plantation, were very different in the sixteenth century. England, then, was just one of the countries whose tastes and manners influenced changing Irish material culture in this period and new commodities came to Ireland not only via English trade and markets but via well-established and sustained continental networks. In this context emergent Irish attitudes to 'civility' and manners were, no doubt, influenced by continental modes as well as by English modes.

On the other hand, it is also evident that there is much to be learned by comparing aspects of English and Irish diet in this period. Despite claims of the 'barbarous' nature of Irish dietary tastes and practices, evolving trends in Irish consumption in some respects mirrored those of its nearest neighbour. Attitudes to diet in Ireland were shaped by the semi-colonised nature of Irish society and demand was driven by a set of circumstances which included practicality, regionalism and social and political affiliation. In Ireland, the widening world of goods served to integrate communities, mediate social boundaries and differentiate social groups.

Based on this analysis, future studies of Irish material culture in this period, especially those attempting to explore the political and cultural interpretation of this widening world of goods, must widen the frame of reference to consider not the extent to which Irish consumers emulated 'English' practices, but rather how individual regions within the British Isles assimilated and interpreted changing European trends in consumption, and what this suggests about their comparative economies and societies.

These findings are, of course, provisional, but demonstrate the analytical importance of addressing the role of food in Ireland beyond its subsistence value, as well as the importance of acknowledging and addressing Irish social development and its integration with the wider world of goods in this period.

# 12

# Retreat from the borough: Castle and community in the early modern Nugent lordship

EVE CAMPBELL

## Introduction

Writing in the 1680s, the Westmeath gentleman Sir Henry Piers described Castletowndelvin, the medieval seat of the Nugent barons of Delvin, and later Earls of Westmeath, as: 'A large oblong square castle, high raised ... a structure speaking of ancient magnificence ... now wholly waste, without roof or inhabitants'.[1] The ruined castle had already become a subject of antiquarian discourse, another gutted edifice scarring the late seventeenth-century Irish landscape.[2] Like many other ruins, the building had suffered during the upheavals of the 1640s, when it was burnt by the kinsmen of the Baron of Delvin.[3] However, its abandonment as the principal residence of the Nugent barons had happened decades earlier, in the latter half of the sixteenth century when they relocated to a residence in the adjoining townland of Clonyn.

In the medieval world, the castle was a locus of becoming and belonging par excellence. It was a place where social relationships and identities were forged, reiterated and renegotiated. The physical presence and prominence of a castle in the landscape signified claim and attachment to place, but more than that, it signified belonging to dynasty, to family, to parish, to lordship. Within its walls relationships were made and re-made, between lords and followers, retainers, tenants, women, men, servants and children. It was a place of rule, power, submission, defiance, justice, hospitality and display.[4] In that context, the Nugents' abandonment of Castletowndelvin as their primary residence in the second half of the sixteenth century had profound implications for their sense of belonging and for what they were becoming. The abandonment of the castle for a new, more secluded dwelling at Clonyn speaks to the shifting dynamic between lordship and community, the reframing of nobility[5] and the renegotiation of vertical social ties. This chapter explores how these changes were expressed materially in building and landscape at the Nugent *caput* of Castletowndelvin.

## The Nugents of Delvin: a marcher lordship

The core territory of the Nugent lordship was located in the easternmost part of what is now County Westmeath and focused on the settlement of Castletowndelvin at the centre of the barony of Delvin. The barony was coterminous with the kingdom of Delbhna, which in the mid-twelfth century was held by the Ó Findalláin kings of Delbhna Mór.[6] During the fifteenth and sixteenth centuries, the territory of the sept's senior branch had expanded substantially to the north and west, acquiring land in adjacent baronies and counties. At the time of the Down Survey, the principal landholding of the second Nugent earl of Westmeath lay in the baronies of Delvin and Fore. He held additional lands in counties Longford, Leitrim, Cavan, Roscommon and Dublin. Much of this land was gained from the mid-fifteenth century as Crown grants and later as dissolved monastic land. In 1476 Christopher Nugent, eleventh Baron of Delvin, was granted the manors of Fore and Belgard and by 1557 Richard, the thirteenth baron, was given the manors in fee.[7] The sept benefitted from the dissolution of the monastic houses. They acquired the lands of the Benedictine monastery of Fore and the Cistercian monastery at Granard, County Longford.[8] In 1641, Richard Nugent held 40,346 Plantation acres, placing him among the largest landholders in Ireland.[9] His widow, Jane Plunkett, reckoned that the 'proffitts of their mannors Lands & meanes hereditantes' was worth £3,000 sterling per annum.[10] In addition to the large swath of land held by the senior branch of the family, cadet branches held much of the barony of Corkerry as well as land in Delvin, Fore, Moygashel and Magheradernon.[11]

The Nugent family came to Ireland during the twelfth-century Anglo-Norman settlement. Guilbert de Nogent, the family's progenitor, was among the knights in the service of Hugh de Lacy. De Lacy granted de Nogent the barony of Delvin,[12] 'which the O Finilians held in the time of the Irish' for the service of five knights to be rendered to the manor of Trim.[13] Upon de Nogent's marriage to de Lacy's sister Rosa, de Lacy gave the couple the barony of Delvin and built a motte castle for them at what would become Castletowndelvin.[14]

It was there, on the northwest marches of the Pale, that the Nugents forged their patrimony.[15] Physically and culturally, they lay between the 'civilised' English Pale to the east and the Gaelic Ó Raghallaigh and Ó Fearghail lordships of south Ulster to the north. Echoing other marcher septs, the senior branch of the Nugents negotiated a pragmatic position between the 'two nations'.[16] As members of the titular peerage, the family were close to the heart of politics and society in the English lordship and looked to England as their cultural home.[17] Yet, like other Anglo-Norman septs, they were bicultural, borrowing from Gaelic customs and patronising the Gaelic arts.[18]

The Nugents of Delvin were patrons of the Ó Cobhthaigh poets.[19] *Duanaire na Nuinseannach*, housed in the National Library of Ireland,[20] is late sixteenth century in date and features poems dating from the thirteenth century onwards. The compilation features two poems by Muircheartach Ó Cobhthaigh commissioned by Christopher Nugent (fourteenth baron).[21] The late sixteenth-century date is of note, particularly in the context of a letter from Christopher Nugent, the fourteenth Lord Delvin, to Lord Burghley in 1591, relating that much of his time was spent in 'books and building'.[22]

The question of Gaelicisation of the Old English has proved historiographically contentious. Ellis has warned against reading all departures from 'English civility' as Gaelicisation, arguing that they can also be seen as a response to marcher conditions.[23] While some septs, like the Burkes in Connacht, especially Clann Uilliam Íochtair (Lower or Mayo Burkes), embraced Gaelic titles, inauguration and election practices, others were more conservative, arguably adopting or 'tolerating' certain customs to 'cut a figure in Gaelic society as a means of strengthening colonial dominance'.[24] The Nugents arguably belonged to the latter category.[25] In the later medieval and early modern period, for example, the senior line's choice of marriage partners came exclusively from fellow Old English families, particularly the daughters of the FitzGeralds and the Viscounts Gormanstown.[26]

Throughout the fifteenth century, members of the Nugent sept served as justices of the peace for Delvin and adjacent baronies.[27] As well as participating in local administration, members of the sept served in the highest offices in the lordship. Richard Nugent, tenth Baron of Delvin, had a distinguished career, serving as sheriff and seneschal of Meath in 1424 and 1452 and as Deputy Lieutenant of the Lordship of Ireland *c.*1448–49.[28] The barons' engagement in politics was not restricted to the English lordship. Throughout the later medieval period, they and their followers partook in the internecine feuding and raiding that characterised those parts of the island outside the Crown's dominion.[29]

## CASTLETOWNDELVIN, THE NUGENT *CAPUT*

The *caput* of the Nugent lordship was at Castletowndelvin in the townland of the same name, at the centre of the barony of Delvin, County Westmeath. Long before the incursion of Hugh de Lacy and his followers into the kingdom of Midhe, Delvin was marked as an important place in the landscape. It was the site of a pre-twelfth-century Ó Findalláin stronghold, which was probably appropriated by de Lacy's men as the site of the earth and timber castle built at the site in the 1180s as part of the process of subinfeudation.[30]

### *Delvin Castle*

By the fifteenth century the earth and timber castle was superseded by an edifice of stone (Fig. 1).[31] Both McNeill and O'Keeffe attribute a fifteenth-century date to the castle. The presence of wicker centring on the corner towers and punch-dressed architectural detail support this date. A construction date sometime in the fifteenth century makes sense in the context of the Nugent re-assumption of the title

1. View of Delvin castle looking north. The northeast half of the castle has been truncated and is the site of a historic market house. Note the later windows on the ground floor from the period when the castle served as a prison (image: author).

of Baron of Delvin in the 1380s.[32] The likely builder of the castle was Richard Nugent, tenth Baron of Delvin. Richard was long-lived, serving numerous roles in local government, as well as being deputy lieutenant in the 1440s as noted above. After his death in 1475, the Annals of Ulster eulogised him as 'an eminent leader and a man who was the best in charity and humanity and who was best in knowledge of every art that was of the Foreigners of Ireland in his

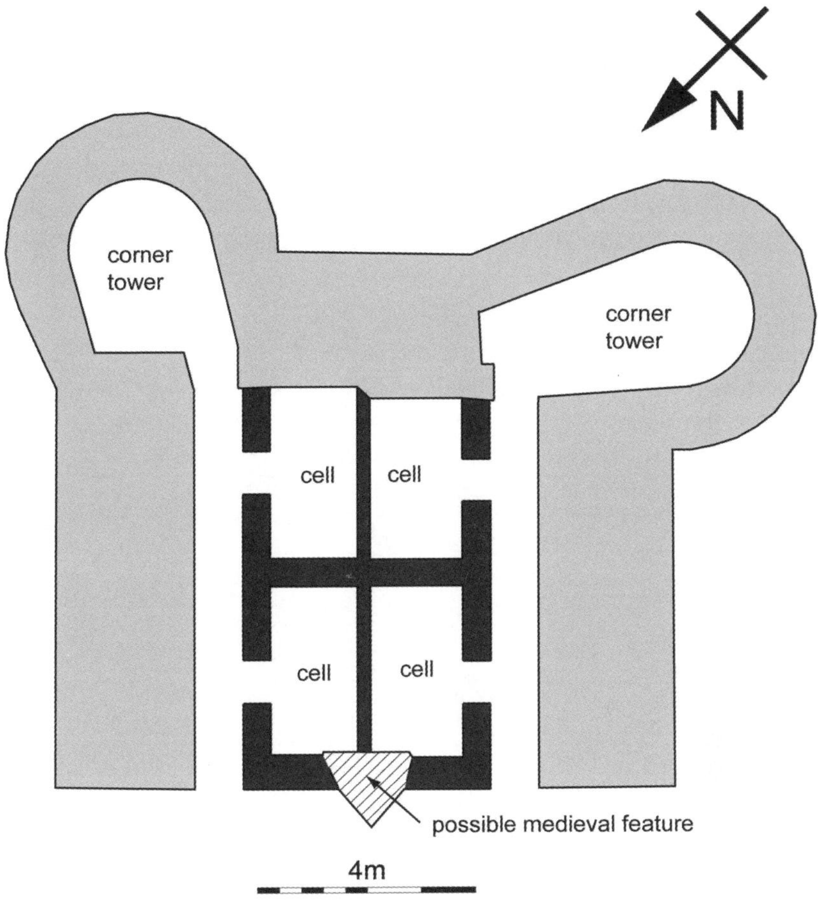


2. Floor plan of Delvin castle showing the original outline and the later inserted prison cells (image: author).

time'.[33] Richard's castle comprised a rectangular masonry structure (6.7m wide internally) with corner drum-towers (Fig. 2). It was built west of the motte and aligned northeast–southwest in the direction of the main street (Fig. 4). Delvin castle is now only partially extant, its northern extent having been truncated by a nineteenth-century market house. It survives to a length of *c.*6.8m southeast–northwest, but was originally *c.*10–12m long. The original doorway was in the destroyed northern half of the castle. Some indication of its original form can be garnered from Piers' late seventeenth-century account of the building. He described the castle as 'a large oblong square castle, high raised, having at each corner a large round tower'.[34]

3. Photograph of the interior of the castle looking southwest, and showing the upper stories of the building. Note the mural fireplaces (image: author).

The central block of the castle has three stories. The ground floor was sparsely lit, and boasted massively thick walls, some 2.5m wide. This was converted into a prison in the eighteenth or nineteenth century with the insertion of four small cells (*c*.3.2m x 1.6m), reached by two corridors, all roofed with brick and stone vaults (Fig. 2). The vaults would appear to be a later insertion, although a diamond-shaped column feature protruding from the northwest wall may be an original feature, perhaps serving as a supporting column for the first floor. Additional windows were cut through the walls of the corner towers as part of this phase of activity (Fig. 1). The first floor of the castle had an amply lit and heated room (Fig. 3). Two fireplaces survive, one in the southwest wall and one in the southeast wall. Four narrow, square-headed, single-light windows remain, two in the southwest wall, one in the southeast wall and one in the northeast wall. Substantial beam holes set into the southwest and northeast walls indicate the ceiling level. An intramural stair in the southeast wall provided communication between the first and second floors, and two door opes in the south and east corners led to the corner towers.

The largest chamber was on the second, and uppermost, floor. As noted above, it was reached via an intra-mural stair in the southeast wall, and two square-headed door-opes in the south and east corners led to rooms in the corner tower. It is probable that the room originally had an additional entrance, perhaps from a stair in one of the demolished towers. The room was well lit, and features four surviving single-light windows featuring a combination of round-headed and square-headed stone-cut frames. There is a small rectangular wall cupboard in the southwest wall. In contrast to the first floor, mural fireplaces are absent from the second-floor chamber. There may have been mural fireplaces in the demolished northwest portion of the castle, but the alternative possibility is that the room was heated by a central hearth. This room had a high ceiling which was open to the gabled roof. The southeast wall is raised to a gable and has a small ogee-headed window, which looked down on the room below from a gallery located in the thickness of the wall.

The combination of open roof space and central hearth strongly suggests that the upper floor served as the castle's hall. The central hearth was an enduring feature of the medieval hall and imbued with immense symbolic significance. Thompson has characterised it as a deliberate archaism designed to conjure an 'immemorial past' of the open fire with all its mythological connotations.[35] The open roof space was connected to the demands of the open hearth, allowing the smoke to rise and leave the building via a smoke-hole or vent, sometimes fitted with a *louver*.[36] The central hearth and open roof were two architectural elements prominent in late medieval Irish castle halls. In his in-depth study of social space in Irish tower houses,[37] Sherlock has identified them as 'critical elements of hall design'.[38] If the room was a hall, then perhaps the east and west towers served as the buttery and the pantry in line with typical English arrangements.[39]

In addition to the presence of these features, the location of the room on the uppermost floor of Delvin castle further supports its identification as a hall. In England, the hall tended to be on the ground floor, largely for safety reasons connected with the open hearth.[40] In contrast, in Ireland there was a strong propensity among tower house builders to place the hall on the highest floor of the buildings. Sherlock attributes this tendency to the desire to maintain the iconic open roof space and the central hearth.[41] Safety concerns were usually addressed by the presence of a stone vault below the hall, although this was not always the case.[42] In other cases the hall was built adjacent to the castle, often being constructed from cob or other perishable materials.

The hall was perhaps the defining feature of the architecture of medieval Christendom.[43] As an architectural form, it was identified with tradition and ancient custom.[44] In this context it is especially relevant that McNeill notes that the castle, while built in the fifteenth century, has stylistic affinities with thirteenth-century buildings.[45] In his book *Castles in Ireland*, McNeill discusses the building alongside hall houses, a castle type that is more usually dated to before the first half of the fourteenth century.[46] Delvin does have affinity with such buildings, namely its scale, horizontality and lack of an original vault. It also bears resemblance to a group of thirteenth-century buildings referred to by Leask as 'towered keeps', owing to their form of a rectangular block with three-quarter drum towers at each corner.[47] These affinities suggest deliberate anachronism on the part of the castle's patrons. The citing of older architectural forms in the fifteenth-century castle indicates the desire of the Nugent barons of Delvin to express the antiquity of their family, and their long-held claim to their territory.

The castle comprised one aspect of the seigneurial landscape of the Nugent *caput*, the residential, administrative and defensive focus of the lordship. The castle was not set apart from the broader manorial landscape, but was at its heart.[48] The stone edifice that Nugent built at Delvin nestled between the original motte castle and the medieval parish church. The settlement was on a regionally important crossroads of the routes from Ardee to Mullingar and from Drogheda to Longford.

### *The parish church*

By at least the end of the thirteenth century, the settlement had a parish church (Fig. 4).[49] St Mary's church at Delvin was assessed at twelve marks for the purposes of the 1302 Papal taxation, while its attendant vicarage was valued at six marks.[50] The extant church incorporates much later medieval fabric.[51] The western facade contains the remains of a blocked-in two-light, round-headed window and a similar single-light window. The windows have a number of parallels in County Meath, where O'Neill has dated the style to the very late fifteenth or early sixteenth century.[52] In 1600, the church was among those reported to be 'in repair' by Thomas Jones, Protestant bishop of Meath.[53] In 1602 Christopher Nugent, fourteenth Baron of Delvin, stipulated in his will that he be buried 'in the Sowthe side of or la:[dy's] Churche in Castletowne of Delvin where I leave a Chappell and a Tumbbe for myself my wyfe and or posteritie'.[54] In 1680 Piers noted that Delvin church was 'fair and large' and in 'good repair' and that 'divine service according to the rites of the church of England ... [was] constantly celebrated'.[55] The medieval church was twice augmented in the nineteenth century – in 1810 and again in 1860 – with the addition of a transept designed by Joseph Wellard.[56]

### *The manorial village or borough*

As the name 'Castletowndelvin' suggests, the castle was surrounded by a settlement, the antecedent of the modern town of Delvin (Fig. 4). This nucleated settlement that grew up around the castles at Castletowndelvin can, at least, be described as a manorial village,[57] which may have had borough status. There is no surviving evidence that the settlement was granted a borough charter, or a fair or market patent prior to 1715.[58] However, as Otway-Ruthven has pointed out, the survival of borough charters is poor, and prior to the fifteenth century 'not only the greatest lords with semi-regal powers ... but even the sub-tenants of their sub-tenants freely created boroughs' without Crown authority.[59] The site was listed among six 'market towns' in Westmeath in 1598, and the Down Survey noted that Delvin was 'formerly a market town'.[60]

The layout of the settlement is suggestive of borough planning. It has a linear street plan reminiscent of other Anglo-Norman foundations (Fig. 4).[61] The settlement is divided into two distinct parts, with the manorial core of castle and parish church at its south end and the dwellings of the inhabitants to the north. The manorial core occupied the highest point in the settlement, sitting atop a gentle hill, emphasising its prominence in the landscape. As the settlement developed, the manorial core expanded south from

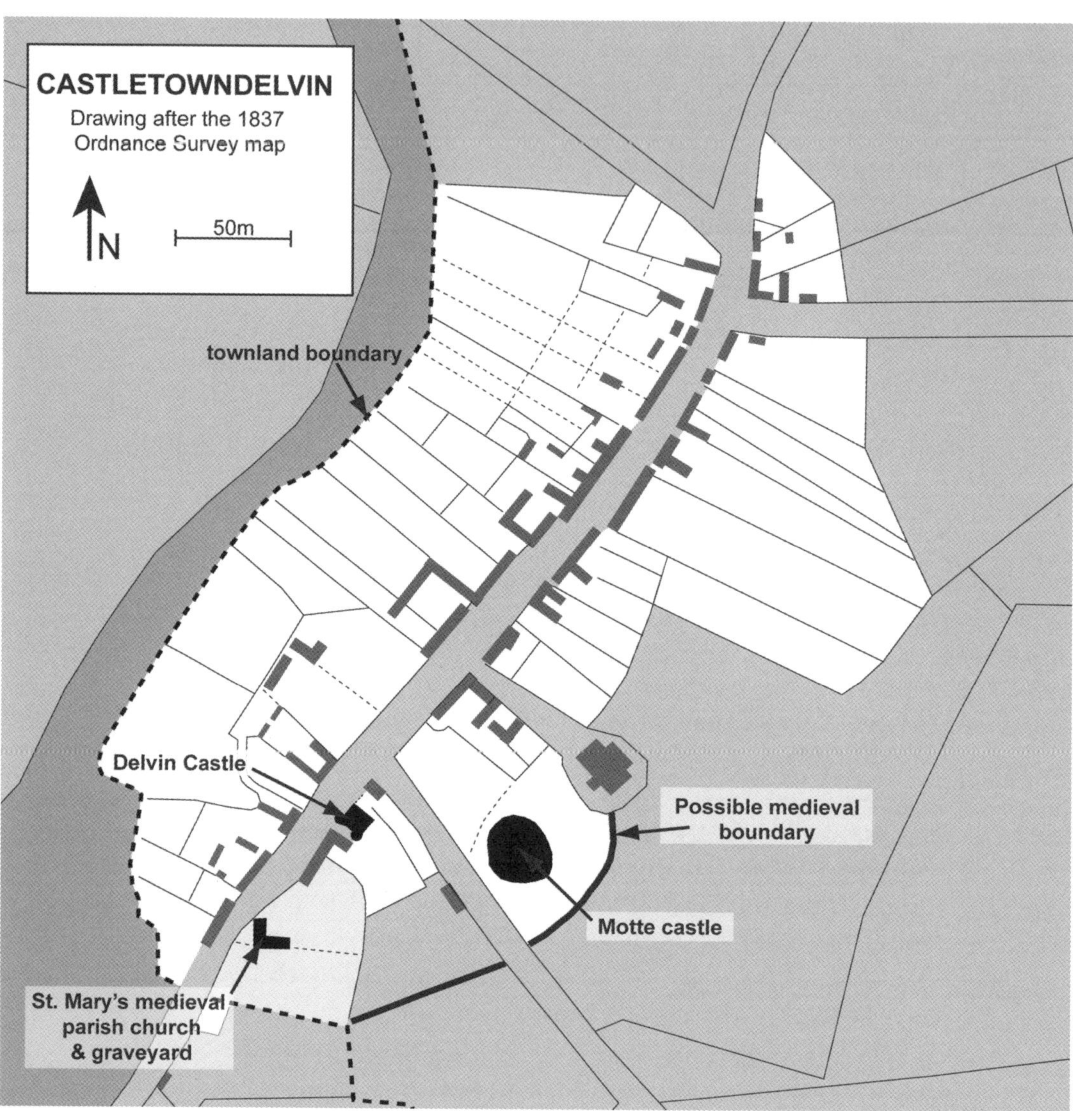


4. Drawing of Castletowndelvin after the first-edition Ordnance Survey map (1837)(image: author).

the original earth and timber castle, with the construction of the parish church and the masonry castle. There is a suggestion of a (now destroyed) boundary around this core area on the first-edition six-inch Ordnance Survey map (Fig. 4). The line extends from the east side of the timber castle southward to the parish church. It is expected that this area originally held a suite of buildings associated with the castle constructed from perishable materials.[62]

The north of the settlement would appear to have comprised the dwellings of the settlement's inhabitants. Both the first-edition six-inch and the twenty-five-inch Ordnance Survey maps depict long, narrow strips of enclosed land, which may be the remains of burgage plots, flanking the main street. It is difficult to know how significant the manorial village or borough of Castletowndelvin was. Its fate was bound up with its vulnerable position in the marches of the Englishry, which left it prone to the cyclical raiding that characterised Gaelic and marcher society. The chronicles note a series of raids *(creacha)* on the territory of the 'Barún Delbna'. In 1461, the Méig Eochagáin and the Ledwiches (Ledúsachaibh) raided the baron's territory as far as the River Inny (in the west of County Westmeath).[63] The town was burned in 1475 by Ó Domhnaill on a foray into Meath to extract an *éiric* (compensation) for his father who 'fell by the foreigners'. The chronicles record that 'much of Meath was destroyed by him and the castle-town of Delvin (*baile caislein Delbna*) was burned'.[64] How the settlement was impacted by the great mid-fourteenth-century plague is undocumented, but that it may have suffered from the sporadic episodes of disease that visited Ireland in the fifteenth century is suggested by the death of Christopher, eleventh Baron of Delvin in 1478, during a great plague (*pláigh mhór*).[65]

The fiants are largely silent about residents of the settlement with the exception of one Richard Nugent, who was listed as of Delvin in 1544–45.[66] In 1603, an inquisition post mortem into Christopher (fourteenth baron) Nugent's lands recorded the settlement as containing 'a castle, 8 messuages, 4 gardens, and 120a. land'.[67] The Down Survey described the settlement as containing 'diverse small cabins'.[68] In 1659, the village returned a population of eighty, one of the highest in the county, following only the boroughs of Mullingar (334) and Kilbeggan (ninety-nine) and the villages of Multifarnham (eighty-one) and Ballymore (eighty-two).[69]

For travellers who passed through the town on the road from Ardee to Athlone, or for the retainers, tenants and kin of the barons, who lived and worked in or around Delvin, the castle stood as a powerful reminder of Nugent lordship. The building itself was a physical expression of that lordship and, along with the adjacent parish church of St Mary's, it was the locus in which bonds of lordship were made and re-remade through rituals of hospitality, commensality, patronage, justice and submission.[70] It was there that some of the overlapping communities to which the barons of Delvin belonged, namely those of borough, dynasty, parish and manor, were repeatedly created. Tenants paid dues, poets recited odes, men gathered for military service, seasonal feasts were given, babies were baptised and the dead were buried.[71] It was the architectural backdrop against which the Nugent barons played out their active military and judicial roles within their lordship. The status of the castle as a social and economic nexus was fundamentally changed in the sixteenth century with its abandonment as the residence of the Nugent barons.

## Retreat from the borough

By the close of the sixteenth century, the masonry castle no longer served as the Nugent barons' principal residence. Instead, they had removed to the adjacent townland of Clonyn, which remained the principal family seat into the nineteenth century (Fig. 6). The precise date of this new construction is unclear. The first reference to occupancy at Clonyn is in an inquisition post mortem of Richard Nugent, twelfth Baron of Delvin (d.1537), which was taken at Trim in 1538.[72] The inquisition listed 'a castle and 160a arable worth £8' in the denomination of 'Clonyne'. Clonyn was listed second only to Castletowndelvin (£6) in the inquisition, but significantly, Clonyn was given a greater value.[73] By the turn of the century, it is evident that the Baron of Delvin's primary residence was Clonyn. Writing in 1598, Sir Henry Folliott listed 'Killean' (*recte* Clonyn) as the 'chief Hous' of the baron of Delvin with 'Castle toune delvin' relegated to a secondary possession.[74] The 'castle' at Clonyn was again listed in an inquisition post mortem of Christopher, fifteenth Baron of Delvin in 1603.[75] Westmeath's 'castle' or 'house' at Clonyn was burnt in the 1641 rebellion. By the middle of the seventeenth century, the Clonyn residence was described by the Down Survey as a 'fayre house' complete with a 'fayre orchard … garden [and] grove of trees', indicating that from at least the first half of the seventeenth century the house was surrounded by a landscaped garden.[76]

The form and character of the sixteenth-century building in the townland, when it was built, and how it initially related to the older castle at Delvin are unclear. Unfortunately, the Down Survey parish map of Castletowndelvin does not depict any buildings or associated features, noting only the townland boundaries.[77] Elsewhere in the Nugent lordship, the Down Survey suggests that tower houses were the most common form of elite residence in the mid-seventeenth century. 'Castles' recorded in the Down Survey correlate with sketches of narrow tower-like structures on the maps and with tower houses on the ground. There were a number of other residence forms in the lordship. In Delvin barony, a 'house with a bawn' was noted at Dervotstown and a 'house' at Rosmeade. At Donowire, Multifernan parish, there was a 'very handsome English-like house'.[78] The sketch of James Nugent's 'castle' at Drumcree appears to depict a tower house with an appended house. The original residence at Clonyn may well have been a tower house, but no trace remains.

The earliest identifiable structure in Clonyn townland comprises the remains of an early modern building concealed within the ruins of Clonyn House (Fig. 5).[79] Clonyn House is a multi-period edifice that was occupied until the 1870s, when the newer Clonyn Castle, a Gothic Revival-style pile, was built to replace the older structure.[80] Clonyn House comprises a central block, orientated north–south, which was augmented at either end by the addition of perpendicular wings to the back (west) and a Gothic-style tower to the south. The earliest surviving phase of the house is a five-bay, single-pile, rectangular plan building, *c.*22.5m by *c.*7.5m. No characteristically early modern cut or dressed stonework could be detected in the building.

A carved armorial plaque, set into the later Gothic Revival tower, appended to the southern end of the original structure, is likely to date from this period. The plaque is rectangular and made from limestone, now heavily eroded. The crest of the Nugent arms, a cockatrice surmounted by a crown, is carved in high relief at the top of the plaque. No further inscriptions could be discerned on the plaque, but the Irish Architectural Archive's assessment of the building reported that the date 1680 was engraved on it.[81] If this date is correct it must relate to the Restoration rebuilding of the earlier house after its destruction in 1641. According to the deposition of Jane Plunkett, Countess of Westmeath and widow of the first earl, the destruction wrought in that episode was substantial. She testified

5. Clonyn house, looking southwest. The building is now heavily vegetated (image: author).

that she 'hadd three faire Castles or howses burned & demolished'. Her losses were estimated to be in the region of £20,025.[82] The extant architectural remains support a post-Restoration date for the core of Clonyn House. Loeber has noted the long rectangular form of the building as more characteristic of the later part of the century.[83]

If the earliest phase of Clonyn House post-dates the Restoration, where was the original sixteenth-century structure and what did it look like? The early sixteenth-century reference to a 'castle' in the denomination might suggest an original tower house that was later remodelled, perhaps in the later part of the century. The sole definitive trace of the pre-Cromwellian building is an armorial plaque dated 1639, set into the staircase of the later nineteenth-century Clonyn castle.[84] It is possible that the construction of the later post-Cromwellian house (the current Clonyn house) erased all trace of the earlier burnt-out building. Alternatively, the first Clonyn House may have been located elsewhere in the townland.

## The Clonyn landscape

Clonyn House is set within a designed demesne landscape (Fig. 6) with roots at least as old as the first half of the seventeenth century. The Down Survey noted 'fayre orchard ... garden ... [and] grove of trees' in the townland.[85] As at many Irish and British demesnes, the earlier formal geometric landscape was largely swept away in the late eighteenth century to make room for the creation of open parklands.[86] This later designed landscape was again transformed in the twentieth century with the construction of a golf course. Traces of early modern landscape features can, however, be identified at Clonyn using a combination of the first-edition six-inch OS map and aerial photography. Characteristic of pre-Brownian demesne landscapes, the earlier phase comprises a series of avenues, enclosures, *bosquets* and gardens laid out on a common grid aligned east-northeast – west-southwest.

Gardens, orchards and forestry were essential elements of early modern estates; they were at once displays of power, taste and civility as well as essential hubs of production, provisioning the owner's table and local markets.[87] While orchards, gardens and woodlands were all important features of later medieval demesnes,[88] in the early modern period their layout, design and relationship to the castle or house took on new significances. From the late sixteenth century onwards, but particularly towards the latter part of the seventeenth century, there was a tendency for the house and garden to form part of a unified design, arranged on a common geometrical grid.[89] Initially this approach manifested itself in the arrangement of a series of courts or walled, sometimes defended, gardens around the immediate environs of the house. Towards the latter end of the seventeenth century, the designed garden began to expand beyond the confines of walled courts and extended into the landscape, organised around long avenues axially arranged on the house.[90] In Ireland, the Baroque garden has largely been characterised as a post-Restoration feature.[91] Following this broad interpretation, the designed landscape at Clonyn may date to the post-Cromwellian period.

What then of the 'fayre orchard … garden … [and] grove of trees' that the Down Survey noted in the 1650s? Much rests on the extent to which the second earl or his grandson and successor, the fourth earl, remodelled the gardens alongside the construction of Clonyn House, to replace the building that was destroyed in 1641. The mention of 'grove of trees' suggests that the designed landscape had been in existence for some time. Were these trees planted specially, or were they remnants of an older medieval landscape? It is worth noting that by the time of the Down Survey, most woodland in Delvin was to be found adjacent to the developing parks surrounding the residences of the barony's elites. There was a grove of trees at Clonyn and 'diverse ash trees and a wood of staple oakes and other underwood' at Rosmeade. Cavetstown too had a wood of staple oaks with other underwood. Ash trees were also noted at Bracklin and Archerstown.[92]

### *Horses in the landscape*

In addition to gardens, orchards and avenues, appurtenances for horses made a mark on the landscape. In early modern Ireland horses served not just a practical role, as a means of transport or a beast of burden, but they also had agency in the creation and expression of elite identities. For the upper classes, horse riding was a leisure pursuit as well as a mark of distinction. While other sectors of society also rode horses, what set them apart was 'the quality of the horses they rode and the skill they displayed while doing so'.[93] The act of horse riding was itself a metaphor of male aristocratic rule and a demarcation of prosperity and rank.[94]

In England, horses were generally kept in a home close or in a park.[95] Within the park at Clonyn there was ample ground on which horses could be pastured. The presence of a purpose-specific area for grazing or racing horses is suggested by the small townland of Clonnagapple, bordering Clonyn (Fig. 6). This narrow townland is located immediately north of Clonyn and, on the first-edition OS map, part of the townland is included in Clonyn demesne. The place-name was first recorded in 1659 as 'Cloon Capull',[96] a corruption of the Irish *Cluain na gCapall*, meaning 'the pasture or meadow of the horses'.[97] The townland is *c.*1,450m long, *c.*140m wide at its western end and *c.*200m wide at its eastern end. Today, it is bisected into eastern and western portions by the road from Delvin to Castlepollard, and bounded to the north by a wet fosse running parallel to the minor road, and to the south by a stream that flows west into Lough Analla. There are no recorded archaeological monuments in Cloonagapple, but there is a probable *ráth* (*c.*47m in diameter) in the denomination.

## *Clonyn before the Nugent residence*

What was Clonyn's role in the Nugent settlement prior to the construction of the sixteenth-century residence? The placename Clonyn derives from the Irish *An Cluainín*, the little meadow or pasture land.[98] The name element *cluain* indicates land suitable for grazing. It is an element found in several instances in the barony of Delvin, where the underlying carboniferous limestone helped to create rich pasture and meadow lands. Indeed, the Down Survey described the barony as 'being good arable land having good meadow & sheep walks with other pasturable grounds'.[99] It would appear that in the Nugent lordship, as in most cases, the demesne land of the lord lay separate to that of the tenants.[100] The inquisitions *post mortem* of Richard (1538) and Christopher (1603) indicate that Clonyn formed part of the demesne or personal land of the Nugent barons.[101] It may have contained grazing land for horses and other animals.

There is no clear evidence as to how Delvin castle was used once the Nugents abandoned it as a residence. It may have maintained an administrative or judicial function, for example, serving as the venue for the manor court or as a place where tenants paid rents. Its use as a prison in the nineteenth century is interesting in this regard. There is evidence that it was used as a meeting place during 1641. A servant of the Earl of Westmeath, one William Baker, deposed that the castle was used as a meeting place for some of the Earl of Westmeath's kinsmen who were active in the events of 1641.[102]

The removal to Clonyn had profound implications. Unlike Delvin castle, Clonyn was secluded in what developed into a landscape park at a distance from the settlement of Castletowndelvin (Fig. 6). Where the original castle was highly visible and easily accessible, the residence at Clonyn was hidden and removed. This must have had an immense impact on the way in which the broader community would have accessed and interacted with the Nugent residence. No longer did travellers along the Ardee to Athlone road pass by the foot of the Nugent baron's residence. For residents in the borough or those who flocked to the town from the hinterland on market days, the meaning of the castle must have changed. If they wished to visit the baron's house, they now had to make their way a kilometre west of the castle through Clonyn. This literal distancing of themselves from their tenants expressed their altered role and what that implied for their interactions with their tenants, kin and followers. This, in part, may be explained by their increasing prominence in the high politics of the lordship, perhaps helping to forge a sense of belonging that was more rooted in a community of elite Catholics in the Kingdom of Ireland.

## Who built Clonyn?

In order to understand the abandonment of the old castle and the construction of the new house, it is necessary to look at the two most likely protagonists in the move to Clonyn. Richard (1522–1559) and Christopher Nugent (1544–1602), the respective thirteenth and fourteenth barons, both succeeded their predecessors before reaching their majority and consequently were made wards, the former of Thomas Cromwell and the latter of the Earl of Sussex.[103] Both men were educated in England. Richard served Henry VIII as deputy governor (to Kildare) in 1527–28 and as governor in 1534.[104] His patrimony was augmented by the acquisition of dissolved monastic land.

The Nugent patrimony was again extended under Richard's successor, Christopher, with Crown grants of land and monastic leases in Westmeath, Longford and King's County. Christopher entered Cambridge in 1563 aged nineteen.[105] He is remembered for his primer on the Irish language, which he presented to Queen Elizabeth.[106] The 1570s were a tumultuous period for the Palesmen as they attempted to resist the encroachments of a sometimes hostile New English administration and to maintain loyalty to the Crown, from which they held their lands. Delvin's refusal to sign a proclamation against the earl of Desmond, and his leadership in the Pale resistance to the cess in the late 1570s, cast him under suspicion.[107] He was implicated in the Baltinglass rebellion and subsequently imprisoned, spurring an unsuccessful attempt by his brother, William, to secure the baron's freedom by force of arms.[108] After a sojourn in England under the custody of Nicholas Bagenal, Delvin was allowed to return to Ireland in 1585, where he attempted to resume an orderly life at Clonyn. He emerged as an important military commander against the rebels at the outset of the

Nine Years' War, but was forced to submit to Ó Néill in 1600, as his armies marched through Nugent's land. This capitulation confirmed Dublin officials' long-standing distrust of his loyalties and in 1602 he was arrested and imprisoned in Dublin castle. Delvin died in custody in October 1602.[109]

As Fenlon has noted, exposure to architectural innovations in England was one avenue by which Irish nobles gathered ideas for the re-edification of their residences in Ireland.[110] Both Richard and Christopher had been educated in England, where they had been exposed to current architectural discourses and fine examples of Tudor architecture including the substantial refurbishments that Henry VIII had carried out at Hampton Court Palace and his other residences.[111] As noted above, the fourteenth Lord Delvin mentioned in a letter of 1591 that much of his time was spent in 'books and building'.[112]

## Material expressions of nobility

The dwelling at Clonyn and its designed landscape was one expression of nobility by the Nugents of Delvin. Both in the rich furnishing of the house and the deployment of heraldry they underscored the message. Heraldry has its roots in the early twelfth century; it developed from the use of devices as personal or family identifiers by knights in tournament or battle. Gradually, the devices were systemised and became hereditary, out of which emerged official heralds and a King of Arms to oversee the granting of arms. While their origin was martial, arms came to be regarded as evidence of privilege, dignity or nobility, and their use spread beyond the battlefield. The development of heraldry in the lordship of Ireland followed a similar course to the rest of feudal Europe, although it was not until 1552, when Ireland had been declared a kingdom, that a King of Arms was appointed to the polity.[113] In the sixteenth and seventeenth centuries, heraldry constituted 'iconography of hono[u]r' and the 'recognition of gentility'.[114] Its cultivation among older, established nobles like the Nugents served to 'reassure themselves of their innate superiority' over the parvenu elements of the landed classes.[115]

Heraldry could be materialised in a wide variety of contexts. As well as the shields, coats of arms, flags and banners associated with its original military context, it was also displayed on seals, funerary monuments, buildings, glass, textiles and furniture.[116] It found expression in the burgeoning accoutrements of polite living and in the products of newly industrialising crafts: coaches, silverware, glassware and fine textiles.[117] While armorials were a common feature of medieval Gothic architecture, they took on a new significance in the early modern period. Carved stone panels containing coats of arms are found in prominent positions above doorways at a number of late sixteenth- and seventeenth-century houses.[118] Reflective of broader European trends, coats of arms were often accompanied by dates or initials of the builders, a practice which both Mytum and Ronnes have characterised as distinctly 'post-medieval'.[119] In addition to the armorial plaques at Clonyn house, another public display of heraldry by the Earl of Westmeath was at Finnea on the Westmeath–Cavan border, where he and his wife, Jane Plunkett, built a bridge over the River Inny. The limestone plaque depicts the joint arms of Nugent and Plunkett, flanked to the left by a cockatrice and to the right by a pegasus. The heraldic shield is surmounted by an earl's coronet.

Perhaps the most blatant display of heraldry was the heraldic funeral. The institution of the heraldic funeral served to publicly underscore the social position of the deceased and their family in the local and national community. Just as important as the elaborate funeral procession and ceremony was the registering of funeral certificates, which served to detail the social position of the dead in a permanent form.[120] The broader Nugent family are well represented in the folios of the Ulster King of Arms' 'funeral entries' and, unsurprisingly, the most detailed entries refer to the titled members of the family, notably Christopher Nugent (fourteenth baron) and his grandson also Christopher (d.1625).[121] In the case of the latter, the mourners and their servants were listed in the certificate.

The country house was an arena for the display of power and taste, and a locus of conspicuous consumption, one of the discriminating attributes of the early modern nobility.[122] While the detailed inventories that have allowed investigation of the material worlds of the Ormonds and the FitzGeralds do not survive for the Nugents, a number of other sources make mention of material culture.[123] The will of Lady Mary Nugent[124] (d.1610) details dining accoutrements. It included a 'white silver salt' and a 'diaper tablecloth'.[125] Salts were large and elaborate containers, often made from silver, silver gilt or pewter.[126] The Nugent collection of fine plate was augmented in 1620, when a warrant was granted to the port at Chester to allow Lord Delvin to transport £300 worth of gilt and silver plate to Ireland for his own use.[127] The vast bulk of surviving or recorded early seventeenth-century silver in Ireland is in the form of church plate. Of the pre-Cromwellian domestic or household items, spoons are the most numerous, followed by porringers, tankards, goblets, salts and candlesticks.[128] Significantly, most of these items are connected with eating and drinking, underlining the role of commensality in conspicuous consumption and display.

In addition to the accoutrements of fine dining, references to costly items of personal adornment also survive. Lady Mary Nugent's will also listed 'two gold ring', 'a diamond ring', 'two rings', and her daughter-in-law Jane Plunkett included apparel and furniture among the items destroyed or stolen from Clonyn in 1641.[129] As Fenlon's study of early modern household inventories indicates, furniture and soft furnishings accounted for some of the most expensive items in elite seventeenth-century households.[130] Sir Richard Nugent willed his parliamentary robes to his grandson.[131]

## The archaeology of closure

The retreat of the family from Castletowndelvin to Clonyn was a significant move, reflective of broader vertical cleavages in society. The polarisation within society in early modern Ireland was in line with trends outside of the island. Simms, for example, has located the 'transformation of the Gaelic ruling classes' firmly within a European context.[132] One useful paradigm for understanding the shifts is that of the 'withdrawal of the upper classes' proposed by Peter Burke.[133] Burke posits that from *c.*1500 the nobility, clergy, merchants and professionals began to abandon popular culture to the 'lower classes'.

> The nobles [adopted] more 'polished' manners, and a new and more self-conscious style of behaviour modelled on courtesy books ... [they] stopped eating in great halls with their retainers and withdrew into separate dining rooms ... they stopped

> wrestling with their peasants ... [and] learned to speak and write 'correctly' according to formal rules.[134]

This phenomenon was intimately bound up with shifting social relationships. They were backgrounded by a complex bundle of social changes encompassing but not limited to the expansion and centralisation of the state and the attendant redefinition of nobility, the emergence of the relationship of private property, struggles over custom rights, and the reformations (both Protestant and Catholic). Studies of these processes in the English metropole have frequently focused on the battles over custom and the multifaceted enclosure movement, initially referring to the physical enclosure of the landscape, but expanded by Matthew Johnson to encompass a series of interlocking processes of closure and re-ordering manifest in different aspects of material culture from elite and vernacular dwellings to churches and fields.[135] Johnson's notion of closure is part of his archaeology of capitalism, a framework which speaks to one of the enduring questions of the humanities, namely the rise of modernity and the genesis of capitalism. These enclosures, for example, were often premised on dispossession and interpreted by Marx as part of the process of 'primitive accumulation' that was central to the birth of capitalism.[136]

In the case of the Nugents, it is tempting to connect the construction of Clonyn House with swelling incomes derived from late fifteenth- and early sixteenth-century land grants bestowed upon the family. In England, the privatisation of monastic land had helped to fuel the sixteenth-century building boom.[137] In Ireland, this post-dissolution period saw the substantial refurbishment or rebuilding of the residences of a number of Irish magnates and wealthy merchants.[138] The tenth Earl of Ormond substantially remodelled Carrick-on-Shannon castle in the 1560s and 1570s, and appended a mansion house to his chief seat, Kilkenny castle.[139] The mid-sixteenth century witnessed a period of urban rebuilding in cities like Kilkenny and Galway, spearheaded by merchant oligarchs.[140]

Beyond the houses of the great magnates, changes were afoot in the way that tower houses were being used. Sherlock has identified a tendency towards privacy in tower houses, linked to shifts in social relationships, realised through remodelling as well as new building design from the sixteenth century onwards. These changes were largely focused on the hall. Sherlock has identified a tendency whereby the hall is divided into two rooms, with mural fireplaces inserted to replace the central hearth. This pattern of change served to privatise the building, transforming it from a semi-public space to one that was more private.[141]

The relocation and seclusion of elite dwellings, as at Clonyn, is a pattern echoing developments in England, where in the course of the sixteenth and seventeenth centuries certain manor houses were relocated from their manorial villages to an isolated position within the medieval deer park, while elsewhere the deer park was extended to encompass the manor house. In some instances, new parks were created to surround the house, often necessitating the total or partial clearance of existing settlements around the elite residence.[142] Judging from comments by contemporary commentators, the top stratum of Irish landholders were creating parks as part of their estate landscapes by the late sixteenth or early seventeenth century. Miles Symner[143] reported that before the Cromwellian war, the Earls of Ormond, Clanricarde, Thomond, Cork and Sir Robert King were in possession of 'parks and in them fallow deer … all planted within 50 or 60 years'.[144] Fynes Moryson noted 'closed in Parkes' at Maynooth (Earl of Kildare), Munster (Earl of Ormond) and 'the North' by the lord of Belfast.[145] At Portumna, the principal residence was located inside the eastern boundary of the park, which extended west, utilising the marshy callow ground flanking Lough Derg. Thomond's seat, at Bunratty, was described by Dinely as adjoined by a 'very fair park with deer'.[146]

## Conclusion

The removal of the Nugents from the borough and their retreat to the seclusion of Clonyn articulated their changing sense of belonging and reflected shifts in vertical social relationships, as well as reinforcements of those shifts. While they remained close to the heart of their old *caput* they were now at a physical remove from the borough. This process was about the reordering of social relationships, both within the community at Castletowndelvin and within the Nugent lordship. The occupation of the medieval castle was no longer in keeping with what the Nugents of Delvin were becoming. Nobility was no longer expressed through collective rituals conducted in the semi-public arena of the castle with its high-roofed hall. The focus had moved to a more private setting where nobility was materialised through new architectural forms, sumptuous furnishing and chattels. These shifts were bound up with changes afoot at the level of the state. The period witnessed the forging of an elite Irish Catholic identity, as the upper tiers of Gaelic and Old English society closed ranks against a hostile Protestant administration. This refashioning of elite identity was physically expressed in Delvin by the abandonment of the old castle and the construction of the new secluded house in Clonyn.

13

# All things to all men: Aodh Ó Néill and the construction of identity

PAUL LOGUE

## Introduction

From relatively small landholding beginnings in the Armagh barony of Oneilland, Aodh Ó Néill, known to history as Ó Néill Mór or 'the Great O'Neill', rose to become one of the most powerful men in Elizabethan Britain and Ireland. Variously, Baron of Dungannon, Earl of Tyrone and The Ó Néill, Aodh lived in a world where cultural differences had to be continually managed. Much of his success can be attributed to his pragmatic approach of being all things to all men, the traditionalist Gaelic noble and the Anglophile-Irish lord. Hiram Morgan has described Aodh Ó Néill as 'a consummate liar' weaving an 'elaborate campaign of disinformation' so successful that it has confounded modern historians as much as it did his contemporaries.[1] This paper examines one part of that campaign as waged through the use of buildings, sites and settings by Ó Néill, suggesting how he manipulated an appreciation of his identity and displayed various messages of belonging throughout his lifetime.

## A LIFE IN BUILDINGS

Aodh Ó Néill was the son of Mathghamhain, or Ferdorcha Ó Néill, an affiliated son of the first Earl of Tyrone (Tír Eoghain), Conn Bacach Ó Néill. In 1542/43 Conn Bacach undertook the process known as 'surrender and regrant' by submitting his lands to Henry VIII and, in turn, receiving them back with the title Earl of Tyrone. Conn overlooked his legitimate sons and nominated Mathghamhain as his heir, having him bestowed with the title Baron of Dungannon. This act destabilised the Gaelic lordship of Tír Eoghain and eventually led to conflict amongst Conn and his sons. By 1558/59, Conn's youngest son, Seaghán, had come to the fore by killing Mathghamhain Ó Néill and driving his father to death and exile in the Pale.[2] Seaghán claimed the title of Ó Néill and declared that Mathghamhain was in fact the son of a blacksmith from Dundalk and not a natural son of Conn Ó Néill at all.[3] Mathghamhain had three legitimate sons, Brian, Aodh and Cormac, plus one notable illegitimate son, Art. Born around 1550,[4] Aodh Ó Néill was Mathghamhain's second son, and prior to the later 1550s he would have been brought up in fosterage with the Uí Ágáin and Uí Chuinn of the *lucht tighe* (mensal lands; see FitzPatrick, Chapter 9).[5] However, following the death of his father, he was raised in the Pale. Aodh's older brother, Brian, was killed by Toirdhealbhach Luinneach Ó Néill in 1562 leaving Aodh, 'not twelve years old', as heir to Matthew.[6] Fynes Moryson took the view that Aodh and Cormac had been 'preserved ... by the English'[7] and Aodh wrote later to Elizabeth I that, at the time of his brother's murder in 1562, he was only 'an infant of tender years and in your Highness' ward'.[8] This statement may well link to the 1583 claim by Sir Henry Sidney that he had bred Aodh Ó Néill 'in my house from a little boy, then very poor of goods and full feebly friended'.[9] Morgan points out that, if true, this need not have been in England, as Sidney spent most of the 1560s in Ireland and he gives further support to that line of argument by showing that Aodh Ó Néill was actually a ward of the Hovenden family in the Pale.[10]

In 1567 Seaghán Ó Néill was killed by Clann Domhnaill and was succeeded as The Ó Néill by Toirdhealbhach Luinneach. The same year Aodh went to the English court in the company of Sir Henry Sidney[11] and Elizabeth I ordered that he should 'be planted in the south part' of Tír Eoghain.[12] Aodh now also assumed his father's title, the Baron of Dungannon. The plan to locate Aodh in Oneilland, southern Tír Eoghain (now in modern County Armagh), had evidently been achieved by October of that year[13] and by 1571 Aodh had improved his position as it was reported that there were then '50,000 cattle under the Baron of Dungannon'.[14] However, this development, along with his lineage, brought him ever more to the attention of Toirdhealbhach Luinneach, who crossed the Blackwater in April 1573 and raided the lands of Aodh Ó Néill along with the adjacent territory of his half-brother, Art Ó Néill. While Art was taken prisoner, Aodh avoided capture, but lost 30,000 head of cattle.[15] Toirdhealbhach Luinneach kept the pressure on, demanding that Aodh give up all his lands in Tír Eoghain.[16] It was perhaps becoming too much for the Baron for he left his Crown allies in no doubt as to his thoughts; in May 1573 Marshal Bagenall and Justice Dowdall wrote to the Lord Deputy that the young Baron was threatening to 'burn his islands and depart' Tír Eoghain.[17]

The situation was saved through the intervention of the Earl of Essex and his military adventure in eastern Ulster from 1573–75. Aodh Ó Néill campaigned with Essex throughout 1573–75,[18] being paid £2,876 for his services.[19] He was a popular and useful member of Essex's entourage in Ulster, with Barnaby Googe describing him as 'a valiant fellow'.[20] The earl's campaign kept Toirdhealbhach Luinneach in check and even allowed Aodh to expand his influence east of the Blackwater. In an effort to control the main fording points of the Blackwater River and to provide a base from which to attack westwards, Essex's forces built a fort at Blackwatertown, County Armagh. It was reported that the new fort would 'be a great stay to the Baron of Dungannon' in his ongoing battle with Toirdhealbhach Luinneach.[21]

## *A timber tower on the Blackwater*

A depiction of Essex's fort (Fig. 1) was undertaken in 1587 showing, on the eastern (now County Armagh) side of the River Blackwater, an earthwork fort with a large tower in the southwest corner, set beside a bridge.[22] The western (now County Tyrone) side of the bridge is shown guarded by a stone-built tower. The tower within the fort has a rectangular plan and is four storeys in height with a gabled and pitched cap-house at parapet level. There are two doorways into the tower, one at ground level and one at first-floor level, leading onto the western stretch of the fort's rampart. In addition to the doorways the visible sides of the tower are pierced by windows and loops. The parapet is crowned by a battlemented wall-walk supported by auxiliary timbers, and the centrally positioned cap-house appears to have a slated roof with a chimney behind, rising from the wall head. However, the main point of note is that the Blackwater Fort tower is clearly shown to be a timber tower house. The point is reinforced by the author of the drawing, through the deliberate juxtaposition of the partially rendered timber castle with the un-rendered stonework of the opposite tower. If further proof were needed, in February 1595 the forces of Aodh Ó Néill attacked the Blackwater fort lying 'around about the wooden castle, assaulting it both within the fort and without'.[23]

In July 1575 the Earl of Essex recorded that the fort 'at Blackwater [was] finished, the bridge and stone tower'.[24] Notably, while the other details of the 1587 drawing were included, he did not mention the timber castle. The reason for this became clear in 1579, as it was then that the timber castle was erected by Aodh Ó Néill, when he was 'content to give £40 to build up the castle at the bridge foot of the Blackwater'.[25] Thereafter Aodh petitioned regularly for ownership of the fort, making a small breakthrough in 1583 when he was given permission 'to resort, abide, and lodge within the fort at such times as he shall desire'.[26] While Aodh was allowed to live at the Blackwater Fort, his motives in helping build it included the wish to protect his home to the east of the river, but where was his home?

### *The Baron's Islands*

In 1568 the seventeen- or eighteen-year-old Aodh Ó Néill was planted in the territory of Oneilland by Sir Henry Sidney. His half-brother, Art Ó Néill, was based close by at Loughgall.[27] Aodh was to be a buffer against raiding by Toirdhealbhach Luinneach into southeast Ulster and the Pale and a potential rival for power in Tír Eoghain. When under pressure from Toirdhealbhach Luinneach in 1573 Aodh had threatened to 'burn his islands and depart'; but where were these islands?

To begin that examination we must first jump forward in time to Bagenall's 'The Description and Present State of Ulster in 1586'.[28] In this, Oneilland is said by Bagenall to be claimed by the Baron

1. Detail of the timber tower house, bridge and stone tower at the Blackwater Fort as depicted in 1587 (TNA, MPF 1/99).

and, further, that he 'hath placed there some of the Quins [Uí Chuinn] and Hagans [Uí Ágáin] who fostered him, and sometimes he dwelleth himself amongst them there in a little island, Loch Coe'.[29] In September 1580, the Baron wrote from 'Magher Lagh Coo' to Lord Deputy Grey that his 'brother Art, McDonnell, and O'Hanlon' were 'gone to Turlough Lynagh' taking with them, most of his cattle.[30] He wrote that Toirdhealbhach Luinneach 'sent hourly for him' and that he was reduced to hiding in the 'woods of Macher lagh coo with but 20 men'.[31] 'Macher lagh coo' is just one of several variant spellings of this place-name that include Magheraloughcoo, Maherlacoo, Maharyloghcoo, Magherlowni and Magherlocowe, found in the state papers for the period 1580–1602. The variations represent the contemporary place-name of Machaire Locha Cubha mentioned in *Leabhar Eoghanach*.[32] The modern-day spelling is Marlacoo, County Armagh and it refers to a small lake on the road between Armagh and Tandragee, which was a home to Aodh Ó Néill for thirty-four years.

Marlacoo is recorded by Bodley's Survey of 1609 as a lough surrounded by the townlands of Loghcoomor, Loghcoobeg and Teemore. Although no *crannóg* was indicated by Bodley, the existence of a *crannóg* below the surface of the water at the northeastern end of the lake has been reported since at least 1884.[33] The first two townland names seem to refer back to the place-name Locha Cubha, and the third may point to a large house (*tigh mór*) adjacent to the lough shore, probably with the accompanying houses or village of retainers and churls of Aodh Ó Néill. These place-names have survived at Marlacoo in the modern townlands of Marlacoo More, Marlacoo Beg and Teemore. The *crannóg* is sometimes locally called Teemore *crannóg* (its presence being known from a timber which pokes out of the water at times). Marlacoo is shown as a *crannóg* on Bartlett's general map of Ulster and the more detailed map of southeast Ulster, both dated to 1602/03.[34] It is shown in more detail on a map drawn in 1600 or early 1601 (and probably connected with Ralph Lane) where it is depicted as a tower house and enclosure on a *crannóg* (Fig. 2).[35] Just over 1km south of Marlacoo another *crannóg* is depicted in a lake on Bartlett's maps and on the Lane map as 'Lough Rorcan'. That *crannóg* is recorded in the state papers 1599–1601 and variously spelt Loughrorken, Loughlurcan, Lough Lorkan and Logh-rorcan; the modern name is Moyrourkan Lough. The Lane map shows Moyrourkan *crannóg* with a wooden tower on it but the artist is not trying to depict a castle as they had with Marlacoo. Parallels for both the Marlacoo tower house and Moyrourkan tower are found in another of Richard Bartlett's drawings, that of Inisloughlin in 1602.[36] That image shows Inisloughlin under attack by the Crown forces and depicted as being a ditched and palisaded enclosure containing five smaller houses, a large house (*tigh mór*?) and two wooden towers. The tower which guards the entrance to the enclosure is round in plan and tall, perhaps three or four storeys, but only pierced with lights or loopholes on one floor close to the conical roof. The Moyrourkan tower appears to have been of identical build. At Inisloughlin the

2. Detail of Marlacoo and Moyrourkan *crannóga* and their buildings from Lane map, *c.*1600–01 (NMM, MS P.49/25).

second wooden tower is square in plan and also three or four storeys in height. The uppermost storey is shown as a frame and is either under construction or has been dismantled. Below this there is a row of triangular-shaped loops, the same as those shown on the timber tower house at the Blackwater Fort; the Inisloughlin square-plan tower is another timber castle. As both the Inisloughlin and Blackwater Fort timber towers were built under the control of Aodh Ó Néill, it is likely that the tower house on his *crannóg* at Marlacoo was also of timber construction. Support for this argument comes from another of Richard Bartlett's illustrations, which shows a *crannóg* under attack and the base frame of a timber tower house on the *crannóg*.[37] It is the second of two *crannóga* shown by Bartlett under attack from the Crown forces. The first has generally been accepted as representing Roughan *crannóg* north of Dungannon.[38] The second is thought to be the only other Ulster *crannóg* mentioned as being captured by the Crown army at the time (1602), a site called 'Magherlocowe'.[39] This is, of course, Marlacoo, and Bartlett's drawing of it shows the base of the timber tower house of Aodh Ó Néill (Fig. 3). It had been dismantled, just as the stone castle at Dungannon was, in order to prohibit its capture by Crown forces.

We have seen that one of the townlands recorded in Bodley's 1609 survey was called Teemore and it is suggested that this may point to the presence of a *tigh mór* or large house adjacent to the lake shores. Fynes-Moryson reported that, in April 1601, Captain Josias Bodley and Captain Edward Blaney had led a surprise attack on the *crannóg* of Moyrourkan.[40] The English used 'arrows with wildfier' to set the houses on the *crannóg* alight and to force the occupants to swim for their lives. Bodley and Blaney's men then 'fired a great house upon their side of the shoare' and 'after the burning of other houses also, they brought away some Cowes and Sheepe, with other pillage'. From a prisoner they learned that 'great store of butter, corne, meale, and powder, was burnt and spoiled in the Iland, which all the rebels of that Countrey made their magasine'.[41] This and other contemporary references show that while Aodh Ó Néill lived at Marlacoo, he had kept Moyrourkan as a supply depot or magazine. The 'great house' and other houses on the shores of Moyrourkan lend further credence to the proposed *tigh mór* and village on the shores surrounding the home *crannóg* at Marlacoo. However, Moyrourkan is in Orior not Oneilland and Ó Néill would have had to take it from the Uí Anluain as he grew his power base from Marlacoo. It is likely that his original storage depot was on another *crannóg* in the vicinity called Loch na nAireadh, which lies within Oneilland and is mentioned in association with Marlacoo in the *Leabhar Eoghanach*.[42] This is present-day Ballynewry Lough, 1.25km southeast of Marlacoo, in which a *crannóg* was recorded by Richard Bartlett and in more recent times by the Northern Ireland Sites and Monuments Record.[43]

## *One foot in the Pale*

As the young Aodh Ó Néill struggled to gain a foothold at Marlacoo and the surrounding lands, he also maintained a home in the march of the Pale. This was at present-day Ballymascanlon, County Louth, where he rented a castle and lands from the Moore family. The senior branch of the Moore family was then based at their country house fashioned from the Cistercian abbey of Mellifont, one of the largest

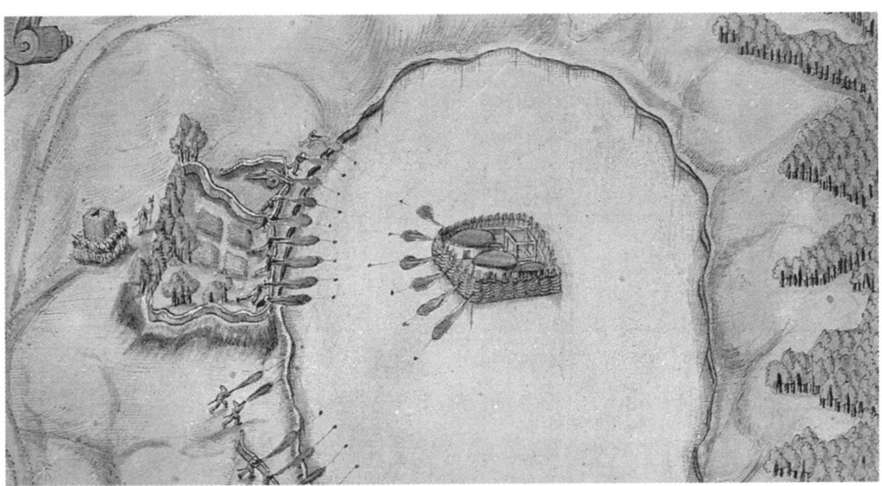

3. Detail of Richard Bartlett's illustrations showing Marlacoo *crannóg* (above), with a timber tower house base frame to the right of the houses, and Inisloughlin timber tower house (below), with an open frame at the uppermost storey and a timber tower guarding the enclosure entrance (NLI, MS 2656, xi; NLI, MS 2656, vi).

and finest houses of the time in Ireland. The owner, Sir Edward Moore, was a 'valiant campaigner' against the Queen's enemies and was very well known to key establishment figures in Ireland and England, such as Adam Loftus and William Cecil.[44] Moore served in the Queen's Irish forces with Aodh Ó Néill and, like his son Garret, was a close friend of the Baron.[45] Indeed, in May 1583 when the Baron was under threat from the sons of Seaghán Ó Néill and their Scots mercenaries, Sir Edward Moore repaired 'to the Baron's aid with 300 foot and 100 horse'.[46]

The site at Ballymascanlon is shown on several contemporary maps as a tower house with an accompanying village. Ruins of the site survived until the twentieth century enabling records to be made of two upstanding stone walls *c*.13m by 15m in length, 2m in width and 4m in height.[47] Although Salter seems hesitant to term the remains a definite tower house, the width of the walls leave little option as to what else it could be; we know that there was a tower house in the vicinity, and the medieval church is at the Church of Ireland site several hundred metres away.

There is no certainty as to when Aodh began living at Ballymascanlon, but it was at least from 1578 when he wrote a letter from 'Ballyscanlane' on 22 December of that year. In it he desired 'that an additional 100 soldiers ... may be sent to his aid' in the fight for his home at Marlacoo.[48] In August 1580, he was again writing from 'Ballyscanlan', this time to Lord Deputy Grey warning that he had better 'send forces to the northern borders of the pale as Toirdhealbhach Luinneach was about to invade' and that he, the Baron, had but twenty-five 'horsemen in pay'.[49] Aodh must have become friendly with the Moore family during his upbringing with the Hovendens, and just as Sir Henry Sidney planted him in Oneilland in 1568, Sir Edward Moore helped out the young man by offering him the castle and lands of Ballymascanlon as a suitable home for Pale society.

Ballymascanlon was an ideal location for the young Baron, as he was also sometimes paid to defend the borders of the Pale.[50] Thomas Lee pointed out that Ballymascanlon was a perfect location to counter Irish raiding into the Pale 'because it is scituate nere the straite of that passage [the Moyry Pass] where the Traytors ... use to goe over either to offend the subjectes or to fetch provision'.[51] In short it was the closest place to Marlacoo where Aodh Ó Néill could live safely amongst his friends in Pale society. That it was a place of reasonable size is shown by Thomas Lee's suggestion that 'Balliemoscanlon which towne and castle was sometymes the dwelling place of Tyrone ... is able to receive one third part of the soldiers assigned for Dondalke'.[52] By May of 1596, when Aodh had

4. Dungannon Castle Hill as depicted by Richard Bartlett in 1602 (NLI, MS 2656, vi).

drifted into open war with the Crown, Sir Henry Bagenall had seized Ballymascanlon, asking that he 'be continued in the possession of Ballynescanlan until it be re-delivered to the earl, or the possession of it evicted from him, Bagenall, by Garrett Moore'.[53] By then, Dungannon had become the focus of Aodh Ó Néill's activity.

## *'The Hill of O'Neill'*

Much has been written of the Ó Néill dynasty's occupancy of Castle Hill, Dungannon, or as it is sometimes now called, 'The Hill of O'Neill'. Generally, the historiography of Dungannon is that the Uí Néill occupied it from the fourteenth century, making it their dynastic centre, and that they lived in various defensive enclosures and castles on the hill from then until 1607.[54] Aodh Ó Néill's grandfather lived at Dungannon and he himself may well have been born there; one could understand his wish to occupy the site.

It is not until 1585 that there is firm evidence that the Baron had control of Dungannon. This had come through increasing his military pressure on Toirdhealbhach Luinneach along with constant lobbying of the Elizabethan government to grant him Conn Bacach's title and lands.[55] By August of 1585 the Baron had been granted his grandfather's title of Earl of Tyrone, and Lord Deputy Perrot was encamped close to Dungannon to confirm 'the order and composition made by indenture between O'Neill (T. Lynagh), the Earl of Tyrone, and Sir Arthur O'Neill'.[56] This agreement gave the new earl control over eastern Tír Eoghain on both sides of the Blackwater River and allowed him to occupy Dungannon. On 31 October 1585 he wrote from Dungannon to Lord Burghley, styling himself 'Hugh, Earl of Teirone'.[57] Thus we now connect with the ubiquitous Bartlett drawing of the ruined castle on the hill of Dungannon.[58] It has been established that Aodh Ó Néill built that castle in 1585/86, as a line in Bagenall's 1586 description of Ulster states that the 'new castle upon the Earl's part is Dungannon'.[59] Over the next twenty years, Aodh slighted and rebuilt Dungannon Castle several times. As seen in Bartlett's 1602 view, the castle at Dungannon is a ruined tower house which had been built in stone to a height of four storeys. Adjacent to the castle remains, there is a bawn enclosed by a looped stone wall. To the right of the castle and bawn there is a lower terrace occupied by houses, and the entire site is surrounded by a wide and deep ditch crossed by a timber bridge (Fig. 4).

The houses shown by Bartlett on the lower terrace are normally interpreted as the town of Dungannon, but this is not correct. In June 1602 Aodh Ó Néill burnt Dungannon and retreated towards Glenconkeyne;[60] he would not have demolished his castle and left the houses of the town for the Crown garrison to occupy. The houses are those of the new Crown garrison. There was another important building at Dungannon that is not shown on Bartlett's drawing as it was destroyed in a raid on Dungannon in August 1597. The raid took place as the earl's attention was focused elsewhere on the building of a new Crown fort at the Blackwater by Lord Deputy Burgh. Some of Sir Henry Bagenall's men undertook the raid and are said to have burned the earl's 'hall' along with 'Dungannon town and the rebels' mills'.[61] The hall in question was a manor house built by the earl from 1591 for his new bride, Mabel Bagenall. The hall would have been built on the hill within the existing complex of lordly buildings and its site may be shown on the Bartlett map as the patch of bare earth running at an angle from the castle and bawn, then occupied by an English cannon. All other such brown patches in Bartlett drawings are associated with buildings and it may be that he was marking this spot for an accompanying narrative. The hall and tower house will be further discussed below, but there is one more site to be mentioned if Dungannon is to be properly understood: the *crannóg* of Ballysaggart Lough.

### *The island of Dungannon*

In March of 1601 a Scotsman visited Dungannon and spoke at length with Aodh Ó Néill over several days. During this time the Scotsman was housed on a *crannóg* there, stating that two Jesuits, his servant and himself 'lay in one chamber within the lake where his [Ó Néill's] house is, which is but made of timber and all covered over with rushes, very easy to be fired'.[62] On the *crannóg*, Ó Néill was also storing match, ammunition and gunpowder. The Scotsman was a double-agent and one night set a fire 'next to the kitchen', which started a conflagration that burnt Ó Néill's 'match with his whole houses', the powder barrels only being saved by being hurled into 'the water'.[63] Later that same year, in July 1601, an adventurous Englishman, Thomas Walker, met Aodh Ó Néill at the Blackwater River. Walker pretended to be sympathetic to Ó Néill's cause but later portrayed himself to Sir Robert Cecil as being on a self-imposed mission to assassinate Ó Néill.[64] Walker stated that Aodh Ó Néill accepted him but would not let him take part in an engagement then being prepared against the Crown. Ó Néill told Walker that he would not have him harmed and, instead, he would send him 'with my lady to my house'. Walker was then sent along with Aodh Ó Néill's wife (Caitríona Mág Aonghusa), her mother, guards and the household servants to Dungannon. He recorded that Caitríona and her mother arrived ahead of him at Dungannon and when he came there he found Lady Ó Néill 'in a cott, where she made me drink, and then sent me before with her servants to her island in a canoe'.[65] In neither entry from 1601 is the home of

Ó Néill at Dungannon portrayed as being in a stone castle on the hill; in both it is a house on a *crannóg*. The *crannóg* is still extant at Dungannon today. It is oval in plan (54m northeast–southwest by 46m northwest–southwest) and rises out of the water to a height of around 1.5m.[66] It is situated in Ballysaggart Lough, *c.*1km south of the location of Aodh Ó Néill's new tower house of 1585/86 on Castle Hill, the significance of which will be discussed below.

## Becoming and Belonging

The scene for the buildings that Aodh Ó Néill chose to construct and live in during his life has been set; this section will examine why he did so. For at least thirty-four years Aodh Ó Néill can be shown to have used the *crannóg* at Marlacoo Lough, County Armagh as one of his main residences, and on it he had a wooden tower house. But why would someone brought up in Pale society choose to live in a timber tower house on a *crannóg*? The answer comes when Aodh Ó Néill's situation and the deeper Gaelic ancestry he claimed is examined. He was settled in Oneilland by the Crown, as the Baron of Dungannon, as their man planted upon a Gaelic territory as a buffer against Toirdhealbhach Luinneach and the sons of Seaghán Ó Néill. His father, Mathghamhain, was claimed to have been the son of a blacksmith from Dundalk and not an Ó Néill at all. In 1592, when commenting on Tír Eoghain and the office of The Ó Néill, Myler McGrath, Archbishop of Cashel and a native of Ulster, noted that the 'Earl of Tyrone is thought by the Irishry to have his nomination and authority, rather by English government than by any right to the principality after the manner of that country. The said sons of Shane O'Neill are taken amongst the Irishry to have more right than any other to the principality in that country, for that they have descended by the right line from O'Neill's principal house by many descents'.[67]

### *The quest for antiquity*

On his return to Oneilland in 1568 detractors in Tír Eoghain could easily have categorised Aodh as an outsider. To counter this he had to look the part of a Gaelic noble with deep roots in Ulster's native past; he had to belong. This he did by living in a timber building

5. Lough Marlacoo, County Armagh. The *crannóg* of Aodh Ó Néill is situated just below the surface in the upper part of the lake closest to the viewer (image: Terence Reeves-Smyth).

on a *crannóg* (Fig. 5). In doing so, he was deliberately drawing on symbolism from the Ó Néill lineage going back several hundred years. One of the most famous of the Uí Néill was Brian 'Catha an Duin', who regained power for the Uí Néill by defeating the Mic Lochlainn at the battle of Caimeirghe in 1241 and was subsequently killed in 1260 while leading a northern Gaelic army against the Anglo-Normans at Downpatrick, County Down. Through Conn Bacach, Aodh would have claimed direct descent from this great Ó Néill of the distant past. The latter was also known as Brian 'Locha Laoghaire', associating him with the *crannóg* on Lough Laoghaire, now called Lough Catherine, County Tyrone.[68] Brian's son, Domhnall Caol Ó Néill, was also associated with the *crannóg* on Lough Laoghaire, dying there in 1325.[69] Donall Caol's son, Aodh

Reamhar Ó Néill, is described in the *Leabhar Eoghanach* as having his residence and hereditary home at 'Fraochmhagh',[70] which is identified by the *Annals of the Four Masters* as being the *crannóg* at Augher, County Tyrone.[71] Ciarán Devlin points out that while it has been asserted that Domhnall Caol was the Ó Néill who built the first castle at Dungannon, the fact that his son lived at Augher and he and his father lived at Lough Catherine leaves 'the matter of the size and importance of contemporary Dungannon' as an open question.[72] To answer that open question we look to the newly significant Ballysaggart *crannóg* and see that in the medieval period Dungannon too was an Ó Néill *crannóg*, not a stone castle on the hill as tradition asserts. Thus by living on his *crannóg* at Marlacoo, Aodh Ó Néill displayed his Uí Néill lineage: he was descended from men who had fought to keep Tír Eoghain free of English rule, men who were based at ancient sites on lakes where legitimate Gaelic lordship was at home. It was inescapable that, when the opportunity arose, he would also occupy the *crannóg* at Dungannon and base his brother, Cormac, at the other *crannóg* of Augher; his half-brother, Art, was already based at the *crannóg* of Loughgall. While there was clearly also a security aspect to living on a *crannóg*, the main reason that Aodh Ó Néill and his family occupied *crannóga* was to display a sense of belonging; it was what an Ó Néill lord did.

The presence of buildings on the shores of lakes where *crannóga* were situated was mentioned above, with a 'great house' noted on the shores of Moyrourkan Lough and postulated for the shore of Marlacoo Lough. The Bartlett drawing of Lough Roughan and the Ó Cuinn *crannóg* there shows three vernacular houses in various states on the lake shore, at the bottom of the illustration. The Marlacoo illustration shows one such vernacular house, but both maps also include lake-shore enclosures from which the Crown forces are firing at the *crannóga* (see Fig. 3 above). These enclosures are square to rectangular in plan and appear to be earthen. When compared with the Bartlett drawing of Tulach Óg, it seems to measure *c.*50–80m across. Just like the Ó Néill inauguration site at Tulach Óg, the enclosures are shown to have large trees growing on their boundaries and slightly within, which implies that they are of considerable age and not newly made by Crown soldiers. The Roughan example has a gated entrance top left and the Marlacoo enclosure has the hint of the same just blocked from sight by a tree. Based on the depiction of corn growing within the enclosure at Roughan, Hayes-McCoy suggested that both enclosures may have been gardens.[73] However, both enclosures are separated into two parts – one part with bare earth surface, one part with grassed surface – and where Bartlett draws such areas of bare earth it is normally at the site of an existing or ruined building. The message in the illustrations then is that in 1602 the buildings that once stood within these lake-side enclosures had been taken down and the sites abandoned but for some agricultural use for the last-ditch garrisons defending the adjacent *crannóga*. In quieter times the 'great houses' of the Gaelic nobles stood within such enclosures and it was from them that access to the *crannóg* was negotiated. This is implied in the 1601 state papers entry, which records that Thomas Walker was given hospitality by Lady Caitríona Ó Néill on the lake shore at Dungannon. Only then did Walker cross to the *crannóg*. This marks out the lake shore as the hospitality boundary, not the entrance to the *crannóg*. In turn, this shows that there must have been a mechanism of controlling access to lordly *crannóga* from a specific point on the shore within sight of the *crannóg*, from which someone would have accompanied a visitor across to the landing point on the *crannóg*; the lake-side enclosure (*crannóg*-bawn) performs this role. The Walker passage has strong similarities to one written by Luke Gernon, an early seventeenth-century traveller in Ireland, who recorded a visit to a tower house thus:

> The castles are built very strong, and with narow stayres, for security. The hall is the uppermost room, lett us go up, you shall not come downe agayne till tomorrow ... The lady of the house meets you with her trayne ... When you are disposing of yourself to depart, they call for Dogh a dores, that is, to drink at the doore, there you are presented agayne with all the drinkes in the house, as at your first entrance.[74]

As noted by Colm Donnelly, the passage implies that an alcoholic drink was offered at the entrance to the tower house on the arrival and exit of guests as part of hospitality etiquette.[75] At this boundary a guest accepted the drink and moved to and from the hospitality and protection of the host family. The hospitality threshold would have been guarded by a retainer and this is shown in a later record from

County Limerick for the 1640s. There, the tower house of Castle Mahon was captured through the actions of one Robert Casey, 'who early in the morning after he had given a whistle from the top of the castle went down from the upper rooms when all the people were asleep and went to the porter and asked him to let him go forth'.[76] Once the door was opened Casey held it and let in waiting rebels to take the castle by surprise. That the tower of Ó Néill at Dungannon was also secured at night by such guards is shown in a visit in 1599 by ecclesiastical student Thomas Mulcloy, who wrote that he arrived at 'the town of the Earl of Tyrone after the night fell, and could not get into his house because his doors were made fast and the watch set'.[77]

Presumably, if a castle had a bawn, and we should assume that most did, there would have been a preliminary check at the gate with differing levels of access and hospitality within the lordly complex as would be expected of an Anglo-Norman castle. The initial hospitality threshold for a *crannóg* was in its accompanying land-based *crannóg*-bawn. It would have been from such a *crannóg*-bawn that Thomas Walker was admitted to the *crannóg* of Dungannon. That *crannóg*-bawn has now no upstanding remains but its likely location on the western shores of the lough is suggested by the presence of an earlier platform *ráth* on the 1609 survey of Dungannon lands by Josias Bodley. A Franciscan friary was founded at Dungannon *c.*1489 by Conn Ó Néill and it was given lands to the south, east and west of the *crannóg*.[78] Bodley plotted these lands as the balliboes (*baile bó*) of Mallanahay, Tanagh, Moyleboy and Kilnemaddy, but showed that Ó Néill had left out of the grant a *baile bó* called Doongorman, which contained the lake and at least its western shores. The retention of Doongorman within the secular lands at Dungannon meant that an access route between Castle Hill and the lake shore (and therefore the *crannóg*) was maintained outside of the church lands. Above this access route to the west there is a large platform *ráth* that overlooks the *crannóg*. It is *c.*300m from the lake shore and measures 45m northeast–southwest x 47m northwest–southeast and up to 1.2m in height.[79] The platform *ráth* and the *crannóg* must mark the early medieval lordly complex taken over by the Uí Néill and then modified with the addition of a shoreline *crannóg*-bawn (Fig. 6).

6. The *crannóg* of Dungannon at modern-day Ballysaggart Lough, County Tyrone, looking northwest. The position of the early medieval *ráth* is marked by the trees on the skyline at the top left of the photograph (image: Terence Reeves-Smyth).

## *The quest for civility*

It has been shown that Aodh Ó Néill maintained a home at Ballymascanlon, County Louth and that it was a stone tower house with accompanying buildings and a village, depicted later by Richard Bartlett on his maps dating to 1600–1602.[80] The site is now destroyed but it is safe to assume that the tower house and other lordly buildings were of a design, finish and layout easily recognisable to Pale society. At Ballymascanlon, Aodh would have set aside his overtly Gaelic persona and become what contemporary English writers would have described as 'civilised'. In simplest terms this meant that he would have adopted the language, customs and laws of the Pale, as distinct from the life he would have been careful to be seen to live at Marlacoo. The level to which Aodh was inculcated into Anglo-Irish society is shown in one letter written by him from Ballymascanlon in February 1589, in which he requested Sir Francis Walsyngham to be his patron, writing that by 'the death of my honourable patron, the Earl of Leicester, who from my youth had a special care of my bringing up and welldoing, I am destitute of a friend to patronize my good actions'.[81]

On taking Dungannon in 1585, Aodh built a new stone castle there. On Bartlett's drawing of Dungannon Castle, he depicts an intact large first-floor window with a second possible ruined large window adjacent to the left as one views the image (see Fig. 4). This may indicate that the tower house had a first-floor hall. If the hall sat on a vault then the Dungannon tower house built by Aodh Ó Néill would be classified by Rory Sherlock as one of his Type B Irish tower houses.[82] The Type B towers are the predominant form in Leinster and east Ulster and the majority date to the sixteenth century. However, if no vault was present (which is a feature common in late Irish towers) this would put the Dungannon tower house into Sherlock's Type E. Type B and E towers tend to have less elaborately designed main halls, heated with mural fireplaces. They represent a move away in design from the earlier Irish tower houses (Sherlock's Types A, C and D), which had elaborate halls, sometimes open to the roof, heated by central fireplaces. The latter types of tower house are also seen by Sherlock as being of western distribution in Ireland. At Dungannon the evidence points to Aodh Ó Néill having built the type of castle with which he was familiar in the Pale and its marches, not the more elaborate and earlier 'Gaelic' western type that he could have used to generate a sense of ancestral attachment to particular settlement forms such as the *crannóg* at Marlacoo. This most likely reflects his more dominant position in Tír Eoghain from 1585; he had a lesser need to portray himself as an Ó Néill of old when it was becoming obvious that he was highly likely to succeed as the Ó Néill of the future. His new Dungannon Castle was also a symbol to the Crown; it was the type of building they could readily relate to and, as a stone castle on a hill, something even New English administrators could identify as a place fit for an important ally of the state. At Dungannon Castle Aodh set out his stall to live 'civilly' and fulfil the role the Crown expected from him. Just as the familiar design and layout of the Pale-type castle gave the

Crown visitor confidence that he was their man, so Ó Néill also used internal furnishings to reinforce the message to Dublin and London. Following his visit to London in 1590 it was recorded that at:

> his departure the more to make this state secuer of his good intentions, that he meant to leive civilie and honourable accordinge to the English manner, he bought riche furniture for his howse, of beddinge, arras {wall tapestries}, carpettes and the lyke, whereof he would not have the state here to be ignorante, in so much that the Lord Burley, Lord Treasorer of England, sayd he was glade to see such furniture goe into Ulster as a goode hope conceved that the Erle would reduce this contrie onto civilitie.[83]

Andrew Murphy quotes this reference along with another passage from Fynes Moryson which stated, with regard to Ó Néill, that while 'pretending to build a faire house (which our State thinkes a tye of civilitie) he got license to transport to Dungannon a great quantitie of Lead to cover the Battlements of his house: but ere long imployed the same only to make bullets for the warre'.[84] However, the Moryson reference refers to the house that Aodh built for Mabel Bagenall from 1591 on, over a year later. The 1590 reference is to an attempt by Ó Néill to deck his tower house at Dungannon with the internal trappings of civility, to show the Crown that he was living an English life as an example to his countrymen; Lord Burghley's response showed that the message was appreciated and understood.

In August 1591, Ó Néill stepped up his quest for dominance in Ulster by seeking to neutralise his constant rival for power in the province, Sir Henry Bagenall, by marrying the latter's younger sister, Mabel, and building her the house referred to by Fynes Moryson.[85] The marriage was bitterly opposed by Sir Henry Bagenall. Writing to Lord Burghley about Sir Henry's continued opposition, Hugh sought to bring the former onside by appealing to his earlier rhetoric of civility, stating that it 'is known to your Lordship that I have taken to wife Sir Henry Bagenall's sister, which I did chiefly to bring civility into my house, and among the country people, which I thank God by her good means is well begun, both in my house and in the country abroad'.[86] That Ó Néill was overtly playing the civility card is further evidenced in Sir William Fitzwilliam's letter to Lord Burghley, in

December 1591, mentioning that 'the Earl since his marriage has bestowed great cost of building at Dungannon, as also at London, to furnish and deck that house at Dungannon'.[87] While Fitzwilliam's letter was supportive of Aodh Ó Néill and his perceived progression towards civility, it was very critical of Aodh's rival, Toirdhealbhach Luinneach Ó Néill, and one wonders whether it was confirmation of Thomas Lee's claim that the 'Earle of Tyrone, soe longe as he fedd Sir William Fitzwilliams, with one Riche jewell or other, was accompted of him, the honorablest gentleman in the Worlde'.[88] That the earl is said to have 'bestowed great cost of building at Dungannon', 'since his marriage', leaves little doubt that the house was being built for his new bride Mabel, not earlier. Although we cannot be certain as to what precise design the house built for Mabel took, it must have been within the broader Elizabethan-style that would have sent the correct message to Dublin and London. A contemporary drawing of Dundalk[89] shows several Elizabethan urban houses that could have served as templates, but the pre-eminent Elizabethan Irish courtier of the time was the Earl of Ormond and his house at Carrick-on-Suir would have provided the perfect model from which the ambitious Earl of Tyrone could design his new hall at Dungannon. When he visited London, Ó Néill had stayed with Ormond[90] and surely must have learned from him how to comport himself at the highest levels of society through manners, home and decor. As noted above, this new house at Dungannon was burnt by the soldiers of Sir Henry Bagenall in a lightning raid in August 1597. As by this time Mabel had died after parting from Ó Néill due to his womanising, it is tempting to suggest that Bagenall had given a special order to his men to be sure to burn the 'Earl of Tyrone's famous house',[91] it being a standing symbol of the marriage he felt so dishonoured by. Aodh Ó Néill sustained his semblance of English-style civility even during his war with the Crown. In April 1599 Sir John Harrington met Ó Néill, commenting that 'the earl used far greater respect to me than I expected; and began debasing his own manner of hard life, comparing himself to wolves, that fill their bellies sometime, and fast as long for it'.[92] This passage could be taken literally to mean that Ó Néill was suggesting that he did not eat well or often at that time, but he was an immensely wealthy man, being both The Ó Néill and the Earl of Tyrone, and such an obviously false claim would have drawn comment from Harrington. It is much more likely that

Ó Néill was actually referring to a lack of what could be termed 'civil' contact and dealings with other 'civil' persons. This is further highlighted by Harrington's record that he:

> took occasion the while to entertain his [O'Neill's] two sons, … finding the two children … in English cloths like a nobleman's sons; with velvet gerkins and gold lace; … both of them [learning] the English tongue; I gave them … my English translation of 'Ariosto' which I got at Dublin; which their teachers took very thankfully, and soon after shewed it the earl, who called to see it openly, and would needs hear some part of it read … [and] he solemnly swore his boys should read all the book over to him.[93]

Ó Néill clearly revelled in the chance to show that, while he may have been then at odds with the Crown, he and his sons still espoused the language, dress and learning of English civility. That the English elite could accept that view is shown in a contemporary statement by William Lithgow. He remarked that the Gaelic gentry, 'such as are brought up here at London, learn to become a great deal more civil than those who are brought up at home, after their own rude and accustomable manner'.[94] His upbringing in the society of the Pale, with influences from persons such as the Earl of Ormond and Sir Henry Sidney, would have qualified Aodh Ó Néill as being 'a great deal more civil' than his contemporary Gaelic lords.

## Conclusion

Living on a *crannóg* at Marlacoo, Aodh Ó Néill set out his stall as a Gaelic lord descended from a long line of Uí Néill who had based themselves on lakes in the lordship of Tír Eoghain for centuries. When he travelled back over the Moyry Pass to Ballymascanlon, Aodh Ó Néill became a gentleman of the Pale, the civilised face of Tír Eoghain and the Crown's man for the future in Ulster. After taking Dungannon in 1585, Aodh continued his nod to civility in the buildings he erected on the hill there and in how he furnished them. While he built the 'English' part of his Dungannon lordly complex on the top of Castle Hill, out of sight from the Crown, he maintained his Gaelic roots with the *crannóg* and *crannóg*-bawn of Ballysaggart

Lough at the base of the same hill; depending on the audience and the occasion he had the stage at hand to be Aodh Ó Néill, Chief of Tír Eoghain, or Hugh O'Neill, Earl of Tyrone. Lord Burghley chose to associate Marlacoo with Aodh Ó Néill and 'the uncivilised', as, though he well knew that site was a home to Ó Néill, he discounted it in 1593 when he wrote that the houses of the 'Earl Tirone' were at Dungannon, Ballymascanlon and Castle Roe.[95] Later, Aodh 'Earl of Teirone' became the arch-traitor who turned the very trappings of civility against his benefactors. When he was accused of plotting to 'join in arms' with the Spanish against the Crown, the alleged crime was made all the worse because he is said to have devised it amongst polite society from within his house at Ballymascanlon.[96] Fynes Moryson saw more of that betrayal in the transformation of the roof lead from Lady Mabel's Dungannon manor house into bullets – literally firing the gift of civility straight back at the Crown. Stephen Greenblatt states that sixteenth-century society had begun to recognise that there were 'always some elements of deliberate shaping in the formation and expression of identity' and that there was then 'an increased self-consciousness about the fashioning of human identity as a manipulable, artful process'.[97] Aodh Ó Néill was certainly self-conscious about his image, manipulating settings throughout his lifetime where he formed and expressed different identities, retaining 'the title of O'Neill with the Irishry and with the State the title of his earldom'.[98] His 'elaborate campaign of disinformation'[99] was played out upon the scenery he created at places such as Marlacoo, Ballymascanlon and Dungannon. As another contemporary of Ó Néill wrote, 'all the world's a stage, and all the men and women merely players: They have their exits and their entrances; and one man in his time plays many parts'.

14

# 'Their skill and practise therein far exceeding their wonted usage': The Irish military revolution, 1593–1603

JAMES O'NEILL

The Nine Years' War and its aftermath is without question one of the great turning points of Irish history. In addition to witnessing the zenith of Gaelic military power and sophistication, perversely, it also led to the final destruction of native military and political power. Despite the apparent modernisation of the native Irish forces, it is not hard to find articles and attitudes which view the war as a contest of the backward and militarily weak Irish, against the modern armies of Elizabeth I.[1] As noted by the historian John Keegan, the way a person fought was a cultural expression.[2] Following on from this, the image of primitive and obsolete styles of warfare by the native Irish could imply a moribund culture which was also archaic and resistant to alteration. Moreover, contemporary descriptions and illustrations of the Irish presented an uncouth visage, and a society in need of outside (English) help to move beyond their primitive native culture. However, the Nine Years' War was not a clash of cultures with the pike and shot forces of the English being initially bested by the noble but yet primitive Irish in a courageous but inevitably doomed effort to throw off English rule; instead, it was one which bore many hallmarks of the type of warfare raging in France and the Low Countries. In the last decade of the sixteenth century Irish military society, under the leadership of Aodh Ó Néill, second Earl of Tyrone, dramatically transformed both its arms and military methods. The force created by Tyrone was not only modern, it went beyond the changes of the 'military revolution' in Europe to create a powerful hybrid which maximised firepower while retaining mobility in the restrictive Irish landscape. If war is a cultural expression, then the military transformation of the 1590s suggested a dynamic and highly flexible native society which was open to revolutionary changes. Indeed, the proclivity to or rejection of change has been an ongoing debate in the historiography of early modern Ireland.

At the end of the sixteenth century, continental warfare was experiencing what some have called the Military Revolution. The key indicators of this revolution was the growth of army size, development of disciplined firepower-centric infantry, construction of *trace itallienne* fortifications, and ocean-going broadside sailing ships.[3] Though Ireland was geographically on the periphery of Europe, Ireland and the course of the Nine Years' War was profoundly influenced by the transformations taking place in continental Europe. The stereotypical native hosts of armoured *gallóglaigh*, *ceatharnaigh* and Scottish mercenary redshanks had little part to play in a war where, for the most part, military pragmatism and innovation dominated. The reality was so different that one wonders how or why this confusion continues to occur. Thomas Bartlett raised this issue in his 2002 O'Donnell lecture, in which he suggested that Irish military history of this period had been marginalised by a perception that Gaelic warfare was primitive and had nothing to do with the innovation in military methods occurring in continental Europe.[4] Modern assessments of warfare in early-modern Ireland have suggested that, despite the construction of some modern fortifications and the occasional deployment of artillery, Ireland was generally unaffected by the military revolution.[5] Such assessments, therefore, promote the notion of Gaelic culture as static and archaic in character.

## Gaelic military and the mythic ideal

We should not be too critical, as in many ways the iconic Irish primitive warrior has been maintained by Irish nationalist movements

1. Irish soldiers shown in the *Códice de Trajes*, 1547.

which idealised pre-conquest Ireland. The Celticisim of the nineteenth century created a cultural history that imagined an idealised identity.[6] Murals across Northern Ireland deploy this imagery to promote modern political and social agendas. The image of the primitive Irish suited both nationalist and unionist interpretations of history. It fitted into the pure Celtic ideal, and it confirmed the backwardness of Ireland and the need for outside intervention to the ultimate benefit of the natives. The image of a modernising Gaelic Ireland did not suit either narrative and may have fallen down the cracks between nationalist and unionist conceptions of late sixteenth-century Ireland.

Contemporary illustrations have helped reinforce modern perceptions of the Irish military as unsophisticated and primitive.

The detailed drawings of *gallóglaigh* and *ceatharnaigh* by Albrecht Durer in 1521 showed Irish troops as positively anachronistic.[7] They were clad in medieval-style gambeson and chain mail, armed with axes, spears, bows and great-swords, and supported by the uncouth *ceatharnaigh*. This presented a most un-soldierly appearance, at a time when battles in Europe were being fought with cannons, firearms and pikes. The *Códice de Trajes*, again from Germany, but written in 1547, continued to show the Irish as crude and unrefined in comparison to other Europeans.[8] One of the most commonly used set of illustrations showing the interactions of the Irish and English is the set of woodcuts from John Derricke's *Image of Irelande* (1581).[9] The illustrations accompanied a work which was primarily intended to glorify the campaigns of Sir Henry Sidney but, as Morgan has pointed out, they illustrated the continuing struggle between the civilising English and the stubborn and barbarous Irish papists.[10] The illustrations show the Irish as craven and cowardly and easily swept aside when confronted by the Crown's forces. Moreover, in arms and dress, the Irish are decidedly archaic.

If the visual media of sixteenth-century illustrations were not enough to portray the general crudeness of the Irish, contemporary writers settled the issue. Frequently quoted authors have provided thorough accounts of the native Irish soldiery. Edmund Spenser vividly described native warfare in *A View of the State of Ireland*. Written in 1596, Spenser noted how the Irish *ceatharnaigh* ran into battle with a terrible yell and hubbub, and were armed with little more than swords, bows and shields. They were unarmoured save a thick lock of hair called glibbs, which were said to be able to bear 'a good stroke'.[11] In battle tactics, Spenser accorded the Irish little skill as, 'Their confused kind of march in heaps, without any order or array, their clashing of swords together, their fierce running upon their enemies, and their manner of fight, resembles altogether that which is read in all histories to have been used of the Scythians'.[12]

Misconceptions about the nature of the Irish did little to assuage the pain of repeated English defeat in the coming war. The shock of Irish victories and the extreme effort required to defeat the Irish lords shook the English military establishment to its core and almost bankrupted the state. By the end of the war, even their harshest Irish critics recognised that the Irish soldiery had changed; Lord Deputy Mountjoy's secretary, Fynes Moryson, considered the Irish under Ó

Néill to be as good as the forces fielded by the Crown, but with time, the old primitive caricature returned. The 1610 revision of William Camden's *Britannia* described the Irish as fighting with spears and axes.[13] As easy as it would be to blame stereotyping on English bias, Irish chroniclers retrenched the myth.

This negative view was compounded by contemporary Irish writers whose prose harked back to a golden age of Irish warrior myth, and therefore the native representation of Irish warfare was deliberately archaised.[14] This is evident in the account of the English and Irish preparations before the Battle of Yellow Ford (1598), as documented in *The Life of Red Hugh O'Donnell* by Lughaidh Ó Cléirigh. He noted that:

> The English proceeded to clothe themselves with strange tunics of iron, and high-crested, shining helmets, and foreign shields of well-tempered, refined iron. They seized their broad-shouldered, firmly-riveted spears, their wide-edged axes ... their straight two-edged swords, and their long single-edged blades, and their loud-voiced shot-firing guns.[15]

In contrast:

> The Irish did not wear armour like them, except a few, and they were unarmed in comparison with the English, but they had sufficient wide-bladed spears and broad grey lances with strong handles of good ash. They had straight two-edged swords and slender flashing axes ... implements for shooting which they had were darts of carved wood and powerful bows, with sharp pointed arrows, and the English generally had quick firing guns.[16]

This was anything but true, as at the Battle of the Yellow Ford the Irish were more dependent on firepower than the English.[17]

## The transformation of Irish warfare

If the Irish forces were modernised by the end of the war in 1603, when did the changes begin to appear? The weapons technology was available long before the 1590s and despite Ireland's position at the edge of Europe, it was not immune to the spread of firearms technology throughout the fifteenth and sixteenth centuries. Henry VIII made good use of Irish shot.[18] There were enough firearms in native hands to give rise to concerns in Dublin, but new technology did not automatically lead to new ways of fighting. Shane Ó Néill armed husbandmen and churls with firearms, but there were no apparent tactical changes, and firearms were just another weapon in support of the traditional Irish host of *gallóglaigh* and *ceatharnaigh*. Two of the major battles fought by Shane, Glentaisie (1565) and Farsetmore (1567), were decided by the clash of heavy infantry, not by disciplined firepower.[19] Transfer of technology was rarely enough to cause substantive changes in military methods. Military expertise and a willingness to use new methods were also needed. Knowledge of new techniques of continental warfare was available, but did not start any broad revision of Gaelic Irish military methods. Many native Irish leaders returned from the continental wars but felt no need to alter their forces of *gallóglaigh* and *ceatharnaigh*.[20]

When did the Irish begin to transform their forces independently of English sponsorship? After the catastrophe of the Spanish Armada in September 1588, some Irish lords in Connacht attempted to adopt European infantry methods by exploiting the windfall of arms and military experience of the survivors of Spanish wrecks. The Uí Fhlaithbheartaigh kept several Spanish captains to train their household troops. When engaged by Crown forces in March 1589, they deployed pike and shot infantry led by a Spanish officer.[21] By the time the Uí Fhlaithbheartaigh had joined with the Burkes in rebellion, the council in Dublin reported that in addition to twenty Spaniards, their combined forces had 2,000 men armed and equipped with arms and ordnance recovered from the Armada wrecks.[22] Aodh Ó Néill, second Earl of Tyrone, was another beneficiary of Spanish expertise from the Armada wrecks. It was Ó Néill who created a force which would bring English power in Ireland to the point of collapse by 1599.

Aodh Ó Néill instigated a profound transformation of native Irish forces. He developed infantry which utilised the fundamental precepts of the military revolution by building pike- and shot-based formations, which relied on firearms as the mainstay of their combat power. This made them more in keeping with continental practices than English, as the Crown force's willingness to enter melee with pikemen was inconsistent with accepted practice in Europe, which viewed firepower as superior to the pike.[23] Ó Néill, however, did not slavishly copy European methods, but created a hybrid force that combined the advantages of modern firepower-oriented infantry with the flexible and highly mobile nature of Irish warfare. Furthermore, his military tactics recognised that the landscape of Ireland placed limitations on how and where troops could march and fight. Much of the Irish landscape was covered in scrub woods and bogland, with roads or tracks traversing defiles, passes and rivers. Vegetation and woods inhibited the use of close order pike. Therefore, rather than attempt to impose the new system of infantry onto a landscape unsuited to it, Ó Néill adapted the reforms to minimise the restrictive effects of the Irish terrain. This was a feat which the English were unable to match for most of the war.

The pike and shot units of Ó Néill took part in the raids of Aodh Mág Uidhir into Connacht, in May and June 1593, but there were still significant contingents of old-style Irish soldiers. At the battle of the Erne fords near Belleek in October 1593, *gallóglaigh* and *ceatharnaigh* were deployed. This can be clearly seen in John Thomas's illustration of the battle, where the Irish are shown armed with swords, axes and bows.[24] There were firearms present, but they were not the dominant weapon in this particular force. The following year the coordinated use of pike and shot destroyed Sir Henry Duke's relief force at the Ford of the Biscuits, south of Enniskillen, in the lordship of Fir Mhanach. Cormac Mac Baron Ó Néill used close-range gunfire to disrupt the English units and then deployed his pikemen to rout the rear and main battle of the army.[25]

The true power of Ó Néill's modernised army was not seen until the Battle of Clontibret in May 1595. Marshall Henry Bagenal led 1,500 foot and 250 horse to relieve the beleaguered garrison in Monaghan town. After being forced to fight their way to Monaghan via the pass at Crossdall, Bagenal's army took a more southerly route for their return home to Newry. Ó Néill attacked with his pike, shot and cavalry. They assailed the flanks of English army for eight hours until mutual exhaustion of gunpowder allowed Bagenal and his men to escape. The discipline and arms of the Irish moved Lord Deputy Russell to comment that:

> Their arms and weapons, their skill and practise therein far exceeding their wonted usage, having not only great force of pikes and muskets, but also many trained and experienced leaders as appeared by their manner of coming to the fight, and their orderly carriage therein.[26]

While it was apparent that Ó Néill was developing pike and shot formations, he was not creating an analogue of his English adversaries. English infantry formations were based upon a combination of pike and shot, with the shot armed with a mixture of muskets and lighter calivers. The troops of Ó Néill were overwhelmingly equipped with firearms, specifically calivers, which were lighter weapons than muskets, and suited to ambushes and fighting in trenches, woods or generally constricted terrain where manageability was more important than long-range firepower. Calivers had a shorter effective range and less penetrating power than muskets, but calivermen were more mobile. English infantry companies comprised 30–60 per cent shot, with the rest primarily pikemen.[27] By comparison, the formations of Ó Néill had a more pronounced dependence upon firepower, as 80 per cent or more of his infantry were equipped with firearms.[28] For the Irish, firepower, and not melee action, had become the primary means to effect battlefield success.

From the outset of the war, both sides experienced difficulty in distinguishing friend from foe, as the Irish came to resemble English both in equipment and formation on the march. This was not surprising as there were frequent references to Irish troops being trained in English ranks, only to defect.[29] In addition, much of the Irish equipment was bought from English deserters and the ostensibly 'loyal' merchants in Galway and Limerick, and even Dublin and London.[30] Examples of near-fatal confusion can be found in the early stages of the war. Aodh Mág Uidhir almost fell into an ambush by Captain Dowdall in late 1593 because he thought Dowdall's men were his own. Dowdall placed a troop of shot at the riverbank, but Mág Uidhir thought they were his men and continued to approach them in a small boat, only to be welcomed by a volley of fire which killed two of his companions.[31] This problem could be greatly exacerbated by the chaos and confusion of battle; therefore Captain Richard Cuney could be forgiven for his uncertainty during the English retreat at the Battle of the Yellow Ford in 1598. Captain

Roger Billings commanded the lead regiment during the withdrawal to Armagh, but his men got so far ahead of the rest of the army that Cuney and other English officers mistook them for Ó Néill's men.[32] During a close encounter in January 1600, Sir Arthur Savage and Captain Francis Shane misidentified Irish troops for their own. While conveying munitions, they thought a column of approaching infantry was Captain Shane's company. It was only as they got closer that it became obvious that these were not Shane's men, as he did not have so many. That they were Irish confederates was revealed by their numbers, not their appearance.[33]

Despite the sartorial similarities and unexpected tactical and operational proficiency of Ó Néill and his allies, the myth of Irish primitiveness remained common in England, which resulted in some degree of surprise to newcomers to the war in Ireland. In 1599 Robert Osborne, who was part of the reinforcements despatched with the Earl of Essex, reported that 'In England they say they be but naked rogues, but we find them as good men as those which are sent us, and better'.[34]

## Fighting Techniques

Despite the praise of their enemies, some of the Irish fighting techniques with firearms appear strange if not wasteful or ill-disciplined. Fire from long range and retreat into cover was a common feature of combat with Ó Néill's forces during the Nine Years' War. Sir John Norreys saw this in Armagh in 1595; Essex experienced it during his sojourn in Munster in 1599 and Mountjoy's men were regularly engaged by apparently ineffective distant gunfire. As already noted above, the caliver was a short-range weapon. Why would this occur when the Irish shot was considered more effective and better ordered than their English opponents?[35] It would be easy to ascribe this to poor fire discipline on the part of the Irish, but this would be incongruous with their tightly controlled actions at Crossdall, Clontibret and Mullaghbrack (all 1595). The answer may be found by considering who was training Ó Néill's troops. Spanish officers had been retained by Ó Néill since the Armada of 1588 and Spanish officers were training Irish troops at Dungannon in 1601, but how would this cause this profligate use of firearms? Sir John

Smyth may give a clue, when he described Spanish skirmishing methods as involving shooting from beyond effective range solely to draw in their targets or trick them into wasting their ammunition, which the Spanish described as '*disparese de lejos, para atraher y engañar bobos*', translated by Smythe as 'discharged afar off to draw on and deceive the fools'.[36]

Spanish training may have also been responsible for the different tactics used by the Irish pikemen. The only description of Irish pike training was that of a Spanish officer exercising troops at Dungannon in 1601, and it was clear Ó Néill's men were not copying their English counterparts. Thomas Douglas, a Scottish merchant (and spy for Sir Robert Cecil), observed Spanish captains training pikemen, but noted that despite their long experience in war, the soldiers were only instructed to 'discharge their pikes and run up and down'.[37] Douglas was surprised that they did not deploy in close order, but the Spanish captain answered that the terrain prevalent in Ireland made the use of close order irrelevant. In 1593, Matthew Sutcliffe wrote in *The Practice, Proceedings and Laws of Armes* that pikes were unwieldy in woods, shrubby ground and straights 'where they could not be managed'.[38] They were also vulnerable to shot or targeteers if not backed by their own shot. However, pikes were an essential element in deploying shot, as when firearm-equipped troops were reloading, they became highly vulnerable to attack by cavalry. In 1598 Robert Barret wrote of pike and shot that 'the armed pike is the strength; the shot the fury, one without the other is weakened'.[39] Given the swiftness of the Irish shot, it was essential for their supporting pike to keep pace; therefore, slow, dense formations were superfluous. Unfortunately this also instilled a critical weakness as light pike in loose order were primarily defensive, with no real shock value and useless against close-order pike forces. Sir John Smith observed that the close order pike will 'overthrow, disorder and break them [loose-order pike] with as great facility, as if they were but a flock of geese'.[40]

Another variance from English infantry training was the Irish confederates' adoption of the Spanish use of targeteers or sword-and-buckler men. By the outbreak of the war in 1593 their use in the Elizabethan armies in Ireland had practically ceased.[41] This was not true of continental Spanish units, who continued to deploy them. Sir Roger Williams wrote of their utility in breaches, trenches and, most

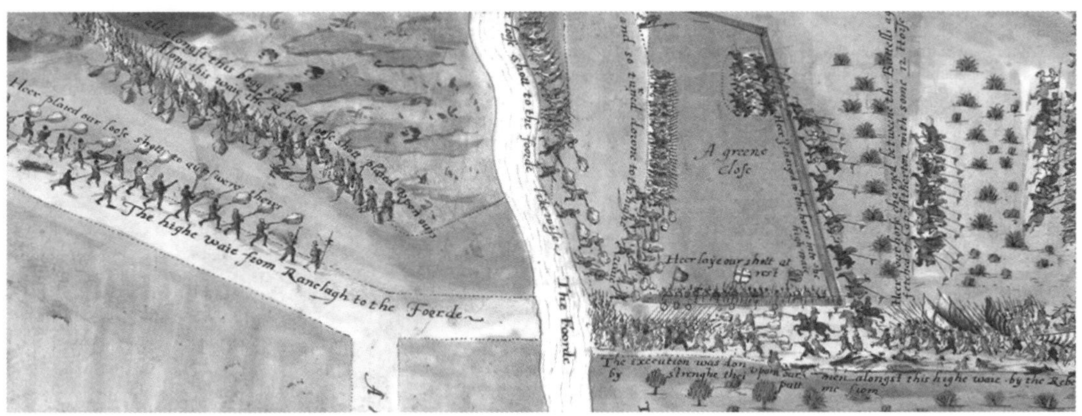


4. Firepower and disciplined skirmishing were central features of the modernised Irish tactics, seen here at the defeat of Sir Henry Harrington's men near Wicklow, 29 May 1599 (TCD, MS 1209/12).

importantly with regards to their use by the Irish, 'to cover shot that skirmishes in straights'.[42] They were most evident at the Battle of the Yellow Ford in 1598, when targeteers, deployed in accordance with Spanish methods, protected the Irish loose shot as they harried the English flanks.[43]

## Skirmish warfare

Skirmishing was a common feature of combat during the war. Indeed, it often appears as the orthodox fighting method of the Irish in early modern Ireland. Quite often it has been used pejoratively to suggest this was inferior to, or something other than, the historically-acceptable 'regular war'. On the contrary, skirmishing was more taxing on the individual soldier and required a higher degree of training and motivation than was expected from soldiers in tight formation. Fighting in line and battle required order, drill and discipline under fire, whereas skirmishing required flexibility, independence and good individual weapon skills. Furthermore, skirmishers had to be able to operate effectively while beyond the control or sight of their officers. One of Phillip II's most trusted commanders, Fernando Alvarez de Toledo, Duke of Alba, had no doubt about the demanding nature of skirmishing. He believed that any troops could be used in a battle, whereas skirmishing required veterans to prevail.[44] If this was true, then what was happening in Ireland?

Skirmishing in Ireland has rarely, if ever, been examined, despite the fact that there are numerous and, in many cases, detailed descriptions available. The engagements at Crossdall and Clontibret in 1595 were described as skirmishes lasting four and six hours respectively.[45] In June 1597, Captain Francis Croft related the skirmishing with Captain Richard Tyrell wherein the Irish conduct was 'as good discretion as Croft ever saw for loose skirmishes'.[46] The bloody stalemate at the Moyry Pass during September–October 1600 witnessed skirmishing which drew in hundreds, if not thousands, of troops. Lord Deputy Mountjoy described the fighting in the Moyry Pass on 2 October 1600 as 'one of the greatest skirmishes and best maintained in all places, that hath been in this kingdom, and continued for three hours'.[47] What was actually happening? One could assume that it was dispersed infantrymen taking pot shots at each other from behind cover, but the conduct of disciplined skirmishing was more complex.

The English soldier and diplomat Sir John Smythe gave a detailed explanation of skirmishing techniques.[48] He noted how loose shot separated themselves into groups of three and four where one advances to fire while the others made their weapons ready. After discharging his weapon, the soldier retired behind or to the side of his companions and one of them took his place to fire. This cycle continued through the course of the engagement. This was carried out by what Smythe described as 'of many societies of threes dispersed in the field'. He suggested that groups of four were better than three, as there would always be at least two loaded weapons and it lessened the chance of a weapon overheating. A second skirmishing method involved alternate 'societies' of three or four advancing and firing volleys, then retiring while those on their flanks advanced to fire. These were the proficient and orderly manners of skirmishing, but Smythe also described the actions of poorly trained or disciplined shot. He explained how badly trained soldiers moved in crowds, discharged their weapons whenever they chose, overheated their weapons and failed to provide mutual support to their comrades. It was clear that the Irish shot fighting at Clontibret, Moyry and elsewhere did not fall into the last category.

## Irish warfare: aberrant or not?

How does all this skirmishing fit into the conduct of continental warfare? Regular warfare has normally been conceived of as set-piece battles, where armies faced each other in ordered ranks or battallia.[49] Sir Charles Oman's classic text *A History of the Art of War in the Sixteenth Century* focused almost exclusively on set-piece battles as the defining experience of war in Renaissance Europe.[50] Opposing forces engaged with infantry, cavalry and artillery until one side broke contact or was routed from the field. This remains the epitome of armed action in popular and, in many cases, academic imagination, but examination of contemporary warfare suggests that the notion of massed infantry or serried ranks of pikes and muskets does not accurately reflect how most western European warfare was fought at the end of the sixteenth century.

The Earl of Essex described the war in Ireland as a 'miserable and beggarly ... war', but a direct parallel with contemporary European experience is clear.[51] War at the end of the sixteenth century was dominated by small-scale actions and skirmishing. Aside from sieges, which were the most high-profile military actions in the Low Countries, contemporary commentators noted that their service was marked by persistent skirmishing and petty actions. The majority of engagements described by Sir Roger Williams in the Low Countries were skirmishes and ambushes.[52] This was the type of war against which Sir John Smythe railed in 1590. He wrote how continental warfare was 'greatly altered' and had become 'disordered and tumultuary'.[53]

The opinion that 'small' war was ascendant over large, regular battle was articulated by Blaise de Montluc, Maréchal de France, who summarised war as a series of 'fights, encounters, skirmishes, ambushes, an occasional battle, minor sieges, assaults, escalades, captures and surprises of towns'.[54] The battle of Coutras in 1587 ended an eighteen-year hiatus of pitched battles in France.[55] In his account of the conflict in Mayenne and Burgundy during 1587–96, Henri Drouot described how war had fragmented into a series of local conflicts of small units pitting neighbour against neighbour. Small garrisons of twelve, ten or even five men fought '*la guerre aux vaches*' or 'the war on cows'.[56] In the seventeenth century, small actions were still far more common than large encounters. During the English Civil War, which is synonymous with battles such as Edgehill (1642) and Naseby (1645), 47 per cent of combat deaths were incurred in local engagements.[57]

## Passes, fastness and constricted terrain

Fighting in passes, woods along rivers and bogs is commonly associated with engagements during the Nine Years' War. Many were also fought at river crossings, at the edge of woods or on ground which restricted mobility. Examples of these include the battles at the Ford of the Biscuits (1594), Crossdall and Clontibret (1595), Mullaghbrack (1595), even at the Yellow Ford (1598); all saw Irish forces engage in constricted terrain. Generally, this has been interpreted as evidence of relative weakness on the part of the Irish forces or an inability of the Irish to fight the English on open ground.[58] While it is true that Ó Néill and his allies used terrain to neutralise the threat posed by English cavalry, the Irish ability to deploy and fight near woods and bogs was not symptomatic of weakness, but evidence of their superior training and discipline. Limited lines of sight restricted a commander's ability to control troops, therefore engagements in these situations required forces which could be relied upon to function without close supervision of senior officers. This was referred to by the Italian general Raimondo Montecuccoli.[59] Though writing in the mid-seventeenth century, his opinion on fighting in defiles and woods is relevant to Ó Néill's forces some sixty years earlier. Montecuccoli wrote that if a general wished to protect his army from the possibility of rout he could order his army to a location which offered refuge nearby, such as swamps, mountains or forests. However, he cautioned that this tactic could only be used if one had a well-trained army: 'The proximity of refuge destroys the will to resist. If the route of escape is made known from the start, either impatience or natural fear of the men will cause them to seek the means of flight once the slightest misfortune occurred.' Throughout the Nine Years' War, Ó Néill's forces were able to function in proximity to obvious lines of retreat, without any appreciable effect on his men's ability or willingness to engage the enemy.

In contemporary reports and subsequent historical analysis, discussion of the war in Ireland has included pejorative terms suggesting that the Irish conflict was fought differently from the way war was practised on the continent.[60] As stated above, the predominant type of warfare fought in Ireland during the war was one of skirmishes and ambush, but the Irish did also engage in large actions involving substantial field armies, with both the Crown and confederates deploying thousands of troops. Despite the large numbers involved, modern descriptions of these battles have tended to attach provisos which appear deprecatory, such as the use of terms like 'running fights' or 'ambushes' on difficult ground or in passes.[61] However, examination of contemporary battles in France and the Low Countries suggests that many engagements were not in the stereotypical lines of battle, but were themselves a complex series of ambushes, traps and skirmishes. The Battle of Heiligerlee in May 1568, which is seen as the start of military resistance in the Dutch revolt, was in effect an elaborate ambush. A feigned cavalry withdrawal by the Dutch drew the Spanish army into an ambuscade by 300–400 shot hidden in peat holes, which flanked the road the Spanish advanced along. The resulting rout killed almost half the Spanish force with little loss to the Dutch.[62] The duke of Alba's annihilation of the Dutch at Jemmingen the same year involved prolonged skirmishing and concealed troop movements in order to draw Louis of Nassau's men out of their trenches, before overwhelming them with attacks from multiple directions.[63]

## Eschewing battle

Ó Néill's Fabian strategy of refusing to meet the crown's army in a pitched battle is well known. He avoided battle in the open, preferring to use conventional troops to suit his prevailing operational or tactical needs.[64] References to Ó Néill's averseness to open battle implied that this tactic was different from the European norm, but examination of campaigns in Europe indicates that battle avoidance was the preferred option for waging war.[65] Warfare in Europe in the sixteenth century saw a decline in set-piece battles, which was reflected in the growing corpus of published material on the theory and conduct of war.

For many contemporary authors, avoiding battle and its inherent risks, in favour of waiting out enemies in the field and exhausting them with constant movement and frequent skirmishing, was preferable, and indeed a characteristic, of a good and prudent commander. Writing in 1549, Raymond Beccarie de Pavie, sieur de Fourquevaux, advised that battle should never be entered into unless a general was sure to have the advantage.[66] The Austrian general Lazarus Schwendi believed a commander to be a fool to choose battle if he could defeat an enemy by waiting. The Spanish Captain-General Bernadino de Mendoza also cautioned against battle and recommended in his *Theorique and Practise of Warre* that battle should be approached with a 'leaden foot'.[67] This tract may have special relevance to Ireland as it was later translated by Sir Edward Hoby, who dedicated it to Sir George Carew in 1597, three years before Carew was tasked with the pacification of Munster. Carew took just under a year to subdue the revolt in Munster without fighting a single battle.

The duke of Alba frequently avoided direct battles, despite having a numerical superiority over his opponents. His use of disciplined and regularly paid troops allowed the Spanish to shadow enemy forces until shortages caused them to disperse. He used this stratagem against the army of the Prince of Orange in 1568. William's troops were continually harassed by Alba's skirmishers all the way into France, where William's mercenary army broke up, with little cost in blood to Alba.[68] English soldiers had first-hand experience of battle-shy enemies in the Low Countries. Captain John Ogle noted how he had marched to where the enemy was encamped and offered battle, but was ignored by the Spanish who were content to remain within their defences. Ogle reported that there were few encounters with the enemy during the march, and that the greatest threat to his men was food shortages and the hot weather.[69]

## Rapid rate of transformation

While Irish warfare mirrored many aspects of the military modernisation process in other parts of Europe, the adoption by the Irish of military reforms and the accompanying change in equipment, arms and methodology was exceptionally fast. Prior to

1588, native Irish infantry was generally composed of *gallóglaigh* and *ceatharnaigh*. Following the Spanish Armada in 1588, unarmoured pikemen and shot infantry started to take the field against the Crown. The transformation of the Irish infantry was rapid, whereby pike, shot and supporting swordsmen became the primary infantry force deployed by the Irish by the end of the war in 1603. The speed of this change was noted by contemporary English commentators.[70] This was made more remarkable as it occurred despite the vested interests of traditional hereditary institutions such as the *gallóglaigh*. The melee-orientated and shock-based combat exemplified by the *gallóglaigh*, which took years for an individual to master and had served as the core of Irish military power for three and a half centuries, was swept away in less than a decade without any apparent resistance, suggesting that at least in military terms, the Irish were highly adaptive and open to change.

In comparison to the native Irish acceptance of Ó Néill's reforms, the English military community proved substantially more resistant to change. The introduction of shot and pike infantry as the mainstay of English armies had been slow and was met with opposition from professional soldiers.[71] The longbow was rooted in the English imagination as something quintessentially English and was associated with victories such as at Crésy (1346) and Agincourt (1415). While government reasons for maintaining the bow were not just military, publications such as *Certain Discourses Military* by Sir John Smythe showed that some military men had remained enthusiastic supporters of the time-honoured and battle-proven English longbow.[72] Despite the presence of shot in Henry VIII's armies, it took until 1589 for bows to be declared unfit for use.[73] Nevertheless, English armies were reformed; for some states modernisation appeared near impossible.

As technology and innovation spread from Western Europe, through Africa, Eastern Europe and the Near East, the impulse to modernise faced resistance from military professionals and elites, who were unwilling to relinquish their prestige or traditional martial skills, even though they were becoming obsolete. This was the case in Russia, where conservatism restricted military modernisation.[74] In order to field effective pike and shot units, the Russian crown was forced to raise foreign-style troops in parallel with the traditional military institutions.[75] For the Ottomans, modifying their infantry to cope with the prevailing modes of warfare proved impossible in the sixteenth and seventeenth centuries. The outbreak of war in Hungary demonstrated that Ottoman field tactics were obsolete when faced with modernised Austrian infantry.[76] Despite the presence of thousands of western veterans in the Muslim armies of the period, there is no evidence to suggest that the new tactics were adopted; weapons technology spread, but tactical techniques did not.[77]

## Revolution to a fault

Irish adoption of new methods and technology was swift and widespread and in that lay the seeds of Irish defeat. The melee-driven attacks of the *ceatharnaigh* and *gallóglaigh* had been swept aside, to be replaced by tactics which relied upon firepower to achieve battlefield success. The new Irish infantry's dependence on firepower was so complete that tactical situations arose where access to traditional Irish methods would have been advantageous. At Clontibret in 1595, when a charge into hand-to-hand combat may have sealed the issue in favour of Ó Néill, the attack stalled when his troop's supply of gunpowder was exhausted. Indeed, Sir Robert Salesbury suggested that it would have been a much bloodier affair if Ó Néill's pike had advanced like his shot.[78] Irish pikemen were present at Clifford's retreat from Ballyshannon (1597) and at the Battle of the Yellow Ford (1598), but throughout those engagements they never closed with unbroken English infantry. When rain extinguished the match for both the English and Irish shot at Ballyshannon, Clifford's unbroken pike deterred any further attacks.[79] The clearest reference to the Irish pikemen's reluctance to offensively engage came from Captain Richard Cuney, after the disaster at the Yellow Ford, who wrote that his men would have been totally routed if the Irish had charged at the closing stages of the battle.[80]

This weakness was critically exposed in 1600 after the arrival of Lord Mountjoy in Ireland. The Ulster lords monopolised critical military supplies, one of which was gunpowder. The main ports for offloading munitions were Killybegs, County Donegal and Strangford, County Down, both of which were in Ulster and under the charge of Ó Néill and his ally Aodh Ruadh Ó Domhnaill.

Control of munitions allowed Ó Néill to secure his direction of the war and domination of other centres of Irish military power, but it also concentrated crucial supplies in the northern extremity of Ireland.

Ó Néill's Munster allies were repeatedly required to request reinforcement and resupply out of Ulster. The precarious supply of gunpowder to Munster confederates was recognised in 1599, when it was noted that the Munster Irish had only two days' reserves of gunpowder.[81] Lord Deputy Mountjoy quickly identified the Irish midlands as key to the Irish war effort, therefore English operations from March to August 1600 interdicted the normal land routes from Ulster to Munster, causing many of Ó Néill's erstwhile allies to defect to the Crown. The submission of the Uí Mag Lochlainn in August 1600 effectively blocked north–south communications through Westmeath.[82] Mountjoy's stranglehold on north–south communications starved Ó Néill's southern allies of crucial munitions, which fatally compromised the southern Irish force's combat power. They were compelled to engage in melee actions with pikes, but this was a type of combat in which the light Irish pikemen were unsuited and untrained, and repeated defeats were followed by military collapse.

## Conclusion

The war in Ireland shared many characteristics of contemporary warfare on the continent. Skirmishes, ambushes and surprise assaults were typical of the experience of combat in Ireland and continental Europe. Small-unit actions were the norm in France and the Low Countries. Battle was eschewed at the highest levels of command. The most competent commanders based their strategies on exhausting their enemy's resources, rather than trusting to the vagaries of chance in battle. With respect to the effects of the military revolution, the war in Ireland was heavily influenced by the changes occurring in Europe. The principal attribute of the Irish reforms was the replacement of melee combat by firepower. The *ceatharnaigh* and *gallóglaigh* were rapidly supplanted by shot and pikemen. The transformation was so complete, and the primacy of firearms so total in Ó Néill's army, that whenever the occasion for shock action arose, his men generally demurred unless the enemy became disordered or started to rout. The new Irish forces were not slavish copies of continental models, but a hybrid, which relied on firepower but retained the Irish advantage of mobility. However, this compromise left them critically vulnerable when compelled to enter a melee with unbroken enemies. The neutralising of the Irish infantry's combat power was a first step on the road that would eventually bring the edifice of Irish military power crashing down.

The ultimate defeat of Ó Néill and his allies has obscured the sweeping changes across the island that almost eradicated English authority in Ireland. Native Irish soldiers and officers did not cling to their obsolete weapons and tactics but wholeheartedly and with great speed adopted the weapons and military methodology of the continent. This was recognised by the queen's officer during the war, but later accounts returned the Irish primitive to the narrative of the conflict. This iconic caricature was later appropriated by both unionists and nationalists for their own political ends, concealing the reality of this moment of dynamic change in native Irish society.

15

# Fugitive identities: Selves, narratives and disregarded lives in early modern Ireland

PATRICIA PALMER

In the spring of 1535, at the height of his rebellion, 'Silken' Thomas FitzGerald marched towards Maynooth with a levy of Connachtmen. FitzGerald was hoping to liberate his castle, which he believed to be still besieged by the Lord Deputy, Thomas Skeffington. As he approached Maynooth, however, he learnt that Skeffington had, in fact, taken the Kildare stronghold, executed its ward and now held it for the King. At this news, 'the better part of his company gaue him the slippe'. Meanwhile, Skeffington, 'hauing intelligence of [FitzGerald's] approach', intercepted some of 'Silken' Thomas's *gallóglaigh* at Naas. He led his 'seauen score' captives, 'all vnarmed toward Ionestowne'.[1] There followed what David Edwards calls 'the first definite massacre of the sixteenth century' in Ireland.[2] In his *Chronicle* account of what happened next, Richard Stanihurst skates over the slaughter of the 'seauen score'; instead, he concentrates on the one 'word-kerne // [who] Escaped from the massacre':[3] Skeffington's 'skoutewatch, espying Thomas to march neere, imparted it to the gouernour, who incontinently commaunded eache man to kyll hys prisoner before the charge, whyche was dispatcht, only Edmond Oleyn escaping mother naked by flight to Thomas his companie, leauing his shyrt in his keepers hande'.[4]

'Edmond Oleyn' slips not only out of his keeper's hand but out of history. We are left with nothing to clutch at but a piece of torn shirt.

When it comes to the 'foot-people'[5] of early modern Ireland, we get only such scraps: a name, perhaps a date, and the vaguest outline of a life-transforming story.

Reports from early modern Ireland are full of such one-off sightings. Individuals, often unnamed, swing momentarily into view, then slip for ever from the historical record. Given that they are so often sighted at moments of extremity, we are left to infer that they slipped – or were violently pushed – not just from the pages of the state papers but from the page of life itself. Their first appearance is also their last; there is no before, no afterwards. We simply get one tantalising glimpse of a life which is, otherwise, completely beyond our grasp. Three lives that, between them, must have involved extraordinary journeying, unfamiliar world views, incomprehension and suffering necessarily lie behind Lord Deputy Drury's wry report on the court sessions which he convened in Kilkenny in 1578: '36 persons were executed, among which some good ones ... a blackamoor, and two witches'. These are 'good ones' insomuch as they are good for adding a splash of anecdotal colour; the only additional information we get about them is legalistic: the 'witches', Drury goes on, were tried 'by natural law, for that we found no law to try them by in this realm'.[6] Elsewhere, a Captain Romley swims briefly in – and out – of view in an account of Bagenal's army retreating from the rout at the Yellow Ford: 'they marched that night to the Newry, without hurt of any savinge one, Captayne Romley, whoe had his throate cutte under a bush whilst he was aloane takinge of tobacco'.[7] As the reports of Romley, the 'witches' and the African confirm, many of these characters enter the record posthumously, their lives surviving merely as back-projections from their deaths and their sometimes lurid afterlives, and so it is with

> one *Con Mackmeloeg*, who before caused maister Smithe to be eaten vp with Dogges, after he had been boiled, and this same *Con Mackmeloeg* beyng slaine, was lefte emong wolues v. daies, and was had into a house, where his freendes howled, and cried ouer his dedde bodie so long, that by mischaunce a greate deale of pouder caught fire, and sett the house in a flame: the Dogges in the toune smellyng this ded bodie ranne in, and tooke it out of the house, and so tore it in peeces, and fedde vppon his carraine fleshe openly.[8]

Early modern Ireland provided the raw material for a significant range of fictionalised and often highly aestheticised accounts of violence which I have written about elsewhere.[9] In this chapter, however, I focus on 'factual' accounts, largely taken from the State Papers, where the telling is balder and often shocking in its terseness. So, while, for example in the stage-play world of *King Lear*, the 'pluck[ing] out'[10] of Gloucester's eyes brings us to a place of pity and terror, a real-life blinding in the Pale enters the record as just another charge in the list of accusations levelled against Captain Thomas Lee by Captain Montagu. As an illustration of Lee's indiscipline, Montagu instanced his capture of a young Wicklow gentleman, Art O'Toole, 'within seven miles from Dublin'. Then, despite the fact that O'Toole was allied to the English and was travelling under their protection, Lee 'bound him to a Maypole, and (the soldiers refusing to be the actors of so barbarous a cruelty dangerous to themselves), at his commandment, and for reward of Art's horse and weapons, a base man of Leix with his thumbs did thrust out both his eyes'.[11]

The spectral quality of those caught, almost accidentally, in the unsteady lantern-beam of history piques an interest that cannot be satisfied. There is no back story, and there is no sequel. These are identities without narratives. We are left to wonder, for example, about what became of the young boy mentioned in John Hooker's account of Captain Davells' assassination during the second Desmond War in Munster. Sir John of Desmond, we learn, burst into Rice's lodging house in Tralee and found Davells and his companions asleep. Sir John peremptorily woke them up; then he and his men set about slaughtering the rudely awakened lodgers. Davells' servant, a boy called 'Smolkin', who had acted as 'a continuall messenger' between the captain and Sir John, rushed in to save his master: 'This boie seeing his maister to be thus murthered ran vpon Iohn of Desmond, and held him by the armes as well as he could, crieng; What wilt thou kill my maister?' Sir John urged him aside: 'Go thy waies Smolkin; thou shalt haue no harme.' But, 'the boie seeing blowes still to be giuen, cast himselfe downe vpon his maister, crieng; If thou wilt kill him, then kill me also. And so saued him as well, and so long as he could. But it auailed not, for slaine and most cruellie *he* was there murthered' [my italics].[12] It is clear from the context that the final 'he' refers to Davells, as Hooker switches seamlessly from recording that 'he was there murthered' into eulogising the dead captain. 'Smolkin' slips out of the historical record, just as Hooker's slipshod third-person pronoun slides from 'Smolkin' ('*he* could') to Davells ('*he* was'). A casualty of Hooker's pronominal inattention, as well as Sir John's frenzy, the boy remains stranded, like all these characters, in one moment in time, in the eternal present of his unstoried life.

In all these cases, we get only one vignette from a life that was otherwise lived in the penumbra beyond the historical record. Sir George Carew, Lord President of Munster, fearing that the late Earl of Desmond's sister was contracting marriage with Aodh Ó Domhnaill of Tír Conaill, mentions in an aside that he has interrogated 'the Countess of Desmond's woman', one 'Mary ny Shee', and made her 'close prisoner in [Limerick] gaol, til leisure better serve for farther examination'.[13] 'Examination' has an ominous ring; the terms of Carew's commission allowed him to put suspects 'to tortures'.[14] Unsurprisingly, 'Mary ny Shee' is never heard of again, but her brief appearance, as a victim caught up in the machiavellianisms of dynastic match-making, reminds us that women figured disproportionately among those who lived outside the identity-confirming realm of public record. Moreover, they entered it without any power to shape its *grand récit*.

All too often, it is violence that hauls such women into the public realm. A girl is dragged by soldiers into Lord Deputy Russell's camp; Russell's logbook merely records that she was seized for shrieking a warning to six kerns, enabling them to escape just as his soldiers were about to close in on them.[15] There is no further mention of her. Such figures streak across the narrative like those damsels in distress who, contemporaneously, were making similarly incidental appearances in Edmund Spenser's *The Faerie Queene*:[16] damsels like Florimell, for example, who is already in flight when she bursts into the text and who exits it just as quickly, hotly pursued (as such damsels so frequently are) by a lascivious dastard. In Book 3, Prince Arthur and Sir Guyon are ambling through a forest when,

> All suddenly out of the thickest brush,
> Vpon a milk-white Palfrey all alone,
> A goodly Ladie did foreby them rush,
> Whose face did seeme as cleare as Christall stone,
> And eke through feare as white as whales bone:

> Her garments all were wrought of beaten gold,
> And all her steed with tinsell trappings shone,
> Which fled so fast, that nothing mote him hold,
> And scarse them leasure gaue, her passing to behold (3.1.15).[17]

Florimell's trajectory – and even the direction of her gaze – are determined by her pursuer:

> Still as she fled, her eye she backward threw,
> As fearing euill, that pursewd her fast (3.1.16.1–2).

Florimell escapes from this 'griesly Foster' who comes 'Breathing out beastly lust her to defile' (3.1.17.2–3), but only to find herself trapped in the ominously phallic 'cock-bote' of the 'Forcyng' Fisher; later still, Proteus locks her in a dungeon and tries to 'compell' her 'by cruelty' (3.8.26.7, 4.11.2.9). As is so often the case, Spenser's poem takes us to a dark place which the prose record shrouds in euphemism and silence. Rapes are almost never mentioned in the state papers. We know, however, that the breach between James FitzMaurice and Sir John of Desmond arose from FitzMaurice's insistence on hanging one of Sir John's followers for raping and murdering a camp-follower; and that an 'orgy of rape' preceded Sir Edmund Butler's burning of Slaney in 1569.[18] Sadly, the threat of rape that hangs over almost every female figure in *The Faerie Queene*[19] is probably an accurate enough pointer to how the story of the shrieking girl dragged back to Lord Russell's camp ended.

Sometimes, the anecdotes embedded in contemporary accounts seem poised to explode into fully fledged narratives. Fynes Moryson provides a skeletal summary of an event that cries out for a fuller explanation than he, relying on hearsay accounts, can supply:

> Capt. *Trever* and many honest Gentlemen lying in the *Newry* can witness, that some old Women of those Parts, used to make a Fire in the Fields, and divers little Children driving out the Cattle in the cold Mornings, and coming thither to warm them, were by them surprized, killed, and eaten, which at last was discovered by a great Girl breaking from them by Strength of her Body, and Capt. *Trever* sending out Soldiers to know the Truth, they found the Childrens Skulls and Bones, who were executed for the Fact.[20]

Behind Moryson's shocking soundbite about these cannibal-*caillí*[21] lies the unexplored landscape of a man-made famine, the bitter fruit of Lord Deputy Arthur Chichester's scorched-earth policy.[22] Another snippet, from the state papers this time, offers only the bare bones of a complex domestic drama of violence and betrayal. We learn that Maud Plunkett, widow of Christopher Plunkett, Baron Dunsany, was murdered 'with sundrie stroakes of an axe'. When the neighbours, alerted by her screams, rushed in, they found Maud dying in the arms of her nurse, 'Honora Caffra'; a horse-boy named 'Tyrrelagh mac ne Moyster' was standing by. The neighbours immediately planted the suspicion that Honora was Maud's killer. The nurse was duly tried, found guilty and burnt on Gallows Hill, though she continued to plead innocence 'euen to the laste gaspe of breath'. Tyrrelagh, meanwhile, languished in prison; but at night he 'would dream and raue, and crye out in his sleepe holde me, holde me, saue me, looke whear she comes, oh she pulles me and pintsheth mee, with sundrie the like outcries'. The prisoner to whom he was chained, weary of having his rest broken by such sleep-talk, complained to his jailers. Tyrrelagh was examined by the Constable and the troubled horse-boy confessed that it was indeed he who had murdered Maud.[23]

In her short-story collection, *Astray*, Emma Donoghue takes precisely these kinds of anecdotal fragments – snippets of real lives garnered, in her case, from letters, scrapbooks, legal records and 'a clipping from the *Tucson Star*' – and turns them into compelling fictions.[24] But my interest is not in projecting endings – or even stories – onto one-off sightings. There is no way of recovering, for example, an identity for the woman from whom Henry Bagenal learnt that Aodh Ó Néill, Earl and Lord of Tír Eoghain, and Aodh Mag Uidhir, Lord of Fir Mhanach, were plotting together; she will have to remain forever as merely the 'woman of that country which was found by his soldiers' and who subsequently escaped.[25] Nor will we ever know anything further about the 'lewd woman' who came aboard Sir Henry Dowcra's ship while it lay at anchor in Lough Foyle and who made her way to the cabin of Mac Suibhne na dTuath, chief of Tuatha Toraighe. Mac Suibhne, who Dowcra was holding captive amidships, 'kept his bed of a disease', according to Dowcra's diary, but the unidentified 'lewd woman' managed to create a commotion which allowed Mac Suibhne to rise from his sick bed and escape.[26]

These are lives and identities left to inference. These individuals are no more than disregarded extras to the main, history-making action. In 1586, after an ill-fated encounter with a Captain Merriman, Alasdair Mac Somhairle Mac Domhnaill managed, though gravely wounded, to swim to a *crannóg* where unidentified accomplices staged his mock-burial, to give the impression he had been killed in the encounter. The 'grave' was covered with rushes and, to complete the effect, 'six owld calliops' knelt around it, 'weepinge'.[27] Captain Merriman, still in pursuit of Mac Somhairle, made his way onto the *crannóg* and he came upon this tableau of simulated lamentation. But, 'At the length an olde woman (whoe satte very mournefull), beinge examined what became of hym, and threatned by the soldiers, for feare of death, she poynted to the place where he lay hidden'.[28] The violence against women, which is only implicit in that reference to examination and threats, breaks closer to the surface in the report of Captain Mackworth's storming of Carrigafoyle Castle during the Desmond War. After a sustained bombardment, Mackworth breached the wall and, pursuing the defenders to the battlements, put fifty of them to the sword and 'six others he tooke, whereof one was a woman, which were executed in the campe'.[29]

The temptation with such figures is to give them an identity as members of a group; they attract interest not on their own terms but as representative figures. As emblematic types, they become part of a collective, the faces – albeit blank, unidentified faces – that fill out (or challenge) the generalisations foisted on the general population in a time of conflict. Robert Devereux, the second Earl of Essex, newly arrived in Ireland, found himself among, as he baldly informed Privy Council, 'savages': how 'unequal a wager' it was, he complained, 'to adventure the lives of noblemen and gentlemen against rogues and naked beggars'.[30] But, of course, rogues and naked beggars have their identities, too, and there is a perfectly understandable desire to extrapolate from these one-off appearances and to fit such stray individuals into broad categories and classes.[31] The temptation is to weave that throwaway reference to 'a blackamoor, and two witches' condemned at the sessions in Kilkenny, for example, into a more general account of witchcraft or of ethnic others in early modern Ireland. We could, for example, work towards accommodating the two Kilkenny witches within a broader collective identity by aggregating a number of other one-off sightings (or imaginings): Sir

George Carew complaining, as he struggled through terrible storms on the way to Dunboy, that 'The country of Beare is full of witches'; or Cathair Mac Art Caomhánach sealing his good relationship with Anthony St Leger, in 1544, by sending the Lord Deputy a witch for examination.[32]

But we should resist the rush to collectivise the identities of characters who faced their fate – and entered the historical record – on their own, in the solitude with which any individual faces a moment of crisis or terror. We need to think, first, about what these individuals have to say to us on their own terms. To do so, we must resist both the group identity projected onto them by early modern observers ('witches', 'rebels', 'savages'), or by our own critical discourses (marginalised women, masterless men, members of the landless underclass). In *Cruel Optimism*, Lauren Berlant surveys the singularity of our own present and our attempts to make sense of the imploding paradigms – economic, political and philosophical – by which, until very recently, we lived. She argues that 'all generality ... derives from stories constituted by a collective catching up to what is already happening in ordinary worlds, shaped in a crisis-defined and continuing now'.[33]

Berlant's concern is with genre and artistic expression, with how 'the aesthetic or formal rendition of affective experience provides [the first] evidence of historical processes'. She is concerned, in short, with the way the formlessness of real lives, 'play[ed] out in lived time', gets turned into patterns and categories.[34] I would argue that the fragmentary little vignettes we have been looking at function in a very similar way. If Berlant is concerned with the movement from the individual's lived experience into genres which can represent 'the emerging event', I am concerned with the event itself, rather than, say, that event's representation in the state papers. In short, I am concerned with what she calls 'a state of things in which *something* that will perhaps matter is unfolding amid the usual activity of life'.[35] That 'something' is, in her words, 'a genre of social time and practice in which a relation of persons and worlds is sensed to be changing but the rules of habitation and the genres of storytelling about it are unstable'.[36] Moreover, the crisis of the present (and we must remember that what is, for us, the historical past was for our characters their very real, existential present) is also a crisis of *presence*, or presenting.[37] That is, it is a crisis about being fully able to experience the moment and to give it aesthetic form. So, given that double crisis – the actual crisis and the crisis of representing it – the imperative, Berlant argues, must be to attend first 'to what is already happening in ordinary worlds shaped in a crisis-defined and continuing now'; we should not, she insists, move too swiftly on to the 'generality'. For all that these early modern characters – these random, unfortunate souls who wander in to the archive – are caught up in the sweep of historical events, they are, in the first instance, living (or being dispatched from) lives that are precarious, contingent and, in that moment of extremity, solitary.

Like Berlant, I am suspicious of the kind of historicism that uses the individual story as – in her words – a 'hyperlink to an untold history that can justify, if the archive is thick enough, a "reading" that must not stray too far from some version of the historical record'.[38] The individual story just becomes grist to the mill of the bigger story, and gets devoured by it. Two of the discourses which might seem best placed to attend to these characters on their own terms, New Historicism and Subaltern Studies, seem to me too disposed to rush on, instead, to the 'generalities'. Gayatri Spivak in 'Can the Subaltern Speak?' memorably describes the subaltern women of whom she writes as occupying 'the points of fadeout' in 'the writing of disciplinary history'. But, of course, they also occupy 'the points of fadeout' in the archive on which the writing of disciplinary history *really* depends. Spivak, however, is not particularly interested in this – archival – 'fadeout'. In an implicit warning against the kind of activity which I am conducting here, she defines her marginal figures as 'footprints of the trace (of someone? something? – we are obliged mistakenly to ask) that efface as they disclose'.[39] Having cautioned herself against taking these footprints literally and, 'mistakenly', searching for the 'someone' to whom they belonged, Spivak, too, presses on to the generalities, to the larger questions of 'the subaltern as female' and 'the broader narratives of imperialism'.[40]

Of course, 'the broader narratives of imperialism' weigh heavily on the lives with which we are concerned; a great many of those who enter the record as its victims are subaltern women. But, in defiance of Spivak's warning, I would argue that it is only by thinking about all those 'someones' that we can begin to get a fix on what those generalities really mean, and on the real cost of imperialism or subalternity. The number of lives lost during the Elizabethan conquest was so great that, for the Four Masters, compilers of the *Annals of the Kingdom of Ireland*, they were simply 'countless and indescribable';[41] the number of the dead in the Second Desmond war alone seemed unquantifiable, as John Hooker concluded: 'the numbers of them are infinit, whose blouds the earth dranke vp, and whose carcases the foules of the aire and the rauening beasts of the feeld did consume and deuoure'.[42]

The crushing ability of war to reduce lives to statistics reaches its apotheosis when even statistics fail and the lives lost become 'infinit' and *un*computable. In a fascinating study of minor characters in the novel, Alex Woloch remarks that 'the distinction between counting and naming occurs precisely at the fault line where an individual ceases to command attention as a *qualitatively* distinct being and begins to be viewed as a *quantitative* unit' [my italics].[43] The faultline – or point of fadeout – with which we are concerned seems very close to this, but its dynamic moves in the opposite direction: our characters occupy the faultline where an individual steps out of the quantitative unit – the 'countless', the 'infinit' – and begins 'to command attention as a qualitatively distinct being'.

Woloch's 'minor characters ... simply through their subordinated multiplicity, hover vulnerably on the borderline between name and number'.[44] Our fugitive apparitions from the archive hover in just the same way. Even establishing these characters' names is tricky. When Don Juan Del Águila lands in Kinsale, he dispatches 'a Fryar in a soldier's Habit' with papal bulls granting indulgences to anyone who will join the rebellion; in Clonmel the disguised friar goes by the name of 'James Fleming', in Waterford he 'named himself Richard Galloway'.[45] Fixed identities were imperilled – or could lead to peril – in a world where solidities dissolved under the pressure of war and the shifting alliances it imposed. In particular, the subaltern army of go-betweens, messengers, informers and spies that weaves in and out of the official reports of the Elizabethan conquest hovers between anonymity and identity, disguise and disclosure. Captain Nicholas Dawtrey declared the Irish to be 'as slippery as an eele' and warned the Queen that spies, in particular, 'deale slipperly'.[46] Informers and double-crossing spies cast not just identity but identification itself into question. An informer writes to Robert Cecil, explaining that he had met a Galway man of Irish blood when they were both in prison. The Irishman went by the name of Blackcadell but also used the alias

'Capt Blague'. The informer recognised that someone occupying such a fluid identity – and Blackcadell, as 'a good linguist', was particularly well equipped to play the chameleon's part – was always likely to be 'a cross intelligencer', however 'useful' he might be in other ways.[47] Women, too, could be involved in these little dramas of disguise and fanciful misnaming. While the Earl of Ormond was being held hostage by Eoghan mac Ruaidhrí Ó Mórdha, Geoffrey Fenton, the Chief Secretary and spymaster general, contrived to infiltrate a 'gentlewoman' called Honora into the Earl's presence. Distracting his guards, Honora overcame Ormond's suspicions by describing, as a 'token' of her credentials, a green silk bookbag belonging to Fenton. For her subsequent missions, Fenton tells Cecil, Honora would 'pass under the name of *Imperia Romana*'. Sometime later, he records that 'Imperia Romana' had returned from the borders of Laois with word that Ó Mórdha had died of gunshot wounds; he subsequently sends her back to confirm the report, and she disappears into the anonymity and puzzlement which her unlikely soubriquet only intensifies.[48]

So often in these cases, we are left struggling with the basic question of identification rather than engaging with the more profound issue of identity. Valentin Groebner, in *Who Are You? Identification, Deception and Surveillance in Early Modern Europe*, explores that crucial distinction between identification and identity. Identity, he declares, 'blurs the boundaries between self-definition and external definition'. Identification, on the other hand, is not intrinsic to the individual but rests solely on 'a set of collectively used signs' – sartorial, racial, physical, physiognomic, vocal, linguistic – 'whose specific combination enables identification'. 'Identifications,' he concludes, 'always amount to what regulates relations between the interior and exterior.'[49] What we repeatedly seem to be offered in the case of our fleetingly encountered figures is an externally projected identification which is, in a crucial sense, not an identity at all; it is merely, like the spymaster's codenames, a convenient moniker. These are individuals reported on from the outside, across barriers of culture, sympathy, ideology and language. Sir William Brereton, visiting Dublin in 1635, recalled passing a house on Bridge Street where an Irish merchant had just died; he reported that 'we heard either his wife or sister roaring out as though she were violently distracted; this they say is very ordinary with the Irish'.[50] Everything about this report is second-hand: the 'roaring out' is merely a sound overheard from the street; the linguistic incomprehension of the Anglophone eavesdropper turns Hibernophone lamentation into 'roaring';[51] the gloss he puts on it ('this they say is very ordinary with the Irish') rests on the authority of an unidentified third party.

So, the newcomer, plunged into an unfamiliar world, struggles even with identification. Recognising the identity of the other is entirely beyond his ken. Groebner stresses the importance of sartorial markers in establishing identification, and the inability of the New English to distinguish individuals or pick them out from the undifferentiated collective explains their obsession with Irish dress (see Horning, Chapter 1). Instead of operating, as clothing did in England, as a livery which manifested one's class and station, Irish dress *disguised* identity. That is the source of Spenser's anxiety about the Irish predilection for 'long glibbes, which is a thicke curled bush of haire, hanging downe of their eyes, and monstrously disguising them';[52] and that is why William Herbert compared to the Irish mantle 'as to a hedgehog his skin, or to a snail her shell'.[53]

The distinction between identification and identity rests, in large measure, on the distinction between having an identity projected onto one – a generic, externally generated identity – and, as Groebner puts it, 'an individual's subjective self-definition ... the identity of the self'.[54] Access to such self-definition presumes self-disclosure and the opportunity, ability and willingness to tell one's own story. There was precious little space, however, for telling one's own story – or for listening to the story of the other – amid the upheaval of the Elizabethan conquest. Indeed, one of the few arenas of self-disclosure in early modern Ireland is the interrogation chamber, as those passing references to 'examination' above attest. We have already met Sir George Carew, the Lord President of Munster, examining the unfortunate 'Mary ny Shee'. Later, as he approached Dunboy Castle, in the lordship of Ó Súilleabháin Bhéara, he subjected another woman to 'examination'. The woman is unnamed; she is simply identified as a 'silly woman', in the early modern sense of 'silly' meaning simple or unsophisticated. But when Carew takes over her 'examination' from Lord Barry (Carew's initial reliance on the Hibernophone Lord Barry points to a language barrier which he never mentions), he confronts an identity that clearly made an impression on him: he reports, in a tone of mild wonderment, that

'I never spake with a woman (of her rude education) that was so sharp and ready'.[55] But no trace of that identity survives; who she was, or why she was interrogated, or what she had to say goes unrecorded.

Time and again, the individual subjected to 'examination' fails to have his story officially recorded. One 'Niall O'Quinn', taken prisoner by Sir Griffin Markham, gets his chance to enter the historical record when he is taken for examination but, we learn, 'drink had made him both so senseless and speechless' that nothing more is heard from him.[56] A priest called 'Dennis O'Roughan' gets his moment in the limelight when taken prisoner by Lord Deputy Fitzwilliam. Fitzwilliam assures Lord Burghley that the priest is composing a book of informations against the disgraced former chief governor, Sir William Perrott. But, Fitzwilliam adds, it will take some time for the priest's disclosures to see the light of day because one of the Constable's men bit off a piece of O'Roughan's nose, 'and he can work only at short fits'.[57] Telling one's story, asserting one's identity, was an uphill battle for the *cosmhuintir* of early modern Ireland.

But behind the vexed question of identity is the even more fraught one of selfhood. If, as Groebner suggests, identity straddles 'the boundaries between self-definition and external definition', the idea of 'selfhood' speaks exclusively of interiority. As Michael Schoenfeld has so convincingly shown in his study of emerging discourses of selfhood among English writers (including Edmund Spenser), the body itself, scrutinised psychologically and physiologically, becomes the site of inwardness.[58] It is ironic that the very period with which we are concerned – and where we are struggling to get even from identification to identity – is also one animated by intense developments in the examination, 'discovery' and writing of the self.[59] Focusing, as the title of his book declares, on *Bodies and Selves in Early Modern England*, Schoenfeld counters the New Historicists' argument that a new emphasis on the disciplined self ultimately worked to empower the state rather than the self-disciplined individual. On the contrary, Schoenfeld insists, the Renaissance's new emphasis on 'self-control' was about 'how to fortify a self, not police a state'. But Schoenfeld's distinction cannot so effortlessly remove the power dynamic from the equation. 'It is,' Schoenfeld goes on, 'the disordered, undisciplined self, subject to a variety of internal and external forces, that is the site of subjugation.'[60] But, of course, it was not just 'the disordered, undisciplined self' that was subject to subjugation. Subjugation – including colonial subjugation – was also meted out to individuals and groups whom those in possession of a putatively 'ordered' self could portray as sufficiently '*dis*ordered' to require conquering and colonising. The self-examination and the discourse of inwardness, which Schoenfeld studies, produced what he calls 'the self-control that authorizes authority'. But that 'authority', of course, would also be exercised over those whose selfhood seemed less compelling.[61] To cultivate one's selfhood is not always to sharpen one's recognition of the other as also, potentially, a self.

Indeed, the harsh discipline of conquest and colonial dispossession left little space for the cultivation or expression of selfhood among the individuals whom we have been following. Identity, as distinct from selfhood, migrates, as Groebner reminds us, between 'an individual's subjective self-definition' and a collective, group identity.[62] While the upheavals convulsing early modern Ireland left little space for the cultivation of identity in the first sense – in the sense of selfhood defined by Schoenfeld – it accelerated the development of identity in the second, collective sense. Powerful forces were coalescing to forge that collective identity: the conquest itself and the resistance it generated, the intensified confessional sectarianism triggered by the Reformation and Counter-Reformation, the realignment and redefinition of both Gaelic and Old English communities all helped to launch what Susan Iwanisziw calls the 'precursive stage of Irish national identity'.[63] But while it is easy to trace the emergence of a discourse of Irish identity in the collective, national sense,[64] there is no corresponding discourse articulating an emerging sense of selfhood. Bardic poetry, for example, continued to articulate a formulaic and communal rather than an individual identity. The arresting lyric voice of the individual would emerge only in the wake of defeat.[65]

It is all too easy to conscript the fugitive figures, who find themselves astray in the State Papers, to identity in the second, national and collective, sense, either as victims or villains. But their real interest, it seems to me, is that they occupy a space between both identity in the sense of selfhood and identity in the collective sense. These are individuals astray in a world in flux, where collective identities are being dissolved and re-formed. Although not 'individuals' in the sense of self-consciously cultivated selfhood examined by Schoenfeld, their journeys and sufferings are individual; and they give us access to a precious singularity that helps us resist the anomie and anonymity which the de-personalising statistics of war reportage produce. Instead of nameless, faceless victims, the 'countless' infinities of the anonymous dead, we are left to wonder about young 'Smolkin' and 'Mary ny Shee' and what it meant to be just that person, in that exact place and time. So we return, at the end, to another fugitive sighting that takes us to a man seen limping suspiciously through Mullingar in 1599. His unusual gait draws the attention of an eagle-eyed Palesman who orders his arrest. The man, Daniel McUillimett, is seized and subsequently – ominously – disappears from the record.[66] But, before that, he is found to have two letters stuffed in the soles of his shoes. One is in Irish and the other, from Captain Tyrrell, in English; both are addressed to the incorrigibly recusant Lord of Delvin.[67] We need to suspend for a moment the larger questions of identity that are being paraded here: the shifting allegiances of the Old English, the observant Palesman's loyalism, the Lord of Delvin's confessionally inspired flirtation with rebellion, the complex bilingualism which compounded that plasticity of identity. Instead, we need, for just one moment, simply to put ourselves in the uncomfortable shoes of 'Daniel McUillimett'.

16

# Popular politics and the legitimacy of power in early modern Ireland

BRENDAN KANE

This chapter is about two things – popular politics and legitimacy in Tudor and early Stuart Ireland – and assuming both exist, how they might be related. Ethan Shagan's definition of popular politics, used in his *Popular Politics and the English Reformation*, is a useful place to start: 'the presence of ordinary, non-elite subjects as the audience for or interlocutors with a political action', and additionally that, 'What defined popular politics … was not the social class of the people politicking, but rather the extent to which the governed played a role in their own governance'.[1] I am interested in the politics of the commons for a few reasons. The first is simply evidentiary. When reading the sources of Tudor and early Stuart Ireland, there are occasional reports of the 'people', or the 'commonalty', acting in ways that are either expressly politically engaged or at least of concern to those in authority. Thus, one goal of this essay is merely to report on a more systematic trawl through those sources and make an initial assessment of whether there is something of a pattern of politicisation and political action by non-elites, those below the level of the grandees with whom we typically associate politics in this period.[2] Doing so should tell us something about the social depth and character of political identity, and thus about the theory and practice of becoming and belonging in early modern Ireland.

A further reason for this interest in popular politics is a historiographical and/or framing one. In many ways the Irish pleb is truly subaltern, having left no – or almost no – voice in the archive. Again, there are contemporary commentaries on the 'people' and their various doings, but none of their own authorship. In that absence, however, we can at least be attentive to how we frame and contextualise those intermittent reports of popular agency that do appear in the usually hostile sources. To that end, we ought to think carefully about those expressions as potentially demonstrating a political awareness that is not simply subsumable under the meta-category of 'resistance', which one encounters so frequently in the literature concerning this period.[3] Thus, the chapter's first concern is to ask whether the fragmentary record of political action by non-elites might rise to the level of evidence for an operative non-elite politics in early modern Ireland.

The chapter's second concern is legitimacy, in particular the legitimacy of authority.[4] Most histories of the period approach English–Irish relations in this chaotic, indeed traumatic, time through attention to the high-political contest over preponderate power.[5] Crudely speaking, that approach focuses on English and Irish under the Tudors, in a struggle over control of the island, a story that would eventually play out with the former emerging victorious post-1607, upon the 'collapse of the Gaelic order'. That narrative is, of course, the fundamental one for understanding the age: this was a colonial setting, one in which a traditional authority and culture was largely eliminated by an external one, frequently with tremendous violence.[6] Beneath that metanarrative, however, existed the lives and hopes of individual people, and there is strong evidence that Gaelic Irish and Old English, at all levels of society, believed there was room for manoeuvre and aspiration beyond the level of mere survival within the new dispensation. Balancing sensitivity to the trauma of the age with acknowledgement of the fact that there was – as there always must be in societies – a bewildering range of interests, motivations and perceptions amongst the people who lived through it, and long stretches of peace between outbreaks of war, is a difficult and potentially fraught undertaking.[7] It is a necessary one, however. Having attempted elsewhere to explore those dynamics at the elite level, here I argue that there was a contemporaneous popular politics in this period and that it was active less in determining matters of *de jure* power – the sorts of constitutional and legal issues fought over by the great – but with determining the legitimacy of *de facto* power on the ground.[8] This could take the form of resistance to official authority, or of loyalty, or of many positions in between. Thus, it is unlikely that there existed a collective voice of non-elites expressive of a shared identity as 'the people', but simply that commoners were able – at times collectively, at others individually – to act politically. Moreover, such political action was not simply 'negotiation', a scholar's term of art that can leave the impression that almost all power lay on one side of an interaction and that something of a 'moral economy' governed state and subject relations. Negotiation there certainly was, but it frequently was the result of real political contestation, across the social hierarchy, over what constituted legitimate power and its expression in the colonial setting of early modern Ireland.

Popular politics are intimately connected to investigation of the complex dynamics of interaction and accommodation that the editors of this volume have succinctly labelled 'becoming and belonging'. In part they relate simply by allowing insight into how emergent identities – here of non-elites as political actors – were expressed in quotidian interactions during a chaotic period of fundamental social and cultural dislocation and transformation. Additionally, however, I wish to engage with the volume's theme on a more abstract level, to think about becoming and belonging as it relates to participation in an expanding state. At the risk of oversimplification, but in the interest of suggestively pushing to reorient how we think of early modern colonial Ireland, an exploration of popular politics reveals how Irish commoners were becoming 'modern' in that the language and organisation of a more 'democratic' or at least demotic, engagement with government was taking shape.

The historiographical background to this study is primarily an English one. Our understanding of England in this period has been transformed by studies of popular politics. Perhaps most famously, and already noted above, is the work of Ethan Shagan, which has demonstrated the role of non-elites in the establishment of 'Reformation': religious, political, legal and so on. Shagan has also demonstrated the vital role that a – at least professed – concern for the commons played in high politics and the legitimacy of governance. His study of the fall of Protector Somerset argues that being seen as too much a friend of the people – as members of the Edwardian political nation deemed the Protector to be, given his negotiation with rebels in 1549 – was a political liability, and in his case a terminal one.[9] Andy Woods' work on the rebels themselves is a groundbreaking study of plebeian political awareness and agency.[10] Moving forward in time, we find similar studies by Krista Kesselring on the 1569 rebellion, by John Walter on the Colchester plunderers at the outbreak of the English Civil War, and Tim Harris on London crowd action during the Restoration.[11] Collectively, these works, among others, have recast our understanding of practical politics *and* of political thought; the commons had agency, however limited, and it was always a factor in the thoughts, calculations and anxieties of the mighty.

There is no analogous tradition in Irish historiography. There is of course work on such 'politics out of doors' for the eighteenth century, and bits for the late seventeenth, but very little for the early seventeenth and the sixteenth.[12] As to why that is the case, part of the answer is likely historical, namely that there simply does not seem to have been a tradition of *en masse* political agitation in Ireland. Medieval England was full of such collective actions, 1381 and 1450 to take two obvious examples. But for Ireland? Neither my experience with Old Irish and pre-1500 early modern Irish sources, nor reading of the relevant secondary literature, reveals evidence of an analogous situation.[13] This 'conclusion' might simply be a trick of the sources, namely that there are significantly fewer textual records surviving from medieval Ireland and those that survive do not happen to mention such things. Nevertheless, it does seem noteworthy that seemingly *no* evidence of popular action exists for the period. That said, part of the reason is likely historiographical in origin, for there is record of non-elites rebelling in the sixteenth and early seventeenth centuries. It just does not seem to be talked about in the language of popular politics as encountered in the English historiography. Rather, it tends to be subsumed under collective action framed as anti-colonial resistance, typically done under the leadership of some elite or another, if it is mentioned at all.[14]

Thus, the first aim is to demonstrate that the people had a place in contemporary Irish politics and political theory. To begin with the latter, the well-being of the commons was of fundamental importance to English notions of legitimate governance, both in England and

Ireland. Indeed, the chief complaint state minions harboured against Irish lords was their supposed tyranny over inferiors, those whom they should have been protecting. This was both a practical and conceptual concern; tyrants, generally speaking, abused the weak and thus were not legitimate governors but rather affronts to God. Irish chiefs demonstrated their tyranny most notoriously through coyne (*coinnmheadh*) and livery, and rare is the English device or treatise that failed to condemn it. George Wyse's letter to Cecil in 1567 is a particularly robust example of both attack on the practice, and claim that its elimination will lead to prosperity:

> The commonwealth has never prospered so well as since the coming of (Lord Deputy) Sidney who has ended coigne and livery under which no man could be accounted master of his own. The poor people begin to savour what it is to live under a more worthy prince, where they are subjects and not slaves ... The honest husbandman that was impoverished can now support his family and servants. The idle man now falls to husbandry ... Where before they lived under the miserable yoke of their Irish lords, they now know that there is a God and under him a prince by whom they are preserved to live in better estate than ever their ancestors did.[15]

Wyse's commentary raises a number of themes important to the politics of legitimacy within the context of becoming and belonging. On the one hand, it registers a sentiment hardly describable as 'belonging', in the sense that it is a bald statement of conflict and socio-cultural destruction. Yet on the other hand, it simultaneously suggests that there was some coming together of peoples from rather different communities in the forging of a new one. Of course this is a grossly biased source, but at least on a rhetorical level it is a claim that Irish non-elites were embracing some civic identity as property owners with the rights of subjects. What some of the 'realities' connected with that identity may have been are briefly explored below. However, it is the duality of the comment's political register that makes it particularly helpful in understanding the period. Truthful or otherwise, Wyse's observation is not one of mere social historical value; it tells us more than whether or not Irish husbandmen were entering a cash economy, for, as Mark Kishlansky has written, in this period there was no separation between the social and the political.[16] If Irish commoners were undertaking new economic and social roles, doing so was a political act in the most tangible, 'practical' sense.

There is also a more abstract political question hinted at in Wyse's words, namely to what extent were Irish non-elites becoming politicised to think of the London-centered state as something promising certain advantages and, crucially, certain rights. Thus, while I want to make a case for tangible political action on the part of the people, I also want to argue that that action was a vital factor in legitimating, or de-legitimating, the state and its representatives. The commoners of Ireland were, in many ways, the chief victims in the clashes between the powerful as Ireland was 'reduced', to use contemporary parlance, to a subordinate kingdom under the Tudor and Stuart monarchies. They were not entirely without agency, however. Furthermore, when considered collectively as a category, they were of great practical and theoretical concern to those who wished to govern in their name. Working from Wyse's claim that the 'honest husbandman' was becoming anglicised, there does seem to be quite a bit of material to support this. In May of 1572, Sir John Perrott reported to Lord Deputy Fitzwilliam that 'The commonalty is beginning to turn away from the tyranny of the lords',[17] and later that year that 'The people are willing to report of great numbers of traitors'.[18] They were also seemingly willing to play more active roles in furthering Crown interests, for instance when the Castle of Glin was noted in 1600 as having been taken by Sir George Carew 'buy the halpe of the common wch made it assaultable'.[19] In Gaelic sources we see numerous examples of a complementary hybridisation and syncretism though invariably this is frowned upon with even the most innocent or unintended instances of anglicisation cast as outrages of cultural treason. The literature of the day included vicious satires of Irish upstarts aping English ways. The great example is the anonymous prose satire 'Pairlement Chloinne Tomáis', a cruel and bawdy destruction of the actions and pretentions of a family who worked their way into the ranks of the nobility under James I and VI. One of the leaders of the clan extorts his fellows to 'set about acquiring riches and wealth, and by virtue of your riches mingle your lowly stock with aristocratic stock … and let there be no master nor superior over you except yourselves

… and dress yourselves in collars, ruffs and gloves'.[20] This snobbery was a phenomenon that spanned genres, and the poetry of the period includes numerous examples of attacks on upstart commoners, Gaels who have adopted English ways, and the like.[21]

We might doubt the reality of such claims for Irish commoners supporting the state in words and deed, and see them as nothing more than rhetorical moves done for whatever variety of purposes. Alternatively, we might accept their social reality, but doubt their sincerity, preferring to see such apparent 'belonging' to an inchoate anglicised culture as little more than survival strategy in the face of coercion, or simply an example of false consciousness.[22] We might even wish to flatly say that whatever the truth value of these statements, from English and Irish commentators, they are not representative and that most non-elites likely were neither politically aware nor operating much outside of traditional socio-cultural norms.

There is corroborating evidence for this sort of agency, however, in the ways in which people availed themselves – in times of peace as well as war – of more mundane state offices and mechanisms in pursuit of their interests. Most commonly we see this sort of quotidian popular political action in the courts. As Tim Stretton has written, Elizabethans and Jacobeans experienced the 'most dramatic per capita increase in litigation levels in English history'.[23] It seems that litigiousness was not lost on residents of the western realm. 'Mór idir na haimsearabih', Muiris MacGearailt's long Ovidean complaint about the social and cultural liberty of the commons, includes charges that Irish subjects were so dependent on the courts that lawyers were something of the new masters. He laments bitterly of having travelled himself to Dublin, from Kerry, pursuing some legal matter only to be put off by a promise of *nisi prius*, or the promise to initiate suit at some future point.[24] Mid-seventeenth-century poems also include complaints over the oppressive rule of law. Donnchadh Mac an Chaoilfhiaclach famously bewailed the enslaving effects of interconnected English courts – including the Court of Wards, Excheqeur, Star Chamber (*an tSeómra Réaltach*), King's Bench, The Bishops' Court (*Cúirt na nEaspog*) and assizes – all of which worked cooperatively to enslave the Irish by means of false charge and judgment ('Braighde 'na gcúirt fa bhréagchoir/

is coistí i ndaoirse trí n-a saora').[25] But if *nisi prius* denotes the origination of suits, the records of the Court of Chancery – many of which are thankfully still extant – demonstrate that Irish people of relatively modest status carried their suits through initial hearing to appeal in this very busy equity court. In those records we see a range of actions by the 'mere Irish', from commons to well-to-do to nobles, seeking justice for a bewilderingly broad range of grievances. For instance, Mac Conchobhair, a mason who had gone to Dublin seeking work, initiated a suit there claiming that, in his absence, he had been cheated out of an inheritance of land at home.[26] Indeed, Chancery was an arena in which Gaels pitched legal battle against fellow Gaels, even family members, as evidenced in a land dispute between two persons of the name Ó Cearbhaill.[27] Curiously, we do see in some of these proceedings the awkwardness of synthesising cultural and social forms. An Ó Laoghaire, for instance, entered the court to protect his right to the surname, claiming to be 'worthiest of the blood'; a case involving the Mic Dhiarmada seems to have been intended to press the rights of privileges of fosterage.[28] A state court in the seventeenth century seems an odd place in which to pursue rights related to tanistry or fosterage, and yet it seems to have served in that manner. Conversely, however, it appears that the Irish were picking up some of the tricks of English landowners, for John Donellan (Ó Domhnalláin) brought suit against local Irish for enclosing and improving commonage that he, being the agent of the earl of Clanricard, deemed the property of his lord.[29]

Of course, the court of Chancery existed long before the Tudors and had been used by Irish of high and modest status for centuries. Unique to this particular period, however, was its existence alongside proliferating common law courts as a site of justice and the backdrop of the Crown's need to win the hearts and minds of those it was seeking to govern. Functioning and efficient courts were vital to that task, corrupt ones a disaster; a major theme running through contemporary English comments on Ireland was fear that justice promised but not delivered would alienate the people. Burghley fretted constantly over this point, and he was particularly concerned about the abuse of martial law.[30] Later in the reign, Sir Thomas Lee attacked the Lord Deputy Sir William Fitzwilliam for abusing the legal system for private gain, claiming that

> … uppon slender informacion giuen against your maiesties poorest and best subiects, the husbandmen, caused them to be apprehended, and sent to prison without bayle, or Mancepryse for Bodye or goodes, and giuen awaye the poore mens goodes, for satisfaccion of his owne olde debts …[31]

In his later 'Brief declaration', Lee generalised this concern over corruption of the legal process, declaring that 'what pity it is that so gracious a prince, as is your majesty, cannot help it! For these many years past your poor subjects have been crying out for justice, and could never get it …'.[32] Indeed, people were known to initiate suits in Chancery out of belief that they could not get justice in common law courts they deemed corrupted by the mighty, just as Lee had claimed. In the words of Nicholas Walsh, he entered a bill in the Dublin equity court against the Viscount Mountgarret, whom he accused of extorting and threatening his tenants and destroying his woods, because the 'said viscount is a nobleman vere greatly allied in the said countrie', whereas he 'as touching allience or kindred [was] utterly a stranger theare' and thus it may be 'p[er]ilous for him to trie withe the said viscount by order of the comen laws of this land'.[33] Yet in time Chancery became distrusted as well, notorious as a fiefdom of the Lord Chancellor. In the 1630s Lord Chancellor Adam Loftus was accused of a host of outrages corruptive of the court's ability to dispense justice. These included insulting the ancient aristocracy (here, the Earl of Kildare), non-attendance at church, charging exorbitant fees of litigants, and even of imprisoning suitors against their will.[34] Charles I, primarily through his Lord Deputy, Sir Thomas Wentworth, was forced to step in to adjudicate the situation. Corruption of the courts seemed a political and social crisis affecting those from top to bottom of society and from province to capital.

It is against this background of justice sought and denied that we may wish to circle back to popular politics as an out-of-doors phenomenon. Again, there were numerous reports of Irish non-elites availing themselves of the law courts – the very act of which helped legitimate those courts and the authority that undergirded them – and even during times of social unrest acting loyally toward the Crown. However, there are as many, and most likely many more, examples of acts we might wish to describe crudely as disloyal, or at least antithetical to Crown interests.[35] The historiography typically treats such instances as ancillary details to high politics, namely the conflict between a local grandee and the Crown. The 'rebellious' action of the earl of Desmond's tenants, for instance, is simply rolled into an understanding of anti-colonial resistance writ large and directed by elites.[36] We may be able to read a bit more political agency in the actions of the plebs, however, and to see that agency conceptualised as something greater than protest: an emergent political consciousness which sought to shape the character of state and governance, not simply to rebuff certain of its local manifestations that those on the ground found objectionable.

Looking at rumours and how they spread might prove a useful starting place for identifying that agency and political awareness. It is well known that English officials, across the early modern period, feared the rapid spread of gossip, news and prophecy among the Irish.[37] This was a phenomenon that reached to the lowest rungs of the social order. Fitzwilliam complained to Burghley in 1572 how

> The words of the people illustrate the level of rumour and expectation of war that prevails in Munster, which day of war all await, and there is no one among them who does not have such expectation, whether old or young, male or female.[38]

These concerns were much more than matters of official handwringing, and people up and down the social hierarchy knew what was at stake. In the last stages of the conflict that would come to be known as the Nine Years' War, for instance, Captain Thomas Boys wrote to the Chief Commissioner for Munster about mopping up rebels and of the supreme violence he intended to visit upon those who would not give intelligence, including – as he expressly stated – 'the poor'.[39] Whatever official claims for legitimate rule as arising in large part from proper treatment of the commons, as discussed above, once people involved themselves in matters of war and state they became reclassified as enemy combatants, just as were their putative leaders. Of course, these 'common' rebels may have wished to be treated as their superiors were and not as Boys intended, for whereas the rebel leaders, Ó Néill and Ó Domhnaill, were punished for their transgressions with the taking of earldoms, Boys' rebels faced a much grimmer, and shorter, future.

Where were Irish non-elites getting the information that enabled their entry into the life-and-death politics of state centralisation? Certainly from preaching clergy of Tridentine influence, and the sources are rife with governmental anxiety over members of the orders firing up the base with thoughts of rebellion. These agents of Counter-Reformation Catholicism worked not merely to spur the faithful to acts of resistance, but also to inculcate a confessional, ideological justification for the same, namely a sense of the right to resist an illegitimate regime. Edward White, clerk to the earl of Clanricard (himself a Catholic), wrote to Deputy Fitzwilliam with alarm at how friars, emboldened by news of the St Bartholomew's Day massacre in France (1572), were preaching rebellion to the commons throughout Ulster and Connacht and in doing so were 'so bold as though the pope were king of England and Ireland'. While clerical sway seemed to White a particularly frequent occurrence in the towns, it was not a solely urban or non-elite phenomenon, for he noted how 'The poor country men, seeing them so embraced in the town, dare say nothing not even the earl himself'.[40] Seemingly, the bards too were a potential source of mass politicisation, a fact that helped fuel the Crown's vicious persecution of them as a class.[41] The author of one early seventeenth-century tract on the problem of governing Ireland noted that even in the Pale the people listened to the bards as if listening to a sermon, and he claimed the poets were the chief fomenters of popular unrest.[42] This seems a particularly interesting case, for the bards were in many ways the guarantors of social justice in the medieval period, and wrongs done to the commonalty were one accepted spur to satire.[43] But they were not in the practice of inspiring collective resistance to an errant lord, but rather lobbying and chastising that lord, in the name of the people, to uphold the practices of good lordship. In the example given above, however, we encounter evidence of direct politicisation with an interest to agitate; if lords and courts could not be moved through traditional means and mechanisms to dispense justice, then it might be sought in arms and action.

And action there was. In 1603 reports rolled into the London and Dublin administrations that people in cities across the realm had publicly celebrated the Queen's death, expressing their views that right rule and liberty of conscience would be swept in with the new Stuart monarch, and generally being obnoxious to local officials in doing so.[44] Sometimes the 'people' were deemed to be acting on their own, as in the case of Waterford, where they were depicted as having rioted in defence of Catholicism and in the face of mayoral authority.[45] In Cork, by contrast, the mayor and recorder were deemed to be parties to this plague of disloyalty, one which had spread quickly, and much to the state's distress, out into the countryside.[46] In spite of the initial elation their accession elicited, the Stuarts would prove little better in the eyes of at least some proportion of the urban citizenry, and in the 1630s Lord Deputy Wentworth complained bitterly of being hounded and heckled in the streets of Dublin on account of his perceived tyrannical rule, lamenting to Charles I how he was 'unable without amazement to hear myself reported, nay cried out aloud in the Streets, to be Outrageous, where verily I take myself to be the Patient; and that intirely for the Service of my Master'.[47]

These actions were clearly not straightforward resistance by colonised against coloniser, or examples of confessional or proto-national conflict inherent to Irish–English relations and destined inevitably to surface. For the evidence adduced above about the pursuit of justice through the mechanisms of the state, examples of loyal action and at least perceived shared interest between subject and Crown, and even of anglicisation (if selective), suggest something more complex.[48] Issues of legitimacy and justice seem key factors in what appears to have been an increasingly widespread and sophisticated popular politics among Irish non-elites. We might consider two rural examples to illustrate the case. In 1571 a bill was brought against one John Thomas, the charge seemingly related to action we associate more with the eighteenth century, namely secret society intimidation as a form of extra-legal justice. Thomas was said to have sent a threatening notice stating that

> 'Tom Truth and his parliament will so blase you and your name that you shall hardly show your crabtree face and if it were not for fear of the queen's laws we would pluck your skin over your ears and take your spoiled good out of your hands': signed Tom Truth and John Justifier[49]

The mention here of 'parliament' and of respect for – or at least fear of – the Queen's law suggests something of the loyal rebellion whereby the state is deemed legitimate, but its current representatives not. Secondly, a report on the state of the realm in 1597 declared Munster to be the 'best tempered' province at that moment, with the exception that some of the 'McShees' and Lord Roche's base sons had become, as the report stated it, 'Robin Hoods' and slain some of the Plantation undertakers. Now, these are not exactly non-elite actors, but the mode of politics is a seemingly populist one done in the interests of the commonalty deemed ill-treated by the state.[50] This example seems to reveal greater animus toward the state than does the first. Together, however, they suggest that modes of political agitation typically associated with later periods may have lineage back to the Elizabethan period.

I wish to conclude this preliminary investigation by briefly looking ahead into the seventeenth century to think about the development of this popular politics and its role in legitimising or delegitimising the state, on the one hand, and within the dynamics of 'becoming and belonging', on the other. Both of the ensuing cases involve political action, but would seem to suggest that difference and conflict would be the operative descriptors of interactions between natives and newcomers, and that any aspiration for becoming and belonging had failed, which would accord with the general thrust of historiographical tradition that sees the seventeenth century as the crucial period in the crystallisation of Irish–English conflict and difference. However, I would argue that even in a war-torn and colonised society there existed modes of community and identities that spanned potential divisions.

The Rising of 1641 is the great example of the popular politics of resistance, a resistance drawn along confessional, ethnic and national lines. What may have started as something of a loyal rebellion aimed at restoring Sir Phelim Ó Néill and his co-conspirators to positions in the local Irish administration quickly escalated to popular rebellion as commoners took advantage of the breakdown in order to rid their communities of planters and other newcomers.[51] Nevertheless, it may also provide some interesting examples of belonging, and in places we might not typically think to look. We tend to search for becoming and belonging in instances of social harmony, but perhaps we should also pay attention to crime? Work on the events of 1641 has detailed numerous examples of people protecting and aiding their neighbours of different faith and national origin, clearly a sign of community.[52] But if harbouring an at-risk neighbour put oneself at risk, the choice to engage in acts of crime with that person was riskier still. In studying the early days of rebellion in Offaly and Kildare, the latter appears to have been much the more chaotic, with more instances of petty crime and more people of artisanal and skilled working status named as offenders in the depositions than in the more recently planted Offaly (or King's): carpenter, merchant, innkeeper, barber, bricklayer, chapman, cobbler, cooper and victualler. Additionally, we also see a greater range of surnames, Irish and English in origin, and reports of crime and outrage committed while not under the leadership of some elite. And most curiously for present purposes is the fact that Irish and English, men and women, took the plunge into crime together. Thus an English woman simply referred to as Katherine, a servant of the Countess of Kildare, teamed up with an Irish accomplice and 'privately imbeizilled and conveyed away from Maynooth divers of the said Countess' lynen, broke up her cabinette and did divers other outrages'.[53]

In the countryside roamed lawless bands, which were a matter of concern, even for the natives. An Irish man captured at the fall of the castle of Clongowes Wood pleaded that he was not a rebel and had only entered the castle because he was terrified to travel out of his local surroundings for fear of being easy prey to outlaws.[54] In spite of Kildare not having been planted, it was plagued by disorganised and opportunistic crime and brigandage, but in a way that suggests integration was deep enough over the long centuries following the Normans' arrival that the grave decision to trust a partner in crime was based on personal factors unique to the members of those communities and was not beholden to macro categories of ethnicity (let alone race), confession or nation. In looking for becoming and belonging, then, even the seemingly counterintuitive examples like crime and survival strategy might be revealing.

The second example comes from the Restoration and involves Catholic petitioning in Down. In 1663 a 'Remonstrance and Petition of the Gentry and inhabitants of Down' was submitted to the 'Most R. Convocation of the Catholique Clergy now assembled at Dublin'.[55] At issue were problems of becoming and belonging, and their attempted resolution involved popular politics as the means to legitimate and thus adjudicate. The Remonstrance complained of newcomers disrupting community and violating history and tradition. The reason it was sent to Convocation was because the offending blow-ins were not English or Scots Protestant planters, but rather Dominicans, interlopers into what the petitioners claimed was long Franciscan territory. Some of the language in what became an ongoing campaign is extraordinary: the begging for alms of the Dominicans was likely to 'overburden the poor inhabitants' and the petitioners sought relief from their 'present molestation'.[56] More remarkable still was the illegitimate origin myth attached to the Dominicans' arrival; it was said that their 'most horrible Intrusions' came in the 'days of the late usurper, Oliver Cromvell'.[57] While the Franciscans had been administering to persecuted Catholics, so the petitioners claimed, their rivals used the opportunity of interregnum to expand their range and feed their own interests. Clearly this was a campaign organised by elites of some variety and which hid a dispute between orders behind a professed concern for the common good. Nevertheless, it was a community campaign and the number of names attached to the petitions runs well over 1,000, and these are of English and Irish origin. In fact, some of the petitions were in Irish. Here, then, I think we may have another unexpected site of becoming and belonging. For, curiously, the outsiders were Catholics, the political actors common as well as elite, and the adjudicating body a Catholic Convocation in the capital under sanction of a legitimate state based in London and under the eye of a Protestant monarch.

The editors of this collection asked us to think about how peoples on the island of Ireland constructed and transformed self and group identities in this key period, and how their senses of belonging were made manifest through their cultural practices. With that in mind, I want to end by thinking – if only briefly and speculatively – over the medieval to modern eras about becoming and belonging and changes in popular politics. As noted above, it is curious that there seems to have been no tradition of mass popular politics in Ireland throughout the medieval period.[58] By 1641 it is there, and explosively so. Come the eighteenth century it is one of the most important elements of Irish political life, urban and rural.[59] By the nineteenth century, with Daniel O'Connell and his 'monster meetings' and the Land League and their boycotts, it has become naturalised, a mode of political organisation and action seen as largely an Irish invention and influential globally, from the English Chartists to American ward politics, from Gandhi to Martin Luther King.[60] That is a remarkable transformation: from nothing to something, to natural and to global. It seems that the early modern period is crucial to that development and that that story remains largely untold; politics out of doors does not emerge fully formed with rapparees, White Boys, Fenians and the rest. Yet earlier political actions are still typically discussed in the register of colonialism and resistance. I hope, however, to have suggested that there is more to be said on the issue, and that an understanding of Irish history of the *longue dureé* demands it.

What the mechanisms of such political development are remains to be determined, though undoubtedly they were an amalgam of indigenous and imported sources. As suggested above, bards and clerics seem to have been important vectors of politicisation – not just simple mobilisation, but rather the actual investing of non-elite people with a sense of political understanding and possibility. Perhaps more controversially, however, I wish to suggest that the Tudor and Stuart states also played a crucial role in this process. We might consider the possibility that the politicisation of the people was one of the great unintended consequences of the bridling of Gaelic lords; as Irish aristocratic culture became less democratic (in the sense that primogeniture cut out the extended male network of the *deirbhfhine* from the lines of succession), plebian culture became more so, and over time proved the more difficult to manage. In essence, representatives of the Crown may have been too successful for their own good in convincing Irish audiences of the promises of subjecthood under a 'modern' state, for at some point, some portion of them believed it enough to at least make use of its mechanisms, such as the courts. In doing so they helped legitimate the state. But when court and state failed them, a politicised people pursued other means of satisfaction. This did not necessarily mean that the state as an abstract, or practical system of government, was deemed inherently illegitimate. It might simply mean that the present office holders, not the offices themselves, required resistance; plebs too could perhaps organise a loyal rebellion. In the end they, of course, experienced immense difficulty in becoming equal subjects of the state. Yet through the traumas of that fraught process Irish non-elites may have forged a sense of belonging with other politicised peoples well beyond the world of the Atlantic archipelago.

# Glossary of Gaelic language terms used in the text

*Compiled by Elizabeth FitzPatrick*

| | |
|---|---|
| *airchinneach* (pl. *airchinnigh*) | in later medieval terms, a hereditary church tenant and un-ordained layman, sometimes with quasi-clerical status, responsible for dispensing hospitality, up-keeping a church and stewarding church land (anglicised, erenagh).[1] |
| *ardfheadhmontaigh* | a sheriff.[2] |
| *ardmhaoir* | a fiscal officer, tax collector, high-collector of dues.[3] |
| *baile biataigh* | a food-provider's estate.[4] |
| *baile bó* | cow land, townland, also known as tate and poll in Ulster.[5] |
| *bìrlinn* | a seafaring term meaning a galley. Borrowed from the Norse in the mid-Gaelic period.[6] |
| *brat* | also *bratt*, a mantle or cloak.[7] |
| *buaile* | a seasonally occupied building connected with cattle herding.[8] |
| *cailleach* (pl. *caillí*) | hag, old woman, but also a sovereignty figure.[9] |
| *caiseal* | a strong, stone-built enclosure (anglicised cashel). Generally referred to as *cathair* (anglicised caher) in the west of Ireland.[10] |
| *camán* | a hurley stick.[11] |
| *caoraigheacht* | a herd of livestock including its keepers.[12] |
| *ceatharnaigh* | Gaelic Irish mercenary foot-soldiers, usually light-armed (anglicised kern, kerne).[13] |
| *cluain* | meadow, water-meadow.[14] |
| *coinnmheadh* | free quartering or billeting of a chief's soldiers and retinue upon the country (anglicised coyne).[15] |
| *comharba* | originally an abbot, or layman in that office, who was deemed the 'heir' of the founder saint of a church. In later medieval terms, a chief tenant on termon or church lands.[16] |
| *cosmhuintir* | dependants, poor people.[17] |

*crannóg* (pl. *crannóga*) usually, an artificial island in a lake shallow.[18]

*creach* cattle raid, predatory expedition.[19]

*creat* rib of a house roof.[20] In the later medieval period used to describe a house with portable crucks.

*deirbhfhine* kinship group of descendants of a common ancestor in four generations, technically eligible for election to the office of chief.[21]

*díberga* also *féinnidi*, young aristocrats, vagrant and without property, and generally in conflict with settled society represented by the *túath*.[22]

*dindshenchas* 'lore of prominent or famous places'.[23]

*duanaire* an anthology of bardic poetry composed for a chief or his family.[24]

*dumha selga* hunting mound.[25]

*éiric* legal fine, penalty clause, compensation.[26]

*fían* warrior band.[27]

*fircheithearnn* true mercenaries, a chief's permanent cohort of mercenaries.[28]

*gallóglach* (pl. *gallóglaigh*) 'Scottish mercenaries who fought as heavy armed foot in Ireland'.[29]

*gossiprid* a pledge of fraternal association between a lord and his client whereby the lord received some service in return for offering the client patronage and protection.[30]

*inis* island, or a small natural island settlement.[31]

*liaig* physician.[32]

*lucht tighe* in a later medieval context, mensal lands set aside for the provision of the chief's household and occupied by service families.[33]

*marasgál* marshal.[34]

*meadar* a wooden drinking vessel, often with two or more handles for group drinking (anglicised mether).[35]

*ollamh* 'master of a learned or skilled profession in the native tradition'.[36]

*pailís* a palace, palisade or stockade. In late thirteenth- and fourteenth-century usage, a chief's hall within a moated site or a *ráth*, usually located on a boundary and probably used for hunting and feasting.[37]

*rannaire* also *ronnadóir*, a spenser in charge of distributing food at a feast.[38]

*ráth* (pl. *ráthanna*) in a later medieval context, an earthen enclosing bank and ditch, the space enclosed and the house within.[39]

*reachtaire* a royal official in the role of steward, overseer.[40]

*senchas* history, traditional Irish historical lore and genealogy.[41]

| | |
|---|---|
| *scian* | an Irish knife-dagger of the sixteenth to seventeenth centuries characterised by the absence of a pommel or guard (anglicised skean and skayne).[42] |
| *stocaire* | trumpeter, blower of a hunting horn. From the root *stoc* meaning trumpet, bugle, horn.[43] |
| *tigh mór* | OI *tech mór*, principal building.[44] |
| *tánaiste* | second in position or rank, usually 'the successor-designate' of a chief.[45] |
| *taoiseach* | leader, chief.[46] |
| *taoiseach teaghlaigh* | leader of the household.[47] |
| *trian* | a division or quarter.[48] |
| *tríocha céad* | usually a local kingdom ruled by a petty king; 'a spatial unit of royal tenure, taxation, local government, and a military levy' established by the eleventh century (OI *trícha cét*).[49] |
| *triubhas* | Scottish Gaelic, trousers, from OI *triubus*, trousers, breeches, hose, borrowed into Older Scots as trewis and later trews.[50] |
| *túath* | a political community and its territory, which by the twelfth century was a sub-unit of the *trícha cét*.[51] |

# Endnotes

*1. Constructing selves, constructing others: Becoming and belonging in Ireland*

1 See E. FitzPatrick, 'The Last Kings of Ireland: Material Expressions of Gaelic lordship *c.*1300–1400 AD', in K. Buchanan, L. H. S. Dean and M. Penman (eds), *Medieval and Early Modern Representations of Authority in Scotland and the British Isles* (Oxford and New York: Routledge, 2016), pp. 197–212, for a sophisticated analysis of the role of kingly pretension in medieval Gaelic Ireland, which challenges the more traditional concept of a Gaelic resurgence.

2 The landmark volume on Gaelic Ireland, P. J. Duffy, D. Edwards and E. FitzPatrick (eds), *Gaelic Ireland c.1250–c.1650: Land, Lordship and Settlement* (Dublin: Four Courts Press, 2001), both collated and inspired much research on the period and still remains as a definitive statement for the topic.

3 Selected sources for settlement forms and landscape analysis include N. Brady, 'When Mounds Become Castles: A Case for the Later Usage of Early Medieval Sites', in C. C. Corlett and M. Potterton (eds), *Rural Settlement in Medieval Ireland in the Light of Recent Archaeological Excavations* (Dublin: Wordwell, 2009), pp. 19–25; C. Breen, *The Gaelic Lordship of the O'Sullivan Beare: A Landscape Cultural History* (Dublin: Four Courts Press, 2005); M. Comber and G. Hull, 'Excavations at Caherconnell Cashel, the Burren, Co. Clare: Implications for Cashel Chronology and Gaelic Settlement', *Proceedings of the Royal Irish Academy,* vol. 110C, 2010, pp. 133–171; T. Finan and K. O'Conor, 'The Moated Site at Cloonfree, Co. Roscommon', *Journal of the Galway Archaeological and Historical Society*, vol. 54, 2002, pp. 72–87; T. Finan, 'Medieval Moated Sites in County Roscommon, Ireland: A Statistical Approach', *Chateau Gaillard*, vol. 26, 2014, pp. 177–180; E. FitzPatrick, E. Murphy, C. Donnelly and C. Foley, 'Evoking the White Mare: The Cult Landscape of Sgiath Gabhra and its Medieval Perception in Gaelic Fir Mhanach', in R. Schot, C. Newman and E. Bhreathnach (eds), *Landscapes of Cult and Kingship* (Dublin: Four Courts Press, 2011), pp. 163–191; E. FitzPatrick, '*Ollamh, Biatach, Comharba*: Lifeways of Gaelic Learned Families in Medieval and Early Modern Ireland', in L. Breatnach, R. Ó hUiginn, D. McManus and K. Simms (eds), *Proceedings of the XIVth Celtic Congress, Maynooth, 2011* (Dublin: Institute for Advanced Studies, 2015), pp. 165–189; E. FitzPatrick, 'Native Enclosed Settlement and the Problem of the Irish "Ring–fort"', *Medieval Archaeology*, vol. 53, 2009, pp. 271–307; E. FitzPatrick, '*Formaoil na Fiann*: Hunting Preserves and Assembly Places in Gaelic Ireland, in D. Furchtgott, G. Henley and M. Holmberg (eds), *Proceedings of Harvard Celtic*

*Colloquium*, vol. 32, 2012, pp. 95–118; E. FitzPatrick, *Royal Inauguration in Gaelic Ireland c.1100–1600* (Woodbridge: The Boydell Press, 2004); S. McDermott, 'The Archaeology of the Twelve Tates of McKenna, *c.*1591', *Clogher Record*, vol. 20, no. 2, 2010, pp. 373–406; K. D. O'Conor and N. Brady, 'The Later Medieval Use of Crannogs in Ireland, *Ruralia*, vol. 5, 2005, pp. 127–136; K. D. O'Conor, N. Brady, A. Connon and C. Fidalgo-Romo, 'The Rock of Lough Cé, Co. Roscommon', in T. Finan (ed.), *Medieval Lough Cé: History, Archaeology, Landscape* (Dublin: Four Courts Press, 2010), pp. 15–40. For buildings, see J. Lyttleton, 'The MacCoghlans of Delvin Eathra: The Transformation of a Late Medieval Lordship in Early Modern Ireland', in L. Doran, and J. Lyttleton (eds), *Lordship in Medieval Ireland: Image and Reality* (Dublin: Four Courts Press, 2007), pp. 236–265; P. Naessens, 'Gaelic Lords of the Sea: The Coastal Tower Houses of South Connemara', in Doran and Lyttleton (eds), *Lordship in Medieval Ireland*, pp. 217–235; P. Naessens, 'The Uí Fhlaithbheartaigh Gaelic Lordship of Iarchonnacht: Medieval Lordly Settlement on the Atlantic Seaboard', Unpublished PhD Thesis, National University of Ireland, Galway, 2009; R. Sherlock, 'The Social Environment of the Irish Tower House', Unpublished PhD Thesis, National University of Ireland, Galway, 2008; R. Sherlock, 'The Evolution of the Irish Tower–House as a Domestic Space', *Proceedings of the Royal Irish Academy*, vol. 111C, 2011, pp. 115–140; K. D. O'Conor, 'Housing in Later Medieval Ireland, *Ruralia*, vol. 4, 2002, pp. 197–206; C. J. Donnelly, 'Architecture and Conflict: Limerick's Tower Houses. *c.*1400 to *c.*1650', in L. Irwin, G. Ó Tuathaigh and M. Potter (eds), *Limerick: History and Society* (Dublin: Geography Publications, 2009), pp. 71–89. For material culture and trade see E. Gray, 'Material Culture of Gaelic High-Status Drinking Ritual in Medieval and Early Modern Ireland', Unpublished PhD Thesis, National University of Ireland, Galway, 2016; A. Horning, 'Clothing and Colonialism: The Dungiven Costume and the Fashioning of Early Modern Identities', *Journal of Social Archaeology*, vol. 14, no. 3, 2014, pp. 296–318; S. Flavin, 'Consumption and Material Culture in Sixteenth-Century Ireland', *Economic History Review*, vol. 64, no. 4, November 2011, pp. 1144–1174 and also S. Flavin, *Consumption and Culture in Sixteenth-Century Ireland: Saffron, Stockings and Silk* (Woodbridge: The Boydell Press, 2014); S. Flavin, 'Consumption and Material Culture in Sixteenth-Century Ireland', Unpublished PhD Thesis, University of Bristol, 2011.

4 N. Ní Dhomhnaill, *Pharaoh's Daughter* (Oldcastle, County Meath: Gallery, 1990).

5 The terms were first coined by Kenneth Pike in the 1950s and published in K. Pike, *Language in Relation to a Unified Theory of the Structures of Human Behavior* (The Hague: Mouton, 1967). See discussions in T. N. Headland, K. L. Pike and M. Harris (eds), *Emics and Etics: The Insider/Outsider Debate* (Newbury Park, CA: Sage, 1990); M. Harris, 'History and Significance of the Emic/Etic Distinction', *Annual Review of Anthropology*, vol. 5, 1976, pp. 329–350.

6 See also P. Palmer, *Language and Conquest in Early Modern Ireland: English Renaissance Literature and Elizabethan Imperial Expansion* (Cambridge: Cambridge University Press, 2001).

7 For archaeological considerations of identity and agency, see for example M. Diaz-Andreu, 'Constructing Identities Through Culture: The Past

in the Forging of Europe', in P. Graves-Brown, S. Jones and C. Gamble (eds), *Cultural Identity and Archaeology: The Construction of European Communities* (London: Routledge, 1996), pp 48–61; J. Thomas, 'Comments on "Past Practices: Rethinking Individuals and Agents in Archaeology" by A. G. Knapp and P. Van Dommelen', *Cambridge Archaeological Journal*, vol. 18, no. 1, 2008, pp. 26–28; J. Robb, 'Beyond Agency', *World Archaeology*, vol. 42, no. 4, 2010, pp. 493–520; S. Jones, *The Archaeology of Ethnicity: Constructing Identities in the Past and Present* (London: Routledge, 1997).

8 M. Heidegger, *Identity and Difference* (Chicago: University of Chicago Press, 1969).

9 Francis Bacon (1608), 'Certain considerations touching the Plantation in Ireland', in C. Maxwell, *Irish History from Contemporary Sources: 1509–1610* (London: George Allen & Unwin Ltd, 1923), pp. 269–273; Francis Bacon (1617) in J. Spedding's *Life of Bacon* VI (London: Longman, Green, Reader & Dyer, 1872).

10 See contributions in T. Herron and M. Potterton (eds), *Ireland in the Renaissance c.1540–1660* (Dublin: Four Courts Press, 2007); D. Ó Catháin, 'Some Reflexes of Latin Learning and of the Renaissance in Ireland *c.*1450–*c.*1600', in J. Harris and K. Sidwell (eds), *Making Ireland Roman: Irish Neo-Latin Writers and the Republic of Letters* (Cork: Cork University Press, 2009).

11 See discussions in K. Buchanan, L. H. S. Dean and M. Penman (eds), *Medieval and Early Modern Representations of Authority in Scotland and the British Isles* (Oxford: Routledge, 2016) and in P. J. Duffy, D. Edwards and E. FitzPatrick (eds), *Gaelic Ireland c.1250–c.1650: Land, Lordship and Settlement* (Dublin: Four Courts Press, 2001), especially the introduction, pp. 39–45.

12 See for example the contributions in L. Doran and L. James (eds), *Lordship in Medieval Ireland: Image and Reality* (Dublin: Four Courts Press, 2007) and especially the Foreword by Bernadette Cunningham, pp. 21–46.

13 For example, brothers-in-law Sir Thomas Phillips and Sir Edward Doddington each acquired Ó Catháin castles in what was constructed as the Londonderry Plantation in the early seventeenth century. Rather than destroying the old as a symbol of conquest, both re-edified the tower houses and employed the spaces as a means of materialising their power and place in the existing Gaelic landscape. Accompanying their tower houses were new manor houses built after the English fashion. Which space was employed by the men was dependent upon the identity and expectations of those they entertained. See discussion in A. Horning, *Ireland in the Virginian Sea: Colonialism in the British Atlantic* (Chapel Hill: The University of North Carolina Press, 2013), chapter three.

14 G. Howell, *Gertrude Bell: Queen of the Desert, Shaper of Nations* (New York: Farrar, Straus & Giroux, 2006). See also discussions by B. Trigger, *A History of Archaeological Thought* (Cambridge: Cambridge University Press, 1989); P. Kohl, 'Nationalism and Archaeology: On the Constructions of Nations and the Reconstructions of the Remote Past', *Annual Review of Anthropology*, vol. 27, 1998, pp. 223–246 and J. A. Atkinson, I. Banks and J. O'Sullivan (eds), *Nationalism and Archaeology* (Glasgow: Cruithne, 1996).

15 I. Pikirayi, *The Zimbabwe Culture: Origins and Decline in Southern Zambezian States* (Walnut Creek: AltaMira, 2001).

16 J. Agnew, 'No Borders, No Nations: Making Greece in Macedonia', *Annals of the Association of American Geographers*, vol. 97, no. 2, 2007, pp. 398–422; K. S. Brown, 'Contests of Heritage and the Politics of Preservation in the Former Yugoslav Republic of Macedonia', in L. Meskell (ed.), *Archaeology Under Fire: Nationalism, Politics and Heritage in the Eastern Mediterranean and Middle East* (London: Routledge 1998), pp. 68–86; J. Cowan (ed.), *Macedonia: The Politics of Identity and Difference: Anthropology, Culture and Society* (London: Pluto Press, 2000).

17 For discussions of identity politics and Irish archaeology, see G. Cooney, 'European and Global Archaeologies', *World Archaeology*, vol. 41, no. 4, 2009, pp. 626–628; A. Horning, 'Archaeology, Conflict, and Contemporary Identity in the North of Ireland: Implications for Theory and Practice in Irish Historical Archaeology', *Archaeological Dialogues*, vol. 13, no. 2, 2006, pp. 183–199; A. Horning, C. Breen and N. Brannon, 'From the Past to the Future: Integrating Archaeology and Conflict Resolution in Northern Ireland', *Conservation and Management of Archaeological Sites*, vol. 17, no. 1, 2015, pp. 5–21.

18 H. Morgan, *Tyrone's Rebellion: The Outbreak of the Nine Years War in Tudor Ireland* (Woodbridge: The Boydell Press, 1993); J. Marshall, 'The Hovendens: Fosterbrothers of Hugh O'Neill, Prince of Ulster', *Ulster Journal of Archaeology*, 2nd series, vol. 13, 1907, pp. 73–83. Sir John Harrington (1699) reported on a visit to O'Neill's household where he noted the presence of an English tutor and the fact that the O'Neill children were dressed in English clothing: J. Harrington, 'Report of a Journey into the North of Ireland to Justice Carey', in C. Maxwell, *Irish History from Contemporary Sources* (London: George Allen, 1923), p. 338.

19 The portrait of Lee by Marcus Gheeraerts has been analysed by a number of scholars, for example I. Leask, 'Sex on (Bare) Legs? Thomas Lee and Irishness', *Irish Review*, vol. 42, 2010, pp. 72–84; D. Kiberd, *Inventing Ireland: The Literature of the Modern Nation* (London: Jonathan Cape, 1995), p. 10; and H. Morgan, 'Tom Lee: The Posing Peacemaker', in B. Bradshaw, A. Hadfield and W. Maley (eds), *Representing Ireland: Literature and the Origins of Conflict, 1534–1660* (Cambridge: Cambridge University Press, 1993), pp. 132–165.

20 P. Logue and J. O'Neill, 'The Battlefield Archaeology of the Yellow Ford', in A. Horning and N. Brannon (eds), *Ireland and Britain in the Atlantic World* (Dublin: Wordwell, 2009), pp. 7–30.

21 E. Durkeim, *The Rules of the Sociological Method* (Glencoe: Free Press, 1958); B. Malinowski, 'The Group and Individual in Functional Analysis', *American Journal of Sociology,* vol. 44, 1939, pp. 938–64; A. R. Radcliffe-Brown, *Structure and Function in Primitive Society* (New York: Free Press, 1952).

22 See the early warning by M. Pluciennik, 'Genetics, Archaeology and the Wider World', *Antiquity*, vol. 70, no. 267, 1996, pp. 13–14, as well as a series of exchanges in *Archaeology Ireland*, volumes 14–15, including D. Croke, 'Ancient DNA: Synergy or Culture Clash', *Archaeology Ireland*, vol. 15, no. 4, 2001, pp. 36–37; G. Cooney, 'Is it all in the Genes?', *Archaeology Ireland*, vol. 15, no. 1, 2001, pp. 34–35.

23 K. Simms, 'Gaelic Lordships in Ulster in the Later Middle Ages', Unpublished PhD Thesis, Trinity College Dublin, 1976, abstract, unpaginated.

24 P. Parkes 'Celtic Fosterage: Adoptive Kinship and Clientage in Northwest Europe', *Comparative Studies in Society and History*, vol. 48, no. 2, 2006, p. 368; F. Fitzsimons, 'Fosterage and Gossiprid in Late Medieval Ireland: Some New Evidence', in Duffy, Edwards and FitzPatrick (eds), *Gaelic Ireland*, pp. 138–49.

25 P. Bourdieu, *Outline of a Theory of Practice* (Cambridge: Cambridge University Press, 1977).

26 F. Barth, *Ethnic Groups and Boundaries: The Social Organisation of Cultural Difference* (Boston: Little, Brown, 1969); Jones, *The Archaeology of Ethnicity*; J. Yaeger and M. Canuto (eds), *The Archaeology of Communities* (London: Routledge 2002).

27 For an extended discussion, see Horning, 'Clothing and Colonialism'.

28 See E. G. Quin (ed.), *Dictionary of the Irish Language: Based Mainly on Old and Middle Irish Materials*, Compact Edition (Dublin: Royal Irish Academy, 1990), p. 81.

29 C. Maxwell, *Irish History from Contemporary Sources: 1509–1610* (London: George Allen & Unwin, 1923), p. 112.

30 S.P., 63/43/6 i, Justice Walsh to Lord Deputie, 24th November 1573; S. Flavin, 'Consumption and Material Culture in Sixteenth-Century Ireland', Unpublished PhD Thesis, University of Bristol, 2011, p. 106.

31 For the linkage between Ulster Scots identity and Presbyterianism, see A. Holmes, 'Presbyterian Religion, Historiography, and Ulster Scots Identity, *c.*1800 to 1914', *The Historical Journal*, vol. 52, no. 3, 2009, pp. 615–640. For considerations of contemporary Northern Ireland politics and Ulster Scots heritage, see T. Crowley, 'The Political Production of a Language: The Case of Ulster Scots', *Journal of Linguistic Anthropology*, vol. 16, no. 1, 2006, pp. 23–35 and also M. Dowling, 'Confusing Culture and Politics: Ulster Scots Culture and Music', *New Hibernia Review*, vol. 11, no. 3, 2007, pp. 51–80.

32 H. K. Bhabha, *The Location of Culture* (London and New York: Routledge, 1994); H. K. Bhabha, 'Signs Taken for Wonders: Questions of Ambivalence and Authority Under a Tree Outside Delhi, May 1817', *Critical Inquiry*, vol. 12, no. 1, 1985, pp. 144–165.

33 R. Ó Baoill, 'Carrickfergus and Belfast', in A. Horning, R. Ó Baoill, C. Donnelly and P. Logue (eds), *The Archaeology of Post-Medieval Ireland c.1550–1750* (Dublin: Wordwell, 2007), pp. 91–116; R. Ó Baoill, *Carrickfergus: The Story of the Castle and Walled Town* (Belfast: TSO, 2008); N. F. Brannon, 'Carrickfergus', in A. Hamlin and C. Lynn (eds), *Pieces of the Past: Archaeological Excavations by the Department of the Environment for Northern Ireland 1970–1986* (Belfast: HMSO, 1986).

34 M. O'Dowd, 'Piers, William (*d.* 1603)', *Oxford Dictionary of National Biography* (Oxford: Oxford University Press, 2004) online edn, Jan 2008 [http://www.oxforddnb.com/view/article/22236] Accessed 28 July 2014; *Cal. S.P. Ire. 1509–1573*, p. 522. Piers' activities are also discussed in C. Brady, *The Chief Governors: The Rise and Fall of Reform Government in Tudor Ireland 1536–1588* (Cambridge: Cambridge University Press, 1994), pp. 258–259 and Horning, *Ireland in the Virginian Sea*, pp. 62–63.

The accuracy of the claim that Piers' brother-in-law was in the Scots forces is uncertain, as Mrs. Piers (Anne Holt) was formerly of Cheshire and came to Ireland as a servant in the household of Sir Henry Sydney.

35 M. Taussig, *Mimesis and Alterity: A Particular History of the Senses* (New York: Psychology Press, 1993), p. xiii.

36 C. M. O'Sullivan, *Hospitality in Medieval Ireland, 900–1500* (Dublin: Four Courts Press, 2004); K. Simms, 'Guesting and Feasting in Gaelic Ireland', *Journal of the Royal Society of Antiquaries of Ireland,* vol. 108, 1978, pp. 67–100.

37 See discussion in B. Cunningham and R. Gillespie, *Stories from Gaelic Ireland* (Dublin: Four Courts Press, 2003), pp. 48–49, 54–55.

38 O'Sullivan, *Hospitality in Medieval Ireland,* pp. 104, 110.

39 Tadhg Dall Ó hUiginn (1589); C. Maxwell, *Irish History from Contemporary Sources 1509–1610*, p. 337; Cunningham and Gillespie, *Stories from Gaelic Ireland*, p. 29.

40 Possibly a now destroyed tower house within the settlement of Downpatrick.

41 J. Bodley, 'A Visit to Lecale', *Ulster Journal of Archaeology*, vol. 2, 1854 [1602], pp. 78–79.

42 F. McCormick, 'Struell Wells: Pagan Past and Christian Present,' *Journal of the Royal Society of Antiquaries of Ireland*, vol. 139, 2009, pp. 45–62.

43 In the estimation of S. Connolly, *Contested Island: Ireland 1460–1630* (Oxford: Oxford University Press, 2007), p. 401, de Renzy 'used his knowledge of Irish annals and mythology to legitimize plantation', a theme developed further by B. Mac Cuarta, 'Sword and Word in the 1620s: Matthew De Renzy and Irish Reform', in B. Mac Cuarta (ed.), *Reshaping Ireland 1550–1700* (Dublin: Four Courts Press, 2011), pp. 101–130. J. Lyttleton (2013) discussed De Renzy's use of the Clonony More tower house in *The Jacobean Plantations in Seventeenth-Century Offaly* (Dublin: Four Courts Press, 2013), pp. 64–65. See also B. Mac Cuarta, 'Mathew De Renzy's Letters on Irish Affairs 1613–1620', *Analecta Hibernica*, vol. 34, 1987, pp. 107–182.

44 N. Canny, *Elizabethan Conquest of Ireland: A Pattern Established, 1565–76* (Hassocks: Harvester Press, 1976), pp. 88–89, 130; M. Dewar, *Sir Thomas Smith: A Tudor Intellectual in Office* (University of London, 1964); C. Lennon, *Sixteenth Century Ireland: The Incomplete Conquest* (Dublin: Gill & Macmillan, 2005), pp. 282–284.

45 *Cal. S.P. Ire. 1509–1573*, p. 530.

46 *Cal. S.P. Ire. 1571–1575*, p. 688.

47 See Palmer, *Language and Conquest in Early Modern Ireland.*

48 Lyttleton, *The Jacobean Plantations*, p. 267.

49 R. A. S. Macalister, *The Archaeology of Ireland* (London: Methuen, 1928), p. 356.

50 See extended discussion in A. Horning, 'Crossing the Battlefield: Archaeology, Nationalism, and Practice in Irish Historical Archaeology', in A. Brooks and N. Mehler (eds), *The Country Where My Heart Is: Historical Archaeologies of Nationalism and National Identity* (Gainesville, FL: University of Florida Press, 2017), pp. 172–201. See also B. J. Graham, 'The Search for the "Common Ground": Estyn Evans's Ireland', *Transactions of the British Institute of Geographers*, vol. 19, no. 2, 1994, pp. 183–201; M.

Burgess, 'Mapping the Narrow Ground: Geography, History and Partition', *Field Day Review*, vol. 1, 2005, pp. 121–131.

51 As recently discussed in M. Gardiner and T. E. McNeill, 'Seaborne Trade and the Commercialisation of Fifteenth- and Sixteenth-century Gaelic Ulster', *Proceedings of the Royal Irish Academy*, vol. 116C, 2016, pp. 1–34. See also Naessens, 'Gaelic Lords of the Sea' and C. Kelleher, 'The Gaelic O'Driscoll Lords of Baltimore, Co. Cork', in L. Doran and J. Lyttleton (eds), *Lordship in Medieval Ireland: Image and Reality* (Dublin: Four Courts Press, 2007) pp. 130–159.

2. *Identity among the Mac Diarmada lords of Magh Luirg in the thirteenth century*

1 N. Ní Shéaghdha (ed. and trans.), 'The Rights of Mac Diarmada', *Celtica*, vol. 6, 1963, pp. 156–72.

2 AC 1253.16.

3 AC 1256.14.

4 T. Finan, *A Nation in Medieval Ireland? Perspectives on Medieval Gaelic National Identity in the Middle Ages* (Oxford: Archaeopress, 2004).

5 D. McCarthy, *The Irish Annals: Their Genesis, Evolution and History* (Dublin: Four Courts Press, 2008).

6 T. Finan, 'O'Conor "Grand Strategy" and the Connacht Chronicle in the Thirteenth Century', in T. Finan (ed.), *Medieval Lough Cé: History, Archaeology, Landscape* (Dublin: Four Courts Press, 2010), pp. 159–180.

7 T. Barry, 'The Origins of Irish Castles: A Contribution to the Debate', in C. Manning (ed.), *From Ringforts to Fortified Houses* (Bray: Wordwell, 2008), pp. 33–40.

8 The Mac Diarmada change in status over the thirteenth century is exemplified in the somewhat passing reference to Mac Diarmada, in J. O'Daly and J. O'Donovan, 'Inauguration of Cathal Crobhdhearg O'Conor, King of Connaught', *Transactions of the Kilkenny Archaeological Society*, vol. 2, no. 2, 1853, pp. 335–47, and the position of primacy as found in 'The Rights of Mac Dermot' a century later.

9 G. Parker, *The Grand Strategy of Phillip II* (New Haven: Yale University Press, 2000); E. Luttwak, *The Grand Strategy of Phillip II* (Baltimore: Johns Hopkins University Press, 1979).

10 Finan, 'O'Conor "Grand Strategy"', pp. 159–161.

11 G. Orpen, *Ireland under the Normans, 1169–1333* (Dublin: Four Courts Press, 2005), p. 375.

12 Finan, 'O'Conor "Grand Strategy"', pp. 170–171.

13 B. J. Graham, 'Medieval Settlement in County Roscommon', *Proceedings of the Royal Irish Academy*, vol. 88C, 1988, pp. 19–36.

14 H. Perros, 'Crossing the Shannon Frontier: Connacht and the Anglo-Normans, 1170–1224', in T. Barry, R. Frame and K. Simms (eds), *Colony and Frontier in Medieval Ireland* (London: The Hambledon Press, 1995), pp. 117–138.

15 Finan, *A Nation in Medieval Ireland*, pp.14–19.

16 Ibid., pp. 14–17.

17 AC 1257.13; AC 1259.6.

18 E. FitzPatrick, *Royal Inauguration in Gaelic Ireland,* c.*1100–1600: A Cultural Landscape Study* (Woodbridge: The Boydell Press, 2004), p. 181.
19 K. Simms, 'Native Sources for Gaelic Settlement: The House Poems', in P. J. Duffy, D. Edwards and E. FitzPatrick (eds), *Gaelic Ireland* c.*1250–1650: Land, Lordship and Settlement* (Dublin: Four Courts Press, 2001), pp. 246–267.
20 Finan, *A Nation in Medieval Ireland,* pp, 10–37.
21 Ibid., pp. 25–37.
22 A. Gwynn and R. N. Hadcock, *Medieval Religious Houses: Ireland* (Harlow: Longmans, 1970), pp. 166, 229.
23 B. Kalkreuter, *Boyle Abbey and the School of the West* (Bray: Wordwell, 2001), pp. 23–27; M. Clyne, 'The Rental of Holy Trinity Abbey, Lough Cé', in T. Finan (ed.), *Medieval Lough Cé: History, Archaeology and Landscape* (Dublin: Four Courts Press, 2010), pp. 67–96.
24 Kalkreuter, *Boyle Abbey,* p. 26.
25 E. O'Byrne, *War, Politics, and the Irish of Leinster, 1156–1606* (Dublin: Four Courts Press, 2003), pp. 124–126.
26 AC 1229.4.
27 AC 1231.2.
28 AC 1243.2.
29 AC 1269.9.
30 AC 1243.2.
31 AC 1233.3.
32 AC 1235.8.
33 AC 1235.17.
34 K. D. O'Conor, N. Brady, A. Connon and C. Fidalgo-Romo, 'The Rock of Lough Cé, Co. Roscommon', in T. Finan (ed.), *Medieval Lough Cé: History, Archaeology and Landscape* (Dublin: Four Courts Press, 2010), pp. 15–40.
35 Rock of Lough Key Survey License: 13R68.
36 Ibid.
37 N. Brady and K. D. O'Conor, 'The Later Medieval Usage of Crannogs in Ireland', *Ruralia*, vol. 5, 2005, pp. 127–136; A. O'Sullivan, 'Crannogs in Late Medieval Gaelic Ireland, *c.*1350–1650', in P. J. Duffy, D. Edwards and E. FitzPatrick (eds), *Gaelic Ireland,* c.*1250–*c.*1650, Land, Lordship and Settlement* (Dublin: Four Courts Press, 2001), pp. 397–417; P. Naessens, 'The Uí Fhlaithbheartaigh Gaelic Lordship of Iarchonnacht: Medieval Lordly Settlement on the Atlantic Seaboard', Unpublished PhD Thesis, National University of Ireland, Galway, 2009.
38 AC 1231.12; ALC 1231.11.
39 AC 1235.17.
40 AC 1230.8.
41 AC 1235.20.
42 Rockingham Moated Site Survey License: 13R69.
43 T. Finan, 'The Moated Sites of Co. Roscommon, Ireland: A Statistical Approach', *Chateau Gaillard*, vol. 24, 2014, pp. 177–180.
44 T. Finan and K. D. O'Conor, 'The Moated Site at Cloonfree', *Journal of the Galway Historical and Archaeological Society,* vol. 54, 2002, pp. 72–87.
45 Rockingham Moated Site Survey License: 13R69.
46 J. J. Parnell, R. Terry, Z. Nelson, 'Soil Chemical Analysis Applied as an Interpretive Tool for Ancient Human Activities in Piedras Negras, Guatemala', *Journal of Archaeological Science,* vol. 29, no. 4, 2002, pp. 379–404.

47 Readings were taken at ten-metre intervals, and the amount of phosphorus at each station was recorded in parts per million. Those readings were then plotted on a grid corresponding to the grid used for gradiometry.
48 ALC, 1231.11.

3. *Milling of cereals in Gaelic and Anglo-Norman Ireland* c.*1200–1500: Technology and cultural choice*

1 O. R. Constable, 'Food and Meaning: Christian Understandings of Muslim Food and Food Ways in Spain, 1250–1550', *Viator*, vol. 44, no. 3, 2013, pp. 213–214.
2 N. Jackman, C. Moore and C. Rynne, *The Mill at Kilbegly: An Archaeological Investigation on the Route of the M6 Ballinasloe to Athlone National Road Scheme* (Dublin: Wordwell, 2013), p. 115.
3 G. MacNiocaill, 'Tír Cumaile', *Eriu*, vol. 22, 1971, pp. 81–86; F. Kelly, *Early Irish Farming: A Study Based Mainly on the Law Texts of the 7th and 8th Centuries AD* (Dublin: Institute for Advanced Studies, 1997), pp. 394–397.
4 C. Rynne, *Technological Change in Anglo-Norman Munster*, The Barryscourt Lectures, vol. III (Cork: Barryscourt Trust, 1998), pp. 82–84.
5 C. Rynne, 'The Patrick Street Watermills: Their Technological Context and a Note on the Reconstruction', in C. Walsh, *Archaeological Excavations at Patrick, Nicholas and Winetavern Streets Dublin* (Dingle: Brandon, 1997), pp. 81–89; C. Rynne, 'A Medieval Watermill at Ballyine, County Limerick', *Journal of the Cork Historical and Archaeological Society*, vol. 112, 2007, pp. 23–28. A probable later medieval millrace has also been excavated at Killegland near Ashbourne, County Meath: see W. O. Frazer, 'A Medieval Farmstead at Killegland, Asbourne, County Meath', in C. Corlett and M. Potterton (eds), *Rural Settlement in Medieval Ireland in the Light of Recent Archaeological Excavations* (Bray: Wordwell, 2009), pp. 109–124.
6 For examples of pre-Norman keyhole kilns see Curtaun, County Galway, kilns 1–3, C14 674–947; S. Delaney et al., 'Crops, Iron and Water', in S. Delaney, E. Lyne, S. McNamara, J. Nunan and K. Molloy (eds), *Borderlands: Archaeological Investigations on the Route of the M18 Gort to Crusheen Road Scheme*, NRA Monographs, No. 9 (Dublin: Wordwell, 2012), pp. 139–145. See also kiln F.11 at Killeen Castle, County Meath, C14 AD 690–900; C. Baker, *The Archaeology of Killeen Castle, County Meath* (Dublin: Wordwell, 2009), pp. 77–79.
7 F. McCormick, T. Kerr, M. McLatchie and A. O'Sullivan, 'The Archaeology of Livestock and Cereal Production in Early Medieval Ireland, AD 400–1100', Early Medieval Archaeology Project, Report 5:1, 2011; Kelly, *Early Irish Farming*, p. 219.
8 See P. A. Kozmin, *Flour Milling*, trans. M. Falkner and T. Fjelstrup (London: D. Van Nostrand Company, 1917), p. 162, who noted that 'grinders of sandstone are used almost exclusively on simple farm mills'.
9 Kozmin, *Flour Milling*, p. 161.
10 Nonetheless, granite millstones continued to be quarried in the Mourne Mountains in the eighteenth and nineteenth centuries: see E. E. Evans, *Mourne County: Landscape and Life in South Down* (Dundalk: Dundalgan Press, 1967), pp. 165–166 and T. McErlean, 'The Millstones and Millhouses', in T. McErlean and N. Crothers, *Harnessing the Tides: The Early Medieval*

*Tide Mills at Nendrum Monastery, Strangford Lough* (London: Stationery Office, 2007), p. 199. Elsewhere in Ireland conglomerate sandstones were almost universally employed as shelling stones: C. Rynne, *Industrial Ireland 1750–1930: An Archaeology* (Cork: The Collins Press, 2006). In Europe, the use of granite millstones appears to have been a matter of convenience rather than choice. In northern Spain, for example *berroqueña*, a local granite, was commonly used for millstones: see J. M. Alonso Gonzalez, *Los Molinos Tradicionales en la Provincia de Léon* (Léon: Leonesas, 1993), p. 62. Granite millstones are also common in northern Portugal (*mós negreiras*), where this stone occurs naturally. It was, however, traditionally used mostly for coarse grinding or for processing maize: see E. Viega de Oliviera, F. Galhano, and B. Pereira, *Tecnologia Tradicional Portuguesa: Sistemas de Moagem*, vol. 2 (Lisbon: Instituto Nacional de Investigação Científica, 1983), pp. 347–348. There are, in addition, written sources that attest to the use of granite millstones in mid-fourteenth-century Portugal, Viega de Oliviera et al., *Tecnologia Tradicional Portuguesa*, p. 349, and medieval Tuscany, J. Muendel, 'The Horizontal Mills of Medieval Pistoia', *Technology and Culture*, vol. 15, 1974, p. 195.

11 The upper or runner stone (Old Irish *liae*) was between 0.55 and 1.07m in diameter, 6–25cm in general thickness and with a central eye 10–16cm in diameter. The lower or bed stone (Old Irish *indeoin*) was 0.55–1.0m in diameter and 8.2cm to 32cm thick.

12 McErlean, 'The Millstones and Millhouses', pp. 184–186.

13 Ibid., p. 191.

14 I. Russell, C. Moore, A. O'Sullivan and V. Ginn, 'Killoteran 9 – Early Medieval Vertical Watermill', in J. Eogan and E. Shee Twohig (eds), *Cois tSiúre – Nine Thousand Years of Human Activity in the Lower Suir Valley. Archaeological Excavations on the Route of the N25 Waterford City Bypass*, NRA Scheme Monographs 8 (Dublin: National Roads Authority, 2011), p. 45.

15 McErlean, 'The Millstones and Millhouses', p. 199.

16 D. Power et al., *Archaeological Inventory of County Cork. Vol. 2, East and South Cork* (Dublin: Stationery Office, 1994), p. 166.

17 S. Connolly and J. M. Picard, 'Cogitosus Life of St. Brigit', *Journal of the Royal Society of Antiquaries of Ireland*, vol. 117, 1987, pp. 5–27.

18 McErlean,'The Millstones and Millhouses', p. 195, based on 'the small size of the fragments' of the runner stone and bed stone recovered from Mashanaglass, casts doubt on the upper estimate for their original diameters. However, I have personally examined these stones and have concluded that Fahy's estimates are quite plausible.

19 S. Wright, 'Millstones', in P. Rahtz and R. Meeson, *An Anglo-Saxon Watermill at Tamworth: Excavations in the Boleridge Street area of Tamworth, Staffordshire in 1971 and 1978*, CBA Research Report no. 83 (London: Council for British Archaeology, 1992), pp. 70–79; B. Arnau and J. Martí, 'Aigua i Desenvoluament Urbá a Madinat Balansiya (Valéncia): L'Excavació d'un Molí Hidráulic de l'Epoca Califal', in T. F. Glick and E. Guinot (eds), *Els Molins Hidràulics Valencians: Tecnologia, Història i Context Social* (Valencia: Institución Alfons el Magnànim de la Diputación de Valencia, 2000), p. 170.

20 V. Lagardère, 'Moulins d'Occident Musulman au Moyen Age (IX au XV Siècles): Al-Andalus', *Al Qantara*, vol. 12, 1991, p. 109; S. Selma, 'De la Construcció Islàmica al Casalici Modern: l'Evolució Molí Hidràulic Valencia', in T. F. Glick and E. Guinot (eds), *Els Molins Hidráulics Valencians. Tecnologia, História i Context Social* (Institución Alfons el Magnànim de la Diputación de Valencia, 2000), p. 108; M. Harverson, *Mills of the Muslim World* (London: SPAB Mills Section, 2000), p. 13.

21 They are 0.55m, 0.61m, 0.65m, 0.70m, 0.73m, 0.78m, 0.80m, 0.81m and 0.82m in diameter.

22 W. Czysz, *Die Ältesten Wassermühlen: Archäologische Entdeckungen im Paartal bei Dasing* (Thierhaupten: Klostermühlenmuseum, 1998); P. Rohmer, 'Le Moulin Carolingien d'Audun-le-Tiche', *L'Archéologue*, vol. 22, 1996, pp. 6–8.

23 R. Cresswell, 'Of Mills and Waterwheels: The Hidden Parameters of Technological Choice', in P. Lemonnier (ed.), *Technological Choices: Transformation in Material Cultures since the Neolithic* (London and New York: Psychology Press, 2002), p. 185.

24 Viega de Oliviera et al., *Tecnologia Tradicional Portuguesa*, p. 347.

25 Ibid.

26 R. Córdoba de la Llave, 'Aceñas, Tahonas y Almazaras: Técnicas Industriales y Procesos Productivos de Sector Agroalimentario en la Córdoba de Siglo XV', *Hispania: Revista Española de Historia*, vol. 48, 1988, pp. 827–874: p. 842; L. Martínez Carillo and M. Martínez Martínez, *Origenes y Expansion de los Molinos Hidráulicos en la Ciudad y Huerta de Murcia (Siglos XII–XV)* (Ayuntamiento de Murcia, 2000), p. 104.

27 S. Selma, *Els Molins d'Aigua Medievals a Sharq al-Andalus* (Ajuntament d'Onda, 1993), p. 38, n. 27; Selma, 'De la Construcció Islàmica', pp. 112–115.

28 A. Guiffrida, 'Permanenza Tecnologia ed Espansione Territoriale del Mulino ad Acqua Siciliano (secc. XIV–XVI)', in S. Mariotti (ed.), *Produttivita e Tecnologie Nei Secoli XII–XVII* (Firenze, 1981), p. 211.

29 Selma, 'De la Construcció Islàmica', p. 111.

30 T. F. Glick and L. P. Martínez, 'La Molineria Hidràulica Valenciana: Questions Obertes', in T. F. Glick and E. Guinot (eds), *Els Molins Hidráulics Valencians: Tecnologia, História i Context Social* (Institución Alfons el Magnànim de la Diputación de Valencia, 2000), pp. 87–88. For the ethnic context of *couscous* in later medieval and early modern Spain see Constable, 'Food and Meaning', pp. 213–214.

31 A. Belmont, 'Why Dig a Millstone Quarry? The Case of Claix in the South West of France', in D. Williams and D. Peacock (eds), *Bread for the People: The Archaeology of Mills and Milling*, British Archaeological Report, International Series, 2274 (Oxford: Archaeopress, 2011), p. 10.

32 T. J. Andersen, T. Grenn and J. M. Fernández Soler, 'Volcanic Quern and Millstone Quarries in Cabo de Gata (Almería) and Campo de Calatrava (Ciudad Real), Spain', in D. Williams and D. Peacock (eds), *Bread for the People: The Archaeology of Mills and Milling*, British Archaeological Report, International Series, 2274 (Oxford: Archaeopress, 2011), p. 154. See also D. P. S. Peacock, 'The Roman Millstone Trade: A Petrological Sketch', *World Archaeology*, vol. 12, no. 1, 1980, pp. 43–53.

33 Czysz, *Die Ältesten Wassermühlen*, p. 14; J. Berthold, 'Eine Hochmittelalterliche Wassermühle, in Elfgen: Befunde, Funde, Reconstruktion',

*Bonner Jahrbucher des LVR–Landesmuseums Bonn und des LVR–Amtes*, vol. 208, 2008, pp. 173–237; A. Chapman, 'Millstones and Querns', in A. Chapman, *West Cotton, Rounds: A Study of Medieval Settlement Dynamics AD 450–1450. Excavation of a Deserted Medieval Hamlet in Northhamptonshire, 1985–89* (Oxford and Oakville: Oxbow, 2010), pp. 395–405; P. Clay, 'Querns and Millstones', in P. Clay and C. R. Salisbury, 'A Norman Mill Dam and Other Sites at Hemington Fields, Castle Donington, Leicestershire', *Archaeological Journal*, vol. 147, 1990, pp. 295–298.

34 H. Amouric, 'L'Anille et les Meules', in D. Meeks and D. Garcia (eds), *Techniques et Économies Antiques et Médiévales, le Temps de l'Innovation, Colloque d'Aix-en-Provence* (Paris: Travaux du Centre Camille, 1996), pp. 39–47; Anderson et al., 'Volcanic Quern and Millstone Quarries', p. 163.

35 Amouric, 'L'Anille et les Meules', pp. 46–47.

36 Anderson et al., 'Volcanic Quern and Millstone Quarries', p. 163.

37 J. P. Brunand and M. Borréani, 'Deux Moulins Hydrauliques du Haut-Empire Romain en Narbonnaise: Villae des Mesclans à la Crau et de Saint-Pierre/Les Laurons aux Ares (Var)', *Gallia: Archéologie de la France antique*, vol. 55, 1998, p. 301.

38 O. Höckman, 'Post-Roman Boat Timbers and a Floating Mill from the Upper Rhine', in C. Westerdahl (ed), *Crossroads in Ancient Shipbuilding: Proceedings of the Sixth International Symposium on Boat and Ship Archaeology, Roskilde 1991* (Oxford: Oxbow, 1994), p. 112; O. Höckman, 'Eine Schiffsmühle aus den Jahren um 760 n.Chr., in Gimbsheim, Kr. Alzey-Worms', *Mainzer Archäologische Zeitschrift*, vol. 1, 1994, p. 197; P. Tutlies, 'Eine Karolingisches Wassermühle in Rotbachtal', *Archäologie in Rheinland*, 2005, p. 107; Berthold, 'Eine Hochmittelalterliche Wassermühle in Elfgen', p. 189; H. Issleib, 'Die Betriebsanlagen der Alten Wassermühle im Ahrensfelder Teich', *Hammaburg*, vol. 4, 1953–1955, p. 70, n. 3.

39 R. Hodges, *Dark Age Economics: The Origins of Towns and Trade, AD 600–1000* (London: Bloomsbury Academic, 1982); J. Parkhouse, 'The Distribution and Exchange of Mayen Lava Quernstones in Early Medieval Europe', in G. de Boc and F. Verhaege (eds), *Exchange and Trade in Medieval Europe. Papers of the Medieval Europe Brugge Conference 1997: Conference III* (Zellik: Institut vor het Archeologisch Patrimonium, 1997), pp. 97–106; C. Coulter, 'Of Cakes and Kings: Breadmaking in Early Medieval England', in Williams and Peacock (eds), *Bread for the People*, pp. 181–182.

40 E. Campbell, 'A Cross-Marked Quern from Dunadd', *Proceedings of the Society of Antiquaries of Scotland*, vol. 117, 1987, pp. 105–117.

41 M. Pohl, 'Querns as Markers for the Determination of Medieval European Trade Spheres', in Williams and Peacock (eds), *Bread for the People*, p. 171.

42 Parkhouse, 'The Distribution and Exchange of Mayen Lava Quernstones', p. 102; F. Mangartz, *Römischer Basaltlava-Abbau Zwischen Eifel und Rhein* (Mainz: Römisch Germanisches Zentralmuseum, 2008), p. 125; Pohl, 'Querns as Markers', p. 173.

43 Chapman, 'Millstones and Querns', p. 142.

44 John Langdon, *Mills in the Medieval Economy* (Oxford: Oxford University Press, 2014), pp. 166–168, suggests that, the technical superiority of French millstones over German lava stones and indigenous types aside, 'overriding

cultural considerations' stemming from consumer expectations and preferences for consistent type of milled products were at play.

45 Pohl, 'Querns as Markers', p. 169.

46 D. L. Farmer, 'Millstones for Medieval Manors', *Agricultural History Review*, vol. 40, no. II, 1992, p. 97. As Farmer notes, 'a single French stone often cost more than the mill's multure sales yielded on the manor from its lease, in a whole year' (ibid., p. 103).

47 Farmer, 'Millstones for Medieval Manors', p. 103; M. Watts, *The Archaeology of Mills and Milling* (Stroud: Tempus, 2002), p. 99.

48 Czysz, *Die Ältesten Wassermühlen*, p. 31.

49 In English mills of the thirteenth and fourteenth centuries, up to one-third of the construction and maintenance costs was accounted for by millstones: see Langdon, *Mills in the Medieval Economy*, p. 162.

50 But see Langdon, *Mills in the Medieval Economy*, pp. 166–168.

51 Arnau and Martí, 'Aigua i Desenvoluament Urbá', p. 170.

52 Ö. Wikander, 'The Water-Mill', in Ö. Wikander (ed.), *Handbook of Ancient Water Technology* (Leiden, Boston, Köln, 2000), p. 392.

53 E. C. Curwen, 'Querns', *Antiquity*, vol. 11, 1937, p. 144; Ö. Wikander, 'Archaeological Evidence for Early Water-Mills an Interim Report', *History of Technology*, vol. 11, 1985, pp. 163–165; A. Wilson, 'Late Antique Water-Mills on the Palatine', *Papers of the British School at Rome*, vol. 71, 2003, pp. 88, 97; C. Krause, *Domus Tiberiana, I: Gli Scavi (Bollettino di Archeologia)*, vols 25–7 (Rome: Istituto Poligrafico e Zecca dello Stato, 1994), figs 132–134.

54 R. Spain and I. Riddler, 'Millstones', in P. Bennett, I. Riddler and C. Sparey Green (eds), *The Roman Watermills and Settlement at Ickham, Kent: The Archaeology of Canterbury, Vol. V* (Canterbury Archaeological Trust, 2010), p. 283.

55 P. Lorquet, 'Decouverte d'un Moulin Carolingien á Belle–Eglise, "Le Pré des Paillards (Oise)"', *Revue Archéologique de Picardie*, vols 3–4, 1994, pp. 51–57; Paul Stevens, pers. comm.; Fischer, *Tidlige Danske Vandmøller*, p. 47.

56 L. C. Nielsen, 'Omgård: The Viking Age Water-Mill Complex. A Provisional Report on the 1986 Excavations', *Acta Archaeologica*, vol. 57, 1987, p. 193.

57 Czysz, *Die Ältesten Wassermühlen*, p. 31; Clay, 'Querns and Millstones', p. 295.

58 Langdon, *Mills in the Medieval Economy*, p. 172. J. Schoonhoven ('Grinding with Stones', *Transactions of the International Molinological Society*, vol. 4, 1978, p. 277) notes the existence of German lava stones in more recent windmills in southern Holland with diameters of 1.3m–1.5m, while as late as 1917 Peter Kozmin can cite 1–1.6m as a typical range of millstone sizes. The largest millstone diameter in Russia in the early twentieth century, according to Kozmin, was 56 inches or 1.42m (see Kozmin, *Flour Milling*, p. 164, Table XVI).

59 C. Lynn, 'The Excavation of Rathmullan, a Raised Rath and Motte in County Down', *Ulster Journal of Archaeology*, vols 44–45, 1982, pp. 65–171.

60 C. Manning, *The History and Archaeology of Glanworth Castle, County Cork* (Dublin: Wordwell, 2009), p. 81; A. Carey, 'The Grinding Stones', in M. Clyne, *Kells Priory, County Kilkenny: Archaeological Excavations by*

*Tom Fanning and Miriam Clyne* (Dublin: Stationery Office, 2007), pp. 436–440.

61 J. Lydon, 'The Mills at Ardee in 1304', *Journal of the County Louth Archaeological and Historical Society*, vol. 19, no. 4, 1980, pp. 259–263: 260; T. O'Neill, *Merchants and Mariners in Medieval Ireland* (Dublin: Irish Academic Press, 1987), p. 92.

62 M. Lyons, 'Manorial Administration and the Manorial Economy in Ireland, *c.*1200–*c.*1377', Unpublished PhD Thesis, Trinity College Dublin, 1984, p. 32.

63 O'Neill, *Merchants and Mariners*, p. 92; M. Murphy and M. Potterton, *The Dublin Region in the Middle Ages: Settlement, Land-use and Economy* (Dublin: Four Courts Press, 2010), p. 425.

64 D. M. Waterman, 'Somersetshire and Other Foreign Building Stone in Ireland, *c.*1175–1400', *Ulster Journal of Archaeology*, vol. 33, 1970, pp. 63–75.

65 Pers. comm. Derek O'Brien, Department of Archaeology, UCC.

66 O'Neill, *Merchants and Mariners*, p. 92.

67 Lyons, 'Manorial Administration', p. 157.

68 Ibid., p. 279.

69 C. Rynne, 'Technological Continuity, Technological "Survival": The Use of Horizontal Mills in Western Ireland, *c.*1632–1940', *Industrial Archaeology Review*, vol. 33, no. 2, 2011, p. 101.

70 Glick and Martínez, 'La Molineria Hidràulica Valenciana', p. 88.

71 Constable, 'Food and Meaning', p. 201.

## 4. *Archaeologies of female monasticism in Ireland: Becoming and belonging c.1200–1600*

1 The term 'master narrative' has multiple meanings. Here, it is used to refer to a male-dominated version of the past. For further explanation see M. C. Erler and M. Kowaleski, 'A New Economy of Power Relations: Female Agency in the Middle Ages', in M. C. Erler and M. Kowaleski (eds), *Gendering the Master Narrative: Women and Power in the Middle Ages* (Ithaca: Cornell University Press, 2003), p. 7.

2 J. F. Hamburger, 'Introduction', in J. F. Hamburger and S. Marti (eds), *Crown and Veil, Female Monasticism from the Fifth to the Fifteenth Centuries* (New York: Columbia University Press, 2008), p. 1; K. Perkins-Curran, '"Quhat Say Ye Now My Lady Priores? How Have Ye Usit Your Office, Can Ye Ges?" Politics, Power and Realities of the Office of a Prioress in Her Community in Late Medieval Scotland', in J. Burton and K. Stöber (eds), *Monasteries and Society in the British Isles in the Later Middle Ages* (Woodbridge: The Boydell Press, 2008), p. 124; L. M. Bitel, 'Introduction, Convent Ruins and Christian Profession: Toward a Methodology for the History of Religion and Gender', in L. M. Bitel and F. Lifshitz (eds), *Gender and Christianity in Medieval Europe: New Perspectives* (Philadelphia: Pennsylvania University Press, 2008), p. 3.

3 R. Gilchrist, *Gender and Material Culture: The Archaeology of Religious Women* (London: Routledge, 1994).

4 C. Harrington, *Women in a Celtic Church, Ireland 450–1150* (Oxford: Oxford University Press, 2002), p. 9.

5 For discussion of this wider debate in a pre-modern context see K. Giles, 'Seeing and Believing: Visuality and Space in Pre-Modern England', *World Archaeology*, vol. 39, no. 1, 2007, p. 109; C. P. Graves, 'Sensing and Believing: Exploring Worlds of Difference in Pre-Modern England: A Contribution to the Debate Opened by Kate Giles', *World Archaeology*, vol. 39, no. 4, 2007.
6 Bitel, 'Introduction', pp. 1–15.
7 P. Ó Riain, *A Dictionary of Irish Saints* (Dublin: Four Courts Press, 2011), p. 319; M. Potterton, *Medieval Trim: History and Archaeology* (Dublin: Four Courts Press, 2005), p. 56.
8 M. Moore, *Archaeological Inventory of County Meath* (Dublin: Stationery Office, 1987), p. 127.
9 Ó Riain, *Dictionary*, pp. 320, 356–357.
10 N. Hadcock, 'The Origin of the Augustinian Order in Meath', *Records of the Meath Archaeological and Historical Society*, vol. 3, no. 2, 1964, p. 125.
11 J. Brady, 'The Nunnery of Clonard', *Records of the Meath Archaeological and Historical Society*, vol. 2, no. 2, 1960, p. 5; A. Gwynn and R. N. Hadcock, *Medieval Religious Houses: Ireland* (Dublin: Longman, 1970).
12 Brady, 'Clonard', p. 6.
13 Moore, *Inventory*, p. 127; Department of Arts, Heritage, Rural, Regional and Gaeltacht Affairs, Historic Environment Viewer [http://webgis.archaeology.ie/historicenvironment/], Accessed 28 February 2014.
14 D. Sweetman, 'Excavation of Medieval "Field Boundaries" at Clonard, County Meath', *Journal of the Royal Society of Antiquaries of Ireland*, vol. 108, 1978, p. 10; P. J. Gibson and D. M. George, 'Geophysical Investigation of the Site of the Former Monastic Settlement, Clonard, County Meath, Ireland', *Archaeological Prospection*, vol. 13, 2006, pp. 45–56.
15 R. Ó Floinn, 'A Crozier Head from Clonard', in T. Condit and C. Corlett (eds), *Above and Beyond: Essays in Memory of Leo Swan* (Dublin: Wordwell, 2005), pp. 333–342; R. Ó Floinn, 'A Fragmentary House-Shaped Shrine from Clonard, Co. Meath', *Journal of Irish Archaeology*, vol. 5, 1989/1990, pp. 49–55; H. Roe, *Medieval Fonts of Meath* (Meath Archaeological and Historical Society, 1968).
16 Gilchrist, *Gender and Material Culture*, pp. 19, 59, 115, 125.
17 Lord Killanin and M. V. Duignan, *The Shell Guide to Ireland* (London: Ebury Press, 1967), p. 87; Gwynn and Hadcock *Religious Houses Ireland,* p. 406.
18 T. J. Westropp, 'The Termon Cross of Kilnaboy, County Clare Sketched in 1854', *Journal of the Royal Society of Antiquaries of Ireland*, vol. 39, 1909, p. 85. This cross bears two female faces interpreted as possible religious women: see G. MacNamara, 'The Ancient Stone Crosses of Uí Fearmaic County Clare: Part II: The Cross of Kilnaboy', *Journal of the Royal Society of Antiquaries of Ireland*, vol. 30, 1900, p. 25.
19 J. O'Donovan, 'Letters Containing Information Relative to the Antiquities of the County of Kildare Collected During the Progress of the Ordnance Survey in 1837', comp. M. O'Flanagan, typescript in 2 vols, vol. 1, p. 73 [206] (Bray, 1930). This site is marked on the first-edition six-inch Ordnance Survey map, sheet 30 (1838) as 'nunnery'.
20 M. MacCurtain, 'Late Medieval Nunneries of the Irish Pale', in H. B. Clarke, J. Prunty and M. Hennessy (eds), *Surveying Ireland's Past: Multidisciplinary*

*Essays in Honour of Anngret Simms* (Dublin: Geography Publications, 2004), p. 133.

21 Gwynn and Hadcock, *Religious Houses Ireland*, p. 321; E. FitzPatrick and C. O'Brien, *The Medieval Churches of County Offaly* (Dublin: Dúchas, 1998), pp. 87–88.

22 Gywnn and Hadcock, *Religious Houses Ireland*, p. 324; D. Hall, *Women and the Church in Medieval Ireland c.1140–1540* (Dublin: Four Courts Press, 2003), p. 152.

23 M. Archdall, *Monasticon Hibernicum: or a History of the Abbeys, Priories and Other Religious Houses in Ireland*, ed. Patrick F. Moran, 3 vols (Dublin: W. B. Kelly, 1876), vol. 2, pp. 84–86; C. Baker, *Antiquities of Old Fingal: The Archaeology of North County Dublin* (Dublin: Wordwell, 2010), p. 99.

24 Gywnn and Hadcock, *Religious Houses Ireland*, p. 307. Only eleven nunneries are listed in the dissolution surveys. N. B. White (ed.), *Extents of Irish Monastic Possessions 1540–41 from Manuscripts in the PRO London* (Dublin: Stationery Office, 1943), pp. 68–77, 123–125, 163–164, 171, 203–206, 209, 234–235, 255–259, 260–262, 336–337.

25 Hall, *Women and the Church*, p. 16.

26 S. Thompson, *Women Religious: The Founding of English Nunneries after the Norman Conquest* (Oxford: Clarendon Press, 1991), p. 177; M. Oliva, *The Convent and the Community in Late Medieval England: Female Monasteries in the Diocese of Norwich, 1350–1540* (Woodbridge: The Boydell Press, 1998); K. A. Curran, 'Religious Women and their Communities in Late Medieval Scotland', Unpublished PhD Thesis, University of Glasgow, 2005, pp. 104–173; K. Stöber, *Late Medieval Monasteries and their Patrons: England and Wales, c.1300–1540* (Woodbridge: The Boydell Press, 2007); J. Cartwright, *Feminine Sanctity and Spirituality in Medieval Wales* (Cardiff: University of Wales Press, 2008); Perkins-Curran, 'Politics, Power and Realities', pp. 124–141.

27 Hall, *Women and the Church*, pp. 63–91.

28 Moran, *Monasticon*, pp. 219–220; R. J. Kelly, 'Notes on the Round Tower of Kilbannon and on Kilcreevanty, County Galway', *Journal of the Royal Society of Antiquaries of Ireland*, vol. 31, 1901, p. 381.

29 S. Lewis, *A Topographical Dictionary of Ireland,* 3 vols (Dublin: S. Lewis & Co., 1837), vol. 2, p. 626; Hall, *Women and the Church*, pp. 63–91; T. Collins, 'Timolin: A Case Study of a Nunnery Estate in Later Medieval Ireland', *Anuario de Studios Medievales*, vol. 44, no. 1, 2014, pp. 51–80.

30 J. T. Gilbert, *A History of the City of Dublin,* 3 vols (Dublin: J. McGlashan, 1854–9), vol. 2, p. 2.

31 Curran, 'Religious Women and their Communities', p. 108.

32 D. Hall, 'Towards a Prosopography of Nuns in Medieval Ireland', *Archivium Hibernicum*, vol. 53, 1999, pp. 3–15; Hall, *Women and the Church,* pp. 211–220.

33 Oliva, *The Convent and the Community,* p. 168. For royal patronage of nunneries in the Anglo-Saxon period see B. Yorke, *Nunneries and the Anglo-Saxon Royal Houses* (London: Bloomsbury Academic, 2003).

34 D. Hall, 'The Nuns of the Medieval Convent of Lismullin, County Meath and their Secular Connections', *Records of the Meath Archaeological and Historical Society,* vol. 10, 1999, p. 58.

35 J. Ní Ghrádaigh, '"But What Exactly Did She Give?": Derbforgaill and the Nuns' Church at Clonmacnoise', in H. A. King (ed.), *Clonmacnoise Studies Volume 2 Seminar Papers 1998* (Dublin: Dept. of Environment, Heritage and Local Government, 2003), pp. 175–207.
36 Gywnn and Hadcock, *Religious Houses Ireland*, pp. 315–316.
37 Thompson, *Women Religious*, p. 177.
38 Stöber, *Late Medieval Monasteries and their Patrons*, pp. 147–189.
39 M. T. Flanagan, *The Transformation of the Irish Church in the Twelfth Century* (Woodbridge: The Boydell Press, 2010), pp. 200–201.
40 Ibid., p. 244.
41 Ibid., pp. 149–154; Hall, *Women and the Church*, pp. 63–91; G. Kenny, *Anglo-Irish and Gaelic Women in Ireland c.1170–1540* (Dublin: Four Courts Press, 2007), pp. 170–173.
42 Gilchrist, *Gender and Material Culture*, p. 41; Hall, *Women and the Church*, p. 81.
43 Gywnn and Hadcock, *Religious Houses Ireland*, pp. 321–322; B. Ó Dálaigh, 'Mistress, Mother and Abbess: Renalda Ní Bhriain *c.*1447–1510', *North Munster Antiquarian Journal*, vol. 32, 1990, p. 58.
44 Gywnn and Hadcock, *Religious Houses Ireland*, p. 130; R. Stalley, *The Cistercian Monasteries of Ireland* (New Haven: Yale University Press, 1987), p. 244; B. Doran and L. Doran, 'St Mary's Cistercian Abbey, Dublin: A Ghost in the Alleyways', in J. Bradley, A. J. Fletcher and A. Simms (eds), *Dublin in the Medieval World: Studies in Honour of Howard B. Clarke* (Dublin: Four Courts Press, 2009), pp. 188–201.
45 Thompson, *Women Religious*, pp. 95–96; J. Burton, 'Looking for Medieval Nuns', in J. Burton and K. Stöber (eds), *Monasteries and Society in the British Isles in the Later Middle Ages* (Woodbridge: The Boydell Press, 2008), pp. 113–123; C. Jäggi and U. Lobbedey, 'Church and Cloister: The Architecture of Female Monasticism in the Middle Ages', in J. F. Hamburger and S. Marti (eds), *Crown and Veil: Female Monasticism from the Fifth to the Fifteenth Centuries* (New York: Columbia University Press, 2008), pp. 109–131.
46 J. Burton, *Monastic and Religious Orders in Britain, 1000–1300* (Cambridge: Cambridge University Press, 1994), pp. 85, 86, 105.
47 P. J. Dunning, 'The Arroasian Order in Medieval Ireland', *Irish Historical Studies*, vol. 4, no. 16, 1945, pp. 297–315; M. T. Flanagan, 'St Mary's Abbey, Louth and the Introduction of the Arrouaisian Observance into Ireland', *The Clogher Record*, vol. 10, no. 2, 1980, pp. 223–234; Flanagan, *Transformation of the Irish Church*, pp. 118–168; T. Ó Carragáin, *Churches in Medieval Ireland* (New Haven: Yale University Press, 2010), pp. 11–12; T. O'Keeffe, *An Anglo-Norman Monastery: Bridgetown Priory and the Architecture of the Augustinian Canons Regular in Ireland* (Cork County Council, 1999), pp. 17–20.
48 On Augustinian male identity see T. O'Keeffe, 'Augustinian Regular Canons in Twelfth- and Thirteenth-Century Ireland: History, Architecture and Identity', in J. Burton and K. Stöber (eds), *The Regular Canons in the Medieval British Isles* (Turnhout: Brepolis, 2011), pp. 469–484.
49 For continental examples of the ethos of an order having a defining role in the affiliation of houses of religious women see C. M. Mooney, 'Nuns, Tertiaries and Quasi-Religious: The Religious Identities of Late Medieval Holy Women', *Medieval Feminist Forum*, vol. 41, 2006, pp. 68–92.

50 P. D. Johnson, *Equal in Monastic Profession: Religious Women in Medieval France* (Chicago: The University of Chicago Press, 1991), pp. 225–229; P. D. Johnson, 'The Cloistering of Medieval Nuns', in D. O. Helly and S. M. Reverby (eds), *Gendered Domains: Rethinking Public and Private in Women's History* (New York: Cornell University Press, 1992), pp. 36–39.
51 For a discussion of this change in a post-medieval and early modern context, but one which has its origins in the medieval period, see D. Rives, 'Taking the Veil: Clothing and the Transformation of Identity', *Proceedings of the Western Society for French History*, vol. 33, 2005, pp. 465–486.
52 For examples, see Ó Dálaigh, 'Mistress, Mother and Abbess', pp. 50–63; Hall, *Women and the Church*, pp. 191–200 on Elicia Butler, abbess of Kilculliheen. For continental examples, see G. Signori, 'Wanderers Between Worlds: Visitors, Letters, Wills, and Gifts as a Means of Communication in Exchanges between Cloister and the World', in J. F. Hamburger and S. Marti (eds), *Crown and Veil, Female Monasticism From the Fifth to the Fifteenth Centuries* (New York: Columbia University Press, 2008), pp. 259–273; C. Schleif and V. Schier, *Katerina's Windows: Donation and Devotion, Art and Music as Heard and Seen Through the Writings of a Birgittine Nun* (Philadelphia: The Pennsylvania State University Press, 2009).
53 Gywnn and Hadcock, *Religious Houses Ireland*, p. 307.
54 Stalley, *Cistercian Monasteries,* p. 31; C. Ó Clabaigh, *The Friars in Ireland 1224–1540* (Dublin: Four Courts Press, 2012), p. 87.
55 J. A. K. McNamara, *Sisters in Arms: Catholic Nuns Through Two Millennia* (Harvard University Press, 1996), p. 263.
56 E. Power, *Medieval English Nunneries* (Cambridge: Cambridge University Press, 1922), pp. 96–130.
57 Oliva, *The Convent and the Community,* pp. 90–99.
58 J. Burton, *The Yorkshire Nunneries in the Twelfth and Thirteenth Centuries* (York: Borthwick Publications, 1979), pp. 11–17.
59 Gilchrist, *Gender and Material Culture*, pp. 70–71, 76, 85.
60 Ibid., p. 90.
61 Hall, *Women and the Church*, p. 137.
62 G. Carville, *The Impact of the Cistercians on the Landscape of Ireland 1142–1541* (Wicklow: KB Publications, 2002), p. 247.
63 Gilchrist, *Gender and Material Culture,* pp. 85–90.
64 Power, *Nunneries*, p. 342; J. M. Howe, 'Cistercian Monastic Life/Vows: A Vision', in J. A. Nichols and L. Thomas Shank (eds), *Peace Weavers: Medieval Religious Women* (Kalamazoo: Cistercian Publications, 1987), p. 368; McNamara, *Sisters in Arms*, pp. 274, 286–288.
65 H. G. Leask, *Irish Churches and Monastic Buildings,* 3 vols (Dundalk: Dundalgan Press, 1960), vol. 2, pp. 1–17; Stalley, *Cistercian Monasteries,* pp. 51–75. For a comprehensive discussion on the origins of this layout see W. Horn, 'On the Origins of the Medieval Cloister', *Gesta*, vol. 12, 1973, pp. 13–52; J. McNeill, 'The Continent Context', *Journal of the British Archaeological Association*, vol. 159, 2006, pp. 1–47.
66 C. McNeill (ed.), *Calendar of Archbishop Alen's Register c.1172–1534* (Dublin: Royal Society of Antiquaries of Ireland, 1950), p. 180.
67 White (ed.), *Monastic Possessions,* p. 255.
68 For an overview of Augustinians in England and Wales see D. M. Robinson, *The Geography of Augustinian Settlement,* British Archaeological Report,

British Series, 80, 2 vols (Oxford: Archaeopress, 1980), pp. 155–171. See also J. Burton and K. Stöber (eds), *The Regular Canons in the Medieval British Isles* (Turnhout: Brepolis, 2011); K. Stöber and D. Austin, 'Culdees to Canons: The Augustinian Houses of North Wales', in J. Burton and K. Stöber (eds), *Monastic Wales: New Approaches* (Cardiff: University of Wales Press, 2013), pp. 39–54.

69 O'Keeffe, *An Anglo-Norman Monastery*, p. 12.

70 J. Bond, 'Medieval Nunneries in England and Wales: Buildings, Precincts and Estates', in D. Wood (ed.), *Women and Religion in Medieval England* (Oxford: Oxbow, 2003), p. 86.

71 T. Collins, 'Archaeological Excavations at St Catherine's, Old Abbey, County Limerick', Unpublished Report, 2010.

72 T. J. Westropp, 'Proceedings: Canons' Island', *Journal of the Royal Society of Antiquaries of Ireland*, vol. 27, 1897, pp. 286–290; T. J. Westropp, 'The Augustinian Houses of the County of Clare: Clare, Killone and Inchicronan', *Journal of the Royal Society of Antiquaries of Ireland*, vol. 30, 1900, pp. 118–135; T. J. Westropp, 'Prehistoric Remains (Forts and Dolmens) in the Burren and its South Western Border', *Journal of the Royal Society of Antiquaries of Ireland*, vol. 45, 1915, p. 217.

73 Power, *Nunneries*, p. 342; R. Gilchrist, *Contemplation and Action: The Other Monasticism* (London: Continuum International Publishing Group, 1995), p. 108; E. Makowski, 'Mulieres Religiosae, Strictly Speaking: Some Fourteenth-Century Canonical Opinions', *The Catholic Historical Review*, vol. 85, no. 1, 1999, pp. 1–14.

74 The writer is grateful to Brian Golding for discussing his forthcoming translation with her in this regard. Brian Golding (trans.), *Speculum Ecclesie* (Oxford, forthcoming).

75 The writer is grateful to Professor Marie Therese Flanagan for drawing this manuscript illustration and the following citation to her attention. The manuscript referred to is NLI MS 700, fol. 31r. For a discussion of Gerald of Wales's influence over illustration used in works attributed to him see M. P. Brown, 'Marvels of the West: Giraldus Cambrensis and the Role of the Author in the Development of Marginal Illustration', in A. S. G. Edwards (ed.), *English Manuscript Studies 1100–1700: Decoration and Illustration in Medieval English Manuscripts, Volume 10* (London: British Library, 2002), pp. 34–59.

76 K. Villiers-Tuthill, 'The Irish Benedictine Nuns: from Ypres to Kylemore', in M. Browne and C. Ó Clabaigh (eds), *The Irish Benedictines: A History* (Dublin: Columba Press, 2005), p. 136; R. Bradley, *An Archaeology of Natural Places* (London: Routledge, 2000).

77 E. de Paermentier, 'Experiencing Space Through Women's Convent Rules: The Rich Clares in Medieval Ghent, Thirteenth to Fourteenth Centuries', *Medieval Feminist Forum*, vol. 44, no. 1, 2008, p. 58.

78 Johnson, 'The Cloistering of Medieval Nuns', pp. 27–39.

79 B. Golding, *Gilbert of Sempringham and the Gilbertine Order* (Oxford: Clarendon Press, 1995); B. M. Kerr, *Religious Life for Women c.1100–c.1350: Fontevraud in England* (Oxford: Clarendon Press, 1999).

80 C. Neuman de Vegvar, '"Romanitas and Realpolitik in Cogitosus": Description of the Church of St Brigit, Kildare', in M. Carver (ed.), *The*

*Cross Goes North: Processes of Conversion in Northern Europe AD 300–1300* (York: Medieval Press, 2003), pp. 153–170.

81 Flanagan, *Transformation of the Irish Church*, pp. 150–154.

82 B. O'Dwyer (trans.), *Stephen of Lexington, Letters from Ireland 1228–1229* (Kalamzoo: Cistercian Publications, 1982); Stalley, *Cistercian Monasteries*, p. 46.

83 J. Burton and J. Kerr, *The Cistercians in the Middle Ages* (Woodbridge: The Boydell Press, 2011), pp. 21–55.

84 Annotated plan reproduced in Gilchrist, *Gender and Material Culture*, p. 75.

85 K. Brady and C. Corlett, 'Ships on Plaster: Evidence for Ships in Medieval Ireland', in C. Manning (ed.), *From Ringforts to Fortified Houses: Studies on Castles and Other Monuments in Honour of David Sweetman* (Bray: Wordwell, 2007), pp. 323–324.

86 T. Collins, 'Missing the Boat…', *Archaeology Ireland*, vol. 4, 2010, pp. 9–11.

87 M. Gardiner, 'Graffiti and their Use in Late Medieval England', *Ruralia*, vol. 6, 2005, pp. 267, 273.

88 For examples from an Irish context see M. Delaney, 'The Human Remains', in M. Clyne, *Kells Priory, Co. Kilkenny: Archaeological Excavations by T. Fanning and M. Clyne* (Dublin: Stationery Office, 2007), pp. 467–482; B. Ó Donnobháin, 'The Human Remains', in A. Lynch, *Tintern Abbey, Co. Wexford: Cistercians and Colcloughs. Excavations 1982–2007. Archaeological Monograph Series: 5* (Dublin: Stationery Office, 2010), pp. 105–125. For a comprehensive synthesis of monastic burial which includes nunneries see R. Gilchrist and B. Sloane, *Requiem: the Medieval Monastic Cemetery in Britain* (Museum of London Archaeology Service, 2005).

89 The writer is grateful to Martin Byrne of Byrne, Mullins and Associates for providing the unpublished report on the archaeological works he carried out in 2000 at Graney East, County Kildare and also the specialist reports on the human remains and the medieval pottery.

90 D. Watt (ed.), *Medieval Women in their Communities* (Toronto: University of Toronto Press, 1997), p. 4

91 Curran, 'Religious Women and their Communities', p. 1.

5. *The Uí Fhlaithbheartaigh of Mag Seóla and Iarchonnacht: From inland kings to sea-lords*

1 F. J. Byrne, *Irish Kings and High-Kings* (London: B.T. Batsford Ltd, 1973), pp. 234–235.

2 D. Ó Corráin, *Ireland before the Normans* (Dublin: Gill & Macmillan, 1972), p. 9.

3 Old Irish *drech* meaning face, front or surface. See E. G. Quin (ed.), *Dictionary of the Irish Language, Based Mostly on Old and Middle Irish Materials* (Dublin: Royal Irish Academy, 1983), p. 248 [390].

4 AFM 990.7.

5 AFM 1061.12.

6 AFM 1061.13.

7 AU 1062.3.

8 AU 1065.6.

9 ALC 1092.2.

10 AFM 1098.15.
11 AFM 1121.7
12 The battle of the ditch.
13 MIA 1132.1
14 J. Hardiman (ed.), *West or h-Iar Connaught by Roderic O'Flaherty: with Notes and Illustrations by Hardiman, J.* (Dublin: The Irish Archaeological Society, 1846), pp. 368–372. See also J. O'Donovan, Letters Containing Information Relative to the Antiquities of the County of Galway Collected during the Progress of the Ordnance Survey in 1839, comp. M. O'Flanagan, typescript in 3 vols (Bray, 1927), vol. 3, pp. 148–151.
15 G. H. Orpen, *Ireland under the Normans 1169–1333* (Dublin: Four Courts Press, 2005), p. 430.
16 ALC 1121.3.
17 AT 1124.3
18 B. J. Graham, 'Medieval Timber and Earthwork Fortifications in Western Ireland', *Medieval Archaeology*, vol. 32, 1988, pp. 110–129; P. Naessens and K. D. O'Conor, 'Pre-Norman Fortification in Eleventh- and Twelfth-century Connacht', *Chateau Gaillard,* vol. 25, 2012, pp. 259–268.
19 P. Walsh, 'Galway: A Summary History', in E. FitzPatrick, M. O'Brien and P. Walsh (eds), *Archaeological Investigations in Galway City, 1987–1998* (Bray: Wordwell, 2004), pp. 272–273.
20 See P. Naessens, The Uí Fhlaithbheartaigh Gaelic Lordship of Iarchonnacht: Medieval Lordly Settlement on the Atlantic Seaboard. Unpublished PhD Thesis, National University of Ireland, Galway, 2009, chapter 4.
21 M. Dillon (ed. and trans.), 'The Inauguration of O'Conor', in F. X. Martin, J. B. Morall and J. A. Watt (eds), *Medieval Studies Presented to Aubrey Gwynn* (Dublin: Three Candles, 1961), pp. 186–202; M. T. Flanagan, 'Irish and Anglo-Norman Warfare in Twelfth-century Ireland', in T. Bartlett and K. Jeffery (eds), *A Military History of Ireland* (Cambridge: Cambridge University Press, 1996), pp. 52–75.
22 ALC 1196.4.
23 ALC 1196.6.
24 ALC 1235.13; See also Hardiman, *West or h-Iar Connaught*, pp. 51–52.
25 See J. Bannerman, *The Beatons: A Medical Kindred in the Classical Tradition* (Edinburgh: John Donald Publishers Ltd, 1998), pp. 116–117 who refers to the activities of the O'Canavans in Connacht during the sixteenth century. See also A. Nic Dhonnchadha, *Medical Writing in Ireland 1400–1700*, published online at http://www.dias.ie/rcsi1.html [accessed 18 August 2015], for the Mac an Leagha.
26 P. MacCotter, *Medieval Ireland: Territorial, Political and Economic Divisions* (Dublin: Four Courts Press, 2008), pp. 133–134, 137.
27 Dillon, 'The Inauguration of O'Conor', p. 202.
28 AFM 1384.6; AC 1417.4; AFM 1503.21.
29 Cormac, the Rotund.
30 AFM 1384.6.
31 AC 1417.4.
32 See P. Naessens, 'Gaelic Lords of the Sea: The Coastal Tower Houses of South Connemara', in L. Doran and J. Lyttleton (eds), *Lordship in Medieval Ireland: Image and Reality* (Dublin: Four Courts Press, 2007), pp. 217–235.

33 K. D. O'Conor, *The Archaeology of Medieval Rural Settlement in Ireland*, Discovery Programme Monographs 3 (Dublin: Royal Irish Academy, 1998), p. 73.
34 E. FitzPatrick, '*Ollamh, Biatach, Comharba*: Lifeways of Gaelic Learned Families in Medieval and Early Modern Ireland', in L. Breatnach, R. Ó hUiginn, D. McManus and K. Simms (eds), *Proceedings of the XIV International Congress of Celtic Studies, held in Maynooth University, 1–5 August 2011* (Dublin: Institute for Advanced Studies, 2015), pp. 182–185.
35 C. Kelleher, 'The Gaelic O'Driscoll Lords of Baltimore, Co. Cork', in L. Doran and J. Lyttleton (eds), *Lordship in Medieval Ireland: Image and Reality* (Dublin: Four Courts Press, 2007), pp. 130–159.
36 O. Davies, *Excavations at Island MacHugh* (Belfast Natural History and Philosophical Society, 1950); C. Fredengren, *A Study of People's Interaction with Lakes, with Particular Reference to Lough Gara in the North-West of Ireland* (Dublin: Wordwell, 2002).
37 Fredengren, *Crannogs*, pp. 273–274.
38 J. J. O'Meara (ed. and trans.), *The History and Topography* of *Ireland* (Dublin: Dolmen Press; Harmondsworth: Penguin 1982), p. 37.
39 O'Conor, *The Archaeology of Medieval Rural Settlement*, p. 82.
40 Ibid., p. 84; T. Finan and K. D. O'Conor, 'The Moated Site at Cloonfree, Co. Roscommon', *Journal of the Galway Archaeological and Historical Society*, vol. 54, 2002, p. 73.
41 O'Conor, *The Archaeology of Medieval Rural Settlement*, p. 88.
42 E. FitzPatrick, *Royal Inauguration in Gaelic Ireland c.1100–1600: A Cultural Landscape Study* (Woodbridge: The Boydell Press, 2004), p. 91.
43 W. G. Wood-Martin, *The Lake Dwellings of Ireland: or Ancient Lacustrine Habitations of Erin, Commonly Called Crannogs* (Dublin: Crannog Editions, 1886), p. 224.
44 Wood-Martin, *The Lake Dwellings*, p. 225.
45 J. P. Nolan, 'Galway Castles and Owners in 1574', *Journal of the Galway Archaeological and Historical Society*, vol. 1, p. 115.
46 A. Gwynn and R. N. Hadcock, *Medieval Religious Houses: Ireland* (Dublin: Irish Academic Press, 1970), p. 287.
47 T. S. Flynn, *The Irish Dominicans, 1536–1641* (Dublin: Four Courts Press, 1993), p. 4.
48 K. D. O'Conor, N. Brady, A. Connon and C. Fidalgo-Romo, 'The Rock of Lough Cé, Co. Roscommon', in T. Finan (ed.), *Medieval Lough Cé: History, Archaeology and Landscape* (Dublin: Four Courts Press, 2010), p. 22.
49 T. Collins and A. Cummins, *Excavation of a Medieval Ringwork at Ballysimon, Co. Limerick* (Dublin: Wordwell, 2001), p. 31.
50 I am grateful to Dr Katharine Simms, TCD, for communicating this important point to me.
51 D. Caldwell, 'Finlaggan, Islay: Stones and Inauguration Ceremonies', in R. Welander, D. J. Breeze and T. O. Clancy (eds), *The Stone of Destiny: Artefact and Icon* (Edinburgh: Society of Antiquaries of Scotland, 2003), p. 62; Kelleher, 'The Gaelic O'Driscoll Lords of Baltimore', p. 156.
52 Hardiman, *West or h-Iar Connaught*, p. 109.

*6. Violence in later medieval Ireland: The osteoarchaeological evidence and its historical context*

1 F. Fitzsimons, 'Wolsey, the Native Affinities, and the Failure of Reform in Henrician Ireland', in D. Edwards (ed.), *Regions and Rulers in Ireland, 1100–1650* (Dublin: Four Courts Press, 2004), p. 84.
2 Great Britain, Public Record Office, State Papers Published under the Authority of His Majesty's Commission: Henry the Eighth, 6 vols (London: His Majesty's Commission for State Papers, 1830–52), vol. 2, p. 1.
3 *State Papers of His Majesty's Commission*, vol. 2, p. 1.
4 J. Lydon, 'The Middle Nation', in J. Lydon (ed.), *The English in Medieval Ireland* (Dublin: Royal Irish Academy, 1984), pp. 1–2.
5 *State Papers of His Majesty's Commission*, vol. 2, p. 6.
6 Fitzsimons, 'Wolsey, the Native Affinities', p. 84.
7 Lydon, 'The Middle Nation', pp. 6–7.
8 R. Frame, 'War and Peace in the Medieval Lordship of Ireland', in J. Lydon (ed.), *The English in Medieval Ireland* (Dublin: Royal Irish Academy, 1984), p. 123.
9 C. J. Donnelly, 'The Tower Houses of County Limerick', in R. Stalley (ed.), *Limerick and South-West Ireland: Medieval Art and Architecture*, British Archaeological Association Conference Transactions 34 (Leeds: Maney Publishing, 2011), p. 189.
10 A. Bliss, 'Language and Literature', in J. Lydon (ed.), *The English in Medieval Ireland* (Dublin: Royal Irish Academy, 1984), pp. 28–30.
11 K. Simms, 'Warfare in the Medieval Gaelic Lordships', *Irish Sword*, vol. 12, 1975, pp. 100–102; C. J. Donnelly, 'Architecture and Conflict: Limerick's Tower Houses, *c.*1400 to *c.*1650', in L. Irwin, G. Ó Tuathaigh and M. Potter (eds), *Limerick: History and Society* (Dublin: Geography Publications, 2009), pp. 80–81.
12 É. Ó Doibhlín, *O'Neill's 'Own Country' and Its Families* (Donaghmore Historical Society, 1998), p. 30.
13 Simms, 'Warfare in the Medieval Gaelic Lordships', p. 100.
14 C. Knüsel and A. Boylston, 'How has the Towton Project Contributed to our Knowledge of Medieval and Later Warfare?', in V. Fiorato, A. Boylston and C. Knüsel (eds), *Blood Red Roses: The Archaeology of a Mass Grave from the Battle of Towton, AD1461* (Oxford: Oxford University Press, 2000), p. 170.
15 A. Boylston, M. Holst and J. Coughlan, 'Physical Anthropology', in V. Fiorato, A. Boylston and C. Knüsel (eds), *Blood Red Roses: The Archaeology of a Mass Grave from the Battle of Towton, AD1461* (Oxford: Oxford University Press, 2000), pp. 45, 51–52.
16 S. A. Novak, 'Battle-related Trauma', in V. Fiorato, A. Boylston and C. Knüsel (eds), *Blood Red Roses: The Archaeology of a Mass Grave from the Battle of Towton, AD1461* (Oxford: Oxford University Press, 2000), pp. 91, 95–99.
17 Knüsel and Boylston, 'How has the Towton Project Contributed', p. 186.
18 G. A. Hayes-McCoy, *Irish Battles: A Military History of Ireland* (Belfast: Appletree Press, 1969), pp. 61–62.
19 Edwards, 'The Escalation of Violence', pp. 43–44.
20 Ibid., p. 40.

21 Ibid., p. 44.
22 D. Seward, *The Last White Rose: The Secret War of the Tudors* (London: Constable & Robinson, 2010).
23 AFM 1452.1
24 AFM 1434.2
25 AFM 1434.7
26 AFM 1439.2
27 AFM 1505.5
28 K. Simms, 'The Barefoot Kings: Literary Image and Reality in Later Medieval Ireland', *Proceedings of the Harvard Celtic Colloquium*, vol. 30, 2010, pp. 13–14.
29 AFM 1454.1
30 AU 1461.1
31 AFM 1488.4
32 AFM 1497.10
33 AU 1505.4
34 O'Donovan, *Annals of the Kingdom of Ireland*, vol. 5, p. 1283.
35 K. W. Nicholls, *Gaelic and Gaelicised Ireland in the Middle Ages* (Dublin: Lilliput Press, 2003), p. 12.
36 J. Hogan, 'The Irish Law of Kingship, with Special Reference to Ailech and Cenél Eoghain', *Proceedings of the Royal Irish Academy*, vol. 40C, 1931–2, p. 251.
37 Hogan, 'The Irish Law of Kingship', p. 249.
38 Ibid., p. 250.
39 AU 1492.35
40 J. Geber, 'Comparative Study of Perimortem Weapon Trauma in Two Early Medieval Skeletal Populations (AD 400–1200) from Ireland', *International Journal of Osteoarchaeology*, vol. 25, 2015, pp. 253–264.
41 Mapping Death 1st to 8th Centuries AD: People, Boundaries and Territories in Ireland, Online Database [http://www.mappingdeathdb.ie/ (accessed 28 August 2017)]; Geber, 'Comparative Study of Perimortem Weapon Trauma', p. 257.
42 E. Murphy and A. Russell, 'Osteological and Palaeopathological Analysis of the Human Remains from Kilroot, Co. Antrim Part 1 – Report', Unpublished Report, Queens University Belfast, 2011.
43 E. Murphy, 'Human Remains from Saint Patrick's Church, Armoy, County Antrim', in E. Murray and P. Logue (eds), *Battles, Bones and Boats: Archaeological Discoveries in Northern Ireland 1987–2008* (Belfast: Stationery Office, 2010).
44 C. McKenzie, 'Life in Medieval Ballyhanna: Insights from the Osteological and Palaeopathological Analysis of the Adult Skeletons', in C. McKenzie, E. Murphy and C. Donnelly (eds), *The Science of a Lost Medieval Gaelic Graveyard: The Ballyhanna Research Project* (Dublin: Transport Infrastructure Ireland, 2015), pp. 94–97; C. McKenzie and E. Murphy, *Life and Death in Medieval Gaelic Ireland: The Skeletons from Ballyhanna, Co. Donegal* (Dublin: Four Courts Press, forthcoming); E. Murphy, 'Lives Cut Short: Insights from the Osteological and Palaeopathological Analysis of the Ballyhanna Juveniles', in C. McKenzie, E. Murphy and C. Donnelly (eds), *The Science of a Lost Medieval Graveyard: The Ballyhanna Research Project* (Dublin: Transport Infrastructure Ireland, 2015), pp. 119–120.

45 G. Dawkes and L. Buckley, 'Before Bagenal's Castle: Evidence of the Medieval Cistercian Abbey at Newry, County Down', *Ulster Journal Of Archaeology*, Third Series, vol. 68, 2009, pp. 124–140.
46 C. Troy, 'Final Report on the Human Remains from Ardreigh, Co. Kildare', Unpublished Report to Headland Archaeology Ltd on behalf of Kildare County Council, 2010; N. Carty, 'Evidence for Cranial Trauma and Treatment in Medieval Kildare', *Journal of the Kildare Archaeological Society*, vol. 10, 2013, pp. 46–76.
47 Geber, 'Comparative Study of Perimortem Weapon Trauma', p. 257.
48 S. Gilmore and E. Murphy, 'Reconstructing the Dead Man's Face: A Violent Death from Medieval Armagh', *Archaeology Ireland*, vol. 15, no. 2, 2001, pp. 16–18.
49 C. J. Lynn, 'Grim Fortress or Picturesque Ruin? Greencastle, County Down', in A. Hamlin and C. Lynn (eds), *Pieces of the Past: Archaeological Excavations by the Department of the Environment for Northern Ireland, 1970-1986* (Belfast: HMSO, 1988), pp. 66–69; E. M. Murphy, 'Osteological Analysis of the Human Remains from Greencastle, Co. Down', Unpublished Report, Northern Ireland Environment Agency, 2013.
50 E. M. Murphy, 'Osteological Report on the Human Remains from Carrickfergus, Co. Antrim', Unpublished Report, Northern Ireland Environment Agency, 2012.
51 B. O'Donnabhain, 'The Social Lives of Severed Heads: Skull Collection and Display in Medieval and Early Modern Ireland', in M. Bonogofsky (ed.), *The Bioarchaeology of the Human Head: Decapitation, Decoration and Deformation* (Gainesville: University Press of Florida, 2011), pp. 122–138.
52 Ibid., p. 132. It should be noted that a left parietal and occipital, which had originated from an adolescent, were recovered from the post-medieval town ditch at Carrickfergus (CF27:F83). Although no evidence for trauma was apparent on the cranial bones, their discovery in the fill of the town ditch is suggestive of the remains of a decapitated head. Since no injuries were apparent on the bones, however, they have been excluded from the main discussion.
53 McKenzie, 'Life in Medieval Ballyhanna', pp. 94–97; Murphy, 'Lives Cut Short', pp. 119–120. Three adults, two males and a female from Ballyhanna also displayed evidence of healed sharp-force injuries but these are not included in the current study since the focus is on injuries that were probably responsible for the death of an individual.
54 Murphy, 'Human Remains from Armoy, Co. Antrim'.
55 Murphy and Russell, 'Human Remains from Kilroot, Co. Antrim'.
56 Dawkes and Buckley, 'Before Bagenal's Castle', pp. 133–136. A tibia with evidence of weapon trauma was also recovered from among the disarticulated remains but since we cannot be certain that it did not belong to one of the individuals with the skull trauma it has been excluded from the calculations used in this study.
57 Carty, 'Evidence for Cranial Trauma and Treatment in Medieval Kildare', p. 49.
58 Two individuals of indeterminable sex have been excluded from this count, one from Ballyhanna and one from Newry.
59 Geber, 'Comparative Study of Perimortem Weapon Trauma', p. 257.

60 S. Mays, 'The Human Remains', in S. Mays, C. Harding and C. Heighway, *The Churchyard (Wharram: A Study of Settlement on the Yorkshire Wolds IX)* (New York University Archaeological Publications, 2007), pp. 77–192.
61 Novak, 'Battle-related Trauma', pp. 91, 95–97.
62 T. Finan, 'Violence in Thirteenth-Century Ireland', *Eolas: The Journal of the American Society of Irish Medieval Studies* vol. 4, 2010, p. 90.
63 Ibid., p. 92.
64 Hogan, 'The Irish Law of Kingship', p. 250.
65 Edwards, 'The Escalation of Violence', p. 44.
66 C. J. McKenzie and E. M. Murphy, 'Health in Medieval Ireland: The Evidence from Ballyhanna, Co. Donegal', in S. Conran, E. Danaher and M. Stanley (eds), *Past Times, Changing Fortunes: Proceedings of a Public Seminar on Archaeological Discoveries on National Road Schemes, August 2010* (Dublin: National Roads Authority Monograph 8, 2011), pp. 140–143.
67 C. J. McKenzie, E. M. Murphy and C. J. Donnelly, 'Conclusions – Ordinary Lives: The Medieval Gaelic People of Ballyhanna', in C. J. McKenzie, E. M. Murphy and C. J. Donnelly (eds), *The Science of a Lost Medieval Gaelic Graveyard: The Ballyhanna Research Project* (Dublin: Transport Infrastructure Ireland, 2015), p. 164.
68 K. Simms, 'The Archbishops of Armagh and the O'Neills 1347–1471', *Irish Historical Studies*, vol. 19, 1974, p. 41.
69 AFM 1505.5.

7. *Scottish, Irish or other? Negotiating identity in late medieval north Ulster*

1 J. Hutchinson, *Dynamics of Cultural Nationalism: The Gaelic Revival and the Creation of the Irish Nation State* (London: Allen & Unwin, 1987), p. 1.
2 C. Breen, *The Gaelic Lordship of the O'Sullivan Beare: A Landscape Cultural History* (Dublin: Four Courts Press, 2005), p. 21; P. Naessens, 'Gaelic Lords of the Sea: The Coastal Tower Houses of South Connemara', in L. Doran and J. Lyttleton (eds), *Lordship in Medieval Ireland: Image and Reality* (Dublin: Four Courts Press, 2007) p. 224.
3 J. Hutchinson, 'Archaeology and the Irish Rediscovery of the Celtic Past', *Nations and Nationalism*, vol. 7, no. 4, 2001, pp. 505–519; Hutchinson, *Dynamics*, p. 506.
4 Breen, *Gaelic Lordship*, pp. 113–121.
5 W. McLeod, *Divided Gaels: Gaelic Cultural Identities in Scotland and Ireland, c.1200–c.1650* (Oxford: Oxford University Press, 2004), p. 1.
6 G. Hill, *An Historical Account of the MacDonnells of Antrim* (Belfast: Archer 1873), p. 18; K. Simms, 'Late Medieval Donegal', in W. Nolan et al. (eds), *Donegal: History and Society* (Dublin: Geography Publications, 1995), pp. 183–201.
7 I. Ralston and I. Armit, *Scotland after the Ice Age: Environment, Archaeology and History, 8000 BC–AD 1000* (Edinburgh: Edinburgh University Press, 2003), p. 217.
8 Simms, 'Late Medieval', p. 187.
9 S. Kingston, *Ulster and the Isles in the Fifteenth Century* (Dublin: Four Courts Press, 2004), p. 49.
10 C. Breen, *Dunluce Castle: History and Archaeology* (Dublin: Four Courts Press, 2012), p. 70.

11 Simms, 'Late Medieval', pp. 183–190.
12 K. W. Nicholls, 'Scottish Mercenary Kindreds in Ireland 1250–1600', in S. Duffy (ed.), *The World of the Galloglass: Kings and Warriors in Ireland and Scotland, 1250–1600* (Dublin: Four Courts Press, 2007) pp. 86–105.
13 Simms, 'Late Medieval', p. 188.
14 M. Johnson, *Behind the Castle Gate: From Medieval to Renaissance* (London: Routledge, 2002), pp. 181–182.
15 See, for example, D. Caldwell, *Islay: The Land of Lordship* (Edinburgh: Birlinn, 2008), p 174.
16 T. E. McNeill, *Castles in Ireland: Feudal Power in a Gaelic World* (London: Routledge, 1997).
17 P. Walsh, *Leabhar Chlainne Suibhne: An Account of the MacSweeney Families in Ireland* (Dublin: Dollard, 1920).
18 K. D. O'Conor, *The Archaeology of Medieval Rural Settlement in Ireland,* Discovery Programme Monograph 3 (Dublin: Royal Irish Academy, 1998), p. 90.
19 E. FitzPatrick, 'Native Enclosed Settlement and the Problem of the Irish "Ring-Fort"', *Medieval Archaeology*, vol. 53, no. 1, 2009, p. 277.
20 Breen, *Dunluce*, p.65.
21 B. Lacy (ed.), *The Archaeological Survey of County Donegal* (Dublin: Government Stationery Office, 1983), p. 356.
22 M. Loingsigh, 'An Assessment of Castles and Landownership in Late Medieval North Donegal', *Ulster Journal of Archaeology*, vol. 57, 1994, p. 148.
23 W. Kelly (ed.), *Docwra's Derry: A Narration of Events in North-West Ulster, 1600–1604* (Belfast: Ulster Historical Foundation, 2008), p. 1.
24 Lacy, *Donegal*, p. 374.
25 K.A. Steer, J.O.W. Bannerman and G.H. Collings, *Late Medieval Monumental Sculpture in the West Highlands* (Edinburgh: Royal Commission on the Ancient and Historical Monuments of Scotland, 1977), p. 1.
26 H. Lanigan-Wood and E. Verling, 'Stone Sculpture in Donegal', in W. Nolan, L. Ronayne and M. Dunlevy (eds), *Donegal: History and Society* (Dublin: Geography Publications, 1995), pp. 51–84.
27 F. J. Bigger, 'The MacSwyne Grave Slab', *Ulster Journal of Archaeology,* vol. 9, no. 3, 1905, p. 139.
28 I. Hodder, *Symbols in Action* (Cambridge: Cambridge University Press, 1982), p. 10.
29 S. Jones, *The Archaeology of Ethnicity: Constructing Identities in the Past and Present* (London: Routledge, 1997), p. 129.
30 M. Comber and G. Hull, 'Excavations at Caherconnell Cashel, the Burren, County Clare: Implications for Cashel Chronology and Gaelic Settlement', *Proceedings of the Royal Irish Academy,* vol. 110C, no. 1, 2010, p. 133.
31 N. Brady, R. McNeary, B. Shanahan and R. Shaw, 'Unravelling Medieval Landscapes from the Air', *Peritia*, vol. 22, no. 1, 2011, p. 295.
32 C. McSparron, 'A Potted History: Medieval Ulster Coarse Pottery', *Archaeology Ireland,* vol. 23, no. 1, 2009, pp. 13–15.
33 D. Caldwell, 'Having the Right Kit: West Highlanders Fighting in Ireland', in S. Duffy (ed.), *The World of the Galloglass: Kings and Warriors in Ireland and Scotland, 1250–1600* (Dublin: Four Courts Press, 2007), p. 160.
34 A. Halpin, 'Weapons, Arms and Armour', in S. Duffy (ed.), *Medieval Ireland: An Encyclopaedia* (Oxford: Oxford University Press, 2005), p. 845.

35 P. Harbison, 'Native Irish Arms and Armour in Medieval Gaelic Literature, 1170–1600', *Irish Sword,* vol. 12, no. 8, 1975, p. 279.
36 Caldwell, 'Galloglass Fighting', p. 23.
37 Simms, 'Late Medieval', p. 188; E. FitzPatrick, *Royal Inauguration in Gaelic Ireland c.1100–1600: A Cultural Landscape Study* (Woodbridge: The Boydell Press, 2004), pp. 182–193.
38 K. Simms, *Medieval Gaelic Sources* (Dublin: Four Courts Press, 2009), p. 57.
39 W. McLeod, 'Images of Scottish Warriors in Later Irish Bardic Poetry', in S. Duffy (ed.), *The World of the Galloglass: Kings and Warriors in Ireland and Scotland, 1250–1600* (Dublin: Four Courts Press, 2007), pp. 169–187.
40 McLeod, 'Images', p. 172.
41 Ibid., p. 184.
42 T. Finan, *A Nation in Medieval Ireland: Perspectives on Gaelic National Identity in the Middle Ages,* British Archaeological Report, British Series, 367 (Oxford: Archaeopress, 2004), p. 28.
43 C. O'Halloran, *Golden Ages and Barbarous Nations: Antiquarian Debate and Cultural Politics in Ireland, c.1750–1800* (Cork: Cork University Press, 2004), p. 172.
44 S. G. Ellis, 'Nationalist Historiography and the English and Gaelic Worlds in the Late Middle Ages', *Irish Historical Studies,* vol. 25, no. 97, 1986, p. 14.

8. Crannóga *in later medieval Ireland: Continuity and change*

1 K. D. O'Conor, *The Archaeology of Medieval Rural Settlement in Ireland,* Discovery Programme Monograph 3 (Dublin: Royal Irish Academy, 1998), pp. 41–44, 57–58.
2 O'Conor, *Archaeology of Medieval Rural Settlement in Ireland,* pp. 57–58. In this respect, see J. Eogan, 'A Betagh Settlement at Attyflin, County Limerick', in C. Corlett and M. Potterton (eds), *Rural Settlement in Medieval Ireland* (Dublin: Wordwell, 2009), pp. 67–77.
3 T. E. McNeill, *Anglo-Norman Ulster: The History and Archaeology of an Irish Barony 1177–1400* (Edinburgh: John Donald, 1980), pp. 84–88.
4 O'Conor, *Archaeology of Medieval Rural Settlement in Ireland,* p. 45.
5 The term 'elite' in this chapter is taken to refer not just to the princely and aristocratic class of later medieval Gaelic Ireland, but also to minor lords and members of service families. For a discussion on the use of *crannóga* as the residences and/or guest houses of some members of service families during the later medieval period, see E. FitzPatrick, '*Ollamh, Biatach, Comharba*: Lifeways of Gaelic Learned Families in Medieval and Early Modern Ireland', in L. Breatnach, R. Ó hUiginn, D. McManus and K. Simms (eds), *Proceedings XIV International Congress of Celtic Studies, Maynooth 2011* (Dublin: Dublin Institute for Advanced Studies, 2015), pp. 182–185.
6 See, for example, K. Simms, *Medieval Gaelic Sources* (Dublin: Four Courts Press), p. 9.
7 O'Conor, *Archaeology of Medieval Rural Settlement in Ireland*, pp. 73–75.
8 K.D. O'Conor, 'Gaelic Lordly Settlement in 13th- and 14th-Century Ireland', in I. Holm, S. Innselet and I. Øye (eds), '*Utmark': The Outfield as Industry and Ideology in the Iron Age and the Middle Ages* (Department of Archaeology, University of Bergen, 2005), pp. 209–221.

9 See K.W. Nicholls, *Gaelic and Gaelicized Ireland in the Middle Ages* (Dublin: Lilliput Press, 2003) for an overview of the social, political and economic background to later medieval Gaelic Ireland.

10 The relative intensity of the archaeological work carried out in the Dublin region over the decades is apparent, for example, in M. Murphy and M. Potterton, *The Dublin Region in the Middle Ages* (Dublin: Four Courts Press, 2010).

11 T. Barry, *The Archaeology of Medieval Ireland* (London and New York: Routledge, 1988); T. O'Keeffe, *Medieval Ireland: An Archaeology* (Stroud: Tempus, 2000). However, see T. O'Keeffe, 'Rural Settlement and Cultural Identity in Gaelic Ireland', *Ruralia*, vol. 1, 1996, pp. 142–153.

12 For example, P.J. Duffy, D. Edwards and E. FitzPatrick, 'Introduction: Recovering Gaelic Ireland, *c*.1250–*c*.1650', in P.J. Duffy, D. Edwards and E. FitzPatrick (eds), *Gaelic Ireland,* c.*1250*–c.*1650: Land, Lordship and Settlement* (Dublin: Four Courts Press, 2001), pp. 21–73; K.D. O'Conor, 'The Morphology of Gaelic Lordly Sites in North Connacht', in P.J. Duffy, D. Edwards and E. FitzPatrick (eds), *Gaelic Ireland,* c.*1250*–c.*1650: Land, Lordship and Settlement* (Dublin: Four Courts Press, 2001), pp. 329–331.

13 O'Conor, 'The Morphology of Gaelic Lordly Sites', pp. 329–330.

14 O'Conor, *Archaeology of Medieval Rural Settlement in Ireland*, pp. 73–107.

15 P.J. Duffy, D. Edwards and E. FitzPatrick (eds), *Gaelic Ireland,* c.*1250*–c.*1650, Land: Lordship and Settlement* (Dublin: Four Courts Press, 2001), pp. 271–435.

16 E. FitzPatrick, *Royal Inauguration in Gaelic Ireland, c.1100–1600: A Cultural Landscape Study* (Woodbridge: The Boydell Press, 2004).

17 C. Breen, *The Gaelic Lordship of the O'Sullivan Beare: A Landscape Cultural History* (Dublin: Four Courts Press, 2005).

18 T. Finan (ed.), *Medieval Lough Cé: History, Archaeology and Landscape* (Dublin: Four Courts Press, 2010).

19 N. Brady, 'The Medieval Rural Project: An Overview for 2002–2004', *Discovery Programme Report* 7 (Dublin: The Discovery Programme, 2005), pp. 1–2; R. McNeary and B. Shanahan, 'Medieval Settlement, Society and Land Use in Medieval Roscommon, 1100–1650AD', *Discovery Programme Report* 7 (Dublin: The Discovery Programme, 2005), pp. 3–22; N. Brady, A. Connon, R. McNeary, B. Shanahan and R. Shaw, 'A Survey of the Priory and Graveyard at Tulsk, County Roscommon', *Discovery Programme Report* 7 (Dublin: The Discovery Programme, 2005), pp. 40–64; N. Brady and P. Gibson, 'The Earthwork at Tulsk: Topographical and Geophysical Excavations and Preliminary Excavations', *Discovery Programme Report* 7 (Dublin: The Discovery Programme, 2005), pp. 65–76; see also N. Brady, *Discovering Irish Medieval Landscapes: The Discovery Programme's Medieval Rural Settlement Project, 2002–2008* (Dublin: The Discovery Programme, 2003).

20 M. Comber and G. Hull, 'Excavations at Caherconnell Cashel, the Burren, Co. Clare: Implications for Cashel Chronology and Gaelic Settlement', *Proceedings of the Royal Irish Academy*, vol. 110, 2010, pp. 133–173; M. Comber, *Caherconnell Archaeological Project: Summary of Fieldwork to Date* (Burren: Burren Forts Ltd, 2014).

21 C.J. McKenzie, E.M. Murphy and C.J. Donnelly (eds), *The Science of a Lost Medieval Graveyard: The Ballyhanna Research Project* (Dublin: Transport Infrastructure Ireland, 2015).

22 For example, see O'Conor, 'The Morphology of Gaelic Lordly Sites', pp. 331–345; A. Horning, '"Dwelling Houses in the Old Irish Barbarous Manner": Archaeological Evidence for Gaelic Architecture in an Ulster Plantation Village', in Duffy, Edwards and FitzPatrick (eds), *Gaelic Ireland,* pp. 375–396; T. Finan and K. D. O'Conor, 'The Moated Site at Cloonfree, County Roscommon', *Journal of the Galway Archaeological and Historical Society*, vol. 54, 2002, pp. 72–87; P. Naessens, 'Gaelic Lords of the Sea: the Coastal Tower Houses of South Connemara', in L. Doran and J. Lyttleton (eds), *Lordship in Medieval Ireland: Image and Reality* (Dublin: Four Courts Press, 2007), pp. 217–235; E. FitzPatrick, 'Native Enclosed Settlement and the Problem of the Irish "Ring-Fort"', *Medieval Archaeology*, vol. 53, no. 1, 2009, pp. 271–307. K. D. O'Conor, N. Brady, A. Connon and C. Fidalgo-Romo, 'The Rock of Lough Cé, County Roscommon', in T. Finan (ed.), *Medieval Lough Cé: History, Archaeology and Landscape* (Dublin: Four Courts Press, 2010), pp. 15–40; S. McDermott, 'The Archaeology of the Twelve Tates of McKenna, *c.*1591', *Clogher Record*, vol. 20, no. 2, 2010, pp. 373–406; E. FitzPatrick, E. Murphy, R. McHugh and C.J. Donnelly, 'Evoking the White Mare: The Cult Landscape of Sgiath Gabhra and its Medieval Perception in Gaelic Fir Mhanach', in R. Schot, C. Newman and E. Bhreathnach (eds), *Landscapes of Cult and Kingship* (Dublin: Four Courts Press, 2011), pp. 163–191; P. Naessens and K.D. O'Conor, 'Pre-Norman Fortification in Eleventh- and Twelfth-Century Connacht', *Chateau Gaillard*, vol. 25, 2012, pp. 259–268; E. FitzPatrick, '*Formaoil na Fiann*: Hunting Preserves and Assembly Places in Gaelic Ireland', in D. Furchtgott, G. Henley and M. Holmberg (eds), *Proceedings of Harvard Celtic Colloquium,* vol. 32, 2012, pp. 95–118; E. FitzPatrick, 'The Landscape and Settlements of the Uí Dhálaigh Poets of Muinter Bháire', in S. Duffy (ed.), *Princes, Prelates and Poets in Medieval Ireland: Essays in Honour of Katharine Simms* (Dublin: Four Courts Press, 2013), pp. 460–480; A. Horning, 'Challenging Colonial Equations? The Gaelic Experience in Early Modern Ireland', in N. Ferris, R. Harrison and M. V. Wilcox (eds), *Rethinking Colonial Pasts Through Archaeology* (Oxford: Oxford University Press, 2014), pp. 293–314; E. FitzPatrick, 'Assembly Places and Elite Collective Identities in Medieval Ireland', *Journal of the North Atlantic*, vol. 8, 2015, pp. 52–68; P. Naessens, 'Murchadha O'Flaithbheartaigh and the Aggrandisement of Aughnanure Castle', in Richard Oram (ed.), *A House That Thieves Might Knock At: Proceedings of the 2010 Stirling and 2011 Dundee Conferences (Tower Studies 1 and 2)* (Doington: Shaun Tyas, 2015), pp. 214–230; E. FitzPatrick, 'The Last Kings of Ireland: Material Expressions of Gaelic Lordship, *c.*1300–1400', in K. Buchanan, L. H. S. Dean and M. Penman (eds), *Medieval and Early Modern Representations of Authority in Scotland and the British Isles* (Oxford: Routledge, 2016), pp. 197–213.

23 K. Simms, 'Native Sources for Gaelic Settlement: The House Poems', in Duffy, Edwards and FitzPatrick (eds), *Gaelic Ireland, c.1250–c.1650: Land, Lordship and Settlement* (Dublin: Four Courts Press, 2001), pp. 246–267; Finan and O'Conor, 'The Moated Site at Cloonfree', pp. 74–76; T. Finan, *A Nation in Medieval Ireland? Perspectives on Gaelic National Identity in*

*the Middle Ages*, British Archaeological Report, British Series 367 (Oxford: Archaeopress, 2004), pp. 10–37.

24 T. Finan, 'Introduction', in Finan (ed.), *Medieval Lough Cé*, p. 11.

25 K. D. O'Conor, 'Crannogs', in B. Lalor (ed.), *The Encyclopaedia of Ireland* (Dublin: Gill & Macmillan, 2003), p. 253.

26 Ibid., p. 253.

27 O'Conor, *Archaeology of Medieval Rural Settlement in Ireland*, pp. 82–83; O'Conor, 'The Morphology of Gaelic Lordly Sites', pp. 336–337.

28 O'Conor, Brady, Connon and Fidalgo-Romo, 'The Rock of Lough Cé', p. 22.

29 Ibid., pp. 21–23.

30 O'Conor, *Archaeology of Medieval Rural Settlement in Ireland*, p. 82.

31 For example, see S. P. Ó Riordáin, *Antiquities of the Irish Countryside* (Cork: Cork University Press, 1942), pp. 89–99; M. de Paor and L. de Paor, *Early Christian Ireland* (London: Thames & Hudson, 1958), pp. 84–86; C. J. Lynn, 'Some "Early" Ringforts and Crannogs', *Journal of Irish Archaeology*, vol. 1, 1983, pp. 51–52; N. Edwards, *The Archaeology of Early Medieval Ireland* (London: Routledge, 1990), pp. 34–41; E. P. Kelly, 'Observations on Irish Lake Dwellings', in C. Karkov and R. T. Farrell (eds), *Studies in Insular Art and Archaeology*, American Medieval Studies 1 (Oxford, Ohio: American Early Medieval Studies and the Miami University School of Fine Arts, 1991), pp. 81–98; E. P. Kelly, 'Crannogs', in M. Ryan (ed.), *The Illustrated Archaeology of Ireland* (Dublin: Country House, 1991), pp. 120–123.

32 C. Fredengren, *Crannogs: A Study of People's Interaction with Lakes, with Particular Reference to Lough Gara in the North-West of Ireland* (Dublin: Wordwell, 2002).

33 O'Conor, *Archaeology of Medieval Rural Settlement in Ireland*, pp. 77–84; O'Conor, 'The Morphology of Gaelic Lordly Sites', pp. 337–338; A. O'Sullivan, *The Archaeology of Lake Settlement in Ireland* (Dublin: Royal Irish Academy, 1998), pp. 152–155, 167–176; O'Sullivan, 'Crannogs in Late Medieval Gaelic Ireland, *c.*1350–1650', in Duffy, Edwards and FitzPatrick (eds), *Gaelic Ireland,* pp. 397–417; Fredengren, *Crannogs*, pp. 265–276, 282, 287; N. Brady and K. D. O'Conor, 'The Later Medieval Usage of Crannogs in Ireland', *Ruralia*, vol. 5, 2005, pp. 127–136.

34 C. Foley and B. Williams, 'The Crannogs of County Fermanagh', in Marion Meek (ed.), *The Modern Traveller to Our Past: Festschrift in Honour of Ann Hamlin* (Dublin: DPK, 2006), pp. 53–64.

35 J. O'Hara, 'A Landscape Archaeology of Later Medieval Fermanagh', Unpublished PhD Thesis, National University of Ireland, Galway, 2009.

36 O'Conor, 'The Morphology of Gaelic Lordly Sites', pp. 337–338; Brady and O'Conor, 'The Later Medieval Usage of Crannogs in Ireland', p. 134.

37 *Cal. S. P. Ire. 1588–1592*, pp. 374–375.

38 W. M. Hennessey (ed.), *The Annals of Lough Cé*, 2 vols (Dublin, 1871), vol. 2, p. 450; A. M. Freeman (ed.), *The Compossicion Booke of Conought* (Dublin: Irish Manuscripts Commission, 1936), p. 163.

39 K. D. O'Conor, 'English Settlement and Change in Roscommon During the Late Sixteenth and Seventeenth Century', in A. Horning, R. Ó Baoill, C. Donnelly and P. Logue (eds), *The Post-Medieval Archaeology of Ireland, 1550–1850* (Dublin: Wordwell, 2007), pp. 200–201.

40 Liam Ó hAisibéil, pers. comm.; see L. Ó hAisibéil, 'Logainmneacha Mhagh Loirg agus Uachtar Thíre, Contae Ros Comáin: Anailis ar Ainmneachta Bhailte Fearainn na Seanduíchi Sin', Unpublished PhD Thesis, National University of Ireland, Galway, 2013.

41 Royal Irish Academy, MS M 14 F 11, Ordnance Survey (1861); Copies of Inquisitions Relating to the County of Roscommon deposited in the Record Tower, Dublin Castle.

42 K. D. O'Conor, 'Kilronan Parish in the Medieval Period (*c.*AD 400–*c.*AD 1600)', in *Kilronan: Then and Now* (Keadue: Kilronan Parish, 2010), pp. 21–24.

43 However, alternatively, FitzPatrick has argued that this particular *crannóg* may have functioned as the residence and guest house of the Ó Duibhgeannáin learned family during the later medieval period. See FitzPatrick, 'Lifeways of Gaelic Learned Families', p. 185. At least one, if not two, other *crannóga* can be seen towards the western end of Lough Meelagh. One possible interpretation of the field and historical evidence is that at least two *crannóga* on the lake were occupied during later medieval times – one by the latter family and the other by the Mac Maghnusa lords of *Tir Tuathail.*

44 R. Moss, 'Romanesque Sculpture in North Roscommon', in T. Finan (ed.), *Medieval Lough Cé: History, Archaeology and Landscape* (Dublin: Four Courts Press, 2010), pp. 141–144.

45 J. J. O'Meara (ed.), *Topographia Hibernica: The History and Topography of Ireland by Gerald of Wales* (Harmondsworth: Penguin Classics, 1982), p. 37.

46 Excavation has taken place here (2016) and confirmed that the moated site was constructed on top of an existing ringfort, in the late thirteenth or very early fourteenth century. Thomas Finan and Paul Naessens, pers. comm.

47 O'Conor, Brady, Connon and Fidalgo-Romo, 'The Rock of Lough Cé', pp. 30–31.

48 Ibid., pp. 338–339; Brady and O'Conor, 'The Later Medieval Usage of Crannogs in Ireland', pp. 130–131, 134.

49 Brian Shanahan, pers. comm.; see Brady and O'Conor, 'The Later Medieval Usage of Crannogs in Ireland', p. 134.

50 T. E. McNeill, *Castles in Ireland: Feudal Power in a Gaelic World* (London: Routledge, 1997), p. 9.

51 Brady and O'Conor, 'The Later Medieval Usage of Crannogs in Ireland', pp. 127–128; O'Conor, 'Gaelic Lordly Settlement in 13th- and 14th-Century Ireland', pp. 212–213.

52 Brady and O'Conor, 'The Later Medieval Usage of Crannogs in Ireland', pp. 127–128; see the discussion, for example, in K. R. Lilley, 'Imagined Geographies of the "Celtic Fringe" and the Cultural Construction of the "Other" in medieval Wales and Ireland', in D. Harvey, R. Jones, N. McInroy and C. Milligan (eds), *Celtic Geographies: Old Cultures, New Times* (London: Psychology Press, 2002), pp. 21–36.

53 Brady and O'Conor, 'The Later Medieval Usage of Crannogs in Ireland', pp. 127–128; O'Conor, 'Gaelic Lordly Settlement in 13th- and 14th-Century Ireland', pp. 212–213.

54 C. Donnelly, P. Logue, J. O'Neill and J. O'Neill, 'Timber Castles and Towers in Sixteenth-Century Ireland: Some Evidence from Ulster', *Archaeology Ireland*, vol. 21, no. 2, 2007, pp. 22–25.

55 E. FitzPatrick, 'The Material World of the Parish', in E. FitzPatrick and R. Gillespie (eds), *The Parish in Medieval and Early Modern Ireland: Community, Territory and Building* (Dublin: Four Courts Press, 2006), pp. 70–72; E. FitzPatrick, 'Native Enclosed Settlement', p. 302. See also FitzPatrick, 'Assembly Places and Elite Collective Identities in Medieval Ireland', pp. 52–68.
56 O'Conor, Brady, Connon and Fidalgo-Romo, 'The Rock of Lough Cé', pp. 24–27
57 Ibid., p. 33.
58 O'Conor, 'The Morphology of Gaelic Lordly Sites', pp. 331–336; O'Conor, Brady, Connon and Fidalgo-Romo, 'The Rock of Lough Cé', pp. 24–27.
59 For example, see O'Conor, 'The Morphology of Gaelic Lordly Sites', p. 336; O'Conor, Brady, Connon and Fidalgo-Romo, 'The Rock of Lough Cé', p. 28; M. Moore, *The Archaeological Survey of County Leitrim* (Dublin: Stationery Office, 2003), pp. 40, 51, 209–210.
60 O'Conor, Brady, Connon and Fidalgo-Romo, 'The Rock of Lough Cé', pp. 27–28.
61 Breen, *The Gaelic Lordship of the O'Sullivan Beare*, pp. 69–72.
62 Donnelly, Logue, O'Neill and O'Neill, 'Timber Castles and Towers in Sixteenth-Century Ireland', p. 25.
63 See, for example, O'Sullivan, 'Crannogs in Later Medieval Gaelic Ireland', pp. 414, 416.
64 K. D. O'Conor and Brian Shanahan, *Roscommon Abbey: A Visitor's Guide* (Boyle: Roscommon County Council, 2013), pp. 8–30.
65 Ibid., pp. 31–38.
66 O'Conor, *Archaeology of Medieval Rural Settlement in Ireland*, p. 83.
67 McNeill, *Castles in Ireland*, pp. 72–74; O'Conor, *Archaeology of Medieval Rural Settlement in Ireland*, pp. 75–77; O'Conor, 'Gaelic Lordly Settlement in 13th- and 14th-Century Ireland', pp. 213–215.
68 O'Conor, *Archaeology of Medieval Rural Settlement in Ireland*, pp. 95, 98–100; O'Conor, 'Gaelic Lordly Settlement in 13th- and 14th-Century Ireland', pp. 216–217.
69 Simms, 'Native Sources for Gaelic Settlement', pp. 250–253; Finan and O'Conor, 'The Moated Site at Cloonfree', p. 206; K. D. O'Conor, 'Housing in Later Medieval Gaelic Ireland', *Ruralia*, vol. 4, 2002, pp. 201–210.
70 J. P. Mahaffy, 'Two Early Tours in Ireland', *Hermathena,* vol. 18, no. 40, 1914, pp. 3–9; H. Allingham (ed.), *Captain Cuellar's Adventures* (London: Elliot Stock, 1897).
71 McNeill, *Castles in Ireland*, p. 168; O'Conor, *Archaeology of Medieval Rural Settlement in Ireland*, pp. 94–101; O'Conor, 'Gaelic Lordly Settlement in 13th- and 14th-Century Ireland', pp. 217–218.
72 O'Conor, *Archaeology of Medieval Rural Settlement in Ireland*, pp. 99–101.
73 R. Higham and P. Barker, *Timber Castles* (London: University of Exeter Press, 1992), p. 100.
74 For example, R. Liddiard, *'Landscapes of Lordship': Norman Castles and the Countryside in Medieval Norfolk, 1066–1200* (Oxford: Archaeopress, 2000); O. Creighton, *Castles and Landscapes: Power, Community and Fortification in Medieval England* (London and New York: Equinox, 2002); O. Creighton, *Designs Upon the Land: Elite*

*Landscapes of the Middle Ages* (Woodbridge: Boydell Press, 2009); C. Coulson, *Castles in Medieval Society: Fortresses in England, France, and Ireland in the Central Middle Ages* (Oxford: Oxford University Press, 2003).

75 For example, P. Dixon, 'The Donjon of Knaresborough: The Castle as Theatre', *Château Gaillard*, vol. 14, 1990, pp. 121–139; M. Johnson, *Behind the Castle Gate* (London and New York: Routledge, 2002), pp. 12–15, 55–92 and passim.

76 K. D. O'Conor, 'Castle Studies in Ireland: The Way Forward', *Château Gaillard*, vol. 23, 2008, pp. 334–335.

77 C. Orser, 'Symbolic Violence, Resistance and the Vectors of Improvement in Early Nineteenth-Century Ireland', *World Archaeology*, vol. 37, no. 3, 2005, pp. 392–407; C. Orser, 'Symbolic Violence and Landscape Pedagogy: An Illustration from the Irish Countryside', *Historical Archaeology,* vol. 40, no. 2, 2006, pp. 28–44.

78 Creighton, *Designs Upon the Land*, pp. 217–218.

79 Ibid., p. 218.

80 Ibid., pp. 17, 21.

81 R. K. Morris, 'The Architecture of Arthurian Enthusiasm: Castle Symbolism in the Reigns of Edward I and his Successors', in M. Strickland (ed.), *Armies, Chivalry and Warfare in Medieval Britain and France* (Stamford: Paul Watkins, 1998), pp. 63–81; Creighton, *Designs Upon the Land*, p. 21.

82 A. Saunders, 'Lydford Castle, Devon', *Medieval Archaeology*, vol. 24, 1980, pp. 123–186; Creighton, *Designs Upon the Land*, p. 21.

83 Creighton, *Designs Upon the Land*, pp. 21, 217–218.

84 O. Creighton, 'Castle, Landscape and Townscape in Thirteenth-Century England: Wallingford, Oxfordshire and the "Princely Building Strategies" of Richard, Earl of Cornwall', in J. Peltzer (ed.), *Rank and Order: The Formation of Aristocratic Elites in Western and Central Europe, 500–1500* (Ostfildern: Jan Thorbecke Verlag 2015), pp. 309–341.

85 FitzPatrick, *Royal Inauguration in Gaelic Ireland*, passim; FitzPatrick, 'The Material World of the Parish', pp. 70–72; FitzPatrick, 'Native Enclosed Settlement', p. 302; FitzPatrick, 'Assembly Places and Collective Identities in Medieval Ireland, pp. 52–68.

86 Rory Sherlock, pers. comm.; G. Eadie, 'Reflections of a Divided Country? The Role of Tower Houses in Late Medieval Ireland', *Château Gaillard*, vol. 26, 2014, p. 143.

87 Simms, 'Native Sources for Gaelic Settlement', p. 248; Finan and O'Conor, 'The Moated Site at Cloonfree', pp. 74–76.

88 Finan and O'Conor, 'The Moated Site at Cloonfree', p. 75.

89 Simms, 'Native Sources for Gaelic Settlement', p. 248; Finan and O'Conor, 'The Moated Site at Cloonfree', pp. 74–76.

90 B. W. O'Dwyer (ed.), *Stephen of Lexington, Letters from Ireland, 1228–1229* (Kalamazoo: Cistercian Publications, 1982), p. 112; O'Conor, 'Housing in Later Medieval Gaelic Ireland', pp. 206–208; Interestingly, as late as the end of the eighteenth century, commentators drew attention to the fact that houses belonging to many Irish gentry were considerably less impressive and far smaller in size than those built by Englishmen of the exact same rank and wealth. For example, see A. Young, *A Tour in Ireland* (London: Whitestone, 1780), p. 185.

91 Finan and O'Conor, 'The Moated Site at Cloonfree', pp. 81–82.
92 Creighton, 'Castle, Landscape and Townscape in Thirteenth-Century England', pp. 321–323.

9. *Gaelic service kindreds and the landscape identity of* lucht tighe

1 K. Simms, *From Kings to Warlords: The Changing Political Structure of Gaelic Ireland in the Later Middle Ages* (Woodbridge: Boydell Press, 1987), p. 176, translates *ollamh* as 'master of poetry, or other learned or skilled profession in the native tradition, such as law, history, medicine, music, smithcraft'.
2 Simms, *From Kings to Warlords*, p. 170 translates the later medieval *airchinneach* as 'an official, normally hereditary, under the authority of the local bishop, with responsibility for maintaining the fabric of a church and providing for the celebration of divine service when not himself ordained'.
3 C. Vallancey, *Collectanea de Rebus Hibernicis: Number II* (Dublin: Luke White, 1786), pp. 163–165; P. Palmer, *Language and Conquest in Early Modern Ireland: English Renaissance Literature and Elizabethan Imperial Expansion* (Cambridge: Cambridge University Press, 2001), pp. 71–72.
4 P. J. Duffy, 'Social and Spatial Order in the MacMahon Lordship of Airghialla in the Late Sixteenth Century', in P. J. Duffy, D. Edwards and E. FitzPatrick (eds), *Gaelic Ireland c.1250–c.1650: Land, Lordship and Settlement* (Dublin: Four Courts Press, 2001) p. 129; L. McInerney, 'The West Clann Chuiléin Lordship in 1586: Evidence from a Forgotten Inquisition', *North Munster Antiquarian Journal*, vol. 48, 2008, pp. 35–37.
5 Simms, *From Kings to* Warlords, pp. 94, 176.
6 For a discussion of the concept of liminality as an intermediate state of being 'in between' during rites of passage (inauguration, for instance) connected with changes in social status, see A. van Gennep, *Les Rites de Passage* (Paris: E. Nourry, 1909) and V. Turner, *The Ritual Process: Structure and Anti-Structure* (New York: Cornell University Press, 1977). For an understanding of how liminality is contrived and conveyed in medieval Irish literature see J. F. Nagy, 'Liminality and Knowledge in Irish Tradition', *Studia Celtica*, vols 16–17, 1981–2, pp. 135–143; Laura Feldt discusses wilderness as a spatial expression of liminality, in L. Feldt (ed.), *Wilderness in Mythology and Religion: Approaching Religious Spatialities, Cosmologies, and Ideas of Wild Nature,* Religion and Society vol. 55 (Boston and Berlin: De Gruyter, 2012), pp. 1–9, and Bjorn Thomassen discusses liminal landscapes in 'Revisiting Liminality: The Danger of Empty Spaces', in H. Andrews and L. Roberts (eds), *Liminal Landscapes: Travel, Experience and Spaces In-Between* (London and New York: Routledge, 2012), pp. 21–35.
7 É. Ó Doibhlin, 'Ceart Uí Néill: A Discussion and Translation of the Document', *Seanchas Ardmhacha: Journal of the Armagh Diocesan Historical Society,* vol. 5, no. 2, 1970, pp. 356–357; E. FitzPatrick, *Royal Inauguration in Gaelic Ireland c.1100–1600: A Cultural Landscape Study* (Woodbridge: The Boydell Press, 2001), pp. 140–143.
8 Eleanor Knott (ed. and trans.), *The Bardic Poems of Tadhg Dall Ó hUiginn*, 2 vols (London: Irish Text Society, 1926), vol. 2, p. 34.
9 For descriptions of many of these roles see Simms, *From Kings to Warlords*, pp. 170–178.

10 C. Ó Scea, 'Erenachs, Erenachships and Church Landholding in Gaelic Fermanagh, 1270–1609', *Proceedings of the Royal Irish Academy*, vol. 112C, 2012, pp. 273–274; P. Mac Cana, 'The Rise of the Later Schools of *Filidheacht*', *Ériu*, vol. 25, 1974, pp. 127–130; M. Dillon, D. A. Binchy and D. Greene (eds), *Robin Flower: The Irish Tradition* (Oxford: Clarendon, 1947; repr. 1948), p. 84.

11 See, for instance, the landholding of the Mac Bruaideadha poet-chroniclers of Lettermoylan and Formoyle at Slieve Callan, County Clare, which constituted episcopal mensal land of the Bishop of Killaloe to whom the learned family paid a rent. L. McInerney, 'Lettermoylan of Clann Bhruaideadha: A Résumé of their Landholding, Topography and History', *North Munster Antiquarian Journal*, vol. 52, 2012, p. 86.

12 AFM 1578.4; E. FitzPatrick, '*Ollamh, Biatach, Comharba*: Lifeways of Gaelic Learned Families in Medieval and Early Modern Ireland', in L. Breatnach, R. Ó hUiginn, D. McManus and K. Simms (eds), *Proceedings of the XIVth Celtic Congress, Maynooth, 2011* (Dublin: Dublin Institute for Advanced Studies, 2015), pp. 173–174.

13 M. Dillon, 'The Inauguration of O'Conor', in J. A. Watt, J. B. Morrall and F. X. Martin (eds), *Medieval Studies Presented to Aubrey Gwynn, S.J.* (Dublin: The Three Candles, 1961), pp. 190, 198, 199; K. Simms, '*Gabh Umad a Fheidhlimidh*: A Fifteenth-Century Inauguration Ode?', *Ériu*, vol. 31, 1980, pp. 132–145.

14 S. H. O'Grady, *Silva Gadelica: A Collection of Tales in Irish with Extracts Illustrating Persons and Places*, 2 vols (London and Edinburgh: Williams & Norgate, 1892), vol. 1, p. 92, vol. 2, p. 99.

15 Myles Dillon (ed. and trans.), 'Ceart Uí Néill', *Studia Celtica*, vol. 1, 1966, pp. 1, 2, 6, 7; Ó Doibhlin, 'Ceart Uí Néill', pp. 326–58.

16 Ó Doibhlin, 'Ceart Uí Néill', pp. 354–355.

17 Simms, *From Kings to Warlords*, pp. 143–145, 172.

18 Palmer, *Language and Conquest in Early Modern Ireland*, p. 74.

19 PRO London SP 63/226 No. 8; H. Morgan (ed.),'The Lawes of Irelande: A Tract by Sir John Davies', *Irish Jurist*, vols 28–30, 1993–5, p. 311.

20 P. MacCotter, *Medieval Ireland: Territorial, Political and Economic Divisions* (Dublin: Four Courts Press, 2008), p. 224; S. Ó Ceallaigh, *Gleanings from Ulster History* (Cork: Cork University Press, 1951; Reprint Draperstown: Ballinasreen Historical Society, 1994), p. 21.

21 É. Ó Doibhlin, 'O Neill's "Own Country" and Its Families', *Seanchas Ardmhacha: Journal of the Armagh Diocesan Historical Society*, vol. 6, no. 1, 1971, p. 3.

22 In *Royal Inauguration*, pp. 195–196, I was incorrect in stating that 'Tulach Óg, although close to the western side of Lough Neagh, could not be considered a boundary site of Tír Eoghain'. It was, of course, a short distance south of the Ballinderry River which, in that area, formed part of the boundary between the lordships of Tír Eoghain and Clann Aodha Buidhe. The presence of the Elagh Fault just south of the Ballinderry River and the location of the assembly place of Tulach Óg in close proximity to the river and the fault suggests that they may have constituted a natural boundary zone for the northern extent of the early medieval kingdom of Tulach Óg. As Pádraig Ó Riain observed in 'Boundary Association

in Early Irish Society', *Studia Celtica*, vol. 7, 1972, pp. 24, 25, assembly places of early medieval territories are often found in boundary zones. Paul MacCotter, however, in *Medieval Ireland*, p. 259, shows the *trícha cét* of Tulach Óg extending into what is now south Derry.

23 TNA, MPF 36.
24 TNA, MPF 35.
25 TNA, MPF 36.
26 Ó Doibhlin, 'Ceart Uí Néill', pp. 328, 331.
27 Ibid., pp. 345–347.
28 Oxford, Bodleian Library, Carte MS no 55, fo. 591; Ó Doibhlin, 'Ceart Uí Néill', p. 353–358.
29 R. Bartlett, Southeast Ulster, TNA, MPF 36.
30 Geological Survey of Northern Ireland, *Geological Map of Northern Ireland: Solid Geology 1:250,000* (Surrey: 1997).
31 E. FitzPatrick, R. Hennessy, P. Naessens and J. F. Nagy, 'Decoding Finn Mac Cumaill's Places', *Archaeology Ireland*, vol. 29, no. 3, 2015, pp. 26–31; E. FitzPatrick, '*Formaoil na Fiann*: Hunting Preserves and Assembly Places in Gaelic Ireland', in D. Furchtgott, G. Henley and M. Holmberg (eds), *Proceedings of the Harvard Celtic Colloquium*, vol. 32 (Cambridge, MA: Harvard University Press 2013), pp. 95–118; FitzPatrick, 'The Mountain Seat of Fionn', in FitzPatrick, *Royal Inauguration*, p. 131.
32 K. McCone, 'The Celtic and Indo-European Origins of the *Fían*', in S. J. Arbuthnot and G. Parsons (eds), *The Gaelic Finn Tradition* (Dublin: Four Courts Press, 2012), pp. 20, 22; K. McCone, *Pagan Past and Christian Present in Early Irish Literature*, Maynooth Monographs, vol. 3 (Maynooth: An Sagart, 1990), pp. 205–206.
33 AI 1111.6; AU 1111.6; FitzPatrick, *Royal Inauguration*, p. 141.
34 B. Sloan, *Community Excavation Adjacent to Tullaghoge Fort, Cookstown, County Tyrone,* Data Structure Report No. 109, Centre for Archaeological Fieldwork, School of Geography Archaeology and Palaeoecology, Queen's University Belfast (Belfast: Northern Ireland Environmental Agency, 2014), p. 2.
35 T. Herron, 'Orpheus in Ulster: Richard Bartlett's Colonial Art', in T. Herron and M. Potterton (eds), *Ireland in the Renaissance c.1540–1660* (Dublin: Four Courts Press, 2007), p. 299.
36 Herron, 'Orpheus', p. 303.
37 Ibid., p. 308.
38 P. Borgeaud, *The Cult of Pan in Ancient Greece*, trans. K. Atlass and J. Redfield (Chicago and London: The University of Chicago Press, 1988), argues (pp. 9–10) that the rustic or brutish nature of the Arcadians was explained by their considerable antiquity.
39 FitzPatrick, *Royal Inauguration*, pp. 105–106, 149–156.
40 NLI, MS 2656[5].
41 Annotation by Richard Bartlett on his map of southeast Ulster 1603, TNA, MPF 36.
42 S. McDermott, 'Magnetometry Survey, Tullaghoge Fort, County Tyrone'. Geophysical Survey Report No. 31. Unpublished Geophysical Report Prepared by the Centre for Archaeological Fieldwork, QUB (Belfast: Northern Ireland Environment Agency, 2014).

43 Geological Survey of Northern Ireland, *Geological Map of Northern Ireland.*
44 FitzPatrick, *Royal Inauguration*, p. 56.
45 M.J. Simms, 'Provenancing the Chair of Clann Aodha Buidhe', in E. FitzPatrick, *Royal Inauguration*, pp. 243–248.
46 É. Ó Doibhlin, 'Ceart Uí Néill', pp. 328, 331; Edmond Oge O'Hagan was cited as being of 'Tullioge', in a general pardon granted to him by James I in 1608. *Cal. Pat. Rolls Jas. I*, 23 Feb. 1608.
47 Ó Doibhlín, 'O Neill's "Own Country"', p. 6.
48 AU 1056.7.
49 G. Hill, *An Historical Account of the Plantation in Ulster at the Commencement of the Seventeenth Century, 1608–1620* (Belfast: McCaw, Stevenson & Orr, 1877), p. 549; FitzPatrick, *Royal Inauguration*, pp. 198–200.
50 FitzPatrick, '*Ollamh, Biatach, Comharba*', p. 4.
51 Research undertaken by Shane McGivern, 'Gaelic Secular Settlement in South-east Tyrone in the Late Medieval Period', Unpublished Thesis, Queen's University Belfast, 2007 argues, convincingly, that the Uí Dhonnghaile residence is likely to have been a *crannóg* in Lough Aughlish, *c.*1km to the west of Castle Caulfield, and not Mullygruen Lough, southwest of Donaghmore, which I suggested in *Royal Inauguration*, p. 199; N. Carver and C.J. Donnelly, *Investigations at Castle Caulfield, Lisnamonaghan, County Tyrone* (Belfast: Centre for Archaeological Fieldwork, Northern Ireland Envrionment Agency, 2011), pp. 73–74.
52 Ó Doibhlín, 'O Neill's "Own Country"', p. 6.
53 FitzPatrick, *Royal Inauguration*, pp. 142–143.
54 M. Vejby and J. Ahlers, 'Land, Myth and Language: The Preservation of Social Memories', in A.M. Chadwick and C.D. Gibson (eds), *Memory, Myth and Long-term Landscape Inhabitation* (Oxford and Oakville: Oxbow, 2013), pp. 276–278.
55 AC 1384.2; FitzPatrick, *Royal Inauguration*, pp. 210–211.
56 F. Verstraten, 'Ua Conchobair', in S. Duffy (ed.), *Medieval Ireland: An Encyclopedia* (New York: Routledge, 2005), p. 772.
57 Dillon, 'The Inauguration of O'Conor', p. 190.
58 MacCotter, *Medieval Ireland,* pp. 148–149, 208–209.
59 F.J. Byrne, *Irish Kings and High-Kings* (London: Batsford, 1973), pp. 251–253.
60 For the landscape of Ard Caoin see 'Survey at Carn Láma, Carnfree and Duma Selga', in J. Waddell, J. Fenwick and K. Barton (eds), *Rathcroghan: Archaeological and Geophysical Survey in a Ritual Landscape* (Dublin: Wordwell, 2009), pp. 113–135; R. McNeary and B. Shanahan, 'Carns Townland, County Roscommon: Excavations by the Medieval Rural Settlement Project in 2006', in C. Corlett and M. Potterton (eds), *Rural Settlement in Medieval Ireland in the Light of Recent Excavations* (Dublin: Wordwell, 2009), pp. 125–137; FitzPatrick, *Royal Inauguration*, pp. 60–68.
61 AC 1306.4; K. Simms, 'Native Sources for Gaelic Settlement: The House Poems', in P.J. Duffy, D. Edwards and E. FitzPatrick (eds), *Gaelic Ireland*, p. 257; L. McKenna (ed. and trans.), 'Poem to Clonfree Castle', *Irish Monthly*, vol. 51, 1923, p. 644; E. Crosby Quiggin (ed. and trans.),

'O'Conor's House at Cloonfree', in E. Crosby Quiggin (ed.), *Essays and Studies Presented to William Ridgeway* (Cambridge: Cambridge University Press, 1913), pp. 336, 337.

62 K. Ferguson, 'Castles and the Pallas Placename: A German Insight', *The Irish Sword*, vol. 22, no. 89, 2001, p. 247; E. FitzPatrick, 'The Last Kings of Ireland: Material Expressions of Gaelic Lordship *c.*1300–1400 AD', in K. Buchanan, L. H. S. Dean and M. Penman (eds), *Medieval and Early Modern Representations of Authority in Scotland and the British Isles* (Oxford: Routledge, 2016), pp. 197–213.

63 B. Shanahan, 'Roscommon Landscape: Cloonybeirne: O'Conor Roe Lordship' (Dublin: Discovery Programme, 2010), outlines the features of the O'Conor Roe lordship centre at Cloonybeirne identified by him during systematic mapping of relict earthworks in the townland.

64 Simms, *From Kings to Warlords*, p. 178.

65 A. M. Freeman (ed.), *The Compossicion Booke of Conought* (Dublin: Irish Manuscripts Commission, 1936), pp. 155, 156, 162–163.

66 Dillon, 'The Inauguration of O'Conor', pp. 196, 202; Simms, '*Gabh umad a Fheidhlimidh*', *Ériu*, vol. 31, 1980, pp. 132–145.

67 The term 'stokaghe' is possibly a corruption of the Irish *stocaire* which according to E. G. Quin (ed.), *Dictionary of the Irish Language: Based Mainly on Old and Middle Irish Materials* (Dublin: Royal Irish Academy, 1984), p. 390, means 'trumpeter'. The root *stoc* translates as trumpet, bugle, horn. It probably refers to hunting horns and to those whose hereditary position it was to blow the hunting horns for Ó Conchobhair.

68 K. W. Nicholls (ed.), *Irish Fiants of the Tudor Sovereigns 1586–1603*, 4 vols (Dublin: Éamonn de Búrca for Edmund Burke, 1994), p. 242 [5888].

69 AFM 1101.13 records the death in that year of Giolla na Naomh Ó Donnabhair, 'Chief Poet of Connacht'.

70 Dillon, 'The Inauguration of O'Conor', pp. 189, 197; FitzPatrick, *Royal Inauguration*, p. 181.

71 Dillon, 'The Inauguration of O'Conor', pp. 190, 195, 197–198, 202.

72 U. Rublack, *Dressing Up: Cultural Identity in Renaissance Europe* (Oxford: Oxford University Press, 2010), pp. 27–31, 182–187.

73 Ibid., p.183.

74 Dillon, 'The Inauguration of O'Conor', pp. 196, 202.

75 A. Harrison, 'The Shower of Hell', *Éigse*, vol. 18, part 2, 1981, p. 304; K. Simms, 'Gaelic Warfare in the Middle Ages', in T. Bartlett and K. Jeffery (eds), *A Military History of Ireland* (Cambridge: Cambridge University Press, 1996), pp. 100–101.

76 Dillon, 'The Inauguration of O'Conor', pp. 190, 198.

77 Ibid., pp. 196, 202.

78 AFM 1448.10.

79 J. O'Donovan, 'Letters Containing Information Relative to the Antiquities of the County of Roscommon Collected During the Progress of the Ordnance Survey in 1837', compiled by M. O'Flanagan, typescript in 2 vols (Bray, 1927), pp. 27–28. In FitzPatrick, *Royal Inauguration*, pp. 63–67, I suggested that Dumha Selga was probably identifiable as a conjoined earthwork straddling the Lismurtagh and Carrowgarve townland boundary. That suggestion was subsequently adopted by Waddell, Fenwick and Barton,

*Rathcroghan*, p. 113. However, in view of Mac Firbisigh's record and a new understanding about the hybrid identity of assembly mounds (for which see FitzPatrick, '*Formaoil na Fiann*', pp. 115–117), I am now convinced that Dumha Selga and Carn Fraoich are the same site and identifiable as the mound on the highest point of the ridge in Carns townland.

80 M. V. Duignan (ed. and trans.),'The Uí Briúin Bréifni Genealogies', *Journal of the Royal Society of Antiquaries of Ireland*, vol. 64, 1934, pp. 103–104.

81 E. Gwynn (ed. and trans.), *The Metrical Dindshenchas: Text, Translation and Commentary*, Part 3, Todd Lecture Series 10 (Dublin: Royal Irish Academy, 1913; repr. Dublin Institute for Advanced Studies, 1991), pp. 386–387.

82 [https://www.logainm.ie/en/43714?s=Bunnamucka]. Accessed 4 July 2016.

83 Irish *cullach* generally translates as a boar but can also mean a stallion; see E. G. Quin (ed.), *Dictionary of the Irish Language: Based Mainly on Old and Middle Irish Materials, Compact Edition* (Dublin: Royal Irish Academy, 1990), p. 168, 613.

84 FitzPatrick, '*Ollamh, Biatach, Comharba*', pp. 169–171.

85 I am grateful to Brian Shanahan for discussion about this feature.

86 J. Fletcher, *Gardens of Earthly Delight: The History of Deer Parks* (Oxford: Windgather Press, 2011), pp. 109–115; J. Stuhmiller, 'Hunting, Fowling and Fishing', in A. Classen (ed.), *Handbook of Medieval Culture: Fundamental Aspects and Conditions of the European Middle Ages*, vol. 2 (Berlin and Boston: Walter de Gruyter, 2015), pp. 697–721; Chris Taylor, in 'Ravensdale Park, Derbyshire, and Medieval Deer Coursing', *Landscape History*, vol. 26, no. 1, 2004, pp. 37–57 has identified what he believes is a deer course within the deer park in the forest of Duffield Frith, at Ravensdale in Derbyshire Park. The park itself was first recorded *c.*1230. The trackway which Taylor identified is formed by two parallel banks with hedges 70–80m apart and 1.6km long. Taylor argues that paddock coursing was so well established by the sixteenth century that it must have developed earlier in the medieval period.

10. *Buildings, rural landscape and space in sixteenth-century Gaelic Ulster*

1 Great Britain, Record Commission, *State Papers During the Reign of Henry the Eighth Published Under the Authority of his Majesty's Commission*, 11 vols (London: His Majesty's Commission for State Papers, 1830–52), vol. 3, pp. 154–156, 435–436.

2 N. Canny, *The Elizabethan Conquest of Ireland: A Pattern Established, 1565–76* (Hassocks: Harvester Press, 1976), p. 6; S. McSkimin, *The History and Antiquitites of the County of the Town of Carrickfergus*, 2nd edn (Belfast: Mullan, J. Cleeland, Davidson & M'Cormack, 1909), p. 384.

3 D. B. Quinn, 'Anglo-Irish Ulster in the Early Sixteenth Century', *Proceedings and Reports of the Belfast Natural History and Philosophical Society, Session 1933–34* (Belfast: 1935) p. 77.

4 P. Robinson, *Irish Historic Towns Atlas: Carrickfergus* (Dublin: Royal Irish Academy, 1986), p. 2.

5 Great Britain, Record Commission, *State Papers Published Under the Authority of his Majesty's Commission*, vol. 2, p. 100.

6 D. B. Quinn, 'Sir Thomas Smith (1513–77) and the Beginnings of English Colonial Theory', *Proceedings of the American Philosophical Society*, vol. 89, no. 4, 1945, pp. 547–550; R. Dunlop, 'Sixteenth Century Schemes for the Plantation of Ulster', *Scottish Historical Review*, vol. 22, 1925, pp. 115–126, 199–212; H. Morgan, 'The Colonial Venture of Sir Thomas Smith in Ulster, 1571–1575', *Historical Journal*, vol. 28, 1985, pp. 261–278. For the concept of the forward policy in Ulster, see D. B. Quinn, 'Ireland and Sixteenth Century European Expansion', in T. D. Williams (ed.), *Historical Studies: Papers Read Before the Second Irish Conference of Historians* (London: Bowes & Bowes, 1958), p. 27.

7 The maps are listed in R. Dunlop, 'Sixteenth-Century Maps of Ireland', *English Historical Review*, vol. 20, no. 78, 1905, pp. 326–327.

8 BL, Cotton MS Augustus I, ii, 42.

9 TCD, MS 1209 (26); J. H. Andrews, *The Irish Surveys of Robert Lythe*, *Imago Mundi*, vol. 19, 1965, vol. 22, no. 30 (no. I).

10 TNA, MPF 1/98 (formerly with the call-mark SP 64/1/31).

11 TNA, MPF 1/82. The buildings are discussed briefly in G. Camblin, *The Town in Ulster* (Belfast: Wm. Mullan & Son Publishers, Ltd, 1951), pp. 13–14 and in C. Foley, 'Bagenal's Castle, Newry, County Down: Discovery and Re-use', *Ulster Journal of Archaeology*, third series, vol. 68, 2009, p. 142; H. O'Sullivan, 'A 1575 Rent-Roll, with Contemporaneous Maps, of the Bagenal Estate in the Carlingford Lough District', *Journal of the County Louth Archaeological and Historical Society*, vol. 21, 1985, pp. 36, 46.

12 P. Logue, forthcoming paper, in T. Reeves-Smith and P. Logue (eds), *Beyond the Horizon of Memory*.

13 G. A. Hayes-McCoy, *Ulster and Other Irish Maps* c. *1600* (Dublin: Irish Manuscripts Commission, 1964), map III; C. Ó Danachair, 'Representations of Houses on Some Irish Maps of *c.*1600', in G. Jenkins (ed.), *Studies in Folklife: Essays in Honour of Iorwerth C. Peate* (New York: Barnes & Noble, 1969), p. 95.

14 Hayes-McCoy, *Ulster and Other Irish Maps*, maps II, V, VI, IX. The buildings shown outside the fort at Monaghan were apparently those 'possessed by the cast soldiers of that garrison' according to Sir John Davies' account (ibid., p. 17).

15 H. K. Bhabha, *The Location of Culture* (London and New York: Routledge, 1994), p. 162; the complexity of such hybrid encounters and spaces is discussed in F. Fahlander, 'Third Space Encounters: Hybridity, Mimicry and Interstitial Practice', in P. Cornell and F. Fahlander (eds), *Encounters | Materialities | Confrontations: Archaeologies of Social Space and Interaction* (Newcastle: Cambridge Scholars Press, 2007), pp. 22–25.

16 A. J. Horning, '"Dwelling Houses in the Old Irish Barbarous Manner": Archaeological Evidence for Gaelic Architecture in an Ulster Plantation Village', in P. J. Duffy, D. Edwards and E. FitzPatrick (eds), *Gaelic Ireland c.1250–c.1650: Land, Lordship and Settlement* (Dublin: Four Courts Press, 2001), pp. 385–388.

17 PRONI T/510 copied from Lambeth Palace Library, Carew MS 634.

18 Hayes-McCoy, *Ulster and Other Irish Maps*, map I.

19 P. J. Duffy, 'Farney in 1634: An Examination of John Raven's Survey of the Essex Estate', *Clogher Record*, vol. 11, 1983, p. 248.

20 *Cal. S.P. Ire. 1598–1599*, pp. 328, 333; *Cal. S.P. Ire. 1600*, p. 94. For the cultivation of crops near Lifford, see D. Murphy (ed.), *Beatha Aodha Ruaidh Uí Dhomhnaill. The Life of Hugh Roe O'Donnell, Prince of Tirconnell* (Dublin: Fallon, 1895), pp. 254–255.
21 J. McGurk, *Sir Henry Docwra, 1564–1631: Derry's Second Founder* (Dublin: Four Courts Press, 2006), pp. 21, 23–24; A. Horning, *Ireland in the Virginian Sea: Colonialism in the British Atlantic* (Chapel Hill: The University of North Carolina Press, 2013), p. 33.
22 G. O'Brien (ed.), *Advertisements for Ireland: Being a Description of the State of Ireland in the Reign of James I* (Dublin: Royal Society of Antiquaries, 1923), p. 33.
23 E. A. Currie, 'Land Tenures, Enclosures and Field-Patterns in County Derry in the Eighteenth and Nineteenth Centuries', *Irish Geography*, vol. 9, 1976, pp. 53–56; P. Robinson, 'The Spread of Hedged Enclosure in Ulster', *Ulster Folklife*, vol. 23, 1977, pp. 57–59.
24 R. H. Buchanan, 'Field Systems of Ireland', in A. R. H. Baker and R. A. Butlin (eds), *Studies of Field Systems in the British Isles* (Cambridge: Cambridge University Press, 1973), pp. 601–603.
25 T. Yager, 'What was Rundale and Where Did It Come From?', *Béaloideas*, vol. 70, 2002, pp. 177–180; Currie, 'Land Tenures, Enclosures and Field-Patterns', pp. 55–56; E. A. Currie, 'Landscape Development in South Derry in the Eighteenth Century', *Studia Hibernica*, vol. 19, 1979, pp. 88–89.
26 N. Canny, 'Hugh O'Neill, Earl of Tyrone, and the Changing Face of Gaelic Ulster', *Studia Hibernica*, vol. 10, 1970, p. 27; F. Moryson, *An Itinerary*, 4 vols (Glasgow: James MacLehose, 1907), vol. 2, pp. 2, 329, 338, 350, 356, 374, 387, 399, 412, 413, 420–421, 434; *Cal. S.P. Ire. 1598–1599*, p. 333; Murphy, *Beatha Aodha Ruaidh Uí Dhomhnaill*, pp. 254–255.
27 Hayes-McCoy, *Ulster and Other Irish Maps, c.1600*, map VI.
28 *Cal. S.P. Ire. 1608–1610*, p. 65; *Cal. S.P. Ire. 1615–1625*, p. 412; T. W. Moody, 'Ulster Plantation Papers', *Analecta Hibernica*, vol. 8, 1938, pp. 179, 181–187, 189–297, 285–286.
29 *Cal. S.P. Ire. 1600*, p. 94.
30 K. Simms, 'The Medieval Kingdom of Lough Erne', *Clogher Record*, vol. 9, no. 2, 1977, pp. 139–140; K. W. Nicholls, *Gaelic and Gaelicized Ireland in the Middle Ages* (Dublin: Lilliput Press, 2003), pp. 135–137.
31 K. Simms, 'Nomadry in Medieval Ireland: The Origins of the Creaght or Caoraigheacht', *Peritia*, vol. 5, 1986, p. 380; K. Simms, 'The Origins of the Creaght: Farming System or Social Unit?', in M. Murphy and M. Stout (eds), *Agriculture and Settlement in Ireland* (Dublin: Four Courts Press, 2015), pp. 101–118.
32 *Cal. S.P. Ire. 1608–1610*, pp. 532–534; H. Morley, *Ireland Under Elizabeth and James the First Described by Edmund Spenser, by Sir John Davies and by Fynes Moryson* (London: George Routledge & Sons, 1890), p. 369.
33 P. J. Duffy, D. Edwards and E. FitzPatrick, 'Introduction: Recovering Gaelic Ireland, *c.*1250–*c.*1650', in P. J. Duffy, D. Edwards and E. FitzPatrick (eds), *Gaelic Ireland* c.*1250–*c.*1650: Land, Lordship and Settlement* (Dublin: Four Courts Press, 2001), p. 50 argue that terms such as 'rent' and 'tenant' obscure the meaning.
34 *Cal. S.P. Ire. 1588–1592*, p. 141.

35 *Cal. S.P. Ire. 1608–1610*, pp. 532–533; Canny, 'Hugh O'Neill, Earl of Tyrone', p. 28.
36 Nicholls, *Gaelic and Gaelicized Ireland*, pp. 77–80.
37 Canny, *The Elizabethan Conquest of Ireland*, pp. 12–13; G. Hill, *An Historical Account of the MacDonnells of Antrim* (Belfast: Archer, 1873), pp. 35–37.
38 B. Cunningham and R. Gillespie, *Stories from Gaelic Ireland: Microhistories from the Sixteenth-Century Irish Annals* (Dublin: Four Courts Press, 2003), pp. 31, 45.
39 H. Morgan, 'The End of Gaelic Ulster: A Thematic Interpretation of Events Between 1534 and 1610', *Irish Historical Studies,* vol. 26, 1988, pp. 20–21.
40 M. Gardiner, 'A Preliminary List of Booley Huts in the Mourne Mountains, County Down', *Ulster Journal of Archaeology*, third series, vol. 67, 2008, pp. 142–152; A. Horning, 'Materiality and Mutable Landscapes: Rethinking Seasonality and Marginality in Rural Ireland', *International Journal of Historical Archaeology*, vol. 11, 2007, pp. 365–368; K. D. O'Conor, 'Housing in Later Medieval Gaelic Ireland', *Ruralia*, vol. 4, 2002, pp. 201–204.
41 M. Gardiner, 'Excavations on a Late Medieval or Early Modern House at Gortin, Ardclinis, County Antrim: Data Structure Report', Queen's University Belfast, 2010. [http://www.qub.ac.uk/sites/ExcavationandSurveyReports/FileStore/Filetoupload,201994,en.pdf]. Accessed 31 August 2017.
42 B. Williams and P. S. Robinson, 'The Excavations of Bronze Age Cists and a Medieval Booley House at Glenmakeeran, County Antrim, and a Discussion of Booleying in North Antrim', *Ulster Journal of Archaeology*, third series, vol. 46, 1983, pp. 29–40.
43 B. Williams, 'A Late Medieval Rural Settlement at Craigs, County Antrim', *Ulster Journal of Archaeology*, third series, vol. 51, 1988, pp. 91–102.
44 L. Belton, 'Experimental Study to Determine Whether Structural Details of Buildings can be Inferred from Earthworks: Study of Leean Mountain, County Leitrim', Unpublished Master's Thesis, Queen's University Belfast, 2008, pp. 38–40; T. Kytmannow, M. Gardiner and T. Kahlert, 'Leean Mountain Prehistoric Landscape Survey, Second Year: Final Report to the Heritage Council of Ireland', Unpublished Report Lodged with The Heritage Council, 2008.
45 At Irish Grid Reference (IGR) C74062542.
46 IGR C68613104.
47 IGR D29592372.
48 Morely, *Ireland Under Elizabeth and James*, p. 430.
49 O'Conor, 'Housing in Late Medieval Gaelic Ireland', pp. 201–204.
50 P. F. Wallace, *The Viking Age Buildings of Dublin*, Medieval Dublin Excavations, vol. 1 (Dublin: National Museum of Ireland, 1992), pp. 7–23, 46; M. Hurley, O. Scully and S. McCutcheon, *Late Viking Age and Medieval Waterford: Excavations 1986–1992* (Waterford Corporation, 1997), pp. 34–39; G. Eogan, *Excavations at Knowth, Volume 5: The Archaeology of Knowth in the First and Second Millennia AD* (Dublin: Royal Irish Academy, 2012), pp. 95–156; T. E. McNeill, 'Excavations at Dunsilly, County Antrim', *Ulster Journal of Archaeology,* third series, vol. 54/55, 1991/92, pp. 83–85, 109–110.
51 T. Nicholl, 'The Use of Domestic Space in Early Medieval Round Houses: An Experimental Archaeological Approach, *Trowel,* vol. 10, 2005,

pp. 27–32, cited in A. O'Sullivan, F. McCormick, T. Kerr and L. Harney, *Early Medieval Ireland AD 400–1100: The Evidence from Archaeological Excavations* (Dublin: Royal Irish Academy, 2013), p. 94.

52 C. J. Lynn and J. A. McDowell, *Deer Park Farms: The Excavation of a Raised Rath in the Glenarm Valley, County Antrim* (Belfast: Stationery Office, 2011), p. 615; Wallace, *The Viking Age Buildings of Dublin*, p. 8.

53 Gardiner, 'A Preliminary List of Booley Huts', pp. 138–139.

54 A. Horning, 'Archaeological Explorations of Cultural Identity and Rural Economy in the North of Ireland: Goodland, County Antrim', *International Journal of Historical Archaeology*, vol. 8, 2004, p. 206 makes a similar point about the lack of evidence for rebuilding at Goodland in her argument that it was not a seasonally occupied site.

55 K. W. Nicholls, *Land, Law and Society in Sixteenth-Century Ireland: O'Donnell Lecture Delivered at University College Cork* (Dublin: National University of Ireland, 1976), p. 9.

56 I argue elsewhere that there were three types of booleying in Ireland: M. Gardiner, 'The Role of Transhumance within Rundale Agriculture', *Ulster Folklife*, vol. 58, 2015, p. 57.

57 This issue is investigated in rather different contexts in M. Gardiner, 'Oral Tradition, Landscape and the Social Life of Place-Names', in R. Jones and S. Semple (eds), *Sense of Place in Anglo-Saxon England* (Donington: Oxbow, 2012), p. 21.

58 T. McErlean, 'The Irish Townland System of Landscape Organisation', in T. Reeves-Smyth and F. Hammond (eds), *Landscape Archaeology in Ireland*, British Archaeological Reports, International Series, 116 (Oxford: Archaeopress, 1983), pp. 315–339.

59 Record Commission, *Inquisitionum in Officio Rotulorum Cancellariae Hiberniae Asservatarum Repertorium*, 2 vols (Dublin: Commissioners of the Public Records of Ireland, 1826–9), vol. 2, unpaginated: Inquisitions County Tyrone, p. 15.

60 Canny, *The Elizabethan Conquest of Ireland*, p. 2.

61 H. Sidney, 'Sir Henry Sidney's Memoir of his Government of Ireland', *Ulster Journal of Archaeology*, first series, vol. 3, 1855, pp. 39, 104.

62 Record Commission, *Inquisitionum in Officio Rotulorum*, vol. 2, unpaginated: Inquisitions County Donegal, p. 3; G. Hatchell (ed.), *Irish Patent Rolls of James I: Facsimile of the Irish Record Commission's Calendar, Prepared Prior to 1830* (Dublin: Stationery Office, 1966), p. 107.

63 A. T. Lucas, 'Toghers or Causeways: Some Evidence from Archaeological, Literary, Historical and Place-Name Sources', *Proceedings of the Royal Irish Academy*, vol. 85C, 1985, pp. 37–60. For the location of the togher on the road to the Gap of the North, see H. G. Tempest, 'The Moyry Pass', *Journal of the County Louth Archaeological Society*, vol. 4, 1958, p. 85.

64 For roads in Ireland in general, C. Ó Lochlainn, 'Roadways in Ancient Ireland', in J. Ryan (ed.), *Essays and Studies Presented to Professor Eoin MacNeill* (Dublin: The Sign of the Three Candles, 1940), pp. 465–474. See also R. Gillespie, *Colonial Ulster: The Settlement of East Ulster 1600–1641* (Cork: Cork University Press, 1985), pp. 21–22.

65 P. O'Keeffe and T. Simington, *Irish Stone Bridges: History and Heritage* (Dublin: Irish Academic Press, 1991), pp. 111–124, 134–136, 145–147,

186–188; M. Murphy and M. Potterton, *The Dublin Region in the Middle Ages: Settlement, Land-Use and Economy* (Dublin: Four Courts Press, 2010), pp. 296, 472–474.

66 D. Harrison, *The Bridges of Medieval England* (Oxford: Oxford Historical Monographs, 2004), pp. 136–140; J. Masschaele, *Peasants, Merchants and Markets: Inland Trade in Medieval England, 1150–1350* (New York: Macmillan, 1997), pp. 189–212.

67 Gillespie, *Colonial Ulster,* p. 14; E. McCracken, *The Irish Woods Since Tudor Times: Their Distribution and Exploitation* (Newton Abbot: David & Charles, 1971), pp. 35–42, but compare with V. Hall and L. Bunting, 'Tephra-Dated Pollen Studies of Medieval Landscapes in the North of Ireland', in P. J. Duffy, D. Edwards and E. FitzPatrick (eds), *Gaelic Ireland c.1250–c.1650: Land, Lordship and Settlement* (Dublin: Four Courts Press, 2001), pp. 219–221. For comments on the fuel-rich character of Ireland, see T. C. Smount, 'Energy Rich, Energy Poor: Scotland, Ireland and Iceland, 1600–1800', in D. Dickson and C. Ó Gráda (eds), *Refiguring Ireland: Essays in Honour of L. M. Cullen* (Dublin: Lilliput Press, 2003), pp. 19–36.

68 However, the period of grass growth would have been affected by the prevailing climatic conditions as studies of modern temperature variation have indicated: L. Lemaire and J. Salette, 'The Effects of Temperature and Fertiliser Nitrogen on the Spring Growth of Tall Fescue and Cocksfoot', *Grass and Forage Science*, vol. 37, 1982, pp. 191–198.

69 Record Commission, *Inquisitionum in Officio Rotulorum*, vol. 2, pp. xli–xliv.

70 M. Gardiner and T. E. McNeill, 'Sea-Borne Trade and the Commercialization of Fifteenth- and Sixteenth-Century Ulster', *Proceedings of the Royal Irish Academy,* vol. 116C, 2016, 229–62.

71 K. Simms, 'Guesting and Feasting in Gaelic Ireland', *Journal of the Royal Society of Antiquaries of Ireland,* vol. 108, 1978, pp. 67–78.

72 R. Faith, 'Forces and Relations of Production in Early Medieval England', *Journal of Agrarian Change*, vol. 9, 2009, pp. 38, 39.

73 Gardiner, 'Oral Tradition, Landscape and the Social Life of Place-Names', pp. 21–22.

74 H. Morgan, 'The End of Gaelic Ulster', *Irish Historical Studies*, vol. 25, 1988, pp. 20–24.

75 Murphy and Potterton, *The Dublin Region in the Middle Ages.*

## 11. *Food, drink and society in sixteenth-century Ireland: Cultures of consumption*

1 HCA, 13/22 (1575/77), printed in J. C. Appleby, *A Calendar Material Relating to Ireland: From the High Court of Admiralty Examinations, 1536–1641* (Dublin: Irish Manuscripts Commission, 1992), p. 84.

2 E. Muir, *Ritual in Early Modern Europe* (Cambridge: Cambridge University Press, 2005), p. 134.

3 Historians have explored, for example, the link between diet and nationalism in England; the impact of religious change on food consumption and dietary rituals; the evolving role of food and drink in marking social and political distinctions and in the construction of elite identity in England. See in particular F. Heal, *Hospitality in Early Modern England* (Oxford: Oxford University Press, 1990); J. Nicholls, *The Politics of Alcohol: A History of*

*the Drink Question in England* (Manchester: Manchester University Press, 2010) and M. Dawson, *Plenti and Grase: Food and Drink in a Sixteenth-Century Household* (Totnes: Prospect Books, 2009).

4 T. Barnard, *A Guide to the Sources for Irish Material Culture: 1500–1900* (Dublin: Four Courts Press, 2005), pp. 16–17.

5 Ibid., p. 17.

6 For a detailed bibliography see Susan Flavin, 'Consumption and Material Culture in Sixteenth-Century Ireland', Unpublished PhD Thesis, University of Bristol, 2011, p. 139. For earlier general studies on Irish food see A. T. Lucas, 'Irish Food Before the Potato', *Gwerin*, vol. 3, 1960, pp. 8–43; P. Weston Joyce, *A Social History of Ancient Ireland* (London: Longmans, Green & Co., 1903). See also K. Connell, *The Population of Ireland 1750–1845* (Oxford: Clarendon Press, 1950).

7 For the medieval period, Catherine O'Sullivan has examined key aspects of the practice of hospitality in Gaelic society, including guesting, feasting and gift-giving. See C. O'Sullivan, *Hospitality in Medieval Ireland, 900–1500* (Dublin: Four Courts Press, 2004). See also K. Simms, 'Guesting and Feasting in Gaelic Ireland', *Journal of the Royal Society of Antiquities of Ireland*, vol. 108, 1978, pp. 67–100. As with consumption studies in general, the seventeenth and eighteenth centuries have received the greatest attention. An example of some excellent new work in the field is Madeline Shanahan's research on early modern recipe books. See M. Shanahan, 'Dining on Words: Manuscript Recipe Books, Culinary Change and Elite Food Culture in Ireland, 1660–1830', *Irish Architectural & Decorative Studies*, vol. 15, 2012. Other important studies of the material culture of food and drink include T. Barnard, *Making the Grand Figure: Lives and Possessions in Ireland 1641–1770* (New Haven: Yale University Press, 2004), pp. 122–150, which explores elite dining. See also a recent study by Jane Fenlon on the changing use of rooms in elite Irish houses, which places Irish domestic developments in the context of wider changes in attitudes to issues like privacy, civility and individuality. See J. Fenlon, 'Moving Towards the Formal House: Room Usage in Early Modern Ireland', in E. FitzPatrick and J. Kelly (eds), *Domestic Life in Ireland* (Dublin: Royal Irish Academy, 2011).

8 One exception to this is the examination by Clarkson and Crawford of diet and nutrition in Ireland between 1500 and 1920 which included a chapter on changing patterns of consumption in the sixteenth and seventeenth centuries and utilised evidence from contemporary writings, army purveyancing records and two elite household accounts. The authors concluded that late sixteenth-century colonisation wrought fundamental changes in Irish dietary patterns, reversing the process of acculturation and imposing on the native population the dietary values of the settlers. This process of adaptation, they noted, took a long time. See L. Clarkson and M. Crawford, *Feast and Famine: A History of Food and Nutrition in Ireland 1500–1920* (Oxford: Oxford University Press, 2001).

9 R. Gillespie, *The Transformation of the Irish Economy, 1500–1700* (Dundalk: Dundalgan Press, 1991), p. 31.

10 L. Cullen, *The Emergence of Modern Ireland 1600–1900* (London: Gill & Macmillan, 1981), pp. 25, 107.

11 For details see E. Jones and S. Flavin, 'Ireland–Bristol Trade in the Sixteenth Century', Project Website, Department of History, University of Bristol [http://www.bris.ac.uk/Depts/History/Ireland/research.htm]. Accessed 20 April 2015.
12 W. Childs, 'Ireland's Trade with England in the Later Middle Ages', *Irish Economic & Social History*, vol. 9, 1982, pp. 8–10; E. Carus-Wilson, 'The Overseas Trade of Bristol', in E. Power and M. Postan (eds), *Studies in English Trade in the Fifteenth Century* (London: Routledge, 1933), p. 192.
13 For a more detailed discussion see S. Flavin, 'Consumption and Material Culture in Sixteenth-Century Ireland', *Economic History Review*, vol. 64, no. 4, 2011, and also S. Flavin, *Consumption and Culture in Sixteenth-Century Ireland: Saffron, Stockings and Silk* (Woodbridge: The Boydell Press, 2014).
14 J. Thirsk, *Economic Policy and Projects: The Development of a Consumer Society in Early Modern England* (Oxford: Clarendon Press, 1978), p. 127.
15 S. Ellis, 'Historical Revision XIX: The Irish Customs Administration Under the Early Tudors', *Irish Historical Studies*, vol. 22, 1980–81, p. 271.
16 C. Lennon, *Sixteenth-Century Ireland: The Incomplete Conquest* (Dublin: Gill & Macmillan, 1994), p. 40.
17 See, for example, T. Barnard, 'Integration or Separation? Hospitality and Display in Protestant Ireland, 1660–1800', in L. Brockliss and D. Eastwood (eds), *A Union of Multiple Identities: The British Isles, c.1750–c.1850* (Manchester: Manchester University Press, 1997), p. 128; M. Powell, *The Politics of Consumption in Eighteenth-Century Ireland* (Hampshire: Palgrave Macmillan, 2005).
18 Thirsk, *Economic Policy*, p. 125.
19 Gillespie, *Transformation*, p. 9.
20 *Cal. Carew MSS, 1601–1603*, p. 388.
21 E. Jones and S. Flavin, *Bristol's Trade with Ireland and the Continent 1503–1601: The Evidence of the Exchequer Customs Accounts* (Dublin: Four Courts Press, 2009), p. 5.
22 Jones and Flavin, *Bristol's Trade*, p. 773.
23 P. Croft, 'Trading with the Enemy', *The Historical Journal*, vol. 32, no. 2, 1989, pp. 281–302.
24 Croft, 'Trading', p. 287.
25 Thirsk, *Economic Policy*, p. 127.
26 Ibid.
27 J. Stow, *Annales of England ... Continued by Edmund Howes* (London: Thomas Dawson, 1615), p. 948.
28 This trend is also noted with regards to other essential everyday items such as pins and needles.
29 N. Elias, *The Civilizing Process: The History of Manners and State Formation and Civilization*, trans. E. Jephcott (Oxford: Blackwell, 1994), p. 175. Elias has discussed the evolution of both the role and design of the knife in the early modern period, as related to his theory of the 'civilising process'. One of the key changes was the development of a less threatening rounded tip.
30 HCA 13/32 (1595–8), 393 in Appleby, *Calendar of Material*, p. 84.
31 HCA 13/30 (1592–4) ff. 30–31, printed in Appleby, *Calendar of Material*, pp. 68–69. The *Mary of Waterford* was laded at Lisbon with a range of

luxury items, including suckets and marmalade, calico, sugar, silver cups, green ginger, Spanish silk, conserved rose flowers, silk lace and gold jewels, Spanish taffeta and spices to the value of a staggering £800.

32 BL, Add MSS. 5754, fol. 180. Victualling accounts, *c.*1580–1600, cited by Clarkson and Crawford, *Feast*, p. 18.

33 F. Moryson, 'An Itinerary', in J. Myers (ed.), *Elizabethan Ireland: A Selection of Writings by Elizabethan Writers on Ireland* (Connecticut: Archon Books, 1983), p. 186.

34 Ibid., p. 189.

35 AFM 1592.9.

36 Ibid.

37 A recipe for beer from 1502 shows that 40 lbs of hops was used to make 60 barrels of single beer. This, of course, would have varied. See R. Arnold, *Customs of London* (Antwerp: A. van Berghen, 1503), p. 247.

38 L. Gernon, 'A Discourse of Ireland Anno 1620', in C. Litton Falkiner (ed.), *Illustrations of Irish History and Topography, Mainly of the Seventeenth Century* (London, New York, Bombay: Longmans, Green & Co., 1904), p. 360.

39 C. A. Wilson, *Food and Drink in Britain* (London: Constable, 1973), p. 376.

40 A. Boorde, *A Compendyous Regyment or a Dyetary of Healthe* (London: Wyllyam Powell, 1547), p. 18.

41 Thirsk, *Food*, p. 306.

42 For a detailed analysis see S. Flavin, *Consumption and Culture*.

43 P. Hammond *Food and Feast in Medieval England* (Gloucestershire: Sutton, 1993), p. 107; Dawson, *Plenti*, p. 215.

44 Hammond, *Food*, p. 108.

45 Ibid., p. 107; Dawson, *Plenti*, p. 215.

46 From 'Treacle box – Trough', *Dictionary of Traded Goods and Commodities, 1550–1820* (2007). Available from [http://www.british-history.ac.uk/report.aspx?compid=58900] Accessed 19 February 2014.

47 G. F. Dow, *Every Day Life in the Massachusetts Bay Colony* (Maryland: Courier Corporation, 2007), p. 84.

48 For a discussion of the role of social emulation in Irish consumption see Flavin, *Consumption and Culture*.

49 Elias, *The Civilizing Process*.

50 'The Little Children's Little Book', British Library, Harley 541. For imports see, for example, TNA E190112912 f9v; TNA E190113110 f49r; f50r; TNA E190113211 f 24 r &v; f26v; f27v; f29r; f 30r; f32r; f 34r & v.

51 A. Haskell and M. Lewis, *Infantilia: The Archaeology of the Nursery* (London: Dobson, 1971), p. 30.

52 Ibid., p. 33; E. E Stevens, 'A History of Infant Feeding', *Journal of Perinatal Education,* vol. 18, no. 2, 2009, pp. 32–39.

53 Jones and Flavin, *Bristol's Trade*, p. 785.

54 T. Phaer, *The Boke of Chyldren* (1544), ed. R. Bowers (Tempe: Arizona Centre for Medieval and Renaissance Studies, 1999), p. 33.

55 M. S. Osborn, 'The Rent Breasts, Part II', *Midwife, Health Visitor & Community Nurse*, vol. 15, no. 9, 1979, p. 347; Stevens, 'A History of Infant Feeding', pp. 32–3.

56 J. Guillemeau, *Child-birth or, the Happy Deliuerie of Vvomen* (London: A. Hatfield, 1612).

57 J. Davies, 'A Discovery of the True Causes Why Ireland Was Never Entirely Subdued', in J. Myers (ed.), *Elizabethan Ireland: A Selection of Writings by Elizabethan Writers on Ireland* (Connecticut: Archon Books, 1983), p. 161; Moryson, *Itinerary*, p. 318; W. Good, 'Descriptions and Customs of the Wild Irish', in W. Camden, *Britannia* (1586), trans. E. Gibson (London: Awnsham Churchill, 1722), vol. II, p. 1418.
58 E. Spenser, 'A View of the Present State of Ireland', in J. Myers (ed.), *Elizabethan Ireland: A Selection of Writings by Elizabethan Writers on Ireland* (Connecticut: Archon Books, 1983), p. 97.
59 See B. Rich, 'A New Description of Ireland', in J. Myers (ed.), *Elizabethan Ireland: A Selection of Writings by Elizabethan Writers on Ireland* (Connecticut: Archon Books, 1983), and Moryson, 'Itinerary'.
60 J. Myers (ed.), *Elizabethan Ireland: A Selection of Writings by Elizabethan Writers on Ireland* (Connecticut: Archon Books, 1983), p. 97.

12. *Retreat from the borough: Castle and community in the early modern Nugent lordship*

1 H. Piers, 'A Chorographical Description of the County of West-Meath written A.D. 1682', in C. Vallancey (ed.), *Collectanea de Rebus Hibernicis* (Dublin: Luke White, 1776), p. 62.
2 M. Johnson, *Behind the Castle Gate: From Medieval to Renaissance* (London and New York: Routledge, 2002), p. 127.
3 TCD, 1641 Depositions Project, online transcript January 1970 [http://1641.tcd.ie/deposition.php?depID<?php echo 817022r038?>] Accessed 27 February 2014.
4 M. Girouard, *Life in the English Country House* (Harmondsworth: Penguin Books, 1980), p. 16.
5 B. Kane, 'From Irish *Eineach* to British Honor? Noble Honor and High Politics in Early Modern Ireland, 1500–1650', *History Compass,* vol. 7, no. 2, 2009, passim.
6 AFM 1144.21; AFM 1174.8.
7 R. Masterson, 'The Early Anglo Norman Colonisation of Fore, County Westmeath', *Ríocht na Midhe*, vol. 13, 2002, p. 52; J. F. Ainsworth and Edward Mac Lysaght, 'Survey of Documents in Private Keeping, Second Series', *Analecta Hibernica*, vol. 20, 1958, p. 129.
8 N. B. White, *Extents of Irish Monastic Possessions, 1540–1541: From Manuscripts in the Public Record Office, London* (Dublin: Irish Manuscripts Commission, 1943), p. 280.
9 J. Ohlmeyer, '"Making Ireland English": The Seventeenth-century Irish Peerage', in B. Mac Cuarta (ed.), *Reshaping Ireland 1550–1700: Colonisation and its Consequences* (Dublin: Four Courts Press, 2011), p. 139.
10 TCD, 1641 Depositions Project, online transcript January 1970 [http://1641.tcd.ie/deposition.php?depID<?php echo 817022r038?>] Accessed 15 June 2012.
11 The Books of Survey and Distribution: Being Abstracts from Various Surveys and Instruments of Title, 1636–1703 (1962) (microform, Stationery Office for the Irish Manuscripts Commission), 10 microfilm reels: negative, 35mm.

12 Westmeath was shired in 1543. D.B. Quinn and K.W. Nicholls, 'Ireland in 1534', in T.W. Moody, F.X. Martin and F.J. Byrne (eds), *Early Modern Ireland 1534–1691* (Oxford: Oxford University Press, 2009), p. 5.

13 G.H. Orpen, 'Motes and Norman Castles in Ireland', *The Journal of the Royal Society of Antiquaries of Ireland*, vol. 37, no. 2, 1907, p. 236; W. Lynch, *A View of the Legal Institutions, Honorary Hereditary Offices and Feudal Baronies Established in Ireland during the Reign of Henry the Second* (London: Longman, Rees, Orme, Browne & Green, 1830), p. 150.

14 G.H. Orpen, *Ireland Under the Normans 1169–1333*, 3 vols (Dublin: Four Courts Press, 2005), vol. 2, p. 87.

15 C. Lennon, 'The Nugent Family and the Diocese of Kilmore in the Sixteenth and Early Seventeenth Centuries', *Breifne*, vol. 10, 2001, p. 361.

16 S. G. Ellis, *Ireland in the Age of the Tudors 1447–1603: English Expansion and the End of Gaelic Rule* (London: Routledge, 1998), p. 106.

17 N. Canny, *The Formation of the Old English Elite in Ireland: O'Donnell Lecture Delivered at University College Galway, 6 September 1974* (Dublin: National University of Ireland, 1975), p. 4.

18 K.W. Nicholls, *Gaelic and Gaelicized Ireland in the Middle Ages* (Dublin: Lilliput Press, 2003), p. 73; C. Lennon, 'Nugent, Christopher, Fifth Baron Delvin (1544–1602)', *Oxford Dictionary of National Biography* (Oxford: Oxford University Press, 2004). [http://www.oxforddnb.com/view/article/20387] Accessed 27 Feb 2014; K. Simms, 'Bards and Barons: The Anglo-Irish Aristocracy and the Native Culture', in R. Bartlett and A. MacKay (eds), *Medieval Frontier Societies* (Oxford: Oxford University Press, 1989), pp. 177–197.

19 Simms, 'Bards and Barons', p. 180; B. Iske, *The Green Cockatrice* (Dublin: Meath Archaeological and Historical Society, 1978), p. 179; T. Ua Brádaigh, 'Clann Cobhthaigh', *Ríocht na Midhe*, vol. 4, 1967, 2, p. 26.

20 NLI Ms. G992. *Duanaire na Nuinseannach* [http://www.isos.dias.ie/english/index.html] Accessed 13 January 2012.

21 [http://bardic.celt.dias.ie/main.html] Accessed 13 January 2012.

22 Lennon, 'Nugent, Christopher' [http://www.oxforddnb.com/view/article/20387] Accessed 28 Feb 2014; *Cal. S.P. Ire. 1588–1592*, p. 420.

23 Ellis, *Ireland in the Age of the Tudors*, p. 48.

24 E. FitzPatrick, 'Assembly and Inauguration Places of the Burkes in Late Medieval Connacht', in P.J. Duffy, D. Edwards and E. FitzPatrick (eds), *Gaelic Ireland* c.*1250*–c.*1650: Land, Lordship and Settlement* (Dublin: Fourt Courts Press, 2004), p. 357; Ellis, *Ireland in the Age of the Tudors*, p. 47.

25 Ellis, *Ireland in the Age of the Tudors,* p. 48.

26 Anonymous, *Historical Sketch of the Nugent Family* (Ledestown: John Charles Lyons, 1853), passim.

27 In 1382 three members of the sept were appointed as keepers of the peace and, another, Thomas Nugent, was appointed as supervisor of the keepers of the peace in 'Lune, Delvin, Ferbill, Moyeshell, Feartolagh, Mullingar [and] Foure'. See P. Crooks (ed.), *A Calendar of Irish Chancery Letters, c.1244–1509*, Patent Roll 5 Richard II, §236. [https://chancery.tcd.ie/document/patent/5-richard-ii/236] Accessed 28 June 2012. Again in 1388 two Nugents were appointed as keepers of the peace: Crook (ed.), *Chancery*

*Letters,* Patent Roll 12 Richard II, §193. [https://chancery.tcd.ie/document/patent/12-richard-ii/193] Accessed 28 June 2012; A. J. Otway-Ruthven, *A History of Medieval Ireland* (London: E. Benn, 1980), p. 180.

28 D. Beresford, 'Nugent, Richard 10th lord of Delvin', in J. McGuire and J. Quinn (ed.), *Dictionary of Irish Biography* (Cambridge: Cambridge University Press, 2009) [http://dib.cambridge.org/viewReadPage.do?articleId=a6256] Accessed 28 June 2012; K. Abraham, 'Upward Mobility in Later Medieval Meath', *History Ireland*, vol. 5, no. 4, 1997, p. 16.

29 Canny, *The Formation of the Old English Elite,* p. 4.

30 M. T. Flanagan, 'Anglo-Norman Change and Continuity: The Castle of Telach Cail in Delbna', *Irish Historical Studies* vol. 28, no. 113, 1993, p. 385; B. J. Graham, 'The Mottes of the Norman Liberty of Meath', in H. Murtagh (ed.), *Irish Midland Studies: Essays in Commemoration of N. W. English* (Athlone: Old Athlone Society, 1980), p. 45.

31 T. E. McNeill, *Castles in Ireland: Feudal Power in a Gaelic World* (London: Routledge, 1997), pp. 261, 240; T. O'Keeffe, *Medieval Ireland: An Archaeology* (Stroud: Tempus, 2000), p. 39.

32 Anonymous, *Historical Sketch of the Nugent Family*, p. 4.

33 AU 1475.3

34 Piers, 'A Chorographical Description', p. 62.

35 M. Thompson, *The Medieval Hall, the Basis of Secular Domestic Life 600–1600AD* (Aldershot: Scolar Press, 1995), p. 101.

36 Ibid., p. 102.

37 Buildings that were largely contemporary with Delvin castle.

38 R. Sherlock, 'The Evolution of the Irish Tower-House as a Domestic Space', *Proceedings of the Royal Irish Academy,* 111C, 2011, p. 133.

39 Thompson, *The Medieval Hall*, p. 107.

40 Ibid., p. 101.

41 Sherlock, 'The Evolution of the Irish Tower-house as a Domestic Space', pp. 122–124.

42 Ibid., p. 128.

43 M. Johnson, *English Houses 1300–1800* (Harlow: Pearson, 2010), p. 69.

44 Ibid., p. 70.

45 McNeill, *Castles in Ireland*, p. 118.

46 Ibid., p. 149.

47 Ibid., p. 118.

48 O. Creighton and T. Barry, 'Seigneurial and Elite Sites in the Medieval Landscape', in N. Christie and P. Stamper (eds), Medieval Rural Settlement: Britain and Ireland, AD 800–1600 (Oxford: Windgather Press, 2012), p. 64.

49 The church at Delvin is first mentioned in 1293 in H. S. Sweetman and G. F. Handcock (eds), *Calendar of Documents, Relating to Ireland,* 5 vols (London: Longman & Co., 1875), vol. 4, p. 18.

50 Ibid., vol. 5, p. 259.

51 M. O'Neill, 'The Medieval Parish Churches in County Meath', *Journal of the Royal Society of Antiquaries of Ireland*, vol. 132, 2002, pp. 30–31.

52 Ibid., pp. 10, 15; A. Empey, 'The Layperson in the Parish: The Medieval Inheritance, 1169–1536', in R. Gillespie and W. G. Neely (eds), *The Laity and the Church of Ireland, 1000–2000* (Dublin: Four Courts Press, 2002), p. 16.

53 J. Brady, 'Documents Concerning the Diocese of Meath', *Archivium Hibernicum,* vol. 8, 1941, pp. 242–243.
54 Ainsworth and Mac Lysaght, 'Survey of Documents in Private Keeping', p. 133.
55 Piers, 'A Chorographical Description', p. 63.
56 [http://www.buildingsofireland.ie/niah/search.jsp?type=record&county=WM®no=15308017] Accessed 8 June 2012.
57 A manorial village can be defined as 'a settlement from where the lord's manor was administered, where his home farm was located and where some tenants lived. It was focused on a church and usually also a castle and a mill': K. J. Edwards, F. W. Hamond and A. Simms, 'The Medieval Settlement of Newcastle Lyons, County Dublin: An Interdisciplinary Approach', *Proceedings of the Royal Irish Academy*, vol. 83C, 1983, p. 14.
58 H. G. R. Robinson and J. Macbeth, *Fairs and Markets' Commission, Ireland. Report of the Commissioners Appointed to Inquire into the State of the Fairs and Markets in Ireland. Part II. Minutes of Evidence* (Dublin: His Majesty's Stationery Office, 1852–53), p. 139.
59 A. J. Otway-Ruthven, 'The Character of Norman Settlement in Ireland', in J. L. McCracken et al. (eds), *Historical Studies*, vol. 5 (London: Bowes & Bowes, 1965), p. 79; B. J. Graham, 'The Towns of Medieval Ireland', in R. A. Butlin (ed.), *The Development of the Irish Town* (London: Rowman & Littlefield, 1977), p. 29.
60 E. Hogan (ed.), *The Description of Ireland and the State thereof as it is at this Present in Anno 1598* (Dublin and London: M. H. Gill, 1878), p. 102; NLI Ms 724, f. 9, Reeves Down Survey.
61 J. Bradley, 'Planned Anglo-Norman Towns in Ireland', in H. B. Clarke and A. Simms (eds), *The Comparative History of Urban Origins 900–1250: Ireland, Wales, Denmark, Germany, Poland and Russia*, British Archaeological Reports, International Series, 255 (Oxford: Archaeopress, 1985), p. 434.
62 Creighton and Barry, 'Seigneurial and Elite Sites', p. 74.
63 AFM 1461.14
64 AU 1475.2
65 According to the Annals of the Kingdom of Ireland, 'the plague was brought by a ship into the harbour of Assaroe … and spread through Fermanagh, Tirconnell and the province in general': AFM 1478.11.
66 K. W. Nicholls (ed.), *The Irish Fiants of the Tudor Sovereigns: During the Reigns of Henry VIII, Edward VI, Philip and Mary, and Elizabeth I*, 4 vols (Dublin: Edmund Burke, 1994), vol. 1, p. 51.
67 Ainsworth and Mac Lysaght, 'Survey of Documents in Private Keeping', p. 134.
68 NLI Ms 724, f. 9, Reeves Down Survey maps.
69 S. Pender, *A Census of Ireland, circa 1659. With Supplementary Material from the Poll Money Ordinances, 1660–1661* (Dublin: Stationery Office, 1939), pp. 513, 516, 519, 526, 527.
70 B. Cunningham, 'Foreword', in L. Doran and J. Lyttleton (eds), *Lordship in Medieval Ireland: Image and Reality* (Dublin: Four Courts Press, 2007), pp. 17–18.
71 Creighton and Barry, 'Seigneurial and Elite Sites', p. 64.

72 Ainsworth and Mac Lysaght, 'Survey of Documents in Private Keeping', p. 126.

73 Ibid.

74 Hogan, *The Description of Ireland,* p. 103.

75 Ainsworth and Mac Lysaght, 'Survey of Documents in Private Keeping', p. 134.

76 NLI MS 724, f.8. Down Survey maps, County Westmeath.

77 Ibid.

78 NLI MS 724 f. 26. Down Survey maps, County Westmeath.

79 RMP (WM013-014----). See also C. Casey and A. Rowan, *North Leinster, the Counties of Longford, Louth, Meath and Westmeath* (London: Penguin, 1993), pp. 214–216.

80 [http://www.buildingsofireland.ie/niah/search.jsp?type=record&county=WM®no=15308017] Accessed 8 June 2012.

81 [http://www.buildingsofireland.ie/niah/search.jsp?type=record&county=WM®no=15308017 ] Accessed 25 February 2014.

82 TCD, 1641 Depositions Project, online transcript January 1970 [http://1641.tcd.ie/deposition.php?depID<?php echo 817022r038?>] Accessed 15 June 2012.

83 R. Loeber, 'Irish Country Houses and Castles of the Late Caroline Period: An Unremembered Past Recaptured?' *Quarterly Bulletin of the Irish Georgian Society*, vol. 16, nos 1 & 2, 1973.

84 Casey and Rowan, *North Leinster*, p. 216.

85 NLI Ms 724, f. 9, Down Survey maps, County Westmeath.

86 T. Reeves Smith, 'The Natural History of Demesnes', in J. Wilson Foster and H. C. G. Chesney (eds), *Nature in Ireland: A Scientific and Cultural History* (Dublin: Lilliput Press, 2007), p. 550; T. Barnard, *Making the Grand Figure: Lives and Possessions in Ireland, 1641–1770* (New Haven: Yale University Press, 2004), p. 186; T. Williamson and L. Bellamy, *Property and Landscape: A Social History of Land Ownership and the English Countryside* (London: George Philip, 1987), p. 140.

87 Barnard, *Making the Grand Figure*, p. 190; T. Barnard, 'Gardening, Diet and Improvement in Later Seventeenth Century Ireland', *Irish Protestant Ascents and Descents, 1641–1770* (Dublin: Four Courts Press, 2004), p. 224.

88 T. Reeves-Smith, 'Irish Gardens and Gardening before Cromwell', in J. Ludlow and N. Jameson (eds), *Medieval Ireland: The Barryscourt Lectures I–X* (Kinsale: Gandon Editions, 1999), p. 116–118.

89 Ibid., p. 121; P. Bowe, 'The Renaissance Garden in Ireland', *Irish Arts Review Yearbook*, vol. 11, 1995, p. 74.

90 Williamson and Bellamy, *Property and Landscape*, p. 139; Reeves-Smith, 'Irish Gardens and Gardening', p. 131; Reeves-Smyth, 'The Natural History of Demesnes', p. 550; Loeber, 'Irish Country Houses and Castles of the Late Caroline Period', p. 47; C. McKean, 'The Scottish Renaissance Country Seat in its Setting', *Garden History*, vol. 31, no. 2, 2003, p. 156.

91 Barnard, 'Gardening, Diet and Improvement'; Reeves-Smyth, 'The Natural History of Demesnes', p. 550.

92 NLI, MS 720–1. Down Survey Maps, County Westmeath.

93 P. Edwards, *Horse and Man in Early Modern England* (Cornwall: Bloomsbury Academic, 2007), p. 82.

94 Ibid.

95 Ibid., p. 37.

96 Pender, *A Census of Ireland*, p. 527.

97 [http://www.logainm.ie/51306.aspx] Accessed 13 October 2011.

98 [http://www.logainm.ie/51307.aspx] Accessed 25 February 2014; D. Flanagan and L. Flanagan, *Irish Place Names* (Dublin: Gill & Macmillan, 1994), p. 56.

99 NLI MS 724, f. 9, Reeves Down Survey maps, County Westmeath.

100 A. J. Otway-Ruthven, 'The Organization of Anglo-Irish Agriculture in the Middle Ages', *The Journal of the Royal Society of Antiquaries of Ireland*, vol. 81, no. 1, 1951, p. 3.

101 Ainsworth and Mac Lysaght, 'Survey of Documents in Private Keeping', pp. 126, 134.

102 TCD, 1641 Depositions Project, online transcript January 1970 [http://1641.tcd.ie/deposition.php?depID<?php echo 817065r067?>] Accessed 28 February 2014.

103 Iske, *The Green Cockatrice*, pp. 16, 20.

104 Ellis, *Ireland in the Age of the Tudors*, pp. 367–368. For more details on the role of governor see Ellis, *Ireland in the Age of the Tudors*, pp. 161–165.

105 Iske, *The Green Cockatrice*, p. 20.

106 Ibid., p. 20.

107 Ellis, *Ireland in the Age of the Tudors*, p. 308.

108 Ibid., p. 315.

109 NLI, GO MS 64 f.39, funeral entries; NLI GO MS 65 f.62, funeral entries.

110 J. Fenlon, 'Moving Towards the Formal House: Room Usage in Early Modern Ireland', *Proceedings of the Royal Irish Academy*, vol. 111C, 2011, p. 142.

111 Ibid., p. 143.

112 Lennon, 'Nugent, Christopher'; *Cal. S. P. Ire. 1588-92*, p. 420.

113 J. Barry, 'Guide to Records of the Genealogical Office, Dublin, with a Commentary on Heraldry in Ireland and on the History of the Office', *Analecta Hibernica*, vol. 26, 1970, pp. 21, 23.

114 J. F. R. Day, 'Primers of Honor: Heraldry, Heraldry Books, and English Renaissance Literature', *Sixteenth Century Journal*, vol. 21, no. 1, 1990, p. 93.

115 L. Stone, *The Crisis of the Aristocracy, 1558–1641* (Oxford: Clarendon Press, 1965), p. 16.

116 Barry, 'Guide to Records of the Genealogical Office', pp. 3, 13; N. R. Wilkinson, 'Heraldry in its Relation to Archaeology', *Journal of the Royal Society of Antiquaries of Ireland*, vol. 40, no. 1, 1909, p. 53; D. Jenkins (ed.), *The Cambridge History of Western Textiles* (Cambridge: Cambridge University Press, 2003), pp. 352, 366; Knight of Glin and J. Peill, *Irish Furniture* (New Haven, CT: Yale University Press, 2007), pp. 15, 41; C. Boutell and A. C. Fox-Davies, *English Heraldry* (Edinburgh: Reeves & Turner, 1908), p. 316.

117 Wilkinson, 'Heraldry in Relation to Archaeology', p. 54; B. Carver Wees, *English, Irish and Scottish Silver at the Sterling and Francine Clark Art*

*Institute* (New York: Hudson Hills Press, 1997), p. 11; P. Glanville, *Silver in England* (Oxton: Routledge, 1987), p. 197.

118 T. Reeves-Smyth, 'Community to Privacy: Late Tudor and Jacobean Manorial Architecture in Ireland, 1560–1640', in A. Horning, et al. (eds), *The Post-Medieval Archaeology of Ireland, 1550–1850* (Dublin: Wordwell, 2007).

119 H. Ronnes, 'Continental Traces at Carrick-on-Suir and Contemporary Irish Castles', in T. Herron and M. Potterton (eds), *Ireland in the Renaissance c.1540–1660* (Dublin: Four Courts Press, 2007), p. 270; Harold Mytum, 'Materiality and Memory: An Archaeological Perspective on the Popular Adoption of Linear Time in Britain', *Antiquity,* vol. 81, 2007, pp. 384–388.

120 R. Gillespie, 'Funerals and Society in Early Seventeenth Century Ireland', *Journal of the Royal Society of Antiquaries of Ireland,* vol. 115, 1985, pp. 90, 87.

121 NLI, GO MS 64, f.39, funeral entries; NLI GO MS 68, f.89, funeral entries.

122 J. A. Sharpe, *Early Modern England: A Social History 1550–1760* (London: Bloomsbury Academic, 2003), p. 172.

123 J. Fenlon, *Goods and Chattels: A Survey of Early Household Inventories in Ireland* (Dublin: Stationery Office, 2003).

124 Wife of the fourteenth Baron, Christopher Nugent, and daughter of the eleventh Earl of Kildare.

125 Ainsworth and Mac Lysaght, 'Survey of Documents in Private Keeping', p. 137.

126 A. Fearn, 'From the Salt to the Centrepieces, 1580–1780', in P. Glanville and H. Young (eds), *Elegant Eating: Four Hundred Years of Dining in Style* (London: V & A Publications, 2002), p. 64.

127 M. A. Everett Green, *Calendar of State Papers, Domestic Series of the Reign of James I,* 5 vols (London: Longman, 1858), vol. 3, p. 150.

128 T. Sweeney, *Irish Stuart Silver: A Short Descriptive Catalogue of Surviving Irish Church, Civic and Ceremonial & Domestic Plate Dating from the Reigns of James I, Charles I, the Commonwealth, Charles II, James II, William & Mary, William III and Queen Anne: 1603–1714* (Dublin: Edmund Burke, 1995).

129 TCD, 1641 Depositions Project, online transcript January 1970 [http://1641.tcd.ie/deposition.php?depID<?php echo 817022r038?>] Accessed 15 June 2012.

130 Fenlon, *Goods and Chattels,* passim.

131 Ainsworth and Mac Lysaght, 'Survey of Documents in Private Keeping', p. 144.

132 K. Simms, *From Kings to Warlords: The Changing Political Structure of Gaelic Ireland in the Later Middle Ages* (Woodbridge: The Boydell Press, 2000), p. 147.

133 P. Burke, *Popular Culture in Early Modern Europe* (Aldershot: Scolar Press, 1994), p. 270.

134 Ibid., p. 271.

135 M. Johnson, *The Archaeology of Capitalism* (Oxford: Wiley, 1996), passim.

136 K. Marx, *Capital: A Critique of Political Economy* (London: Penguin, 1990), p. 873.

137 M. Airs, 'Architecture, Politics and Society', in R. Tittler (ed.), *A Companion to Tudor Britain* (Oxford: Blackwell, 2004), pp. 471–472; M. Johnson, 'Meanings of Polite Architecture in Sixteenth-century England', *Historical Archaeology*, vol. 26, no. 3, 1992, pp. 45–56.
138 Fenlon, 'Moving Towards the Formal House', p. 145.
139 J. Fenlon, 'Episodes of Magnificence: The Material Worlds of the Dukes of Ormonde', in T. Barnard and J. Fenlon (eds), *The Dukes of Ormonde, 1610–1745* (Woodbridge: The Boydell Press, 2000), p. 138.
140 G. M. Keane, '"Great Stone Houses": Kilkenny and its Early Modern Townhouses 1550–1650', Unpublished MA Thesis, University College Dublin, 2010, pp. 11–12; E. FitzPatrick, M. O'Brien and P. Walsh (eds), *Archaeological Investigations in Galway City, 1987–1998* (Bray: Wordwell, 2004), p. 349.
141 R. Sherlock, 'The Social Environment of the Irish Tower House', Unpublished PhD Thesis, National University of Ireland, Galway, 2008, p. 231.
142 Williamson and Bellamy, *Property and Landscape*, pp. 136–137; C. Taylor, *Village and Farmstead: A History of Rural Settlement in England* (London: George Philip, 1983), p. 202.
143 Symner was appointed a commissioner for setting out lands to soldiers by the Cromwellian government, and was subsequently appointed as a professor of mathematics at Trinity College: T. Barnard, 'Miles Symner and the New Learning in Seventeenth-Century Ireland', *Journal of the Royal Society of Antiquaries of Ireland*, vol. 102, no. 2, 1972, pp. 129–130.
144 Barnard, 'Gardening, Diet and Improvement', p. 213.
145 G. Kew, 'The Irish Sections of Fynes Moryson's Unpublished "Itinerary"', *Analecta Hibernica,* vol. 37, 1998, pp. 112–113. For a discussion of the park at Maynooth see F. Beglane, *Anglo-Norman Parks in Medieval Ireland* (Dublin: Four Courts Press, 2015), p. 167.
146 E. P. Shirley et al., 'Extracts from the Journal of Thomas Dineley, Esquire, Giving Some Account of his Visit to Ireland in the Reign of Charles II (continued)', *The Journal of the Kilkenny and South-East of Ireland Archaeological Society*, vol. 6, no. 1, 1867, pp. 87–88.

13. *All things to all men: Aodh Ó Néill and the construction of identity*

1 H. Morgan, *Tyrone's Rebellion* (Woodbridge: Boydell Press,1993), p. 217.
2 S. Connolly, *Contested Island* (Oxford: Oxford University Press, 2007), pp. 139–141.
3 *Cal. Carew MSS,* 1515–1574, p. 305.
4 J. K. Graham, 'The Birth-Date of Hugh O'Neill, Second Earl of Tyrone', *Irish Historical Studies*, vol. 1, no. 1, 1938, pp. 58–59.
5 *Cal. Carew MSS, 1515–1574,* p. 436.
6 Joseph Stephenson (ed.), *Calendar of State Papers: Foreign Series, of the Reign of Elizabeth 1562* (London: Longman, Green, Reader & Dyer, 1867), p. 82.
7 F. Moryson, *An Itinerary*, 4 vols (Glasgow: James MacLehose & Sons, 1907), vol. 2, p. 178.
8 *Cal. S. P. Ire. 1586–1588*, pp. 290–291.
9 Morgan, *Tyrone's Rebellion*, p. 93.

10 Ibid.
11 Ibid.
12 Ibid., pp. 340–341.
13 Ibid., p. 390.
14 Ibid., p. 460.
15 Ibid., p. 500.
16 Ibid., p. 505.
17 Ibid., p. 505.
18 Ibid., p. 525; *Cal. S. P. Ire. 1574–1585*, pp. 22–52.
19 Connolly, *Contested Island*, p. 228.
20 *Cal. S. P. Ire. 1574–1585*, p. 18.
21 Ibid., p. 71.
22 TNA, MPF 1/99, Plot of the Fort at the Black-water, March 27 1587; *Cal. S. P. Ire.*, p. 288.
23 *Cal. S. P. Ire., 1592–1596 June*, p. 298.
24 *Cal. S. P. Ire. 1574–1585*, p. 72.
25 Ibid., p. 160.
26 Ibid., p. 451.
27 Morgan, *Tyrone's Rebellion*, p. 95.
28 *Cal. Carew MSS*, 1515–1574, pp. 435–439.
29 Ibid., p. 436.
30 *Cal. S. P. Ire. 1574–1585*, p. 248.
31 Ibid.
32 M. O'Neill, 'An Leabhar Eoghanach – An Abridged Translation of the Book of the Descendants of Eoghan', *Dúiche Néill*, no. 19, 2011, p. 54.
33 Northern Ireland Sites and Monuments Record (NISMR) ARM-15-13; H. W. Lett, 'Report on Ancient Monuments in the County of Armagh', *The Journal of the Royal Historical and Archaeological Association of Ireland*, Fourth Series, vol. 6, 59, 1884, pp. 431–434.
34 TNA, 'A Generalle Description of Ulster' [1602–3], MPF, 1/35; TNA, Map of the southern part of Ulster, Ireland, showing mountains and woods in perspective, MPF, 1/36.
35 NMM, London, MS P/49(25) [East Part of Ulster]; Audrey Horning suggested the Lane connection to me.
36 NLI, MS 2656 (6), Drawing of Enish Loughan Fort, County Antrim. By Richard Barthelet. *c.*1602.
37 NLI, MS 2656 (11), Drawings of Attacks on Crannogs in Ulster, by Richard Barthelet *c.*1602; C. J. Donnelly, P. Logue, J. O'Neill and J. O'Neill, 'Timber Castles and Towers in Sixteenth-Century Ireland: Some Evidence from Ulster', *Archaeology Ireland*, vol. 21, no. 2, 2007, p. 25.
38 NLI, Drawings of Attacks on Crannogs in Ulster, by Richard Barthelet *c.*1602, MS 2656 (5).
39 J. H. Andrews, *The Queen's Last Map-Maker: Richard Bartlett in Ireland, 1600–03* (Dublin: Geography Publications, 2008), p. 32; G. A. Hayes-McCoy, *Ulster and Other Irish Maps* (Dublin: Irish Manuscripts Commission, 1964), pp. 9–10; A. O'Sullivan, *The Archaeology of Lake Settlement in Ireland* (Dublin: Royal Irish Academy, 1998), p. 173.
40 Moryson, *An Itinerary*, vol. 2, pp. 372–373.
41 Ibid.

42 O'Neill, 'An Leabhar Eoghanach', p. 54.
43 NISMR, ARM-13-28.
44 *Cal. S. P. Ire. 1586–1588*, p. 281; *Cal. S. P. Ire. 1586–1588*, p. 281.
45 *Cal. S. P. Ire. 1586–1588*, p. 51.
46 *Cal. S. P. Ire. 1574–1585*, p. 446.
47 National Monuments Service (Ireland) LH007–115; M. Salter, *The Castles of Leinster* (Malvern: Folly Publications, 2004), p. 109.
48 *Cal. S. P. Ire. 1574–1585*, p. 154.
49 Ibid., p. 247.
50 Connolly, *Contested Island*, p. 228.
51 T. Lee, *The Discovery and Recovery of Ireland with the Author's Apology*, comp. B. Färber and R. Murphy (University College Cork: CELT, 2009) [http://www.ucc.ie/celt/published/E590001–005/index.html]. Accessed 4 June 2013.
52 Lee, *Discovery and Recovery*, ff. 48–49.
53 *Cal. S. P. Ire. 1592–1596*, p. 524.
54 Hayes-McCoy, *Ulster and Other Irish Maps*, p. 8; R. M. Chapple, 'Don't Let it get you Down, it's Only Castles Burning: A History of the Fortifications at Dungannon', *Duiche Néill*, vol. 16, 2007, pp. 96–135.
55 *Cal. S. P. Ire. 1574–1585*, p. 481; *Cal. S. P. Ire. 1574–1585*, p. 570.
56 Ibid., p. 575.
57 Ibid., p. 584.
58 NLI, MS 2656 (5), Drawing of Dungannon Castle and the Stone Chair at Tullaghoge, County Tyrone, by Richard Barthelet. *c.*1602.
59 *Cal. Carew MSS, 1515–1574*, p. 435.
60 *Cal. S. P. Ire. 1601–1603*, p. 415; *Cal. S. P. Ire. 1601–1603*, p. 417.
61 *Cal. S. P. Ire. 1596–1597*, p. 365; Hayes-McCoy, *Ulster and Other Maps*, p. 8.
62 *Cal. S. P. Ire. 1601–1603*, pp. 338–342.
63 Ibid., p. 342.
64 T. Walker, *Documents on Thomas Walker's plot against Tyrone in 1601*, comp. B. Färbertext (University College Cork: CELT, 2010) [http://www.ucc.ie/celt/published/E600001–003/index.html]. Accessed 20 May 2013.
65 Hatfield House, Cecil Papers 88/121–2; Walker, *Documents*.
66 NISMR, TYR-54-28.
67 *Cal. S. P. Ire., 1588–1592*, p. 497.
68 NISMR TYR-17-33.
69 AFM 1325.1.
70 O'Neill, 'An Leabhar Eoghanach', pp. 51–52.
71 AFM 1602.19.
72 C. Devlin, 'The Rise and Fall of a Dynasty: Medieval West Tyrone as Reported in the Annals Source', *Clogher Record*, vol. 16, no. 3, 1999, pp. 75–76.
73 Hayes-McCoy, *Ulster and Other Irish Maps*, p. 20.
74 L. Gernon, *A Discourse of Ireland, anno 1620*, ed. C. Litton Falkiner (University College Cork: CELT, 2007) [http://www.ucc.ie/celt/published/E620001/index.html]. Accessed 20 May 2013.
75 C. J. Donnelly, 'Passage or Barrier? Communication between Bawn and Tower House in Late Medieval Ireland: The Evidence from County Limerick', *Chateau Gaillard*, vol. 21, 2002, pp. 57–64.

76 TCD, 'Deposition of Mourish fitz Gerrald, Concerning the Irish Insurrection in County Limerick, 1642', MSS 829, f. 161v [http://1641.tcd.ie/deposition.php?depID=829161r097].
77 Royal Commission on Historical Manuscripts, *Calendar of the Manuscripts of the Most Honourable the Marquess of Salisbury ... Preserved at Hatfield House, Hertfordshire, Part IX* (London: His Majesty's Stationery Office, 1902), pp. 155–156.
78 C. Mooney, 'The Franciscan Third Order Friary at Dungannon', *Seanchas Ardmhacha: Journal of the Armagh Diocesan Historical Society*, vol. 1, no. 1, 1954, pp. 12–23.
79 NISMR, TYR-54-13
80 NLI, MS 2656 (1), Map of the District Between Dundalk and Newry. By Richard Barthelet *c.*1602, MS 2656 (1); BL, Cotton MS, Aug. I, ii, 37.
81 *Cal. S. P. Ire. 1588–1592*, p. 119.
82 R. Sherlock, 'The Evolution of the Irish Tower-House as a Domestic Space', *Proceedings of the Royal Irish Academy,* vol. 111C, pp. 115–140.
83 A. Murphy, *But the Irish Sea Betwixt Us: Ireland, Colonialism and Renaissance Literature* (Lexington, KY: University Press of Kentucky, 1999), p. 103.
84 Moryson, *An Itinerary*, vol. 2, p. 189.
85 *Cal. S. P. Ire. 1588–1592*, p. 433.
86 Ibid., pp. 565–566.
87 Ibid., p. 446.
88 T. Lee, *Infformacion giuen to Queen Elizabeth against Sir William Fitzwilliams, his gouernmente in Irelande*, comp. B. Hazard (University College Cork: CELT, 2007) [http://www.ucc.ie/celt/published/E590001–002/index.html]. Accessed 15 February 2014.
89 H. O'Sullivan, 'Rothe's Castle, Dundalk and Hugh O'Neill: A Sixteenth-Century Map', *Journal of the County Louth Archaeological Society*, vol. 15, no. 3, 1963, p. 284.
90 Sir J. Harrington, *Nugae Antiquae*, ed. Thomas Park, 2 vols (London: His Majesty's Stationery Office, 1804), vol. 1, p. 248.
91 *Cal. S. P. Ire. 1596–1597*, p. 366.
92 Harrington, *Nugae Antiquae*, vol. 1, p. 248.
93 Ibid., p. 249.
94 W. Lithgow, *Rare Adventures in Ireland in 1619,* comp. R. Murphy (University College Cork: CELT, 2012) [http://www.ucc.ie/celt/published/E610003–001/index.html]. Accessed 13 February 2014.
95 *Cal. S. P. Ire. 1592–1596*, p. 121.
96 Ibid., p. 94; *Cal. S. P. Ire. 1592–1596*, pp. 111–112.
97 E. O'Neill and I. Portela, 'Prince of Ulster or Arch Traitor? The Self-Fashioning of Hugh O'Neill', *Brazilian Journal of Irish Studies*, vol. 2, 2000, p. 91, quoting Stephen Greenblatt, *Renaissance Self-Fashioning: From More to Shakespeare* (Chicago: University of Chicago Press, 1980), pp. 1–2.
98 *Cal. S. P. Ire. 1592–1596*, p. 529.
99 Morgan, *Tyrone's Rebellion*, p. 217.

14. *'Their skill and practise therein far exceeding their wonted usage': The Irish military revolution, 1593–1603*

1 J. M. Hill, 'Gaelic Warfare, 1453–1815', in J. Black (ed.), *European Warfare 1453 1815* (New York: Palgrave Macmillan, 1999), pp. 201–223; M. C. Fissel, *English Warfare, 1511–1642* (London: Psychology Press, 2001), pp. 222–223; R. G. Haycock, 'Review of Celtic Warfare 1595–1763, by James Michael Hill', *Military Affairs*, vol. 51, no. 4, 1987, p. 209; W. E. Lee, 'Indigenes as "Counterinsurgents" in the British Atlantic, 1500–1800', *Defence Studies*, vol. 10, nos 1–2, 2010, p. 88.
2 J. Keegan, *A History of Warfare* (London: Random House, 1993), pp. 11, 27.
3 For an exhaustive discussion on this see C. J. Rogers (ed.), *The Military Revolution Debate: Readings on the Military Transformation of Early-Modern Europe* (Oxford: Westview Press, 1995).
4 T. Bartlett, *The Academy of Warre: Military Affairs in Ireland, 1600 to 1800. The 30th O'Donnell Lecture 2002* (Dublin: National University of Ireland, 2002), p. 9.
5 R. Loeber and G. Parker, 'The Military Revolution in Seventeenth-Century Ireland', in J. Ohlmeyer (ed.), *Ireland from Independence to Occupation 1641–1660* (Cambridge: Cambridge University Press, 1995), p. 71.
6 G. J. Watson, 'Celticisim: Macpherson, Matthew Arnold and Ireland', in S. Ó Síocháin (ed.), *Social Thought on Ireland in the Nineteenth* Century (Dublin: University College Dublin Press, 2009), p. 148.
7 *Irish Soldiers and Poor People* by Albrecht Dürer, 1521, Preußischer Kulturbesitz, Berlin (KdZ 37).
8 Biblioteca Nacional de España (MS Res 285, f. 64v), *Códice de Trajes*, 1547.
9 J. Derricke, *The Image of Irelande with a Discovery of Wood Kerne, Wherein is Most Lively Expressed, the Nature, and Quality of the said Wild Irish Wood Kerne, their Notable Aptness, Celerity, and Proness to Rebellion* (London, 1581).
10 H. Morgan, 'The Messenger in John Derricke's "Image of Irelande" (1581)', *History Ireland*, vol. 15, no. 1, 2007, p. 6.
11 E. Spenser, *A View of the State of Ireland*, ed. A. Hadfield and W. Maley (Oxford: Blackwell, 1997), p. 62.
12 Ibid., p. 62.
13 W. Camden, *Britain, or A Chorographicall Description of the Most Flourishing Kingdomes, England, Scotland, and Ireland, and the Ilands Adioyning, out of the Depth of Antiquitie Beautified Vvith Mappes of the Severall Shires of England: Vvritten First in Latine by William Camden Clarenceux K. of A. Translated Newly into English by Philémon Holland Doctour in Physick: Finally, Revised, Amended, and Enlarged with Sundry Additions by the Said Author*, part 2 (London, 1610), p. 147.
14 K. Simms, 'Images of Warfare in Bardic Poetry', *Celtica*, vol. 21, 1990, p. 612.
15 L. Ó Cléirigh, *The Life of Aodh Ruadh Ó Domhnaill,* ed. and trans. P. Walsh (Dublin: Irish Texts Society, 1948), p. 175.
16 Ibid., p. 177.
17 G. A. Hayes-McCoy, 'History of Guns in Ireland', *Journal of the Galway Archaeological and Historical Society*, vol. 18, 1938, p. 61.

18 D. G. White, 'Henry VIII's Irish Kerne in France and Scotland, 1544–1545', *Irish Sword*, vol. 3, 1958, pp. 213–225.
19 J. M. Hill, 'Shane O'Neill's Campaign Against the MacDonalds of Antrim, 1564–5', *Irish Sword*, vol. 17, 1991, p. 137; G. A. Hayes-McCoy, *Irish Battles: A Military History of Ireland* (Belfast: Appletree Press, 1990), pp. 68–86.
20 One such leader was Florence MacCarthy, who served with Sir William Stanley. When O'Neill's men reached Munster in 1598, MacCarthy's men still fought in the traditional manner. See G. Henry, *The Irish Military Community in Spanish Flanders, 1586–1621* (Dublin: Irish Academic Press, 1992), pp. 120–121; TNA, SP 63/202 pt. 3, f. 297.
21 *Cal. S. P. Ire. 1588–92*, pp. 146–147; TNA, SP 63/143, f. 148.
22 TNA, SP 63/143, f. 41.
23 T. F. Arnold, 'War in Sixteenth-Century Europe: Revolution and Renaissance', in Jeremy Black (ed.), *European Warfare 1453–1815* (New York: Macmillan, 1999), pp. 40–41.
24 BL, Cottonian Augustus I/ii, f. 38. The Battle of the Erne Ford, 10 Oct. 1593, by John Thomas.
25 P. O'Sullivan Beare, *Ireland Under Elizabeth: Chapters Towards a History of Ireland Under Elizabeth*, trans. M. J. Byrne (Dublin: Sealy, Bryers & Walker, 1903), pp. 80–81.
26 TNA, SP 63/180, f. 9.
27 C. G. Cruickshank, *Elizabeth's Army,* 2nd edn (Oxford: Oxford University Press, 1966), pp. 114–115.
28 HHA, C.P. 139/54.
29 *Cal. S.P. Ire., 1599–1600*, pp. 132–133.
30 TNA, SP 63/207 pt 4, f. 9; *Cal. S. P. Ire., 1600*, pp. 182–185. Prohibition of the trade in arms to the native Irish was not new; Perrot had tried to have it stopped but with no lasting effect. See Anon, *The Government of Ireland Under the Honourable, Just and Wise Sir John Perrot* (London, 1626), c.4.
31 *Cal. S. P. Ire., 1592–6*, pp. 203–204.
32 HHA, C.P. 177/131.
33 *Cal. S. P. Ire., 1599–1600*, pp. 462–464.
34 HHA, C.P. 179/74.
35 J. Perrot, *The Chronicle of Ireland 1584–1608*, ed. H. Wood (Dublin: Irish Manuscripts Commission, 1933), p. 161; *Cal. S. P. Ire., 1600–01*, pp. 303–305.
36 J. Smythe, *Certain Discourses Military*, ed. J. R. Hale (Ithaca: Associated University Press, 1964), p. 6.
37 TNA, SP 63/210, f. 192. This manuscript was erroneously dated to 1602 in the Irish calendar, but the Scottish calendars have identified the author as Thomas Douglas and more convincingly dated the letter to 1601. See *Cal. S. P. Scot., 1597–1603, part* 2, pp. 1138–43.
38 M. Sutcliffe, *The Practice and Proceedings and Laws of Armes* (London, 1593), pp. 185–186.
39 R. Barret, *The Theorike and Practike of Moderne Warre* (London, 1598), p. 69.
40 J. Smythe, *Instructions, Observations, and Orders Mylitarie* (London, 1594), pp. 25–26.
41 H. J. Webb, *Elizabethan Military Science: The Books and Practice* (Madison: University of Wisconsin Press, 1965), pp. 89–90.

42 J. X. Evans (ed.), *The Works of Sir Roger Williams* (Oxford: Clarendon, 1972), p. 39.
43 TCD, MS 1209/35, 'The description of the army which was defeated by the earle of Tyrone', 14 August 1598.
44 Cited in G. Parker, *The Army of Flanders and the Spanish Road, 1567–1659*, 2nd edn (Cambridge: Cambridge University Press, 2004), p. 10.
45 TNA, 63/180, f. 66; *Cal. Carew MSS, 1589–1600*, pp. 109–110.
46 TNA, SP 63/199, f. 298.
47 *Cal. S. P. Ire., 1600*, pp. 472–473.
48 Smythe, *Instructions, Observations, and Orders Mylitarie*, pp. 133–141.
49 Parker, *The Army of Flanders and the Spanish Road*, pp. 9–10.
50 C. Oman, *A History of the Art of War in the Sixteenth Century* (New York: AMS Press, 1979).
51 R. Devereux, 2nd Earl of Essex, *An Apology of the Earl of Essex. Against Those which Falsely and Maliciously Tax him to be the Only Hinderer of the Peace and Quiet of his Country* (London, 1603), pp. E1v.
52 Evans, *Sir Roger Williams*, pp. cxliii, 72, 77, 87–88, 93, 109, 111, 113, 137.
53 Smythe, *Certain Discourses Military*, p. 6.
54 Quoted in G. Parker, *The Military Revolution: Military Innovation and the Rise of the West 1500–1800* (New York: Cambridge University Press, 1996), p. 41. This phrase was on the title page of H. Brome, *The Commentaries of Messire Blaize de Montluc, Marshal of France* (London, 1674).
55 R. J. Knecht, *The French Religious Wars 1562–1598* (Oxford: Osprey, 2002), p. 60.
56 H. Drouot, *Mayenne et la Bourgogne* (Paris: Picard, 1937), p. 333.
57 J. Landers, *The Field and the Forge: Population, Production and Power in the Pre-Industrial West* (Oxford: Oxford University Press, 2003), p. 224.
58 C. Falls, *Elizabeth's Irish Wars* (London: Syracuse University Press, 1996), p. 75. Falls erroneously claimed that apart from Yellow Ford (1598), all O'Neill victories were fought in defiles or restricted terrain.
59 T. M. Barker (ed.), *The Military Intellectual and Battle: Raimondo Montecuccoli and the Thirty Years War* (Albany: State University of New York Press, 1975), p. 76.
60 *Cal. S. P. Ire., 1596–1597*, pp. 381–382; A. Fletcher and D. MacCulloch, *Tudor Rebellions*, 4th edn (Harlow: Pearson Educational, 1997), p. 114; Falls, *Elizabeth's Irish Wars*, p. 75.
61 J. McGurk, 'Terrain and Conquest', in Padráig Lenihan (ed.), *Conquest and Resistance: War in Seventeenth-Century Ireland* (Leiden: Brill, 2001), p. 110; B. Lenman, *England's Colonial Wars 1550–1688: Conflicts, Empire and National Identity* (Harlow: Longman, 2001), pp. 112, 115; C. Carlton, *This Seat of Mars: War and the British Isles 1485–1746* (London: Yale University Press, 2010), pp. 48–49.
62 L. L. Doedens, '"The Day the Nation was Born": The Battle of Heiligerlee, 1568', in M. Van der Hoeven (ed.), *Exercise of Arms: Warfare in the Netherlands, 1569–1648* (Leiden: Brill, 1997), pp. 63–64.
63 Oman, *A History of the Art of War in the Sixteenth Century*, pp. 555–558.
64 McGurk, 'Terrain and Conquest 1600–1603', p. 86; D. O'Carroll, 'Change and Continuity in Weapons and Tactics 1594–1691', in P. Lenihan (ed.), *Conquest and Resistance: War in Seventeenth-Century Ireland* (Leiden:

Brill, 2001), p. 225. Eoin Ó Néill attacked some historians' predilection for defining Irish war in battles. He thought this approach was too Clausewitzian and produced a very limited view of the war which obscured the less glamorous aspects of the war, such as logistics or desertion rates. See E. Ó Néill, 'Towards a New Interpretation of the Nine Years' War', *Irish Sword*, vol. 26, 2009, pp. 245–250.

65 Fissel, *English Warfare*, pp. 209, 216.

66 Quoted in B. Heuser, *The Evolution of Strategy: Thinking War from Antiquity to the Present* (Cambridge: Cambridge University Press, 2010), p. 91.

67 B. de Mendoza, *Theorique and Practise of Warre written to Don Philip Prince of Castil,* trans. E. Hoby (Middleburg, 1597), p. 109.

68 W. S. Maltby, *Alba: A Biography of Fernando Alvarez de Toledo, Third Duke of Alba, 1507–1582* (Berkeley: University of California Press, 1983), pp. 177–178.

69 HHA, C.P. 94/26.

70 TNA, SP63/203, f. 349; H. Collier, *The Dialogue of Silvynne and Peregrynne*, transc. H. Morgan (University College Cork: CELT: 2010), [http://www.ucc.ie/celt/published/E590001-001/index.html]. Accessed 16 September 2010; *Cal. S. P. Ire., 1598–1599*, pp. 174–175.

71 Cruickshank, *Elizabeth's Army*, p. 102.

72 Smythe, *Certain Discourses Military*, pp. 81–102.

73 Cruickshank, *Elizabeth's Army*, p. 114.

74 M. C. Paul, 'The Military Revolution in Russia, 1550–1682', *Journal of Military History*, vol. 68, 1, 2004, p. 24.

75 J. H. Keep, *Soldiers of the Tsar: Army and Society in Russia 1462–1874* (Oxford: Clarendon Press, 1985), pp. 80–81.

76 C. Imber, *Ottoman Empire 1300–1650: The Structure of Power* (Basingstoke: Palgrave Macmillan, 2002), pp. 282–283.

77 T. Arnold, *The Renaissance at War* (London: Harper Collins, 2001), pp. 119–120.

78 TNA, SP 63/180, f. 5.

79 *Cal. S. P. Ire., 1596–1597*, pp. 373–377.

80 HHA, C.P. 177/131.

81 *Cal. S. P. Ire., 1599–1600*, pp. 365–370.

82 *Cal. S. P. Ire., 1600–01*, pp. 55–57.

15. *Fugitive identities: Selves, narratives and disregarded lives in early modern Ireland*

1 R. Stanihurst, *Holinshed's Irish Chronicle,* ed. L. Miller and E. E. Power (Dublin: Dolmen Press, 1979), p. 280.

2 D. Edwards, 'The Escalation of Violence in Sixteenth Century Ireland', in D. Edwards, P. Lenihan and C. Tait (eds), *Age of Atrocity: Violence and Political Conflict in Early Modern Ireland* (Dublin: Four Courts Press, 2007), p. 55.

3 S. Heaney, 'Exposure', in *North* (London: Faber, 1975), p. 67. 'Kern' is an anglicisation of '*ceatharnach*', 'mercenary footsoldier'; see K. Simms, *From Kings to Warlords: The Changing Political Structure of Ireland in the Later Middle Ages* (Woodbridge: The Boydell Press, 1987), p. 172 and K. Simms, 'Gaelic Warfare in the Middles Ages', in T. Bartlett and K. Jeffery (eds), *A*

*Military History of Ireland* (Cambridge: Cambridge University Press, 1997), pp. 99–115.

4 Stanihurst, *Irish Chronicle*, pp. 280–281.

5 'Foot-people' is the literal translation of the expressive – and revealing – Irish term 'cosmhuintir' which Ó Dónaill translates as 'hangers-on, followers, dependents ... poor people, proletariat'; in N. Ó Dónaill (ed.), *Foclóir Gaeilge–Béarla* (Baile Átha Cliath: An Gúm, 1977), p. 303.

6 *Cal. Carew MSS, 1575–1588*, p. 144.

7 J. Perrott, *The Chronicle of Ireland, 1584–1608*, ed. H. Wood (Dublin: Irish Manuscripts Commission, 1933), p. 155. Countless others, left entirely nameless, were snuffed out even more unceremoniously. For example, Captain Humphrey Willis records that, within days of Sir Henry Dowcra's arrival in Lough Foyle, soldiers going out to fetch wood, or stragglers who fell behind, were being picked off by the enemy: *Cal. S. P. Ire. 1600*, p. 202.

8 T. Churchyard, *A Generall Rehearsall of Warres* (London: Edward VVhite, 1579), f. iii.v.

9 See P. Palmer, *The Severed Head and the Grafted Tongue: Translating Violence in Early Modern Ireland* (Cambridge: Cambridge University Press, 2014).

10 W. Shakespeare, *The Tragedy of King Lear*, ed. J. L. Halio (Cambridge: Cambridge University Press, 2005), iii.vii.3.

11 *Cal. S. P. Ire. 1598–1599*, p. 102.

12 J. Hooker, 'The Irish Historie Composed and Written by Giraldus Cambrensis, and Translated into English ... Together with the Supplie of the said Historie ... vnto 1587', in R. Holinshed (ed.), *Chronicles of England, Scotland and Ireland*, 6 vols (London: AMS Press, 1807–8), vol. 6, p. 408.

13 *Cal. Carew MSS, 1589–1600*, p. 492. For more on George Carew, see J. Dorsett, 'Sir George Carew: The Study and Conquest of Ireland', Unpublished DPhil Thesis, Oxford, 2000. Hugh O'Donnell, chief of Tír Chonaill, partnered Hugh O'Neill in directing the Nine Years' War (1594–1603).

14 [Thomas Stafford], *Pacata Hibernia: Ireland Appeased and Reduced, or a Historie of the Late Warres of Ireland*, ed. S. H. O'Grady, 2 vols (London: Downey, 1896), vol. 2, p. 327.

15 *Cal. Carew MSS, 1575–88*, p. 226.

16 On Spenser's eighteen years of colonial service in Ireland, see A. Hadfield, *Edmund Spenser: A Life* (Oxford: Oxford University Press, 2012).

17 E. Spenser, *The Faerie Queene*, ed. A. C. Hamilton, 2nd edn (London: Routledge, 2007), p. 291; subsequent references are made parenthetically. On the bleed between the real violence which he witnessed (at Smerwick and elsewhere) and the fictionalised violence against women in *The Faerie Queene*, see Palmer, *The Severed Head*, pp. 66–99.

18 R. Berleth, *The Twilight Lords* (New York: Barnes & Noble, 1978), p. 94; Edwards, *Age of Atrocity*, p. 71. In implicit recognition of the problem, Mountjoy's Army Orders made rape a crime punishable by death, *Cal. Carew MSS, 1589–1600*, p. 503. On the larger question of violence against women in wartime, see E. Heineman (ed.), *Sexual Violence in Conflict Zones: From the Ancient World to the Era of Human Rights* (Philadelphia: University of Pennsylvania Press, 2011).

19 See J. Catty, *Writing Rape, Writing Women in Early Modern England* (Basingstoke: Palgrave Macmillan, 2011), pp. 74–90.
20 F. Moryson, *An History of Ireland, from the Year 1599–1603*, 2 vols (Dublin: George Ewing, 1735), vol. 2, p. 283.
21 *Cailleach* is Irish for 'old woman' or 'hag'; cf. 'calliops' below.
22 See C. Falls, *Elizabeth's Irish Wars* (London: Syracuse University Press, 1950), p. 277, and B. Kiernan, *Blood and Soil: A World History of Genocidal Extermination from Sparta to Darfur* (New Haven, CT: Yale University Press, 2007), p. 210.
23 C. Litton Falkiner (ed.), 'William Farmer's Chronicles of Ireland', *The English Historical Review*, vol. 87, 1907, p. 548.
24 E. Donoghue, *Astray* (London: Pan Macmillan, 2012), p. 72.
25 *Cal. S. P. Ire. 1592–1596*, p. 181.
26 *Cal. S. P. Ire. 1600*, pp. 383–384.
27 William Pinkerton, 'The "Overthrow" of Sir John Chichester at Carrickfergus in 1597', *Ulster Journal of Archaeology*, vol. 5, 1857, p. 194.
28 Perrott, *Chronicle of Ireland*, p. 47.
29 Hooker, 'Irish Historie', vol. 6, p. 431.
30 *Cal. S. P. Ire. 1599–1600*, p. 36.
31 On 'representations' of the Irish, see J. T. Leerssen, *Mere Irish and Fíor-Ghael* (Cork: Cork University Press, 1996); B. Bradshaw, A. Hadfield and W. Maley (eds), *Representing Ireland: Literature and the Origins of the Conflict, 1534–1660* (Cambridge: Cambridge University Press, 1993); E. M. Hinton, *Ireland through Tudor Eyes* (Philadelphia: University of Pennsylvania Press, 1935); P. Palmer, '"Hungry Eyes" and the Rhetoric of Dispossession: English Writing from Early-Modern Ireland', in J. Wright (ed.), *The Blackwell Companion to Irish Literature*, 2 vols (Oxford: Wiley-Blackwell, 2010), vol. 1, pp. 92–107. By the end of the Nine Years' War, Londoners would find themselves 'exceedingly pestered with a multitude of beggars', Irish refugees who were proving to be 'a great eyesore and burden' throughout the capital; see *Cal. S. P. Ire. 1606–1608*, p. 462.
32 *Cal. Carew MSS, 1601–1603*, p. 259; on St Leger and Cahir McArt Kavanagh's machinations against the more senior branch of the Kavanaghs, see E. O'Byrne, 'The Tudor State and the Irish of East Leinster', in M. Potterton and T. Herron (eds), *Dublin and the Pale in the Renaissance c.1540–1660* (Dublin: Four Courts Press, 2011), p. 87.
33 L. Berlant, *Cruel Optimism* (Durham , NC: Duke University Press, 2011), p. 54.
34 Ibid., p. 16.
35 Ibid., p. 5.
36 Ibid., p. 6.
37 Ibid., p. 59.
38 Ibid., p. 67.
39 G. C. Spivak, 'Can the Subaltern Speak?', in R. C. Morris (ed.), *Can the Subaltern Speak? Reflections on the History of an Idea* (New York: Columbia University Press, 2010), p. 21.
40 Ibid., pp. 41, 45.
41 AFM 1580.19.

42 Hooker, 'Irish Historie', vol. 6, pp. 459–460.
43 A. Woloch, *The One vs. the Many: Minor Characters and the Space of the Protagonist in the Novel* (Princeton, NJ: Princeton University Press, 2003), p. 7.
44 Ibid.
45 Moryson, *An History of Ireland,* vol. 1, p. 317.
46 H. Morgan (ed.), 'A Booke of Questions and Answars Concerning the Warrs or Rebellions of the Kingdome of Irelande', *Analecta Hibernica*, vol. 36, 1995, pp. 106–107.
47 *Cal. S. P. Ire. 1598–1599*, p. 53. On the perceived unreliability of bilinguals, see P. Palmer, 'False and Unreliable Interpreters in Sixteenth-Century Ireland', *Irish Historical Studies*, vol. 33, no. 131, 2004, pp. 257–277.
48 *Cal. S. P. Ire. 1600*, pp. 167, 181, 364. As a spymaster, Fenton bustled about in a world of codenames and false identities. He complains that his 'three intelligencers' in Ulster have cost £44.15d from his own pocket. One is a soldier in Tyrone's camp, the second, codenamed Fr Jarkey, is a priest in Dungannon while the third, 'an intelligencer whom I have long time employed in Ulster', is known only as 'PW'. He refers to a Palesman who speaks Spanish and French as his 'Spanish' spy: his 'prymire' education taught him 'some insight' into Latin; he 'knoweth to use his pen in two or three manner of hands' and had been a soldier in Spain for four or five years before returning with Bishop Mateo. *Cal. S. P. Ire. 1599–1600*, pp. 387–388; *Cal. S. P. Ire. 1600*, pp. 169, 365; *Cal. S. P. Ire. 1601–1603*, p. 492.
49 V. Groebner, *Who Are You? Identification, Deception and Surveillance in Early Modern Europe*, trans. M. Kyburz and J. Peck (New York: Zone Books, 2007), p. 29.
50 C. Litton Falkiner (ed.), 'Travels of Sir William Brereton in Ireland', in *Illustrations of Irish History and Topography* (London: Longmans, Green & Co., 1904), p. 386.
51 On the practice of keening (*caoineadh*), see A. O'Connor, 'Keening', in B. Lalor (ed.), *The Encyclopaedia of Ireland* (Dublin: Gill & Macmillan, 2003), p. 579.
52 E. Spenser, *A View of the Present State of Ireland*, ed. A. Hadfield and W. Maley (Oxford: Blackwell, 1997), p. 56.
53 *Cal. Carew MSS, 1601–1603*, p. 192. See A. R. Jones and P. Stallybrass, 'Dismantling Irena: The Sexualising of Ireland in Early Modern England', in A. Parker et al. (eds), *Nationalisms and Sexualities* (New York: Routledge, 1992), pp. 157–171.
54 Groebner, *Who Are You?*, p. 26.
55 *Cal. Carew MSS, 1575–1588*, p. 276.
56 *Cal. S. P. Ire. 1600–1601*, p. 21.
57 *Cal. S. P. Ire. 1588–1592*, p. 305. Fitzwilliam himself discounted the charge that he had knocked a man called Legge senseless 'and struck two of his best teeth out of his head', though he does concede that, 'having seven or eight sheets of paper, holding them longways in my hand … I did so lift up his nose with them as I think the gristle of [it] ached with it, and sure I am it bled' (*Cal. Carew MSS, 1589–1600*, p. 57).
58 M. Schoenfeld, *Bodies and Selves in Early Modern England: Physiology and Inwardness in Spenser, Shakespeare, Herbert, and Milton* (Cambridge: Cambridge University Press, 1999).

59 On early modern notions of selfhood, see P. Burke, 'Representations of the Self from Petrarch to Descartes', and J. Sawday, 'Self and Selfhood in the Seventeenth Century', in R. Porter (ed.), *Rewriting the Self: Histories from the Renaissance to the Present* (London: Routledge, 1997), pp. 17–48.
60 Schoenfeld, *Bodies and Selves*, pp. 11–12.
61 For the *loss* of 'self-control' which the exercise of such 'authority' could entail, see, for example, W. Maley, 'Something Quite Atrocious: English Colonialism beyond the Pale and the Licence to Violence', *Eolas: Journal of the American Society of Irish Mediaeval Studies*, vol. 3, 2009, pp. 82–111.
62 Groebner, *Who Are You?*, p. 26.
63 S. B. Iwanisziw, 'Hugh O'Neill and National Identity in Early Modern Ireland', in D. V. Valone and J. Marie Bradbury (eds), *Anglo-Irish Identities, 1571–1845* (Lewisburg: Bucknell University Press, 2008), p. 31.
64 See, for example, M. Mac Craith, 'Gaelic Ireland and the Renaissance', in G. Williams and R. O. Jones (eds), *The Celts and the Renaissance* (Cardiff: University of Wales Press, 1990), pp. 57–89.
65 See B. Ó Buachalla, *Aisling Ghéar: Na Stíobhartaigh agus an tAos Léinn 1603–1788* (Baile Átha Cliath: Clóchomhar Tta., 1996), and S. McKibben, *Endangered Masculinities in Irish Poetry 1540–1780* (Dublin: University College Dublin Press, 2010).
66 P. Woulfe, in *Sloinnte Gaedhal is Gall: Irish Names and Surnames* (Dublin: M. H. Gill, 1922), p. 414 describes Mac Uilliméid as 'an old, but rare Westmeath surname'. On the wider issue of linguistic colonisation and misnaming, see P. Palmer, *Language and Conquest in Early Modern Ireland: English Renaissance Literature and Elizabethan Imperial Expansion* (Cambridge: Cambridge University Press, 2001).
67 *Cal. S. P. Ire. 1599–1600*, p. 109.

16. *Popular politics and the legitimacy of power in early modern Ireland*

1 E. Shagan, *Popular Politics and the English Reformation* (Cambridge: Cambridge University Press, 2002), pp. 19.
2 This is a preliminary exploration of what I hope will be a longer study, one that will assess more closely the distinctions between the politics and agency of those below the level of the nobility. For present purposes, however, I take a fairly broad definition of 'non-elite' and do so for two reasons. First, that political action by those from the gentry on down in the Irish social hierarchy has received very little attention, and thus I wish to suggest ways in which it might be pursued and to what ends. Second, and as will be seen in some of the evidence cited below, English commentators seem to have been in the habit of considering all those below the level of the aristocracy – that is, those possessing a level of authority that was a rival to state centralisation – as the 'people'.
3 See, for instance, D. Edwards, P. Lenihan and C. Tait (eds), *Age of Atrocity: Violence and Political Conflict in Early Modern Ireland* (Dublin: Four Courts Press, 2007), p. 29. Insightful comments on the prevalence, and at times constraining effects, of a focus on resistance, especially as concerns the application to the early modern of the theories of James Scott, are made in A. Shepard, 'Review of M.J. Braddick and J. Walter (eds), *Negotiating Power in Early Modern Society: Order, Hierarchy and Subordination in*

*Britain and Ireland'*, H-Albion, H-Net Reviews, November, 2002 [http://networks.h-net.org/node/16749/reviews/17727/shepard-braddick-and-walter-negotiating-power-early-modern-society] Accessed 13 September 2017. Applications of Scott's theories can be found, for instance, in C. Tait, 'Disorder and Commotion: Urban Riots and Popular Protest in Ireland, 1570–1640', in W. Sheehan and M. Cronin (eds), *Riotous Assemblies: Rebels, Riots and Revolts in Ireland* (Cork: Mercier Press, 2011), pp. 22–49. I wish to thank Dr Tait for bringing this article to my attention; it is the most detailed and sophisticated discussion of non-elite politicised action. Here I wish to build upon her focus on riots and crowd action as a form of protest against Tudor/Stuart state authority and consider how one effect of 'becoming and belonging' was that Irish non-elites could act politically in a loyal register and, more abstractly, were forming a sense of political identity that complemented the practice of politics seen in crowd action. Moreover, I am interested in the *longue durée* matter of why there is no evidence of popular politics before this period and, thus, why it seems to emerge when it does.

4 For an initial exploration of the politics of legitimacy in post-Flight of the Earls Ireland see B. Kane, 'Languages of Legitimacy? *An Ghaeilge*, the Earl of Thomond and British Politics in the Renaissance Pale, 1600–24', in M. Potterton and T. Herron (eds), *Dublin and the Pale in the Renaissance, c.1540–1660* (Dublin: Four Courts Press, 2011), pp. 267–279.

5 I would argue that this characterises both studies that focus on cooperation, for instance C. Brady, *The Chief Governors: The Rise and Fall of Reform Government in Tudor Ireland, 1536–1588* (Cambridge: Cambridge University Press, 2002), and those concerned with coercion, such as N. Canny, *The Elizabethan Conquest of Ireland: A Pattern Established* (London: Barnes & Noble Books, 1976). On this point see B. Kane, *The Politics and Culture of Honour, 1541–1641* (Cambridge: Cambridge University Press, 2010), Chapter 1; A. Horning, *Ireland in the Virginian Sea: Colonialism in the British Atlantic* (Chapel Hill: The University of North Carolina Press, 2013), Introduction and Chapter 1.

6 Within a large literature on this subject, essential starting points are Canny, *The Elizabethan Conquest* and Edwards, et al. (eds), *Age of Atrocity*.

7 For an example of striking such balance, see Raymond Gillespie, 'Negotiating Order in Early Seventeenth-Century Ireland', in Michael J. Braddick and John Walter (eds), *Negotiating Power in Early Modern Society: Order, Hierarchy and Subordination in Britain and Ireland* (Cambridge: Cambridge University Press, 2001). For debates over the issue of such 'balance' see, for instance, the disagreements revealed in D. Edwards, 'The Escalation of Violence in Sixteenth Century Ireland', in Edwards et al. (eds), *Age of Atrocity*, pp. 34–78 and the reviews of the same by J. Crawford in *The Sixteenth Century Journal*, vol. 40, no. 3, 2009, pp. 929–931 and P. Little in *The English Historical Review*, vol. 74, no. 508, 2009, pp. 708–710.

8 Kane, *The Politics and Culture of Honour*. It should be noted that I do not wish to claim that non-elites were unaware of high political questions and played no role in debates surrounding them. Quite the opposite, I wish to demonstrate that they were increasingly sophisticated in their political

awareness, but that their political voice was one expressed outside corridors of power such as parliaments and privy chambers. Ideally, high and low politics, struggles over *de jure* and *de facto* power, should be seen as interconnected phenomena.

9 E. Shagan, 'Protector Somerset and the 1549 Rebellions: New Sources and New Perspectives', *English Historical Review*, vol. 114, 1999, pp. 34–63.

10 A. Wood, *The 1549 Rebellions and the Making of Early Modern England* (Cambridge: Cambridge University Press, 2007).

11 K. Kesselring, *The Northern Rebellion of 1569: Faith, Politics, and Protest in Elizabethan England* (Basingstoke: Palgrave Macmillan, 2007); J. Walter, *Understanding Popular Violence in the English Revolution: The Colchester Plunderers* (Cambridge: Cambridge University Press, 1999); T. Harris, *London Crowds in the Reign of Charles II: Propaganda and Politics from the Restoration until the Exclusion Crisis* (Cambridge: Cambridge University Press, 1990).

12 The examples that do exist are quite recent, and include, prominently, Gillespie, 'Negotiating Order'; Tait, 'Disorder and Commotion' and M. Empey, '"We Are Not Safe for They Threaten Us with More Violence": A Study of the Cook Street Riot, 1629', in Sheehan and Cronin (eds), *Riotous Assemblies*, pp. 64–79.

13 I wish to thank Liam Breatnach for discussion of this point relative to the evidence of Old Irish materials.

14 The great exception would seem to be the literature on the 1641 Rising, which is much concerned with the 'popular rebellion' aspect of the conflict. Nevertheless, the motivation is characterised as product of colonial dislocation and religious change, and not as expression of an ingrained and developed sense of plebeian political 'right' or expectation. For suggestive comments on this point see, J. Walter, 'Performative Violence and the Politics of Violence in the 1641 Depositions', in J. Ohlmeyer and M. Ó Siochrú (eds), *Ireland, 1641: Contexts and Reactions* (Manchester: Manchester University Press, 2013), pp. 134–152.

15 *Cal. S.P. Ire. 1509–1573*, p. 193.

16 M. Kishlansky, *Parliamentary Selection: Social and Political Choice in Early Modern England* (Cambridge: Cambridge University Press, 1986), p. 15.

17 M. O'Dowd (ed.), *Calendar of State Papers, Ireland, Tudor period 1571–1575* (Kew: Irish Manuscripts Commission, 2000), p. 176.

18 O'Dowd *CSPI 1571–1575*, p. 214.

19 Lambeth Palace Library, Carew Ms. v. 626: f. 93r.

20 N. J. A. Williams (ed. and trans.), *Pairlement Chloinne Tomáis* (Dublin: Institute for Advanced Studies, 1981), p. 75.

21 For discussion of some examples, see Kane, *The Politics and Culture of Honour*, pp. 146–158 and M. Caball, 'Culture, Continuity and Change in Early Seventeenth-Century South-West Munster', *Studia Hibernica*, vol. 38, 2013, pp. 37–56.

22 An excellent example of study of survival strategy is J. Cope, 'The Experience of Survival during the 1641 Irish Rebellion', *The Historical Journal*, vol. 46, no. 2, 2003, pp. 295–316. Nevertheless, our understanding of survival strategies is undeveloped and demands greater attention. On this point see Horning, *Ireland in the Virginian Sea*, p. 31.

23 T. Stretton, 'Written Obligations, Litigation and Neighbourliness, 1580–1680', in S. Hindle, A. Shepard and J. Walter (eds), *Remaking English Society: Social Relations and Social Change in Early Modern England* (Woodbridge: The Boydell Press, 2013), p. 189.
24 'Ar feadh fichid groidthéarma/go hÁth Cliath leis go scíosmhar/do-chuaidh mise ar boidéarma/'s gan liom acht *nisi prius*'. N. Williams (ed.), *Dánta Mhuiris Mhic Dháibhí Dhuibh Mhic Ghearailt* (Dublin: Clóchomhar, 1979) p. 53.
25 Cecile O'Rahilly, *Five Seventeenth-Century Political Poems* (Dublin: Institute for Advanced Studies, 1977), pp. 8–9.
26 NAI, Chancery Bills, G. 68: 13.
27 NAI, Chancery Bills, H. 18.
28 NAI, Chancery Bills, F. 38: 7–8; C. 98: 13–14.
29 NAI, Chancery Bills, D 19: 3–4.
30 C. Maginn, *William Cecil, Ireland, and the Tudor State* (Oxford: Oxford University Press, 2012), p. 203.
31 Captain Thomas Lee, 'Infformacion Giuen to Queen Elizabeth Against Sir William Fitzwilliam, his Gouernmente in Ireland' (Corpus of Electronic Texts, Cork), ff. 260v–261r.
32 Captain T. Lee, 'A Brief Declaration of the Government of Ireland,' in J. Curry (ed.), *An Historical and Critical Review of the Civil Wars in Ireland* (Dublin: R. Conolly, 1810), p. 607.
33 NIA, E 246: 39–40.
34 See for instance William Weston's complaints of financial corruption, Bodleian Library, Oxford, Ms Bankes 18/14 f. 22, 41/51 f. 101, and 42/77 f. 157. On Loftus's struggles with Wentworth, see Kane, *Politics and Culture of Honour*, Chapter 7.
35 Tait, 'Disorder and Commotion'.
36 See, for instance, Anthony McCormick's masterful recounting of the rebellion in his *The Earldom of Desmond, 1463–1583: The Decline and Crisis of a Feudal Lordship* (Dublin: Four Courts Press, 2005), pp. 145–192. It is noteworthy how recent this comprehensive treatment of the rebellion is, the point being that we are only just now working through the high political tale in Ireland. Nevertheless, the call here is to build on the work of McCormick and others in the interest of expanding our understanding of the period.
37 M. Ó Siochrú, 'Propaganda, Rumour and Myth: Oliver Cromwell and the Massacre at Drogheda', in Edwards et al. (eds), *Age of Atrocity*, pp. 266–282. However, it should be pointed out that paranoia on the part of the regime regarding rumours spread amongst the plebs was a characteristic of domestic governance, too. See, for instance, Wood, *The 1549 Rebellions*.
38 O'Dowd (ed.), *CSPI 1571–1575*, p. 184.
39 *Cal. S.P. Ire. 1603–1606*, p. 6.
40 O'Dowd (ed.), *CSPI 1571–1575*, p. 240.
41 Generally on the politics of concentrated state efforts to eliminate the language and its elite practitioners, see P. Palmer, *Language and Conquest in Early Modern Ireland* (Cambridge: Cambridge University Press, 2001).
42 Exeter College, Oxford, Ms 154, f. 57 v.

43 R. McLaughlin, 'A Threat of Satire by Tadhg (Mac Dáire) Mac Bruaideadha', *Ériu*, vol. 55, 2005, pp. 37–57, and for the medieval context, R. McLaughlin, *Early Irish Satire* (Dublin: Institute for Advanced Studies, 2008).
44 *Cal. S.P. Ire. 1603–1606*, p. 19.
45 Ibid.
46 Ibid., p. 22.
47 T. Wentworth, Earl of Strafford, *The Letters and Dispatches of the Earl of Strafforde*, ed. W. Knowler, 2 vols (London: printed for the editor, by William Bowyer, 1739), vol. 2, p. 161.
48 Audrey Horning's observation regarding private versus state administration of colonial efforts is particularly relevant here: 'In contrast to the Roanoke effort and the abortive Ulster Plantations of the 1570s, and perhaps in recognition of the reasons behind their failure, the Munster Plantation was to be directed by the government rather than established and administered via private speculation.' Horning, *Ireland in the Virginian Sea*, p. 85. The crucial point for present purposes is that different forms and modes of colonial organisation can spur rather different forms and modes of political thought and action, or at least allow 'private' disagreements to be expressed in the language of macro politics. For examples of local quarrels being the occasions within which state politics and political theory could penetrate into non-elite politicking and mentalities, see Shagan, *Popular Politics*, p. 24.
49 O'Dowd *CSPI 1571–1575*, p. 120.
50 *Cal. Carew MSS, 1589–1600*, p. 273.
51 The classic study remains N. Canny, 'What Really Happened in Ireland in 1641?', in J. Ohlmeyer (ed.), *Ireland: From Independence to Occupation, 1641–1660* (Cambridge: Cambridge University Press, 1995), pp. 24–42.
52 See, for instance, Cope, 'The Experience of Survival During the 1641 Irish Rebellion'.
53 TCD, Ms 813, Deposition of William Vowells, f. 330.
54 TCD, Ms 813, Deposition of Hugh Cullen, f. 78b.
55 University College Dublin (UCD), Ó Cléirigh Institute Ms D 2, v. I, p. 54. I wish to thank Seamus Helferty for providing me copies of these documents, and for the faculty of the Ó Cléirigh Institute for the generous opportunity to make use of the vast, and still underutilised, Franciscan collection housed at UCD.
56 Ibid., pp. 63, 67.
57 P. J. Campbell, 'The Franciscan Petition Lists: Diocese of Armagh, 1670–1', *Seanchas Ardmhacha: Journal of the Armagh Diocesan Historical Society*, vol. 15, no. 1, 1992, p. 192.
58 The study of popular politics in Ireland, then, is more than the migration of a historiographical approach to a new setting, more than doing for Ireland what historians have done for England and continental polities. Rather, it is both historiographical intervention and investigation of a, perhaps, unique *historical* problem: the seeming absence of large-scale political action by non-elites in Europe, where otherwise it was quite common, and its rapid emergence and development.
59 In a large historiography, useful starting points include J. Donnelly and S. Clark (eds), *Irish Peasants: Violence and Political Unrest, 1780–1914* (Madison: University of Wisconsin Press, 1983) and J. Smyth, *The Men of*

*No Property: Irish Radicals and Popular Politics in the Late 18th Century* (Dublin: Palgrave Macmillan, 1992), and for the international influence, M. J. Bric, 'The United Irishmen, International Republicanism and the Definition of the Polity in the United States of America, 1791–1800', *Proceedings of the Royal Irish Academy*, vol. 104C, 2004, pp. 81–106.

60 In Fergus O'Ferrall's slightly grandiose phrasing, 'Catholic Emancipation inaugurated the liberal democratic era', F. O'Ferrall, *Catholic Emancipation: Daniel O'Connell and the Birth of Irish Democracy, 1820–30* (Dublin: Gill & Macmillan, 1985), p. 273. For a compelling case for the temperance movement's influence on modern mass politics, see P. Townend, *Father Mathew, Temperance, and Irish Identity, 1838–1848* (Dublin: Irish Academic Press, 2002). A recent, troublesome reminder of boycotting's legacy and its complicated moral dimensions can be found in Paul Berman, who expressly notes the Irish origins of this modern form of ostracism: 'Scar of David', *The Chronicle Review*, 7 November 2014, B14–B16.

*Glossary*

1 K. Nicholls, *Gaelic and Gaelicized Ireland in the Middle Ages* (Dublin: Lilliput Press, 1972), pp. 185–186; K. Simms, *From Kings to Warlords: The Changing Political Structure of Gaelic Ireland in the Later Middle Ages* (Woodbridge: The Boydell Press, 1987), p. 170; L. McInerney, *Clerical and Learned Lineages of Medieval Co. Clare: A Survey of the Fifteenth-Century Papal Registers* (Dublin: Four Courts Press, 2014), p. 295.

2 É. Ó Doibhlin, 'Ceart Uí Néill: A Discussion and Translation of the Document', *Seanchas Ardmhacha: Journal of the Armagh Diocesan Historical Society*, vol. 5, no. 2, 1970, pp. 328, 331.

3 Simms, *From Kings to Warlords*, pp. 92, 176.

4 P. J. Duffy, 'Social and Spatial Order in the MacMahon Lordship of Airghialla', in P. J. Duffy, D. Edwards and E. FitzPatrick (eds), *Gaelic Ireland c.1250–1650: Land, Lordship and Settlement* (Dublin: Four Courts Press, 2001), pp. 128–134; P. MacCotter, *Medieval Ireland: Territorial, Political and Economic Divisions* (Dublin: Four Courts Press, 2008), pp. 23–24.

5 T. McErlean, 'The Irish Townland System of Landscape Organisation', in T. Reeves-Smyth and F. Hammond (eds), *Landscape Archaeology in Ireland*, British Archaeological Reports, 116 (Oxford, 1983), pp. 315–339.

6 M. Watson and M. McLeod (eds), *Edinburgh Companion to the Gaelic Language* (Edinburg: Edinburgh University Press, 2010) p. 7.

7 E. G. Quin (ed.), *Dictionary of the Irish Language: Based Mainly on Old and Middle Irish Materials*, Compact Edition (Dublin: Royal Irish Academy, 1990), p. 81.

8 Simms, *From Kings to Warlords*, p. 171.

9 G. Ó Crualaoich, *The Book of the Cailleach* (Cork: Cork University Press, 2007).

10 E. FitzPatrick, 'Native Enclosed Settlement and the Problem of the "Irish Ringfort"', *Medieval Archaeology*, vol. 53, 2009, pp. 271–307 at pp. 274–275.

11 An Roinn Oideachais, *Gearrfhoclóir Gaeilge–Béarla* (Dublin: Rialtais na hÉireann, 1981), p. 102.

12 K. Simms, 'Nomadry in Medieval Ireland: The Origins of the Creaght or *Caoraigheacht*', *Peritia*, vol. 5, 1986, pp. 379–391.
13 Simms, *From Kings to Warlords*, pp. 125–126.
14 Quin (ed.), *Dictionary of the Irish Language*, pp. 124, 257.
15 Nicholls, *Gaelic and Gaelicized Ireland*, p. 185.
16 Simms, *From Kings to Warlords*, p. 173; McInerney, *Clerical and Learned Lineages*, p. 297.
17 An Roinn Oideachais, *Gearrfhoclóir*, p. 168.
18 A. O'Sullivan, 'Crannogs in Late Medieval Gaelic Ireland, *c.*1350–*c.*1650', in Duffy, Edwards and FitzPatrick (eds) *Gaelic Ireland*, p. 397.
19 A. T. Lucas, *Cattle in Ancient Ireland* (Kilkenny: Boethius Press, 1989) p. 146.
20 An Roinn Oideachais, *Gearrfhoclóir*, p. 176.
21 Nicholls, *Gaelic and Gaelicized Ireland*, pp. 26–27.
22 K. McCone, 'The Celtic and Indo-European Origins of the *Fían*', in S. H. Arbuthnot and G. Parsons (eds), *The Gaelic Finn Tradition* (Dublin: Four Courts Press, 2012), pp. 14–30 at pp. 20–22.
23 N. Ó Muraíle, 'Dinnshenchas', in S. Duffy (ed.), *Medieval Ireland: An Encyclopedia* (New York and London: Routledge, 2005), pp. 132–133.
24 K. Simms, 'Duanairí', in Duffy (ed.), *Medieval Ireland*, pp. 134–135.
25 E. FitzPatrick, '*Formaoil na Fiann*: Hunting Preserves and Assembly Places in Gaelic Ireland', in D. Furchtgott, G. Henley and M. Holmberg (eds), *Proceedings of the Harvard Celtic Colloquium*, vol. 32 (Harvard: Harvard University Press, 2013), pp. 95–118 at pp. 113–116.
26 Simms, *From Kings to Warlords*, p. 174.
27 K. Murray, 'Fenian Cycle', in Duffy (ed.), *Medieval Ireland*, p. 166.
28 Simms, *From Kings to Warlords*, pp. 172, 175.
29 D. McGettigan, 'MacSweeney', in Duffy (ed.), *Medieval Ireland*, pp. 305–307.
30 F. Fitzsimons, 'Fosterage and Gossiprid in Late Medieval Ireland: Some New Evidence', in Duffy, Edwards and FitzPatrick (eds) *Gaelic Ireland*, pp. 138–149 at p. 143.
31 K. O'Conor, *The Archaeology of Medieval Rural Settlement in Ireland* (Dublin: Discovery Programme and Royal Irish Academy, 1998), p. 82.
32 F. Kelly, *A Guide to Early Irish Law* (Dublin: Institute for Advanced Studies, 1988), pp. 57–59.
33 Simms, *From Kings to Warlords*, p. 176.
34 Ibid.
35 For an account of the *meadar*, see E. Gray, 'Material Culture of High-status Drinking Ritual in Medieval and Early Modern Gaelic Ireland', Unpublished PhD Thesis, National University of Ireland, Galway, 2016.
36 Simms, *From Kings to Warlords*, p. 176.
37 E. FitzPatrick, 'The Last Kings of Ireland: Material Expressions of Gaelic Lordship *c.*1300–1400 AD', in K. Buchanan, L. H. S. Dean and M. Penman (eds), *Medieval and Early Modern Representations of Authority in Scotland and the British Isles* (Routledge: Oxford, 2016), pp. 197–213 at pp. 201–209.
38 Simms, *From Kings to Warlords*, p. 177.
39 FitzPatrick, 'Native Enclosed Settlement', p. 273.

40 Simms, *From Kings to Warlords*, p. 177.
41 Simms, 'Bardic Schools, Learned Families', in Duffy (ed.), *Medieval Ireland*, p. 36.
42 E. Rynne, 'Three Irish Knife-daggers (from Mayo)', *Journal of the Royal Society of Antiquaries of Ireland*, vol. 99, part 2, 1969, pp. 137–143.
43 Quin (ed.), *Dictionary of the Irish Language*, p. 390.
44 Ibid., p. 581.
45 Nicholls, *Gaelic and Gaelicized Ireland*, p. 187.
46 Simms, *From Kings to Warlords*, p. 178.
47 Ibid., p. 82.
48 An Roinn Oideachais, *Gearrfhoclóir*, p. 782.
49 MacCotter, *Medieval Ireland*, p. 22.
50 Quin (ed.), *Dictionary of the Irish Language*, p. 608; P. Durkin, *Borrowed Words: A History of Loanwords in English* (Oxford: Oxford University Press, 2014), p. 93.
51 MacCotter, *Medieval Ireland* pp. 22–23.

# Bibliography


Abraham, K., 'Upward Mobility in Later Medieval Meath', *History Ireland*, vol. 5, no. 4, 1997, pp. 15–20.

Agnew, J., 'No Borders, No Nations: Making Greece in Macedonia', *Annals of the Association of American Geographers*, vol. 97, no. 2, 2007, pp. 398–422.

Ainsworth, J. F. and E. Mac Lysaght, 'Survey of Documents in Private Keeping, Second Series', *Analecta Hibernica*, vol. 20, 1958, pp. 1, 3–361, 363–393.

Airs, M., 'Architecture, Politics and Society', in R. Tittler (ed.), *A Companion to Tudor Britain* (Oxford: Blackwell, 2004), pp. 470–491.

Allingham, H. (ed.), *Captain Cuellar's Adventures* (London: Elliot Stock, 1897).

Alonso Gonzalez, J. M., *Los Molinos Tradicionales en la Provincia de Léon* (Léon: Leonesas, 1993).

Amouric, H., 'L'Anille et les Meules', in D. Meeks and D. Garcia (eds), *Techniques et Économies Antiques et Médiévales, le Temps de l'Innovation, Colloque d'Aix en Provence* (Paris: Travaux du Centre Camille, 1996), pp. 33–47.

Andersen, T. J., T. Grenn and J. M. Fernández Soler, 'Volcanic Quern and Millstone Quarries in Cabo de Gata (Almería) and Campo de Calatrava (Ciudad Real), Spain', in D. Williams and D. Peacock (eds), *Bread for the People: The Archaeology of Mills and Milling*, British Archaeological Report, International Series, 2274 (Oxford: Archaeopress, 2011), pp. 151–167.

Andrews, J. H., 'The Irish Surveys of Robert Lythe', *Imago Mundi*, vol. 19, 1965, pp. 22–31.

Andrews, J. H., *The Queen's Last Map-Maker: Richard Bartlett in Ireland, 1600–03* (Dublin: Geography Publications, 2008).

Anon., *Historical Sketch of the Nugent Family* (Ledestown: John Charles Lyons, 1853).

Anon., *The Government of Ireland Under the Honourable, Just and Wise Sir John Perrot Knight, One of the Privy Council to Queen Elizabeth, Beginning 1584, and Ending 1588* (London, 1626).

An Roinn Oideachais, *Gearrfhoclóir Gaeilge–Béarla* (Dublin: Rialtas na hÉireann, 1981).

Appleby, J. C., *A Calendar of Material Relating to Ireland: From the High Court of Admiralty Examinations, 1536–1641* (Dublin: Irish Manuscripts Commission, 1992).

Archdall, M., *Monasticon Hibernicum: or a History of the Abbeys, Priories and Other Religious Houses in Ireland*, ed. P. F. Moran, 3 vols (Dublin: W. B. Kelly, 1876).

Arnau, B. and J. Martí, 'Aigua i Desenvoluament Urbà a Madinat Balansiya (València): L'Excavació d'un Molí Hidràulic de l'Època Califal', in T. F. Glick and E. Guinot (eds), *Els Molins Hidràulics Valencians: Tecnologia, Història i Context Social* (Valencia: Institución Alfons el Magnànim de la Diputación de Valencia, 2000), pp. 165–192.

Arnold, R., *Customs of London* (Antwerp: A. Van Berghen, 1503).

Arnold, T. F., 'War in Sixteenth Century Europe: Revolution and Renaissance', in J. Black (ed.), *European Warfare 1453–1815* (New York: Macmillan, 1999), pp. 23–44.

Arnold, T. F., *The Renaissance at War* (London: Harper Collins, 2001).

Atkinson, J. A., I. Banks and J. O'Sullivan (eds), *Nationalism and Archaeology* (Glasgow: Cruithne 1996).

Bacon, F., 'Certain Considerations Touching the Plantation in Ireland', in C. Maxwell, *Irish History from Contemporary Sources: 1509–1610* (London: George Allen & Unwin Ltd, 1923), pp. 269–273.

Bain, J., W. K. Boyd, A. I. Cameron, M. S. Giuseppi, H. W. Meikle and J. D. Mackie (eds), *Calendar of the State Papers Relating to Scotland and Mary, Queen of Scots, 1547–1603*, 13 vols (Glasgow, 1898–1969).

Baker, C., *The Archaeology of Killeen Castle, County Meath* (Dublin: Wordwell, 2009).

Baker, C., *Antiquities of Old Fingal: The Archaeology of North County Dublin* (Dublin: Wordwell, 2010).

Balé, M. and E. Purcell (comp.), *The Annals of Ulster* (University College Cork: CELT, 2010) [http://www.ucc.ie/celt/published/T100001C/index.html].

Bambury, P. (comp.), *Annála Connacht* (University College Cork: CELT, 2008) [http://www.ucc.ie/celt/published/T100011/index.html].

Bannerman, J., *The Beatons: A Medical Kindred in the Classical Tradition* (Edinburgh: John Donald Publishers Ltd, 1998).

Barker, T. M., *The Military Intellectual and Battle: Raimondo Montecuccoli and the Thirty Years War* (Albany: State University of New York Press, 1975).

Barnard, T., 'Miles Symner and the New Learning in Seventeenth-Century Ireland', *Journal of the Royal Society of Antiquaries of Ireland*, vol. 102, no. 2, 1972, pp. 129–142.

Barnard, T., 'Integration or Separation? Hospitality and Display in Protestant Ireland, 1660–1800', in L. Brockliss and D. Eastwood (eds), *A Union of Multiple Identities: The British Isles, c.1750–c.1850* (Manchester: Manchester University Press, 1997), pp. 127–146.

Barnard, T., 'Gardening, Diet and Improvement in Later Seventeenth Century Ireland', in T. Barnard, *Irish Protestant Ascents and Descents, 1641–1770* (Dublin: Four Courts Press, 2004).

Barnard, T., *Making the Grand Figure: Lives and Possessions in Ireland, 1641–1770* (New Haven: Yale University Press, 2004).

Barnard, T., *A Guide to the Sources for Irish Material Culture: 1500–1900* (Maynooth: Four Courts Press, 2005).

Barret, R., *The Theorike and Practike of Moderne Warre* (London, 1598).

Barry, J., 'Guide to Records of the Genealogical Office, Dublin, with a Commentary on Heraldry in Ireland and on the History of the Office', *Analecta Hibernica*, vol. 26, 1970, pp. 1–43.

Barry, T., *The Archaeology of Medieval Ireland* (London and New York: Routledge, 1988).

Barry, T., 'The Origins of Irish Castles: A Contribution to the Debate', in C. Manning (ed.), *From Ringforts to Fortified Houses* (Dublin: Wordwell, 2008), pp. 33–40.

Barth, F., *Ethnic Groups and Boundaries: The Social Organisation of Cultural Difference* (Boston: Little, Brown, 1969).

Bartlett, T., *The Academy of Warre: Military Affairs in Ireland, 1600 to 1800: The 30th O'Donnell Lecture 2002* (Dublin: National University of Ireland, 2002).

Beglane, F., *Anglo-Norman Parks in Medieval Ireland* (Dublin: Four Courts Press, 2015).

Belmont, A., 'Why Dig a Millstone Quarry? The Case of Claix in the South West of France', in D. Williams and D. Peacock (eds), *Bread for the People: The Archaeology of Mills and Milling*, British Archaeological Report, International Series, 2274 (Oxford: Archaeopress, 2011), pp. 1–18.

Belton, L., 'Experimental Study to Determine Whether Structural Details of Buildings Can Be Inferred from Earthworks: Study of Leean Mountain, Co. Leitrim', Unpublished MA Thesis, Queen's University Belfast, 2008.

Beresford, D., 'Nugent, Richard 10th Lord of Delvin', in J. McGuire and J. Quinn (ed.), *Dictionary of Irish Biography* (Cambridge: Cambridge University Press, 2009) [http://dib.cambridge.org/viewReadPage.do?articleId=a6256].

Berlant, L., *Cruel Optimism* (Durham, NC: Duke University Press, 2011).

Berleth, R., *The Twilight Lords* (New York: Barnes & Noble, 1978).

Berman, P., 'Scar of David', *The Chronicle Review* (7 November 2014), B14–B16.

Berthold, J., 'Eine Hochmittelalterliche Wassermühle in Elfgen. Befunde, Funde, Reconstruktion', *Bonner Jahrbucher des LVR–Landesmuseums Bonn und des LVR–Amtes*, vol. 208, 2008, pp. 173–237.

Bhabha, H. K., 'Signs Taken for Wonders: Questions of Ambivalence and Authority Under a Tree Outside Delhi, May 1817', *Critical Inquiry*, vol. 12, no. 1, 1985, pp. 144–165.

Bhabha, H. K., *The Location of Culture* (London and New York: Routledge, 1994).

Bigger, F. J., 'The MacSwyne Grave Slab', *Ulster Journal of Archaeology*, vol. 9, no. 3, 1905, pp. 139–140.

Bitel, M., 'Introduction, Convent Ruins and Christian Profession: Toward a Methodology for the History of Religion and Gender', in L. M. Bitel and F. Lifshitz (eds), *Gender and Christianity in Medieval Europe: New Perspectives* (Philadelphia: Pennsylvania University Press, 2008), pp. 1–15.

Black, J. (ed.), *European Warfare 1453–1815* (New York: Palgrave Macmillan, 1999).

Bliss, A., 'Language and Literature', in J. Lydon (ed.), *The English in Medieval Ireland* (Dublin: Royal Irish Academy, 1984), pp. 27–45.

Bodley, J., 'A Visit to Lecale', *Ulster Journal of Archaeology*, vol. 2, 1854 [1602], pp. 73–99.

Bond, J., 'Medieval Nunneries in England and Wales: Buildings, Precincts and Estates', in D. Wood (ed.), *Women and Religion in Medieval England* (Oxford: Oxbow, 2003), pp. 46–90.

Boorde, A., *A Compendyous Regyment or a Dyetary of Healthe* (London: Wyllyam Powell, 1547).

Bordieu, P., *Outline of a Theory of Practice* (Cambridge: Cambridge University Press, 1977).

Borgeaud, P., *The Cult of Pan in Ancient Greece*, trans. K. Atlass and J. Redfield (Chicago and London: The University of Chicago Press, 1988).

Boutell, C. and A. C. Fox-Davies, *English Heraldry* (Edinburgh: Reeves & Turner, 1908).

Bowe, P., 'The Renaissance Garden in Ireland', *Irish Arts Review Yearbook*, vol. 11, 1995, pp. 74–81.

Boylston, A., M. Holst and J. Coughlan, 'Physical Anthropology', in V. Fiorato, A. Boylston and C. Knüsel (eds), *Blood Red Roses: The Archaeology of a Mass Grave from the Battle of Towton, AD1461* (Oxford: Oxford University Press, 2000), pp. 45–59.

Bradshaw, B., A. Hadfield and W. Maley (eds), *Representing Ireland: Literature and the Origins of the Conflict, 1534–1660* (Cambridge: Cambridge University Press, 1993).

Bradley, J., 'Planned Anglo-Norman Towns in Ireland', in H. B. Clarke and A. Simms (eds), *The Comparative History of Urban Origins 900–1250: Ireland, Wales, Denmark, Germany, Poland and Russia*, British Archaeological Reports, International Series, 255 (Oxford: Archaeopress, 1985), pp. 411–487.

Bradley, R., *An Archaeology of Natural Places* (London: Routledge, 2000).

Brady, C., *The Chief Governors: The Rise and Fall of Reform Government in Tudor Ireland, 1536–1588* (Cambridge: Cambridge University Press, 1994).

Brady, J., 'The Nunnery of Clonard', *Records of the Meath Archaeological and Historical Society*, vol. 2, no. 2, 1960, pp. 4–7.

Brady, J., 'Documents Concerning the Diocese of Meath', *Archivium Hibernicum,* vol. 8, 1941, pp. 242–243.

Brady, K. and C. Corlett, 'Ships on Plaster: Evidence for Ships in Medieval Ireland', in C. Manning (ed.), *From Ringforts to Fortified Houses: Studies on Castles and Other Monuments in Honour of David Sweetman* (Dublin: Wordwell, 2007), pp. 28–31.

Brady, N., *Discovering Irish Medieval Landscapes: The Discovery Programme's Medieval Rural Settlement Project, 2002–2008* (Dublin: The Discovery Programme, 2003).

Brady, N., 'The Medieval Rural Project: An Overview for 2002–2004', *Discovery Programme Report 7* (Dublin: The Discovery Programme, 2005), pp. 1–2.

Brady, N., 'When Mounds Become Castles: A Case for the Later Usage of Early Medieval Sites', in C. C. Corlett and M. Potterton (eds), *Rural Settlement in Ireland in the Light of Recent Archaeological Excavations* (Dublin: Wordwell, 2009), pp. 19–25.

Brady, N., A. Connon, R. McNeary, B. Shanahan and R. Shaw, 'A Survey of the Priory and Graveyard at Tulsk, Co. Roscommon', *Discovery Programme Report 7* (Dublin: The Discovery Programme, 2005), pp. 40–64.

Brady, N. and P. Gibson, 'The Earthwork at Tulsk: Topographical and Geophysical Excavations and Preliminary Excavations', *Discovery Programme Report 7* (Dublin: The Discovery Programme, 2005), pp. 65–76.

Brady, N., R. McNeary, B. Shanahan and R. Shaw, 'Unravelling Medieval Landscapes from the Air', *Peritia*, vol. 22, no. 1, 2011, pp. 295–316.

Brady, N. and K. D. O'Conor, 'The Later Medieval Usage of Crannogs in Ireland', *Ruralia*, vol. 5, 2005, pp. 127–136.

Brannon, N.F., 'Carrickfergus', in A. Hamlin and C. Lynn (eds), *Pieces of the Past: Archaeological Excavations by the Department of the Environment for Northern Ireland 1970–1986* (Belfast: HMSO, 1986), pp 64–66.

Breen, C., *The Gaelic Lordship of the O'Sullivan Beare: A Landscape Cultural History* (Dublin: Four Courts Press, 2005).

Breen, C., *Dunluce Castle: History and Archaeology* (Dublin: Four Courts Press, 2012).

Brewer, J. S. and W. Bullen (eds), *Calendar of the Carew Manuscripts Preserved in the Archiepiscopal Library at Lambeth*, 6 vols (London: Longmans Green & Co., 1867–73).

Bric, M. J., 'The United Irishmen, International Republicanism and the Definition of the Polity in the United States of America, 1791–1800', *Proceedings of the Royal Irish Academy,* vol. 104C, no. 4, 2004, pp. 81–106.

Brome, H., *The Commentaries of Messire Blaize de Montluc, Mareschal of France* (London, 1674).

Brown, K. S., 'Contests of Heritage and the Politics of Preservation in the Former Yugoslav Republic of Macedonia', in Lynn Meskell (ed.), *Archaeology Under Fire: Nationalism, Politics and Heritage in the Eastern Mediterranean and Middle East* (London: Routledge 1998), pp. 68–86.

Brown, M. P., 'Marvels of the West: Giraldus Cambrensis and the Role of the Author in the Development of Marginal Illustration', in A. S. G. Edwards (ed.), *English Manuscript Studies 1100–1700, Volume 10: Decoration and Illustration in Medieval English Manuscripts* (London: British Library, 2002), pp. 35–59.

Brunand, J. P. and M. Borréani, 'Deux Moulins Hydrauliques du Haut-Empire Romain en Narbonnaise: Villae des Mesclans à la Crau et de Saint-Pierre/Les Laurons aux Ares (Var)', *Gallia: Archéologie de la France Antique*, vol. 55, 1998, pp. 279–326.

Buchanan, K., L. H. S. Dean and M. Penman (eds), *Medieval and Early Modern Representations of Authority in Scotland and the British Isles* (Oxford: Routledge, 2016).

Buchanan, R. H., 'Field Systems of Ireland', in A. R. H. Baker and R. A. Butlin (eds), *Studies of Field Systems in the British Isles* (Cambridge: Cambridge University Press, 1973), pp. 616–626.

Burgess, M., 'Mapping the Narrow Ground: Geography, History and Partition', *Field Day Review*, vol. 1, 2005, pp. 121–131.

Burke, P., *Popular Culture in Early Modern Europe* (Aldershot: Scolar Press, 1994).

Burke, P., 'Representations of the Self from Petrarch to Descartes', in R. Porter (ed.), *Rewriting the Self: Histories from the Renaissance to the Present* (London: Routledge, 1997), pp. 17–28.

Burton, J., *The Yorkshire Nunneries in the Twelfth and Thirteenth Centuries* (York: Borthwick Publications, 1979).

Burton, J., *Monastic and Religious Orders in Britain, 1000–1300* (Cambridge: Cambridge University Press, 1994).

Burton, J., 'Looking for Medieval Nuns', in J. Burton and K. Stöber (eds), *Monasteries and Society in the British Isles in the Later Middle Ages* (Woodbridge: The Boydell Press, 2008), pp. 113–123.

Burton, J. and J. Kerr, *The Cistercians in the Middle Ages* (Woodbridge: The Boydell Press, 2011).

Burton, J. and K. Stöber (eds), *The Regular Canons in the Medieval British Isles* (Turnhout: Brepolis, 2011).

Byrne, F.J., *Irish Kings and High-Kings* (London: B.T. Batsford Ltd, 1973).

Caball, M., 'Culture, Continuity and Change in Early Seventeenth-Century South-West Munster', *Studia Hibernica*, vol. 38, 2013, pp. 37–56.

Caldwell, D., 'Finlaggan, Islay: Stones and Inauguration Ceremonies', in R. Welander, D. J. Breeze and T. O. Clancy (eds), *The Stone of Destiny:*

*Artefact and Icon* (Edinburgh: Society of Antiquaries of Scotland, 2003), pp. 61–75.

Caldwell, D., 'Having the Right Kit: West Highlanders Fighting in Ireland', in S. Duffy (ed.), *The World of the Galloglass: Kings and Warriors in Ireland and Scotland, 1250–1600* (Dublin: Four Courts Press, 2007), pp. 144–168.

Caldwell, D., *Islay, The Land of Lordship* (Edinburgh: Birlinn, 2008).

Camblin, G., *The Town in Ulster* (Belfast: Wm. Mullan & Son Publishers, Ltd, 1951).

Camden, W., *Britain, or A Chorographicall Description of the Most Flourishing Kingdoms, England, Scotland, and Ireland, and the Islands Adjoining, out of the Depth of Antiquity Beautified with Maps of the Several Shires of England: Written First in Latin by William Camden Clarenceux K. of A. Translated Newly into English by Philémon Holland Doctour in Physick: Finally, Revised, Amended, and Enlarged with Sundry Additions by the said Author* (London, 1610).

Camden, W., *Britannia* (1586), trans. E. Gibson (London: Awnsham Churchill, 1722).

Campbell, E., 'A Cross-Marked Quern from Dunadd', *Proceedings of the Society of Antiquaries Scotland*, vol. 117, 1987, pp. 105–117.

Campbell, P. J., 'The Franciscan Petition Lists: Diocese of Armagh, 1670–1', *Seanchas Ardmhacha: Journal of the Armagh Diocesan Historical Society*, vol. 15, no. 1, 1992, pp. 186–216.

Canny, N., 'Hugh O'Neill, Earl of Tyrone, and the Changing Face of Gaelic Ulster', *Studia Hibernica*, vol. 10, 1970, pp. 7–35.

Canny, N., *The Formation of the Old English Elite in Ireland: O'Donnell Lecture Delivered at University College Galway, 6 September 1974* (Dublin: National University of Ireland, 1975).

Canny, N., *The Elizabethan Conquest of Ireland: A Pattern Established* (Hassocks: Harvester Press, 1976).

Canny, N., 'What Really Happened in Ireland in 1641?', in J. Ohlmeyer (ed.), *Ireland: From Independence to Occupation, 1641–1660* (Cambridge: Cambridge University Press, 1995), pp. 24–42.

Carey, A., 'The Grinding Stones', in M. Clyne, *Kells Priory, County Kilkenny: Archaeological Excavations by Tom Fanning and Miriam Clyne* (Dublin: Stationery Office, 2007).

Carleton, C., *This Seat of Mars: War and the British Isles 1485–1746* (New Haven, CT: Yale University Press, 2010).

Cartwright, J., *Feminine Sanctity and Spirituality in Medieval Wales* (Cardiff: University of Wales Press, 2008).

Carty, N., 'Evidence for Cranial Trauma and Treatment in Medieval Kildare', *Journal of the Kildare Archaeological Society*, vol. 10, 2013, pp. 46–76.

Carus-Wilson, E., 'The Overseas Trade of Bristol', in E. Power and M. Postan (eds), *Studies in English Trade in the Fifteenth Century* (London: Routledge, 1933), pp. 143–183.

Carver Wees, B., *English, Irish and Scottish Silver at the Sterling and Francine Clark Art Institute* (New York: Hudson Hills Press, 1997).

Carver, N. and C. J. Donnelly, *Investigations at Castle Caufield, Lisnamonaghan, Co. Tyrone* (Belfast: Centre for Archaeological Fieldwork, QUB, 2011).

Carville, G., *The Impact of the Cistercians on the Landscape of Ireland 1142–1541* (Wicklow: KB Publications, 2002).

Casey, C. and A. Rowan, *North Leinster, the Counties of Longford, Louth, Meath and Westmeath* (London: Penguin, 1993).

Catty, J., *Writing Rape, Writing Women in Early Modern England* (Basingstoke: Palgrave Macmillan, 2011).

Chapman, A., 'Millstones and Querns', in A. Chapman, *West Cotton, Rounds: A Study of Medieval Settlement Dynamics AD450–1450: Excavation of a Deserted Medieval Hamlet in Northhamptonshire, 1985–89* (Oxford and Oakville: Oxbow, 2010), pp. 395–405.

Chapple, R. M., 'Don't Let It Get You Down, It's Only Castles Burning: A History of the Fortifications at Dungannon', *Dúiche Néill*, no. 16, 2007, pp. 96–135.

Childs, W., 'Ireland's Trade with England in the Later Middle Ages', *Irish Economic and Social History*, vol. 9, 1982, pp. 8–10.

Churchyard, T., *A Generall Rehearsall of Warres* (London: Edward VVhite, 1579).

Clarkson, L. and M. Crawford, *Feast and Famine: A History of Food and Nutrition in Ireland 1500–1920* (Oxford: Oxford University Press, 2001).

Clay, P., 'Querns and Millstones', in P. Clay and C. R. Salisbury, 'A Norman Mill Dam and Other Sites at Hemington Fields, Castle Donington, Leicestershire', *Archaeological Journal*, vol. 147, 1990, pp. 276–307.

Clyne, M., 'The Rental of Holy Trinity Abbey, Lough Cé', in T. Finan (ed.), *Medieval Lough Cé: History, Archaeology and Landscape* (Dublin: Four Courts Press, 2010), pp. 67–96.

Crosby Quinn, E. (ed. and trans.), 'O'Conor's House at Cloonfree', in E. Crosby Quinn (ed.), *Essays and Studies Presented to William Ridgeway* (Cambridge: Cambridge University Press, 1913), pp. 333–352.

Collier, H., *The Dialogue of Silvynne and Peregrynne*, transc. H. Morgan (University College Cork: CELT: 2010) [http://www.ucc.ie/celt/published/E590001-001/index.html].

Collins, T., 'Archaeological Excavations at St Catherine's, Old Abbey, County Limerick', Unpublished Report, 2010.

Collins, T., 'Missing the Boat ...', *Archaeology Ireland*, vol. 4, 2010, pp. 9–11.

Collins, T., 'Timolin: A Case Study of a Nunnery Estate in Later Medieval Ireland', *Anuario de Studios Medievales*, vol. 44, no. 1, 2014, pp. 51–80.

Collins, T. and A. Cummins, *Excavation of a Medieval Ringwork at Ballysimon, Co. Limerick* (Dublin: Wordwell, 2001).

Comber, M., *Caherconnell Archaeological Project: Summary of Fieldwork to Date* (Burren: Burren Forts Ltd, 2014).

Comber, M. and G. Hull, 'Excavations at Caherconnell Cashel, the Burren, Co. Clare: Implications for Cashel Chronology and Gaelic Settlement', *Proceedings of the Royal Irish Academy,* vol. 110C, no. 1, 2010, pp. 133–171.

Connell, K., *The Population of Ireland 1750–1845* (Oxford: Clarendon Press, 1950).

Connolly, S., *Contested Island* (Oxford: Oxford University Press, 2007).

Connolly, S., and J.M. Picard, 'Cogitosus Life of St. Brigit', *Journal of the Royal Society of Antiquaries of Ireland*, vol. 117, 1987, pp. 5–27.

Constable, O. R., 'Food and Meaning: Christian Understandings of Muslim Food and Food Ways in Spain, 1250–1550', *Viator*, vol. 44, no. 3, 2013, pp. 199–236.

Cooney, G., 'Is it all in the Genes?', *Archaeology Ireland*, vol. 15, no. 1, 2001, pp. 34–35.

Cooney, G., 'European and Global Archaeologies', *World Archaeology*, vol. 41, no. 4, 2009, pp. 626–628.

Cope, J., 'The Experience of Survival during the 1641 Irish Rebellion', *The Historical Journal*, vol. 46, no. 2, 2003, pp. 295–316.

Córdoba de la Llave, R., 'Aceñas, Tahonas y Almazaras: Técnicas Industriales y Procesos Productivos de Sector Agroalimentario en la Córdoba de Siglo XV', *Hispania: Revista Española de Historia*, vol. 48, 1988, pp. 827–874.

Coulson, C., *Castles in Medieval Society: Fortresses in England, France, and Ireland in the Central Middle Ages* (Oxford: Oxford University Press, 2003).

Coulter, C., 'Of Cakes and Kings: Breadmaking in Early Medieval England', in D. Williams and D. Peacock (eds), *Bread for the People: The Archaeology of Mills and Milling,* British Archaeological Report, International Series, 2274 (Oxford: Archaeopress, 2011), pp. 181–182.

Cowan, J. (ed.), *Macedonia: The Politics of Identity and Difference: Anthropology, Culture and Society* (London: Pluto Press, 2000).

Crawford, J., 'Age of Atrocity', *The Sixteenth Century Journal*, vol. 40, no. 3, 2009, pp. 34–78.

Creighton, O., *Castles and Landscapes: Power, Community and Fortification in Medieval England* (London and New York: Equinox, 2002).

Creighton, O., *Designs Upon the Land: Elite Landscapes of the Middle Ages* (Woodbridge: Boydell Press, 2009).

Creighton, O., 'Castles, Landscapes and Townscapes in Thirteenth-Century England: Wallingford, Oxfordshire and the "Princely Building Strategies" of Richard, Earl of Cornwall', in J. Peltzer (ed.), *Rank and Order: The Formation of Aristocratic Elites in Western and Central Europe, 500–1500* (Ostfildern: Jan Thorbecke Verlag, 2015), pp. 309–341.

Creighton, O., and T. Barry, 'Seigneurial and Elite Sites in the Medieval Landscape', in N. Christie and P. Stamper (eds), *Medieval Rural Settlement: Britain and Ireland, AD 800–1600* (Oxford: Windgather Press, 2012), pp. 63–80.

Cresswell, R., 'Of Mills and Waterwheels: The Hidden Parameters of Technological Choice', in P. Lemonnier (ed.), *Technological Choices: Transformation in Material Cultures Since the Neolithic* (London and New York: Psychology Press, 2002), pp. 181–213.

Croft, P., 'Trading with the Enemy', *The Historical Journal*, vol. 32, no. 2, 1989, pp. 281–302.

Croke, D., 'Ancient DNA: Synergy or Culture Clash', *Archaeology Ireland*, vol. 15, no. 4, 2001, pp. 36–37.

Crowley, T., 'The Political Production of a Language: The Case of Ulster Scots', *Journal of Linguistic Anthropology*, vol. 16, no. 1, 2006, pp. 23–35.

Cruickshank, C. G., *Elizabeth's Army,* 2nd edn (Oxford: Oxford University Press, 1966).

Cullen, L., *The Emergence of Modern Ireland 1600–1900* (Dublin: Gill & Macmillian, 1981).

Cunningham, B., 'Foreword', in L. Doran and J. Lyttleton (eds), *Lordship in Medieval Ireland: Image and Reality* (Dublin: Four Courts Press, 2007), pp. 17–18.

Cunningham, B. and R. Gillespie, *Stories from Gaelic Ireland: Microhistories from the Sixteenth-Century Irish Annals* (Dublin: Four Courts Press, 2003).

Curran, K. A., 'Religious Women and their Communities in Late Medieval Scotland', Unpublished PhD Thesis, University of Glasgow, 2005.

Currie, E. A., 'Land Tenures, Enclosures and Field-Patterns in Co. Derry in the Eighteenth and Nineteenth Centuries', *Irish Geography*, vol. 9, 1976, pp. 50–62.

Currie, E. A., 'Landscape Development in South Derry in the Eighteenth Century, *Studia Hibernica,* vol. 19, 1979, pp. 78–101.

Curwen, E. C., 'Querns', *Antiquity*, vol. 11, 1937, pp. 133–151.

Czysz, W., *Die Ältesten Wassermühlen: Archäologische Entdeckungen im Paartal bei Dasing* (Thierhaupten: Klostermühlenmuseum, 1998).

Davies, J., 'A Discovery of the True Causes Why Ireland Was Never Entirely Subdued', in J. Myers (ed.), *Elizabethan Ireland: A Selection of Writings by Elizabethan Writers on Ireland* (Connecticut: Archon Books, 1983).

Davies, O., *Excavations at Island MacHugh* (Belfast: Belfast Natural History and Philosophical Society, 1950).

Dawkes, G. and L. Buckley, 'Before Bagenal's Castle: Evidence of the Medieval Cistercian Abbey At Newry, County Down', *Ulster Journal Of Archaeology*, Third Series, vol. 68, 2009, pp. 124–140.

Dawson, M., *Plenti and Grase: Food and Drink in a Sixteenth-Century Household* (Totnes: Prospect Books, 2009).

Day, J. F. R., 'Primers of Honor: Heraldry, Heraldry Books, and English Renaissance Literature', *Sixteenth Century Journal,* vol. 21, no. 1, 1990, pp. 93–103.

Delaney, M., 'The Human Remains', in M. Clyne, *Kells Priory, Co. Kilkenny: Archaeological Excavations by T. Fanning and M. Clyne* (Dublin: Stationery Office, 2007), pp. 467–482.

Delaney, S. et al., 'Crops, Iron and Water', in S. Delaney, E. Lyne, S. McNamara, J. Nunan and K. Molloy, *Borderlands: Archaeological Investigations on the Route of the M18 Gort to Crusheen Road Scheme,* NRA Monographs, No. 9 (Dublin: Wordwell, 2012), pp. 139–145.

de Mendoza, B., *Theorique and Practise of Warre Written to Don Philip Prince of Castil,* trans. Sir E. Hoby (Middleburg, 1597).

de Paermentier, E., 'Experiencing Space Through Women's Convent Rules: The Rich Clares in Medieval Ghent, Thirteenth to Fourteenth Centuries', *Medieval Feminist Forum,* vol. 44, no. 1, 2008, pp. 53–68.

de Paor, M. and L. de Paor, *Early Christian Ireland* (London: Thames & Hudson, 1958).

Derricke, J., *The Image of Ireland with a Discovery of Wood Kerne, Wherein is Most Lively Expressed, the Nature, and Quality of the Said Wild Irish Wood Kerne, their Notable Aptness, Celerity, and Proness to Rebellion* (London, 1581).

Devereux, R., 2nd Earl of Essex, *An Apology of the Earl of Essex. Against those which Falsely and Maliciously Tax him to be the Only Hinderer of the Peace and Quiet of his Country* (London, 1603).

Devlin, C., 'The Rise and Fall of a Dynasty: Medieval West Tyrone as Reported in the Annals Source', *Clogher Record,* vol. 16, no. 3, 1999, pp. 75–76.

Dewar, M., *Sir Thomas Smith: A Tudor Intellectual in Office* (London: University of London, 1964).

Diaz-Andreu, M., 'Constructing Identities through Culture: The Past in the Forging of Europe', in P. Graves-Brown, S. Jones and C. Gamble (eds), *Cultural Identity and Archaeology: The Construction of European Communities* (London: Routledge, 1996), pp. 48–61.

Dillon, M. (ed. and trans.), 'The inauguration of O'Conor', in F. X. Martin, J. B. Morall and J. A. Watt (eds), *Medieval Studies Presented to Aubrey Gwynn* (Dublin: Three Candles, 1961), pp. 186–202.

Dillon, M. (ed. and trans.), 'Ceart Uí Néill', *Studia Celtica,* vol. 1, 1966, pp. 1–18.

Dillon, M., D. A. Binchy and D. Greene (eds), *Robin Flower: The Irish Tradition* (Oxford: Clarendon, 1947; repr. 1948).

Dixon, P., 'The Donjon of Knaresborough: The Castle as Theatre', *Château Gaillard,* vol. 14, 1990, pp. 121–139.

Doedens, L. L., '"The Day the Nation was Born." The Battle of Heiligerlee, 1568', in Marco Van der Hoeven (ed.), *Exercise of Arms: Warfare in the Netherlands, 1569–1648* (Leiden: Brill, 1997), pp. 57–68.

Donnelly, C. J., 'Passage or Barrier? Communication between Bawn and Tower House in Late Medieval Ireland: The Evidence from County Limerick', *Chateau Gaillard,* vol. 21, 2002, pp. 57–64.

Donnelly, C. J., 'Architecture and Conflict: Limerick's Tower Houses, *c.*1400 to *c.*1650', in L. Irwin, G. Ó Tuathaigh and M. Potter (eds), *Limerick: History and Society* (Dublin: Geography Publications, 2009), pp. 71–89.

Donnelly, C. J., P. Logue, J. O'Neill and J. O'Neill, 'Timber Castles and Towers in Sixteenth-Century Ireland: Some Evidence from Ulster', *Archaeology Ireland*, vol. 21, no. 2, 2007, pp. 22–25.

Donnelly, C. J., 'The Tower Houses of County Limerick', in R. Stalley (ed.), *Limerick and South-West Ireland: Medieval Art and Architecture*, British Archaeological Association Conference Transactions 34 (Leeds: Maney Publishing, 2011), pp. 189–201.

Donnelly, J. and S. Clark (eds), *Irish Peasants: Violence and Political Unrest, 1780–1914* (Madison: University of Wisconsin Press, 1983).

Donoghue, E., *Astray* (London: Pan Macmillan, 2012).

Doran, B. and L. Doran, 'St Mary's Cistercian Abbey, Dublin: A Ghost in the Alleyways', in J. Bradley, A.J. Fletcher and A. Simms (eds), *Dublin in the Medieval World: Studies in Honour of Howard B. Clarke* (Dublin: Four Courts Press, 2009), pp. 188–201.

Dorsett, J., 'Sir George Carew: The Study and Conquest of Ireland', Unpublished DPhil Thesis, Oxford, 2000.

Dow, G. F., *Every Day Life in the Massachusetts Bay Colony* (Maryland: Courier Corporation, 2007).

Dowling, M., 'Confusing Culture and Politics: Ulster Scots Culture and Music', *New Hibernia Review,* vol. 11, no. 3, 2007, pp. 51–80.

Drouot, H., *Mayenne et la Bourgogne* (Paris: Picard, 1937).

Duffy, P. J., 'Farney in 1634: An Examination of John Raven's Survey of the Essex Estate', *Clogher Record*, vol. 11, 1983, pp. 245–256.

Duffy, P. J., 'Social and Spatial Order in the MacMahon Lordship of Airghialla in the Late Sixteenth Century', in P. J. Duffy, D. Edwards and E. FitzPatrick (eds), *Gaelic Ireland c.1250–c.1650: Land, Lordship and Settlement* (Dublin: Four Courts Press, 2001), pp. 128–134.

Duffy, P. J., D. Edwards and E. FitzPatrick, 'Introduction: Recovering Gaelic Ireland, *c.*1250–*c.*1650', in P. J. Duffy, D. Edwards and E. FitzPatrick (eds), *Gaelic Ireland* c.*1250*–c.*1650: Land, Lordship and Settlement* (Dublin: Four Courts Press, 2001), pp. 21–73.

Duffy, S. (ed.), *Medieval Ireland: An Encyclopedia* (New York and London: Routledge, 2005).

Duignan, M. V. (ed. and trans.), 'The Uí Briúin Bréifni Genealogies', *Journal of the Royal Society of Antiquaries of Ireland*, vol. 64, 1934, pp. 90–137, 213–256.

Dunlop, R., 'Sixteenth-Century Maps of Ireland', *English Historical Review,* vol. 20, no. 78, 1905, pp. 309–337.

Dunlop, R., 'Sixteenth Century Schemes for the Plantation of Ulster', *Scottish Historical Review*, vol. 22, 1925, pp. 115–126, 199–212.

Dunning, P.J., 'The Arroasian Order in Medieval Ireland', *Irish Historical Studies*, vol. 4, no. 16, 1945, pp. 297–315.

Durkeim, E., *The Rules of the Sociological Method* (Glencoe: Free Press, 1958).

Eadie, G., 'Reflections of a Divided Country? The Role of the Tower House in Late Medieval Ireland', *Château Gaillard*, vol. 26, 2014, pp. 135–147.

Edwards, D., P. Lenihan and C. Tait (eds), *Age of Atrocity: Violence and Political Conflict in Early Modern Ireland* (Dublin: Four Courts Press, 2007).

Edwards, D., 'The Escalation of Violence in Sixteenth Century Ireland', in D. Edwards, P. Lenihan and C. Tait (eds), *Age of Atrocity: Violence and Political Conflict in Early Modern Ireland* (Dublin: Four Courts Press, 2007), pp. 34–78.

Edwards, K. J., F. W. Hamond and A. Simms, 'The Medieval Settlement of Newcastle Lyons, County Dublin: An Interdisciplinary Approach', *Proceedings of the Royal Irish Academy*, vol. 83C, 1983, pp. 351–378.

Edwards, N., *The Archaeology of Early Medieval Ireland* (London: Routledge, 1990).

Edwards, P., *Horse and Man in Early Modern England* (Cornwall: Bloomsbury Academic, 2007).

Elias, N., *The Civilizing Process: The History of Manners and State Formation and Civilization,* trans. E. Jephcott (Oxford: Blackwell, 1994).

Ellis, S. G., 'Historical Revision XIX: The Irish Customs Administration Under the Early Tudors', *Irish Historical Studies*, vol. 22, 1980–81, pp. 271–277.

Ellis, S. G., 'Nationalist Historiography and the English and Gaelic Worlds in the Late Middle Ages', *Irish Historical Studies,* vol. 25, no. 97, 1986, pp. 1–18.

Ellis, S. G., *Ireland in the Age of the Tudors 1447–1603: English Expansion and the End of Gaelic Rule* (London: Routledge, 1998).

Empey, A., 'The Layperson in the Parish: The Medieval Inheritance, 1169–1536', in R. Gillespie and W. G. Neely (eds), *The Laity and the Church of Ireland, 1000–2000* (Dublin: Four Courts Press, 2002), pp. 7–48.

Empey, M., '"We Are Not Safe for They Threaten Us with More Violence": A Study of the Cook Street Riot, 1629', in W. Sheehan and M. Cronin (eds), *Riotous Assemblies: Popular Protest in Ireland* (Cork: Mercier Press, 2011), pp. 64–79.

Eogan, G., *Excavations at Knowth, Volume 5: The Archaeology of Knowth in the First and Second Millennia AD* (Dublin: Royal Irish Academy, 2012).

Eogan, J., 'A Betagh Settlement at Attyflin, Co. Limerick', in C. Corlett and M. Potterton (eds), *Rural Settlement in Medieval Ireland* (Dublin: Wordwell, 2009), pp. 66–77.

Erler, M. C. and M. Kowaleski, 'A New Economy of Power Relations: Female Agency in the Middle Ages', in M. C. Erler and M. Kowaleski (eds), *Gendering the Master Narrative: Women and Power in the Middle Ages* (Ithaca: Cornell University Press, 2003), pp. 1–16.

Evans, E. E., *Mourne County: Landscape and Life in South Down* (Dundalk: Dundalgan Press, 1967).

Evans, J. X. (ed.), *The Works of Sir Roger Williams* (Oxford: Clarendon, 1972).

Fahlander, F., 'Third Space Encounters: Hybridity, Mimicry and Interstitial Practice', in P. Cornell and F. Fahlander (eds), *Encounters | Materialities | Confrontations: Archaeologies of Social Space and Interaction* (Newcastle: Cambridge Scholars Press, 2007), pp. 22–25.

Faith, R., 'Forces and Relations of Production in Early Medieval England', *Journal of Agrarian Change*, vol. 9, 2009, pp. 23–24.

Falls, C., *Elizabeth's Irish Wars* (London: Syracuse University Press, 1950).

Farmer, D. L., 'Millstones for Medieval Manors', *Agricultural History Review*, vol. 40, no. 2, 1992, pp. 97–111.

Fearn, A., 'From the Salt to the Centrepieces, 1580–1780', in P. Glanville and H. Young (eds), *Elegant Eating: Four Hundred Years of Dining in Style* (London: V & A Publications, 2002), p. 64.

Feldt, L. (ed.), *Wilderness in Mythology and Religion: Approaching Religious Spatialities, Cosmologies, and Ideas of Wild Nature*, Religion and Society vol. 55 (Boston and Berlin: De Gruyter, 2012), pp. 1–9.

Fenlon, J., 'Episodes of Magnificence: The Material Worlds of the Dukes of Ormonde', in T. Barnard and J. Fenlon (eds), *The Dukes of Ormonde, 1610–1745* (Woodbridge: The Boydell Press, 2000), pp. 137–159.

Fenlon, J., *Goods and Chattels: A Survey of Early Household Inventories in Ireland* (Dublin: Stationery Office, 2003).

Fenlon, J., 'Moving Towards the Formal House: Room Usage in Early Modern Ireland', *Proceedings of the Royal Irish Academy*, vol. 111C, 2011, pp. 141–168.

Ferguson, K., 'Castles and the Pallas Placename: A German Insight', *The Irish Sword*, vol. 22, no. 89, 2001, pp. 241–248.

Finan, T., *A Nation in Medieval Ireland; Perspectives on Gaelic National Identity in the Middle Ages*, British Archaeological Report, British Series, 367 (Oxford: Archaeopress, 2004).

Finan, T. (ed.), *Medieval Lough Cé: History, Archaeology and Landscape* (Dublin: Four Courts Press, 2010).

Finan, T., 'Introduction', in T. Finan (ed.), *Medieval Lough Cé: History, Archaeology and Landscape* (Dublin: Four Courts Press, 2010), p. 11–14.

Finan, T., 'O'Conor "Grand Strategy" and the Connacht Chronicle in the Thirteenth Century', in T. Finan (ed.), *Medieval Lough Cé: History, Archaeology, Landscape* (Dublin: Four Courts Press, 2010), pp. 159–180.

Finan, T., 'Violence in Thirteenth-Century Ireland', *Eolas: The Journal of the American Society of Irish Medieval Studies*, vol. 4, 2010, pp. 86–97.

Finan, T., 'The Moated Sites of Co. Roscommon, Ireland: A Statistical Approach', *Chateau Gaillard*, vol. 24, 2014, pp. 177–180.

Finan, T. and K. D. O'Conor, 'The Moated Site at Cloonfree, Co. Roscommon', *Journal of the Galway Archaeological and Historical Society*, vol. 54, 2002, pp. 72–87.

Fischer, C., *Tidlige Danske Vandmøller* (Aarhus Universitesforlag, 2004).

Fissel, M. C., *English Warfare, 1511–1642* (London: Psychology Press, 2001).

FitzPatrick, E., 'Assembly and Inauguration Places of the Burkes in Late Medieval Connacht', in P. J. Duffy, D. Edwards and E. FitzPatrick (eds), *Gaelic Ireland c.1250–c.1650: Land, Lordship and Settlement* (Dublin: Four Courts Press, 2004), pp. 357–374.

FitzPatrick, E., *Royal Inauguration in Gaelic Ireland c.1100–1600: A Cultural Landscape Study* (Woodbridge: The Boydell Press, 2004).

FitzPatrick, E., 'The Material World of the Parish', in E. FitzPatrick and R. Gillespie (eds), *The Parish in Medieval and Early Modern Ireland: Community, Territory and Building* (Dublin: Four Courts Press, 2006), pp. 62–75.

FitzPatrick, E., 'Native Enclosed Settlement and the Problem of the Irish "Ring-Fort"', *Medieval Archaeology*, vol. 53, no. 1, 2009, pp. 271–307.

FitzPatrick, E., '*Formaoil na Fiann*: Hunting Preserves and Assembly Places in Gaelic Ireland', in D. Furchtgott, G. Henley and M. Holmberg (eds), *Proceedings of Harvard Celtic Colloquium*, vol. 32, 2012, pp. 95–118.

FitzPatrick, E., 'The Landscape and Settlements of the Uí Dhalaigh Poets of Muinter Bhaire', in S. Duffy (ed.), *Princes, Prelates and Poets in Medieval Ireland: Essays in Honour of Katharine Simms* (Dublin: Four Courts Press, 2013), pp. 460–480.

FitzPatrick, E., R. Hennessy, P. Naessens and J. F. Nagy, 'Decoding Finn MacCumaill's Places', *Archaeology Ireland*, vol. 29, no. 3, 2015, pp. 26–31.

FitzPatrick, E., '*Ollamh, Biatach, Comharba*: Lifeways of Gaelic Learned Families in Medieval and Early Modern Ireland', in L. Breatnach, R. Ó hUiginn, D. McManus and K. Simms (eds), *Proceedings of the XIV International Congress of Celtic Studies, held in Maynooth University, 1–5 August 2011* (Dublin: Institute for Advanced Studies, 2015), pp. 165–189.

FitzPatrick, E., 'Assembly Places and Elite Collective Identities in Medieval Ireland', *Journal of North Atlantic Studies*, vol. 8, 2015, pp. 52–68.

FitzPatrick, E., 'The Last Kings of Ireland: Material Expressions of Gaelic Lordship, *c.*1300–1400', in K. Buchanan, L. H. S. Dean and M. Penman (eds), *Medieval and Early Modern Representations of Authority in Scotland and the British Isles* (Oxford: Routledge, 2016), pp. 197–213.

FitzPatrick, E., E. M. Murphy, R. McHugh and C. J. Donnelly, 'Evoking the White Mare: The Cult Landscape of Sgiath Gabhra and its Medieval Perception in Gaelic Fir Mhanach', in R. Schot, C. Newman and E.

Bhreathnach (eds), *Landscapes of Cult and Kingship* (Dublin: Four Courts Press, 2011), pp. 163–191.

FitzPatrick, E. and C. O'Brien, *The Medieval Churches of County Offaly* (Dublin: Dúchas, 1998).

FitzPatrick, E., M. O'Brien and P. Walsh (eds), *Archaeological Investigations in Galway City, 1987–1998* (Dublin: Wordwell, 2004).

Fitzsimons, F., 'Fosterage and Gossiprid in Late Medieval Ireland: Some New Evidence', in P. Duffy, D. Edwards and E. FitzPatrick (eds), *Gaelic Ireland c.1250–c.1650: Land, Lordship and Settlement* (Dublin: Four Courts Press, 2001), pp. 138–149.

Fitzsimons, F., 'Wolsey, the Native Affinities, and the Failure of Reform in Henrician Ireland', in D. Edwards (ed.), *Regions and Rulers in Ireland, 1100–1650* (Dublin: Four Courts Press, 2004), pp. 78–121.

Flanagan, D. and L. Flanagan, *Irish Place Names* (Dublin: Gill & Macmillan, 1994).

Flanagan, M. T., 'St Mary's Abbey, Louth and the Introduction of the Arrouaisian Observance into Ireland', *The Clogher Record*, vol. 10, no. 2, 1980, pp. 223–234.

Flanagan, M. T., 'Anglo-Norman Change and Continuity: The Castle of Telach Cail in Delbna', *Irish Historical Studies,* vol. 28, no. 113, 1993, pp. 385–389.

Flanagan, M. T., 'Irish and Anglo-Norman Warfare in Twelfth-century Ireland', in T. Bartlett and K. Jeffery (eds), *A Military History of Ireland* (Cambridge: Cambridge University Press, 1996), pp. 52–75.

Flanagan, M. T., *The Transformation of the Irish Church in the Twelfth Century* (Woodbridge: The Boydell Press, 2010).

Flavin, S., 'Consumption and Material Culture in Sixteenth-Century Ireland', Unpublished PhD Thesis, University of Bristol, 2011.

Flavin, S., 'Consumption and Material Culture in Sixteenth-Century Ireland', *Economic History Review*, vol. 64, no. 4, 2011, pp. 1144–74.

Flavin, S., *Consumption and Culture in Sixteenth-Century Ireland: Saffron, Stockings and Silk* (Woodbridge: The Boydell Press, 2014).

Fletcher, A. and D. MacCulloch, *Tudor Rebellions,* 4th edn (Harlow: Pearson Educational, 1997).

Fletcher, J., *Gardens of Earthly Delight: The History of Deer Parks* (Oxford: Windgather Press, 2011).

Flynn, T. S., *The Irish Dominicans, 1536–1641* (Dublin: Four Courts Press, 1993).

Foley, C., 'Bagenal's Castle, Newry, County Down: Discovery and Re-Use', *Ulster Journal of Archaeology*, third series, vol. 68, 2009, pp. 141–151.

Foley, C. and B. Williams, 'The Crannogs of County Fermanagh', in M. Meek (ed.), *The Modern Traveller to Our Past: Festschrift in Honour of Ann Hamlin* (Dublin: DPK, 2006), pp. 53–64.

Frame, R., 'War and Peace in the Medieval Lordship of Ireland', in J. Lydon (ed.), *The English in Medieval Ireland* (Dublin: Royal Irish Academy, 1984), pp. 221–239.

Frazer, J. E., *From Caledonia to Pictland: Scotland to 795* (Edinburgh: Edinburgh University Press, 2009).

Frazer, W. O., 'A Medieval Farmstead at Killegland, Asbourne, County Meath', in C. Corlett and M. Potterton (eds), *Rural Settlement in Medieval Ireland in the Light of Recent Archaeological Excavations* (Dublin: Wordwell, 2009), pp. 109–124.

Fredengren, C., *Crannogs: A Study of People's Interaction with Lakes, with Particular Reference to Lough Gara in the North-West of Ireland* (Dublin: Wordwell, 2002).

Freeman, A. M. (ed.), *The Compossicion Booke of Conought* (Dublin: Irish Manuscripts Commission, 1836).

Gardiner, M., 'Graffiti and their Use in Late Medieval England', *Ruralia,* vol. 6, 2005, pp. 265–276.

Gardiner, M., 'A Preliminary List of Booley Huts in the Mourne Mountains, County Down', *Ulster Journal of Archaeology*, third series, vol. 67, 2008, pp. 142–152.

Gardiner, M., 'Excavations on a Late Medieval or Early Modern House at Gortin, Ardclinis, Co. Antrim: Data Structure Report', Queen's University Belfast, 2010 [http://www.qub.ac.uk/sites/ExcavationandSurveyReports/FileStore/Filetoupload,201994,en.pdf].

Gardiner, M., 'Oral Tradition, Landscape and the Social Life of Place-Names', in R. Jones and S. Semple (eds), *Sense of Place in Anglo-Saxon England* (Donington: Oxbow, 2012), pp. 16–30.

Gardiner, M., 'The Role of Transhumance within Rundale Agriculture', *Ulster Folklife*, vol. 58, 2015, pp. 53–63.

Gardiner, M. and T. E. McNeill, 'Sea-Bourne Trade and the Commercialisation of Fifteenth- and Sixteenth-Century Ulster', *Proceedings of the Royal Irish Academy*, vol. 116C, 2016, pp. 1–34.

Geber, J., 'Comparative Study of Perimortem Weapon Trauma in Two Early Medieval Skeletal Populations (AD 400–1200) from Ireland', *International Journal of Osteoarchaeology*, vol. 25, 2015, pp. 253–264.

Geological Survey of Northern Ireland, *Geological Map of Northern Ireland: Solid Geology 1:250,000* (Surrey, 1997).

Gernon, L., 'A Discourse of Ireland Anno 1620', in C. Litton Faulkner (ed.), *Illustrations of Irish History and Topography, Mainly from the Seventeenth Century* (London, New York, Bombay: Longmans, Green & Co., 1904), pp. 345–362.

Gernon, L., *A Discourse of Ireland, Anno 1620*, ed. C. Litton Falkiner (University College Cork: CELT, 2007) [http://www.ucc.ie/celt/published/E620001/index.html].

Gibson, P. J. and D. M. George, 'Geophysical Investigation of the Site of the Former Monastic Settlement, Clonard, County Meath, Ireland', *Archaeological Prospection*, vol. 13, 2006, pp. 45–56.

Gilbert, J. T., *A History of the City of Dublin,* 3 vols (Dublin: J. McGlashan, 1854–9).

Gilchrist, R., *Gender and Material Culture: The Archaeology of Religious Women* (London: Routledge, 1994).
Gilchrist, R., *Contemplation and Action: The Other Monasticism* (London: Continuum International Publishing Group, 1995).
Gilchrist, R. and B. Sloane, *Requiem: The Medieval Monastic Cemetery in Britain* (Museum of London Archaeology Service, 2005).
Giles, K., 'Seeing and Believing: Visuality and Space in Pre-Modern England', *World Archaeology*, vol. 39, no. 1, 2007, pp. 105–121.
Gillespie, R., *Colonial Ulster: The Settlement of East Ulster 1600–1641* (Cork: Cork University Press, 1985).
Gillespie, R., 'Funerals and Society in Early Seventeenth Century Ireland', *Journal of the Royal Society of Antiquaries of Ireland,* vol. 115, 1985, pp. 86–91.
Gillespie, R., *The Transformation of the Irish Economy, 1500–1700* (Dundalk: Dundalgan Press, 1991).
Gillespie, R., 'Negotiating Order in Early Seventeenth-Century Ireland', in M. J. Braddick and J. Walter (eds), *Negotiating Power in Early Modern Society: Order, Hierarchy and Subordination in Britain and Ireland* (Cambridge: Cambridge University Press, 2001), pp. 188–205.
Gilmore, S. and E. M. Murphy, 'Reconstructing the Dead Man's Face: A Violent Death from Medieval Armagh', *Archaeology Ireland*, vol. 15, no. 2, 2001, pp. 16–18.
Girouard, M., *Life in the English Country House* (Harmondsworth: Penguin Books, 1980).
Glanville, P., *Silver in England* (Oxton: Routledge, 1987).
Glick, T. F. and L. P Martínez, 'La Molineria Hidràulica Valenciana: Questions Obertes', in T. F. Glick and E. Guinot (eds), *Els Molins Hidráulics Valencians: Tecnologia, História i Context Social* (Institución Alfons el Magnànim de la Diputación de Valencia, 2000), pp. 22–99.
Glin, Knight of, and J. Peill, *Irish Furniture* (New Haven, CT: Yale University Press, 2007).
Golding, B., *Gilbert of Sempringham and the Gilbertine Order* (Oxford: Clarendon Press, 1995).
Golding, B. (trans.), *Speculum Ecclesiae* (Oxford, forthcoming).
Good, W., 'Descriptions and Customs of the Wild Irish', in W. Camden, *Britannia* (1585), trans. E. Gibson (London: Awnsham Churchill, 1722).
Graham, B. J., 'The Towns of Medieval Ireland', in R. A. Butlin (ed.), *The Development of the Irish Town* (London: Rowman & Littlefield, 1977), pp. 28–60.
Graham, B. J., 'The Mottes of the Norman Liberty of Meath', in H. Murtagh (ed.), *Irish Midland Studies: Essays in Commemoration of N. W. English* (Athlone: Old Athlone Society, 1980), pp. 39–56.
Graham, B. J., 'Medieval Settlement in County Roscommon', *Proceedings of the Royal Irish Academy,* vol. 88C, 1988, pp. 19–36.

Graham, B. J., 'Medieval Timber and Earthwork Fortifications in Western Ireland', *Medieval Archaeology*, vol. 32, 1988, pp. 110–129.

Graham, B. J., 'The Search for the Common Ground: Estyn Evans's Ireland', *Transactions of the Institute of British Geographers*, vol. 19, no. 2, 1994, pp. 183–201.

Graham, J. K., 'The Birth-Date of Hugh O'Neill, Second Earl of Tyrone', *Irish Historical Studies*, vol. 1, no. 1, 1938, pp. 58–59.

Graves, C. P., 'Sensing and Believing: Exploring Worlds of Difference in Pre-Modern England: A Contribution to the Debate Opened by Kate Giles', *World Archaeology*, vol. 39, no. 4, 2007, pp. 515–531.

Gray, E., 'Material Culture of Gaelic High-Status Drinking Ritual in Medieval and Early Modern Ireland', Unpublished PhD Thesis, National University of Ireland, Galway, 2016.

Great Britain, Public Record Office, *State Papers Published under the Authority of His Majesty's Commission: Henry the Eighth*, 6 vols (London: His Majesty's Commission for State Papers, 1830–52).

Green, M. A. E., *Calendar of State Papers, Domestic Series of the Reign of James I*, 5 vols (London: Longman, 1858).

Greenblatt, S., *Renaissance Self-Fashioning: From More to Shakespeare* (Chicago: University of Chicago Press, 2005).

Groebner, V., *Who Are You? Identification, Deception and Surveillance in Early Modern Europe*, trans. M. Kyburz and J. Peck (New York: Zone Books, 2007).

Guiffrida, A., 'Permanenza Tecnologia ed Espansione Territoriale del Mulino ad Acqua Siciliano (secc. XIV–XVI)', in S. Mariotti (ed.), *Produttivita e Tecnologie nei Secoli XII–XVII* (Firenze: Fondazione Istituto Internazionale Di Storia Economica, 1981), pp. 205–221.

Guillemeau, J., *Child-Birth or, the Happy Deliuerie of Vvomen* (London: A. Hatfield, 1612).

Gwynn, A. (ed. and trans.), *The Metrical Dindshenchas: Text, Translation and Commentary*, Part 3, Todd Lecture Series 10 (Dublin: Royal Irish Academy, 1913, repr. Institute for Advanced Studies, 1991).

Gwynn, A. and R. N. Hadcock, *Medieval Religious Houses: Ireland* (Harlow: Longmans, 1970).

Hadcock, N., 'The Origin of the Augustinian Order in Meath', *Records of the Meath Archaeological and Historical Society*, vol. 3, no. 2, 1964, pp. 124–31.

Hadfield, A., *Edmund Spenser: A Life* (Oxford: Oxford University Press, 2012).

Hall, D., 'The Nuns of the Medieval Convent of Lismullin, County Meath and their Secular Connections', *Records of the Meath Archaeological and Historical Society,* vol. 10, 1999, pp. 58–70.

Hall, D., 'Towards a Prosopography of Nuns in Medieval Ireland', *Archivium Hibernicum*, vol. 53, 1999, pp. 3–15.

Hall, D., *Women and the Church in Medieval Ireland* c.*1140–1540* (Dublin: Four Courts Press, 2003).

Hall, V. and L. Bunting, 'Tephra-Dated Pollen Studies of Medieval Landscapes in the North of Ireland', in P. J. Duffy, D. Edwards and E. Fitzpatrick (eds), *Gaelic Ireland* c.*1250*–c.*1650: Land, Lordship and Settlement* (Dublin: Four Courts Press, 2001), pp. 207–222.

Halpin, A., 'Weapons, Arms and Armour', in S. Duffy (ed.), *Medieval Ireland: An Encyclopaedia* (Oxford: Oxford University Press, 2005), pp. 511–514.

Hamburger, J. F., 'Introduction', in J. F. Hamburger and S. Marti (eds), *Crown and Veil: Female Monasticism from the Fifth to the Fifteenth Centuries* (New York: Columbia University Press, 2008), pp. 1–12.

Hamilton, H. C., E. G. Atkinson and R. Pentland Mahaffy, *Calendar of the State Papers Relating to Ireland of the Reigns of Henry VIII, Edward VI, Mary, and Elizabeth, 1509–1603: Preserved in the State Paper Department of Her Majesty's Public Record Office*, 11 vols (Nendeln: Kraus Reprint, 1974).

Hamilton, H. C. (ed.), *Calendar of State Papers Relating to Ireland of the Reign of Elizabeth, 1592, October–1596, June* (London: Her Majesty's Stationery Office, 1890).

Hamilton, H. C. (ed.), *Calendar of State Papers Relating to Ireland of the Reign of Elizabeth, 1588, August–1592, September* (London: Longman & Co, 1885).

Hamilton, H. C. (ed.), *Calendar of State Papers Relating to Ireland of the Reign of Elizabeth, 1586–1588* (London: Longman & Co., 1877).

Hamilton, H. C. (ed.), *Calendar of State Papers Relating to Ireland of the Reign of Elizabeth, 1574–1585* (London: Longman, Green, Reader & Dyer, 1867).

Hamilton, H. C. (ed.), *Calendar of State Papers relating to Ireland of the Reigns of Henry VIII, Edward VI, Mary and Elizabeth, 1509–1573* (Longman, Green, Longman & Roberts, 1860).

Hammond, P., *Food and Feast in Medieval England* (Gloucestershire: Sutton, 1993).

Harbison, P., 'Native Irish Arms and Armour in Medieval Gaelic Literature, 1170–1600', *Irish Sword,* vol. 12, no. 8, 1975, pp. 270–284.

Hardiman, J. (ed.), *West or h-Iar Connaught by Roderic O'Flaherty: With Notes and Illustrations by J. Hardiman* (Dublin: The Irish Archaeological Society, 1846).

Harrington, C., *Women in a Celtic Church, Ireland 450–1150* (Oxford: Oxford University Press, 2002).

Harrington, J., *Nugae Antiquae*, ed. T. Park, 2 vols (London: His Majesty's Stationery Office, 1804).

Harrington, J., 'Report of a Journey into the North of Ireland to Justice Carey', in C. Maxwell, *Irish History from Contemporary Sources* (London: George Allen, 1923), p. 338.

Harris, M., 'History and Significance of the Emic/Etic Distinction', *Annual Review of Anthropology*, vol. 5, 1976, pp. 329–350.

Harris, T., *London Crowds in the Reign of Charles II: Propaganda and Politics from the Restoration until the Exclusion Crisis* (Cambridge: Cambridge University Press, 1990).

Harrison, A., 'The Shower of Hell', *Éigse*, vol. 18, part 2, 1981, p. 304.

Harrison, D., *The Bridges of Medieval England* (Oxford: Oxford Historical Monographs, 2004).

Haskell, A. and M. Lewis, *Infantilia: The Archaeology of the Nursery* (London: Dobson, 1971).

Hatchell, G. (ed.), *Irish Patent Rolls of James I: Facsimile of the Irish Record Commission's Calendar, Prepared Prior to 1830* (Dublin: Stationery Office, 1966).

Harverson, M., *Mills of the Muslim World* (London: SPAB Mills Section, 2000).

Haycock, R. G., 'Review of *Celtic Warfare 1595–1763* by James Michael Hill', *Military Affairs*, vol. 51, no. 4, 1987, p. 209.

Hayes-McCoy, G. A., 'History of Guns in Ireland', *Journal of the Galway Archaeological and Historical Society*, vol. 18, 1938, pp. 43–65.

Hayes-McCoy, G. A., *Ulster and Other Maps* (Dublin: Irish Manuscripts Commission, 1964).

Hayes-McCoy, G. A., *Irish Battles: A Military History of Ireland* (Belfast: Appletree Press, 1990).

Headland, T. N., L. Pike and M. Harris (eds), *Emics and Etics: The Outsider/Insider Debate* (Newbury Park, CA: Sage, 1990).

Heidegger, M., *Identity and Difference* (Chicago: University of Chicago Press, 1969).

Henry, G., *The Irish Military Community in Spanish Flanders, 1586–1621* (Dublin: Irish Academic Press, 1992).

Herron, T. and M. Potterton (eds), *Ireland in the Renaissance c.1540–1660* (Dublin: Four Courts Press, 2007).

Heuser, B., *The Evolution of Strategy: Thinking War from Antiquity to the Present* (Cambridge: Cambridge University Press, 2010).

Higham, R. and P. Barker, *Timber Castles* (London: University of Exeter Press, 1992).

Hill, G., *An Historical Account of the MacDonnells of Antrim* (Belfast: Archer, 1873).

Hill, G., *An Historical Account of the Plantation of Ulster at the Commencement of the Seventeenth Century 1608–1620* (Belfast: McCaw, Stevenson & Orr, 1877).

Hill, J. M., 'Shane O'Neill and the Campaign Against the MacDonalds of Antrim, 1564–5', *Irish Sword*, vol. 18, 1991, pp. 129–138.

Hill, J. M., 'Gaelic Warfare, 1453–1815', in J. Black (ed.), *European Warfare 1453–1815* (New York: Macmillan, 1999), pp. 99–115.

Hodder, I., *Symbols in Action* (Cambridge University Press, 1982).

Hogan, E. (ed.), *The Description of Ireland and the State Thereof as it is at this Present in Anno 1598* (Dublin and London: M.H. Gill, 1878).

Hogan, J., 'The Irish Law of Kingship, with Special Reference to Ailech and Cenél Eoghain', *Proceedings of the Royal Irish Academy*, vol. 40C, 1931–2, pp. 186–254.

Holmes, A., 'Presbyterian Religion, Historiography, and Ulster Scots Identity, *c.*1800 to 1914', *The Historical Journal*, vol. 52, no. 3, 2009, pp. 615–640.

Horn, W., 'On the Origins of the Medieval Cloister', *Gesta*, vol. 12, 1973, pp. 13–52.

Horning, A., '"Dwelling Houses in the Old Irish Barbarous Manner": Archaeological Evidence for Gaelic Architecture in an Ulster Plantation Village', in P. J. Duffy, D. Edwards and E. FitzPatrick (eds), *Gaelic Ireland, c.1250–c.1650: Land, Lordship and Settlement* (Dublin: Four Courts Press, 2001), pp. 374–396.

Horning, A., 'Archaeological Explorations of Cultural Identity and Rural Economy in the North of Ireland: Goodland, Co. Antrim', *International Journal of Historical Archaeology*, vol. 8, 2004, pp. 199–215.

Horning, A., 'Archaeology, Conflict and Contemporary Identity in the North of Ireland: Implications for Theory and Practice in Irish Historical Archaeology', *Archaeological Dialogues,* vol. 13, no. 2, 2006, pp. 183–199.

Horning, A., 'Materiality and Mutable Landscapes: Rethinking Seasonality and Marginality in Rural Ireland', *International Journal of Historical Archaeology*, vol. 11, 2007, pp. 358–378.

Horning, A., *Ireland in the Virginian Sea: Colonialism in the British Atlantic* (Chapel Hill: The University of North Carolina Press, 2013).

Horning, A., 'Clothing and Colonialism: The Dungiven Costume and the Fashioning of Early Modern Identities', *Journal of Social Archaeology*, vol. 14, no. 3, 2014, pp. 296–318.

Horning, A., 'Challenging Colonial Equations? The Gaelic Experience in Early Modern Ireland', in N. Ferris, R. Harrison and M. V. Wilcox (eds), *Rethinking Colonial Pasts Through Archaeology* (Oxford: Oxford University Press, 2014), pp. 293–314.

Horning, A., C. Breen and N. Brannon, 'From the Past to the Future: Integrating Archaeology and Conflict Resolution in Northern Ireland', *Conservation and Management of Archaeological Sites,* vol. 17, no. 1, 2015, pp. 5–21.

Horning, A., 'Crossing the Battlefield: Archaeology, Nationalism and Practice in Irish Historical Archaeology', in A. Brooks and N. Mehler (eds), *The Country Where My Heart Is: Historical Archaeologies of Nationalism and National Identity* (Gainesville, FL: University of Florida Press, 2017), pp. 172–201.

Howell, G., *Gertrude Bell: Queen of the Desert, Shaper of Nations* (New York: Farrer & Giroux, 2006).

Heal, F., *Hospitality in Early Modern England* (Oxford: Oxford University Press, 1990).

Heaney, S., 'Exposure', in *North* (London: Faber, 1975).

Heineman, E., (ed.), *Sexual Violence in Conflict Zones: From the Ancient World to the Era of Human Rights* (Philadelphia: University of Pennsylvania Press, 2011).

Herron, T., 'Orpheus in Ulster: Richard Bartlett's Colonial Art', in T. Herron and M. Potterton (eds), *Ireland in the Renaissance c.1540–1660* (Dublin: Four Courts Press, 2007), pp. 289–310.

Hinton, E. M., *Ireland through Tudor Eyes* (Philadelphia: University of Pennsylvania Press, 1935).

Höckman, O., 'Post-Roman Boat Timbers and a Floating Mill from the Upper Rhine', in C. Westerdahl (ed.), *Crossroads in Ancient Shipbuilding. Proceedings of the Sixth International Symposium on Boat and Ship Archaeology, Roskilde 1991* (Oxford: Oxbow, 1994), pp. 105–115.

Höckman, O., 'Eine Schiffsmühle aus den Jahren um 760 n.Chr. in Gimbsheim, Kr. Alzey–Worms', *Mainzer Archäologische Zeitschrift*, vol. 1, 1994, pp. 191–209.

Hodges, R., *Dark Age Economics: The Origins of Towns and Trade, AD 600–1000* (London: Bloomsbury Academic, 1982).

Hooker, J., 'The Historie Composed and Written by Giraldus Cambrensis, and Translated into English ... Together with the Supplie of the said Historie ... vnto 1587', in R. Holinshed (ed.), *Chronicles of England, Scotland and Ireland*, 6 vols (London: AMS Press, 1807–8).

Howe, J. M., 'Cistercian Monastic Life/Vows: A Vision', in J. A. Nichols and L. Thomas Shank (eds), *Peace Weavers: Medieval Religious Women* (Kalamazoo: Cistercian Publications, 1987), pp. 365–372.

Hurley, M., O. Scully and S. McCutcheon, *Late Viking Age and Medieval Waterford: Excavations 1986–1992* (Waterford Corporation, 1997).

Hutchinson, J., *Dynamics of Cultural Nationalism: The Gaelic Revival and the Creation of the Irish Nation State* (London: Allen & Unwin, 1987).

Hutchinson, J., 'Archaeology and the Irish Rediscovery of the Celtic Past', *Nations and Nationalism*, vol. 7, no. 4, 2001, pp. 505–519.

Imber, C., *Ottoman Empire, 1300–1650: The Structure of Power* (Basingstoke: Palgrave Macmillan, 2002).

Irish Manuscripts Commission, *The Books of Survey and Distribution: Being Abstracts from Various Surveys and Instruments of Title, 1636–1703* (Dublin: Stationery Office for the Irish Manuscripts Commission, 1962), 10 microfilm reels: negative, 35mm.

Iske, B., *The Green Cockatrice* (Dublin: Meath Archaeological and Historical Society, 1978).

Issleib, H., 'Die Betriebsanlagen der Alten Wassermühle im Ahrensfelder Teich', *Hammaburg*, vol. 4, 1953–1955, pp. 68–70.

Iwanisziw, S. B., 'Hugh O'Neill and National Identity in Early Modern Ireland', in D. V. Valone and J. M. Bradbury (eds), *Anglo-Irish Identities, 1571–1845* (Lewisburg: Bucknell University Press, 2008), pp. 30–43.

Jackman, N., C. Moore and C. Rynne, *The Mill at Kilbegly: An Archaeological Investigation on the Route of the M6 Ballinasloe to Athlone National Road Scheme* (Dublin: Wordwell, 2013).

Jenkins, D. (ed.), *The Cambridge History of Western Textiles* (Cambridge: Cambridge University Press, 2003).

Jäggi, C. and U. Lobbedey, 'Church and Cloister: The Architecture of Female Monasticism in the Middle Ages', in J. F. Hamburger and S. Marti (eds), *Crown and Veil: Female Monasticism from the Fifth to the Fifteenth Centuries* (New York: Columbia University Press, 2008), pp. 109–131.

Johnson, M., 'Meanings of Polite Architecture in Sixteenth-Century England', *Historical Archaeology*, vol. 26, no. 3, 1992, pp. 46–56.

Johnson, M., *The Archaeology of Capitalism* (Oxford: Wiley, 1996).

Johnson, M., *Behind the Castle Gate: From Medieval to Renaissance* (London and New York: Routledge, 2002).

Johnson, M., *English Houses 1300–1800* (Harlow: Pearson, 2010).

Johnson, P. D., *Equal in Monastic Profession: Religious Women in Medieval France* (Chicago: The University of Chicago Press, 1991).

Johnson, P. D., 'The Cloistering of Medieval Nuns', in D. O. Helly and S. M. Reverby (eds), *Gendered Domains: Rethinking Public and Private in Women's History* (New York: Cornell University Press, 1992), pp. 27–39.

Jones, A. R. and P. Stallybrass, 'Dismantling Irena: The Sexualising of Ireland in Early Modern England', in A. Parker et al. (eds), *Nationalisms and Sexualities* (New York: Routledge, 1992), pp. 157–171.

Jones, E. and S. Flavin, *Bristol's Trade with Ireland and the Continent, 1503–1601: The Evidence of the Exchequer Customs Accounts* (Dublin: Four Courts Press, 2009).

Jones, S., *The Archaeology of Ethnicity: Constructing Identities in the Past and Present* (London: Routledge, 1997).

Kane, B., 'From Irish *Eineach* to British Honor? Noble Honor and High Politics in Early Modern Ireland, 1500–1650', *History Compass,* vol. 7, no. 2, 2009, pp. 414–430.

Kane, B., *The Politics and Culture of Honour, 1541–1641* (Cambridge: Cambridge University Press, 2010).

Kane, B., 'Languages of Legitimacy? *An Ghaeilge*, the Earl of Thomond and British Politics in the Renaissance Pale, 1600–24', in M. Potterton and T. Herron (eds), *Dublin and the Pale in the Renaissance, c.1540–1660* (Dublin: Four Courts Press, 2011), pp. 267–279.

Keane, G. M., '"Great Stone Houses": Kilkenny and its Early Modern Townhouses 1550–1650', Unpublished MA Thesis, University College Dublin, 2010.

Keegan, J., *A History of Warfare* (London: Random House, 1993).

Keep, J. H., *Soldiers of the Tsar: Army and Society in Russia 1462–1874* (Oxford: Clarendon Press, 1985).

Kelleher, C., 'The Gaelic O'Driscoll Lords of Baltimore, Co. Cork', in L. Doran and J. Lyttleton (eds), *Lordship in Medieval Ireland: Image and Reality* (Dublin: Four Courts Press, 2007), pp. 130–159.

Kelly, E. P., 'Observations on Irish Lake Dwellings', in C. Karkov and R. T. Farrell (eds), *Studies in Insular Art and Archaeology*, American Medieval Studies 1 (Oxford, OH: American Early Medieval Studies and the Miami University School of Fine Arts, 1991), pp. 81–98.

Kelly, F., *A Guide to Early Irish Law* (Dublin: Institute for Advanced Studies, 1988).

Kelly, F., *Early Irish Farming: A Study Based on Law Texts of the 7th and 8th Centuries AD* (Dublin: Institute for Advanced Studies, 1997).

Kelly, R. J., 'Notes on the Round Tower of Kilbannon and on Kilcreevanty, County Galway', *Journal of the Royal Society of Antiquaries of Ireland*, vol. 31, 1901, pp. 379–384.

Kelly, W. (ed.), *Docwra's Derry: A Narration of Events in North-West Ulster, 1600–1604* (Belfast: Ulster Historical Foundation, 2008).

Kenny, G., *Anglo-Irish and Gaelic Women in Ireland* c.*1170–1540* (Dublin: Four Courts Press, 2007).

Kerr, B. M., *Religious Life for Women* c.*1100*–c.*1350: Fontevraud in England* (Oxford: Clarendon Press, 1999).

Kesselring, K., *The Northern Rebellion of 1569: Faith, Politics, and Protest in Elizabethan England* (Basingstoke: Palgrave Macmillan, 2007).

Kew, G., 'The Irish Sections of Fynes Moryson's Unpublished "Itinerary"', *Analecta Hibernica*, vol. 37, 1998, pp. 1–137.

Kiberd, D., *Inventing Ireland: The Literature of the Modern Nation* (London: Jonathan Cape, 1995).

Kiernan, B., *Blood and Soil: A World History of Genocidal Extermination from Sparta to Darfur* (New Haven, CT: Yale University Press, 2007).

Lord Killanin and M.V. Duignan, *The Shell Guide to Ireland* (London: Ebury Press, 1967).

Kingston, S., *Ulster and the Isles in the Fifteenth Century* (Dublin: Four Courts Press, 2004).

Kishlansky, M., *Parliamentary Selection: Social and Political Choice in Early Modern England* (Cambridge: Cambridge University Press, 1986).

Knecht, R. J., *The French Religious Wars 1562–1598* (Oxford: Osprey, 2002).

Knott, E. (ed. and trans.), *The Bardic Poems of Tadhg Dall Ó hUiginn*, 2 vols (London: Irish Texts Society, 1926).

Knüsel, C. and A. Boylston, 'How Has the Towton Project Contributed to our Knowledge of Medieval and Later Warfare?', in V. Fiorato, A. Boylston and C. Knüsel (eds), *Blood Red Roses: The Archaeology of a Mass Grave from the Battle of Towton, AD1461* (Oxford: Oxford University Press, 2000), pp. 169–188.

Kohl, P., 'Nationalism and Archaeology: On the Constructions of Nations and the Reconstructions of the Remote Past', *Annual Review of Anthropology*, vol. 27, 1998, pp. 223–246.

Kozmin, P. A., *Flour Milling*, trans. M. Falkner and T. Fjelstrup (London: D. Van Nostrand Company, 1917).

Krause, C., 'Domus Tiberiana, I: Gli Scavi', *Bollettino di Archeologia*, nos 25–7, 1994.

Kytmannow, T., M. Gardiner and T. Kahlert, 'Leean Mountain Prehistoric Landscape Survey, Second Year: Final Report to the Heritage Council of Ireland', Unpublished Report Lodged with The Heritage Council, 2008.

Lacy, B., *The Archaeological Survey of County Donegal* (Dublin: Government Stationery Office, 1983).

Lagardère, V., 'Moulins d'Occident Musulman au Moyen Age (IX au XV Siècles): Al–Andalus', *Al Qantara*, vol. 12, 1991, pp. 59–118.

Landers, J., *The Field and the Forge: Population, Production and Power in the Pre-Industrial West* (Oxford: Oxford University Press, 2003).

Langdon, J., *Mills and the Medieval Economy: England 1300–1540* (Oxford: Oxford University Press, 2004).

Lanigan-Wood, H. and E. Verling, 'Stone Sculpture in Donegal', in W. Nolan, L. Ronayne and M. Dunlevy (eds), *Donegal History and Society* (Dublin: Geography Publications, 1995), pp. 51–84.

Leask, H. G., *Irish Churches and Monastic Buildings*, 3 vols (Dundalk: Dundalgan Press, 1960).

Leask, I., 'Sex on (Bare) Legs? Thomas Lee and Irishness', *Irish Review*, vol. 42, 2010, pp. 72–84.

Lee, T., *Infformacion giuen to Queen Elizabeth against Sir William Fitzwilliams, his gouernmente in Irelande*, comp. B. Hazard (University College Cork: CELT, 2007) [http://www.ucc.ie/celt/published/E590001–002/index.html].

Lee, T., *A Brief Declaration of the Government of Ireland*, comp. B. Färber (University College Cork: CELT, 2009) [http://www.ucc.ie/celt/published/E590001–004/index.html].

Lee, T., *The Discovery and Recovery of Ireland with the Author's Apology*, comp. B. Färber and R. Murphy (University College Cork: CELT, 2009) [http://www.ucc.ie/celt/published/E590001–005/index.html].

Lee, W. E., 'Indigenes as "Counterinsurgents" in the British Atlantic, 1500–1800', *Defence Studies*, vol. 10, nos 1–2, 2010, pp. 88–105.

Leerssen, J. T., *Mere Irish and Fíor-Ghael* (Cork: Cork University Press, 1996).

Lemaire, L. and J. Salette, 'The Effects of Temperature and Fertiliser Nitrogen on the Spring Growth of Tall Fescue and Cocksfoot', *Grass and Forage Science*, vol. 37, 1982, pp. 191–198.

Lenihan, P. (ed.), *Conquest and Resistance: War in Seventeenth-Century Ireland* (Leiden: Brill, 2001).

Lenman, B., *England's Colonial Wars 1550–1688: Conflicts, Empire and National Identity* (Harlow: Longman, 2001).

Lennon, C., *Sixteenth-Century Ireland: The Incomplete Conquest* (Dublin: Gill & Macmillan, 1994).

Lennon, C., 'The Nugent Family and the Diocese of Kilmore in the Sixteenth and Early Seventeenth Centuries', *Breifne*, vol. 10, 2001, pp. 360–374.

Lennon, C., 'Nugent, Christopher, Fifth Baron Delvin (1544–1602)', *Oxford Dictionary of National Biography* (Oxford University Press, 2004) [http://www.oxforddnb.com/view/article/20387].

Lett, H. W., 'Report on Ancient Monuments in the County of Armagh', *The Journal of the Royal Historical and Archaeological Association of Ireland*, Fourth Series, vol. 6, no. 59, 1884, pp. 431–434.

Lévi-Strauss, C., 'The Culinary Triangle', *New Society,* vol. 22, 1966, pp. 36–43.

Lewis, S., *A Topographical Dictionary of Ireland,* 3 vols (Dublin: S. Lewis & Co., 1837).

Liddiard, R., *'Landscapes of Lordship': Norman Castles and the Countryside in Medieval Norfolk, 1066–1200* (Oxford: Archaeopress, 2000).

Lilley, K. R., 'Imagined Geographies of the "Celtic Fringe" and the Cultural Construction of the "Other" in Medieval Wales and Ireland', in D. Harvey, R. Jones, N. McInroy and C. Milligan (eds), *Celtic Geographies: Old Cultures, New Times* (London: Psychology Press, 2002), pp. 21–36.

Lithgow, W., *Rare Adventures in Ireland in 1619,* comp. R. Murphy (University College Cork: CELT, 2012) [http://www.ucc.ie/celt/published/E610003-001/index.html].

Little, P., 'Age of Atrocity', *The English Historical Review*, vol. 124, no. 508, 2009, pp. 708–710.

Litton Falkiner, C. (ed.), *Illustrations of Irish History and Topography, Mainly of the Seventeenth Century* (London, New York, Bombay: Longmans, Green & Co., 1904).

Litton Falkiner, C. (ed.) 'Travels of Sir William Brereton in Ireland', in *Illustrations of Irish History and Topography* (London: Longmans, Green & Co., 1904), pp. 363–407.

Litton Falkiner, C. (ed.) 'William Farmer's Chronicles of Ireland', *The English Historical Review*, vol. 87, 1907, pp. 527–552.

Loeber, R., 'Irish Country Houses and Castles of the Late Caroline Period: An Unremembered Past Recaptured?', *Quarterly Bulletin of the Irish Georgian Society*, vol. 16, nos 1 and 2, 1973, pp. 1–70.

Loeber, R. and G. Parker, 'The Military Revolution in Seventeenth-Century Ireland', in J. Ohlmeyer (ed.), *Ireland from Independence to Occupation 1641–1660* (Cambridge: Cambridge University Press, 1995), pp. 66–88.

Logue, P., forthcoming in T. Reeves-Smith and P. Logue (eds), *Beyond the Horizon of Memory: A Festschrift for Chris Lynn* (Dublin: Wordwell, forthcoming).

Logue, P. and J. O'Neill, 'The Battlefield Archaeology of the Yellow Ford', in A. Horning and N. Brannon (eds), *Ireland and Britain in the Atlantic World* (Dublin: Wordwell, 2009).

Loingsigh, M., 'An Assessment of Castles and Landownership in Late Medieval North Donegal', *Ulster Journal of Archaeology*, vol. 57, 1994, pp. 145–158.

Lorquet, P., 'Découverte d'un Moulin Carolingien à Belle-Eglise, "Le Pré des Paillards (Oise)"', *Revue Archéologique de Picardie*, vols 3–4, 1994, pp. 51–57.

Lucas, A. T., 'Irish Food Before the Potato', *Gwerin*, vol. 3, 1960, pp. 8–43.

Lucas, A. T., 'Toghers or Causeways: Some Evidence from Archaeological, Literary, Historical and Place-Name Sources', *Proceedings of the Royal Irish Academy,* 85C, 1985, pp. 37–60.

Lucas, A. T., *Cattle in Ancient Ireland* (Kilkenny: Boethius Press, 1989).

Luttwak, E., *The Grand Strategy of Phillip II* (Baltimore: Johns Hopkins University Press, 1979).

Lydon, J., 'The Mills at Ardee in 1304', *Journal of the County Louth Archaeological and Historical Society*, vol. 19, no. 4, 1980, pp. 259–263.

Lydon, J., 'The Middle Nation', in J. Lydon (ed.), *The English in Medieval Ireland* (Dublin: Royal Irish Academy, 1984), pp. 1–26.

Lynch, W., *A View of the Legal Institutions, Honorary Hereditary Offices and Feudal Baronies Established in Ireland during the Reign of Henry the Second* (London: Longman, Rees, Orme, Browne & Green, 1830).

Lynn, C. J., 'The Excavation of Rathmullan, a Raised Rath and Motte in County Down', *Ulster Journal of Archaeology,* vols 44–45, 1982, pp. 65–171.

Lynn, C. J., 'Some "Early" Ringforts and Crannogs', *Journal of Irish Archaeology*, vol. 1, 1983, pp. 51–52.

Lynn, C. J., 'Grim Fortress or Picturesque Ruin? Greencastle, County Down', in A. Hamlin and C. Lynn (eds), *Pieces of the Past: Archaeological Excavations by the Department of the Environment for Northern Ireland, 1970–1986* (Belfast: HMSO, 1988), pp. 66–69.

Lynn, C. J. and J. A. McDowell, *Deer Park Farms: The Excavation of a Raised Rath in the Glenarm Valley, Co. Antrim* (Belfast: Stationery Office, 2011).

Lyons, M., 'Manorial Administration and the Manorial Economy in Ireland, *c.*1200–*c.*1377', Unpublished PhD Thesis, Trinity College Dublin, 1984.

Lyttleton, J., 'The MacCoghlans of Delvin Eathra: The Transformation of a Late Medieval Lordship in Early Modern Ireland', in L. Doran and J. Lyttleton (eds), *Lordship in Medieval Ireland: Image and Reality* (Dublin: Four Courts Press, 2007), pp. 236–265.

Lyttleton, J., *The Jacobean Plantations in Seventeenth-Century Offaly* (Dublin: Four Courts Press, 2013).

Macalister, R. A. S., *The Archaeology of Ireland* (London: Methuen, 1928).
Mac Cana, P., 'The Rise of the Later Schools of *Filidheacht*', *Ériu*, vol. 25, 1974, pp. 127–130.
MacCotter, P., *Medieval Ireland: Territorial, Political and Economic Divisions* (Dublin: Four Courts Press, 2008).
MacCraith, M., 'Gaelic Ireland and the Renaissance', in G. Williams and R. O. Jones (eds), *The Celts and the Renaissance* (Cardiff: University of Wales Press, 1990), pp. 57–89.
Mac Cuarta, B., 'Mathew De Renzy's Letters on Irish Affairs 1613–1620', *Analecta Hibernica*, vol. 34, 1987, pp. 107–182.
Mac Cuarta, B., 'Sword and Word in the 1620s: Matthew De Renzy and Irish Reform', in B. Mac Cuarta (ed.), *Reshaping Ireland 1550–1700* (Dublin: Four Courts Press, 2011), pp. 101–130.
MacCurtain, M., 'Late Medieval Nunneries of the Irish Pale', in H. B. Clarke, J. Prunty and M. Hennessy (eds), *Surveying Ireland's Past: Multidisciplinary Essays in Honour of Anngret Simms* (Dublin: Geography Publications, 2004), pp. 129–143.
MacNamara, G., 'The Ancient Stone Crosses of Uí Fearmaic, County Clare. Part II: The Cross of Kilnaboy', *Journal of the Royal Society of Antiquaries of Ireland*, vol. 30, 1900, pp. 22–33.
Mac Niocaill, G., 'Tír Cumaile', *Ériu*, vol. 22, 1971, pp. 81–86.
Mac Niocaill, G. (trans.), *The Annals of Tigernach,* comp. E. Purcell and D. Ó Corráin (University College Cork: CELT, 2010) [http://www.ucc.ie/celt/published/T100002A/index.html].
Maginn, C., *William Cecil, Ireland, and the Tudor State* (Oxford: Oxford University Press, 2012).
Mahaffy, J. P., 'Two Early Tours in Ireland', *Hermathena,* vol. 18, no. 40, 1914, pp. 3–9.
Makowski, E., 'Mulieres Religiosae, Strictly Speaking: Some Fourteenth-Century Canonical Opinions', *The Catholic Historical Review*, vol. 85, no. 1, 1999, pp. 1–14.
Maley, W., 'Something Quite Atrocious: English Colonialism beyond the Pale and the Licence to Violence', *Eolas: Journal of the American Society of Irish Mediaeval Studies*, vol. 3, 2009, pp. 82–111.
Malinowski, B., 'The Group and Individual in Functional Analysis', *American Journal of Sociology,* vol. 44, 1939, pp. 938–964.
Maltby, W. S., *Alba: A Biography of Fernando Alvarez de Toledo, Third Duke of Alba 1507–1582* (Berkeley: University of California Press, 1983).
Mangartz, F., *Römischer Basaltlava-Abbau Zwischen Eifel und Rhein* (Mainz: Römisch Germanisches Zentralmuseum, 2008).
Manning, C., *The History and Archaeology of Glanworth Castle, County Cork* (Dublin: Wordwell, 2009).
Marshall, J., 'The Hovendens: Fosterbrothers of Hugh O'Neill, Prince of Ulster', *Ulster Journal of Archaeology*, 2nd series, vol. 13, 1907, pp. 73–83.

Martínez Carillo, L. and M. Martínez Martínez, *Origenes y Expansion de los Molinos Hidráulicos en la Ciudad y Huerta de Murcia (Siglos XII–XV)* (Ayuntamiento de Murcia, 2000).

Marx, K., *Capital: A Critique of Political Economy* (London: Penguin, 1990).

Masschaele, J., *Peasants, Merchants and Markets: Inland Trade in Medieval England, 1150–1350* (New York: Macmillan, 1997).

Masterson, R., 'The Early Anglo Norman Colonisation of Fore, Co. Westmeath', *Ríocht na Midhe*, vol. 13, 2002, pp. 44–60.

Maxwell, C., *Irish History from Contemporary Sources 1509–1610* (London: George Allen 1923).

Mays, S., 'The Human Remains', in S. Mays, C. Harding and C. Heighway, *The Churchyard (Wharram: A Study of Settlement on the Yorkshire Wolds IX)* (York: York University Archaeological Publications, 2007), pp. 77–192.

McCarthy, D., *The Irish Annals: Their Genesis, Evolution and History* (Dublin: Four Courts Press, 2008).

McCone, K., *Pagan Past and Christian Present in Early Irish Literature*, Maynooth Monographs, vol. 3 (Maynooth: An Sagart, 1990).

McCone, K., 'The Celtic and Indo-European Origins of the *Fían*', in S. J. Arbuthnot and G. Parsons (eds), *The Gaelic Finn Tradition* (Dublin: Four Courts Press, 2012), pp. 14–30.

McCormick, A., *The Earldom of Desmond, 1463–1583: The Decline and Crisis of a Feudal Lordship* (Dublin: Four Courts Press, 2005).

McCormick, F., 'Struell Wells: Pagan Past and Christian Present', *Journal of the Royal Society of Antiquaries of Ireland*, vol. 139, 2009, pp. 45–62.

McCormick, F., T. Kerr, M. McLatchie and A. O'Sullivan, 'The Archaeology of Livestock and Cereal Production in Early Medieval Ireland, AD 400–1100', *Early Medieval Archaeology Project Report 5.1*, 2011.

McCracken, E., *The Irish Woods Since Tudor Times: Their Distribution and Exploitation* (Newton Abbot: David & Charles, 1971).

McDermott, S., 'The Archaeology of the Twelve Tates of McKenna, *c.*1591', *Clogher Record*, vol. 20, no. 2, 2010, pp. 373–406.

McDermott, S., 'Magnetometry Survey, Tullahoge Fort, Co. Tyrone. Geophysical Survey Report No. 31', Unpublished Geophysical Report Prepared by the Centre for Archaeological Fieldwork, QUB (Belfast: Northern Ireland Environmental Agency, 2014).

McErlean, T., 'The Irish Townland System of Landscape Organisation', in T. Reeves-Smyth and F. Hammond (eds), *Landscape Archaeology in Ireland*, British Archaeological Reports, International Series, 116 (Oxford: Archaeopress, 1983), pp. 315–339.

McErlean, T. and N. Crothers, *Harnessing the Tides: The Early Medieval Tide Mills at Nendrum Monastery, Strangford Lough* (London: Stationery Office, 2007).

McGettigan, D., 'MacSweeney', in S. Duffy (ed), *Medieval Ireland: An Encyclopedia* (New York and London: Routledge, 2005), pp. 305–307.

McGivern, S., 'Gaelic Secular Settlement in South-East Tyrone in the Late Medieval Period', Unpublished Thesis, Queen's University Belfast, 2007.

McGurk, J., 'Terrain and Conquest 1600–1603', in P. Lenihan (ed.), *Conquest and Resistance: War in Seventeenth-Century Ireland* (Leiden: Brill, 2001), pp. 87–114.

McGurk, J., *Sir Henry Docwra, 1564–1631: Derry's Second Founder* (Dublin: Four Courts Press, 2006).

McInerney, L., 'The West Clann Chuiléin Lordship in 1586: Evidence from a Forgotten Inquisition', *North Munster Antiquarian Journal*, vol. 48, 2008, pp. 35–37.

McInerney, L., 'Lettermoylan of Clann Bhruaideadha: A Résumé of their Landholding, Topography and History', *North Munster Antiquarian Journal*, vol. 52, 2012, pp. 81–113.

McInerney, L., *Clerical and Learned Lineages of Medieval Co. Clare: A Survey of the Fifteenth-Century Papal Registers* (Dublin: Four Courts Press, 2014).

McKean, C., 'The Scottish Renaissance Country Seat in its Setting', *Garden History*, vol. 31, no. 2, 2003, pp. 141–162.

McKenna, L. (ed. and trans.), 'Poems to Clonfree Castle', *Irish Monthly*, vol. 51, 1923, pp. 639–645.

McKenzie, C. J., 'Life in Medieval Ballyhanna: Insights from the Osteological and Palaeopathological Analysis of the Adult Skeletons', in C. J. McKenzie, E. M. Murphy and C. J. Donnelly (eds), *The Science of a Lost Medieval Gaelic Graveyard: The Ballyhanna Research Project* (Dublin: Transport Infrastructure Ireland, 2015), pp. 94–97.

McKenzie, C. J. and E. M. Murphy, *Life and Death in Medieval Gaelic Ireland: The Skeletons from Ballyhanna, Co. Donegal* (Dublin: Four Courts Press, 2018).

McKenzie, C. J. and E. M. Murphy, 'Health in Medieval Ireland: The Evidence from Ballyhanna, Co. Donegal', in S. Conran, E. Danaher and M. Stanley (eds), *Past Times, Changing Fortunes: Proceedings of a Public Seminar on Archaeological Discoveries on National Road Schemes, August 2010* (Dublin: National Roads Authority Monograph 8, 2011), pp. 140–143.

McKenzie, C. J., E. M. Murphy and C. J. Donnelly, 'Conclusions – Ordinary Lives: The Medieval Gaelic People of Ballyhanna', in C. J. McKenzie, E. M. Murphy and C. J. Donnelly (eds), *The Science of a Lost Medieval Gaelic Graveyard: The Ballyhanna Research Project* (Dublin: Transport Infrastructure Ireland, 2015), pp. 161–167.

McKenzie, C. J., E. M. Murphy and C. J. Donnelly (eds), *The Science of a Lost Medieval Graveyard: The Ballyhanna Research Project* (Dublin: Transport Infrastructure Ireland, 2015).

McKibben, S., *Endangered Masculinities in Irish Poetry 1540–1780* (University College Dublin Press, 2010).

McLaughlin, R., 'A Threat of Satire by Tadhg (Mac Dáire) Mac Bruaideadha', *Ériu,* vol. 55, 2005, pp. 37–57.

McLaughlin, R., *Early Irish Satire* (Dublin: Institute for Advanced Studies, 2008).

McLeod, W., *Divided Gaels: Gaelic Cultural Identities in Scotland and Ireland,* c.*1200*–c.*1650* (Oxford: Oxford University Press, 2004).

McLeod, W., 'Images of Scottish Warriors in Later Irish Bardic Poetry', in S. Duffy (ed.), *The World of the Galloglass: Kings and Warriors in Ireland and Scotland, 1250–1600* (Dublin: Four Courts Press, 2007).

McNamara, J. A. K., *Sisters in Arms: Catholic Nuns through Two Millennia* (Cambridge, MA: Harvard University Press, 1996).

McNeary, R. and B. Shanahan, 'Medieval Settlement, Society and Land Use in Medieval Roscommon, 1100–1650 AD', *Discovery Programme Report 7* (Dublin: The Discovery Programme, 2005).

McNeary, R. and B. Shanahan, 'Carns Townland, Co. Roscommon: Excavations by the Medieval Rural Settlement Project 2006', in C. Corlett and M. Potterton (eds), *Rural Settlement in Medieval Ireland in the Light of Recent Excavations* (Dublin: Wordwell, 2009), pp. 125–137.

McNeill, C. (ed.), *Calendar of Archbishop Alen's Register* c.*1172–1534* (Dublin: Royal Society of Antiquaries of Ireland, 1950).

McNeill, J., 'The Continent Context', *Journal of the British Archaeological Association*, vol. 159, 2006, pp. 1–47.

McNeill, T. E., *The History and Archaeology of the Anglo-Norman Earldom of Ulster*, Unpublished PhD Thesis, Queen's University Belfast, 1974.

McNeill, T. E., *Anglo-Norman Ulster: The History and Archaeology of an Irish Barony 1177–1400* (Edinburgh: John Donald, 1980).

McNeill, T. E., 'Excavations at Dunsilly, County Antrim', *Ulster Journal of Archaeology*, third series, vols 54/55, 1991/92, pp. 78–122.

McNeill, T. E., *Castles in Ireland: Feudal Power in a Gaelic World* (London: Routledge, 1997).

McNeill, T. E., 'Where Should We Place the Boundary Between the Medieval and Post-Medieval Periods in Ireland?', in A. Horning, R. Ó Baoill, C. Donnelly and P. Logue (eds), *The Post-Medieval Archaeology of Ireland, 1550–1850* (Dublin: Wordwell, 2007), pp. 7–13.

McSkimin, S., *The History and Antiquitites of the County of the Town of Carrickfergus,* 2nd edn (Belfast: Mullan, J. Cleeland, Davidson & M'Cormack, 1909).

McSparron, C., 'A Potted History: Medieval Ulster Coarse Pottery', *Archaeology Ireland,* vol. 23, no. 1, 2009, pp. 13–15.

McSparron, C., 'The Medieval Coarse Pottery of Ulster', *Journal of Irish Archaeology,* vol. 20, 2011, pp. 101–121.

Moody, T. W., 'Ulster Plantation Papers', *Analecta Hibernica,* vol. 8, 1938, pp. 179–311.

Mooney, C., 'The Franciscan Third Order Friary at Dungannon', *Seanchas Ardmhacha: Journal of the Armagh Diocesan Historical Society*, vol. 1, no. 1, 1954, pp. 12–23.

Mooney, C. M., 'Nuns, Tertiaries and Quasi–Religious: The Religious Identities of Late Medieval Holy Women', *Medieval Feminist Forum,* vol. 41, 2006, pp. 68–92.

Moore, M., *Archaeological Inventory of County Meath* (Dublin: Stationery Office, 1987).

Moore, M., *The Archaeological Survey of County Leitrim* (Dublin: Stationery Office, 2003).

Morgan, H., 'The Colonial Venture of Sir Thomas Smith in Ulster, 1571–1575', *Historical Journal*, vol. 28, 1985, pp. 261–278.

Morgan, H., 'The End of Gaelic Ulster: A Thematic Interpretation of Events Between 1534 and 1610', *Irish Historical Studies,* vol. 26, 1988, pp. 8–32.

Morgan, H., 'Tom Lee: The Posing Peacemaker', in B. Bradshaw, A. Hadfield and W. Maley (eds), *Representing Ireland: Literature and the Origins of Conflict, 1534–1660* (Cambridge: Cambridge University Press, 1993).

Morgan, H., *Tyrone's Rebellion: The Outbreak of the Nine Years War in Tudor Ireland* (Woodbridge: The Boydell Press, 1993).

Morgan, H., 'The Lawes of Irelande: A Tract by Sir John Davies', *Irish Jurist*, vols 28–30, 1993–5, pp. 307–313.

Morgan, H. (ed.), 'A Booke of Questions and Answars Concerning the Warrs or Rebellions of the Kingdome of Irelande', *Analecta Hibernica*, vol. 36, 1995, pp. 79–132.

Morgan, H., 'The Messenger in John Derricke's "Image of Irelande" (1581)', *History Ireland*, vol. 15, no. 1, 2007, pp. 6–7.

Morley, H., *Ireland Under Elizabeth and James the First Described by Edmund Spenser, by Sir John Davies and by Fynes Moryson* (London: George Routledge & Sons, 1890).

Morris, R. K., 'The Architecture of Arthurian Enthusiasm: Castle Symbolism in the Reigns of Edward I and his Successors', in M. Strickland (ed.), *Armies, Chivalry and Warfare in Medieval Britain and France* (Stamford: Paul Watkins, 1998), pp. 63–81.

Moryson, F., *An History of Ireland, from the Year 1599–1603*, 2 vols (Dublin: George Ewing, 1735).

Moryson, F., *An Itinerary*, 4 vols (Glasgow: James MacLehose & Sons, 1907).

Moss, R., 'Romanesque Sculpture in North Roscommon', in T. Finan (ed.), *Medieval Lough Cé: History, Archaeology and Landscape* (Dublin: Four Courts Press, 2010), pp. 141–144.

Muendel, J., 'The Horizontal Mills of Medieval Pistoia', *Technology and Culture,* vol. 15, 1974, pp. 194–225.

Muir, E., *Ritual in Early Modern Europe* (Cambridge: Cambridge University Press, 2005).

Murphy, A., *But the Irish Sea Betwixt Us: Ireland, Colonialism and Renaissance Literature* (Lexington, KY: University Press of Kentucky, 1999).

Murphy, D., *Beatha Aodha Ruaidh Uí Dhomhnaill: The Life of Hugh Roe O'Donnell, Prince of Tirconnell (1586–1602)* (Dublin: Fallon, 1895).

Murphy, E. M., 'Human Remains from Saint Patrick's Church, Armoy, County Antrim', in E. Murray and P. Logue (eds), *Battles, Bones and Boats: Archaeological Discoveries in Northern Ireland 1987–2008* (Belfast: Stationery Office, 2010).

Murphy, E. M., 'Osteological Report on the Human Remains from Carrickfergus, Co. Antrim', Unpublished Report, Northern Ireland Environment Agency, 2012.

Murphy, E. M., 'Osteological Analysis of the Human Remains from Greencastle, Co. Down', Unpublished Report, Northern Ireland Environment Agency, 2013.

Murphy, E. M., 'Lives Cut Short: Insights from the Osteological and Palaeopathological Analysis of the Ballyhanna Juveniles', in C. J. McKenzie, E. M. Murphy and C. J. Donnelly (eds), *The Science of a Lost Medieval Graveyard: The Ballyhanna Research Project* (Dublin: Transport Infrastructure Ireland, 2015), pp. 103–120.

Murphy, E. M. and A. Russell, 'Osteological and Palaeopathological Analysis of the Human Remains from Kilroot, Co. Antrim, Part 1 – Report', Unpublished Report, Queen's University Belfast, 2011.

Murphy, M. and M. Potterton, *The Dublin Region in the Middle Ages* (Dublin: Four Courts Press, 2010).

Murray, K., 'Fenian Cycle', in S. Duffy (ed), *Medieval Ireland: An Encyclopedia* (New York and London: Routledge, 2005), pp. 166–167.

Myers, J. (ed.), *Elizabethan Ireland: A Selection of Writings by Elizabethan Writers on Ireland* (Connecticut: Archon Books, 1983).

Mytum, H., 'Materiality and Memory: An Archaeological Perspective on the Popular Adoption of Linear Time in Britain', *Antiquity,* vol. 81, 2007, pp. 381–396.

Naessens, P., 'Gaelic Lords of the Sea: The Coastal Tower Houses of South Connemara', in L. Doran and J. Lyttleton (eds), *Lordship in Medieval Ireland: Image and Reality* (Dublin: Four Courts Press, 2007), pp. 217–235.

Naessens, P., 'The Uí Fhlaithbheartaigh Gaelic Lordship of Iarchonnacht: Medieval Lordly Settlement on the Atlantic Seaboard', Unpublished PhD Thesis, National University of Ireland, Galway, 2009.

Naessens, P., 'Murchadha O'Flaithbheartaigh and the Aggrandisement of Aughnanure Castle', in Richard Oram (ed.), *A House That Thieves Might Knock At: Proceedings of the 2010 Stirling and 2011 Dundee Conferences* (*Tower Studies 1 and 2*) (Donington: Shaun Tyas, 2015), pp. 214–230.

Naessens, P. and K. D. O'Conor, 'Pre-Norman Fortification in Eleventh- and Twelfth-century Connacht', *Chateau Gaillard,* vol. 25, 2012, pp. 259–268.

Nagy, J. F., 'Liminality and Knowledge in Irish Tradition', *Studia Celtica*, vols 16–17, 1981–2, pp. 135–143.

Neuman de Vegvar, C., '"Romanitas and Realpolitik in Cogitosus": Description of the Church of St Brigit, Kildare', in M. Carver (ed.), *The Cross Goes North: Processes of Conversion in Northern Europe AD 300–1300* (York: York Medieval Press, 2003), pp. 153–170.

Nic Dhonnchadha, A., *Medical Writing in Ireland 1400–1700* [http://www.dias.ie/rcsi1.html].

Nicholl, T., 'The Use of Domestic Space in Early Medieval Round Houses: An Experimental Archaeological Approach', *Trowel*, vol. 10, 2005, pp. 27–32.

Nicholls, J., *The Politics of Alcohol: A History of the Drink Question in England* (Manchester: Manchester University Press, 2010).

Nicholls, K. W., *Land, Law and Society in Sixteenth-Century Ireland: O'Donnell Lecture Delivered at University College Cork* (Dublin: National University of Ireland, 1976).

Nicholls, K. W. (ed.), *The Irish Fiants of the Tudor Sovereigns: During the Reigns of Henry VIII, Edward VI, Philip and Mary, and Elizabeth I*, 4 vols (Dublin: Edmund Burke, 1994).

Nicholls, K. W., *Gaelic and Gaelicized Ireland in the Middle Ages* (Dublin: Lilliput Press, 2003).

Nicholls, K. W., 'Scottish Mercenary Kindreds in Ireland 1250–1600', in S. Duffy (ed.), *The World of the Galloglass: Kings and Warriors in Ireland and Scotland, 1250–1600* (Dublin: Four Courts Press, 2007), pp. 86–105.

Ní Dhomhnaill, N., *Pharaoh's Daughter* (Oldcastle, Co. Meath: Gallery Press, 1990).

Nielsen, L. C., 'Omgård, The Viking Age Water-Mill Complex: A Provisional Report on the 1986 Excavations', *Acta Archaeologica*, vol. 57, 1987, pp. 177–210.

Ní Ghrádaigh, J., '"But What Exactly Did She Give?": Derbforgaill and the Nuns' Church at Clonmacnoise', in Heather A. King (ed.), *Clonmacnoise Studies, Volume 2, Seminar Papers 1998* (Dublin: Dept. of Environment, Heritage and Local Government, 2003).

Ní Shéaghdha, N., (ed. and trans.), 'The Rights of Mac Diarmada', *Celtica,* vol. 6, 1963, pp. 156–172.

Nolan, J. P., 'Galway Castles and Owners in 1574', *Journal of the Galway Archaeological and Historical Society*, vol. 1, 1900–1, pp. 109–123.

Novak, S. A., 'Battle-related Trauma', in V. Fiorato, A. Boylston and C. Knüsel (eds), *Blood Red Roses: The Archaeology of a Mass Grave from the Battle of Towton, AD1461* (Oxford: Oxford University Press, 2000).

Ó Baoill, R., 'Carrickfergus and Belfast', in A. Horning, R. Ó Baoill, C. Donnelly and P. Logue (eds), *The Archaeology of Post-Medieval Ireland* c.*1550–1750* (Dublin: Wordwell, 2007), pp. 91–116.

Ó Baoill, R., *Carrickfergus: The Story of the Castle and Walled Town* (Belfast: TSO, 2008).

O'Brien, G. (ed.), *Advertisements for Ireland: Being a Description of the State of Ireland in the Reign of James I* (Dublin: Royal Society of Antiquaries, 1923).

Ó Buachalla, B., *Aisling Ghéar: Na Stíobhartaigh agus an tAos Léinn 1603–1788* (Baile Átha Cliath: Clóchomhar Tta., 1996).

O'Byrne, E., *War, Politics and the Irish of Leinster, 1156–1606* (Dublin: Four Courts Press, 2003).

O'Byrne, E., 'The Tudor State and the Irish of East Leinster', in M. Potterton and T. Herron (eds), *Dublin and the Pale in the Renaissance* c.*1540–1660* (Dublin: Four Courts Press, 2011).

Ó Carragáin, T., *Churches in Medieval Ireland* (New Haven, CT: Yale University Press, 2010).

O'Carroll, D. 'Change and Continuity in Weapons and Tactics 1594–1691', in P. Lenihan (ed.), *Conquest and Resistance: War in Seventeenth-Century Ireland* (Leiden: Brill, 2001), pp. 211–256.

Ó Catháin, D., 'Some Reflexes of Latin Learning and of the Renaissance in Ireland *c.*1450–*c.*1600', in J. Harris and K. Sidwell (eds), *Making Ireland Roman: Irish Neo-Latin Writers and the Republic of Letters* (Cork: Cork University Press, 2009), pp. 1–13.

Ó Ceallaigh, S., *Gleanings from Ulster History* (Cork: Cork University Press, 1951; Reprint 2008).

Ó Clabaigh, C., *The Friars in Ireland 1224–1540* (Dublin: Four Courts Press, 2012).

Ó Clérigh, L., *The Life of Aodh Ruadh O'Domhnaill*, ed. and trans. P. Walsh (Dublin: Irish Texts Society, 1948).

O'Connor, A., 'Keening', in B. Lalor (ed.), *The Encyclopaedia of Ireland* (Dublin: Gill & Macmillan, 2003), p. 579.

O'Conor, K. D., N. Brady, A. Connon and C. Fidalgo-Romo, 'The Rock of Lough Cé, Co. Roscommon', in T. Finan (ed.), *Medieval Lough Cé: History, Archaeology and Landscape* (Dublin: Four Courts Press, 2010), pp. 15–40.

O'Conor, K. D. and B. Shanahan, *Roscommon Abbey: A Visitor's Guide* (Boyle: Roscommon County Council, 2013).

O'Conor, K. D., 'Crannogs', in M. Ryan (ed.), *The Illustrated Archaeology of Ireland* (Dublin: Country House, 1991), pp. 120–123.

O'Conor, K. D., *The Archaeology of Medieval Rural Settlement in Ireland*, Discovery Programme Monograph 3 (Dublin: Royal Irish Academy, 1998).

O'Conor, K. D., 'The Morphology of Gaelic Lordly Sites in North Connacht', in P. J. Duffy, D. Edwards and E. FitzPatrick (eds), *Gaelic*

*Ireland, c.1250–c.1650: Land, Lordship and Settlement* (Dublin: Four Courts Press, 2001), pp. 329–345.

O'Conor, K. D., 'Housing in Later Medieval Gaelic Ireland', *Ruralia*, vol. 4, 2002, pp. 201–210.

O'Conor, K. D., 'Crannogs', in B. Lalor (ed.), *The Encyclopaedia of Ireland* (Dublin: Gill & Macmillan, 2003).

O'Conor, K. D., 'Gaelic Lordly Settlement in 13th- and 14th-Century Ireland', in I. Holm, S. Innselet and I. Øye (eds), *'Utmark': The Outfield as Industry and Ideology in the Iron Age and the Middle Ages* (Department of Archaeology, University of Bergen, 2005).

O'Conor, K. D., 'English Settlement and Change in Roscommon During the Late Sixteenth and Seventeenth Century', in A. Horning, R. Ó Baoill, C. Donnelly and P. Logue (eds), *The Post-Medieval Archaeology of Ireland, 1550–1850* (Dublin: Wordwell, 2007).

O'Conor, K. D., 'Castle Studies in Ireland: The Way Forward', *Château Gaillard*, vol. 23, 2008, pp. 334–335.

O'Conor, K. D., 'Kilronan Parish in the Medieval Period (*c.*AD 400–*c.*AD 1600)', in *Kilronan: Then and Now* (Keadue: Kilronan Parish, 2010).

Ó Corráin, D., *Ireland before the Normans* (Dublin: Gill & Macmillan, 1972).

Ó Corráin, D. (comp.), *Annals of Loch Cé AD 1014–1590* (University College Cork: CELT, 2002) [http://www.ucc.ie/celt/published/G100010A/index.html].

Ó Dálaigh, B., 'Mistress, Mother and Abbess: Renalda Ní Bhriain *c.*1447–1510', *North Munster Antiquarian Journal,* vol. 32, 1990, pp. 50–63.

O'Daly, J. and J. O'Donovan, 'Inauguration of Cathal Crobhdhearg O'Conor, King of Connaught', *Transactions of the Kilkenny Archaeological Society,* vol. 2, no. 2, 1853, pp. 335–347.

Ó Danachair, C., 'Representations of Houses on Some Irish Maps of *c.*1600', in G. Jenkins (ed.), *Studies in Folklife: Essays in Honour of Iorwerth C. Peate* (New York: Barnes & Noble, 1969), pp. 91–103.

Ó Doibhlin, É., 'Ceart Uí Néill: A Discussion and Translation of the Document', *Seanchas Ardmhacha: Journal of the Armagh Diocesan Historical Society,* vol. 5, no. 2, 1970, pp. 324–358.

Ó Doibhlin, É., 'O Neill's "Own Country" and its Families', *Seanchas Ardmhacha: Journal of the Armagh Diocesan Historical Society,* vol. 6, no. 1, 1971, pp. 3–23.

Ó Doibhlin, É., *O'Neill's 'Own Country' and its Families* (Donaghmore Historical Society, 1998).

Ó Dónaill, N. (ed.), *Foclóir Gaeilge–Béarla* (Baile Átha Cliath: An Gúm, 1977).

Ó Donnobháin, B., 'The Human Remains', in A. Lynch, *Tintern Abbey, Co. Wexford: Cistercians and Colcloughs. Excavations 1982–2007. Archaeological Monograph Series: 5* (Dublin: Stationery Office, 2010).

O'Donnabhain, B., 'The Social Lives of Severed Heads: Skull Collection and Display in Medieval and Early Modern Ireland', in M. Bonogofsky (ed.), *The Bioarchaeology of the Human Head: Decapitation, Decoration and Deformation* (Gainesville FL: University Press of Florida, 2011), pp. 122–138.

O'Donovan, J., 'Letters Containing Information Relative to the Antiquities of the County of Kildare Collected During the Progress of the Ordnance Survey in 1837', comp. M. O'Flanagan, typescript in 2 vols (Bray, 1930).

O'Donovan, J., 'Letters Containing Information Relative to the Antiquities of the County of Galway Collected during the Progress of the Ordnance Survey in 1839', comp. M. O'Flanagan, typescript in 3 vols (Bray, 1927).

O'Donovan, J. (trans.), *Annals of the Four Masters*, comp. E. Ryan (University College Cork: CELT, 2002) [http://www.ucc.ie/celt/published/T100005A/index.html].

O'Dowd, M., 'Piers, William (*d.* 1603)', *Oxford Dictionary of National Biography* (Oxford: Oxford University Press, 2004) online edn [http://www.oxforddnb.com/view/article/22236].

O'Dowd, M. (ed.), *Calendar of State Papers, Ireland, Tudor period 1571–1575* (Dublin: Irish Manuscripts Commission; London: Public Record Office, 2000).

O'Dwyer, B. (trans.), *Stephen of Lexington, Letters from Ireland 1228–1229* (Kalamzoo: Cistercian Publications, 1982).

O'Ferrall, F., *Catholic Emancipation: Daniel O'Connell and the Birth of Irish Democracy, 1820–30* (Dublin: Gill & Macmillan, 1985).

Ó Floinn, R., 'A Fragmentary House-Shaped Shrine from Clonard, Co. Meath', *Journal of Irish Archaeology*, vol. 5, 1989/1990, pp. 49–55.

Ó Floinn, R., 'A Crozier Head from Clonard', in T. Condit and C. Corlett (eds), *Above and Beyond: Essays in Memory of Leo Swan* (Dublin: Wordwell, 2005), pp. 333–342.

O'Grady, S. H., *Silva Gadelica: A Collection of Tales in Irish with Extracts Illustrating Persons and Places*, 2 vols (London and Edinburgh: Williams & Norgate, 1892).

Ó hAisibéil, L., 'Logainmneacha Mhagh Loirg agus Uachtar Thíre, Contae Ros Comáin: Anailis ar Ainmneachta Bhailte Fearainn na Seanduíchi Sin', Unpublished PhD Thesis, National University of Ireland, Galway, 2013.

O'Halloran, C., *Golden Ages and Barbarous Nations: Antiquarian Debate and Cultural Politics in Ireland, c.1750–1800* (Cork: Cork University Press, 2004).

O'Hara, J., 'A Landscape Archaeology of Later Medieval Fermanagh', Unpublished PhD Thesis, National University of Ireland, Galway, 2009.

Ó hInnse, S., *Miscellaneous Irish Annals, Fragment I (Mac Carthaigh's Book)*, comp. B. Färber and P. Bambury (University College Cork: CELT, 2010) [http://www.ucc.ie/celt/published/T100013/index.html].

Ohlmeyer, J. (ed.), *Ireland from Independence to Occupation 1641–1660* (Cambridge: Cambridge University Press, 1995).

Ohlmeyer, J., '"Making Ireland English": The Seventeenth-Century Irish Peerage', in B. Mac Cuarta (ed.), *Reshaping Ireland 1550–1700, Colonisation and its Consequences* (Dublin: Four Courts Press, 2011), pp. 131–146.

Kalkreuter, B., *Boyle Abbey and the School of the West* (Dublin: Wordwell, 2001).

O'Keeffe, P. and T. Simington, *Irish Stone Bridges: History and Heritage* (Dublin: Irish Academic Press, 1991).

O'Keeffe, T., 'Augustinian Regular Canons in Twelfth- and Thirteenth-Century Ireland: History, Architecture and Identity', in J. Burton and K. Stöber (eds), *The Regular Canons in the Medieval British Isles* (Turnhout: Brepolis, 2011), pp. 107–145.

O'Keeffe, T., *Medieval Ireland: An Archaeology* (Stroud: Tempus, 2000).

O'Keeffe, T., *An Anglo-Norman Monastery: Bridgetown Priory and the Architecture of the Augustinian Canons Regular in Ireland* (Cork: Cork County Council, 1999).

O'Keeffe, T., 'Rural Settlement and Cultural Identity in Gaelic Ireland', *Ruralia*, vol. 1, 1996, pp. 142–153.

Oliva, M., *The Convent and the Community in Late Medieval England: Female Monasteries in the Diocese of Norwich, 1350–1540* (Woodbridge: The Boydell Press, 1998).

Ó Lochlainn, C., 'Roadways in Ancient Ireland', in J. Ryan (ed.), *Essays and Studies Presented to Professor Eoin MacNeill* (Dublin: The Sign of the Three Candles, 1940), pp. 465–474.

Oman, C., *A History of the Art of War in the Sixteenth Century* (New York: AMS Press, 1979).

O'Meara, J. J. (ed. and trans.), *The History and Topography* of *Ireland* (Dublin: Dolmen Press; Harmondsworth: Penguin, 1982).

O'Meara, J. J. (ed.), *Topographia Hibernica: The History and Topography of Ireland by Gerald of Wales* (Harmondsworth: Penguin Classics, 1982).

Ó Muraíle, N., 'Dinnshenchas', in S. Duffy (ed), *Medieval Ireland: An Encyclopedia* (New York and London: Routledge, 2005), pp. 132–133.

Ó Néill, E., 'Towards A New History of the Nine Years' War', *Irish Sword*, vol. 26, 2009, pp. 241–262.

Ó Néill, E. and I. Portela, 'Prince of Ulster or Arch Traitor? The Self-Fashioning of Hugh O'Neill', *Brazilian Journal of Irish Studies*, vol. 2, 2000, pp. 87–96.

O'Neill, M., 'An Leabhar Eoghanach: An Abridged Translation of the Book of the Descendants of Eoghan', *Dúiche Néill*, no. 19, 2011.

O'Neill, M., 'The Medieval Parish Churches in County Meath', *Journal of the Royal Society of Antiquaries of Ireland*, vol. 132, 2002, pp. 1–56.

O'Neill, T., *Merchants and Mariners in Medieval Ireland* (Dublin: Irish Academic Press, 1987).

O'Rahilly, C., *Five Seventeenth-Century Political Poems* (Dublin: Institute for Advanced Studies, 1977).

Ó Riain, P., 'Boundary Association in Early Irish Society', *Studia Celtica*, vol. 7, 1972, pp. 12–29.

Ó Riain, P., *A Dictionary of Irish Saints* (Dublin: Four Courts Press, 2011).

Ó Riordáin, S. P., *Antiquities of the Irish Countryside* (Cork: Cork University Press, 1942).

Orpen, G. H., 'Motes and Norman Castles in Ireland', *The Journal of the Royal Society of Antiquaries of Ireland*, vol. 37, no. 2, 1907, pp. 123–152.

Orpen, G. H., *Ireland under the Normans 1169–1333*, 3 vols (Oxford: Clarendon Press, 1911; reprint Dublin: Four Courts Press, 2005).

Orser, C., 'Symbolic Violence, Resistence and the Vectors of Improvement in Early Nineteenth-Century Ireland', *World Archaeology*, vol. 37, no. 3, 2005, pp. 392–407.

Orser, C., 'Symbolic Violence and Landscape Pedagogy: An Illustration from the Irish Countryside', *Historical Archaeology*, vol. 40, no. 2, 2006, pp. 28–44.

Osborn, M. S., 'The Rent Breasts, Part II', *Midwife, Health Visitor and Community Nurse*, vol. 15, no. 9, 1979, pp. 347–348.

Ó Scea, C., 'Erenachs, Erenachships and Church Landholding in Gaelic Fermanagh, 1270–1609', *Proceedings of the Royal Irish Academy*, vol. 112C, 2012, pp. 273–274

Ó Síocháin, S. (ed.), *Social Thought on Ireland in the Nineteenth Century* (Dublin: University College Dublin Press, 2009).

Ó Siochrú, M., 'Propaganda, Rumour and Myth: Oliver Cromwell and the Massacre at Drogheda', in D. Edwards, P. Lenihan and C. Tait (eds), *Age of Atrocity: Violence and Political Conflict in Early Modern Ireland* (Dublin: Four Courts Press, 2007), pp. 266–282.

O'Sullivan, A., F. McCormick, T. Kerr and L. Harney, *Early Medieval Ireland AD 400–1100: The Evidence from Archaeological Excavations* (Dublin: Royal Irish Academy, 2013).

O'Sullivan, A., 'Crannogs in Late Medieval Gaelic Ireland, *c.*1350–1650', in P. J. Duffy, D. Edwards and E. FitzPatrick (eds), *Gaelic Ireland, c.1250–c.1650: Land, Lordship and Settlement* (Dublin: Four Courts Press, 2001), pp. 397–417.

O'Sullivan, A., *The Archaeology of Lake Settlement in Ireland* (Dublin: Royal Irish Academy, 1998).

O'Sullivan, C., *Hospitality in Medieval Ireland, 900–1500* (Dublin: Four Courts Press, 2004).

O'Sullivan, H., 'A 1575 Rent-Roll, with Contemporaneous Maps, of the Bagenal Estate in the Carlingford Lough District', *Journal of the County Louth Archaeological and Historical Society*, vol. 21, 1985, pp. 31–47.

O'Sullivan, H., 'Rothe's Castle, Dundalk and Hugh O'Neill: A Sixteenth-Century Map', *Journal of the County Louth Archaeological Society*, vol. 15, no. 3, 1963, pp. 281–291.

O'Sullivan Beare, P., *Ireland under Elizabeth: Chapters Towards a History of Ireland Under Elizabeth*, trans. M. J. Byrne (Dublin: Sealy, Bryers & Walker, 1903).

Otway-Ruthven, A. J., 'The Organization of Anglo-Irish Agriculture in the Middle Ages', *The Journal of the Royal Society of Antiquaries of Ireland*, vol. 81, no. 1, 1951, pp. 1–13.

Otway-Ruthven, A. J., 'The Character of Norman Settlement in Ireland', in J. L. McCracken et al. (eds), *Historical Studies*, vol. 5 (London: Bowes & Bowes, 1965), pp. 162–177.

Otway-Ruthven, A. J., *A History of Medieval Ireland* (London: E. Benn, 1980).

Palmer, P., *Language and Conquest in Early Modern Ireland: English Renaissance Literature and Elizabethan Imperial Expansion* (Cambridge: Cambridge University Press, 2001).

Palmer, P., 'False and Unreliable Interpreters in Sixteenth-Century Ireland', *Irish Historical Studies*, vol. 33, no. 131, 2004, pp. 257–277.

Palmer, P., '"Hungry Eyes" and the Rhetoric of Dispossession: English Writing from Early-Modern Ireland', in J. Wright (ed.), *The Blackwell Companion to Irish Literature*, 2 vols (Oxford: Wiley-Blackwell, 2010), pp. 92–107.

Palmer, P., *The Severed Head and the Grafted Tongue: Translating Violence in Early Modern Ireland* (Cambridge: Cambridge University Press, 2014).

Parker, G., *The Military Revolution: Military Innovation and the Rise of the West 1500–1800*, 2nd edn (Cambridge: Cambridge University Press, 1999).

Parker, G., *The Grand Strategy of Phillip II* (New Haven CT: Yale University Press, 2000).

Parker, G., *The Army of Flanders and the Spanish Road 1567–1659*, 2nd edn (Cambridge: Cambridge University Press, 2004).

Parkhouse, J., 'The Distribution and Exchange of Mayen Lava Quernstones in Early Medieval Europe', in G. de Boc and F. Verhaege (eds), *Exchange and Trade in Medieval Europe. Papers of the Medieval Europe Brugge Conference 1997. Conference III* (Zellik: Institut vor het Archeologisch Patrimonium, 1997), pp. 97–106.

Parkes, P., 'Celtic Fosterage: Adoptive Kinship and Clientage in Northwest Europe', *Comparative Studies in Society and History*, vol. 48, no. 2, 2006, pp. 359–395.

Parnell, J. J., R. Terry and Z. Nelson, 'Soil Chemical Analysis Applied as an Interpretive Tool for Ancient Human Activities in Piedras Negras, Guatemala', *Journal of Archaeological Science*, vol. 29, no. 4, 2002, pp. 379–404.

Paul, M. C., 'The Military Revolution in Russia, 1550–1682', *Journal of Military History*, vol. 68, no. 1, 2004, pp. 9–45.

Peacock, D. P. S., 'The Roman Millstone Trade: A Petrological Sketch', *World Archaeology*, vol. 12, no. 1, 1980, pp. 43–53.

Pender, S., *A Census of Ireland, Circa 1659. With Supplementary Material from the Poll Money Ordinances, 1660–1661* (Dublin: Stationery Office, 1939).

Pentland Mahaffy, R. (ed.), *Calendar of State Papers Relating to Ireland 1601–1603* (London: His Majesty's Stationery Office, 1912).

Perkins-Curran, K., '"Quhat Say Ye Now My Lady Priores? How Have Ye Usit Your Office, Can Ye Ges?" Politics, Power and Realities of the Office of a Prioress in Her Community in Late Medieval Scotland', in J. Burton and K. Stöber (eds), *Monasteries and Society in the British Isles in the Later Middle Ages* (Woodbridge: The Boydell Press, 2008), pp. 124–144.

Perros, H., 'Crossing the Shannon Frontier: Connacht and the Anglo-Normans, 1170–1224', in T. Barry, R. Frame and K. Simms (eds), *Colony and Frontier in Medieval Ireland* (London: The Hambledon Press, 1995), pp. 117–138.

Perrott, J., *The Chronicle of Ireland, 1584–1608*, ed. H. Wood (Dublin: Irish Manuscripts Commission, 1933).

Phaer, T., *The Boke of Chyldren* (1544), ed. R. Bowers (Tempe, AZ: Centre for Medieval and Renaissance Studies, 1999).

Phillips, J. R. S., 'The Irish Remonstrance of 1317: An International Perspective', *Irish Historical Studies*, vol. 27, 1990, pp. 112–129.

Piers, H., 'A Chorographical Description of the County of West-Meath Written A.D. 1682', in C. Vallancey (ed.), *Collectanea de Rebus Hibernicis* (Dublin: Luke White, 1776).

Pike, K., *Language in Relation to a Unified Theory of the Structure of Human Behaviour* (The Hague: Mouton, 1967).

Pikirayi, I., *The Zimbabwe Culture: Origins and Decline in Southern Zambezian States* (Walnut Creek: AltaMira, 2001).

Pinkerton, W., 'The "Overthrow" of Sir John Chichester at Carrickfergus in 1597', *Ulster Journal of Archaeology*, vol. 5, 1857, pp. 188–209.

Pluciennik, M., 'Genetics, Archaeology and the Wider World', *Antiquity*, vol. 70, no. 267, 1996, pp. 13–14.

Pohl, M., 'Querns as Markers for the Determination of Medieval European Trade Spheres', in D. Williams and D. Peacock (eds), *Bread for the People: The Archaeology of Mills and Milling,* British Archaeological Report, International Series, 2274 (Oxford: Archaeopress, 2011), pp. 169–178.

Potterton, M., *Medieval Trim: History and Archaeology* (Dublin: Four Courts Press, 2005).

Powell, M., *The Politics of Consumption in Eighteenth-Century Ireland* (Hampshire: Palgrave Macmillan, 2005).

Power, D. et al., *Archaeological Inventory of County Cork. Vol. 2: East and South Cork* (Dublin: Stationery Office, 1994).

Power, E., *Medieval English Nunneries* (Cambridge: Cambridge University Press, 1922).

Quinn, D. B., 'Anglo-Irish Ulster in the Early Sixteenth Century', *Proceedings and Reports of the Belfast Natural History and Philosophical Society, Session 1933–34* (Belfast, 1935), pp. 56–78.

Quinn, D. B., 'Sir Thomas Smith (1513–77) and the Beginnings of English Colonial Theory', *Proceedings of the American Philosophical Society*, vol. 89, no. 4, 1945, pp. 543–560.

Quinn, D. B., 'Ireland and Sixteenth Century European Expansion', in T. Desmond Williams (ed.), *Historical Studies: Papers Read Before the Second Irish Conference of Historians* (London: Bowes & Bowes, 1958).

Quinn, D. B. and K. W. Nicholls, 'Ireland in 1534', in T. W. Moody, F. X. Martin and F. J. Byrne (eds), *Early Modern Ireland 1534–1691* (Oxford: Oxford University Press, 2009).

Quin, E. G. (ed.), *Dictionary of the Irish Language, Based Mostly on Old and Middle Irish Materials* (Dublin: Royal Irish Academy, 1984).

Radcliffe-Brown, A. R., *Structure and Function in Primitive Society* (New York: Free Press, 1952).

Ralston, I. and I. Armit, *Scotland After the Ice Age: Environment, Archaeology and History, 8000 BC–AD 1000* (Edinburgh: Edinburgh University Press, 2003).

Record Commission, *Inquisitionum in Officio Rotulorum Cancellariae Hiberniae Asservatarum Repertorium*, 2 vols (Dublin: Commissioners of the Public Records of Ireland, 1826–9).

Reeves-Smith, T., *Irish Gardens and Gardening Before Cromwell* (Kinsale: Gandon Editions, 1999).

Reeves-Smith, T., 'Community to Privacy: Late Tudor and Jacobean Manorial Architecture in Ireland, 1560–1640', in A. Horning et al. (eds), *The Post-Medieval Archaeology of Ireland, 1550–1850* (Dublin: Wordwell, 2007), pp. 289–326.

Reeves-Smith, T., 'The Natural History of Demesnes', in J. W. Foster and H. C. G. Chesney (eds), *Nature in Ireland: A Scientific and Cultural History* (Dublin: Lilliput Press, 2007), pp. 549–572.

Rich, B., 'A New Description of Ireland', in J. Myers (ed.), *Elizabethan Ireland: A Selection of Writings by Elizabethan Writers on Ireland* (Connecticut: Archon Books, 1983).

Rives, D., 'Taking the Veil: Clothing and the Transformation of Identity', *Proceedings of the Western Society for French History*, vol. 33, 2005, pp. 465–486.

Robinson, D. M., *The Geography of Augustinian Settlement*, British Archaeological Report, British Series, 80, 2 vols (Oxford: Archaeopress, 1980).

Robinson, H. G. R. and J. Macbeth, *Fairs and Markets' Commission, Ireland. Report of the Commissioners Appointed to Inquire into the State of the Fairs and Markets in Ireland. Part II: Minutes of Evidence* (Dublin: His Majesty's Stationery Office, 1852–53).

Robinson, P., 'The Spread of Hedged Enclosure in Ulster', *Ulster Folklife*, vol. 23, 1977, pp. 57–69.

Robinson, P., *Irish Historic Towns Atlas: Carrickfergus* (Dublin: Royal Irish Academy, 1986).

Roe, H., *Medieval Fonts of Meath* (Meath Archaeological and Historical Society, 1968).

Rogers, C. J. (ed.), *The Military Revolution Debate: Readings on the Military Transformation of Early-Modern Europe* (Oxford: Westview Press, 1995).

Rohmer, P., 'Le Moulin Carolingien d'Audun-le-Tiche', *L'Archéologue*, vol. 22, 1996, pp. 6–8.

Ronnes, H., 'Continental Traces at Carrick-on-Suir and Contemporary Irish Castles', in T. Herron and M. Potterton (eds), *Ireland in the Renaissance c.1540–1660* (Dublin: Four Courts Press, 2007), pp. 255–273.

Royal Commission on Historical Manuscripts, *Calendar of the Manuscripts of the Most Honourable the Marquess of Salisbury … Preserved at Hatfield House, Hertfordshire, Part IX* (London: His Majesty's Stationery Office, 1902).

Rublack, U., *Dressing Up: Cultural Identity in Renaissance Europe* (Oxford: Oxford University Press, 2010).

Russell, I., C. Moore, A. O'Sullivan and V. Ginn, 'Killoteran 9: Early Medieval Vertical Watermill', in J. Eogan and E. Shee Twohig (eds), *Cois tSiúre: Nine Thousand Years of Human Activity in the Lower Suir Valley. Archaeological Excavations on the Route of the N25 Waterford City Bypass*, NRA Scheme Monographs 8 (Dublin: National Roads Authority, 2011), pp. 37–48.

Ryan, M. (ed.), *The Illustrated Archaeology of Ireland* (Dublin: Country House, 1991).

Rynne, C., 'The Patrick Street Watermills: Their Technological Context and a Note on the Reconstruction', in C. Walsh, *Archaeological Excavations at Patrick, Nicholas and Winetavern Streets, Dublin* (Dingle: Brandon, 1997), pp. 81–89.

Rynne, C., *Technological Change in Anglo-Norman Munster*, The Barryscourt Lectures, vol. III (Cork: Barryscourt Trust, 1998).

Rynne, C., *Industrial Ireland 1750–1930: An Archaeology* (Cork: The Collins Press, 2006).

Rynne, C., 'A Medieval Watermill at Ballyine, County Limerick', *Journal of the Cork Historical and Archaeological Society*, vol. 112, 2007, pp. 23–28.

Rynne, C., 'Technological Continuity, Technological "Survival": The Use of Horizontal Mills in Western Ireland, *c.*1632–1940', *Industrial Archaeology Review*, vol. 33, no. 2, 2011, pp. 96–105.

Rynne, E., 'Three Knife-Daggers (from Mayo)', *Journal of the Royal Society of Antiquaries of Ireland*, vol. 99, part 2, 1969, pp. 137–143.

Salter, M., *The Castles of Leinster* (Malvern: Folly Publications, 2004).

Salter, M., *Abbeys and Friaries of Ireland* (Malvern: Folly Publications, 2009).

Saunders, A., 'Lyford Castle, Devon', *Medieval Archaeology*, vol. 24, 1980, pp. 123–186.

Sawday, J., 'Self and Selfhood in the Seventeenth Century', in R. Porter (ed.), *Rewriting the Self: Histories from the Renaissance to the Present* (London: Routledge, 1997), pp. 29–49.

Schleif, C. and V. Schier, *Katerina's Windows: Donation and Devotion, Art and Music as Heard and Seen Through the Writings of a Birgittine Nun* (Philadelphia: Pennsylvania State University Press, 2009).

Schoenfeld, M., *Bodies and Selves in Early Modern England: Physiology and Inwardness in Spenser, Shakespeare, Herbert and Milton* (Cambridge: Cambridge University Press, 1999).

Schoonhoven, J., 'Grinding with Stones', *Transactions of the International Molinological Society*, vol. 4, 1978, pp. 269–283.

Selma, S., *Els Molins d'Aigua Medievals a Sharq al-Andalus* (Ajuntament d'Onda, 1993).

Selma, S., 'De la Construcció Islàmica al Casalici Modern: l'Evolució Molí Hidràulic Valencia', in T. F. Glick and E. Guinot (eds), *Els Molins Hidráulics Valencians: Tecnologia, História i Context Social* (Institución Alfons el Magnànim de la Diputación de Valencia, 2000), pp. 101–163.

Seward, D., *The Last White Rose: The Secret War of the Tudors* (London: Constable & Robinson, 2010).

Shagan, E., 'Protector Somerset and the 1549 Rebellions: New Sources and New Perspectives', *English Historical Review*, vol. 114, 1999, pp. 34–63.

Shagan, E., *Popular Politics and the English Reformation* (Cambridge: Cambridge University Press, 2002).

Shakespeare, W., *The Tragedy of King Lear*, ed. Jay L. Halio (Cambridge: Cambridge University Press, 2005).

Shanahan, B., *Roscommon Landscape: Cloonybeirne – O'Conor Roe Lordship* (Dublin: Discovery Programme, 2010).

Shanahan, M., 'Dining on Words: Manuscript Recipe Books, Culinary Change and Elite Food Culture in Ireland, 1660–1830', *Irish Architectural and Decorative Studies*, vol. 15, 2012, pp. 82–97.

Sharpe, J. A., *Early Modern England: A Social History 1550–1760* (London: Bloomsbury Academic, 2003).

Shennan, S. J., 'Cultural Approaches to Cultural Identity', in S. J. Shennan (ed.), *Cultural Approaches to Cultural Identity* (London: Unwin, 1989), pp. 1–32.

Shepard, A., Review of M. J. Braddick and J. Walter (eds), *Negotiating Power in Early Modern Society: Order, Hierarchy and Subordination in Britain and Ireland*, H-Albion, H-Net Reviews, November 2002. [http://www.h–net.org/reviews/showrev.php?id=6884].

Sherlock, R., 'The Social Environment of the Irish Tower House', Unpublished PhD Thesis, National University of Ireland, Galway, 2008.

Sherlock, R., 'The Evolution of the Irish Tower-House as a Domestic Space', *Proceedings of the Royal Irish Academy,* vol. 111C, 2011, pp. 115–140.

Shirley, E. P. et al., 'Extracts from the Journal of Thomas Dineley, Esquire, Giving Some Account of his Visit to Ireland in the Reign of Charles II (continued)', *The Journal of the Kilkenny and South-East of Ireland Archaeological Society*, vol. 6, no. 1, 1867, pp. 73–91, 176–204.

Sidney, H., 'Sir Henry Sidney's Memoir of his Government of Ireland', *Ulster Journal of Archaeology*, First Series, vol. 3, 1855, pp. 33–52, 85–109, 336–357.

Signori, G., 'Wanderers Between Worlds: Visitors, Letters, Wills and Gifts as a Means of Communication in Exchanges between Cloister and the World', in J. F. Hamburger and S. Marti (eds), *Crown and Veil: Female Monasticism From the Fifth to the Fifteenth Centuries* (New York: Columbia University Press, 2008), pp. 259–274.

Simms, K., 'The Archbishops of Armagh and the O'Neills 1347–1471', *Irish Historical Studies*, vol. 19, 1974, pp. 38–55.

Simms, K., 'Warfare in the Medieval Gaelic Lordships', *Irish Sword*, vol. 12, 1975, pp. 100–102.

Simms, K., 'Gaelic Lordship in Ulster in the Later Middle Ages', Unpublished PhD Thesis, Trinity College Dublin, 1976.

Simms, K., 'The Medieval Kingdom of Lough Erne', *Clogher Record*, vol. 9, no. 2, 1977, pp. 126–141.

Simms, K., 'Guesting and Feasting in Gaelic Ireland', *Journal of the Royal Society of Antiquities of Ireland*, vol. 108, 1978, pp. 67–100.

Simms, K., 'Gabh Umad a Fheidhlimidh: A Fifteenth Century Inauguration Ode?', *Ériu*, vol. 31, 1980, pp. 132–145.

Simms, K., 'Nomadry in Medieval Ireland: The Origins of the Creaght or Caoraigheacht', *Peritia*, vol.5, 1986, pp. 379–391.

Simms, K., 'Bards and Barons: The Anglo-Irish Aristocracy and the Native Culture', in R. Bartlett and A. MacKay (eds), *Medieval Frontier Societies* (Oxford: Oxford University Press, 1989), pp. 177–197.

Simms, K., 'Images of Warfare in Bardic Poetry', *Celtica*, vol. 21, 1990, pp. 608–619.

Simms, K., 'Late Medieval Donegal', in W. Nolan et al. (eds), *Donegal History and Society* (Dublin: Geography Publications, 1995), pp. 183–202.

Simms, K., 'Gaelic Warfare in the Middles Ages', in T. Bartlett and K. Jeffery (eds), *A Military History of Ireland* (Cambridge: Cambridge University Press, 1996), pp. 99–115.

Simms, K., *From Kings to Warlords: The Changing Political Structure of Gaelic Ireland in the Later Middle Ages* (Woodbridge: The Boydell Press, 1987).

Simms, K., 'Native Sources for Gaelic Settlement: The House Poems', in P. J. Duffy, D. Edwards and E. FitzPatrick (eds), *Gaelic Ireland, c.1250–c.1650: Land, Lordship and Settlement* (Dublin: Four Courts Press, 2001), pp. 246–270.

Simms, K., 'Dunairí', in S. Duffy (ed), *Medieval Ireland: An Encyclopedia* (New York and London: Routledge, 2005), pp. 134–135.

Simms, K., 'Bardic Schools, Learned Families', in S. Duffy (ed), *Medieval Ireland: An Encyclopedia* (New York and London: Routledge, 2005), pp. 35–37.

Simms, K., *Medieval Gaelic Sources* (Dublin: Four Courts Press, 2009).

Simms, K., 'The Barefoot Kings: Literary Image and Reality in Later Medieval Ireland', *Proceedings of the Harvard Celtic Colloquium*, vol. 30, 2010, pp. 13–14.

Simms, K., 'The Origins of the Creaght: Farming System or Social Unit?', in M. Murphy and M. Stout (eds), *Agriculture and Settlement in Ireland* (Dublin: Four Courts Press, 2015), pp. 379–391.

Sloan, B., *Community Excavation Adjacent to Tullaghoge Fort, Cookstown, Co. Tyrone,* Data Structure Report No. 109, Centre for Archaeological Fieldwork, School of Geography, Archaeology and Palaeoecology, Queen's University Belfast (Belfast: Northern Ireland Environmental Agency, 2014).

Small, J. (ed.), *The Image of Ireland by John Derricke* (Edinburgh: Adam & Charles Black, 1883).

Smount, T. C., 'Energy Rich, Energy Poor: Scotland, Ireland and Iceland, 1600–1800', in D. Dickson and C. Ó Gráda (eds), *Refiguring Ireland: Essays in Honour of L. M. Cullen* (Dublin: Lilliput Press, 2003), pp. 19–36.

Smyth, J., *The Men of No Property: Irish Radicals and Popular Politics in the Late 18th Century* (London: Palgrave Macmillan, 1992).

Smythe, J., *Certain Discourses Military* (1590), ed. J. R. Hale (Ithaca: Associated University Press, 1964).

Smythe, J., *Instructions, Observations, and Orders Mylitarie* (London, 1594).

Spain, R. and I. Riddler, 'Millstones', in P. Bennett, I. Riddler and C. Sparey Green (eds), *The Roman Watermills and Settlement at Ickham, Kent: The Archaeology of Canterbury, Vol. V* (Canterbury Archaeological Trust, 2010).

Speeding, J. (ed.), *The Letters and the Life of Francis Bacon*, vol. VI (London: Longman, Green, Reader & Dyer, 1872).

Spenser, E., *A View of the Present State of Ireland*, in J. Myers (ed.), *Elizabethan Ireland: A Selection of Writings by Elizabethan Writers on Ireland* (Connecticut: Archon Books, 1983).

Spenser, E., *A View of the Present State of Ireland*, ed. A. Hadfield and W. Maley (Oxford: Blackwell, 1997).

Spenser, E., *The Faerie Queene*, ed. A. C. Hamilton, 2nd edn (London: Routledge, 2007).

Spivak, G. C., 'Can the Subaltern Speak?', in R. C. Morris (ed.), *Can the Subaltern Speak? Reflections on the History of an Idea* (New York: Columbia University Press, 2010), pp. 21–78.

Strafford, Earl of, *The Letters and Dispatches of the Earl of Strafforde*, 2 vols, ed. W. Knowler (London, 1739).

[Stafford, T.], *Pacata Hibernia: Ireland Appeased and Reduced, or a Historie of the Late Warres of Ireland*, ed. S. H. O'Grady, 2 vols (London: Downey, 1896).

Stalley, R., *The Cistercian Monasteries of Ireland* (New Haven CT: Yale University Press, 1987).

Stanihurst, R., *Holinshed's Irish Chronicle*, ed. L. Miller and E. E. Power (Dublin: Dolmen Press, 1979).

Steer, K. A., J. O. W. Bannerman and G. H. Collings, *Late Medieval Monumental Sculpture in the West Highlands* (Edinburgh: Royal Commission on the Ancient and Historical Monuments of Scotland, 1977).

Stephenson, J. (ed.), *Calendar of State Papers: Foreign Series, of the Reign of Elizabeth 1562* (London: Longman, Green, Reader & Dyer, 1867).

Stevens, E. E., 'A History of Infant Feeding', *Journal of Perinatal Education*, vol. 18, no. 2, 2009, pp. 32–39.

Stöber, K., *Late Medieval Monasteries and their Patrons: England and Wales, c.1300–1540* (Woodbridge: Boydell, 2007).

Stöber, K. and D. Austin, 'Culdees to Canons: The Augustinian Houses of North Wales', in J. Burton and K. Stöber (eds), *Monastic Wales: New Approaches* (Cardiff: University of Wales Press, 2013), pp. 39–54.

Stone, L., *The Crisis of the Aristocracy, 1558–1641* (Oxford: Clarendon Press, 1965).

Stow, J., *Annales of England ... Continued by Edmund Howes* (London: Thomas Dawson, 1615).

Stretton, T., 'Written Obligations, Litigation and Neighbourliness, 1580–1680', in S. Hindle, A. Shepard and J. Walter (eds), *Remaking English Society: Social Relations and Social Change in Early Modern England* (Woodbridge: The Boydell Press, 2013), pp. 189–209.

Stuhmiller, J., 'Hunting, Fowling and Fishing', in A. Classen (ed.), *Handbook of Medieval Culture: Fundamental Aspects and Conditions of the European Middle Ages*, vol. 2 (Berlin and Boston, Walter de Gruyter, 2015), pp. 697–721.

Sutcliffe, M., *The Practice and Proceedings and Laws of Arms* (London, 1593).

Sweeney, T., *Irish Stuart Silver: A Short Descriptive Catalogue of Surviving Irish Church, Civic and Ceremonial and Domestic Plate Dating from the Reigns of James I, Charles I, the Commonwealth, Charles II, James II, William and Mary, William III and Queen Anne: 1603–1714* (Dublin: Edmund Burke, 1995).

Sweetman, D., 'Excavation of Medieval "Field Boundaries" at Clonard, County Meath', *Journal of the Royal Society of Antiquaries of Ireland*, vol. 108, 1978, pp. 10–22.

Sweetman, H. S. and G. F. Handcock, *Calendar of Documents, Relating to Ireland*, 5 vols (London: Longman & Co., 1875).

Tait, C., 'Disorder and Commotion: Urban Riots and Popular Protest in Ireland, 1570–1640', in W. Sheehan and M. Cronin (eds), *Riotous Assemblies: Rebels, Riots and Revolts in Ireland* (Cork: Mercier Press, 2011), pp. 22–49.

Taussig, M., *Mimesis and Alterity: A Particular History of the Senses* (New York: Psychology Press, 1993).

Taylor, C., *Village and Farmstead: A History of Rural Settlement in England* (London: George Philip, 1983).

Taylor, C., 'Ravensdale Park, Derbyshire, and Medieval Deer Coursing', *Landscape History*, vol. 26, no. 1, 2004, pp. 37–47.

Tempest, H. G., 'The Moyry Pass', *Journal of the County Louth Archaeological Society*, vol. 14, 1958, pp. 82–90.

Thirsk, J., *Economic Policy and Projects: The Development of a Consumer Society in Early Modern England* (Oxford: Clarendon Press, 1978).

Thomas, J., 'Comments on "Past Practices: Rethinking Individuals and Agents in Archaeology" by A. G. Knapp and P. Van Dommelen', *Cambridge Archaeological Journal*, vol. 18, no. 1, 2008, pp. 26–28.

Thomassen, B., 'Revisiting Liminality: The Danger of Empty Space', in H. Andrews and L. Roberts (eds), *Liminal Landscapes: Travel, Experience and Spaces In-Between* (London and New York: Routledge, 2012), pp. 21–35.

Thompson, M., *The Medieval Hall, the Basis of Secular Domestic Life 600–1600 AD* (Aldershot: Scolar Press, 1995).

Thompson, S., *Women Religious: The Founding of English Nunneries after the Norman Conquest* (Oxford: Clarendon Press, 1991).

Townend, P., *Father Mathew, Temperance, and Irish Identity, 1838–1848* (Dublin: Irish Academic Press, 2002).

Trigger, B., A *History of Archaeological Thought* (Cambridge: Cambridge University Press, 1989).

Troy, C., 'Final Report on the Human Remains from Ardreigh, Co. Kildare', Unpublished Report to Headland Archaeology Ltd on behalf of Kildare County Council, 2010.

Turner, V., *The Ritual Process: Structure and Anti-Structure* (New York: Cornell University Press, 1977).

Tutlies, P., 'Eine Karolingisches Wassermühle in Rotbachtal', *Archäologie in Rheinland*, 2005, pp. 106–108.

Ua Brádaigh, T., 'Clann Cobhthaigh', *Ríocht na Midhe*, vol. 4, 1967, pp. 26–32.

Vallancey, C., *Collectanea de Rebus Hibernicis: Number II* (Dublin: Luke White, 1786).

Van der Hoeven, M. (ed.), *Exercise of Arms: Warfare in the Netherlands, 1569–1648* (Leiden: Brill, 1997).

Van Gennep, A., *Les Rites de Passage* (Paris: E. Nourry, 1909).

Vejby, M. and J. Ahlers, 'Land, Myth and Language: The Preservation of Social Memories', in A. M. Chadwick and C. D. Gibbons (eds), *Memory, Myth and Long-Term Landscape Inhabitation* (Oxford and Oakville: Oxbow, 2013), pp. 276–290.

Verstraten, F., 'Ua Conchobair', in S. Duffy (ed.), *Medieval Ireland: An Encyclopaedia* (New York: Routledge, 2005), p. 772.

Viega de Oliviera, E., F. Galhano and B. Pereira, *Tecnologia Tradicional Portuguesa: Sistemas de Moagem*, vol. 2 (Lisbon: Instituto Nacional de Investigação Científica, 1983).

Villiers-Tuthill, K., 'The Irish Benedictine Nuns: From Ypres to Kylemore', in M. Browne and C. Ó Clabaigh (eds), *The Irish Benedictines: A History* (Dublin: Columba Press, 2005), pp. 122–139.

Waddell, J., J. Fenwick and K. Barton (eds), *Rathcroghan: Archaeological and Geophysical Survey in a Ritual Landscape* (Dublin: Wordwell, 2009).

Walker, T., *Documents on Thomas Walker's Plot against Tyrone in 1601*, comp. B. Färber (University College Cork: CELT, 2010) [http://www.ucc.ie/celt/published/E600001-003/index.html].

Wallace, P. F., *The Viking Age Buildings of Dublin*, Medieval Dublin Excavations, vol. 1 (Dublin: National Museum of Ireland, 1992).

Walsh, P., *Leabhar Chlainne Suibhne: An Account of the MacSweeney Families in Ireland* (Dublin: Dollard, 1920).

Walsh, P., 'Galway: A Summary History', in E. FitzPatrick, M. O'Brien and P. Walsh (eds), *Archaeological Investigations in Galway City, 1987–1998* (Dublin: Wordwell, 2004), pp. 269–291.

Walter, J., *Understanding Popular Violence in the English Revolution: The Colchester Plunderers* (Cambridge: Cambridge University Press, 1999).

Walter, J., 'Performative Violence and the Politics of Violence in the 1641 Depositions', in J. Ohlmeyer and M. Ó Siochrú (eds), *Ireland, 1641: Contexts and Reactions* (Manchester: Manchester University Press, 2013), pp. 134–152.

Waterman, D. M., 'Somersetshire and Other Foreign Building Stone in Ireland, *c.*1175–1400', *Ulster Journal of Archaeology*, vol. 33, 1970, pp. 63–75.

Watson, G. J., 'Celticisim: Macpherson, Matthew Arnold and Ireland', in S. Ó Síocháin (ed.), *Social Thought on Ireland in the Nineteenth Century* (Dublin: University College Dublin Press, 2009), pp. 147–166.

Watt, D. (ed.), *Medieval Women in their Communities* (Toronto: University of Toronto Press, 1997).

Watts, M., *The Archaeology of Mills and Milling* (Stroud: Tempus, 2002).

Watson, M. and M. McLeod (eds), *Edinburgh Companion to the Gaelic Language* (Edinburgh: Edinburgh University Press, 2010).

Webb, H. J., *Elizabethan Military Science: The Books and Practice* (London: University of Wisconsin Press, 1965).

Weston Joyce, P., *A Social History of Ancient Ireland* (London: Longmans, Green & Co., 1903).

Westropp, T. J., 'Proceedings: Canons' Island', *Journal of the Royal Society of Antiquaries of Ireland*, vol. 27, 1897, pp. 286–290.

Westropp, T. J., 'The Augustinian Houses of the County of Clare: Clare, Killone and Inchicronan', *Journal of the Royal Society of Antiquaries of Ireland*, vol. 30, 1900, pp. 118–135.

Westropp, T. J., 'The Termon Cross of Kilnaboy, County Clare Sketched in 1854', *Journal of the Royal Society of Antiquaries of Ireland*, vol. 39, 1909, pp. 85–88.

Westropp, T. J., 'Prehistoric Remains (Forts and Dolmens) in the Burren and its South Western Border', *Journal of the Royal Society of Antiquaries of Ireland*, vol. 45, 1915, pp. 45–62.

White, D. G., 'Henry VIII's Irish Kerne in France and Scotland, 1544–1545', *Irish Sword*, vol. 3, 1958, pp. 213–225.

White, N. B., *Extents of Irish Monastic Possessions, 1540–1541: From Manuscripts in the Public Record Office, London* (Dublin: Irish Manuscripts Commission, 1943).

Wikander, Ö., 'Archaeological Evidence for Early Water-Mills: An Interim Report', *History of Technology*, vol. 11, 1985, pp. 151–179.

Wikander, Ö., 'The Water-Mill', in Ö. Wikander (ed.), *Handbook of Ancient Water Technology* (Leiden, Boston, Köln: Brill, 2000), p. 392.

Wilkinson, N. R., 'Heraldry in its Relation to Archaeology', *Journal of the Royal Society of Antiquaries of Ireland*, vol. 40, no. 1, 1909, pp. 52–55.

Williams, B., 'A Late Medieval Rural Settlement at Craigs, County Antrim', *Ulster Journal of Archaeology*, third series, vol. 5, 1988, pp. 91–102.

Williams, B. and P. S. Robinson, 'The Excavations of Bronze Age Cists and a Medieval Booley House at Glenmakeeran, County Antrim, and a Discussion of Booleying in North Antrim', *Ulster Journal of Archaeology*, third series, vol. 46, 1983, pp. 29–40.

Williams, N. (ed.), *Dánta Mhuiris Mhic Dháibhí Dhuibh Mhic Ghearailt* (Dublin: Clóchomhar, 1979) p. 53.

Williams, N. J. A. (ed. and trans.), *Pairlement Chloinne Tomáis* (Dublin: Institute for Advanced Studies, 1981).

Williamson, T. and L. Bellamy, *Property and Landscape: A Social History of Land Ownership and the English Countryside* (London: George Philip, 1987).

Wilson, A., 'Late Antique Water-Mills on the Palatine', *Papers of the British School at Rome*, vol. 71, 2003, pp. 85–109.

Wilson, C. A., *Food and Drink in Britain* (London: Constable, 1973).

Woloch, A., *The One vs. the Many: Minor Characters and the Space of the Protagonist in the Novel* (Princeton, NJ: Princeton University Press, 2003).

Wood, A., *The 1549 Rebellions and the Making of Early Modern England* (Cambridge: Cambridge University Press, 2007).

Wood-Martin, W. G., *The Lake Dwellings of Ireland: or Ancient Lacustrine Habitations of Erin, Commonly Called Crannogs* (Dublin: Hodges Figgis, 1886).

Woulfe, P., *Sloinnte Geadhal is Gall: Irish Names and Surnames* (Dublin: M. H. Gill, 1922).

Wright, S., 'Millstones', in P. Rahtz and R. Meesom, *An Anglo-Saxon Watermill at Tamworth. Excavations in the Boleridge Street Area of Tamworth, Staffordshire in 1971 and 1978*, CBA Research Report No. 83 (London: Council for British Archaeology, 1992).

Yaeger, J. and M. Canuto (eds), *The Archaeology of Communities* (London: Routledge, 2002).

Yaeger, J., 'What Was Rundale and Where Did It Come From?', *Béaloideas*, vol. 70, 2002, pp. 153–186.

Yorke, B., *Nunneries and the Anglo-Saxon Royal Houses* (London: Bloomsbury Academic, 2003).

**Digital Sources**

Crooks, P. (ed.), CIRCLE: A Calendar of Irish Chancery Letters *c.*1244–1509 [https://chancery.tcd.ie/].

Cox, N. and K. Dannehl, Dictionary of Traded Goods and Commodities 1550–1820 (Wolverhampton, 2007), British History Online [http://www.british–history.ac.uk/no–series/traded–goods–dictionary/1550–1820].

Department of Arts, Heritage, Rural, Regional and Gaeltacht Affairs, Historic Environment Viewer [http://webgis.archaeology.ie/historic environment/].

Fiontar, Scoil na Gaeilge and The Placenames Branch, Placenames Database of Ireland [https://www.logainm.ie/en/].

Jones, E. and S. Flavin, Ireland–Bristol Trade in the Sixteenth Century, Project Website, Department of History, University of Bristol [http://www.bris.ac.uk/Depts/History/Ireland/research.htm].

National Inventory of Architectural Heritage, Buildings Survey [http://www.buildingsofireland.ie/Surveys/Buildings/].

Northern Ireland Sites and Monuments Record (NISMR) [http://appsc.doeni.gov.uk/ambit/Default.aspx].

Mapping Death 1st to 8th Centuries AD: People, Boundaries and Territories in Ireland, Online Database [http://www.mappingdeathdb.ie].

School of Celtic Studies, Dublin Institute for Advanced Studies, Irish Script on Screen [https://www.isos.dias.ie/].

Simms, K. and M. Hoyne, Bardic Poetry Database [https://bardic.celt.dias.ie/].

Trinity College Dublin, 1641 Depositions Project [http://1641.tcd.ie/].

## Archival and Manuscript Sources

**National Library of Ireland**

NLI, MS 700, Giraldus Cambrensis, Topographia Hibernica: Expugnatio Hibernia.

NLI, MS 724, Reeves Down Survey Maps, Co. Westmeath.

NLI, MS 720–1, Down Survey Maps, Co. Westmeath.

NLI, GO MS 64, Funeral Entries.

NLI, MS 2656 (1), Map of the District Between Dundalk and Newry. By Richard Barthelet *c.*1602.

NLI, MS 2656 (5), Drawings of Attacks on Crannogs in Ulster, by Richard Barthelet *c.*1602.

NLI, MS 2656 (5), Drawing of Dungannon Castle and the Stone Chair at Tullaghoge, Co. Tyrone, by Richard Barthelet. *c.*1602.

NLI, MS 2656 (6), Drawing of Enish Loughan Fort, Co. Antrim, by Richard Barthelet *c.*1602.

NLI, MS 2656 (11), Drawings of Attacks on Crannogs in Ulster, by Richard Barthelet *c.*1602.

NLI, GO MS 65, Funeral Entries.

NLI, GO MS 68, Funeral Entries.

NLI, MS G992, Duanaire na Nuinseannach.

**The National Archives of Ireland**

NAI, Chancery Bills, C. 98: 13–4.

NAI, Chancery Bills, D. 19: 3–4.

NAI, Chancery Bills, E 246: 39–40.

NAI, Chancery Bills, F. 38: 7–8.

NAI, Chancery Bills, G. 68: 13.

NAI, Chancery Bills, H. 18.

**The National Archives, Kew**

TNA, MPF 1/35, A Generalle Description of Ulster [1602–3].

TNA, MPF 1/36, Map of the Southern Part of Ulster, Ireland, Showing Mountains and Woods in Perspective.

TNA, MPF 1/82.

TNA, MPF 1/98 (formerly with the call-mark SP 64/1/31).

TNA, MPF 1/99, Plot of the Fort at the Black-water, 27 March 1587.

TNA, SP 63/180.

TNA, SP 63/143.

TNA, SP 63/180.

TNA, SP 63/202.

TNA, SP 63/203.

TNA, SP 63/207.

TNA, SP 63/210.

TNA, SP 63/180.
TNA, SP 63/199.

**The National Maritime Museum, Greenwich**
NMM, MS P/49(25) [East Part of Ulster].

**The British Library**
BL, Harley 541, 'The Little Children's Little Book'.
BL, Cotton MS, Augustus I, ii, 37.
BL, Cotton MS, Augustus I, ii, 38. The Battle of the Erne Ford, 10 Oct. 1593, by John Thomas.
BL, Cotton MS, Augustus I, ii, 42.

**Trinity College Dublin**
TCD, MS 813, 1641 Depositions.
TCD, MS 829, 1641 Depositions.
TCD, MS 1209 (26), A plan of the town of 'Craggfargus'.
TCD, MS 1209 (35), 'The description of the army which was defeated by the earle of Tyrone', 14 August 1598.

**Hatfield House Archive**
HHA, Cecil Papers, 88/121–2.
HHA, Cecil Papers, 94/26.
HHA, Cecil Papers, 139/54.
HHA, Cecil Papers, 177/131.
HHA, Cecil Papers, 179/74.
HHA, Cecil Papers, 177/131.

**Other Archives**
Biblioteca Nacional de España, Códice de Trajes, 1547 (MS Res 285).
Bodleian Library, Oxford, MS Bankes, 18/14; 41/51; 42/77.
Exeter College, Oxford, MS 154.
Lambeth Palace Library, Carew MSS v. 626.
Public Record Office Northern Ireland, T/510 copied from Lambeth Palace Library, Carew MS 634.
Royal Irish Academy, MS M 14 F 11, Ordnance Survey (1861); copies of Inquisitions relating to the County of Roscommon deposited in the Record Tower, Dublin Castle.
University College Dublin, Ó Cléirigh Institute, MSS D2.

# Index

Note: illustrations are indicated by page numbers in **bold**. Entries for counties refer to general discussion of that county in the text, individual locations within the county are listed separately.